Critical Thinking, Thoughtful Writing

A Rhetoric with Readings

Bruce P. Loomis

Critical Thinking, Thoughtful Writing

A Rhetoric with Readings

SECOND EDITION

John Chaffee, Ph.D.

Director, NY Center for Critical Thinking and Language Learning
LaGuardia College, City University of New York

Christine McMahon
Barbara Stout

English Department, Montgomery College

Houghton Mifflin Company   Boston   New York

For Jessie and Joshua

Senior Sponsoring Editor: Suzanne Phelps Weir
Senior Development Editor: Janet Young
Senior Project Editor: Carol Newman
Senior Manufacturing Coordinator: Priscilla Bailey
Marketing Manager: Cindy Graff Cohen

Cover image: *Expansion of the Lyric, 1913* by Leonardo Dudreville (b. 1885), Richard Miller
    Collection, New York, USA Bridgeman Art Library.
Back cover photo: Jerry Bauer.

Printed in the U.S.A.

Library of Congress Catalog Number: 2001131483
ISBN: 0-618-12411-X

23456789-DOC-05 04 03 02 01

Brief Contents

Contents

Preface

Leo Tolstoy eloquently observed, "The relation of word to thought, and the creation of new concepts, is a complex, delicate, and enigmatic process unfolding in our soul." Writers and teachers of writing have long recognized intricate relationships between the extraordinary human processes of thought and language. In general, textbook writers and publishers have not clearly translated this insight into a comprehensive approach that helps beginning college students become thoughtful writers. Experts in the thinking process (philosophers and psychologists, for example) have not generally concentrated on the complex challenges of teaching writing. Experts in teaching writing have found integrating the critical thinking process into their pedagogy a sometimes problematic endeavor.

Critical Thinking, Thoughtful Writing: A Rhetoric with Readings presents an integrated approach to teaching the thinking, writing, and reading skills that first-year composition students need for success in academic work. As students develop higher-order thinking abilities, they learn to articulate their ideas through writing. And as they develop their abilities to navigate the writing process, they learn to think coherently, precisely, and creatively. This unique approach integrates development of thinking skills with writing skills so that they not only reinforce each other but also become inseparable.

This book stimulates and guides students to think deeply and beyond superficialities, to refuse to be satisfied with the first idea they have, to look objectively at the pros and cons of issues, and to formulate their own informed conclusions. It helps students develop an interest in research and in delving into possibilities rather than into commonplace answers. It encourages students to be independent in their thinking and courageous in their convictions. And it shows them how to organize information, interpret different perspectives, solve challenging problems, analyze complex issues, and communicate their ideas clearly.

Advantages of a Critical Thinking Framework

The critical thinking framework of this text helps instructors and students in the following ways:

- **By providing an intellectual and thematic framework** that helps writing teachers place structural and mechanical concerns in a meaningful context. *Critical Thinking, Thoughtful Writing* challenges and guides students to think and write about important topics that build on their cognitive activities and critical explorations. This process enables students to improve both the technical aspects of their writing (coherence, organization, detail, use of conventions) and the quality of their writing (depth, insight, sophistication).

- **By leading students to understand the reciprocal relationship** between the process of thinking and the process of writing. The text stimulates students to explore their own composing processes and to understand the forms of thought that are the hallmark of mature writing.

- **By helping students to appreciate that reading is a thinking activity** rather than a series of decoding skills. This understanding results in enhanced reading development. Students are better able to understand and develop the interrelated thinking abilities the reading process comprises, including problem solving, forming and applying concepts, and relating ideas to larger conceptual frameworks.

Content and Organization

MOVEMENT FROM THE PERSONAL TO THE SOCIAL

The book moves logically from introducing creative and critical thinking to explaining how these tools can be used in different kinds of writing. In Part One, we aim to help students understand themselves as thinkers and writers; the Writing Projects in this section ask them to write from their own experiences and observations. In Part Two, students explore important thinking patterns and language issues; here, the Writing Projects ask them to incorporate some ideas from others into their expository writing. In Part Three, students must use an increasing number of sources as they work with problem solving, argumentation, and research. This logical progression provides a productive format for pulling students beyond their personal experiences and pushing them to think and write about challenging issues and concepts, while at the same time seeing how social issues are connected with their own lives. The practical strategies that they learn will help students address writing assignments in other academic classes and in the workplace.

1. **Critical Thinking Focus**—Examines the thinking skill central to each chapter. Examples of critical thinking skills are thinking about thinking, creative thinking, decision-making, evaluating perspectives, causal reasoning, conceptualizing, constructing knowledge, solving problems, and developing reasoned arguments.

2. **Reading Focus**—Comprises 55 professional readings (40 of them complete essays, articles, or book chapters) and 21 student essays, on themes including creativity, decision making, intercultural issues, gender issues, language discovery, ecological relationships, problem solving, and arguments on controversial topics. Each chapter offers three or more pieces of professional writing (such as essays, stories, newspaper articles, and poems) and at least one student essay. The readings reflect the critical thinking focus in each chapter and provide the basis for assignments that initiate students' writing.

3. **Writing Focus**—Provides strategies and Thinking-Writing Activities that draw upon the chapter's critical thinking skill.

4. **Writing Project**—Builds on the reading themes and skills developed through the chapter's activities. These carefully structured projects move systematically toward a finished project, providing guidance throughout the writing process. Each chapter includes at least one (usually two) student examples of the completed Writing Project.

Special Features

Practical Critical Thinking Strategies for Writing The concept of "critical thinking" often seems abstract to students, but this book introduces the process of thinking critically as a practical and powerful approach to writing as well as to life in general. For example, in learning a thoughtful approach for making decisions, students apply this process to making decisions about revising drafts as well as to making important decisions in other areas of their lives. By developing their problem-solving abilities, students become able both to write about problems and to be more effective in solving problems beyond the classroom.

Comprehensive Thinking-Writing Model The Thinking-Writing Model introduced in Chapter 1 (page 31) and reinforced throughout the book provides a clear graphic representation of the writing process and of the connections between critical thinking and thoughtful writing, as well as creative thinking and inventive writing.

Creative Thinking to Enrich the Writing Process The book shows that creative thought can and should be an integral part of academic writing. All aspects of the writing process can be approached creatively, including topic selection, generating ideas and drafting, using specific details, and writing introductions and conclusions. In learning to think creatively, students discover strategies to make their writing more inventive, while also infusing creative energy into other areas of their lives.

Emphasis on Collaboration The value of collaboration in thinking and writing is emphasized throughout, with this special icon appearing in the margin highlighting Thinking-Writing Activities and other material specifically designed for collaboration and peer review. Critical thinking is emphasized in actively exploring ideas, listening to others, and carefully evaluating alternative points of view. Students learn to examine their own opinions more analytically and relate their views to those of others, contributing to their development into a community of concerned thinkers and writers.

Cross-Disciplinary Approach Recognizing that first-year composition courses prepare students to write in many of their courses and after college, this book presents examples, selections, and assignments from sociology, psychology, linguistics, history, cultural studies, economics, and the sciences.

Critical Thinking as a Tool for Living The book views learning to think, write, and read as integral dimensions of an individual's personal growth and transformation. While learning how to think and write, students are encouraged to apply critical and creative thinking skills to all facets of their lives, enabling them to make enlightened decisions, solve challenging problems, analyze complex issues, communicate effectively, nurture creative talents, and become more thoughtful and socially aware citizens.

Changes to the Second Edition

The Second Edition provides numerous improvements and additions in response to instructor feedback and in keeping with current instructor needs.

New Research Chapter and MLA Appendix A new Chapter 13 emphasizes the principles behind research processes and citation practices. In keeping with the book's overall approach, the Critical Thinking Focus of this chapter explores the why's of research—why research is valuable and why sources must be documented—and the how's—how to gather, evaluate and select information and how to incorporate that information into a paper. To help students develop more discernment about handling material from the web, a checklist called "Tips for Evaluating the Reliability of a Web Site" offers specific, practical advice. Chapter 13 shows that research is not an isolated activity by pointing out connections with other chapters in this book. In addition, material throughout the book that pertains to research is identified by an icon appearing in the margin. An annotated student paper demonstrates how a topic is developed and how sources are documented. A new appendix provides up-to-date instruction on the MLA documentation system.

Expanded Critical Reading Coverage The opening chapter introduces critical reading as part of the recursive thinking-writing process, with a discussion of Toni Morrison's speech "The Site of Memory." Throughout the text, critical reading questions now follow the reading selections. The questions are designed to guide students in analyzing the central issues in the readings, and also to help them develop the full range of sophisticated critical thinking abilities needed for success in college and beyond.

Expanded Coverage of the Writing Process, Especially Revising Additional examples of revising have been added throughout the book, including both student paragraphs and professional examples such as Roger Garrison's "Revision—Seeing Again" (Chapter 1) and a manuscript version of FDR's "'Day of Infamy' Speech" (Chapter 5). The student research paper in Chapter 13 demonstrates stages of the writing process, complete with student commentary, from brainstorming through revising and editing. The writing process section at the end of each chapter has been improved and expanded, especially with more specific points for revising. Chapter 4 offers a step-by-step method for revising any assignment.

More Material on Collaborative Writing Peer response methods introduced in the writing process sections of Chapters 2 and 3 show students how to comment productively on other students' writing, and students are encouraged to use these methods, with tailored revision questions, for every Writing Project. As mentioned above, specially designed collaborative activities have been added throughout the text and are highlighted with a distinctive icon.

Stronger Argument Coverage Chapter 12 now includes the basic principles of the Toulmin approach to argument and more emphasis on consensus building, as well as an introduction to some classical concepts. This chapter also contains a new pair of readings that offer differing views on assisted suicide.

Over One-Fourth New Readings Fourteen new professional readings include work by Edwidge Danticat, Roger Garrison, and Toni Morrison plus articles on engineering, ecology, and U.S. voting regulations. In response to instructors' desire to draw on and develop students' visual literacy, in Chapter 12 we provide two new visual texts for analysis: the original "Uncle Sam" Army recruitment poster, and screen shots from the U.S. Army's current recruitment web site. The Second Edition also features five new student essays on topics such as logic, youth violence, the creative urge, and definition of friendship. A new argumentative student paper in Chapter 12, by a student with school-age children, makes the case for allowing children to bring cell phones to school.

Updated Two-Color Design with More Visuals An eye-catching new design makes the entire text easier to read and use and highlights annotations and revisions in readings and writing samples. The text now also includes concise guidelines and checklists for key skills, as well as more photographs, diagrams, advertisements, and cartoons, accompanied by thought-provoking captions.

Supplements

Instructor's Resource Manual A revised edition of the manual by Joyce Neff of Old Dominion University offers an essay on critical thinking that explores recent scholarship; sample syllabi; teaching suggestions; handouts and blackline masters for key processes and diagrams as well as a writing inventory and reader response guidelines; biographical notes for all reading selections; and suggestions for additional readings, films, and videos.

Web Site The accompanying web site includes links to sites on critical thinking, creativity, research, and many of the topics discussed in the readings as well as interactive step-by-step directions for completing each of the Writing Projects. Students will enjoy working with "Tom Randall's Halloween Party," an interactive court case that allows them to analyze evidence, devise cross-examination questions, and serve as judge and jury evaluating the case of a college student charged with serving alcohol to an underage guest.

The Authors

Critical Thinking, Thoughtful Writing is the result of collaboration by three authors. John Chaffee is Director of the New York Center for Critical Thinking, and Professor of Philosophy at The City University of New York. As a nationally recognized figure in critical thinking, he conducts workshops and lectures around the country. His best-selling textbook *Thinking Critically*, Sixth Edition, presents a comprehensive, language-based approach to learning that helped define the field of critical thinking. His trade book, *The Thinker's Way*, has been translated into six languages. Barbara Stout and Christine McMahon, both English professors at Montgomery College, used *Thinking Critically* in their composition courses for several years, which made them ideally suited to adapt its critical thinking approach to the teaching of writing, resulting in this text.

Acknowledgments

The following reviewers offered wise insights and suggestions about the manuscript in the First Edition:

Patricia Bizzel, College of the Holy Cross

Paul Bodmer, Bismarck State College

Judith A. Hinman, College of the Redwoods

Frederick T. Janzow, Southeast Missouri State

Shirley Wilson Logan, University of Maryland

Elizabeth A. Nist, Anoka-Ramsey Community College

Isaiah Smithson, Southern Illinois University

Byron Stay, Mount St. Mary's College

Kay Stokes, Hanover College

Michael Thomas, College of the Redwoods

Elizabeth Wahlquist, Brigham Young University

These reviewers provided valuable comments on the Second Edition:

Stephanie Byrd, Cleveland State University

Gina Claywell, Murray State University

Sarah Dangelantonio, Franklin Pierce College

Charlie Davis, Boise State University

Thomas Fink, LaGuardia College

John H. Jones, Jacksonville State University

Jill Kinkade, University of Southern Indiana

Linda McHenry, Fort Hays State University

Joan Mullin, University of Toledo

Kenneth Rosenauer, Missouri Western State College

Nicholas Schevera, College of Lake County

Jane Armstrong Woodman, Northern Arizona University

John Chaffee would like to thank Christine McMahon and Barbara Stout for the dedication and expertise they brought to the unique project of extending his work in critical thinking to the field of composition. Their approaches to teaching writing and their active involvement in the composition field have contributed significantly to a text that is practical, effective, and adaptable to a variety of instructional contexts.

He would like to gratefully acknowledge his editors at Houghton Mifflin for their friendship and their outstanding contributions to this book. Suzanne Phelps Weir brought a creative vision that enabled the book to transcend conventional boundaries, and she has guided its evolution with wise choices and inspiring energy. Janet Young helped to fashion every aspect of this Second Edition, bringing thoughtful insight, subtle wit, and a rare sense of mission to the project. The expert and timely production of this edition was made possible by the talent of Carol Newman, whose unique blend of efficacy and distinctive humor was a pleasure to experience. We are indeed fortunate to benefit from the marketing talents of Cindy Graff Cohen, who has brought fresh ideas and creative energy to the book. Janet Edmonds displayed exceptional wisdom in nurturing the book through its development in the First Edition. And Jill Haber brought technical and art expertise to the text.

We are indebted to Warren Gebert for his inspired illustrations that communicate complex ideas with intellectual clarity and visual creativity. The splendid revision of the Thinking-Writing Model is due to the unique talent of Robin Landa and her design students, Shawn Anderson and Jennifer Sencion. We are also grateful to Trina Sullivan for her knowledgeable work on developing the "Looking Critically@ Internet" activities.

A special acknowledgment goes to Joyce Neff at Old Dominion University for her superb work in writing the Instructor's Resource Manual. John is particularly indebted to the members of the English Department at LaGuardia College for their creative collaboration in linking the writing and critical thinking programs over the last twenty years, which was initially supported with funding from the National Endowment for the Humanities.

John's children, Jessie and Joshua, and his wife, Heide Lange, have provided ongoing love, support, and guidance that have enhanced this book and brought purpose and meaning to his life.

Christine McMahon gratefully acknowledges the W. K. Kellogg Foundation, whose Beacon College Project supported the Critical Literacy Institute at Oakton College, and the faculty at Oakton who introduced her to John Chaffee's work. She is indebted to the administrators at Montgomery College who chose her as the Project Director for the grant and who continue to provide generous support for Montgomery's critical literacy program. She acknowledges John and Barbara as wonderful co-authors. Her students, some of whose work appears in this book, helped her learn how to teach and motivated her to share what she knows. Her very special thanks go to her husband, Michael, her grownup children, Gregory and Beth, and her granddaughter, Brooke.

Barbara Stout is grateful to countless colleagues from many colleges and universities whose scholarship in composition, rhetoric, and writing across the curriculum is the foundation for informed teaching, programs, and textbooks. She is grateful to the Conference on College Composition and Communication, the Two-Year College English Association, and the national Writing Project for providing opportunities for sharing information and ideas. Her thanks also extend to the faculty, staff, and administrators of Montgomery College and to her students, from whom she always learns more than she can teach. She greatly appreciates John's and Chris's friendship and sound thinking. Of course, her most heartfelt thanks are to her family: David, Richard, Rebecca, Sally, Lyn, Mitch, Patrick, Kathleen, Sean, and Florence.

Critical Thinking, Thoughtful Writing

A Rhetoric with Readings

Tools of Thinking and Writing

If you stop to think about it, you will probably notice several ways that thinking and writing are connected. How can you write about a topic unless you have spent time thinking about it? How much better do you understand a topic after you have written about it? Part One of this book sharpens your awareness of the relationships between thinking and writing while introducing you to ways of becoming a critical thinker and a thoughtful writer.

1

Thinking Through Writing

"I write to understand as much as to be understood." —Elie Wiesel

Critical Thinking Focus: Thinking through writing

Writing Focus: The writing process

Reading Themes: Writing as self-expression

Writing Activity: Expressing a deep meaning

Thinking and Writing in College

Thinking and writing exist on many levels, ranging from the basic to the complex and sophisticated. Most people are able to "write," in that they can put words on paper. In your previous education, "good writing" might have meant mastering the basics of organization, grammar, and spelling. Although these are essential, as a college writer, you are expected to do more: to write with depth, insight, and analytical understanding. In order to achieve this level of sophistication in writing, you need to develop comparably advanced thinking abilities. You can't, after all, write better than you think! As the writer E. M. Forster remarked, "How do I know what I think until I see what I say?"

This book is designed to improve your writing abilities while you develop your critical thinking abilities. For example, instead of simply telling you how to write a paper using a problem-solving format, this book is designed to teach you to *think* like a problem solver and then to write like one. Rather than providing you with guidelines on how to write an analytical or argumentative essay, this book will help you to think through the processes of analyzing complex issues and constructing compelling arguments and then to express your understanding in effective writing.

In order to improve your writing abilities, you also need to write on a regular basis, integrating writing into your life as a vital and natural element. Therefore, this book offers you Thinking-Writing Activities. These can be done in various ways: out of class or in, individually or in pairs or groups, and in whatever format your instructor specifies. He or she might ask you to record your responses in a special journal to be reviewed periodically or on separate sheets of paper to be handed in. Your writing may also be shared with classmates or used as a basis for discussion. The thinking you do for the Thinking-Writing Activities will help to prepare you for the Writing Projects that conclude each chapter. These will give you an opportunity to think deeply about important subjects, to express your own distinctive point of view in a thoughtful and organized fashion, and to analyze the ideas of others from a variety of sources.

The Writing Projects in Part One (Chapters 1–5) ask you to draw upon your experiences and observations as you write about topics that help you explore the relationships between thinking and writing. The projects in Part Two and Part Three ask you to incorporate ideas from others into your papers.

Thinking and writing are active processes that all of us learn by engaging in them. By participating in the Thinking-Writing Activities, applying ideas presented in this book to your own experiences, and completing the Writing Projects, you will be sharpening your thinking and writing abilities, and by sharing your ideas with other members of the class, you will expand your own thinking and theirs. Each student has a wealth of experiences and insights to offer the class community, so there will be special Collaborative Activities that will provide the opportunity to enrich your writing by working with other students.

Thinking ↔ Writing Activity

Recalling a Learning Experience

Recall a memorable learning experience that you have had, either in school or outside. Describe that experience and explain why it has had a lasting impact on you. Discuss how the experience has contributed to your development as a thinker and writer.

Becoming an effective writer enables you to represent the rich fabric of your experience with clarity and precision. As you may have learned from your writing experiences thus far, the very process of using language serves to generate ideas. As a vehicle for creating and communicating your ideas, writing can be thought of as a catalyst that stimulates your personal and intellectual development. Since the writing process also enlarges your understanding of the world, becoming an effective writer is at the heart of your college education.

WORKING AT A HIGHER LEVEL

In many ways college is a whole new world. Not only are you expected to do more work in your courses, but you also are expected to work at a higher level: to *write more analytically,* to *think more conceptually,* and to *read more critically* than ever before.

Writing, thinking, and reading are, of course, closely connected. Through reading, literate human beings obtain information to use or to react to in their writing. On the conventional paper pages of books, magazines, and newspapers, and on the computer screens of email or the Internet, we read other people's thoughts, reflect on those thoughts, and deal with them in various ways when we write.

In addition to gathering information, you can improve your writing by analyzing and evaluating the ideas that you read about and by using them more precisely in your own writing. Most people, consciously and unconsciously, emulate as writers what they take in as readers. Therefore, one of this book's goals is to help you analyze how other writers have put their pieces together, leading you to a more analytical reading of your own writing. These techniques are powerful tools for revising your drafts into effective papers.

BECOMING A MORE THOUGHTFUL WRITER

What exactly is "thinking"? **Thinking** is the cognitive process you use every waking moment to make sense of your world as you work toward your goals, make informed decisions, analyze complex issues, and solve problems. However, in order to become a sophisticated thinker, you need to become an accomplished writer. Writing and thought are intimately related. **Writing**, with its power to represent our thoughts, feelings, and experiences symbolically, is the most important tool our thinking process has. Used together, thinking and writing enable us to create and communicate meaning.

Thinking and writing are processes that develop with use over a lifetime. You can improve your thinking and writing by following these three steps:

- *Becoming aware* of your thinking and writing processes. Have you often taken thinking and writing for granted and paid little attention to them? Developing these abilities means that you really have to "think about" the way you think and write.

- *Carefully examining* your thinking and writing processes (and the thinking and writing of others). By analyzing and understanding these complex processes, you can learn to handle them more effectively.

- *Practicing* your thinking and writing processes. To improve your thinking, you have to explore and make sense of thinking situations; to improve your writing, you have to write thoughtfully on an ongoing basis. Although it is important to learn how other people think and use language, there is no substitute for engaging in these activities yourself. As the Greek dramatist Sophocles insightfully observed, "Knowledge must come through action."

Thinking critically by carefully exploring your thinking process is one of the most satisfying aspects of being a mature, educated human being. Analogously, **writing thoughtfully** involves thinking critically as you move through the process of writing so that you can express your ideas effectively.

People are able to think critically and to write thoughtfully because of their natural human ability to *reflect*—to think back on what they are thinking, doing, or feeling. By carefully reflecting on your thinking, you are able to see how that thinking operates, so you learn to think more effectively. In the same way, reflecting on your language use, and particularly on the way you write, enables you to improve and refine your writing abilities. In the following chapters, you will be systematically exploring the many dimensions of how the human mind works.

The Thinking-Writing Model

The paradox of acquiring any complex ability is that in the best of all possible worlds, you would learn all the component parts of the activity at the same time. For example, learning to drive a car requires you to master a variety of component skills that operate simultaneously: watching the road ahead, steering, applying the appropriate pressure on the gas pedal, braking, keeping a proper distance from other vehicles, watching for traffic signs and traffic lights, keeping an eye open for pedestrians, and so on. Yet a book on driving, or a video, focuses on one skill at a time because that is how information is presented most easily. Somehow you have to make the leap from learning all of the skills separately in a linear, step-by-step fashion to using them all at the same time, in complex relationships with one another.

One of the authors of this book remembers his first, bewildering driving lesson with his parents. As he headed directly for a brick wall in the supermarket parking lot, his mother yelled, "Turn right!" while his father screamed, "Turn left!" In the driver's frenzied brain, these contradictory commands canceled each other out, so he continued on his course—with disastrous results.

Learning the complex skills of thinking critically and writing thoughtfully poses a similar dilemma. Although it is essential to learn each of the component parts of these processes, what distinguishes critical thinkers and thoughtful writers is that they can use all of these individual skills simultaneously.

Our approach to solving this problem will be to introduce a visual Thinking-Writing Model that presents the important parts of these processes. As you work on the various chapters and activities in the book, you will become more familiar with the different dimensions of the thinking-writing process as they function in the model we provide and as they function for you. This book offers you opportunities to build on the strengths you have and to grow as a critical thinker and thoughtful writer. The following Thinking-Writing Activity asks you to reflect on your own thinking-writing process as a starting point.

Thinking ↔ Writing Activity

Analyzing a Writing Experience

Describe in detail a writing experience that you found particularly satisfying or successful: for example, a paper you wrote for school, a market analysis you created for your company, or a letter in which you expressed important thoughts and feelings. After completing your description, answer the following questions in your journal or notebook.

- What was your goal or purpose in writing?
- What was the reaction of the people who read it—your audience?
- How did you think of the key ideas you included?
- How did you organize your ideas?
- Did you use other sources (such as readings) to provide support and context for your writing?
- In what ways did you revise your writing?
- How did you feel after completing your writing?

Your analysis will probably demonstrate that you already use many of the abilities that are integral to the Thinking-Writing Model. Carefully examine the Thinking-Writing Model on page 31. Before long, the model will become familiar, and you will be able to use it as a powerful guide to strengthen and clarify your thinking and writing. Let's explore the various dimensions of the Thinking-Writing Model and see how they work together to produce clear thinking and effective writing.

The Writing Situation

Writing always occurs in a **situation** within which the act of writing takes place. Or, to state it another way, no writer works in a vacuum. Writers have reasons to write, someone to whom they wish to write, a subject about which they have something important to say, and a sense of self as a writer which they want to project. Countless contextual factors affect a piece of writing: Is the writing done because it has been assigned? Or is it done because the writer wants to do it? How effective does it need to be, and why? Is it done with a pencil or a Braillewriter or a computer? Is it composed in a native language or in a second or third language? Is the writer working under time pressure? Still, whatever

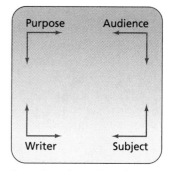

Figure 1.1 The Writing Situation

else contributes to the context, most writing situations are shaped by considering the **purpose, audience, subject,** and **writer**. In Figure 1.1, these four components of the writer's situation appear in the first part of the model because they provide an immediate context for any act of writing.

PURPOSE

Every act of writing has a *purpose*. When you complete a paper for a college course, you hope to show your professor that you can make significant statements about concepts relevant to the class. In a business setting, your aim is to transmit information or requests in a memo or a report; in your social life, you want to communicate with friends through letters or email; in your private life, you write in your journal so that you can later recall your activities and feelings. A crucial part of becoming an accomplished writer is maintaining a clear sense of the specific goals of whatever piece you are working on.

AUDIENCE

Thoughtful writing is shaped by consideration of its *audience*, the intended reader or readers. Although there are some instances when you write only for yourself (a diary entry, for example), you probably intend most of your writing to be read by someone else: the person receiving your letter, the coworkers reading your memo, the friend enjoying your poem, or the instructor grading your paper. The more you think about your audience, the more concerned you will be about making yourself clear, and the better your writing will become. The real skill lies in writing so clearly and coherently that your audience receives exactly the same message that you intended to send.

Effective writers are able to put themselves in their readers' place and to view their own writing through their readers' eyes. This perspective-taking helps them to craft their writing so that it will best communicate the ideas and emotions they seek to convey. In other words, they think about how much background information their audience will need, or won't need, to understand the intended message. Anticipating possible questions that their audience may have, they try to answer such questions at appropriate places. Understanding that the audience may have strong feelings about the topic, they consider those feelings as they write.

Effective writers organize their expository writing so that the audience can easily follow it. They state their main point, their *thesis,* in a clear thesis statement so that the audience will know what the focus is. They use examples so that the audience can "see" what they mean, transitions to help them make connections among ideas, and standard grammar, punctuation, and spelling so that the audience will not become distracted and confused. Such errors cause an audience to stop and reread or, worse yet, require the audience to guess what the writer means.

SUBJECT

Writing has to be about someone or something—a *subject.* Sometimes the subject originates in your own experience, but often it comes from ideas and information provided by others. Much of college writing involves responding to ideas presented in textbooks, class lectures, or research sources. Your writing task is usually to demonstrate your understanding of the ideas presented and also to apply, analyze, synthesize, or evaluate the ideas being expressed. The quality of your writing depends on the quality of your thinking as you process ideas and present them in order to communicate your own informed perspective on the subject.

WRITER

Of course, any writing situation calls for a *writer,* and the characteristics of the writer affect what is written and how it is produced. Experienced writers usually approach writing with more abilities and confidence than the inexperienced. Someone with considerable knowledge sees a subject differently from someone exploring it for the first time. A writer's identity as a woman or a man or as a member of an ethnic or other social group often influences approaches and attitudes. The relationship of the writer to the language or dialect being used makes a difference; whether the writer is tired or energetic, happy or sad, and so forth, makes a difference, too.

This book emphasizes the importance of understanding yourself as a writer. You should be aware of what knowledge—and what biases—you bring to the subject, the audience, and the purpose of an assignment. All writers do have at least one thing in common: They want to succeed in their writing tasks by discussing their subjects appropriately, reaching their audiences, and fulfilling their purposes.

CRITICAL READING: TONI MORRISON, "THE SITE OF MEMORY"

Reading critically is an essential part of becoming an insightful thinker and a proficient writer. It goes beyond simply understanding the information being presented. Reading critically also means *thinking critically* about the information and its source. All writing reflects a point of view, a perspective, a built-in bias. Rather than accepting this point of view without question, a critical reader strives to understand the point of view, analyze the reasons why the author developed it, and evaluate its credibility. This is precisely the subject of a speech by novelist Toni Morrison entitled "The Site of Memory." As you read the passage, think critically about its writing context:

- Who is the *writer*, and what perspective does she bring to the writing selection?
- What is the *subject* of the selection, and how would you evaluate its cogency and reliability?
- Who is the intended *audience*, and what assumptions is the writer making about it?
- What is the *purpose* of the selection, and how is the author trying to achieve it?

Following the Morrison selection are questions designed to stimulate and guide your critical thinking and class discussion.

"The Site of Memory"
BY TONI MORRISON

My inclusion in a series of talks on autobiography and memoir is not entirely a misalliance. Although it's probably true that a fiction writer thinks of his or her work as alien in that company, what I have to say may suggest why I'm not completely out of place here. For one thing, I might throw into relief the differences between self-recollection (memoir) and fiction, and also some of the similarities—the places where those two crafts embrace and where that embrace is symbiotic.

But the authenticity of my presence here lies in the fact that a very large part of my own literary heritage is the autobiography. In this country the print origins of black literature (as distinguished from the oral origins) were slave narratives. These book-length narratives (autobiographies, recollections, memoirs), of which well over a hundred were published, are familiar texts to historians and students of black history. They range from the adventure-packed life of Olaudah Equiano's *The Interesting Narrative of the Life of Olaudah Equiano, or Gustavus Vassa, the African, Written by Himself* (1769) to the quiet desperation of *Incidents in the Life of a Slave Girl: Written by Herself* (1861), in which Harriet Jacob ("Linda Brent") records hiding for seven years in a room too small to stand up in; from the political savvy of Frederick Douglass's *Narrative of the Life of Frederick Douglass, an American Slave, Written by Himself* (1845) to the subtlety and modesty of Henry Bibb, whose voice, in *Life and Adventures of Henry Bibb, an American Slave, Written by Himself* (1849), is surrounded by ("loaded with" is a better phrase) documents attesting to its authenticity. Bibb is careful to note that his formal schooling (three weeks) was short, but that he was "educated in the school of adversity, whips, and chains." Born in Kentucky, he put aside his plans to escape in order to marry. But when he learned that he was the father of a slave and watched the degradation of his wife and child, he reactivated those plans.

Whatever the style and circumstances of these narratives, they were written to say principally two things. One: "This is my historical life—my singular, special example that is personal, but that also represents the race." Two: "I write this text to persuade other people—you, the reader, who is probably not black—that we are human beings worthy of God's grace and the immediate abandonment of slavery." With these two missions in mind, the narratives were clearly pointed.

In Equiano's account, the purpose is quite up-front. Born in 1745 near the Niger River and captured at the age of ten, he survived the Middle Passage, American plantation slavery, wars in Canada and the Mediterranean; learned navigation and clerking from a Quaker named Robert King, and bought his freedom at twenty-one. He lived as a free servant, traveling widely and living most of his latter life in England. Here he is speaking to the British without equivocation: "I hope to have the satisfaction of seeing the renovation of liberty and justice resting on the British government. . . . I hope and expect the attention of gentlemen of power. . . . May the time come—at least the speculation is to me pleasing—when the sable people shall gratefully commemorate the auspicious era of extensive freedom." With typically eighteenth-century reticence he records his singular and representative life for one purpose: to change things. In fact, he and his co-authors *did* change things. Their works gave fuel to the fires that abolitionists were setting everywhere.

5   More difficult was getting the fair appraisal of literary critics. The writings of church martyrs and confessors are and were read for the eloquence of their message as well as their experience of redemption, but the American slaves' autobiographical narratives were frequently scorned as "biased," "inflammatory" and "improbable." These attacks are particularly difficult to understand in view of the fact that it was extremely important, as you can imagine, for the writers of these narratives to appear as objective as possible—not to offend the reader by being too angry, or by showing too much outrage, or by calling the reader names. As recently as 1966, Paul Edwards, who edited and abridged Equiano's story, praises the narrative for its refusal to be "inflammatory."

"As a rule," Edwards writes, "he [Equiano] puts no emotional pressure on the reader other than that which the situation itself contains—his language does not strain after our sympathy, but expects it to be given naturally and at the proper time. This quiet avoidance of emotional display produces many of the best passages in the book." Similarly, an 1836 review of Charles Bell's *Life and Adventures of a Fugitive Slave*, which appeared in the "Quarterly Anti-Slavery

Magazine," praised Bell's account for its objectivity. "We rejoice in the book the more, because it is not a partisan work. . . . It broaches no theory in regard to [slavery], nor proposes any mode or time of emancipation."

As determined as these black writers were to persuade the reader of the evil of slavery, they also complimented him by assuming his nobility of heart and his high-mindedness. They tried to summon up his finer nature in order to encourage him to employ it. They knew that their readers were the people who could make a difference in terminating slavery. Their stories—of brutality, adversity and deliverance—had great popularity in spite of critical hostility in many quarters and patronizing sympathy in others. There was a time when the hunger for "slave stories" was difficult to quiet, as sales figures show. Douglass's *Narrative* sold five thousand copies in four months; by 1847 it had sold eleven thousand copies. Equiano's book had thirty-six editions between 1789 and 1850. Moses Roper's book had ten editions from 1837 to 1856; William Wells Brown's was reprinted four times in its first year. Solomon Northrop's book sold twenty-seven thousand copies before two years had passed. A book by Josiah Henson (argued by some to be the model for the "Tom" of Harriet Beecher Stowe's *Uncle Tom's Cabin*) had a pre-publication sale of five thousand.

In addition to using their own lives to expose the horrors of slavery, they had a companion motive for their efforts. The prohibition against teaching a slave to read and write (which in many Southern states carried severe punishment) and against a slave's learning to read and write had to be scuttled at all costs. These writers knew that literacy was power. Voting, after all, was inextricably connected to the ability to read; literacy was a way of assuming and proving the "humanity" that the Constitution denied them. That is why the narratives carry the subtitle "written by himself," or "herself," and include introductions and prefaces by white sympathizers to authenticate them. Other narratives, "edited by" such well-known anti-slavery figures as Lydia Maria Child and John Greenleaf Whittier, contain prefaces to assure the reader how little editing was needed. A literate slave was supposed to be a contradiction in terms.

One has to remember that the climate in which they wrote reflected not only the Age of Enlightenment but its twin, born at the same time, the Age of Scientific Racism. David Hume, Immanuel Kant and Thomas Jefferson, to mention only a few, had documented their conclusions that blacks were incapable of intelligence. Frederick Douglass knew otherwise, and he wrote refutations of what Jefferson said in "Notes on the State of Virginia": "Never yet could I find that a black had uttered a thought above the level of plain narration, never see even an elementary trait of painting or sculpture." A sentence that I have always thought ought to be engraved at the door to the Rockefeller Collection of African Art. Hegel, in 1813, had said that Africans had no "history" and couldn't write in modern languages. Kant disregarded a perceptive observation by a black man by saying, "This fellow was quite black from head to foot, a clear proof that what he said was stupid."

Yet no slave society in the history of the world wrote more—or more thoughtfully—about its own enslavement. The milieu, however, dictated the purpose and the style. The narratives are instructive, moral and obviously representative.

Some of them are patterned after the sentimental novel that was in vogue at the time. But whatever the level of eloquence or the form, popular taste discouraged the writers from dwelling too long or too carefully on the more sordid details of their experience. Whenever there was an unusually violent incident, or a scatological one, or something "excessive," one finds the writer taking refuge in the literary conventions of the day. "I was left in a state of distraction not to be described" (Equiano). "But let us now leave the rough usage of the field . . . and turn our attention to the less repulsive slave life as it existed in the house of my childhood" (Douglass). "I am not about to harrow the feelings of my readers by a terrific representation of the untold horrors of that fearful system of oppression. . . . It is not my purpose to descend deeply into the dark and noisome caverns of the hell of slavery" (Henry Box Brown).

Over and over, the writers pull the narrative up short with a phrase such as, "But let us drop a veil over these proceedings too terrible to relate." In shaping the experience to make it palatable to those who were in a position to alleviate it, they were silent about many things, and they "forgot" many other things. There was a careful selection of the instances that they would record and a careful rendering of those that they chose to describe. Lydia Maria Child identified the problem in her introduction to "Linda Brent's" tale of sexual abuse: "I am well aware that many will accuse me of indecorum for presenting these pages to the public; for the experiences of this intelligent and much-injured woman belong to a class which some call delicate subjects, and others indelicate. This peculiar phase of Slavery has generally been kept veiled; but the public ought to be made acquainted with its monstrous features, and I am willing to take the responsibility of presenting them with the veil drawn [aside]."

But most importantly—at least for me—there was no mention of their interior life.

For me—a writer in the last quarter of the twentieth century, not much more than a hundred years after Emancipation, a writer who is black and a woman—the exercise is very different. My job becomes how to rip that veil drawn over "proceedings too terrible to relate." The exercise is also critical for any person who is black, or who belongs to any marginalized category, for, historically, we were seldom invited to participate in the discourse even when we were its topic.

Moving that veil aside requires, therefore, certain things. First of all, I must trust my own recollections. I must also depend on the recollections of others. Thus memory weighs heavily in what I write, in how I begin and in what I find to be significant. Zora Neale Hurston said, "Like the dead-seeming cold rocks, I have memories within that came out of the material that went to make me." These "memories within" are the subsoil of my work. But memories and recollections won't give me total access to the unwritten interior life of these people. Only the act of the imagination can help me.

◆

15   If writing is thinking and discovery and selection and order and meaning, it is also awe and reverence and mystery and magic. I suppose I could dispense with

the last four if I were not so deadly serious about fidelity to the milieu out of which I write and in which my ancestors actually lived. Infidelity to that milieu—the absence of the interior life, the deliberate excising of it from the records that the slaves themselves told—is precisely the problem in the discourse that proceeded without us. How I gain access to that interior life is what drives me and is the part of this talk which both distinguishes my fiction from autobiographical strategies and which also embraces certain autobiographical strategies. It's a kind of literary archeology: on the basis of some information and a little bit of guesswork you journey to a site to see what remains were left behind and to reconstruct the world that these remains imply. What makes it fiction is the nature of the imaginative act: my reliance on the image—on the remains—in addition to recollection, to yield up a kind of a truth. By "image," of course, I don't mean "symbol"; I simply mean "picture" and the feelings that accompany the picture.

Fiction, by definition, is distinct from fact. Presumably it's the product of imagination—invention—and it claims the freedom to dispense with "what really happened," or where it really happened, or when it really happened, and nothing in it needs to be publicly verifiable, although much in it can be verified. By contrast, the scholarship of the biographer and the literary critic seems to us only trustworthy when the events of fiction can be traced to some publicly verifiable fact. It's the research of the "Oh, yes, this is where he or she got it from" school, which gets its own credibility from excavating the credibility of the sources of the imagination, not the nature of the imagination.

The work that I do frequently falls, in the minds of most people, into that realm of fiction called fantastic, or mythic, or magical, or unbelievable. I'm not comfortable with these labels. I consider that my single gravest responsibility (in spite of that magic) is not to lie. When I hear someone say, "Truth is stranger than fiction," I think that old chestnut is truer than we know, because it doesn't say that truth is truer than fiction; just that it's stranger, meaning that it's odd. It may be excessive, it may be more interesting, but the important thing is that it's random—and fiction is not random.

Therefore the crucial distinction for me is not the difference between fact and fiction, but the distinction between fact and truth. Because facts can exist without human intelligence, but truth cannot. So if I'm looking to find and expose a truth about the interior life of people who didn't write it (which doesn't mean that they didn't have it); if I'm trying to fill in the blanks that the slave narratives left—to part the veil that was so frequently drawn, to implement the stories that I heard—then the approach that's most productive and most trustworthy for me is the recollection that moves from the image to the text. Not from the text to the image.

Simone de Beauvoir, in *A Very Easy Death*, says, "I don't know why I was so shocked by my mother's death." When she heard her mother's name being called at the funeral by the priest, she says, "Emotion seized me by the throat. . . . 'Françoise de Beauvoir': the words brought her to life; they summed up her history, from birth to marriage to widowhood to the grave. Françoise de Beauvoir—that retiring woman, so rarely named, became an *important* person." The book becomes an exploration both into her own grief and into the images in which the grief lay buried.

20   Unlike Mme. de Beauvoir, Frederick Douglass asks the reader's patience for spending about half a page on the death of his grandmother—easily the most profound loss he had suffered—and he apologizes by saying, in effect, "It really was very important to me. I hope you aren't bored by my indulgence." He makes no attempt to explore that death: its images or its meaning. His narrative is as close to factual as he can make it, which leaves no room for subjective speculation. James Baldwin, on the other hand, in *Notes of a Native Son*, says, in recording his father's life and his own relationship to his father, "All of my father's Biblical texts and songs, which I had decided were meaningless, were ranged before me at his death like empty bottles, waiting to hold the meaning which life would give them for me." And then his text fills those bottles. Like Simone de Beauvoir, he moves from the event to the image that it left. My route is the reverse: the image comes first and tells me what the "memory" is about.

I can't tell you how I felt when my father died. But I was able to write *Song of Solomon* and imagine, not him, and not his specific interior life, but the world that he inhabited and the private or interior life of the people in it. And I can't tell you how I felt reading to my grandmother while she was turning over and over in her bed (because she was dying, and she was not comfortable), but I could try to reconstruct the world that she lived in. And I have suspected, more often than not, that I *know* more than she did, that I *know* more than my grandfather and my great-grandmother did, but I also know that I'm no wiser than they were. And whenever I have tried earnestly to diminish their vision and prove to myself that I know more, and when I have tried to speculate on their interior life and match it up with my own, I have been overwhelmed every time by the richness of theirs compared to my own. Like Frederick Douglass talking about his grandmother, and James Baldwin talking about his father, and Simone de Beauvoir talking about her mother, these people are my access to me; they are my entrance into my own interior life. Which is why the images that float around them—the remains, so to speak, at the archeological site—surface first, and they surface so vividly and so compellingly that I acknowledge them as my route to a reconstruction of a world, to an exploration of an interior life that was not written and to the revelation of a kind of truth.

So the nature of my research begins with something as ineffable and as flexible as a dimly recalled figure, the corner of a room, a voice. I began to write my second book, which was called *Sula*, because of my preoccupation with a picture of a woman and the way in which I heard her name pronounced. Her name was Hannah, and I think she was a friend of my mother's. I don't remember seeing her very much, but what I do remember is the color around her—a kind of violet, a suffusion of something violet—and her eyes, which appeared to be half closed. But what I remember most is how the women said her name: how they said "Hannah Peace" and smiled to themselves, and there was some secret about her that they knew, which they didn't talk about, at least not in my hearing, but it seemed *loaded* in the way in which they said her name. And I suspected that she was a little bit of an outlaw but that they approved in some way.

And then, thinking about their relationship to her and the way in which they talked about her, the way in which they articulated her name, made me think about friendship between women. What is it that they forgive each other for? And what it is that is unforgivable in the world of women. I don't want to know any more about Miss Hannah Peace, and I'm not going to ask my mother who she really was and what did she do and what were you laughing about and why were you smiling? Because my experience when I do this with my mother is so crushing: she will give you *the* most pedestrian information you ever heard, and I would like to keep all of my remains and my images intact in their mystery when I begin. Later I will get to the facts. That way I can explore two worlds—the actual and the possible.

What I want to do this evening is to track an image from picture to meaning to text—a journey which appears in the novel that I'm writing now, which is called *Beloved*.

25   I'm trying to write a particular kind of scene, and I see corn on the cob. To "see" corn on the cob doesn't mean that it suddenly hovers; it only means that it keeps coming back. And in trying to figure out "What is all this corn doing?" I discover what it *is* doing.

I see the house where I grew up in Lorain, Ohio. My parents had a garden some distance away from our house, and they didn't welcome me and my sister there, when we were young, because we were not able to distinguish between the things that they wanted to grow and the things that they didn't, so we were not able to hoe, or weed, until much later.

I see them walking, together, away from me. I'm looking at their backs and what they're carrying in their arms: their tools, and maybe a peck basket. Sometimes when they walk away from me they hold hands, and they go to this other place in the garden. They have to cross some railroad tracks to get there.

I also am aware that my mother and father sleep at odd hours because my father works many jobs and works at night. And these naps are times of pleasure for me and my sister because nobody's giving us chores, or telling us what to do, or nagging us in any way. In addition to which, there is some feeling of pleasure in them that I'm only vaguely aware of. They're very rested when they take these naps.

And later on in the summer we have an opportunity to eat corn, which is the one plant that I can distinguish from the others, and which is the harvest that I like the best; the others are the food that no child likes—the collards, the okra, the strong, violent vegetables that I would give a great deal for now. But I do like the corn because it's sweet, and because we all sit down to eat it, and it's finger food, and it's hot, and it's even good cold, and there are neighbors in, and there are uncles in, and it's easy, and it's nice.

30   The picture of the corn and the nimbus of emotion surrounding it became a powerful one in the manuscript I'm now completing.

Authors arrive at text and subtext in thousands of ways, learning each time they begin anew how to recognize a valuable idea and how to render the texture that accompanies, reveals or displays it to its best advantage. The process by which this is accomplished is endlessly fascinating to me. I have always thought that as an editor for twenty years I understood writers better than their most careful critics, because in examining the manuscript in each of its subsequent stages I knew the author's process, how his or her mind worked, what was effortless, what took time, where the "solution" to a problem came from. The end result—the book—was all that the critic had to go on.

Still, for me, that was the least important aspect of the work. Because, no matter how "fictional" the account of these writers, or how much it was a product of invention, the act of imagination is bound up with memory. You know, they straightened out the Mississippi River in places, to make room for houses and livable acreage. Occasionally the river floods these places. "Floods" is the word they use, but in fact it is not flooding; it is remembering. Remembering where it used to be. All water has a perfect memory and is forever trying to get back to where it was. Writers are like that: remembering where we were, what valley we ran through, what the banks were like, the light that was there and the route back to our original place. It is emotional memory—what the nerves and the skin remember as well as how it appeared. And a rush of imagination is our "flooding."

Along with personal recollection, the matrix of the work I do is the wish to extend, fill in and complement slave autobiographical narratives. But only the matrix. What comes of all that is dictated by other concerns, not least among them the novel's own integrity. Still, like water, I remember where I was before I was "straightened out."

Critical Reading Questions

1. In what ways does Toni Morrison believe that her own writing context is based on the writing situations described in the slave narratives?

2. In describing the slave narratives, Morrison writes, "As determined as these black writers were to persuade the reader of the evil of slavery, they also complimented him by assuming his nobility of heart and his high-mindedness." Evaluate the merits of this approach.

3. In Morrison's essay Thomas Jefferson is quoted as saying, "Never yet could I find that a black had uttered a thought above the level of plain narration, never see even an elementary trait of painting or sculpture." Explain the significance of the slaves' demonstrating that they could read, write, and think at high levels.

4. According to Morrison, the slave narratives do not reveal the interior lives of the authors, their deepest thoughts and most passionate emotions. In contrast, Morrison believes that her "job," as a writer who is black and a woman, is to "rip that veil drawn over 'proceedings too terrible to relate.'" Additionally, she believes that "The exercise is also

critical for any person who is black, or who belongs to any marginalized category." Explain why you agree or disagree with this point of view.

5. Morrison concludes by saying, "Along with personal recollection, the matrix of the work I do is the wish to extend, fill in and complement slave autobiographical narratives." She does this by blending her own experiences with an imaginative leap into the lives of the characters she is creating. Using a personal experience of your own, describe that event as it might have been experienced by someone very different from yourself, perhaps someone in a different place and time.

WRITING THOUGHTFULLY, THINKING CREATIVELY, THINKING CRITICALLY

The next part of the Thinking-Writing Model, Figure 1.2, indicates the reciprocal relationships among writing thoughtfully, thinking creatively, and thinking critically. When you first decide to write something, you need to come up with some initial ideas to write about. Your ability to *think creatively* makes producing such ideas possible. When you think creatively, you discover ideas—and connections among ideas—that are illuminating, useful, often exciting, sometimes original, and usually worth developing. We can define **thinking creatively** as discovering and developing ideas that are unusual and worthy of further elaboration.

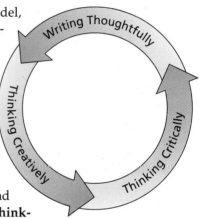

Figure 1.2 Core Abilities

Simultaneously (or *almost* simultaneously), these beginning ideas find form in language expressed in writing. Yet the process of writing thoughtfully elaborates and shapes the ideas that you are trying to express, especially if you are to bring your critical thinking abilities to bear on this evolving process. This extraordinarily complex process typically takes place in a very natural fashion, as creative thinking and critical thinking work together to produce thoughtful writing, which in turn gives form to our ideas and communicates them to others.

Effective writers not only use each of these processes but also are able to integrate them. For example, it is impossible to write thoughtfully without creating ideas that reflect your vision of the world or without using your critical thinking abilities to evaluate the accuracy and intelligibility of your writing. Unfortunately, these essential abilities are not always taught explicitly. Too often, writing is emphasized as a way of putting words together in conventional forms, not as a dynamic means of personal expression that liberates us to articulate our creative perspectives—tempered by critical evaluation.

The Writing Process

THE RECURSIVE NATURE OF THE WRITING PROCESS

Despite the many different writing forms and contexts, the basic elements of the writing process remain constant:

- Generating ideas
- Defining a focus (main idea or *thesis*)
- Organizing ideas into various thinking patterns
- Drafting
- Revising, editing, and proofreading
- Collaborating, which can weave through all these activities

These elements of the writing process occur within the writing situation as a result of creative and critical thinking, and they are depicted in the third part of the Thinking-Writing Model (Figure 1.3). For most writers, these activities rarely occur in a neat, orderly sequence. Instead, writers move in different ways, from generating ideas to drafting to more generating to organizing to revising to generating to editing—around and around—as they develop ideas and clarify them.

You have probably discovered that the process of writing does not merely express your thinking; it also stimulates your thoughts, bringing to the surface new ideas and ways to explore them. So although you may begin a writing project by generating some ideas, you may find yourself returning to generate more ideas later on as you work to organize and draft your thoughts, developing new or refined concepts to write about. And as you gain more experience with collaboration, you may find yourself turning to others more frequently to benefit from their ideas and perspectives. Writers always need readers.

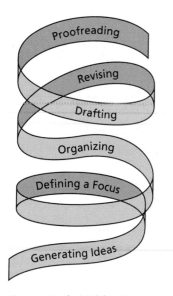

Figure 1.3 The Writing Process

GENERATING IDEAS

Most writing efforts begin with identifying something to write about. Since ideas are not created in isolation but are almost always related to a particular subject, you expand ideas by exploring that subject. Some writing projects have very specific requirements; others may be more open-ended. In most cases, however, you will be expected to come up with your own ideas. Even when you are responding to an assigned topic or a reading selection, you are typically expected to offer an original insight or viewpoint. At this stage of generating ideas, a number of strategies are useful, such as brainstorming, creating mind maps, freewriting, and asking key questions to stimulate your creative thinking.

DEFINING A FOCUS

After generating a number of possible ideas to write about, academic writers need to define a focus. Academic writing is *expected* to have a focus; classmates, professors, and others interested in your subject expect more than a list of facts. Once selected, your main idea—known as a **thesis**—will organize and direct your thinking. Your thesis will also guide your exploration of the subject and suggest new ideas. Of course, a variety of main ideas can develop out of any particular situation, and your initial working thesis will probably need redefining as you draft your paper.

Sometimes you will need to do some drafting and organizing before you are ready to define your focus. And sometimes you will need to refocus your thesis as you do further drafting. Deciding on the right thesis is highly important.

ORGANIZING IDEAS

Once you have a tentative thesis, you can start to plan the organization of your paper. To begin, ask yourself, "What are my main points, and how should they be presented to my audience?" You can use a variety of thinking patterns as you organize your writing, such as reporting chronologically, comparing and contrasting, or dividing and classifying. Your choice of thinking pattern will depend on the subject you are exploring, your purpose, and your audience.

It usually helps to have a tentative organization to guide your drafting, but often your organization changes as you draft and revise. This is a natural and productive part of most people's writing processes.

DRAFTING

Drafting begins when you actually put words on paper. *What* you write reflects your previous work from the initial stages of the writing process: generating ideas, defining a focus, and thinking about an organizational structure. Your writing expresses how far your thinking on the subject has progressed to that point. It is unlikely that your writing will emerge in finished form. In fact, your initial draft may undergo substantial revision until it finally represents your mind's best work. So don't get obsessed with trying to craft the perfect sentence, fashion the ideal metaphor, or secure the optimal word. You'll have time to do that later on. The most important goal in drafting is to *do it*. Get those vague and evolving ideas onto paper, where they can be examined, reflected upon, and refined. If you sit there in front of the blank screen waiting for polished, incisive prose to emerge from your fingertips, you may never get started! The purpose of a draft is to begin the writing process in earnest, with the assumption that you will be returning to rework, refashion, and revise these initial efforts.

Often you will find it useful to draft in sections, according to the plan you established. But be prepared to let the writing process take you to new places that you didn't anticipate. The process of writing is a catalyst for your thinking process, creating new ideas and leading in unexpected directions. Trusting your writing/thinking process leads to creative breakthroughs that will enrich your original plan.

Naturally, what you are drafting—a summary, a news story, an essay—influences the way you express and organize your thinking. Much of your academic writing will be in the form of essays in which you are expected to take a position, analyze a concept, or interpret a subject. The structure normally used to organize ideas in an essay typically reflects the basic questions raised when you discuss ideas with others. As you draft, keep in mind the questions posed by Mina Shaughnessey in her book *Errors and Expectations:*

What is your point? (stating the main idea)

I don't quite get your meaning. (explaining the main idea)

Prove it to me. (providing examples, evidence, and arguments to support the main idea)

So what? (drawing a conclusion)

REVISING, EDITING, AND PROOFREADING

Because thinking and writing are interactive processes, you are continually revising your thinking and writing as you work on almost any paper. An early draft is usually just a starting point. Some writers need to produce multiple drafts with—they hope—increasing levels of effectiveness; other writers can get things on paper in relatively good shape quickly. Whatever your work style, though, once you have expressed your thinking in language, you must be able to go back and "re-see" (the origin of the word *revise*) your drafts as clearly as possible.

Most writers have a hard time looking objectively at their own writing. They know what they mean; they sometimes like certain words, sentences, or clever ideas and don't want to change them. But effective writers have acquired the ability to be critical readers of their own work and to accept the need for making major changes in their drafts.

One way to approach revising is to allow time for drafts to sit; you get away from them in order to see them with fresh eyes. Another way is to have other readers respond to your drafts; be prepared to heed their advice when appropriate.

Revising begins with a rereading of the whole draft and with attention to big questions about it. Does it fulfill its purpose, deal with its subject, address its audience? Does the thesis need to be reformulated? Are ideas supported with sound evidence and explained clearly?

Now might be a good time to create an outline or map of the draft to identify the main ideas and express their relationships. This, in turn, may suggest ways to clarify your thinking by rearranging different parts, developing certain points further, or deleting whatever is repetitious or irrelevant to the paper's main ideas. These activities are at the heart of revision. They often result in a lot of rewriting or perhaps a complete reworking of the draft. Fortunately, word processors make revision easier.

Next, you need to look at smaller components: paragraph division, topic sentences, sentence variety, connections and transitions. Some writers call this *editing*. Then you need to check spelling and punctuation. Some writers call this *proofreading*. And sometimes while you are editing or proofreading, you will see content and organization problems that require more revision!

The model pertains most fully to writing done with enough time for revision. Sometimes you have to write quickly, with little or no time to rethink and rewrite. College examinations often put you in this writing situation. Then the model has to function in a fast-forward mode. Purpose, subject, and audience are usually very clear (pass the test; discuss the subject well; show your instructor what you know). Generating ideas, staying with the focus defined by the question, and organizing ideas are the components most useful to writing that must be done quickly. If you can understand, practice, and improve these abilities in contexts in which you have time to draft and revise, you should be able to cope better with writing that must be done quickly.

The following reading, "Revision—Seeing Again," a chapter from Roger Garrison's book *How A Writer Works*, allows you the unique opportunity to watch a writer going through the stages of drafting and revising during the writing process. The passage concludes with a number of practical suggestions which should help immediately, though the real value of reading the piece is your becoming familiar with the dynamic and creative nature of the writing process.

FROM

Revision—Seeing Again
BY ROGER GARRISON

Writing is learned by writing, and in no other way. No instructor can "teach" you how to write, though he or she can help you learn by being a responsive reader and helpful editor.

Rewriting is the key to good writing. Rewriting you must do alone, since it has to come out of your own head. Revision is your chief writing instructor; you learn to write *as* you write and *re*write.

After prewriting, you do a rough draft—your first try at putting your information together. One writer calls this a "discovery draft," and the term is exactly right. The draft discovers whether you are saying what you mean to say.

Your task is to shape and mold your draft to come as close to your intentions as possible. It would be easy to give you general advice about rewriting. But, as Oliver Wendell Holmes once remarked, "No generalization is worth a damn, including this one." There aren't any simple steps or rules. What you have written belongs to you. Any changes or developments also come from you. No book can read your mind or sense your feelings.

5   If you and I could sit side by side, with your draft between us, I could give you reader-responses and reader-questions: Does your second point follow your first? Does this sentence mean what you want it to? What does this phrase mean? Is this an accurate word, or can you find a more specific one? But for now, you have only this book in front of you.

What I *can* do, however, is reverse the process, and let you into *my* mind as I revise a piece of my own writing. I will share with you exactly my thinking, as nearly as I can reproduce it, as I rewrote a single paragraph. Here is the situation:

I write almost every day, sometimes a line or two, sometimes more. There is always an article or a book in the works. I keep a journal, a workbook where I jot down ideas, bits of experience, thoughts, discussion with myself. The workbook is my personal cultch pile. ("Cultch" is Yankee for discarded odds and ends that may be useful someday: You never know.)

Late in September recently, I visited a friend who lives in New Hampshire's White Mountains. (My own roots, both family and spiritual, are in this spare, hard country.) Her home has been in her family for seven generations. She gave me a room where I could write, and where, looking out a window, I could see the mountains in the distance. Occasionally I took a break from my work and simply stared out the window. Inside myself I felt—I did not think in any coherent way—how deeply *home* New Hampshire was, how I responded to autumn, my favorite season, and how, simply, I *belonged* here. In my journal I wrote:

> Short break from the drudgery. Out the window, hills are hazy-blue in the sunny afternoon. Big bee, striped yellow and black, fat with nectar from the flowers, bats against the screen. Buzzzzz, stop. Buzzzz, stop. A lifetime of these Septembers, these beloved autumns; then winters and brief springs and summers; and my God I get a lump in my throat because I can feel my way back to my great, great-grandfather who saw these brooding hills exactly as I see them now, who smelled the cut hay, who heard another bee at the window.

I chose this entry because, as I write this now, I am in the same New Hampshire house on a September day. The journal paragraph is my way of prewriting. I want you, as a reader, to share my feeling of the season, of my love for a New

England fall. As I revise the entry, I will make notes to myself and to you. I want you to come along with me in the process.

10   As it is with any writer, there are two characters in my head: the Writer (me) and a Reader/Editor (also me), who represents anyone who reads what I write. These two talk to each other.

Reader's question*	Writer's response
1. What are you going to tell me? What's your point?	1. Opening statement; lead.
2. I'm not sure what you mean.	2. Brief qualification of opening, or perhaps an example.
3. Prove it to me. Show me.	3. Information, examples, details.
4. So what?	4. Summary, conclusion, inclusive example.

If you are a beginning writer, you will find it hard, at first, even to recognize this Reader, to say nothing of being able to listen to him. But if you cultivate internal listening, your Reader/Editor will begin to show himself as a creative nag, who pokes you with questions like, "So what?" or "What does that mean?" Think of him as a kind of archeologist who scrapes and digs beneath the surface of your mind to throw up memories and associations, unearthing what you thought you had forgotten. Then the Editor part of him forces you to see what you *have* written, not what you think you have written. Once you get to know him, this Reader/Editor person can be trusted.

You will notice, as you follow the revisions, that the journal entry changes— evolves—into something else. The original entry stressed my sense of continuity with the past. But as I started a draft, I realized that I wanted first to express my feelings about the unfolding of autumn from mid-September to November. If I were to develop the idea of successive generations, it would come in later paragraphs. *Let this changing happen;* it is almost invariably what rewriting does.

Now, back to my journal paragraph.

READER: What's your point here?

WRITER: I want some reader in New Mexico or Nebraska or Oregon, who has never been east—any reader, for that matter—to understand my feelings about a New England autumn.

READER: Your entry doesn't show me much. A bee at the screen and great-grandfathers. Hazy mountains and sentimental stuff about a lump in the throat—cliché, you know.

WRITER: I don't want more than a paragraph. Any more might get sticky.

READER: So put me in place. Where are you and what are you doing when you have these feelings?

---

*Adapted from Mina Shaughnessey, *Errors and Expectations* (Oxford University Press, 1977).

WRITER: I'm at a friend's house in New Hampshire in September. I'm writing. When I look out the window, I can see the mountains.

READER: Show me. Start there, anyway.

WRITER: I want a lead to give you a sense of place and a feeling of time—continuity.

Draft lead. I am writing, and my papers are spread out on a 150-year-old trestle table. The rubbed wood is satiny to the touch. When I look up, I see the mountains, blue-hazy in the distance. They are old mountains, not like the raw upthrust western Rockies.

READER: You're getting off the point. I don't want to see the Rockies. Stick to New Hampshire.

WRITER: OK, you're right. I'll come back to it with more detail. I want you to see the color, too.

NOTES: *Maples and sumac: red-orange; birch and beech, yellow; popple, gold; oak, leather-brown; hackmatack, lighter green; pines shedding showers of brown needles.*

READER: Color?

WRITER: A regional expression: the changing color of the leaves: spectacular. For a brief time, this is one of the most beautiful spots on earth.

READER: Give me more. I've got five senses after all.

NOTES: *Ground hard as iron. Heavy frost on brown grass and shrubs. Grass crackles under foot. Sight and smell of the root cellar under the house—all that harvest down there.*

WRITER: The changes through fall. November, first sleet, snow.

READER: What harvest?

WRITER: Wait. I'm beginning to feel a sequence for this thing. I want to move from September to November. I'm going to try another draft, which usually dredges up useful stuff: details, words, phrases often find themselves.

NOTES: *Forget bee at window. Forget great-great-grandfather. See, touch, smell, hear.*

Second Draft

As I write this, my papers are spread out on a ten-foot trestle table made of two joined pine boards, each 20 inches wide and 3 inches thick. It's a 150-year-old antique, in constant use all that time. The wood feels satiny under my hand. As I look out the window, I can see ranges of mountains receding in the hazy distance. Already, some trees have turned color: red-orange maples, blazing sumac, golden birch. Nowhere do I feel the procession of seasons more than here. Soon, the ground will freeze hard as iron, and the November snows will come down the valleys. In the root cellar of the old house will be the fruits of the harvest.

READER: Your organization is getting into shape. But I want more details.

WRITER: Yes, it's thin. I'll do another draft. I'm beginning to feel the sentences.

NOTES: *List some stuff in the root cellar.*

Ending?

Comment In the next draft, I have underlined added or changed material. The writing is beginning to flow, and sentences start to take on rhythms. There is a slight overlap into the editing stage. None of this is deliberate—yet. It is occurring because *I am writing my way into it*. I now know what I want to say: the movement from late summer, through fall, to winter's beginning. Now I have to find out how I can best say this. The third draft is still "discovering."

Third Draft

As I write, my papers are spread out on an <u>antique</u> trestle table, made of two joined boards, each 20 inches wide and 3 inches thick. <u>Around me are old sideboards, chairs, tables, bookcases, all handmade, sturdy, priceless</u>, with only the satiny shine that <u>rubbed pine can have</u>. Across <u>the long valley, I can see the Presidential and Franconia ranges</u>, and more in the hazy distance. Already <u>some maples and sumac are flaring red-orange, signs of the color when autumn begins to draw its paintbrush across the hills. From mid-September to late October, there is no more beautiful spot on earth. Then, for a brief October period, the color fades and there will be Indian summer, warm and russet-gold, a brief benison</u>. Then the November snows will come down the valleys, <u>and my breath will be white in the morning</u>, and the ground will turn to iron. In the root cellar of the old house will be <u>the smell of apples, of cider in stone jugs, of onions, squash, seed corn hung from the rafters; and potatoes in bins and jars of canned vegetables and all the fall bounty</u>.

READER: Now you're beginning to tell me something. But it's not right yet. The ending, for instance: it's weak.

NOTES: *Earthy smell of potatoes. Dank cellar. Put specific vegetables in jars.*

Comment In the third draft, you see not only added information, you may also have noticed that I have begun to cut and change. "Procession of the seasons" is out, for instance. "Indian summer" is added. Such changes are a central part of the process as you dig more and more into your memory and your store of sense impressions. All of us have these resources. The act of writing allows us to get at them.

In the fourth draft, I've got hold of what I want to say. My Reader turns Editor, and here is where the changes become calculated. The comments to the left of the draft reflect what that internal Editor thought as I began to polish the paragraph.

Fourth Draft

Some last cut-or-add. Editing: sentence cadences; word choices; consistent tense; check grammar.

As I write, my papers are spread ~~out~~

on an antique table made of two joined

"Plank" more accurate than board.

planks
~~boards,~~ each 20 inches wide and 3

Around
inches thick. ~~Surrounding~~ me are old

"Chairs"—one item too much.

sideboards, ~~chairs,~~ tables, bookcases,

"Priceless"—not needed.

handmade, sturdy, ~~priceless,~~ with the

"Patina" is right word: suggests both look and feel.

patina
~~satiny shine~~ that only rubbed pine can

Place names have after-echoes: they resonate, especially in a sequence. Remember Benet's poem about American names. And the line in Thoreau's little poem, "twine, wine, hides, and China teas."

have. Across the valley are the Presidential and Franconia ranges—Mt. Washington, Jefferson, Kinsman, the Nubbles, the Three Graces, and more

Don't over-do adjectives. Confused. Horizon didn't come from Ice Age. Glaciers rubbed down—scoured—the land.

in the ~~blue-~~hazy distance—the
scoured down hills
~~rounded horizon~~ from the last Ice Age.

Already ~~some~~ maples and sumac ~~are~~

Harbinger—old usage: herald of royal progress. *Yes.*

flare   *harbingers*
~~flaring~~ red-orange, ~~forerunner~~ of the

"color" when autumn draws its paint-

Save words.

land   *In*
brush across the ~~hills.~~ ~~For a brief~~ late

Rhythm of adjectives.

October ~~period~~, the color fades, and there is Indian summer, hazed, hushed, [warm,] russet-gold, a brief

"Benison"—wrong tone, archaic.

blessing *sleet*
~~benison.~~ Then the November ~~snows~~

"Come down"—weak. Not snow—"sleet." (Snow is quiet.) "Hissing"—exactly right sound. "Intervales"—New England term for small valleys. "Smoke"—active verb. "Turn to iron"—cliché. Earthy? Winy? Tart?

comes hissing down the intervales,
~~come down the valleys,~~ and my breath
smokes
~~will be white~~ in the morning, and the
muddy ruts in the meadow road *stone*
~~ground~~ will turn to ~~iron~~. In the dank

root cellar of the old house will be the

tart smell of apples, the ~~earthy~~ smell

of potatoes in bins. In stone jugs lining

Succession of nouns to suggest bounty.

the walls, cider turns hard. Onions,

squash, seed corn hang from the

rafters; and long shelves of canned

tomatoes, beets, green beans, zucchini

soup, pickles, nut squash, peaches, are

the fall bounty to stretch winter into

Last sentence, too much: Sentimental. Cut.

May. ~~I have a love affair with New England, and autumn is its climax.~~

Fifth Draft

No draft is "final," but this is the last one I am going to do. My purpose has been to take you through a revision process as clearly as I could, so that you could see what I have meant by "discovery" and "development."

As I write, my papers are spread on an antique table made of two planks, each 20 inches wide and 3 inches thick. Around me are old sideboards, tables, bookcases, handmade, sturdy, with the satin patina that only rubbed pine can have. Across the valley are the Presidential and Franconia ranges—Mt. Washington, Jefferson, Lafayette, Kinsman, the

Nubbles, the Three Graces in the hazy distance—the rounded hills scoured down by the last Ice Age. Already, maples and sumac flare red-orange, harbingers of the color when autumn draws its paintbrush across the land. In late October, the color fades, and there is Indian summer, warm, hazed, hushed, russet-gold, a brief blessing. Soon the November sleet comes hissing down the intervales, my breath smokes in the morning, and the muddy ruts in the meadow road turn to stone. In the dank root cellar of the old house is the tart smell of apples, the earthy smell of potatoes in bins. In stone jugs lining the walls, cider turns hard. Onions, squash, seed corn, hang from the rafters; and long shelves of canned tomatoes, beets, green beans, zucchini soup, pickles, nut squash, peaches, are fall bounty to stretch the winter into May.

Revision-and-editing is hard work, but it is rewarding. You see and feel meaning develop under your pen or typewriter. Even for a beginning writer, there can be mounting excitement. As I rewrote this paragraph, I literally *felt* my way back into the magic of autumn. If you go back to the original journal entry, and then through the drafts, you will see the paragraph moving toward the feeling I wanted to communicate. In each draft, I added *substance*: facts, particulars, details. My internal Reader nagged me for more information, packed in. It is for finding these details that rewriting is most valuable. (If you have too many, you can always cut some out.)

There are other changes to make, not so much revision as editing: finding strong verbs (verbs are the muscle of sentences): "sleet *comes hissing* down the intervales" or "my breath *smokes*" in the morning. And using adjectives and nouns or phrases that evoke sights, sounds, and smells.

Critical Reading Questions

1. "Writing is learned by writing, and in no other way." What do you think Roger Garrison means by this? If the statement is true, what's the point of taking courses in writing or using books on writing? Can you describe a skill you learned for which you had to actually *perform* the skill in order to learn it? What role did "teachers" (knowledgeable people) and books play in your learning the skill?

2. Many people treat their first draft of writing—assignments, letters, emails, papers—as their last draft, one requiring no further revision. Do you think this approach makes sense? Garrison states, "Rewriting is the key to good writing." What reasons support the idea that you should usually try to revise your writing if time permits?

3. Compare the first draft of Garrison's paragraph with the final draft. In what ways do they differ? What additional meaning—ideas and feelings—does the final version communicate that the first doesn't?

4. Garrison uses a journal to jot down ideas, bits of experience, thoughts, and reflections. Have you ever kept a journal? Have you ever used its contents as a resource for writing? If not, this may be a good time to start so that you can capture valuable ideas and experiences that otherwise will likely be lost.

5. When you revise your writing, are you aware of a conversation between two parts of yourself, the Writer and the Reader/Editor? If so, what is this conversation like? What questions does the Reader/Editor tend to ask? If this interaction is not familiar, make a special effort to create these two voices the next time you revise your writing.

6. Revise the writing you did for the Thinking-Writing Activity on page 6, "Analyzing a Writing Experience." Keep in mind Garrison's suggestions, including

   • Create a conversation between the Writer and the Reader/Editor.

   • Add details that communicate your meaning as specifically as possible.

   • Work to discover the essential feelings and ideas that you are trying to express. Pay particular attention to word selection, trying to find precisely the right words to communicate your message.

   • Craft your sentences so that they flow together, embodying a rhythm and working in concert to express a coherent meaning.

COLLABORATING

When you work with other people in the writing process, you participate in collaboration. You can collaborate with others at every stage of the writing process. People can help one another generate ideas, identify a main idea to pursue, or suggest possible approaches and ways of organizing. Some entire pieces of writing, especially in business, are produced collaboratively by a team of writers. Since collaborating can occur in all writing process activities, the line representing collaboration circles around them in the model in Figure 1.3.

We often discover new perspectives when others review drafts of our writing. This is the moment when writers get a sense of how effective their efforts at communication are. No matter how clearly you try to keep your audience in mind as you write, you may not succeed at first. There is no substitute for having your audience (or people like your intended audience) let you know what you have and have not communicated. With their suggestions, you can improve and refine your writing so that it will better convey what you intended. As a critical thinker and informed writer, you will learn to work with others in developing your thinking and writing, welcoming their advice when you are the sole author and contributing well when you are part of a writing team. Opportunities for collaborating are marked throughout the book with the symbol.

Of course, in writing any collaboration, you also have a responsibility to respond critically to the writing of others. *Critical* is related to *criticize*, which means "to question and evaluate." Unfortunately, the ability to criticize is often used destructively to tear down someone else's thinking. Criticism, however, should be *constructive*—analyzing for the purpose of developing better understanding. To develop your abilities to think critically and write thoughtfully, it is important to offer and receive constructive criticism.

Communicating

At the very center of the model is **communicating,** the process by which we share our thoughts, feelings, and experiences. Communication creates miraculous moments when our minds touch and engage other minds, and such moments occur throughout the activities in the Thinking-Writing Model. Figure 1.4 shows the entire Thinking-Writing Model with all its parts.

The word *communicating* comes from the Latin word *communicare*, which means "to share, to impart, to make common." As members of a social species, we need to share thoughts and feelings with other human beings. Also, we often need to communicate more clearly with ourselves. Writing helps us reach both our external and internal audiences. As technologies allow very rapid communication throughout the world, critical thinking and thoughtful writing are ever more vital to the survival and progress of humanity. So, of course, *communicating* is the center.

LOOKING CRITICALLY @ COMMUNICATING ON THE INTERNET

"Since brevity is the soul of wit, and tediousness the limbs and outward flourishes,—I will be brief." So said William Shakespeare in *Hamlet* (II. ii. 90). He may have predicted the coming of the electronic age with its communication tools— email, instant messaging, chat groups, and message boards. The fewer words used to convey an idea, the faster the audience can receive it. And speed is essential in the modern world.

Email   **Email** (electronic mail) generally consists of short writings that are to the point, without formalities, typed into a memo-like template, and sent to one or many addresses via an Internet service. But you need to consider a few things before taking mouse in hand. What kind of letter are you composing (business or personal)? Who will receive it (a friend, a teacher, a prospective employer)? What kind of service will transmit your email, and what kind does your reader use? Let's talk about why these points are important.

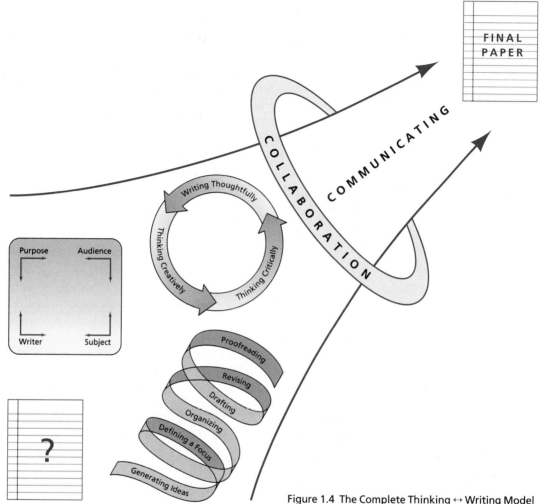

Figure 1.4 The Complete Thinking ↔ Writing Model

Because, for your safety and privacy, some carriers let you adopt a nom de plume (called a *screen name* in cyberspeak), it is important to identify yourself clearly to the recipient—and in formal writings, that means including your full name. Be cautious about what you are trying to say and how you say it: the tone of your thoughts may not be understood if you write casually. Use acronyms and symbols sparingly; not everyone knows the language of cyberspace. Paragraphs peppered with ASCII art (pictures drawn with keyboard letters and symbols) can look like gibberish to the uninitiated.

Why Email Why use email at all? It's fast, it saves time (no more searching for stamps, envelopes, or paper), it lets you communicate at your convenience (at 2 A.M. or 4 P.M.), and it's inexpensive. You can maintain a current, daily correspondence with your friends in Brazil, in Germany, or next door without worrying about losing mail or weighing packages and trekking to a post office. There is usually only a minimal time lag between the moment you press the Send button and the moment the recipient finds out she has mail.

For school and the workplace, email can be a savior. In addition to copying and pasting words into the email template, you can generally attach an electronic file (created in word processing or in a spreadsheet program) as a tagalong. This is a great way to hand in that term paper or take-home test, send your résumé to a prospective employer, or return a completed grant application. Be sure, however, to tell readers which software you used to create the attachment because they will have to use a compatible program to open the file. The days of faxing documents are almost gone; today, employers want your plain text résumé via email. So be sure to lay it out simply, check the spelling and syntax, and include a polite cover letter with your name, address, phone number, and other ways you can be contacted.

Chat Rooms and Bulletin Boards   And what about *chat rooms, forums,* and *conference rooms?* These are ways to communicate "live and in person" while signed onto an Internet service such as America Online. People with common interests (age, hobbies, geographical location) gather together in groups and talk to each other, generally with a host to introduce the "newbies" (newcomers), keep the chatter going, monitor the language, and ensure that behavior stays reasonable. The "room" display resembles a movie script, with a running dialogue shown along with the names of people in the room and a space provided for you to type a brief message and send it to the room for viewing. In some cases, you can also initiate another feature, *Instant Messaging* (IM), which allows you to send a quickly typed message to a friend who is also online. You can then continue conversing with only that person. Think of how much money you both can save on long distance charges.

Another interesting way to communicate on the Internet is to use message or bulletin boards. Much like the old-fashioned cork-board-and-paper displays in school or supermarket lobbies, these boards allow you to post a question or message and put it "out there" for public viewing and response. Such message boards are often organized by topic, so you can find them by searching an online service's index. One of the largest is Usenet, a network of newsgroups or electronic bulletin boards accessible through the Internet. (A newsreader program needs to be installed on your computer system in order to access Usenet.) Selling a car? Arranging a high school reunion? Want to find roommates for a vacation time-share? Having problems with a software application? Moving to a new town and want to find out what community groups are there? Many bulletin boards allow the person responding to your posting to also select a "return by email" feature. So, aside from receiving a personal answer to your question, you can also browse these boards to see if other people have posted questions and/or answers that can help you. These boards can be a great learning and research tool for someone who is just beginning to explore cyberspace. There's nothing like the experience of others to help you with your daily grind!

Netiquette Finally, there is the issue of *netiquette* (a word coined from *Internet* and *etiquette*). As the electronic age expands throughout the world, rules for this new means of communication seem to develop on their own. Typing in all capitals is considered RUDE and means you are SHOUTING. *Scrolling*—typing the same thing over and over while in a chat room, thereby preventing others from "speaking" and making a nuisance of yourself—is also prohibited. Sending unsolicited mass mailings—called *spamming*—or chain letters is also frowned upon. Using foul language or profanity and displaying crass, juvenile behavior can result in your being temporarily cut off from an Internet service or permanently losing online privileges. Of course, doing anything illegal can have the police knocking on your door. The Internet is a public space, and government regulation is only now being developed to deal with those who abuse the freedom of speech. So, the trick is to use common sense when communicating on the Web and to "speak" as you would to someone face to face—with self-control and politeness, exuberance and creativity, and simplicity—so that the message gets across!

Thinking ↔ Writing Activity

Communicating on the Internet

As an assignment before the next class:

- Email at least one other student in the class.
- Participate in at least one chat room.
- Post at least one notice on a message or bulletin board.

If you have trouble performing any of these activities, you can get help in the computer center at your college.

Describe your experiences and reactions to each of these activities and then engage in some critical thinking and write out your responses. How can these forms of electronic communication improve your academic performance? Enrich your social life? Save you time and money? Enhance your communication skills? Now, think critically about some of the potential liabilities or risks involved with this type of communication. Could you spend too much time online—developing a kind of "Net addiction"? How might email contribute to misunderstandings or cause you to express something that you might later regret? What precautions should you take before giving your real name, phone number, or address to someone you have met online? What are some of the dangers of meeting an online friend in person?

Thinking and Writing as a Way of Life

Becoming a critical thinker and thoughtful writer does not simply involve mastering certain skills; it affects the entire way that you view the world and live your life. Your development as a critical thinker and thoughtful writer is revealed in many aspects of your life: how you make decisions, how you relate to others, and how you deal with controversial issues. There is no recipe or bag of tricks for becoming a thoughtful writer. Like other achievements, it requires patience and practice. But you can master certain abilities and strategies that will enable you to express your ideas clearly and coherently, and helping you to master them is the explicit purpose of this book and the course you are taking.

By improving your abilities to think critically and write thoughtfully, you will equip yourself to deal with the challenges that life poses: to solve problems, to establish and achieve goals, and to make sense of complex issues. This foundation will be constructed in the chapters ahead, helping to provide you with a basis for success in college and in your career.

Thinking ↔ Writing Activity

Expressing a Deeper Meaning

This Thinking-Writing Activity gives you an opportunity to apply some of the ideas we have been exploring in this chapter. Situate yourself in a comfortable location, perhaps one that has special meaning to you, much like the one Roger Garrison describes. Your goal is to write a paragraph that effectively communicates *where* you are but also expresses a deeper meaning. What kind of meaning? That's up to you. Use Garrison as a guide: "Inside myself I felt—did not think in any coherent way—how deeply *home* New Hampshire was, how I responded to autumn, my favorite season, and how, simply, I *belonged* here." Reach deep within yourself and discover an analogous feeling to articulate in writing, and then do it. Remember the writing guidelines you have learned in this chapter and in class.

- Consider the audience for whom you are writing and the purpose you would like to accomplish.
- Use Mina Shaughnessey's questions below (and also included in Garrison's selection on page 23) to structure your paragraph:

What is your point?	Stating the main idea
I don't quite get your meaning.	Explaining the main idea
Prove it to me.	Provide examples, evidence, and arguments
So what?	Drawing a conclusion

- After writing your first draft, *rewrite* your paragraph at least two more times to express your original intention—the feelings and ideas that were the original catalyst for the writing—more clearly and effectively. Use Garrison's revision strategies:

  Create a conversation between your Writer and your Reader/Editor.

  Add details that communicate your meaning as specifically as possible.

  Discover the essential feelings and ideas that you are trying to express. Try to find precisely the right words to communicate your message.

  Craft your sentences so that they flow together, embodying a rhythm and working in concert to express a coherent meaning.

- Share the paragraph with your classmates. Ask them what feelings and ideas your writing communicated to them. Respond to their questions and listen carefully to any constructive suggestions for improving your paragraph.

Thinking Critically, Writing Thoughtfully

"The mere process of writing is one of the most powerful tools we have for clarifying our own thinking." —James Van Allen

Critical Thinking Focus: Thinking about thinking

Writing Focus: Reflecting on experiences

Reading Theme: Experiences that have affected beliefs

Writing Project: Recalling the impact of experience on a belief

From Insight to Writing

A thoughtful writer is a person who thinks critically while moving through the process of writing. This writer reflects deeply on the ideas to be expressed and thinks carefully about the language and organization needed to meet the goals of the writing situation. In short, a thoughtful writer is a critical thinker. No collection of writing tips and strategies will ever enable you to write thoughtfully if you're not thinking critically.

But who is a critical thinker, and how do you become one? Traditionally, when people refer to a critical thinker, they mean someone who has developed an understanding of today's complex world, a thoughtful perspective on ideas and issues, the capacity for insight and good judgment, and sophisticated reasoning and language abilities. Critical thinkers are able to

- articulate their ideas clearly and persuasively in writing
- understand and evaluate what they read
- discuss ideas in an informed, productive fashion

These goals of higher education have remained remarkably consistent for several thousand years. In ancient Greece, most advanced students studied rhetoric in order to effect persuasion and studied philosophy in order to achieve wisdom. (The Greek word *philosophos* means "lover of wisdom.") In the modern world, many college students do likewise in order to become informed critical thinkers and capable speakers and writers.

The word *critical* comes from the Greek word *kritikos*, which means "able to perceive, detect, judge, or analyze." By questioning and analyzing, by evaluating and making sense of information, you examine your own thinking and that of others. And by clearly expressing your ideas in writing, you enter a larger community of thinkers and writers who enrich and sharpen your own thoughts through their responses. These thinking and writing activities help us reach the best possible conclusions and decisions.

This chapter explores various qualities that characterize a critical thinker and thoughtful writer, including the following:

- Thinking actively
- Thinking independently
- Viewing a situation from different perspectives
- Supporting diverse perspectives with evidence and reasons

The chapter then presents readings in which authors think critically by reflecting on experiences that have affected their beliefs. Concluding the chapter is a Writing Project which asks you to think critically and write thoughtfully about an experience that had an important impact on a belief that you held or hold. You should keep this Writing Project in mind as you read the chapter and work on Thinking-Writing Activities.

THINKING ACTIVELY AND WRITING

When you think critically, you are *actively* using your intelligence, knowledge, and abilities to deal effectively with life's situations. Similarly, when you write thoughtfully, you act in the following ways:

- You *become involved* in the subject you are writing about, and because the writing process stimulates your thinking, you often discover ideas that you were unaware of until you started writing. Also, if you keep a journal or notebook and make writing part of your daily life, you find yourself more involved in and more reflective about your world.

- You *take initiative* as you develop confidence in your writer's voice, so you express your own perspectives instead of imitating the ideas of others.
- You *follow through* as you revise and edit in order to produce your best effort.
- You *take responsiblity* for your work. That is, you begin assignments promptly and budget enough time to complete them. Though your professors will guide you, and your classmates and writing center tutors will make suggestions about your drafts, you are in charge of your writing, and it is up to you to complete it honestly and well.

When you are thinking actively, you are not just waiting for something to happen. You are engaged in the process of achieving goals, making decisions, analyzing issues, and writing thoughtfully.

INFLUENCES ON YOUR THINKING

As our minds grow and develop, we are exposed to influences that encourage us to think actively. We also, however, have many experiences that encourage us to think passively. For example, some analysts believe that when people, especially children, spend much of their time watching television instead of reading and writing, they are being encouraged to think passively, thus inhibiting their intellectual growth. Listed next are some of the influences we all experience in our lives, along with space for adding others you are aware of. As you read through the list, place an *A* next to items that you believe influence you to think actively and a *P* next to items that make you more passive.

Activities	People
Reading	Family members
Writing	Friends
Watching television	Employers
Surfing the Internet	Advertisers
Drawing and painting	Teachers
Playing video games	Police officers
Playing sports	Religious leaders
Listening to music	Politicians
_____	_____
_____	_____

Of course, certain people or activities can act as either active or passive influences, depending on specific situations and your individual responses. For example, consider employers. If you are performing a routine, repetitive task—such as a summer job in a peanut-butter cracker plant, hand-scooping 2,000 pounds of peanut butter a day—the very nature of the work encourages passive, uncritical thinking (although it might also lead to creative daydreaming!). You are also influenced to think passively if an employer gives you detailed instructions for performing every task that permit no exception or deviation. On the other hand, when an employer gives you general areas of responsibility within which you are expected to make thoughtful and creative decisions, you are being stimulated to think actively and independently.

These contrasting styles of supervision are mirrored in different approaches to raising children. Some parents encourage children to be active thinkers by teaching them to express themselves clearly, make independent decisions, look at different points of view, and choose what they think is right. Other parents influence their children to be passive thinkers by not letting them do things on their own. These parents give detailed instructions to be followed without question and make the important decisions for their children. Such parents, reluctant to give their children significant responsibilities, unintentionally create dependent thinkers who are not well adapted to making independent decisions and assuming responsibility for their own lives.

Similar experiences occur in college. You will probably find that some of your professors will encourage you to think actively by expecting you to apply, analyze, synthesize, and evaluate the information you are acquiring. These professors may assign independent research projects, give essay exams, and require you to write papers in which you must bring your informed perspective to the course material. Other professors may expect you to represent the information from class lectures and the textbooks but not ask for your perspective—an approach that may not encourage active thinking.

Thinking ↔ Writing Activity

Active and Passive Influences

Identify one important influence in your life that stimulates you to think actively; then identify one that encourages you to think passively. Write explanations of how each has affected your thinking. Provide at least two specific examples for each influence.

Developing your ability to think actively rather than passively, to use your mind to take initiative, is crucial for becoming an effective writer. The Thinking-Writing Model (page 31) shows that active, creative, critical thinking is important throughout the writing process, and each chapter in this book deals with some aspect of the thinking-writing connection.

To find topics for your writing, you need to think creatively first to generate a variety of ideas, then to think critically to select the ones that you can use. You can ask yourself what you already know about your topics; then you can think about what you need to find out and how to search for the information. As you decide what to include in your writing, you must evaluate your own ideas and those of others. When you revise drafts, you will be thinking most actively and critically, deciding what to say and how to organize it.

THINKING INDEPENDENTLY

Answer the following questions on the basis of what you believe to be true.

	Yes	No	Not Sure

1. Is the earth flat?
2. Is there a God?
3. Should marijuana be legalized?
4. Should music lyrics and videos be censored?
5. Should men be the breadwinners and women the homemakers?

"I keep my core beliefs written on my palm for easy reference."

Your responses to these questions reveal aspects of the way your mind works, beliefs you have developed that you express in your speaking and writing. How did you arrive at these conclusions? Your views on these and many other issues probably had their beginnings with your family, especially your parents or other adults who raised you. When you were little, you were very dependent on those adults, and you were influenced by the way they saw the world. As you grew up, you learned how to think, feel, and behave in various situations. Very likely your teachers included your brothers and sisters, friends, religious leaders, instructors, books, television, and so on. You absorbed most of what you learned without even being aware of doing so. Many of your ideas about the issues raised in the five questions you just answered probably were shaped by experiences you had while growing up.

As a result of your ongoing experiences, however, your mind—and your thinking—have continued to mature. Instead of simply accepting the views of others, you have gradually developed the ability to examine your earlier thinking and to decide how much of it still makes sense to you and whether you should accept it. Now, when you think through important ideas, use this standard when making a decision: Are there good reasons or evidence that support this thinking? If there are, you can actively decide to adopt the ideas. If not, you can modify or reject them.

Of course, you may not *always* examine your own thinking or the thinking of others so carefully. In fact, people often continue to believe the same ideas they were brought up with, without ever examining and deciding for themselves what to think. Or they may blindly reject the beliefs they were brought up with, without really examining them.

How do you know when you have examined and adopted beliefs yourself instead of simply borrowing them from others? One indication of having thought your beliefs through is being able to explain why you believe in them, telling the reasons that led you to your conclusions.

Still, not all reasons and evidence are equally strong or accurate. For example, in Europe before the fifteenth century, the common belief that the earth was flat was supported by the following reasons and evidence:

People of Authority: Many educational and religious authorities taught that the earth was flat.

Recorded References: The written opinions of scientific experts supported belief in a flat earth.

Observed Evidence: No person had ever circumnavigated the earth.

Personal Experience: From a normal vantage point, the earth *looks* flat.

Thinking ↔ Writing Activity

Evaluating Beliefs

For each of the five beliefs you expressed at the beginning of this section, explain how you arrived at it and state the reasons and evidence that you believe support it.

1. *Example*: Is the earth flat?

   Belief: No, it is round.

   Reasons/Evidence:

   a. People of Authority: My parents and teachers taught me this.

   b. Recorded References: What references support your beliefs? I read about the earth in science textbooks and saw films and videos.

   c. Observed Evidence: I have seen a sequence of photographs taken from outer space that show the earth as a globe.

   d. Personal Experience: When I flew across the country, I could see the horizon line changing.

2. Is there a God?

3. Should marijuana be legalized?

4. Should music lyrics and videos be censored?

5. Should men be the breadwinners and women the homemakers?

To evaluate the strengths and accuracy of the reasons and evidence you identified for holding your beliefs on the five issues, address questions such as the following:

People of Authority: Are the authorities knowledgeable in this area? Are they reliable? Have they ever given inaccurate information? Do other authorities disagree with them?

Recorded References: What references support your belief? What are the credentials of the authors? Do other authors disagree with their opinions? On what reasons and evidence do the authors base their opinions?

Observed Evidence: What is the source and foundation of the evidence? Can the evidence be interpreted differently? Does the evidence support the conclusion?

Personal Experience: What were the circumstances under which the experiences took place? Were distortions or mistakes in perception possible? Have other people had either similar or conflicting experiences? Are there other explanations for your experiences?

As a college writer, you are going to apply these questions to material you encounter while gathering information for papers or reports. The opposite of thinking for yourself is simply accepting the thinking of others without examining or questioning it. Learning to become an independent thinker is a complex, ongoing process.

Viewing a Situation from Different Perspectives

Critical thinkers listen to other views and new ideas and examine them carefully. No one person has *all* the answers! Your beliefs represent just one perspective on whatever problem you want to solve or situation you are trying to understand. In addition to your own particular viewpoint, there may be others, equally important, that you need to consider if you are to develop a more complete understanding of the problem or situation. Learning to think and write at a high level, in fact, requires this.

Perspective-taking is essential to becoming a thoughtful writer. To begin with, exploring topics from a variety of vantage points is often the best way to present a comprehensive analysis of the subject you are writing about. When you are tied to only one perspective, your writing tends to be one-sided and superficial. Second, effective writing depends on always having a clear sense of your readers, the audience for whom you are writing. The ability to remain focused on that audience includes being able to see things from their point of view, to think empathetically within their frame of reference, and to understand their perspective. Finally, in order to produce your most accomplished writing, you need to be open to the informed comments and suggestions of others and flexible enough to use that feedback to refine your writing.

Consider the following situation:

Imagine that you have been employed at a new job for the past six months. Although you enjoy the challenge of your responsibilities and are performing well, you simply cannot complete all your work during office hours. To keep up, you have to work late, take work home, and occasionally even work on weekends. When you explain this to your employer, she says that although she is sorry that the job interferes with your personal life, it has to be done. She suggests that you view this as an investment in your future and try to work more efficiently. She reminds you that many other people would be happy to have your position.

- What is your initial reaction to your employer's response?
- Describe this situation from the employer's standpoint, identifying reasons that might support her views.
- Describe some different approaches that you and your employer might take toward resolving this situation.

For most of the important issues and problems in your life, one viewpoint is simply not adequate to provide a full and satisfactory understanding. To increase and deepen your knowledge, you must seek other perspectives. Sometimes you can accomplish this by using your imagination to visualize other viewpoints. Usually, however, you need to seek actively (and *listen to*) other people's viewpoints. It is often very difficult to see things from points of view other than your own; if you are not careful, you can make the serious mistake of assuming that the way you see things is the way they really are.

In order to identify with perspectives other than your own, then, you also have to work to grasp the reasons for these alternate viewpoints. This approach, which stimulates you to evaluate your beliefs critically, is enhanced by writing. Writing about beliefs encourages people to explain their reasons for holding them and provides a vehicle for sharing their thinking with those who have contrasting points of view.

Thinking ↔ Writing Activity

Two Sides of a Belief

Describe in detail a belief about which you feel very strongly. Then explain the reasons or experiences that led you to this belief. Next, describe a point of view that differs from your belief. Identify some of the reasons why someone would have that point of view. A student example follows.

STUDENT WRITING

Dying with Peace and Dignity
BY OLAVIA HEREDIA

I used to think that we should always try everything in our power to keep a person alive. But now I strongly believe that a person has a right to die in peace and with dignity. I believe this now because of my father's illness and death.

It all started on Christmas Day, December 25, 1987, when my father was admitted to the hospital. The doctors diagnosed his condition as a heart attack. Following this episode, he was readmitted and discharged from several different hospitals. On June 18, 1988, he was hospitalized for what was initially thought to be pneumonia but which turned out to be lung cancer. He began chemotherapy treatments. When complications occurred, he had to be placed on a respirator. At first he couldn't speak or eat. But then they operated on him and placed the tube from the machine in his throat instead of his mouth. He was then able to eat and move his mouth. He underwent radiation therapy when they discovered he had three tumors in his head and that the cancer had spread all over his body. We had to sign a paper which asked us to indicate, if he should stop breathing, whether we would want the hospital to try to revive him or just let him go. We decided to let him go because the doctors couldn't guarantee that he wouldn't become brain-dead. At first they said that there was a forty percent chance that he would get off the machine. But instead of that happening, the percentage went down.

It was hard seeing him like that since I was so close to him. But it was even harder when he didn't want to see me. He said that by seeing me suffer, his suffering was greater. So I had to cut down on seeing him. Everybody that visited him said that he had changed dramatically. They couldn't even recognize him.

The last two days of his life were the worst. I prayed that God would relieve him of his misery. I had come very close to taking him off the machine in order for him not to suffer, but I didn't. Finally he passed away on November 22, 1988, with not the least bit of peace or dignity. The loss was great then and still is, but at least he's not suffering. That's why I believe that when people have terminal diseases with no hope of recovery, they shouldn't place them on machines to prolong their lives of suffering, but instead they should be permitted to die with as much peace and dignity as possible.

Somebody else might believe very strongly that we should try everything in our power to keep people alive. It doesn't matter what kind of illness or disease the people have, what's important is that they are kept alive, especially if they are loved ones. Some people want to keep their loved ones alive with them as long as they can, even if it's by a machine. They also believe it is up to God and medical science to determine whether people should live or die. Sometimes doctors give them hope that their loved ones will recover, and many people wish for a miracle to happen. With these hopes and wishes in mind, they wait and try everything in order to prolong a life, even if the doctors tell them that there is nothing that can be done.

Being open to new ideas and different viewpoints means being *flexible* enough to change or modify one's own ideas in the light of new information or better insight. People do have a tendency to cling to the beliefs they were brought up with and the conclusions they have arrived at. If you are going to continue to grow and develop as a thinker, however, you have to be willing to change or modify your beliefs when evidence suggests that you should.

For example, imagine that you have been brought up with certain views concerning an ethnic group—African American, Euroamerican, Hispanic, Asian, Native American, or any other. As you mature and your experiences increase, you may find that the evidence of your experiences conflicts with those earlier views. As a critical thinker, you will become open to receiving new evidence and flexible enough to change and modify your ideas.

In contrast to open and flexible thinking, *un*critical thinking tends to be one-sided and closed-minded. People who think uncritically are convinced that they alone see things as they really are and that everyone who disagrees with them is wrong. It is very difficult for them to step outside their own viewpoints and look at issues from other people's perspectives. Words often used to describe this type of person include *dogmatic, subjective,* and *egocentric*.

SUPPORTING DIVERSE PERSPECTIVES WITH REASONS AND EVIDENCE

When you are thinking critically, you can offer sound reasons for your views. As a thoughtful writer, you cannot simply take a position on an issue or make a claim; you have to back up your views, reinforce them with information that you feel supports your position. There is an important distinction between *what* you believe and *why* you believe it.

If you want to know all sides of an issue, you have to be able to give supporting reasons and evidence not just for your own views but also for the views of others.

Consider the issue of whether side air bags should be standard equipment for cars. As you try to make sense of this issue, you should attempt to identify not just the reasons for your view but also the reasons for other views. Following are reasons that support each view of this issue.

Issue

Side air bags should be standard equipment.	Side air bags should not be standard equipment.
Supporting Reasons	Supporting Reasons
1. Studies show that side air bags save lives in accidents.	1. Side air bags sometimes injure and even kill children and small adults.
2. Studies show that side air bags reduce injury in accidents.	2. Side air bags should not be forced on citizens of a free country.

Now see if you can identify additional supporting reasons for each position on making air bags standard equipment. For each of the following issues, identify reasons that support each side.

Issues

1. Multiple-choice and true/false exams should be given in college-level courses.	1. Multiple-choice and true/false exams should *not* be given in college-level courses.
2. It is better to live in a society in which the government plays a major role in citizens' lives.	2. It is better to live in a society that minimizes the role of the government in citizens' lives.
3. The best way to deal with crime is to impose long prison sentences.	3. Long prison sentences will not reduce crime.
4. When a couple divorce, the children should choose the parent with whom they wish to live.	4. When a couple divorce, the court should decide all custody issues regarding the children.

As critical thinkers and thoughtful writers we have an obligation to appreciate diverse perspectives on complex issues and develop informed opinions that are supported by compelling reasons. © Hazel Hankin/Stock Boston.

Thinking ↔ Writing Activity

Viewing Different Perspectives

Seeing different perspectives is crucial to getting a more complete understanding of ideas expressed in passages you read. Read the two passages that follow. Then, for each passage, do these four things:

1. Identify the main idea of each passage.
2. List the reasons that support the main idea.
3. Develop another view of the main issue.
4. List the reasons that support the other view.

If we want auto safety but continue to believe in auto profits, sales, styling, and annual obsolescence, there will be no serious accomplishments. The moment we put safety ahead of these other values, something will happen. If we want better municipal hospitals but are unwilling to disturb the level of spending for defense, for highways, or for household appliances, hospital service will not improve. If we want peace but still believe that countries with differing ideologies are threats to one another, we will not get peace. What is confusing is that up to now, while we have wanted such things as conservation, auto safety, hospital care, and peace, we have tried wanting them without changing consciousness; that is, while continuing to accept those underlying values that stand in the way of what we want. The machine can be controlled at the "consumer" level only by people who change their whole value system, their whole world-view, their whole way of life. One cannot favor saving our wildlife and wear a fur coat.

◆

Most wicked deeds are done because the doer proposes some good to himself. The liar lies to gain some end; the swindler and thief want things which, if honestly got, might be good in themselves. Even the murderer may be removing an impediment to normal desires or gaining possession of something his victim keeps from him. None of these people usually does evil for evil's sake. They are selfish or unscrupulous, but their deeds are not gratuitously evil. The killer for sport has no such comprehensible motive. He prefers death to life, darkness to light. He gets nothing except the satisfaction of saying, "Something which wanted to live is dead. There is that much less vitality, consciousness, and, perhaps, joy in the universe. I am the Spirit that Denies." When a human wantonly destroys one of humankind's own works, we call him Vandal. When he wantonly destroys one of the works of God, we call him Sportsman.

Experiences That Affected Beliefs

In the following narratives, four writers reflect on learning experiences that caused them to evaluate and in some cases revise beliefs about themselves, about other people, and about ways to live their lives. Annie Dillard shares the impact of her first scientific observation, N. Scott Momaday describes a loss of childhood innocence, Peter Rondinone writes on the transforming nature of his college experience, and Edwidge Danicat explains how the story of a historical figure continues to shape the beliefs of Haitian women.

As you read the selections, remember to keep in mind the critical reading questions we identified in the first chapter.

- Who is the *writer* and what perspective does he or she bring to the writing selection?

- What is the *subject* of the selection, and how would you evaluate its cogency and reliability?
- Who is the intended *audience,* and what assumptions is the writer making about it?
- What is the *purpose* of the selection, and how is the author trying to achieve it?

Following each selection are questions designed to stimulate and guide your critical thinking and thoughtful writing.

Handed My Own Life

BY ANNIE DILLARD

After I read *The Field Book of Ponds and Streams* several times, I longed for a microscope. Everybody needed a microscope. Detectives used microscopes, both for the FBI and at Scotland Yard. Although usually I had to save my tiny allowance for things I wanted, that year for Christmas my parents gave me a microscope kit.

In a dark basement corner, on a white enamel table, I set up the microscope kit. I supplied a chair, a lamp, a batch of jars, a candle, and a pile of library books. The microscope kit supplied a blunt black three-speed microscope, a booklet, a scalpel, a dropper, an ingenious device for cutting thin segments of fragile tissue, a pile of clean slides and cover slips, and a dandy array of corked test tubes.

One of the test tubes contained "hay infusion." Hay infusion was a wee brown chip of grass blade. You added water to it, and after a week it became a jungle in a drop, full of one-celled animals. This did not work for me. All I saw in the microscope after a week was a wet chip of dried grass, much enlarged.

Another test tube contained "diatomaceous earth." This was, I believed, an actual pinch of the white cliffs of Dover. On my palm it was an airy, friable chalk. The booklet said it was composed of the silicaceous bodies of diatoms—one-celled creatures that lived in, as it were, small glass jewelry boxes with fitted lids. Diatoms, I read, come in a variety of transparent geometrical shapes. Broken and dead and dug out of geological deposits, they made chalk, and a fine abrasive used in silver polish and toothpaste. What I saw in the microscope must have been the fine abrasive—grit enlarged. It was years before I saw a recognizable, whole diatom. The kit's diatomaceous earth was a bust.

5   All that winter I played with the microscope. I prepared slides from things at hand, as the books suggested. I looked at the transparent membrane inside an onion's skin and saw the cells. I looked at a section of cork and saw the cells, and at scrapings from the inside of my cheek, ditto. I looked at my blood and saw not much; I looked at my urine and saw long iridescent crystals, for the drop had dried.

All this was very well, but I wanted to see the wildlife I had read about. I wanted especially to see the famous amoeba, who had eluded me. He was supposed to live in the hay infusion, but I hadn't found him there. He lived outside in warm ponds and streams, too, but I lived in Pittsburgh, and it had been a cold winter.

Finally late that spring I saw an amoeba. The week before, I had gathered puddle water from Frick Park; it had been festering in a jar in the basement. This June night after dinner I figured I had waited long enough. In the basement at my microscope table I spread a scummy drop of Frick Park puddle water on a slide, peeked in, and lo, there was the famous amoeba. He was as blobby and grainy as his picture; I would have known him anywhere.

Before I had watched him at all, I ran upstairs. My parents were still at table, drinking coffee. They, too, could see the famous amoeba. I told them, bursting, that he was all set up, that they should hurry before his water dried. It was the chance of a lifetime.

Father had stretched out his long legs and was tilting back in his chair. Mother sat with her knees crossed, in blue slacks, smoking a Chesterfield. The dessert dishes were still on the table. My sisters were nowhere in evidence. It was a warm evening; the big dining-room windows gave onto blooming rhododendrons.

10 Mother regarded me warmly. She gave me to understand that she was glad I had found what I had been looking for, but that she and Father were happy to sit with their coffee, and would not be coming down.

She did not say, but I understood at once, that they had their pursuits (coffee?) and I had mine. She did not say, but I began to understand then, that you do what you do out of your private passion for the thing itself.

I had essentially been handed my own life. In subsequent years my parents would praise my drawings and poems, and supply me with books, art supplies, and sports equipment, and listen to my troubles and enthusiasms, and supervise my hours, and discuss and inform, but they would not get involved with my detective work, nor hear about my reading, nor inquire about my homework or term papers or exams, nor visit the salamanders I caught, nor listen to me play the piano, nor attend my field hockey games, nor fuss over my insect collection with me, or my poetry collection or stamp collection or rock collection. My days and nights were my own to plan and fill.

When I left the dining room that evening and started down the dark basement stairs, I had a life, I sat with my wonderful amoeba, and there he was, rolling his grains more slowly now, extending an arc of his edge for a foot and drawing himself along by that foot, and absorbing it again and rolling on. I gave him some more pond water.

I had hit pay dirt. For all I knew, there were paramecia, too, in that pond water, or daphniae, or stentors, or any of the many other creatures I had read about and never seen: volvox, the spherical algal colony; euglena with its one red eye; the elusive glassy diatom; hydra, rotifers, water bears, worms. Anything was possible. The sky was the limit.

Critical Reading Questions

1. When Annie Dillard rushed to share her discovery of the amoeba with her parents, they politely declined. What reaction had she expected, and what did this reveal about her beliefs regarding her relationship with her parents?

2. Her parents' lack of interest in this and other passions in her life led her to a conclusion: "I had essentially been handed my own life." Explain why you think she reached this conclusion.

3. Based on your own experience, do you believe that the best way to achieve "your own life" is through your parents' lack of involvement in your life?

4. The author states that "you do what you do out of your private passion for the thing itself." Describe a "private passion" of your own that you pursue not to please others but because of your personal interest and enthusiasm.

The End of My Childhood

BY N. SCOTT MOMADAY

At Jemez I came to the end of my childhood. There were no schools within easy reach. I had to go nearly thirty miles to school at Bernalillo, and one year I lived away in Albuquerque. My mother and father wanted me to have the benefit of a sound preparation for college, and so we read through many high school catalogues. After long deliberation we decided that I should spend my last year of high school at a military academy in Virginia.

The day before I was to leave I went walking across the river to the red mesa, where many times before I had gone to be alone with my thoughts. And I had climbed several times to the top of the mesa and looked among the old ruins there for pottery. This time I chose to climb the north end, perhaps because I had not gone that way before and wanted to see what it was. It was a difficult climb, and when I got to the top I was spent. I lingered among the ruins for more than an hour, I judge, waiting for my strength to return. From there I could see the whole valley below, the fields, the river, and the village. It was all very beautiful, and the sight of it filled me with longing.

I looked for an easier way to come down, and at length I found a broad, smooth runway of rock, a shallow groove winding out like a stream. It appeared to be safe enough, and I started to follow it. There were steps along the way, a stairway, in effect. But the steps became deeper and deeper, and at last I had to drop down the length of my body and more. Still it seemed convenient to follow in the groove of rock. I was more than halfway down when I came upon a deep, funnel-shaped formation in my path. And there I had to make a decision. The slope on either side was extremely steep and forbidding, and yet I thought that I could work my way down on either side. The formation at my feet was something else. It was perhaps ten or twelve feet deep, wide at the top and narrow at the bottom, where there appeared to be a level ledge. If I could get down through the funnel to the ledge, I should be all right; surely the rest of the way down was negotiable. But I realized that there could be no turning back. Once I was down in that rocky chute I could not get up again, for the round wall which nearly encircled the space there was too high and sheer. I elected to go down into it, to try for the ledge directly below. I eased myself down the smooth, nearly vertical wall on my back, pressing my arms and legs outward against the sides. After what seemed a long time I was trapped in the rock. The ledge was no longer there below me; it had been an optical illusion. Now, in this angle of vision, there was nothing but the ground, far, far below, and jagged boulders set there like teeth. I remember that my arms were scraped and bleeding, stretched out against the walls with all the pressure that I could exert. When once I looked down I saw that my legs, also spread out and pressed hard against the walls, were shaking violently. I was in an impossible situation: I could not move in any direction, save downward in a fall, and I could not stay beyond another minute where I was. I believed then that I would die there, and I saw with a terrible clarity the things of the valley below. They were not the less beautiful to me. It seemed to me that I grew suddenly very calm in view of that beloved world. And I remember nothing else of that moment. I passed out of my mind, and the next thing I knew I was sitting down on the ground, very cold in the shadows, and looking up at the rock where I had been within an eyelash of eternity. That was a strange thing in my life, and I think of it as the end of an age. I should never again see the world as I saw it on the other side of that moment, in the bright reflection of time lost. There are such reflections, and for some of them I have the names.

Critical Reading Questions

1. Momaday begins his essay with the statement "At Jemez I came to the end of my childhood." Identify the descriptions of his experience at Jemez that lead him to this conclusion.

2. His essay concludes with this passage: "That was a strange thing in my life, and I think of it as the end of an age. I should never again see the world as I saw it on the other side of that moment, in the bright reflection of time lost." Explain why Momaday sees the world differently as a result of his experiences.

3. Think about an experience that had special meaning for you, one that transformed the way you see the world and your beliefs about it. Write a passage in which you use description to create the atmosphere and meaning that this experience had for you.

Independence and the Inward "I"

BY PETER J. RONDINONE

The fact is, I didn't learn much in high school. I spent my time on the front steps of the building smoking grass with the dudes from the dean's squad. For kicks we'd grab a freshman, tell him we were undercover cops, handcuff him to a banister, and take his money. Then we'd go to the back of the building, cop some "downs," and nod away the day behind the steps in the lobby. The classrooms were overcrowded anyhow, and the teachers knew it. They also knew where to find me when they wanted to make weird deals: If I agreed to read a book and do an oral report, they'd pass me. So I did it and graduated with a "general" diploma. I was a New York City public school kid.

I hung out on a Bronx streetcorner with a group of guys who called themselves "The Davidson Boys" and sang songs like "Daddy-lo-lo." Everything we did could be summed up with the word "snap." That's a "snap." She's a "snap." We had a "snap." Friday nights we'd paint ourselves green and run through the streets swinging baseball bats. Or we'd get into a little rap in the park. It was all very perilous. Even though I'd seen a friend stabbed for wearing the wrong colors and another blown away for "messin'" with some dude's woman, I was too young to realize that my life too might be headed toward a violent end.

Then one night I swallowed a dozen Tuminols and downed two quarts of beer at a bar in Manhattan. I passed out in the gutter. I puked and rolled under a parked car. Two girlfriends found me and carried me home. My overprotective brother answered the door. When he saw me—eyes rolling toward the back of my skull like rubber—he pushed me down a flight of stairs. My skull hit the edge of a marble step with a thud. The girls screamed. My parents came to the door and there I was: a high school graduate, a failure, curled in a ball in a pool of blood.

The next day I woke up with dried blood on my face. I had no idea what had happened. My sister told me. I couldn't believe it. Crying, my mother confirmed the story. I had almost died! That scared hell out of me. I knew I had to do something. I didn't know what. But pills and violence didn't promise much of a future.

5   I went back to a high school counselor for advice. He suggested I go to college.

◆

On the day I received my letter of acceptance, I waited until dinner to tell my folks. I was proud.

"Check out where I'm going," I said. I passed the letter to my father. He looked at it.

"You jerk!" he said. "You wanna sell ties?" My mother grabbed the letter.

"God," she said. "Why don't you go to work already? Like other people."

10   "Later for that," I said. "You should be proud."

At the time, of course, I didn't understand where my parents were coming from. They were immigrants. They believed college was for rich kids, not the ones who dropped downs and sang songs on streetcorners. . . .

Anyhow, I wasn't about to listen to my parents and go to work; for a dude like me, this was a big deal. So I left the dinner table and went to tell my friends about my decision.

◆

The Davidson Boys hung out in a rented storefront. They were sitting around the pool table on milk boxes and broken pinball machines, spare tires and dead batteries. I made my announcement. They stood up and circled me like I was the star of a cockfight. Sucio stepped to the table with a can of beer in one hand and a pool stick in the other.

"Wha' you think you gonna get out of college?" he said.

15   "I don't know, but I bet it beats this," I said. I shoved one of the pool balls across the table. That was a mistake. The others banged their sticks on the wood floor and chanted, "Oooh-ooh—snap, snap." Sucio put his beer on the table.

"Bull!" he yelled. "I wash dishes with college dudes. You're like us—nuttin', man." He pointed the stick at my nose.

Silence.

I couldn't respond. If I let the crowd know I thought their gig was uncool, that I wanted out of the club, they would have taken it personally. And they would have taken me outside and kicked my ass. So I lowered my head. "Aw, hell, gimme a hit of beer," I said, as if it were all a joke. But I left the corner and didn't go back.

◆

I spent that summer alone, reading books like *How to Succeed in College* and *30 Days to a More Powerful Vocabulary*. My vocabulary was limited to a few choice phrases like "Move over, Rover, and let Petey take over." When my friends did call for me I hid behind the curtains. I knew that if I was going to make it, I'd have to push these guys out of my consciousness as if I were doing the breaststroke in a sea of logs. I had work to do, and people were time consuming. As it happened, all my heavy preparations didn't amount to much.

20   On the day of the placement exams I went paranoid. Somehow I got the idea that my admission to college was some ugly practical joke that I wasn't prepared for. So I copped some downs and took the test nodding. The words floated on the page like flies on a crock of cream.

That made freshman year difficult. The administration had placed me in all three remedial programs: basic writing, college skills, and math. I was shocked. I had always thought of myself as smart. I was the only one in the neighborhood who read books. So I gave up the pills and pushed aside another log.

The night before the first day of school, my brother walked into my room and threw a briefcase on my desk. "Good luck, Joe College," he said. He smacked me in the back of the head. Surprised, I went to bed early.

◆

In Basic Writing I the instructor, Regina Sackmary, chalked her name in bold letters on the blackboard. I sat in the front row and reviewed my *How to Succeed* lessons: Sit in front/don't let eyes wander to cracks on ceilings/take notes on a legal pad/make note of all unfamiliar words and books/listen for key phrases like "remember this," they are a professor's signals. The other students held pens over pads in anticipation. Like me, they didn't know what to expect. We were public school kids from lousy neighborhoods and we knew that some of us didn't have a chance; but we were ready to work hard.

Before class we had rapped about our reasons for going to college. Some said they wanted to be the first in the history of their families to have a college education—they said their parents never went to college because they couldn't afford it, or because their parents' parents were too poor—and they said open admissions and free tuition ($65 per semester) were a chance to change that history. Others said they wanted to be educated so they could return to their neighborhoods to help "the people"; they were the idealists. Some foreigners said they wanted to return to their own countries and start schools. And I said I wanted to escape the boredom and the pain I had known as a kid on the streets. But none of them said they expected a job. Or if they did they were reminded that there were no jobs.

25 In math I was in this remedial program for algebra, geometry, and trigonometry. But unlike high school math, which I thought was devised to boggle the mind for the sake of boggling, in this course I found I could make a connection between different mathematical principles and my life. For instance, there were certain basics I had to learn—call them 1, 2, and 3—and unless they added up to 6 I'd probably be a failure. I also got a sense of how math related to the world at large: Unless the sum of the parts of a society equaled the whole there would be chaos. And these insights jammed my head and made me feel like a kid on a ferris wheel looking at the world for the first time. Everything amazed me!

Like biology. In high school I associated this science with stabbing pins in the hearts of frogs for fun. Or getting high snorting small doses of the chloroform used for experiments on fruit flies. But in college biology I began to learn and appreciate not only how my own life processes functioned but how there were thousands of other life processes I'd never known existed. And this gave me a sense of power, because I could deal with questions like, Why do plants grow? not as I had before, with a simple spill of words: "'Cause of the sun, man." I could actually explain that there was a plant cycle and cycles within the plant cycle. You know how the saying goes—a little knowledge is dangerous. Well, the more I learned the more I ran my mouth off, especially with people who didn't know as much as I did.

I remember the day Ms. Sackmary tossed Sartre's *No Exit* in my lap and said, "Find the existential motif." I didn't know what to look for. What was she talking about? I never studied philosophy. I turned to the table of contents, but there was nothing under E. So I went to the library and after much research I discovered the notion of the absurd. I couldn't believe it. I told as many people as I could. I told them they were absurd, their lives were absurd, everything was absurd. I became obsessed with existentialism. I read Kafka, Camus, Dostoevski, and others in my spare time. Then one day I found a line in a book that I believed summed up my unusual admittance to the college and my determination to work hard. I pasted it to the headboard of my bed. It said: "Everything is possible."

To deal with the heavy workload from all my classes, I needed a study schedule, so I referred to my *How to Succeed* book. I gave myself an hour for lunch and reserved the rest of the time between classes and evenings for homework and research. All this left me very little time for friendships. But I stuck to my schedule and by the middle of the first year I was getting straight A's. Nothing else mattered. Not even my family.

◆

When I entered my second year my family began to ask, "What do you want to do?" And I got one of those cards from the registrar that has to be filled out in a week or you're dropped from classes. It asked me to declare my major. I had to make a quick decision. So I checked off BS degree, dentistry, though I didn't enroll in a single science course.

30   One course I did take that semester was *The Writer and the City*. The professor, Ross Alexander, asked the class to keep a daily journal. He said it should be as creative as possible and reflect some aspect of city life. So I wrote about different experiences I had with my friends. For example, I wrote "Miracle on 183rd Street" about the night "Raunchy" Rick jumped a guy in the park and took his portable radio. When the guy tried to fight back Rick slapped him in the face with the radio; then, using the batteries that spilled out, he pounded this guy in the head until the blood began to puddle on the ground. Those of us on the sidelines dragged Rick away. Ross attached notes to my papers that said things like: "You really have a great hit of talent and ought to take courses in creative writing and sharpen your craft! Hang on to it all for dear life."

In my junior year I forgot dentistry and registered as a creative writing major. I also joined a college newspaper, *The Campus*. Though I knew nothing about journalism, I was advised that writing news was a good way to learn the business. And as Ross once pointed out to me, "As a writer you will need an audience."

I was given my first assignment. I collected piles of quotes and facts and scattered the mess on a desk. I remember typing the story under deadline pressure with one finger while the editors watched me struggle, probably thinking back to their own first stories. When I finished, they passed the copy around.

The editor-in-chief looked at it at last and said, "This isn't even English." Yet, they turned it over to a rewrite man and the story appeared with my by-line. Seeing my name in print was like seeing it in lights—flashbulbs popped in my head and I walked into the school cafeteria that day expecting to be recognized by everyone. My mother informed the relatives: "My son is a writer!"

Six months later I quit *The Campus*. A course in New Journalism had made me realize that reporting can be creative. For the first time I read writers like Tom Wolfe and Hunter S. Thompson, and my own news stories began to turn into first-person accounts that read like short stories. *The Campus* refused to publish my stuff, so I joined the *Observation Post*, the only paper on campus that printed first-person material. I wanted to get published.

My first *Post* feature article (a first-person news story on a proposed beer hall at CCNY) was published on the front page. The staff was impressed enough to elect me assistant features editor. However, what they didn't know was that the article had been completely rewritten by the features editor. And the features editor had faith in me, so he never told. He did my share of the work and I kept the title. As he put it: "You'll learn by hanging around and watching. You show talent. You might even get published professionally in 25 years!"

35   God, those early days were painful. Professors would tear up my papers the day they were due and tell me to start over again, with a piece of advice—"Try to say what you really mean." Papers I had spent weeks writing. And I knew I lacked the basic college skills; I was a man reporting to work without his tools. So I smiled when I didn't understand. But sometimes it showed and I paid the price: A professor once told me the only reason I'd pass his course was that I had a nice smile. Yes, those were painful days.

And there were nights I was alone with piles of notebooks and textbooks. I wanted to throw the whole mess out the window; I wanted to give up. Nights the sounds of my friends singing on the corner drifted into my room like fog over a graveyard and I was afraid I would be swept away. And nights I was filled with questions but the answers were like moon shadows on my curtains: I could see them but I could not grasp them.

Yet I had learned a vital lesson from these countless hours of work in isolation: My whole experience from the day I received my letter of acceptance enabled me to understand how in high school my sense of self-importance came from being one of the boys, a member of the pack, while in college the opposite was true. In order to survive, I had to curb my herd instinct.

Nobody, nobody could give me what I needed to overcome my sense of inadequacy. That was a struggle I had to work at on my own. It could never be a group project. In the end, though people could point out what I had to learn and where to learn it, I was always the one who did the work; and what I learned I earned. And that made me feel as good as being one of the boys. In short, college taught me to appreciate the importance of being alone. I found it was the only way I could get any serious work done.

Critical Reading Questions

1. What was Peter Rondinone's view of his life during his high school years? Why did he change his beliefs?

2. "Everything is possible" is the existentialist statement that the author pasted on his headboard. What significance did this have for him? How do you think it might apply to your life?

3. Rondinone's professors advised him, in his writing, to "try to say what you really mean." What did *they* mean by that? How might you apply this insight to your own writing?

4. The author concludes, "In high school my sense of self-importance came from being one of the boys, a member of the pack, while in college the opposite was true. In order to survive, I had to curb my herd instinct." Do you believe that this conclusion applies to you? Why or why not?

We Are Ugly, But We Are Here

EDWIDGE DANTICAT

One of the first people murdered on our land was a queen. Her name was Anacaona and she was an Arawak Indian. She was a poet, dancer, and even a painter. She ruled over the western part of an island so lush and green that the Arawaks called it Ayiti, land of high. When the Spaniards came from across the sea to look for gold, Anacaona was one of their first victims. She was raped and killed and her village pillaged in a tradition of ongoing cruelty and atrocity. Anacaona's land is now the poorest country in the Western hemisphere, a place of continuous political unrest. Thus, for some, it is easy to forget that this land was the first Black Republic, home to the first people of African descent to uproot slavery and create an independent nation in 1804.

I was born under Haiti's dictatorial Duvalier regime. When I was four, my parents left Haiti to seek a better life in the United States. I must admit that their motives were more economic than political. But as anyone who knows Haiti will tell you, economics and politics are very intrinsically related in Haiti. Who is in power determines to a great extent whether or not people will eat.

I am twenty-six years old now and have spent more than half of my life in the United States. My most vivid memories of Haiti involve incidents that represent the general situation there. In Haiti, there are a lot of "blackouts," sudden power failures. At those times, you can't read or study or watch TV, so you sit around a candle and listen to stories from the elders in the house. My grandmother was an old country woman who always felt displaced in the city of Port-au-Prince where we lived and had nothing but her patched-up quilts and her stories to console her. She was the one who told me about Anacaona. I used to share a room with her. I was in the room when she died. She was over a hundred years old. She died with her eyes wide open and I was the one who closed her eyes. I still miss the countless mystical stories that she told us. However, I accepted her death very easily because in Haiti death was always around us.

As a little girl, I attended more than my share of funerals. My uncle and legal guardian was a Baptist minister and his family was expected to attend every funeral he presided over. I went to all the funerals he presided over. I went to all the funerals in the same white lace dress. Perhaps it was because I attended so many funerals that I have such a strong feeling that death is not the end, that the people we bury are going off to live somewhere else. But at the same time, they will always be hovering around to watch over us and guide us through our journeys.

5   When I was eight, my uncle's brother-in-law went on a long journey to cut cane in the Dominican Republic. He came back, deathly ill. I remember his wife twirling feathers inside his nostrils and rubbing black pepper on his upper lip to make him sneeze. She strongly believed that if he sneezed, he would live. At night, it was my job to watch the sky above the house for signs of falling stars. In Haitian folklore, when a star falls out of the sky, it means someone will die. A star did fall out of the sky and he did die.

I have memories of Jean-Claude "Baby Doc" Duvalier and his wife, racing by in their Mercedes Benz and throwing money out of the window to the very poor children in our neighborhood. The children nearly killed each other trying to catch a coin or a glimpse of Baby Doc. One Christmas, they announced on the radio that the first lady, Baby Doc's wife, was giving away free toys at the palace. My cousins and I went and were nearly killed in the mob of children who flooded the palace lawns.

All of this now brings many questions buzzing to my head. Where was really my place in all of this? What was my grandmother's place? What is the legacy of the daughters of Anacaona? What do we all have left to remember, the daughters of Haiti?

Watching the news reports, it is often hard to tell whether there are real living and breathing women in conflict-stricken places like Haiti. The evening news broadcasts only allow us a brief glimpse of presidential coups, rejected boat people, and sabotaged elections. The women's stories never manage to make the front page. However, they do exist.

I know women who, when the soldiers came to their homes in Haiti, would tell their daughters to lie still and play dead. I once met a woman whose sister was shot in her pregnant stomach because she was wearing a t-shirt with an "anti-military image." I know a mother who was arrested and beaten for working with a pro-democracy group. Her body remains laced with scars where the soldiers put out their cigarettes on her flesh. At night, this woman still smells the ashes of the cigarette butts that were stuffed lit inside her nostrils. In the same jail cell, she watched as paramilitary "attachés" raped her fourteen-year-old daughter at gunpoint. When mother and daughter took a tiny boat to the United States, the mother had no idea that her daughter was pregnant. Nor did she know that the child had gotten the HIV virus from one of the paramilitary men who had raped her. The grandchild, the offspring of the rape, was named Anacaona, after the queen, because that family of women is from the same region where Anacaona was murdered. The infant Anacaona has a face which no longer shows any trace of indigenous blood; however, her story echoes back to the first flow of blood on a land that has seen much more than its share.

10   There is a Haitian saying which might upset the aesthetic images of most women. *"Nou led, Nou la,"* it says. We are ugly, but we are here. Like the modesty that is somewhat common in Haitian culture, this saying makes a deeper claim for poor Haitian women than maintaining beauty, be it skin deep or otherwise. For most of us, what is worth celebrating is the fact that we are here, that we against all the odds exist. To the women who might greet each other with this saying when they meet along the countryside, the very essence of life lies in survival. It is always worth reminding our sisters that we have lived yet another day to answer the roll call of an often painful and very difficult life. It is in this spirit that to this day a woman remembers to name her child Anacaona, a name which resonates both the splendor and agony of a past that haunts so many women.

When they were enslaved, our foremothers believed that when they died, their spirits would return to Africa, most specifically to a peaceful land we call Guinin, where gods and goddesses live. The women who came before me were women who spoke half of one language and half another. They spoke the French and Spanish of their captors mixed in with their own African language. These women seemed to be speaking in tongues when they prayed to their old gods, the ancient African spirits. Even though they were afraid that their old deities would no longer understand them, they invented a new language, our Creole *patois*, with which to describe their new surroundings, a language from which colorful phrases blossomed to fit the desperate circumstances. When these women greeted each other, they found themselves speaking in codes.

—How are we today, Sister?

—I am ugly, but I am here.

These days, many of my sisters are greeting each other away from the homelands where they first learned to speak in tongues. Many have made it to other shores, after traveling endless miles on the high seas, on rickety boats that almost took their lives. Two years ago, a mother jumped into the sea when she discovered that her baby daughter had died in her arms on a journey which they had hoped would take them to a brighter future. Mother and child, they sank to the bottom of an ocean which already holds millions of souls from the middle passage, the holocaust of the slave trade that is our legacy. That woman's sacrifice moved then-deposed Haitian President Jean-Bertrand Aristide to the brink of tears. However, like the rest of us, he took comfort in the past sacrifices that were made for all of us so that we could be here.

15   The past is full of examples when our foremothers and forefathers showed such deep trust in the sea that they would jump off slave ships and let the waves

embrace them. They too believed that the sea was the beginning and the end of all things, the road to freedom and their entrance to Guinin. These women have been part of the very construction of my being ever since I was a little girl. Women like my grandmother who had taught me the story of Anacaona, the queen.

My grandmother believed that if a life is lost, then another one springs up replanted somewhere else, the next life even stronger than the last. She believed that no one really dies as long as someone remembers, someone who will acknowledge that this person had in spite of everything been here. We are part of an endless circle, the daughters of Anacaona. We have stumbled, but have not fallen. We are ill-favored, but we still endure. Every once in a while, we must scream this as far as the wind can carry our voices: We are ugly, but we are here! And here to stay.

Critical Reading Questions

1. Ms. Danticat begins her essay with a reference to an ancient queen of Haiti, Anacaona, whose story she learned from her grandmother. What role does the life—and death—of Anacaona have in the author's beliefs about Haitian women?

2. Death and suffering are dominant themes in this essay. Why does the author state, "I have such a strong feeling that death is not the end, that the people we bury are going off to live somewhere else"?

3. In response to the question "What is the legacy of the daughters of Anacaona?" Ms. Danticat offers a common greeting among Haitian women: "*Nou led, Nou la* (We are ugly, but we are here)." Explain the significance of this expression and how it symbolizes the author's deepest beliefs.

4. Ms. Danticat's critical reflection on these issues appears to have deepened the beliefs she was brought up with rather than altering them. Identify a significant belief that your family taught you that has been strengthened by critical evaluation and experience.

Writing Project: An Experience That Affected a Belief

The Thinking-Writing Activities and the readings and questions in this chapter have encouraged you to become an active thinker, to examine your beliefs, and to observe how some thoughtful people have reflected on their learning experiences. As you work on this project, reread what you wrote for the activities and think about the events discussed in the readings.

Write an essay telling of an experience that had an important impact on a belief that you held or hold. The belief might be about yourself, about another person involved in the experience, or about the issue that the experience illustrates. The experience may have helped form your belief, or it may have influenced you to change or revise it. Alternatively, you could describe an experience which deepened and strengthened an important belief of yours by testing it in trying circumstances.

You should explain your belief, of course, and describe the experience, reflecting on what happened as you tell of its effects. You will probably want to discuss the sources of the belief (see page 42). Follow your instructor's directions for length, format, and so forth.

THE WRITING SITUATION

Begin by considering the elements discussed in the Writing Situation section of the Thinking-Writing Model.

Purpose Examining your beliefs is necessary for developing critical thinking abilities. Once you understand and evaluate your own beliefs, you can understand and evaluate other people's perspectives. When you reflect on and write about significant experiences, you begin to view them in a new way. The record that you create allows you to relive the experiences, rethink their significance, share them with others, and profit from others' responses. In the essay you are about to write, you will be explaining your experience and your belief but not trying to convince your readers that they should adopt or reject the belief. You are analyzing the meaning of *your* experience and the impact that it had on *your* life.

Audience When you write reflectively about your own experiences, you are an important part of the audience. This form of writing acts as a catalyst for self-discovery by encouraging you to reflect on your past experiences in a disciplined, analytical way. As you write in this form, your guiding ideas should include these questions:

- How effectively am I communicating the richness and reality of this experience?
- How effectively have I analyzed the significance of this experience and the impact that it had?

You will also be writing for the other readers with whom you'll share this piece of writing. Consider these questions when thinking about their needs:

- How much information about my original belief should I include for my readers to understand it and know where it came from?

- How much would my readers be likely to know about the background of the experience I am writing about? What in that background is essential for them to understand the experience and how or why it affected my belief?
- What details of the experience should I include to make it real for my readers? What details can I leave out?

In other words, you will need to put yourself in your readers' position and view your writing through their eyes.

Subject Autobiographical narratives are often engaging. Most of us like to learn about what other people did and what they think their personal stories mean. If the narrator is famous, readers can satisfy their curiosity about an extraordinary life. If the narrator is an ordinary person, readers often identify with the experiences and use them as warnings or inspirations for their own lives. For instance, consider the natural curiosity that your classmates have about each other's lives.

The story must be well told, with thoughtfully selected events, graphic details, and strong verbs. As you draft and revise, keep your subject and purpose in mind so that the meaning you attach to your experiences becomes clear.

Writer This Writing Project, like the others in Part One of this book, asks you to use your own experience as the basis of an essay. This makes you the authority on the subject, which should give you confidence. Your challenges are to shape your story and to connect it directly to your belief.

THE WRITING PROCESS

One of this book's main goals is to help you think about your own writing process, to tap its strengths and to reduce its weaknesses. This project provides a good opportunity for you to reflect on your writing process as you describe and analyze a significant experience.

Generating Ideas Brainstorm to find a suitable experience to write about. Look for an experience that had a profound effect on your beliefs and that may have implications for other people's lives. Once you have found your topic, ask yourself questions and make notes about your responses. Questions you might ask include these:

- What happened? Outline the major events of the experience.
- How did you respond? What were your thoughts, reactions, feelings?
- What roles did other people play? Was the location important? Recall

specific details about what people did and said, and about the setting, to make your retelling vivid for your audience.

- What was the result of the experience? How did it affect your belief?
- As you reflect on it, what was the experience's value for you? How has it influenced your life?

You may also refer to the questions for generating ideas in Chapter 3.

Defining a Focus   In a few sentences, summarize the main point you wish to make in your essay, given your subject, audience, and purpose. Then evaluate your focus: Is it specific enough for you to convey it clearly in an essay? Is it interesting so that your audience will find it worth reading about? Is it thoughtful so that it serves the purpose of reflection?

At this point, consider whether or not the experience you have chosen is an appropriate subject. If not, you can begin again by brainstorming for another experience to write about.

Organizing Ideas   Think about how you can order the elements of your experience. Will you start at the beginning and describe them chronologically? Or will you start at a later point in time and use a flashback to the beginning of the experience? Where will you include your observations and reflections about the experience: at the end, or at various places throughout?

As you are organizing your ideas and drafting, planning, and revising, you will need to decide whether your paper will have a visible or an invisible structure. With a *visible structure,* the thesis is stated clearly, most paragraphs contain topic sentences, transitional expressions explicitly point out connections among ideas, and the introductory and concluding sections do their jobs of beginning and ending the piece. Visible structure is sometimes called the "no-fail" method of organization because it usually works and because anybody can learn to use it. Much academic and business writing relies on visible structure. The student essay at the end of this chapter, "Using Logic in Study," and those at the end of Chapter 4, "Deciding What to Do About My Hearing Problem" and "A Space Problem," all use visible structures because they have clear thesis statements and topic sentences for each body paragraph that relate to the thesis.

Invisible structure is more subtle and demands artistic crafting from the writer. Professional writers often create beautiful pieces with invisible structure. You may want to try using it in some of your papers, but first you need to master the visible structure mode so that your expository writing will fulfill its purpose. Edwidge Danticat's essay in this chapter uses invisible structure.

Drafting   As you translate your ideas, notes, and early versions into coherent writing, you will need to decide how to draft in ways that will help you revise your work effectively. Because the essay you are about to write will have three distinct components—your belief, your experience, and their connections—you may want to draft each component separately and then think about connecting them.

Drafting Hints

1. Spread out all the work you did while generating ideas and drafting a focus so that you can see it while you write the sections of your draft.

2. Draft briskly. You will revise and correct later.

3. If you stop or are interrupted while drafting, be sure to save what you have written.

4. When you return to drafting, reread what you saved to resume the flow of your ideas.

5. Reward yourself when you complete a section of your draft: Take a short break; exercise; have a snack.

Revising One of the very best strategies is to get an audience's reactions to your draft. Your classmates, or peers, can help you see where your draft is already successful and where it needs improvement. If your instructor allows class time for peer review, be sure to have a draft ready so that you can benefit from this activity.

Revising Strategy: Peer Response Groups This activity works best with groups of three or four.

1. The group selects a timekeeper who allots ten minutes to each writer. Regardless of how many response process steps have been completed, after ten minutes the group goes on to the next writer's work.

2. One person begins by reading aloud his or her draft while group members listen.

3. The writer next reads his or her writing aloud a second time. *Do not skip this step.*

4. Group members listen and write notes or comments.

5. The writer then asks each group member this question and jots down their responses: "What questions do you have about my original belief and its sources?"

6. The writer next asks each member these questions and takes notes as each answers: "What questions do you have about the experience I described? What else do you need to know about it?"

7. The writer then asks each member these questions and records their responses: "Do you understand why my belief changed as a result of this experience and what my belief is now? What could I add to make my writing clearer?"

As soon as possible after peer review, you should revise your draft based on your peers' questions and comments. Then, if possible, put it aside for a day or two before continuing with revision.

Reread your revised draft out loud, slowly. Then think about each of the following questions. As you consider ways to improve your draft based on your answers, stop and make changes to your draft before you move on to the next question.

1. How could you improve the first paragraph? How could you get your readers' attention and make them want to read on?

2. How could you improve the order of your draft? Could you rearrange some paragraphs?

3. How could you improve the flow of your draft? Where would transitions help your audience?

4. How could you improve your sentences? Pay particular attention to sentences that are difficult to read aloud. Your audience will have trouble following them! Could you shorten hard-to-read long sentences or write them as two sentences? Where could you use parallel structure to make your sentences more graceful?

Proofreading After you prepare a final draft, check for standard grammar and punctuation usage. Proofread carefully for omitted words and punctuation marks. Run your spelling checker program, but be aware of its limitations. Proofread again to detect the kinds of errors the computer can't catch.

◆

Your essay should now be completed to the very best of your ability, and, of course, you will need to submit a copy to your instructor by the due date. But also consider other possible audiences for this essay. Would members of your family enjoy reading it? Would other people who were involved in the experience want to know how it affected you? Would someone with whom you currently have a relationship understand you better by reading it?

The following essays show how two students responded to this assignment.

STUDENT WRITING

A Changed Belief: Using Logic in Study

BY HIROMI S. ISHII

When people tackle difficult subjects of study, what kinds of approaches can they take? I used to take an intuitive approach; all I did was to input information as much as possible and to wait for an idea to come out. However, studying English writing and art history in the United States convinced me of the importance of logic.

When I studied in Japan, the results of my study largely depended on an intuitive approach. There were two reasons for my attitude: my university major and my enlightenment experiences. I majored in Chinese poetry at Nanzan University in Japan. Most of the lectures and assignments were readings of Chinese poems and translations of them. We were expected to be open-minded about the words, but we didn't have to analyze them. In addition, I regarded enlightenment as the Almighty of study. When I struggled with a difficult problem, sudden enlightenment often led me to comprehension of the point. I didn't know how I had gotten an idea, but the result was not bad. Therefore, I tended to rely on my inspirations although I felt that something was missing.

Last year, I came to the United States from Japan and began to study at Montgomery College. The way of study there rocked my attitude to its foundation because I had to face logic.

First, I took courses for reading and writing in English simply because I was a nonnative, and these courses demanded that I think about a process that I had skipped previously. I needed to give strong supporting details for my opinions and to understand methods for writing.

In the writing class, I learned to compose my ideas into paragraphs more strategically than before. In Japan, I used to believe that ability in writing was a kind of gift and the only way to improve was to practice. However, in the English class, using the methods consciously, everyone could achieve a certain writing quality. One method I learned was to put a topic sentence and supporting details in every paragraph. I learned to analyze my writing.

After I finished ESL classes, I took an art history class, and I was convinced again how logic was important. To tell the truth, I started the class still thinking that an intuitive approach was more important than a logical approach in certain areas of study, such as arts and humanities.

The art class instructed me to see art works within their context, to identify the techniques that were used in them, and to understand influences from society and other artists. It was fun to be able to say more than "I love it" about a favorite painting. For example, I learned that using perspective techniques was an important theme for many European artists during the Renaissance period. I learned that Leonardo da Vinci's *Last Supper* was not only a famous, well-depicted religious painting but also an experimental artwork with the one-point perspective technique. Then, I could compare and contrast the painting with others that had been made during the same period or on the same subject.

Furthermore, I found that setting my own perspective was a great way of organizing information. Previously, after leaving a museum, sometimes I couldn't remember what I had seen because I tried to be neutral about the paintings. In other words, I didn't have a system of organizing them. If I used a certain perspective, such as the period of art history—like impressionism or modernism, I could pick out key paintings and classify them, so it was easier to consult my memory later.

Now, I believe both intuition and logic are necessary to thinking. I still trust an intuitive approach because experience makes me familiar with a subject and enlightenment can come. However, I realize the importance of a logical approach as a very suitable way to work effectively and objectively. For me, using logic is a new way to explain things, and it leads me to the joy of the academic world. With the discovery of logic, my true study has begun at last.

Money Can't Do It

BY MICHAEL PERSCH

Probably only a couple of events in people's lives cause them to completely change their views on a matter. So far, the biggest one for me was when my father and mother lost their business. Several months later, I realized something: that money doesn't bring true happiness, but that your family, if given the chance, can and will. This thought was like a light bulb that clicked on in my head. Two experiences caused it to click on, and I am sure glad it did. That light bulb helped me become a more real person.

When I was growing up, and all during high school, I was able to get almost anything that I wanted. For example, at Christmas, everyone in my family always received exactly what they asked for, plus a lot of other stuff. On my birthday and Valentine's day my parents usually sent flowers and balloons to me. Finally, whenever I needed money, all I had to do was ask my mom and dad, and they would give it to me. I used to take money for granted and never really thought about it not being there until it wasn't.

Our home was in the most prestigious area to live in. During high school I never had to take the bus because I had my own car to drive after I turned sixteen. My friends and I were by far the coolest guys and girls in the school. I was able to live life to the fullest, or at least I thought I was, because I had these important things.

All of this was because my father owned a large variety store in town, and both it and my father were very successful. He was president of the Chamber of Commerce. The biggest reason that the store was so successful is that there was no competition. That is, until Wal-Mart came to town.

Just toward the end of the summer after graduation, my father resigned from the Chamber of Commerce. Then, he called a family meeting and told us that he was going to shut down the store because the new Wal-Mart had put us out of business.

I was grateful that this happened after I graduated from high school because my whole life changed and seemed to be falling apart. I had to sell my car; I felt that I had lost most of my friends, my money, and my self-respect and esteem. To top it off, now I had to get rides to and from work and college.

I couldn't stand it anymore, so I quit my job, dropped out of college and went to work far away as a server at the Grand Canyon North Rim where I didn't know anybody and nobody knew me! It wasn't too long before I had become particularly good buddies with a couple of guys I worked with, and the three of us decided that it would be cool to move to Seattle. So we quit, packed up our stuff, and moved there.

But in Seattle I hit rock bottom. Now there were new stresses, simple things like paying rent and bills. I began looking for an escape and found it in tobacco, alcohol, and drugs.

However, it was also in Seattle that I did a lot of growing up. Although using drugs and alcohol was a bad part of my life, not all of the effects were negative. I found myself talking with people from all walks of life. These were people who before I would never have been caught dead associating with. Now, not only was I talking with them, but I was learning from them. I began to have an open mind and to see that other people were both worse off and better off than I was.

Then a life-changing event happened. I got sick, really sick. I caught Hepatitis A from something, which put me in the hospital. I just knew that I was going to die.

Consequently, I realized how much I needed and missed my family, and it didn't matter how much I had previously thought that they had failed me. I called my mother and she told me that they would be there as soon as possible. When they arrived the next day, I was very happy to see them! When I could leave the hospital, we stayed together in a hotel for a few more days until I was well enough to fly home. Then I realized just how much I was loved.

Now things are going well for my family. Both of my parents went back to school. My mom is the head of the nursing department at Dixie Medical Center, and my father has become a toxic waste manager for the EPA. They are again able to help me financially with school, but I no longer take their help for granted because I now believe that my parents' love is much more valuable than their money.

ALTERNATIVE WRITING PROJECT: AN AUTHOR'S CHANGE IN BELIEF

Write an essay explaining how one of the authors of the readings in Chapter 2 (Annie Dillard, N. Scott Momaday, Peter Rondinone, Edwidge Danticat) changed or strengthened one or more important beliefs. You should cite the title and author in your introduction and have a thesis indicating the main idea that your essay will develop. Your audience will need to understand what the author's original belief was, what circumstances changed or strengthened it, and what it was after these circumstances. Your audience will also want to know if and how this change or strengthening of belief affected the author's life.

Think carefully about purpose, audience, subject, and writer as you move through the steps of generating ideas, defining a focus, organizing ideas, drafting, revising, editing, and proofreading. Review the discussions in these sections in Chapter 1 and in this chapter.

If you use any of the author's words, be sure to put quotation marks around them. To the extent possible, express the ideas in your own words: Save the direct quotations for very important and powerfully worded statements.

Follow your instructor's directions for length, format, and so forth.

3

Thinking Creatively, Writing Creatively

"You must expect the unexpected, because it cannot be found by search or trail." —Heraclitus

Critical Thinking Focus: The qualities of a creative thinker

Writing Focus: Generating original ideas

Reading Theme: The creative thinking process

Writing Project: Imagining your life lived more creatively

Aspects of Writing Creatively

Creative writing is often thought of as imaginative fiction, poetry, or drama, for which the author invents characters and situations. So the question naturally arises, what part does creativity have in *expository writing*, in which facts, ideas, and concepts are explored, developed, and argued? The answer: a very large part.

You can use your creative thinking in selecting and narrowing your topic (if you are allowed to pick your own topic), in the way you generate and research ideas, in the way you organize your ideas, and in the way you focus on your ideas with your thesis. You can also use creative thinking to develop your ideas with carefully chosen specific details and examples. You can use creative thinking to develop analogies and metaphors to help your readers grasp your ideas. Finally, you can use creative thinking to write imaginative, inviting introductions that will make your readers eager to read further, and you can use it to write carefully crafted conclusions that tie in elegantly with your introductions. Of course, your critical thinking abilities are also involved in all these steps, helping you to decide which of your creative ideas to include and which to discard.

Does all this sound like a large amount of work? Well, you're right. It is. Yet there are good reasons for developing your creativity in writing. If all you do in your expository writing is restate other people's ideas in a dry, formulaic way, you risk boring yourself with your writing—and boring your audience as well.

The challenge to be creative in your writing is a difficult one, but the possibilities for creativity are vast. Focusing on the following four areas for creativity in expository writing will help you further develop the creative writing abilities you may already have.

- Creativity in topic selection

- Creativity in generating ideas, researching, and drafting

- Creativity in using specific details and examples

- Creativity in writing introductions and conclusions

CREATIVITY IN TOPIC SELECTION

Some topics are personal and ask you to draw on your own life experiences, others are impersonal and clearly require research, and still others are a blend of the personal and impersonal. Furthermore, some topics are quite precise; for example, "Write about your father's influence on your religious development" or "Write about the causes of the Crimean War." When given such a specific topic, that is exactly what you must write about. Often, though, assigned topics are general and need to be narrowed to be made more precise. Such topics allow for some creativity on your part: "Write about how some family member influenced you in an important way," "Write about some aspect of the Crimean War," or even "Write a paper on some topic related to this course." When given this type of assignment, you may want to use the creative process to shape it. Begin your topic search by picking a tentative topic, one that interests you and that you would like to think and learn more about. A good strategy is to state a topic as a question. For example, "What, if any, new military strategies were introduced during the Crimean War?" If your topic requires research, read as much as you can about the general topic area, looking for ways to modify your tentative topic question or even for a new question altogether. If you are working with a personal topic, begin making notes that will help you answer your question. Either way, try to gauge whether you have enough information to answer your question or whether you have too little or too much. You can broaden or narrow your topic question as you proceed.

Expect false starts! The fact that your original question needs to be modified or even discarded does not mean that you are doing something wrong. Becoming aware of the need to make these changes is a normal development that most writers experience, so don't become discouraged when it occurs. Instead, congratulate yourself for being willing to put in the time and effort needed for the creative process as you shape your topic.

CREATIVITY IN GENERATING IDEAS, RESEARCHING, AND DRAFTING

Books about writing sometimes speak as though generating ideas, researching, and drafting are three entirely separate stages, and the writer finishes one stage before beginning the next. This may even be true in some cases, but often writers find themselves getting new ideas while researching or beginning to draft only to realize the need for more research or brainstorming. Furthermore, writers find that the order of these stages, as well as the time needed to complete them successfully, may vary from one writing project to another.

Since there is often this back-and-forth movement between stages, there are many opportunities for creative thinking. Here are some general strategies you can use to develop creative ideas in your writing.

Brainstorming   **Brainstorming** is an activity in which, working individually or with a group of people, you write down all the ideas you can think of related to a given theme. The goal is to produce as many ideas as possible in a specific time period. While you are engaged in this idea-generating process, it is important to relax, let your mind run free, build on the ideas of others, and refrain from censoring or evaluating any ideas produced, no matter how marginal they may seem at first. Brainstorming stimulates your creative juices, and you will be surprised at how many ideas you can come up with. And if you work with other people, you will be exposed to fresh perspectives and the synergy of people working as a team.

Imagine, for example, that you are assigned the following topic for a research paper:

> There are many problems that students face on college campuses. Identify one such problem and then write a research paper that analyzes the causes of and possible solutions to the problem. Why does the problem occur, and what can be done to deal with it? Your paper should include relevant research findings as well as your own perspective on this problem.

Using the brainstorming strategy with a friend, you might come up with a list that includes the following student problems on your campus:

parking	poor quality of campus food
cafeteria too noisy	classes too large
library closes too early	no comfortable places to study
racial tensions	date rape
abuse of alcohol	use of other drugs
registration is a nightmare	tests and papers come in clumps
not enough social activities	some teachers just lecture
thefts are increasing	books are too expensive
not sufficient financial aid	the curriculum is not well organized

Can you brainstorm additional problems students on your campus face?

Mind Maps **Mind maps** are visual presentations of the various ways ideas can be related to one another. For example, the Thinking-Writing Model is represented as a mind map in Figure 3.1 on page 74. Mind maps are also a powerful approach for writing, helping you to generate ideas and to begin organizing them into various relationships. They are well suited to the writing process for a number of reasons. First, the organization grows naturally, reflecting the way your mind naturally makes associations and arranges information. Second, the organization can easily be revised to reflect new information and your developing understanding of how it should be organized. Third, you can express a range of relationships among the various ideas. Also, instead of being identified once and then forgotten, each idea remains an active part of the overall pattern, suggesting new possible relationships. Fourth, you do not have to decide initially on a beginning, subpoints, and so on; you can do this after your pattern is complete, so you save time and avoid frustration.

For example, imagine that from your list of problems on campus you select "abuse of alcohol" as a paper topic. Your mind map might resemble Figure 3.1.

Can you add some additional "routes" to the mind map?

Freewriting **Freewriting** is a sort of written brainstorming in which you write with a minimum of conscious reflection. But rather than simply list ideas, freewriters usually write in sentences. The goal is to let your ideas flow freely, without inhibition, giving your mind the opportunity to develop creative ideas in unique combinations. As with brainstorming, freewriting generally works best in a limited time frame. Don't worry about spelling, grammar, or evaluating the ideas you are expressing. Freewriting is an excellent way to "jump-start"

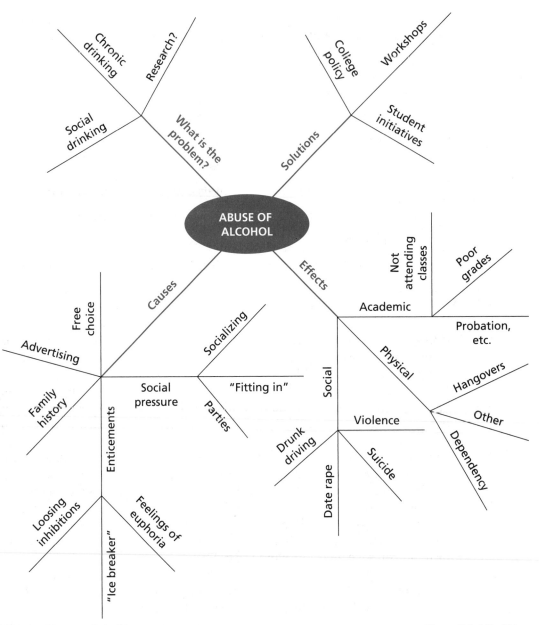

Figure 3.1 Mind Map

your thinking process and prepare for more thoughtful composing. It also helps you realize what information you already have on a subject so that you can decide whether to do more research.

An example of freewriting about the problem of alcohol abuse might begin something like this:

Alcohol is a real problem on campus. Every party, that's all people do, is drink too much and then get silly. I think it's ok for people to drink some if they want to. They say it relaxes them and makes it easier to talk to strangers. But it's out of control, and that's a problem. There are a lot of students that drink all the time. They must be failing their classes, they sleep until noon, and they look lousy. There's got to be a better way to socialize and have fun with people besides getting bombed out of your mind. . . .

Questioning **Asking questions** that explore a topic provides another strategy for generating ideas. In fact, the ability to ask appropriate and penetrating questions is one of the most powerful thinking/language tools we possess. Asking questions enables us to go beyond the obvious, to think and write in ways that are in-depth, complex, and articulate. Questions come in many different forms and are used for many different purposes. For instance, questions can be classified in terms of the ways people organize and interpret information. The following are six such categories of questions:

1. Fact
2. Interpretation
3. Analysis
4. Synthesis
5. Evaluation
6. Application

Thoughtful writers are able to ask appropriate questions from all of these categories in a very natural and flexible way. Listed next is a summary of the six categories of questions, along with sample forms of questions from each category.

1. **Questions of Fact.** Questions of fact seek to determine the basic information of a situation: who, what, when, where, how. These following seek information that is relatively straightforward and objective:

   Who, what, when, where, how?

   Describe _____ .

2. **Questions of Interpretation.** Questions of interpretation seek to select and organize facts and ideas, discovering the relationships among them. Examples of such relationships include the following:

   Chronological relationships—relating things in time sequence

   Process relationships—relating aspects of growth, development, or change

   Comparison/contrast relationships—relating things in terms of their similar or different features

   Causal relationships—relating events in terms of the way some are responsible for causing others

   These questions can help you discover relationships:

   Can you retell _____ in your own words?

What is the *main idea* of _____ ?

What is the *time sequence* relating the following events: _____ ?

What are the steps in the *process of growth* or *development* in _____ ?

How would you *compare* and *contrast* the features of _____ and _____ ?

What was/were the *cause(s)* of _____ ? What was/were the *effect(s)* of _____ ?

3. **Questions of Analysis.** Questions of analysis seek to separate an entire process or situation into its component parts and understand the relation of these parts to the whole. These questions or statements attempt to classify various elements, outline component structures, articulate various possibilities, and clarify the reasoning being presented:

What are the *parts* or *features* of _____ ?

Classify according to _____ .

Outline/diagram/web _____ .

What *evidence* can you present to support _____ ?

What are the *possible alternatives* for _____ ?

Explain the *reasons why* you think _____ .

4. **Questions of Synthesis.** The goal of questions of synthesis is to combine ideas to form a new whole or to arrive at a conclusion, making inferences about future events, creating solutions, and designing plans of action:

What would you *predict/infer* from _____ ?

What ideas can you *add to* _____ ?

How would you *create/design* a new _____ ?

What might happen if you *combined* _____ with _____ ?

What *solutions/decisions* would you suggest for _____ ?

5. **Questions of Evaluation.** The aim of evaluation questions is to help you make informed judgments and decisions by determining the relative value, truth, or reliability of things. The process of evaluation involves identifying your criteria or standards and then determining to what extent the things being evaluated meet those standards.

How would you *evaluate* _____ and what *standards* would you use?

Do you *agree with* _____ ? *Why* or *why not*?

How would you *decide* about _____ ?

What *criteria* would you use to *assess* _____ ?

6. **Questions of Application.** The purpose of application questions is to help you take the knowledge or concepts you have gained in one situation and apply them to other situations.

How is _____ *an example* of _____ ?

How would you *apply* this rule/principle to _____ ?

Thinking ↔ Writing Activity

Generating Ideas

To practice the strategies just presented (brainstorming, mind mapping, freewriting, and asking questions), spend five minutes applying each (choose one set of questions) to a specific subject that you are going to write about for this class, for another class, for your job, or for an organization in which you participate. (If you don't have an assignment, think of a subject that you would like to write about.) Record the ideas you generate.

Tips for Generating Ideas

In addition to the general strategies for finding original ideas to write about, there are also specific strategies you can employ. Here are some strategies that you might use. You should also create some strategies of your own and share them with your fellow students.

- When brainstorming, write down every idea, no matter how unusable it may seem at the time.
- When brainstorming, write each idea on a separate Post-it note. (This makes it easy to rearrange them into groups later when organizing them.)
- Phone your voice mail and leave yourself a message if an idea strikes you while you're away from home.
- Speak into a tape recorder and later listen to what you said.
- Talk to other people about your topic. Knowledgeable people will add information; those unfamiliar with the topic will ask useful questions.
- Ask a librarian for research suggestions.
- Note conflicting information or opinions. They are the heart of academic discussion.

- Look in the Yellow Pages for businesses or organizations that can provide information.
- Identify and interview experts on your topic. (Be sure to acknowledge them as sources.)
- Scan the TV schedule, including cable and PBS channels, for related programs.
- Surf the Internet for sources of information.
- When drafting, don't necessarily begin with the introduction. Instead, begin with whatever section is easiest to write.
- Be willing to modify your thesis as you go along so that you don't lock yourself into a position too early.
- Avoid premature organization; draft sections on separate pages or as separate computer files. Then try arranging them in various orders.
- If you are interrupted while drafting, read what you have already written to get back into the flow.

In other words, immerse yourself in your writing; live in it and with it long enough for the creative process to work. It's important to integrate these general and specific strategies into your normal patterns of thinking and living rather than just using them when you have to write a paper. These strategies will act as catalysts for creativity in your life which will go far beyond simply finding topics to write about. With this in mind, it's a very good idea to use a Writer's Notebook to develop the habit of searching for ideas on an ongoing basis and recording them for future reference. Here are some guidelines for creating and using a Writer's Notebook described by Beth Baruch Joselow from her book *Writing Without the Muse*.

> If you have not been keeping a notebook or a journal, it's time for you to get started with one. Find a notebook that is a convenient size for you to carry with you as often as possible. Choose a format that will make it easy for you to take notes, whether it's a small, spiral-bound notepad or a folded sheaf of papers that you put into a ringbinder or file folder at the end of each day. Carry a pen with you at all times, too.
>
> Now, when you are hit with an idea for something you would like to think about, research, or write about, write it down in your notebook immediately. Use your notebook as well for writing down an interesting bit of dialogue you overhear, a musical line for a poem that pops into your head, or for doodling a description when you are waiting for a train, waiting for an appointment, or when you're stuck in traffic. People doodle pictures all the time—try doodling in words. Use your notebook to "talk" to yourself about ideas you are thinking of developing. Thinking changes when we write things down. Ideas develop in ways

that don't occur when we keep our ideas silently to ourselves. These notes will remain your private notes, but by opening a kind of dialogue with the pages of your notebook, you will expand your thinking ability and be more productive. You will also be making a habit of writing, and that helps keep the writing engine oiled. Try to develop at least one idea from your notebook each week.

CREATIVITY IN USING SPECIFIC DETAILS AND EXAMPLES

Because solid evidence for claims is one of the most important requirements of college writing and one of the essentials in critical thinking, a good thinker will habitually give specific examples for any general statement to show its validity and to make it understandable. However, writers often need to think creatively in order to discover examples and to present them effectively.

A common piece of advice to writers is "Don't tell your readers; show them." Good writers show by providing specific details and relevant examples, often searching through levels of specificity to find what is needed. For example:

Telling:	Michael Jordan is a great basketball player.
Showing:	During the 1995–1996 season, Michael Jordan led the NBA with a scoring average of 30.4 points per game.
	That same season, he ranked second on the Bulls for rebounding and assists.
	He was chosen for the NBA All-Star Team in his first nine seasons.
	He has won four league MVP awards and two Olympic gold medals.

Often one example will lead to another:

Telling:	My brother is an easygoing person.
Showing:	My brother lets me borrow his car whenever I want. When I had an accident while driving his car, all he said was, "That's why we have insurance."

In order to come up with abundant examples, you may need to do research, and you may need to think creatively. Follow the suggestions on being creative when generating ideas, researching, and drafting discussed earlier in this chapter.

Writers can also be creative in generating language for expressing the details that most writing needs. Although writing must always be as accurate as possible, sometimes metaphorical images can be applied; in other instances, clear descriptors are needed. Think of the differences created by describing someone's hair as being *dark,* or *black,* or *like wet pavement,* or *like polished ebony,* or *like a mink.*

Thinking ↔ Writing Activity

Using Your Senses

Our senses are powerful tools we can use to "show" people what we want to communicate. Select a situation you would like to depict in writing. It could be sitting in the cafeteria, riding the bus, attending a concert, worshipping in church, playing pool, or anything else. Then write a detailed description of the situation from your perspective, making full use of your senses:

What sounds do you hear?

What odors do you smell?

What do you taste?

What are the sensations on your skin?

What do you see?

Make a special effort to focus on each sense and identify specific sensations such as the weave of someone's sweater or the clink of ice cubes in glasses, striving to create descriptions that are rich and evocative. For example: "As the pool cue slides smoothly through my encircled finger, stained with blue chalk and white talcum, the cue ball tenderly kisses the eight ball with a soft click and sends it rolling gently down the expanse of green felt to the leather pocket waiting to embrace it."

CREATIVITY IN WRITING INTRODUCTIONS AND CONCLUSIONS

Another time to think creatively while working on a piece of writing is when you are ready to deal with the beginning and ending. It's important to realize that you need not, and probably should not, try to write these sections in order. Many successful writers work on the beginning or introduction last—or they may draft an introduction at an early stage but plan to revise it as they complete the paper.

Explore as many different types of introductions and conclusions as you can if you are writing something for which there can be choices. (Some kinds of writing, such as lab reports, have expected formats that include types of beginnings and endings.)

Following are some types of beginnings:

- Background information or context

- A relevant anecdote

- A quotation or proverb that relates to the topic

- A striking statement (to be contradicted or supported)

- The problem to be addressed in the paper

- Questions connected to the content of the paper

- The who, what, where, when, and why of the paper's focus

- The claim, thesis, or main point

- Combinations of these types

You can use creative thinking to come up with more; then use critical thinking and help from your editors, including peers, to decide which beginning your paper should have.

The same approach works for drafting conclusions. Explore the many possibilities for endings, which include these six:

- A summary of the paper's information

- A recommendation, exhortation, or call for action

- An apt quotation or proverb

- A telling anecdote

- The thesis or main point stated at the end instead of the beginning

- A suggestion of the need for more discussion of the issue

A conclusion must provide a sense of closure to the piece; readers should recognize it as an ending (you should not have to write "The End"!).

Neither introductions nor conclusions should be apologetic ("I don't know much about this, but . . ."); nor should their tone differ from that of the body of the paper. Both should be carefully revised after being creatively prepared.

Thinking ↔ Writing Activity

Creative Introductions and Conclusions

Find two or three articles in a publication that you enjoy. Look at the introductions and conclusions. Are they among the types just listed? If not, how would you describe them? Try to write a different introduction or conclusion for one of the articles and then evaluate its effectiveness.

How Are You Creative?

As effective writers, we are able to express ourselves clearly by *thinking critically*, and we are able to communicate inventive ideas from unique perspectives by *thinking creatively.* Writing is integral to the way we think and live our lives: It gives form to our thoughts and provides a vehicle for expressing our deepest and most passionate beliefs. Writing reveals who we are while helping us explore who we wish to become. In short, becoming a powerful, insightful writer necessarily involves becoming a powerful, insightful thinker, one who can think both critically and creatively.

Thinking critically and thinking creatively are two essential and tightly interwoven dimensions of the thinking process. Both work together as partners to produce effective thinking, leading to informed decisions and eventually to successful lives. Thinking critically and thinking creatively also work as partners in the writing process, enabling us to find and evaluate new approaches and insights, to discover ways to interest readers in our ideas, and to express our ideas in fresh, striking language. **Thinking creatively** involves discovering and developing ideas that are unusual and worthy of further elaboration. **Thinking critically** involves carefully examining our ideas and the thinking of others in order to clarify and improve our understanding.

For example, imagine that you are confronted with a problem to solve. Thinking critically enables you to identify and accept the problem. When you generate alternatives for solving the problem, you are thinking creatively in order to come up with inventive possibilities. When you evaluate the various alternatives and select one or more to pursue, you are thinking critically. Developing ideas for implementing alternatives involves thinking creatively, while constructing a practical plan of action and evaluating its results depends on thinking critically.

Although the first two chapters of this book have emphasized critical thinking abilities, creative thinking has been involved in every part of our explorations of the mind. In this chapter, we shift the emphasis to creative thinking, working to gain insight into this powerful and mysterious dimension of the thinking process, a dimension that can add richness and joy to our lives and to our writing.

Thinking ↔ Writing Activity

Recalling a Creative Writing Experience

1. Write about a time when you expressed yourself creatively in writing. It may have been in an important letter, a memorable poem, or even a paper for a school course. Respond to the following questions as you recall the writing experience.

   • What was the writing situation that required your creativity?

- How did you go about finding a creative idea or approach?
- Was it successful?
- How do you feel as you recall this experience?

2. Share your experience with the class and listen carefully to the experiences of other students. On the basis of your own writing experience and those of your peers, make some inferences or general statements about creativity.

LIVING CREATIVELY

Human beings have a nearly limitless capacity to be creative; our imaginations give us the power to conceive of new possibilities and to put these innovative ideas into action. Using creative resources in this way enriches our lives and brings a special meaning to our activities. Although we might not go to the extreme of saying that the uncreative life is not worth living, it is surely preferable to live a life enriched by the joys of creativity.

Many people think that being creative is beyond them, that creativity is a mysterious gift bestowed on only a chosen few. One reason for this misconception is that people often confuse being "creative" with being "artistic"—skilled at art, music, poetry, imaginative writing, drama, or dance. Although artistic people are certainly creative, there are an infinite number of ways to be creative that are *not* artistic. Being creative is a state of mind and a way of life. As the writer Eric Gill expresses it: "The artist is not a different kind of person, but each one of us is a different kind of artist."

Are you creative? Yes! Think of all the activities that you enjoy: cooking, creating a wardrobe, raising children, playing sports, cutting or braiding hair, dancing, playing music. Whenever you are investing your own personal ideas, applying your own personal stamp, you are being creative. For example, imagine that you are cooking your favorite dish. To the extent that you are expressing your unique ideas developed through inspiration and experimentation, you are being creative. If, of course, you are simply following someone else's recipe without significant modification, your dish may be tasty—but it is not creative. Similarly, if your moves on the dance floor or the basketball court express your distinctive personality, you are being creative, as you are when you stimulate the original thinking of your children or make your friends laugh with your own brand of humor.

Living life creatively means bringing your perspective and creative talents to all of the areas of your life. Following are five passages written by students about creative areas in their lives. After reading the passages, complete the Thinking-Writing Activity, which gives you the opportunity to describe a creative area in your own life.

Creative Cooking

One of the most creative aspects of my life is my diet. I have been a vegetarian for the past five years, while the rest of my family has continued to eat meat. I had to overcome many obstacles to make this lifestyle work for me, including family dissension. The solution was simple: I had to learn how to cook creatively. I have come to realize that my diet is an ongoing learning process. The more I learn about and experiment with different foods, the healthier and happier I become. I feel like an explorer setting out on my own to discover new things about food and nutrition. I slowly evolved from a person who could cook food only if it came from a can into someone who could make bread from scratch and grow yogurt cultures. I find learning new things about nutrition and cooking healthful foods very relaxing and rewarding. I like being alone in my house baking bread; there is something very comforting about the aroma. Most of all, I like to experiment with different ways to prepare foods, because the ideas are my own. Even when an effort is less than successful, I find pleasure in the knowledge that I gained from the experience. I discovered recently, for example, that eggplant is terrible in soup! Making mistakes seems to be a natural way to increase creativity, and I now firmly believe that people who say that they do not like vegetables simply have not been properly introduced to them!

Inventive Child-rearing

As any parent knows, children have an abundance of energy to spend, and toys or television do not always meet their needs. In response, I create activities to stimulate their creativity and preserve my sanity. For example, I involve them in the process of cooking, giving them the skin from peeled vegetables and a pot so they make their own "soup." Using catalogs, we cut out pictures of furniture, rugs, and curtains, and they paste them onto cartons to create their own interior decor: vibrant living rooms, plush bedrooms, colorful family rooms. I make beautiful boats from aluminum paper, and my children spend hours in the bathtub playing with them. We "go bowling" with empty soda cans and a ball, and they star in "track meets" by running an obstacle course we set up. When it comes to raising children, creativity is a way of survival!

Braiding Hair with Originality

My area of creativity is hair braiding, an activity that requires skill, talent, and patience that is difficult for most people to accomplish. Braiding hair in styles that are being worn today consists of braiding small to tiny braids, and it may include adding artificial hair to make the hair look fuller. It takes anywhere from ten to sixteen hours, depending on the type of style that is desired: the smaller the braids, the longer it takes. In order to braid, I had to learn how to determine the right hair and color for people who wanted extensions, pick out the right style that would fit perfectly on my customers' faces, learn to cut hair in an asymmetrical fashion, put curls in the braids, and know the sequence of activities. Doing hair is a rewarding experience for me because when I am through with my work, my customers think the result is gorgeous!

Creative Construction

After quitting the government agency I was working at because of too much bureaucracy, I was hired as a carpenter at a construction site, although I had little knowledge of this profession. I learned to handle a hammer and other tools by watching co-workers, and within a matter of weeks I was skilled enough to organize my own group of workers for projects. Most of my fellow workers used the old-fashioned method of construction carpentry, building panels with inefficient and poorly made bracings. I redesigned the panels in order to save construction time and materials. My supervisor and site engineer were thrilled with my creative ideas, and I was assigned progressively more challenging projects, including the construction of an office building that was completed in record time.

Imaginative Writing

The most creative area in my life is my writing. I love the thrill of inventing a new person or location, and, although I have a host of characters and story lines, there is one character named Pynthe that I am particularly proud of. Pynthe is not only my favorite character; she is also my most creative. When I invented Pynthe, I did more than just arrange a few words on paper. I gave her dimension. I took a daydream, a glimmer of an idea, and turned it into an individual. From my imagination, I created a fantasy world and religion for my character. I also gave her a past with its share of heartaches and happiness, and a future full of dreams. There is nothing more exhilarating than creating with language. In the extreme, I can destroy my character with two words, or let her lead a long and satisfying life. I can best describe this feeling of creation as a euphoric rush. I love letting my imagination roam, and I easily lose myself in writing, absorbed in the process.

Thinking ↔ Writing Activity

A Creative Area of Your Life

1. Describe a creative area of your life in which you are able to express your personality and talents. Be specific and give examples.

2. Analyze your creative area by answering the following questions:

   • Why do you feel that this activity is creative? Give examples.

   • How would you describe the experience of being engaged in this activity? Where do your creative ideas come from? How do they develop?

- What strategies do you use to increase your creativity? What obstacles block your creative efforts? How do you try to overcome these blocks?

The following article from the *Boston Globe* illustrates the far-reaching impact that creativity can have on the everyday lives of people. After reading the article, reflect on the critical reading questions that follow.

Finally, Eye to Eye

"Ibot" May Revolutionize Life in Wheelchair

BY DAVID L. CHANDLER

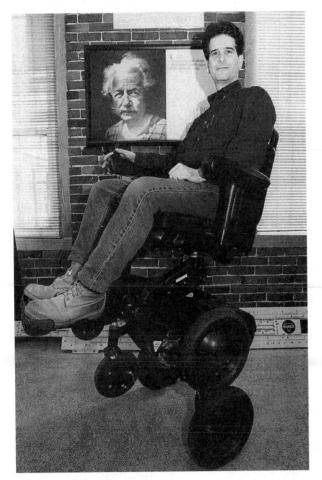

Dean Kamen is determined to make sure that never again will anyone look down on people with disabilities.

Literally.

For people who must use a wheelchair, the obstacles to ordinary life are not just curbs and staircases, steep slopes, or squishy sand that can stop them in their tracks. On a deeper emotional level, there is the constant fact that they are seeing other people at belt-buckle level. And those people are, regardless of attitude, looking down at them.

Kamen, a Manchester-based inventor and entrepreneur and the founder of a popular annual robot-building competition for high school students called FIRST, says he has the answer.

Dean Kamen demonstrating his all-terrain wheelchair invention, which uses space-age technology inside its conventional exterior. © J. Denham

5   Kamen calls his invention the Ibot. Like a wheelchair, it is a device with wheels that a person with disabilities can use to get around. But that's about where the comparison ends.

The Ibot is unfazed by curbs, loose sand, gravel, or a shaggy lawn. Terrain and obstacles that would freeze any wheelchair are no problem for the Ibot, which conceals space-age technology inside its conventional-looking exterior. (When asked how it works, Kamen sometimes answers "magic," but it's really a sophisticated array of motion sensors and gyroscopes similar to those used to stabilize spacecraft.)

Zipping up or down over a curb is nothing. The Ibot can even climb a flight of stairs. Or several flights. One of the prototype chairs, in Kamen's headquarters in an old converted Manchester mill building, sports a bumper sticker saying "This Ibot climbed the Eiffel Tower." And it really did.

Kamen said he was inspired to invent the Ibot after he saw a person in a wheelchair struggling to get on a curb.

Johnson & Johnson, one of the world's leading manufacturers of medical equipment, is financing the commercialization of the Ibot. It hopes to have it on the market next year.

10   The 100 prototypes built so far cost about $1 million each, and 40 of them have been smashed as part of the safety-testing process. Johnson & Johnson hopes to sell them for $25,000, Kamen said. Eventually, in full-scale production, the price may go down.

But even an ordinary motorized wheelchair today can cost $10,000, Kamen said. And, he says, unlike ordinary wheelchairs, the Ibot might save someone from having to modify a staircase in the person's home, or might keep someone from having to move into a nursing home.

People who see the machine in action are enthralled. At a recent satirical ceremony at Harvard University—the annual "Ig Nobel" awards—Kamen made a brief appearance in his Ibot and stole the show.

The event's organizer, Marc Abrahams, former computer engineer and now editor of the satirical Annals of Improbable Research, said he became curious after reading about the Ibot in an engineering magazine. When he first saw the Ibot, he said, "Even though I'd seen a description of it, it just made me stop and stare at it and smile."

It was one of the few times, Abrahams said, he has felt like that on seeing a new technological device. When he saw the Ibot, Abrahams said he thought "there was no one else in the universe who would have thought of this . . . It has the potential to change a little piece of the world in a very big way."

15   NBC News correspondent John Hockenberry, who uses a wheelchair, was initially skeptical of the new device, Kamen said. But once he tried it he became a convert, and has signed up to be part of the clinical trials going on with support from the U.S. Food and Drug Administration.

Scores of people with disabilities have tested the Ibot. More than the Ibot's amazing mobility, Kamen said, wheelchair users are impressed by the machine's capability of standing up to balance on two wheels and bringing its user up to eye level.

When they try it for the first time, "they go up and down a curb and say, 'Wow, that's really neat,'" Kamen said. "Then they go up and down stairs— 'Wow, that's really practical, that's great.' And then they stand up and they cry. All of them."

After spending years being looked down on every time they talk to a standing person, the emotional impact of being able to look someone straight in the eye is so powerful that people are startled by their own reactions.

"Standing up" has a practical side as well. Its users can reach items on high shelves or in kitchen cabinets without having to wait for help. And on streets with traffic whizzing by, standing at full height alleviates the dangers of not being seen by motorists.

20   Kamen's company, Deka Research and Development Corp., mostly develops biomedical devices under contract with various companies. But some devices, including the Ibot, are developed independently because Kamen says he does not want to be bothered with traditional market research.

Another of Kamen's projects, and the one that he most enjoys talking about, is trying to get children excited about science. Ten years ago, he started the For Inspiration and Recognition of Science and Technology (FIRST) program, which pairs high school students with engineers from corporations to build robots for a nationwide competition.

His intention, he says, is to try to give science and engineering the excitement and glamour that youngsters usually associate with athletes and rock stars.

But in terms of affecting people's lives, the Ibot may be Kamen's biggest venture yet. There are 7 million people in the world who use wheelchairs, Kamen said. Virtually all of them could benefit from the independence provided by the Ibot, he said. Kamen hopes that ultimately the cost will be covered by medical insurance.

The device is really about freedom, Kamen said. One of our highest values, he said, is the freedom to go anywhere, and with the Ibot, that freedom can belong to even those with the most extreme disabilities.

25   "The most extraordinary thing about that machine," he said, "is that it lets people do ordinary things."

Critical Reading Questions

1. Describe the experience that served as a creative spark for the invention of the Ibot.

2. What was the inventor of the Ibot, Dean Kamen, trying to accomplish with his invention? Do you think he was successful?

3. Explain the significance of a wheelchair-using person's being able to converse with others "eye to eye."

4. The essence of creativity is to come up with a fresh, inventive way of looking at things. Why do you think that the Ibot (or something like it) was not invented earlier?

5. Describe your own idea for an invention that you believe would make a positive contribution to the lives of people.

BECOMING MORE CREATIVE

Although we each have nearly limitless potential to live creatively, most people use only a small percentage of their creative gifts. In fact, there is research to suggest that people typically achieve their highest creative point as young children, after which there is a long, steady decline into uncreativity. Why? Well, to begin with, young children are immersed in the excitement of exploration and discovery. They are eager to try out new things, act on their impulses, and make unusual connections between disparate ideas. They are not afraid to take risks by trying out untested solutions; they do not feel compelled to identify the socially acceptable "correct answer." They are not afraid to write stories for fear of making grammar or spelling errors. Children are willing to play with ideas, creating improbable scenarios and imaginative ways of thinking, without fear of being ridiculed.

All of this tends to change as we get older. The weight of "reality" begins to smother our imagination, and we increasingly focus our attention on the nuts and bolts of living rather than entertaining possibilities. The social pressure to conform to group expectations increases dramatically. Whether the group is our friends, schoolmates, or fellow employees, there are clearly defined rules for dressing, behaving, speaking, and thinking. When we deviate from these rules, we risk social disapproval, rejection, or ridicule. Most groups have little tolerance for individuals who think independently and creatively. As we become older, we also become more reluctant to pursue untested courses of action because we become increasingly more afraid of failure. Pursuing creativity inevitably involves failure because we are trying to break out of established ruts and go beyond traditional methods. For example, going beyond the safety of a proven recipe to create an innovative dish may involve some disasters, yet it is the only way to create something genuinely unique. Analogously, forcing ourselves to go beyond the predictable safety of conventional writing is the only way to achieve genuine creative expression. The history of creative discoveries is littered with failures, a fact we tend to forget when we are debating whether to risk trying an untested idea.

Thinking ↔ Writing Activity

Inhibitions to Creativity

Reflect on your own creative development and describe some of the fears and pressures that inhibit your own creativity. For example, have you ever been penalized for trying a new idea that didn't work out? Have you ever suffered the wrath of the group for daring to be different and violating the group's unspoken rules? Do you feel that your life is so filled with responsibilities and demands that you don't have time to be creative?

Cultivating the Creative Process

Although the forces that discourage you from being creative are powerful, they can nevertheless be overcome with four productive strategies:

- Understand and trust the creative process.
- Eliminate the "Voice of Judgment."
- Make creativity a priority.
- Establish a creative environment.

UNDERSTAND AND TRUST THE PROCESS

Discovering your creative talents requires that you understand how the creative process operates and then have confidence in the results it produces. There are no fixed procedures or formulas for generating creative ideas because creative ideas by definition go beyond established ways of thinking to the unknown and the innovative. As the ancient Greek philosopher Heraclitus once said, "You must expect the unexpected, because it cannot be found by search or trial."

Although there is no fixed path to creative ideas, there are activities you can pursue that make the birth of creative ideas possible. In this respect, generating creative ideas is similar to gardening. You need to prepare the soil; plant the seeds; ensure proper watering, light, and food; and then be patient until the ideas begin to sprout. Following are some steps for cultivating your creative garden.

Absorb yourself in the task: Creative ideas don't occur in a vacuum. They emerge after a great deal of work, study, and practice. For example, if you want to come up with creative ideas in the kitchen, you need to learn more about the art of cooking. The more knowledgeable you are, the better prepared you will be to create innovative dishes. Similarly, if you are developing a creative perspective for a college research paper, you need to immerse yourself in the subject, gaining an in-depth understanding of the central concepts and issues. Absorbing yourself in the task "prepares the soil" for your creative ideas.

Allow time for ideas to incubate: After absorbing yourself in the task or problem, the next stage is to stop working on it. When your conscious mind stops actively working on the task, the unconscious dimension of your mind continues working—processing, organizing, and ultimately generating innovative ideas and solutions. This process is known as *incubation* because it mirrors the process in which baby chicks gradually evolve inside the egg until the moment when they break out through the shell. In the same way, your creative mind is at work while you are going about your business until the moment of *illumination*, when the incubating idea finally erupts to the surface of your conscious mind. People report that these illuminating moments—when their mental light bulbs go on—often occur when they are engaged in activities completely unrelated to the task. For example, you may suddenly realize how to organize your research paper while you are working out at the gym.

Seize on the ideas when they emerge and follow them through: Generating creative ideas is of little use unless you recognize them when they appear and then act on them. Too often people don't pay much attention to these ideas when they occur, or they dismiss them as too impractical. Have confidence in your ideas, even if they seem a little strange. Many of the most valuable inventions in history began as improbable ideas ridiculed by the popular wisdom. For example, the idea of Velcro started with burrs covering the pants of the inventor as he walked through a field, and Post-it notes resulted from the accidental invention of an adhesive that was weaker than normal. In other words, thinking effectively means thinking creatively and thinking critically. After you use your *creative thinking* abilities to generate innovative ideas, you must employ your *critical thinking* abilities to evaluate and refine those ideas and design a practical plan for implementing them. For example, you should write down your creative idea about organizing your research paper and then begin drafting to see if it will work.

ELIMINATE THE VOICE OF JUDGMENT

The biggest threat to your creativity lies within yourself, the negative **Voice of Judgment (VOJ).** This term was coined by Michael Ray and Rochelle Myers, the authors of *Creativity in Business,* a book based on a Stanford University course. The VOJ can undermine your confidence in every area of your life, including your creative activities. For example, when you are drafting a paper, the VOJ may whisper:

"This is a stupid idea, and no one will like it."

"Even if I could pull this idea off, it probably won't amount to much."

These statements, and countless others like them, have the ongoing effect of making you doubt yourself and the quality of your creative thinking. As you lose confidence, you become more timid, reluctant to follow through on ideas and present them to others. After a while your cumulative insecurity will discourage you from even generating ideas in the first place, and you will end up simply conforming to established ways of thinking and the expectations of others. In so doing, you surrender an important part of yourself, the vital and dynamic creative core of your personality.

How do you eliminate this unwelcome and destructive inner voice? There are a number of effective strategies. Remember, though, that the fight, although worth the effort, will not be easy.

Become aware of the VOJ: You have probably been listening to the negative messages of the VOJ for so long that you may not even consciously be aware of it. To conquer the VOJ, you first need to recognize it when it speaks.

Restate the judgment in a more accurate or constructive way: Sometimes there is an element of truth in our self-judgments, but we may have blown the reality out of proportion. For example, if you receive a low grade on a writing assignment , your VOJ may say, "You're a failure." But you need to assess the situation accurately: "I got a low grade on this paper—I wonder what went wrong and how I can improve my performance in the future."

Get tough with the VOJ: You can't be a wimp if you hope to overcome the VOJ. Instead, you have to be strong and determined, responding as soon as the VOJ appears: "I'm throwing you out and not letting you back in!" You may feel peculiar at first, but this will soon become an automatic response when those negative judgments appear.

Create positive voices and visualizations: The best way to destroy the VOJ for good is to replace it with positive encouragement. As soon as you have stomped on, say, the judgment "You're a jerk," replace it with "No, I'm an intelligent, valuable person with many positive qualities and talents." Similarly, make extensive use of positive visualization—"see" yourself performing well on assignments, being entertaining and insightful with other people, and succeeding gloriously in your courses and activities.

Use other people for independent confirmation: The negative judgments coming from the VOJ are usually irrational, but until they are dragged out into the light of day for examination, they can be very powerful. Sharing your VOJ with people you trust is an effective strategy because they can provide an objective perspective that will reveal the irrationality and destructiveness of negative judgments.

ESTABLISH A CREATIVE ENVIRONMENT

An important part of eliminating the negative voice in your mind is to establish environments in which your creative resources can flourish. This means finding or developing physical environments conducive to creative expression as well as supportive social environments. Sometimes, working with other people can be stimulating and energizing to your creative juices; at other times, you may need a private place to work without distraction. One writer says, "I have a specific location in which I do much of my writing: sitting on a comfortable couch, with a calm, pleasing view, music on the stereo, a cold drink, a supply of Tootsie Roll Pops. I'm ready for creativity to strike me, although I sometimes have to wait for some time." Different environments work for different writers: You have to find the environment(s) best suited to your own creative process; then make a special effort to do your work there.

The people in your life who form your social environment play an even more influential role in encouraging or inhibiting your creative process. When you are surrounded by people who are positive and supportive, their presence will increase your confidence and encourage you to risk expressing your creative vision. They can stimulate your creativity by providing you with fresh ideas and new perspectives. By engaging in brainstorming (described on page 72), they can help you generate ideas and then later can help you figure out how to refine and implement the most valuable ones.

MAKE CREATIVITY A PRIORITY

Having diminished the negative Voice of Judgment in your mind, established a creative environment, and committed yourself to trusting your creative gifts, you are now in a position to live and write more creatively. But how do you actually do this? Start small. Identify some habitual patterns in your life and break out of them. Choose new experiences whenever possible—for example, order unfamiliar items from a menu, get to know people outside your circle of friends, or deliberately choose a new type of introduction for a paper—and strive to develop fresh perspectives on aspects of your life. Resist falling back into the ruts you were in previously; remember that living things are supposed to be continually growing, changing, and evolving, *not* acting in repetitive patterns like machines.

Where Do Ideas Come From?

Creativity is the process we use to discover and develop ideas that are unusual and worthy of further elaboration. But how do we get creative ideas? Where do they come from? The following readings offer us some clues.

FROM

Pizza Tiger

BY TOM MONAGHAN, WITH ROBERT ANDERSON

There are some personal approaches in management that I don't think I could have learned from a book. My method of making decisions is one of them. I don't know that it would work for anyone else. But here, for whatever it's worth, is how I do it:

I reach decisions by making lists on my yellow legal pads. Down one side of a page, I'll write all the reasons I can think of in favor of a given course of action. On the other side, I list every reason I can think of against it. Thinking of arguments for and against a decision is where my ability to dream comes in handy: I *imagine* the decision has been made. I see in my mind's eye how it affects people and the way they react. If it's a complicated issue, with many reasons for it and a lot of others against, I will break each point down into sublists and assign them a kind of point value so I can weigh them against each other.

Sometimes, as I learned from my experience with the proposal that we change our name to Pizza Dispatch, it's good to consider future situations, too. In that case, my list of the benefits of the name Pizza Dispatch were outweighed by the drawbacks of giving up Domino's. But I concentrated on the immediate situation. I didn't ask myself, Okay, five years from now, when we have more than two thousand stores and are in every state in the Union, what will the pros and cons be then? Had I done so, I would have made a better decision.

I also make lists as a way of brainstorming ideas with myself on paper. This is a written version of what I love to do verbally on the occasions when I can get on the same wavelength with another person. Doing it verbally is more fun because it's exciting to share the exploration of ideas. But the written approach is absorbing, too, and it can be extremely fruitful.

5   At the outset I'm often unable to see a good idea because there's a clutter of other things hiding it. There are roads through the clutter, though, and I have to go down them until I find the one that will take me up mentally above the clutter, to a point where I can see a good idea on the horizon. The roads are propositions that I think up, write down on my list, and follow one by one. A proposition might be stupid or obvious, but I take it anyway because I don't know where it will lead and what it might connect with. I say to myself, Why don't we do this? Well, I see that if we did that, it would allow us to do something else, and I just keep adding to it. If I don't go down those roads, I never get to the good idea, because there's a link, and I find the link by following something that may not work or is impossible.

I sometimes compare my brainstorming on paper to the drilling of oil wells. The only way to strike oil is to drill a lot of wells. My lists are wells, and every once in a while I hit a gusher. I'm working away, making lists, and all of a sudden something pops right out. I'll say, Hey, look at that!

Lots of times I'll be writing lists of things I want to do this year or next year, which I do just for the fun of it, and I'll find one item I want to think about some more. So I'll take a separate page, or sometimes even another pad, and start making lists of ideas about that particular thing. I expand on it, and who knows, maybe I'll find other things in *that* list that I want to expand on. It's like fishing. I never know what kind of idea I might catch.

1. The author identifies several strategies he uses to generate creative ideas and solutions, including

   • making pro and con lists • brainstorming • previsualizing alternatives

   Describe examples from your own life in which you have used these strategies to come up with a unique idea or inventive solution.

2. The author uses several analogies to illustrate his creative quest, including:

   • finding roads through the clutter
   • drilling oil wells
   • fishing

   Identify two analogies that illustrate your creative process.

Original Spin

BY LESLEY DORMEN AND PETER EDIDIN

Creativity, somebody once wrote, is the search for the elusive "Aha," that moment of insight when one sees the world, or a problem, or an idea, in a new way. Traditionally, whether the discovery results in a cubist painting or an improved carburetor, we have viewed the creative instant as serendipitous and rare—the product of genius, the property of the elect.

Unfortunately, this attitude has had a number of adverse consequences. It encourages us to accept the myth that the creative energy society requires to address its own problems will never be present in sufficient supply. Beyond that, we have come to believe that "ordinary" people like ourselves can never be truly creative. As John Briggs, author of *Fire in the Crucible: The Alchemy of Creative Genius,* said, "The way we talk about creativity tends to reinforce the notion that it is some kind of arbitrary gift. It's amazing the way 'not having it' becomes wedded to people's self-image. They invariably work up a whole series of rationalizations about why they 'aren't creative,' as if they were damaged goods of some kind." Today, however, researchers are looking at creativity, not as an advantage of the human elite, but as a basic human endowment. As Ruth Richards, a psychiatrist and creativity researcher at McLean Hospital in Belmont, MA, says, "You were being creative when you learned how to walk. And if you are looking for something in the fridge, you're being creative because you have to figure out for yourself where it is." Creativity, in Richards' view, is simply fundamental to getting about in the world. It is "our ability to adapt to change. It is the very essence of human survival."

In an age of rampant social and technological change, such an adaptive capability becomes yet more crucial to the individual's effort to maintain balance in a constantly shifting environment. "People need to recognize that what Alvin Toffler called future shock is our daily reality," says Ellen McGrath, a clinical psychologist who teaches creativity courses at New York University. "Instability is an intrinsic part of our lives, and to deal with it every one of us will need to find new, creative solutions to the challenges of everyday life. I think creativity will be the survival skill of the '90s."

But can you really become more creative? If the word *creative* smacks too much of Picasso at his canvas, then rephrase the question in a less intimidating way: Do you believe you could deal with the challenges of life in a more effective, inventive, and fulfilling manner? If the answer is yes, then the question becomes, "What's stopping you?"

Defining Yourself as a Creative Person

5   People often hesitate to recognize the breakthroughs in their own lives as creative. But who has not felt the elation and surprise that come with the sudden, seemingly inexplicable discovery of a solution to a stubborn problem? In that instant, in "going beyond the information given," as psychologist Jerome Bruner has said, to a solution that was the product of your own mind, you were expressing your creativity.

This impulse to "go beyond" to a new idea is not the preserve of a genius, stresses David Henry Feldman, a developmental psychologist at Tufts University and the author of *Nature's Gambit,* a study of child prodigies. "Not everybody can be Beethoven," he says, "but it is true that all humans, by virtue of being dreamers and fantasizers, have a tendency to take liberties with the world as it exists. Humans are always transforming their inner and outer worlds. It's what I call the 'transformational imperative.'"

The desire to play with reality, however, is highly responsive to social control, and many of us are taught early on to repress the impulse. As Mark Runco, associate professor of psychology at California State University at Fullerton and the founder of the new *Creativity Research Journal,* says, "We put children in groups and make them sit in desks and raise their hands before they talk. We put all the emphasis on conformity and order, then we wonder why they aren't being spontaneous and creative."

Adults too are expected to conform in any number of ways and in a variety of settings. Conformity, after all, creates a sense of order and offers the reassurance of the familiar. But to free one's natural creative impulses, it is necessary, to some extent, to resist the pressure to march in step with the world. Begin small, suggests Richards. "Virtually nothing you do can't be done in a slightly different, slightly better way. This has nothing to do with so-called creative pursuits but simply with breaking with your own mindsets and trying an original way of doing some habitual task. Simply defer judgment on yourself for a little while and try something new. Remember, the essence of life is not getting things right, but taking risks, making mistakes, getting things *wrong*."

But it also must be recognized that the creative life is to some degree, and on some occasions, a solitary one. Psycholinguist Vera John-Steiner, author of *Notebooks of the Mind: Explorations of Thinking,* is one of many creativity researchers who believe that a prerequisite for creative success is "intensity of preoccupation, being pulled into your activity to such an extent that you forget it's dinnertime." Such concentration, John-Steiner believes, is part of our "natural creative bent," but we learn to ignore it because of a fear that it will isolate us from others. To John-Steiner, however, this fear is misplaced. Creative thought, she has written, is a "search for meaning," a way to connect our inner sense of being with some aspect of the world that preoccupies us. And she believes that only by linking these two aspects of reality—the inner and the outer—can we gain "some sense of being in control of life."

Avoiding the Myths

10 David Perkins, co-director of Project Zero at the Harvard Graduate School of Education, asks in *The Mind's Best Work,* "When you have it—creativity, that is—what do you have?" The very impalpability of the subject means that often creativity can be known only by its products. Indeed, the most common way the researchers define creativity is by saying it is whatever produces something that is: a. original; b. adaptive (i.e., useful); c. meaningful to others. But because we don't understand its genesis, we're often blocked or intimidated by the myths that surround and distort this mercurial subject.

One of these myths is, in Perkins's words, that creativity is "a kind of 'stuff' that the creative person has and uses to do creative things, never mind other factors." This bit of folk wisdom, that creativity is a sort of intangible psychic organ—happily present in some and absent in others—so annoys Perkins that he would like to abolish the word itself.

Another prevalent myth about creativity is that it is restricted to those who are "geniuses"—that is, people with inordinately high IQs. Ironically, this has been discredited by a study begun by Stanford psychologist Lewis Terman, the man who adapted the original French IQ test for America. In the early 1920s, Terman had California schoolteachers choose 1,528 "genius" schoolchildren (those with an IQ above 135), whose lives were then tracked year after year. After six decades, researchers found that the putative geniuses, by and large, did well in life. They entered the professions in large numbers and led stable, prosperous lives. But very few made notable creative contributions to society, and none did extraordinary creative work.

According to Dean Simonton, professor of psychology at the University of California at Davis and the author of *Genius, Creativity and Leadership* and *Scientific Genius,* "There just isn't any correlation between creativity and IQ. The average college graduate has an IQ of about 120, and this is high enough to write novels, do scientific research, or any other kind of creative work."

A third myth, voiced eons ago by Socrates, lifts creativity out of our own lives altogether into a mystical realm that makes it all but unapproachable. In this view, the creative individual is a kind of oracle, the passive conduit or channel chosen by God, or the tribal ancestors, or the muse, to communicate sacred knowledge.

15   Although there *are* extraordinary examples of creativity, for which the only explanation seems to be supernatural intervention (Mozart, the story goes, wrote the overture to *Don Giovanni* in only a few hours, after a virtually sleepless night and without revision), by and large, creativity begins with a long and intensive apprenticeship.

Psychologist Howard Gruber believes that it takes at least 10 years of immersion in a given domain before an eminent creator is likely to be able to make a distinctive mark. Einstein, for example, who is popularly thought to have doodled out the theory of relativity at age 26 in his spare time, was in fact compulsively engaged in thinking about the problem at least from the age of 16.

Finally, many who despair of ever being creative do so because they tried once and failed, as though the truly creative always succeed. In fact, just the opposite is true, says Dean Simonton. He sees genius, in a sense, as inseparable from failure. "Great geniuses make tons of mistakes," he says. "They generate lots of ideas and they accept being wrong. They have a kind of internal fortress that allows them to fail and just keep going. Look at Edison. He held over 1,000 patents, but most of them are not only forgotten, they weren't worth much to begin with."

Mindlessness vs. Mindfulness

"Each of us desires to share with others our vision of the world, only most of us have been taught that it's wrong to do things differently or look at things differently," says John Briggs. "We lose confidence in ourselves and begin to look at reality only in terms of the categories by which society orders it."

This is the state of routinized conformity and passive learning that Harvard professor of psychology Ellen Langer calls, appropriately enough, mindlessness. For it is the state of denying the perceptions and promptings of our own minds, our individual selves. Langer and her colleagues' extensive research over the past 15 years has shown that when we act mindlessly, we behave automatically and limit our capacity for creative response. Mired down in a numbing daily routine, we may virtually relinquish our capacity for independent thought and action.

20   By contrast, Langer refers to a life in which we use our affective, responsive, perceptive faculties as "mindful." When we are mindful, her research has shown, we avoid rigid, reflexive behavior in favor of a more improvisational and intuitive response to life. We notice and feel the world around us and then act in accordance with our feelings. "Many, if not all, of the qualities that make up a mindful attitude are characteristic of creative people," Langer writes in her new book, *Mindfulness*. "Those who can free themselves of mindsets, open themselves to new information and surprise, play with perspective and context,

and focus on process rather than outcome are likely to be creative, whether they are scientists, artists, or cooks."

Much of Langer's research has demonstrated the vital relationship between creativity and uncertainty, or conditionality. For instance, in one experiment, Langer and Alison Piper introduced a collection of objects to one group of people by saying, "This is a hair dryer," and "This is a dog's chew toy," and so on. Another group was told "This *could* be a hair dryer," and "This *could* be a dog's chew toy." Later, the experimenters for both groups invented a need for an eraser, but only those people who had been conditionally introduced to the objects thought to use the dog's toy in this new way.

The intuitive understanding that a single thing is, or could be, many things, depending on how you look at it, is at the heart of the attitude Langer calls mindfulness. But can such an amorphous state be cultivated? Langer believes that it can, by consciously discarding the idea that any given moment of your day is fixed in its form. "I teach people to 'componentize' their lives into smaller pieces," she says. "In the morning, instead of mindlessly downing your orange juice, *taste it*. Is it what you want? Try something else if it isn't. When you walk to work, turn left instead of right. You'll notice the street you're on, the buildings and the weather. Mindfulness, like creativity, is nothing more than a return to who you are. By minding your responses to the world, you will come to know yourself again. How you feel. What you want. What you want to do."

Creating the Right Atmosphere

Understanding the genesis of creativity, going beyond the myths to understand your creative potential, and recognizing your ability to break free of old ways of thinking are the three initial steps to a more creative life. The fourth is finding ways to work that encourage personal commitment and expressiveness.

Letting employees learn what they want to do has never been a very high priority in the workplace. There, the dominant regulation has always been, "Do what you are told."

25   Today, however, economic realities are providing a new impetus for change. The pressure on American businesses to become more productive and innovative has made creative thinking a hot commodity in the business community. But innovation, business is now learning, is likely to be found wherever bright and eager people *think* they can find it. And some people are looking in curious places.

Financier Wayne Silby, for example, founded the Calvert Group of funds, which today manages billions of dollars in assets. Silby, whose business card at one point read Chief Daydreamer, occasionally retreats for inspiration to a sensory deprivation tank, where he floats in warm water sealed off from light and sound. "I went into the tank during a time when the government was changing money-market deposit regulations, and I needed to think how to compete with banks. Floating in the tank I got the idea of joining them instead. We wound up creating an $800-million program. Often we already have answers to our problems, but we don't quiet ourselves enough to see the solutions bubbling just below the surface." Those solutions will stay submerged, he says, "unless you create a culture that encourages creative approaches, where it's OK to have bad ideas."

Toward this goal, many companies have turned to creativity consultants, like Synectics, Inc., in Cambridge, MA. Half the battle, according to Synectics facilitator Jeff Mauzy, is to get the clients to relax and accept that they are in a safe place where the cutthroat rules of the workplace don't apply, so they can allow themselves to exercise their creative potential in group idea sessions.

Pamela Webb Moore, director of naming services (she helps companies figure out good names for their products) at Synectics, agrees. One technique she uses to limber up the minds of tightly focused corporate managers is "sleight of head." While working on a particular problem, she'll ask clients to pretend to work on something else. In one real-life example, a Synectics-trained facilitator took a group of product-development and marketing managers from the Etonic shoe corporation on an "excursion," a conscious walk away from the problem—in this case, to come up with a new kind of tennis shoe.

The facilitator asked the Etonic people to imagine they were at their favorite vacation spot. "One guy," Moore says, "was on a tropical island, walking on the beach in his bare feet. He described how wonderful the water and sand felt on his feet, and he said, 'I wish we could play tennis barefoot.' The whole thing would have stopped right there if somebody had complained that while his colleague was wandering around barefoot, they were supposed to come up with a *shoe*. Instead, one of the marketing people there was intrigued, and the whole group decided to go off to play tennis barefoot on a rented court at 10 at night."

30

While the Etonic people played tennis, the facilitator listed everything they said about how it felt. The next morning, the group looked at her assembled list of comments, and they realized that what they liked about playing barefoot was the lightness of being without shoes, and the ability to pivot easily on both the ball of the foot and the heel. Nine months later, the company produced an extremely light shoe called the Catalyst, which featured an innovative two-piece sole that made it easier for players to pivot.

The Payoff

In *The Courage to Create*, Rollo May wrote that for much of this century, researchers had avoided the subject of creativity because they perceived it as "unscientific, mysterious, disturbing and too corruptive of the scientific training of graduate students." But today researchers are coming to see that creativity, at once fugitive and ubiquitous, is the mark of human nature itself.

Whether in business or the arts, politics or personal relationships, creativity involves "going beyond the information given" to create or reveal something new in the world. And almost invariably, when the mind exercises its creative muscle, it also generates a sense of pleasure. The feeling may be powerfully mystical, as it is for New York artist Rhonda Zwillinger, whose embellished artwork appeared in the film *Slaves of New York*. Zwillinger reports, "There are times when I'm working and it is almost as though I'm a vessel and there is a force operating through me. It is the closest I come to having a religious experience."

The creative experience may also be quiet and full of wonder, as it was for Isaac Newton, who compared his lifetime of creative effort to "a boy playing on the seashore and diverting himself and then finding a smoother pebble or prettier shell than ordinary, while the greater ocean of truth lay all undiscovered before me."

But whatever the specific sensation, creativity always carries with it a powerful sense of the mind working at the peak of its ability. Creativity truly is, as David Perkins calls it, the mind's best work, its finest effort. We may never know exactly how the brain does it, but we can feel that it is exactly what the brain was meant to do.

Aha!

Critical Reading Questions

1. According to the authors, "creativity . . . is the search for the elusive 'Aha,' that moment of insight when one sees the world, or a problem, or an idea, in a new way." Describe an "Aha" moment that you have had recently, detailing the origin of your innovative idea and how you implemented it.

2. Identify some of the influences in your life that have inhibited your creative development, including the myths about creativity described in the reading.

3. Using the ideas contained in this chapter and in this reading selection, identify some of the strategies that you intend to use in order to become more creative in your life: for example, becoming more "mindful," destroying the Voice of Judgment, and creating a more conducive atmosphere.

Writing Project: Imagining Your Life Lived More Creatively

This chapter includes a number of Thinking-Writing Activities and readings that encourage you to reflect on the nature of creativity and on your own creativity—past, present, and future. Be sure to reread what you wrote for those activities: You may be able to use or build on the ideas you wrote about to complete this project. You may also want to include material from the chapter readings in your essay. If you do, be sure to document them correctly by citing the authors and acknowledging their ideas. And, of course, use quotation marks or set off a longer quotation by indenting it.

The chapter's Writing Project asks you to think creatively to imagine changes in your life. Doing this can, in fact, be very difficult. But it is important to do to avoid future regrets; often people most regret the things they did not do as they lived their lives. According to a French proverb, "Only he who does nothing makes a mistake."

> Imagine how some part of your life could be more satisfying or exciting. You will need to focus on one or more specific areas of your life, such as an important relationship, your college work, or a job that would be ideal for you. Visualize how your future will be when you creatively transform this part of your life, and think about what you must do in the present to achieve this imagined goal. Alternatively, you could describe a creative breakthrough you had in the past that enabled you to envision your life more creatively. Then write an essay in which you present your vision. Follow your instructor's directions for length, format, and so on.

THE WRITING SITUATION

Begin by considering the key elements of the Thinking-Writing Model.

Purpose Your primary purpose is to employ the strategies for thinking, living, and writing creatively this chapter presents to create a new vision of your own life. Doing this will require you, to some extent, to step back from your life, to become an observer of how you have lived, are living, or might be living, and then to become a creator of a potentially different vision.

Another purpose will be to show, not tell, what the creative changes in your life would be by giving enough examples to let your readers picture what you mean.

Audience You have an interesting and varied audience for this Writing Project. In a real sense, you are your own most important audience, for who else could be more involved with or interested in the subject? Beyond yourself, you may choose to show your writing to key people in your life, especially if any of them would be affected by the creative changes you propose. Their reactions to early drafts could be very helpful as you revise your writing.

At another level, your classmates may be part of your audience, especially if your writing is going to be shared with or reviewed by them. All the readers mentioned so far—you, key people in your life, and your classmates—will be interested in what you say, and especially in the changes you propose, so be sure to include enough background information about how your life was, or is, for them to readily understand the impact of what you are proposing.

Finally, your instructor is also part of your audience, and his or her judgment of your work will matter to you. Therefore, carefully consider both your instructor's directions and the points that have been emphasized in class. Be aware that as a writing teacher, your instructor is interested not only in what you say but also in how you say it.

Subject Thinking and writing about our own lives can be both exciting and challenging. Often we are so busy just living our lives that we don't take time to actually think about them and about how they might be different. We begin to think that whatever *is* has to be.

For this Writing Project, you should try to use as many of the chapter's suggestions as you can to help generate ideas. Doing this will take time, so begin as soon as possible. You may think of changes you aren't sure you want to make in your life, but your critical thinking abilities will help you sort these out.

A potential problem with this subject is that you may believe that there is little in your life that can be changed; if this is the case, think carefully and honestly about how true this really is. If some areas cannot be changed, think creatively to discover other areas to write about. Note that you are not necessarily being asked to propose major changes. What you end up writing about could be a very different life or simply a richer, more fully realized version of what your life is now. For instance, you might envision an ideal job situation for your life after college.

Writer As the expert on your own life, you can feel comfortable as you work on this project. If you are the creative type, you should welcome the chance to let your imagination go! If you consider yourself unimaginative, take this opportunity to develop your creative side. (We are all creative, as this chapter reminds us.)

THE WRITING PROCESS

The following sections will guide you through the stages of generating, planning, drafting, and revising as you work on an essay about adding more creativity to some aspect of your life. Try to be particularly conscious of how creative thinking can help you discover and connect ideas.

Generating Ideas You have already written about your creativity if you've done the Thinking-Writing Activities in this chapter. Review what you wrote. You will probably see that you noted a number of ideas that pertain to this project. Then, to discover more ideas and a possible focus, follow these suggestions and jot down your responses.

- Think about two or three things you do that are particularly important to you. How might they become more satisfying if you became more creative in your approach to them?

- Envision your life five years from now. What activities do you hope to be involved in? How do you believe they could be shaped by creative thinking? What would be your ideal job situation?

- Recall an event from the past in which you experienced a creative break-through. What was your flash of insight? How did it influence the way you envision yourself and your life? Can you apply that creative insight to your current situation or future life?

- Choose a situation and brainstorm or ask questions about it (see pages 72–77 in this chapter).

- Talk to friends or family members about your ideas to see if they have suggestions.

- Ask yourself if you have enough ideas to begin drafting your paper. If not, you may want to try again by examining another aspect of your life.

Defining a Focus Review all the material you created while generating ideas. Consider which area of your life would be most exciting to focus on for creative change. Then write a few sentences about that change. Your passage might look like this:

> I think that I would like to be a more creative cook. Why? How? So that my housemates and I can have more enjoyable meals when it's my turn in the kitchen; so that I can really enjoy cooking. . . . Some ways that I can do this is to take a cooking course, check some really different cook-books out of the library—like from other countries or other regions, or vegan, or barbecue. I should spend some time with my uncle who makes such good one-dish meals, find some tasty web sites, and watch some of those cooking shows instead of surfing away.

It seems that this writer has settled on a focus: becoming a more creative cook. She can now decide how to draft the thesis—as a simple statement or in a "blueprinted" sentence that lays out the organization of the paper.

Simple statement: I want to change my life by becoming a more creative cook.

Blueprinted sentence: I plan to become a more creative cook by taking a cooking course, checking some good cookbooks out of the library, spending more time with my uncle, finding some tasty web sites, and watching some cooking shows.

If you do write a blueprinted sentence, consider whether you have listed the changes in the order that your audience can most easily comprehend. Once you have established an order like this, you must be sure to follow it in your essay.

Organizing Ideas After you have decided whether you will focus on one area, two, or three and have done some drafting, you can

- describe your current or past situation
- describe some changes you would like to make or wish you had made
- describe the improved situation

Does this thinking suggest a method of organization? Is that organization effective, or is it too stodgy for a paper about creative thinking? If this project warrants something other than a regular essay structure, how about narrating the events from a future perspective, after you have made some changes? How about imagining your new (or old) situation from your boyfriend's or mother's or boss's point of view?

Map out an organizational plan that you think might work. Consult with your instructor if you are taking a creative approach to organization.

Drafting As you translate your ideas, notes, and early versions into coherent writing, you will need to decide how you can draft in ways that will help you revise your work effectively. Because the essay you are about to write will have three distinct components—your present situation, the changes you would make, and how your life would be different as a result—you may want to draft each component separately and then think about connecting them.

Drafting Hints

1. If you are drafting on a word processor, double or even triple space. Be sure to save your work every few minutes if your program does not do so automatically.

2. Consider drafting the three components of this essay as three separate files. You could name them "Present Situation," "Changes," and "New and Different Life." Then you can easily copy and paste them to see what organization would work best.

3. If you are drafting by hand, skip lines and write on only one side of the paper. That way you can easily rearrange them if you decide to reorganize.

Revising One of the best revision strategies is to get an audience's reactions to your draft. Your classmates, or peers, can help you see where your draft is already successful and where it needs improvement. If your instructor allows class time for peer review, be sure to have a draft ready so that you can benefit from this activity.

Revising Strategy: Peer Response with Silent Writer This activity, which works best with groups of three or four, introduces a different method for peer review than the one in Chapter 2. In this method, the writer is silent after reading his or her draft aloud twice and simply listens as peers make responses. When you are the writer, listen carefully to your peers' responses and take notes. When you are a peer, try to give the writer useful responses to parts of the draft which could benefit from revision. Follow all the steps of the directions carefully.

1. The group selects a timekeeper, who allots ten minutes to each writer. Regardless of how many steps in the response process have been completed, after ten minutes the group moves on to consider the next writer's work.

2. One person begins by reading his or her draft aloud while group members listen and give the writer their full attention.

3. The writer then reads his or her writing aloud a second time. Group members listen again, this time taking notes.

4. Group members read their comments to the writer. Responses that are stated as "I" messages and that are geared to helping the writer revise work well:

   a. Weak response: "I like it. It sounds okay to me." (no specific help given to writer)

   b. Marginally useful: "I thought the description of your new neighborhood was entertaining." (encouragement for the writer)

   c. Useful: "Can you give me an example of the kind of task you would perform in your new job?" (The writer learns what information the reader needs.)

   d. Very useful: "I was confused when you said your aunt came into the room. I thought you said earlier that you were alone in the house." (Again, the writers hear from someone who wasn't there when it happened, someone who needs more information.)

5. The writer listens to questions and comments and may take notes but does *not* answer or respond aloud.

6. The writer may ask questions after all group members have commented.

7. After each group member has used ten minutes of response time, members may begin revising their own writing.

As soon as possible after peer review, you should revise your draft based on your peers' questions and comments. Then, if possible, put it aside for a day or two before continuing to revise.

Reread your revised draft out loud, slowly. Then think about each of the following questions. Be sure to take advantage of technology by making changes to your draft at each level of revision before moving on to the next level.

1. How could you improve your introduction? It should be creative since this is a paper about creative thinking! Review the suggestions on pages 80 and 81 of this chapter.

2. How could you improve the order of your draft? Here you need to balance creativity against the needs of your readers. Are you providing

information in an order that is easy for your readers to follow? Is there a more creative way to arrange your essay without sacrificing the needs of your readers?

3. Could you provide transitions between sections of your essay to help your readers follow your ideas?

4. Is your use of language creative? Could you provide more specific adjectives and adverbs?

5. Have you given your essay an inventive title that will make your readers want to read it?

Editing and Proofreading   After you prepare a final draft, edit for standard grammar and punctuation usage. Proofread carefully to detect omitted words and punctuation marks. Run your spelling checker program, but be aware of its limitations. Proofread again for the kinds of errors the computer can't catch. Finally, ask someone you trust to proofread after you are finished.

The following essays show how two students responded to the idea of living their lives more creatively.

STUDENT WRITING

Discovering Creativity by Not Looking for It
BY JESSIE LANGE

There have been numerous times when I have sat in front of a blank computer screen, a writing assignment in hand, feeling completely uninspired and uncreative. Without having even begun I think, "Now what?" There have been numerous times when I've just started filling up that screen with meaningless, dry words that really have no effect on me or anyone else. Yes, I'm getting the job done, but not the job I'd like—not my best work, not anywhere near it. One thing that I've found in my life is that in your most uncreative ruts sometimes you can't pull yourself out all on your own. You can't always, sitting in an idea-less vacuum, turn on the creativity. Sometimes you will save yourself time and produce a much more fulfilling piece of work if you take the time out to go *out* of the world of your blank screen. For me this has always meant literally getting outdoors, because somehow it always seems that I find *outside* what I've been looking for *inside*.

It was the first English assignment of my senior year of high school—an interpretation of a Buddhist legend—and I was struggling with its meaning. The legend is about a set of stairs leading to the top of the tower from where you can see the "whole horizon" and the "loveliest landscape"—a symbol of attaining nirvana. The paradox in the legend is that you can only reach the top if you do not believe in the legend itself. How would those who believe, then, ever reach the top? How can you even start the climb without making the conscious decision to do so?

Being in the country on weekends has many benefits, one of them being that I could go outside to clear my head. I lit my Williams Sonoma oil lamp and walked out into the night that offered the occasional drizzle and a strong breeze that ruffled the leaves of the tree I lay down under. I was there for an hour, feeling the drops on my face and the dampness settling into my body, before it happened. I rolled over and looked out into the field, because I sensed something the way that you can and will when you're listening with your entire body. Farther out, right before the lawn becomes high grass and eventually woods, were four white shapes moving across my line of vision. The same deer I casually glance at during the day were like ghosts grazing out there at night. Just faint, light vaporous figures against the pitch black. That moment was like seeing the "whole horizon." Those animals, moving with such grace, were unaware of my presence. For all they knew, I was another tree silently overseeing their nightly ritual. Watching these beasts—because that's what they are, wonderfully wild animals—I was witnessing a scene that could have taken place in this same spot on this same night hundreds or thousands of years before. I reached for my lantern and turned up the flame, holding it in front of me for a better view. This light, however, obstructed my vision rather than illuminating it. It was only when I put the flame aside and cupped my hands around my eyes, creating a deeper darkness, that I could really see the deer. And then I realized that perhaps that was why only those who do not believe the legend ever climb the stairs of the tower—because when you actively search for things, like holding the light, perhaps you prevent yourself from seeing them. Had I not put my writing aside and taken that walk, I would never have found this answer, the answer I was looking for. I wrote my English essay and I also learned something about creativity in my own life. Some of your most creative moments happen when you're not looking. In the journey up the steps of the tower toward creativity, sometimes it is not those who are keenly searching for a victory of sorts, but those who are instead turning down the light, that begin the climb.

The Voice

BY STEPHANIE H. MOSES

I lie in my bed. For the last two hours I have been trying to fall asleep. My roommates are being too loud. It isn't all their fault that I'm still awake, though. It's the voice. From within I hear many different dialogues. Words pop in and out of my head to form sentences that mean nothing to me. Without proper guidance, the voice can be a nuisance. It beckons me to go to my computer. *I am talking to you,* it says. *I want to say something important. Get up and let me be realized!* But I stay in bed. I fight it. I once learned to give the dialogues a representation, and visualize picking them up and putting them in a jar one at a time. Then close the jar, and the voices will be silent. This doesn't work for me. The voice always fights back. *I am stronger than this jar. I can break it to pieces from within, and your head will be filled with pieces of broken glass forever.* So I let it talk to me with the hope that it will either run out of things to say or develop laryngitis. If I am lucky and it stops before three a.m., I can still get five hours of sleep before class in the morning.

Next quarter I will be taking two writing classes, and I know that I will not be kept awake at night by the voice. I will have to go in search of it, and the blank Word document will mock my pain and remind me of the time when the voice came without summons. *Remember when you lay in your bed all night, trying to ignore the voice,* my computer will say. *You had so much to write, but not one single creative writing assignment.* I could've opened my journal and written something. I could've turned on the computer and let the voice free flow. I could've reworked an old piece with the hope of submitting it to a contest or a magazine. Even reading a book would've turned down the voice's tenacious spirit and quenched my creative desires.

For me writing is not only a necessity—the alternative being insanity—it is also a private realm in which I can create an outcome to my liking. I interweave experiences from real life that I dislike with fantasy and the hypothetical. This induces in me a sense of justice. The person who was wronged is avenged. The world is set right once again.

Every person I have met that wants to be a serious writer is intrigued with lying. A poet once told me that he lies about everything when he gives speeches to people that he doesn't know. My fiction professor is the same way: when he meets people, he tells them that he works for NASA. I too am captivated by telling the occasional lie. I have been known to tell people that I am a dentist, my mother is Spanish and this is why I am bilingual, and that I got a perfect score on the SATs. Being able to pull off a lie is living fiction. After all, it is not me that comes up with these ideas; it is the voice inside. It fights with reality and wins.

My voice has a big head. It wants to be doted on, adored; it wants to be the main focus of my life and the only source of my income. This is the path that I want to follow into the future, not the path to insanity. I will submit my short stories to literary magazines. I will apply to MFA programs throughout the country. I will listen to my voice and feed it with creativity. I know it will give me sensational writings in return. If I cannot get by just writing novels, I hope to find a job in which writing is a major component. For me, the type of writing doesn't matter, so long as the voice is being heard and is communicating with me at decent hours.

ALTERNATIVE WRITING PROJECT:
A CREATIVE SOLUTION TO A PHYSICAL PROBLEM

Write an essay explaining your original, creative solution to a physical problem, one involving a piece of equipment, the use of space, overcoming some barrier, and so on. Here are some examples:

- Crowd control or better seating at concerts and sporting events
- A device that makes some activity easier or more accessible for the disabled
- A re-engineering of your dorm or apartment building
- New design or redesign of highways and roads in your area
- An imaginative new tool or transportation device

Review the section about understanding and trusting the creative process on pages 90–91 as you work toward your solution. Your audience will need to understand the problem and the difficulties involved in solving it. You will need to provide a very clear description of your solution so that your audience will understand how and/or why it will work. Think carefully about purpose, audience (it might include others facing the same problem or a company which could market your solution), subject, and writer as you move through the steps of generating ideas, defining a focus, organizing ideas, drafting, revising, and proofreading. Review the ideas under these sections in Chapter 1 and in this chapter.

Follow your instructor's directions for length, format, and so on. Include a drawing or diagram if you wish.

4

Making Decisions

Revising Purposefully

"The strongest principle of growth lies in human choice." —George Eliot

Critical Thinking Focus: Decision making

Writing Focus: Making decisions about drafts

Reading Themes: People making decisions, writers thinking about revision

Writing Project: Analyzing a decision to be made

After professional writers have used creative thinking to generate ideas and early drafts, they bring their critical thinking abilities into play to revise their writing—to "see it again." As writers revise, they keep purpose and audience in mind and make decisions about what to keep and what to change in their drafts. In other words, revision involves identifying possible changes and then deciding whether these changes will help to accomplish the writer's purpose with an audience. Revision is often the key to the success of a piece of writing. Effective writers have the ability to reread drafts critically, to rethink what those drafts are saying, and to rewrite—or revise—when necessary.

Making Decisions

This chapter presents an organized method for making decisions, a way of thinking that will help you revise successfully and also lead to the best possible life decisions. The chapter then applies this method to revising drafts and to a Writing Project which provides you with the opportunity to analyze an important decision in your life.

In order to reach various goals in life, we try to make the best decisions for ourselves or our community. Even so, we don't always make the most *informed* or *intelligent* decisions possible. In fact, most of us regularly end up mentally kicking ourselves after making a poor decision. Many faulty or regrettable decisions involve relatively minor issues such as selecting an unappealing dish in a restaurant, hastily agreeing to go on a blind date, or taking a course that does not meet our expectations. Although these decisions may result in unpleasant consequences, the discomfort is neither life threatening nor long-lasting (although a disappointing course may *seem* to last forever!). However, there also are many significant decisions in which poor choices can result in considerably more damaging and far-reaching consequences. For example, one reason the current divorce rate in the United States stands at 50 percent is poor decisions people make before or after the vow "till death do us part." Similarly, the fact that many employed adults wake up unhappy about going to work, anxiously waiting for the end of the day or the week (TGIF!) when they will be free to do what they really want, suggests that somewhere along the line, they have made poor decisions or felt trapped by circumstances beyond their control.

Thinking ↔ Writing Activity

Analyzing a Previous Decision

Think back to an important decision you made that turned out well and describe the experience as specifically as possible by reconstructing the reasoning process you used to make your decision.

- How did you *define* the decision to be made?
- What *choices* did you consider?
- What were the various *pros and cons* of each possible choice?
- What specific plan of action did you use to implement your ideas?
- How did you review your decision to make any necessary adjustments?

AN ORGANIZED APPROACH TO MAKING DECISIONS

As you were reflecting on the successful decision you wrote about in the previous Thinking-Writing Activity, you probably noticed your mind working in a systematic way as you thought your way through the decision-making process. Of course, we often make important decisions with less thoughtful analysis by acting impulsively and are later forced to cope with the consequences. Our intuitions can be a useful guide to success when they are *informed intuitions*—based on lessons learned from past experience and thoughtful reflection. Naturally, there are no guarantees that careful analysis will lead to a successful result—there are often too many unknown elements and factors beyond our control. But we can certainly improve our success rate as well as our speed by becoming more knowledgeable about the decision-making process.

This approach consists of five steps. As you master these steps, they will become integrated into your way of thinking, and you will be able to apply them in a natural and flexible way.

In 1993, following an extended siege, and spurred by reports of child abuse in the Branch Davidian compound in Waco, Texas, U.S. Attorney General Janet Reno ordered an attack that resulted in death and destruction. "I still don't know if I made the right decision," Reno admitted. © Associated Press.

STEP 1: DEFINE THE DECISION AND ITS GOALS CLEARLY

This seems like an obvious step, but decision making frequently goes wrong at the starting point. For example, imagine that you are trying to decide on a major. In order to make an informed decision, you have to project yourself into the future, imagining the career that will be right for you. Your goals will likely include

- financial security
- personal fulfillment
- an opportunity to make use of your special talents
- employment opportunities and job security

Students who keep these goals in mind as they consider various majors will have the greatest success discovering the field that best suits them. The more specific your definition of the decision—and its goals—is, the clearer your

In an early morning raid, U.S. marshals recovered Elián González from the home of his relatives in Miami in order to reunite him with his Cuban father. The raid culminated months of conflict between the U.S. government and those opposed to the regime of the Cuban dictator, Fidel Castro. © Associated Press.

analysis and the greater the likelihood of your success will be. Here's a strategy you can use to best define your decision:

Strategy: Write a one-page analysis describing your decision-making situation that defines your goals as clearly and specifically as possible.

STEP 2: CONSIDER ALL POSSIBLE CHOICES

Successful decision makers explore all possible choices, not simply the obvious ones. In fact, the less obvious choices often turn out to be the most effective ones. For instance, one student couldn't decide whether to major in accounting or business management. While discussing his situation with other class members, he revealed that his real interest was in graphic design and illustration. Although he was very talented, he considered this area only a hobby, not a possible career choice. Classmates pointed out that design and illustration could prove to be his best career opportunity, but he first needed to see it as a possibility.

Strategy: List as many possible choices for your situation as you can—obvious and not obvious, practical and impractical. Ask other people for additional suggestions and don't censor or prejudge any ideas.

STEP 3: GATHER ALL RELEVANT INFORMATION AND EVALUATE THE PROS AND CONS OF EACH POSSIBLE CHOICE

Each of the possible choices you identified will have certain advantages and disadvantages, so it is essential that you analyze these pros and cons in an organized fashion. In the case of the student discussed in Step 2, the career choice of accounting might on the one hand offer advantages like ready employment opportunities, the flexibility of working in many different situations and geographical locations, a moderate-to-high income, and job security. On the other hand, disadvantages might be that accounting does not reflect the student's deep and abiding interest, that he might become bored with it over time, and that the career might not result in the personal challenge and fulfillment that he needs.

Strategy: Using a format similar to the following, analyze the pros and cons of each of your possible choices.

	Possible Choices	Pros	Cons
1.			
2.			
3.			

In many cases, you may lack sufficient information to make an informed choice. Unfortunately, this has never prevented people from plunging ahead anyway, making a decision that is more a gamble than an informed choice. But it makes much more sense to seek out the information you need in order to determine which of your choices has the best chance of success. In the case of the student, he would need certain crucial information to determine which career would be best for him: What sort of academic preparation and experience is required for the various careers? What are the prospects for employment in these areas, and how well do the positions pay? What are the day-to-day activities in each career? How happy are the people in the various careers?

Strategy: For each possible choice that you have identified, create questions regarding information you need; then obtain that information.

STEP 4: SELECT THE CHOICE THAT SEEMS BEST SUITED TO THE SITUATION

The first three steps are designed to help you analyze your decision situation: to define clearly the decision in terms of your goals, to generate possible choices, and to evaluate the pros and cons of the choices you have identified. In the fourth step, you must synthesize what you have learned, weaving together all the various threads into a conclusion that you consider your best choice. How do you do this? There is no one simple way to identify your best choice, but the following are two useful strategies for guiding your deliberations.

Strategy: Identify and prioritize the goal(s) of your decision situation and determine which of your choices best meets these goals. This process will probably involve reviewing and perhaps refining your definition of the decision situation. For example, for the student we have been discussing, goals included choosing a career that would (a) provide financial security, (b) provide personal fulfillment, (c) make use of special talents, and (d) offer plentiful work opportunities along with job security.

Once identified, these goals can be ranked in order of priority, which will then suggest what the best choice would be. If the student ranks goals *a* and *d* at the top of the list, a choice of accounting or business administration may make sense. However, if the student ranks goals *b* and *c* at the top, pursuing a career in graphic design and illustration may be the best selection.

Strategy: Anticipate the consequences of each choice by "preliving" the choices. Project yourself into the future, imagining as realistically as you can the consequences of each possible choice. As with previous strategies, this process is aided by writing your thoughts down and discussing them with others.

STEP 5: IMPLEMENT A PLAN OF ACTION AND MONITOR THE RESULTS, MAKING NECESSARY ADJUSTMENTS

Once you have made your best choice, you need to develop and implement a specific, concrete plan of action. The more specific and concrete your plan, the greater the likelihood of its success. If, for instance, the student in the example decides to pursue a career in graphic design and illustration, his plan should include reviewing the major that best meets his needs, discussing his situation with students and faculty in that department, planning what courses to take, and perhaps speaking with people working in the field.

Strategy: Create a plan that details the steps you would take to implement your decision, along with a time line for taking these steps. Naturally, your plan is merely a starting point. As you actually begin taking the steps in your plan, you may discover that you need to make changes and adjustments. You might find new information which suggests that your choice may be wrong. For example, as the student takes courses in graphic design and illustration, he may realize that his interest in the field is not as serious as he once thought and that although he liked this area as a hobby, he does not want it to be his life's work. In this case, he should reconsider his other choices, perhaps adding some choices that he did not contemplate before.

Strategy: After implementing your choice, evaluate its success by identifying what is working and what is not; then make the necessary adjustments to improve the situation.

Summary for Making Decisions

1. Define the decision clearly.
2. Consider all possible choices.
3. Gather all relevant information and evaluate the pros and cons of each possible choice.
4. Select the choice that seems best suited to the situation.
5. Implement a plan of action and monitor the results, making necessary adjustments.

APPLYING THE METHOD FOR MAKING DECISIONS

Maintaining objectivity about the lives and decisions of others is sometimes easier than maintaining objectivity about our own lives. To familiarize yourself with applying the five steps just presented, read the following story from Amy Tan's *The Joy Luck Club*. Then review the Critical Reading section which follows on page 129.

FROM *The Joy Luck Club*

The Red Candle
BY AMY TAN

Lindo Jong

I once sacrificed my life to keep my parents' promise. This means nothing to you, because to you promises mean nothing. A daughter can promise to come to dinner, but if she has a headache, if she has a traffic jam, if she wants to watch a favorite movie on TV, she no longer has a promise.

I watched this same movie when you did not come. The American soldier promises to come back and marry the girl. She is crying with a genuine feeling and he says, "Promise! Promise! Honey-sweetheart, my promise is as good as gold." Then he pushes her onto the bed. But he doesn't come back. His gold is like yours, it is only fourteen carats.

To Chinese people, fourteen carats isn't real gold. Feel my bracelets. They must be twenty-four carats, pure inside and out.

It's too late to change you, but I'm telling you this because I worry about your baby. I worry that someday she will say, "Thank you, Grandmother, for the gold bracelet. I'll never forget you." But later, she will forget her promise. She will forget she had a grandmother.

◆

5   In this same war movie, the American soldier goes home and he falls to his knees asking another girl to marry him. And the girl's eyes run back and forth, so shy, as if she had never considered this before. And suddenly!—her eyes look straight down and she knows now she loves him, so much she wants to cry. "Yes," she says at last, and they marry forever.

This was not my case. Instead, the village matchmaker came to my family when I was just two years old. No, nobody told me this, I remember it all. It was summertime, very hot and dusty outside, and I could hear cicadas crying in the yard. We were under some trees in our orchard. The servants and my brothers were picking pears high above me. And I was sitting in my mother's hot sticky arms. I was waving my hand this way and that, because in front of me floated a small bird with horns and colorful paper-thin wings. And then the paper bird flew away and in front of me were two ladies. I remember them because one lady made watery "shrrhh, shrrhh" sounds. When I was older, I came to recognize this as a Peking accent, which sounds quite strange to Taiyuan people's ears.

The two ladies were looking at my face without talking. The lady with the watery voice had a painted face that was melting. The other lady had the dry face of an old tree trunk. She looked first at me, then at the painted lady.

Of course, now I know the tree-trunk lady was the old village matchmaker, and the other was Huang Taitai, the mother of the boy I would be forced to marry. No, it's not true what some Chinese say about girl babies being worthless. It depends on what kind of girl baby you are. In my case, people could see my value. I looked and smelled like a precious buncake, sweet with a good clean color.

The matchmaker bragged about me: "An earth horse for an earth sheep. This is the best marriage combination." She patted my arm and I pushed her hand away. Huang Taitai whispered in her shrrhh-shrrhh voice that perhaps I had an unusually bad *pichi*, a bad temper. But the matchmaker laughed and said, "Not so, not so. She is a strong horse. She will grow up to be a hard worker who serves you well in your old age."

10   And this is when Huang Taitai looked down at me with a cloudy face as though she could penetrate my thoughts and see my future intentions. I will never forget her look. Her eyes opened wide, she searched my face carefully and then she smiled. I could see a large gold tooth staring at me like the blinding sun and then the rest of her teeth opened wide as if she were going to swallow me down in one piece.

    This is how I became betrothed to Huang Taitai's son, who I later discovered was just a baby, one year younger than I. His name was Tyan-yu—*tyan* for "sky," because he was so important, and *yu,* meaning "leftovers," because when he was born his father was very sick and his family thought he might die. Tyan-yu would be the leftover of his father's spirit. But his father lived and his grandmother was scared the ghosts would turn their attention to this baby boy and take him instead. So they watched him carefully, made all his decisions, and he became very spoiled.

    But even if I had known I was getting such a bad husband, I had no choice, now or later. That was how backward families in the country were. We were always the last to give up stupid old-fashioned customs. In other cities already, a man could choose his own wife, with his parents' permission of course. But we were cut off from this type of new thought. You never heard if ideas were better in another city, only if they were worse. We were told stories of sons who were so influenced by bad wives that they threw their old, crying parents out into the street. So, Taiyuanese mothers continued to choose their daughters-in-law, ones who would raise proper sons, care for the old people, and faithfully sweep the family burial grounds long after the old ladies had gone to their graves.

    Because I was promised to the Huangs' son for marriage, my own family began treating me as if I belonged to somebody else. My mother would say to me when the rice bowl went up to my face too many times, "Look how much Huang Taitai's daughter can eat."

    My mother did not treat me this way because she didn't love me. She would say this biting back her tongue, so she wouldn't wish for something that was no longer hers.

15   I was actually a very obedient child, but sometimes I had a sour look on my face—only because I was hot or tired or very ill. This is when my mother would say, "Such an ugly face. The Huangs won't want you and our whole family will be disgraced." And I would cry more to make my face uglier.

    "It's no use," my mother would say. "We have made a contract. It cannot be broken." And I would cry even harder.

    I didn't see my future husband until I was eight or nine. The world that I knew was our family compound in the village outside of Taiyuan. My family lived in a modest two-story house with a smaller house in the same compound, which was really just two side-by-side rooms for our cook, an everyday servant, and their families. Our house sat on a little hill. We called this hill Three Steps to Heaven, but it was really just centuries of hardened layers of mud washed up by the Fen River. On the east wall of our compound was the river, which my father said liked to swallow little children. He said it had once swallowed the whole town of Taiyuan. The river ran brown in the summer. In the winter, the river was blue-green in the narrow fast-moving spots. In the wider places, it was frozen still, white with cold.

Oh, I can remember the new year when my family went to the river and caught many fish—giant slippery creatures plucked while they were still sleeping in their frozen riverbeds—so fresh that even after they were gutted they would dance on their tails when thrown into the hot pan.

That was also the year I first saw my husband as a little boy. When the firecrackers went off, he cried loud—wah!—with a big open mouth even though he was not a baby.

20   Later I would see him at red-egg ceremonies when one-month-old boy babies were given their real names. He would sit on his grandmother's old knees, almost cracking them with his weight. And he would refuse to eat everything offered to him, always turning his nose away as though someone were offering him a stinky pickle and not a sweet cake.

So I didn't have instant love for my future husband the way you see on television today. I thought of this boy more like a troublesome cousin. I learned to be polite to the Huangs and especially to Huang Taitai. My mother would push me toward Huang Taitai and say, "What do you say to your mother?" And I would be confused, not knowing which mother she meant. So I would turn to my real mother and say, "Excuse me, Ma," and then I would turn to Huang Taitai and present her with a little goodie to eat, saying, "For you, Mother." I remember it was once a lump of *syaumei*, a little dumpling I loved to eat. My mother told Huang Taitai I had made this dumpling especially for her, even though I had only poked its steamy sides with my finger when the cook poured it onto the serving plate.

My life changed completely when I was twelve, the summer the heavy rains came. The Fen River which ran through the middle of my family's land flooded the plains. It destroyed all the wheat my family had planted that year and made the land useless for years to come. Even our house on top of the little hill became unlivable. When we came down from the second story, we saw the floors and furniture were covered with sticky mud. The courtyards were littered with uprooted trees, broken bits of walls, and dead chickens. We were so poor in all this mess.

You couldn't go to an insurance company back then and say, Somebody did this damage, pay me a million dollars. In those days, you were unlucky if you had exhausted your own possibilities. My father said we had no choice but to move the family to Wushi, to the south near Shanghai, where my mother's brother owned a small flour mill. My father explained that the whole family, except for me, would leave immediately. I was twelve years old, old enough to separate from my family and live with the Huangs.

The roads were so muddy and filled with giant potholes that no truck was willing to come to the house. All the heavy furniture and bedding had to be left behind, and these were promised to the Huangs as my dowry. In this way, my family was quite practical. The dowry was enough, more than enough, said my father. But he could not stop my mother from giving me her *chang*, a necklace made out of a tablet of red jade. When she put it around my neck, she acted very stern, so I knew she was very sad. "Obey your family. Do not disgrace us," she said. "Act happy when you arrive. Really, you're very lucky."

◆

25   The Huangs' house also sat next to the river. While our house had been flooded, their house was untouched. This is because their house sat higher up in the valley. And this was the first time I realized the Huangs had a much better position than my family. They looked down on us, which made me understand why Huang Taitai and Tyan-yu had such long noses.

When I passed under the Huangs' stone-and-wood gateway arch, I saw a large courtyard with three or four rows of small, low buildings. Some were for storing supplies, others for servants and their families. Behind these modest buildings stood the main house.

I walked closer and stared at the house that would be my home for the rest of my life. The house had been in the family for many generations. It was not really so old or remarkable, but I could see it had grown up along with the family. There were four stories, one for each generation: great-grandparents, grandparents, parents, and children. The house had a confused look. It had been hastily built and then rooms and floors and wings and decorations had been added on in every which manner, reflecting too many opinions. The first level was built of river rocks held together by straw-filled mud. The second and third levels were made of smooth bricks with an exposed walkway to give it the look of a palace tower. And the top level had gray slab walls topped with a red tile roof. To make the house seem important, there were two large round pillars holding up a veranda entrance to the front door. These pillars were painted red, as were the wooden window borders. Someone, probably Huang Taitai, had added imperial dragon heads at the corners of the roof.

Inside the house held a different kind of pretense. The only nice room was a parlor on the first floor, which the Huangs used to receive guests. This room contained tables and chairs carved out of red lacquer, fine pillows embroidered with the Huang family name in the ancient style, and many precious things that gave the look of wealth and old prestige. The rest of the house was plain and uncomfortable and noisy with the complaints of twenty relatives. I think with each generation the house had grown smaller inside, more crowded. Each room had been cut in half to make two.

No big celebration was held when I arrived. Huang Taitai didn't have red banners greeting me in the fancy room on the first floor. Tyan-yu was not there to greet me. Instead, Huang Taitai hurried me upstairs to the second floor and into the kitchen, which was a place where family children didn't usually go. This was a place for cooks and servants. So I knew my standing.

30   That first day, I stood in my best padded dress at the low wooden table and began to chop vegetables. I could not keep my hands steady. I missed my family and my stomach felt bad, knowing I had finally arrived where my life said I

belonged. But I was also determined to honor my parents' words, so Huang Taitai could never accuse my mother of losing face. She would not win that from our family.

As I was thinking this I saw an old servant woman stooping over the same low table gutting a fish, looking at me from the corner of her eye. I was crying and I was afraid she would tell Huang Taitai. So I gave a big smile and shouted, "What a lucky girl I am. I'm going to have the best life." And in this quick-thinking way I must have waved my knife too close to her nose because she cried angrily, *"Shemma bende ren!"*—What kind of fool are you? And I knew right away this was a warning, because when I shouted that declaration of happiness, I almost tricked myself into thinking it might come true.

I saw Tyan-yu at the evening meal. I was still a few inches taller than he, but he acted like a big warlord. I knew what kind of husband he would be, because he made special efforts to make me cry. He complained the soup was not hot enough and then spilled the bowl as if it were an accident. He waited until I had sat down to eat and then would demand another bowl of rice. He asked why I had such an unpleasant face when looking at him.

Over the next few years, Huang Taitai instructed the other servants to teach me how to sew sharp corners on pillowcases and to embroider my future family's name. How can a wife keep her husband's household in order if she has never dirtied her own hands, Huang Taitai used to say as she introduced me to a new task. I don't think Huang Taitai ever soiled her hands, but she was very good at calling out orders and criticism.

"Teach her to wash rice properly so that the water runs clear. Her husband cannot eat muddy rice," she'd say to a cook servant.

35

Another time, she told a servant to show me how to clean a chamber pot: "Make her put her own nose to the barrel to make sure it's clean." That was how I learned to be an obedient wife. I learned to cook so well that I could smell if the meat stuffing was too salty before I even tasted it. I could sew such small stitches it looked as if the embroidery had been painted on. And even Huang Taitai complained in a pretend manner that she could scarcely throw a dirty blouse on the floor before it was cleaned and on her back once again, causing her to wear the same clothes every day.

After a while I didn't think it was a terrible life, no, not really. After a while, I hurt so much I didn't feel any difference. What was happier than seeing everybody gobble down the shiny mushrooms and bamboo shoots I had helped to prepare that day? What was more satisfying than having Huang Taitai nod and pat my head when I had finished combing her hair one hundred strokes? How much happier could I be after seeing Tyan-yu eat a whole bowl of noodles without once complaining about its taste or my looks? It's like those ladies you see on American TV these days, the ones who are so happy they have washed out a stain so the clothes look better than new.

Can you see how the Huangs almost washed their thinking into my skin? I came to think of Tyan-yu as a god, someone whose opinions were worth much more than my own life. I came to think of Huang Taitai as my real mother, someone I wanted to please, someone I should follow and obey without question.

When I turned sixteen on the lunar new year, Huang Taitai told me she was ready to welcome a grandson by next spring. Even if I had not wanted to marry, where would I go live instead? Even though I was strong as a horse, how could I run away? The Japanese were in every corner of China.

◆

"The Japanese showed up as uninvited guests," said Tyan-yu's grandmother, "and that's why nobody else came." Huang Taitai had made elaborate plans, but our wedding was very small.

40

She had asked the entire village and friends and family from other cities as well. In those days, you didn't do RSVP. It was not polite not to come. Huang Taitai didn't think the war would change people's good manners. So the cook and her helpers prepared hundreds of dishes. My family's old furniture had been shined up into an impressive dowry and placed in the front parlor. Huang Taitai had taken care to remove all the water and mud marks. She had even commissioned someone to write felicitous messages on red banners, as if my parents themselves had draped these decorations to congratulate me on my good luck. And she had arranged to rent a red palanquin to carry me from her neighbor's house to the wedding ceremony.

A lot of bad luck fell on our wedding day, even though the matchmaker had chosen a lucky day, the fifteenth day of the eighth moon, when the moon is perfectly round and bigger than any other time of the year. But the week before the moon arrived, the Japanese came. They invaded Shansi province, as well as the provinces bordering us. People were nervous. And the morning of the fifteenth, on the day of the wedding celebration, it began to rain, a very bad sign. When the thunder and lightning began, people confused it with Japanese bombs and would not leave their houses.

I heard later that poor Huang Taitai waited many hours for more people to come, and finally, when she could not wring any more guests out of her hands, she decided to start the ceremony. What could she do? She could not change the war.

I was at the neighbor's house. When they called me to come down and ride the red palanquin, I was sitting at a small dressing table by an open window. I began to cry and thought bitterly about my parents' promise. I wondered why my destiny had been decided, why I should have an unhappy life so someone else could have a happy one. From my seat by the window I could see the Fen River with its muddy brown waters. I thought about throwing my body into this river that had destroyed my family's happiness. A person has very strange thoughts when it seems that life is about to end.

It started to rain again, just a light rain. The people from downstairs called up to me once again to hurry. And my thoughts became more urgent, more strange.

45

I asked myself, What is true about a person? Would I change in the same way the river changes color but still be the same person? And then I saw the curtains blowing wildly, and outside rain was falling harder, causing everyone to scurry and shout. I smiled. And then I realized it was the first time I could see the power of the wind. I couldn't see the wind itself, but I could see it carried the water that filled the rivers and shaped the countryside. It caused men to yelp and dance.

I wiped my eyes and looked in the mirror. I was surprised at what I saw. I had on a beautiful red dress, but what I saw was even more valuable. I was strong. I was pure. I had genuine thoughts inside that no one could see, that no one could ever take away from me. I was like the wind.

I threw my head back and smiled proudly to myself. And then I draped the large embroidered red scarf over my face and covered these thoughts up. But underneath the scarf I still knew who I was. I made a promise to myself: I would always remember my parents' wishes, but I would never forget myself.

When I arrived at the wedding, I had the red scarf over my face and couldn't see anything in front of me. But when I bent my head forward, I could see out the sides. Very few people had come. I saw the Huangs, the same old complaining relatives now embarrassed by this poor showing, the entertainers with their violins and flutes. And there were a few village people who had been brave enough to come out for a free meal. I even saw servants and their children, who must have been added to make the party look bigger.

Someone took my hands and guided me down a path. I was like a blind person walking to my fate. But I was no longer scared. I could see what was inside me.

50   A high official conducted the ceremony and he talked too long about philosophers and models of virtue. Then I heard the matchmaker speak about our birthdates and harmony and fertility. I tipped my veiled head forward and I could see her hands unfolding a red silk scarf and holding up a red candle for everyone to see.

The candle had two ends for lighting. One length had carved gold characters with Tyan-yu's name, the other with mine. The matchmaker lighted both ends and announced, "The marriage has begun." Tyan-yu yanked the scarf off my face and smiled at his friends and family, never even looking at me. He reminded me of a young peacock I once saw that acted as if he had just claimed the entire courtyard by fanning his still-short tail.

I saw the matchmaker place the lighted red candle in a gold holder and then hand it to a nervous-looking servant. This servant was supposed to watch the candle during the banquet and all night to make sure neither end went out. In the morning the matchmaker was supposed to show the result, a little piece of black ash, and then declare, "This candle burned continuously at both ends without going out. This is a marriage that can never be broken."

I still can remember. That candle was a marriage bond that was worth more than a Catholic promise not to divorce. It meant I couldn't divorce and I couldn't ever remarry, even if Tyan-yu died. That red candle was supposed to seal me forever with my husband and his family, no excuses afterward.

And sure enough, the matchmaker made her declaration the next morning and showed she had done her job. But I know what really happened, because I stayed up all night crying about my marriage.

◆

55   After the banquet, our small wedding party pushed us and half carried us up to the third floor to our small bedroom. People were shouting jokes and pulling boys from underneath the bed. The matchmaker helped small children pull red eggs that had been hidden between the blankets. The boys who were about Tyan-yu's age made us sit on the bed side by side and everybody made us kiss so our faces would turn red with passion. Firecrackers exploded on the walkway outside our open window and someone said that this was a good excuse for me to jump into my husband's arms.

After everyone left, we sat there side by side without words for many minutes, still listening to the laughing outside. When it grew quiet, Tyan-yu said, "This is my bed. You sleep on the sofa." He threw a pillow and a thin blanket to me. I was so glad! I waited until he fell asleep and then I got up quietly and went outside, down the stairs and into the dark courtyard.

Outside it smelled as if it would soon rain again. I was crying, walking in my bare feet and feeling the wet heat still inside the bricks. Across the courtyard I could see the matchmaker's servant through a yellow-lit open window. She was sitting at a table, looking very sleepy as the red candle burned in its special gold holder. I sat down by a tree to watch my fate being decided for me.

I must have fallen asleep because I remember being startled awake by the sound of loud cracking thunder. That's when I saw the matchmaker's servant running from the room, scared as a chicken about to lose its head. Oh, she was asleep too, I thought, and now she thinks it's the Japanese. I laughed. The whole sky became light and then more thunder came, and she ran out of the courtyard and down the road, going so fast and hard I could see pebbles kicking up behind her. Where does she think she's running to, I wondered, still laughing. And then I saw the red candle flickering just a little with the breeze.

I was not thinking when my legs lifted me up and my feet ran me across the courtyard to the yellow-lit room. But I was hoping—I was praying to Buddha, the goddess of mercy, and the full moon—to make that candle go out. It fluttered a little and the flame bent down low, but still both ends burned strong. My throat filled with so much hope that it finally burst and blew out my husband's end of the candle.

60   I immediately shivered with fear. I thought a knife would appear and cut me down dead. Or the sky would open up and blow me away. But nothing happened, and when my senses came back, I walked back to my room with fast guilty steps.

The next morning the matchmaker made her proud declaration in front of Tyan-yu, his parents, and myself. "My job is done," she announced, pouring the remaining black ash onto the red cloth. I saw her servant's shame-faced, mournful look.

◆

I learned to love Tyan-yu, but it is not how you think. From the beginning, I would always become sick thinking he would someday climb on top of me and do his business. Every time I went into our bedroom, my hair would already be standing up. But during the first months, he never touched me. He slept in his bed, I slept on my sofa.

In front of his parents, I was an obedient wife, just as they taught me. I instructed the cook to kill a fresh young chicken every morning and cook it until pure juice came out. I would strain this juice myself into a bowl, never adding any water. I gave this to him for breakfast, murmuring good wishes about his health. And every night I would cook a special tonic soup called *tounau*, which was not only very delicious but has eight ingredients that guarantee long life for mothers. This pleased my mother-in-law very much.

But it was not enough to keep her happy. One morning, Huang Taitai and I were sitting in the same room, working on our embroidery. I was dreaming about my childhood, about a pet frog I once kept named Big Wind. Huang Taitai seemed restless, as if she had an itch in the bottom of her shoe. I heard her huffing and then all of a sudden she stood up from her chair, walked over to me, and slapped my face.

65 "Bad wife!" she cried. "If you refuse to sleep with my son, I refuse to feed you or clothe you." So that's how I knew what my husband had said to avoid his mother's anger. I was also boiling with anger, but I said nothing, remembering my promise to my parents to be an obedient wife.

That night I sat on Tyan-yu's bed and waited for him to touch me. But he didn't. I was relieved. The next night, I lay straight down on the bed next to him. And still he didn't touch me. So the next night, I took off my gown.

That's when I could see what was underneath Tyan-yu. He was scared and turned his face. He had no desire for me, but it was his fear that made me think he had no desire for any woman. He was like a little boy who had never grown up. After a while I was no longer afraid. I even began to think differently toward Tyan-yu. It was not like the way a wife loves a husband, but more like the way a sister protects a younger brother. I put my gown back on and lay down next to him and rubbed his back. I knew I no longer had to be afraid. I was sleeping with Tyan-yu. He would never touch me and I had a comfortable bed to sleep on.

After more months had passed and my stomach and breasts remained small and flat, Huang Taitai flew into another kind of rage. "My son says he's planted enough seeds for thousands of grandchildren. Where are they? It must be you are doing something wrong." And after that she confined me to the bed so that her grandchildren's seeds would not spill out so easily.

Oh, you think it is so much fun to lie in bed all day, never getting up. But I tell you it was worse than a prison. I think Huang Taitai became a little crazy.

70 She told the servants to take all sharp things out of the room, thinking scissors and knives were cutting off her next generation. She forbade me from sewing. She said I must concentrate and think of nothing but having babies.

And four times a day, a very nice servant girl would come into my room, apologizing the whole time while making me drink a terrible-tasting medicine.

I envied this girl, the way she could walk out the door. Sometimes as I watched her from my window, I would imagine I was that girl, standing in the courtyard, bargaining with the traveling shoe mender, gossiping with other servant girls, scolding a handsome delivery man in her high teasing voice.

One day, after two months had gone by without any results, Huang Taitai called the old matchmaker to the house. The matchmaker examined me closely, looked up my birthdate and the hour of my birth, and then asked Huang Taitai about my nature. Finally, the matchmaker gave her conclusions: "It's clear what has happened. A woman can have sons only if she is deficient in one of the elements. Your daughter-in-law was born with enough wood, fire, water, and earth, and she was deficient in metal, which was a good sign. But when she was married, you loaded her down with gold bracelets and decorations and now she has all the elements, including metal. She's too balanced to have babies."

This turned out to be joyous news for Huang Taitai, for she liked nothing better than to reclaim all her gold and jewelry to help me become fertile. And it was good news for me too. Because after the gold was removed from my body, I felt lighter, more free. They say this is what happens if you lack metal. You begin to think as an independent person. That day I started to think about how I would escape this marriage without breaking my promise to my family.

It was really quite simple. I made the Huangs think it was their idea to get rid of me, that they would be the ones to say the marriage contract was not valid.

75   I thought about my plan for many days. I observed everyone around me, the thoughts they showed in their faces, and then I was ready. I chose an auspicious day, the third day of the third month. That's the day of the Festival of Pure Brightness. On this day, your thoughts must be clear as you prepare to think about your ancestors. That's the day when everyone goes to the family graves. They bring hoes to clear the weeds and brooms to sweep the stones and they offer dumplings and oranges as spiritual food. Oh, it's not a somber day, more like a picnic, but it has special meaning to someone looking for grandsons.

On the morning of that day, I woke up Tyan-yu and the entire house with my wailing. It took Huang Taitai a long time to come into my room. "What's wrong with her now," she cried from her room. "Go make her be quiet." But finally, after my wailing didn't stop, she rushed into my room, scolding me at the top of her voice.

I was clutching my mouth with one hand and my eyes with another. My body was writhing as if I were seized by a terrible pain. I was quite convincing, because Huang Taitai drew back and grew small like a scared animal.

"What's wrong, little daughter? Tell me quickly," she cried.

"Oh, it's too terrible to think, too terrible to say," I said between gasps and more wailing.

80   After enough wailing, I said what was so unthinkable. "I had a dream," I reported. "Our ancestors came to me and said they wanted to see our wedding.

So Tyan-yu and I held the same ceremony for our ancestors. We saw the matchmaker light the candle and give it to the servant to watch. Our ancestors were so pleased, so pleased . . ."

Huang Taitai looked impatient as I began to cry softly again. "But then the servant left the room with our candle and a big wind came and blew the candle out. And our ancestors became very angry. They shouted that the marriage was doomed! They said that Tyan-yu's end of the candle had blown out! Our ancestors said Tyan-yu would die if he stayed in this marriage!"

Tyan-yu's face turned white. But Huang Taitai only frowned. "What a stupid girl to have such bad dreams!" And then she scolded everybody to go back to bed.

"Mother," I called to her in a hoarse whisper. "Please don't leave me! I am afraid! Our ancestors said if the matter is not settled, they would begin the cycle of destruction."

"What is this nonsense!" cried Huang Taitai, turning back toward me. Tyan-yu followed her, wearing his mother's same frowning face. And I knew they were almost caught, two ducks leaning into the pot.

85 "They knew you would not believe me," I said in a remorseful tone, "because they know I do not want to leave the comforts of my marriage. So our ancestors said they would plant the signs, to show our marriage is now rotting."

"What nonsense from your stupid head," said Huang Taitai, sighing. But she could not resist. "What signs?"

"In my dream, I saw a man with a long beard and a mole on his cheek."

"Tyan-yu's grandfather?" asked Huang Taitai. I nodded, remembering the painting I had observed on the wall.

"He said there are three signs. First, he has drawn a black spot on Tyan-yu's back, and this spot will grow and eat away Tyan-yu's flesh just as it ate away our ancestor's face before he died."

90 Huang Taitai quickly turned to Tyan-yu and pulled his shirt up. "Ai-ya!" She cried, because there it was, the same black mole, the size of a fingertip, just as I had always seen in these past five months of sleeping as sister and brother.

"And then our ancestor touched my mouth," and I patted my cheek as if it already hurt. "He said my teeth would start to fall out one by one, until I could no longer protest leaving this marriage."

Huang Taitai pried open my mouth and gasped upon seeing the open spot in the back of my mouth where a rotted tooth fell out four years ago.

"And finally, I saw him plant a seed in a servant girl's womb. He said this girl only pretends to come from a bad family. But she is really from imperial blood, and . . ."

I lay my head down on the pillow as if too tired to go on. Huang Taitai pushed my shoulder, "What does he say?"

95 "He said the servant girl is Tyan-yu's true spiritual wife. And the seed he has planted will grow into Tyan-yu's child."

By mid-morning they had dragged the matchmaker's servant over to our house and extracted her terrible confession.

And after much searching they found the servant girl I liked so much, the one I had watched from my window every day. I had seen her eyes grow bigger and her teasing voice become smaller whenever the handsome delivery man arrived. And later, I had watched her stomach grow rounder and her face become longer with fear and worry.

So you can imagine how happy she was when they forced her to tell the truth about her imperial ancestry. I heard later she was so struck with this miracle of marrying Tyan-yu she became a very religious person who ordered servants to sweep the ancestors' graves not just once a year, but once a day.

◆

There's no more to the story. They didn't blame me so much. Huang Taitai got her grandson. I got my clothes, a rail ticket to Peking, and enough money to go to America. The Huangs asked only that I never tell anybody of any importance about the story of my doomed marriage.

100   It's a true story, how I kept my promise, how I sacrificed my life. See the gold metal I can now wear. I gave birth to your brothers and then your father gave me these two bracelets. Then I had you. And every few years, when I have a little extra money, I buy another bracelet. I know what I'm worth. They're always twenty-four carats, all genuine.

But I'll never forget. On the day of the Festival of Pure Brightness, I take off all my bracelets. I remember when I finally knew a genuine thought and could follow it where it went. It was the day I was a young girl with my face under a red marriage scarf. I promised not to forget myself.

How nice it is to be that girl again, to take off my scarf, to see what is underneath and feel the lightness come back into my body!

Critical Reading Questions

1. Amy Tan begins this story with the statement, "I once sacrificed my life to keep my parents' promise." What do you think she means by this?

2. Lindo Jong's experiences present a fascinating example of the decision-making process. Having been the subject of an arranged marriage when she was two years old, she states, "But even if I had known I was getting such a bad husband, I had no choice, now or later." Why does she initially believe that this is a decision in which she "has no choice"? What does this belief reveal about how she defines her decision?

3. On the day of her wedding, Lindo Jong experiences a transformational insight which will eventually alter the way she views her situation and her potential choices. She begins her psychic journey in desperation: "I wondered why my destiny had been decided, why I should have an unhappy life so someone else could have a happy one. . . . A person has very strange thoughts when it seems that life is about to end." But Lindo breaks through this feeling of helpless desperation and voices this realization: "I was strong, I was pure. I had genuine

thoughts inside me that no one could see, that no one could ever take away from me. . . . I made a promise to myself: I would always remember my parents' wishes, but I would never forget myself." What effect does this startling insight have on the way in which she views her situation and the choices she can make regarding her destiny?

4. Although Lindo's initial effort to alter "destiny" by blowing out half of the red marriage candle fails, it is a step which eventually leads her to a new feeling of independence with the possibility of personal liberation. Once she is relieved of her gold bracelets and jewelry, she begins to feel "lighter, more free." She explains: "They say this is what happens if you lack metal. You begin to think as an independent person. That day I started to think about how I would escape this marriage without breaking my promise to my family."

   During the initial stages of her decision to accept her arranged marriage, Lindo believed that she had "no choice." What is the choice that she now sees which she previously did not comprehend?

5. Lindo concludes with the eloquent statement, "I remember when I finally knew a genuine thought and could follow it where it went. It was the day I was a young girl with my face under a red marriage scarf. I promised not to forget myself." As you work toward creating yourself through your choices, why is it essential that you think clearly and follow your thoughts wherever they lead you?

Thinking ↔ Writing Activity

Preparing for Decisions

1. Make a list of whatever important decisions in your academic or personal life you have to make now or will have to make in the near future.

2. Select one decision and apply the five-step decision-making method that begins on page 113. As you think through your decision, be sure to identify all of your possible choices and to follow your thoughts wherever they lead.

There are no guarantees in life. Our decisions may or may not turn out well. Still, following an organized method for making decisions can at least assure us of having explored and evaluated many possible choices and then selected the one that seemed to best meet our needs. In other words, we will know that we made the best decision that we could have at the time.

Making Decisions When Revising Drafts

Revising your writing is the key to producing your best possible work. It is very rare for a first draft to represent the most effective writing of which a person is capable. Most accomplished writers expect their work to undergo a number of revisions based on their own re-evaluation and on feedback from others. The difference between outstanding and mediocre writing often depends on revision.

Many of the concepts in the five-step decision-making approach that begins on page 113 can be applied to revising your drafts.

- You *define the decision and your goals* by identifying what in a draft needs to be revised and what should be left as it is.

- You *consider possible choices* for improving a draft, especially with major components such as composing and placing the thesis statement, presenting evidence, and arranging material in sequences, sections, or paragraphs. You also often have various choices among words and sentence patterns when you work at the editing level of revision.

- You *gather relevant information* and *evaluate the pros and cons* of the different choices in order to select the one that best meets the needs of the writing situation. Sometimes you may want to write down the different possibilities; in other instances, you may just try them out in your mind.

- After *implementing* your choices by revising a draft, you *evaluate* your writing by *reading it again,* slowly and completely, to be sure that the whole piece is as good as you can make it.

Collaborating with classmates or other trusted readers in all these decisions will usually be very helpful. Other readers can see your drafts more objectively and can help you "re-see" and revise them.

SPECIFIC CHOICES TO MAKE AT SEVERAL LEVELS

The following suggestions should help you improve your drafts.

Read your entire draft slowly and carefully. You may find, as many writers do, that reading out loud helps you to identify parts that don't sound right. Also, ask someone whose judgment you trust to read the draft and help you to decide what improvement is needed. If your class allows peer review, be prepared for this opportunity by having a draft ready.

If you determine that improvement is required, you need to make a decision immediately. At what level should you begin to make changes? Some people think that revision means correcting grammar, punctuation, and spelling. Revision can indeed include those corrections, but it usually means much more. In fact, those corrections are often made separately, as editing and proofreading, to distinguish them from larger aspects of revision.

A helpful way to decide where to begin revising is to move through the following hierarchy of concerns and questions about your draft. If you find yourself answering any of the questions in a manner that suggests ways to improve your writing, *stop and try to make the changes or additions to your draft before you move on to the next level.* There is no point in worrying about punctuation if your draft lacks focus or good examples.

However, remember that revision, like all activities in a writing process, is recursive. You may detect content, organization, or wording problems while you are checking punctuation; you may fix a typo while you're rewording the thesis statement. The following hierarchy emphasizes the importance of looking first at major concerns, but you should be prepared to move around among the levels of attention as you make your decisions about a draft.

A Step-by-Step Method for Revising Any Assignment

The following method can be used both for revising your own papers and for reviewing your classmates' papers. It can be applied to any assignment. For easy reference as you move through the assignments in this book and those for other courses, an edited version of this method is reprinted on the inside back cover of this text. It will be referred to in the Revising section of each Writing Project in the following chapters.

1. **Think big**. Look at the draft as a whole.

   ❑ Does it fulfill the assignment in terms of topic and length?

   ❑ Does it have a clear focus?

   ❑ What parts of the draft, if any, do not relate to its focus?

   ❑ How could the draft be reorganized to make it more logical?

   ❑ What evidence could be added to help to accomplish your purpose?

   ❑ How could the flow between paragraphs be made smoother?

   ❑ Is your point of view consistent throughout?

   Develop alternatives based on the answers to these questions, decide which alternatives will improve your draft, and then make changes to your draft before proceeding to the next level of revision.

2. **Think medium**. Look at the draft paragraph by paragraph.

   First consider the *introduction*.

   ❑ How could you rewrite your lead to make the audience more interested in reading on? (See the suggestions for being creative with introductions on pages 80 and 81 of Chapter 3.)

   ❑ How could you make the introduction more appropriate for the rest of the draft—that is, can you make the tone of the introduction match the tone of the rest of the draft?

❏ How could you state the focus more effectively if you are working with "visible structure"?

Then look at each of your *body paragraphs.*

❏ Does each support the thesis?

❏ Does each present relevant, specific evidence not presented elsewhere?

❏ Which, if any, body paragraphs should be combined or eliminated?

❏ Which body paragraphs use topic sentences effectively? Which don't?

❏ Where could you use transitions to improve the flow within or between body paragraphs?

Now look at your *conclusion.* This is your last chance to accomplish your purpose with your intended audience.

❏ How could you make your conclusion more effective? (See the suggestions for being creative with conclusions on pages 80 and 81 of Chapter 3.)

❏ Is the tone of the conclusion appropriate?

Again, develop alternatives and make changes to your draft before proceeding to the next level.

3. **Think small.** Look at your draft sentence by sentence.

❏ Which sentences are difficult to understand? How could you reword them?

❏ Which, if any, sentences are so long that your audience could get lost in them?

❏ Where are there short, choppy sentences that can be combined?

❏ Which sentences seem vague? How could you clarify them?

❏ Which, if any, sentences have errors in standard English grammar or usage? How could you correct them?

Make necessary changes to your draft before proceeding to the next level.

4. **Think "picky."** Look at your draft as the fussiest critic might.

❏ Which words are not clear or not quite right for your meaning? What words could you use instead?

❏ Are any words spelled incorrectly? (Run the spelling checker program on your computer, but don't rely on it alone.)

❏ Are the pages numbered consecutively?

❏ Does the physical appearance of your draft make a good impression?

❏ Is there anything else you can do to improve your draft?

To see an example of a writer working through the revision process, see the reading by Roger Garrison on pages 21–29 of Chapter 1.

Thinking ↔ Writing Activity

Using the Revision Method

Apply the revision method to an essay you have written for this course (your instructor will advise you about which one to select). Be sure to complete each of the steps in the method. Although this process may initially seem time-consuming and rather mechanical, you will soon begin to integrate these ideas in a more natural and flexible way. As you become more experienced as a writer, the revision method will eventually become an integral part of your composing process.

Beyond considering your own earlier experiences, you can deepen your understanding of revision by reading the following selections by two expert writers.

The Maker's Eye: Revising Your Own Manuscripts

BY DONALD M. MURRAY

When students complete a first draft, they consider the job of writing done—and their teachers too often agree. When professional writers complete a first draft, they usually feel that they are at the start of the writing process. When a draft is completed, the job of writing can begin.

That difference in attitude is the difference between amateur and professional, inexperience and experience, journeyman and craftsman. Peter F. Drucker, the prolific business writer, calls his first draft "the zero draft"—after that he can start counting. Most writers share the feeling that the first draft, and all of those which follow, are opportunities to discover what they have to say and how best they can say it.

To produce a progression of drafts, each of which says more and says it more clearly, the writer has to develop a special kind of reading skill. In school we are taught to decode what appears on the page as finished writing. Writers, however, face a different category of possibility and responsibility when they read their own drafts. To them the words on the page are never finished. Each can be changed and rearranged, can set off a chain reaction of confusion or clarified meaning. This is a different kind of reading, which is possibly more difficult and certainly more exciting.

Writers must learn to be their own best enemy. They must accept the criticism of others and be suspicious of it; they must accept the praise of others and be even more suspicious of it. Writers cannot depend on others. They must detach themselves from their own pages so that they can apply both their caring and their craft to their own work.

5   Such detachment is not easy. Science fiction writer Ray Bradbury supposedly puts each manuscript away for a year to the day and then rereads it as a stranger. Not many writers have the discipline or the time to do this. We must read when our judgment may be at its worst, when we are close to the euphoric moment of creation.

Then the writer, counsels novelist Nancy Hale, "should be critical of everything that seems to him most delightful in his style. He should excise what he most admires, because he wouldn't thus admire it if he weren't . . . in a sense protecting it from criticism." John Ciardi, the poet, adds, "The last act of writing must be to become one's own reader. It is, I suppose, a schizophrenic process, to begin passionately and to end critically, to begin hot and to end cold; and, more important, to be passion-hot and critic-cold at the same time."

Most people think that the principal problem is that writers are too proud of what they have written. Actually, a greater problem for most professional writers is one shared by the majority of students. They are overly critical, think everything is dreadful, tear up page after page, never complete a draft, see the task as hopeless.

The writer must learn to read critically but constructively, to cut what is bad, to reveal what is good. Eleanor Estes, the children's book author, explains: "The writer must survey his work critically, coolly, as though he were a stranger to it. He must be willing to prune, expertly and hard-heartedly. At the end of each revision, a manuscript may look . . . worked over, torn apart, pinned together, added to, deleted from, words changed and words changed back. Yet the book must maintain its original freshness and spontaneity."

Most readers underestimate the amount of rewriting it usually takes to produce spontaneous reading. This is a great disadvantage to the student writer, who sees only a finished product and never watches the craftsman who takes the necessary steps back, studies the work carefully, returns to the task, steps back, returns, steps back, again and again. Anthony Burgess, one of the most prolific writers in the English-speaking world, admits, "I might revise a page twenty times." Roald Dahl, the popular children's writer, states, "By the time I'm nearing the end of a story, the first part will have been reread and altered and corrected at least 150 times. . . . Good writing is essentially rewriting. I am positive of this."

10   Rewriting isn't virtuous. It isn't something that ought to be done. It is simply something that most writers find they have to do to discover what they have to say and how to say it. It is a condition of the writer's life.

There are, however, a few writers who do little formal rewriting, primarily because they have the capacity and experience to create and review a large number of invisible drafts in their minds before they approach the page. And some writers slowly produce finished pages, performing all the tasks of revision simultaneously, page by page, rather than draft by draft. But it is still possible to see the sequence followed by most writers most of the time in rereading their own work.

Most writers scan their drafts first, reading as quickly as possible to catch the larger problems of subject and form, then move in closer and closer as they read and write, reread and rewrite.

The first thing writers look for in their drafts is *information*. They know that a good piece of writing is built from specific, accurate, and interesting information. The writer must have an abundance of information from which to construct a readable piece of writing.

Next, writers look for meaning in the information. The specifics must build a pattern of significance. Each piece of specific information must carry the reader toward meaning.

15   Writers reading their own drafts are aware of *audience*. They put themselves in the reader's situation and make sure that they deliver information which a reader wants to know or needs to know in a manner which is easily digested. Writers try to be sure that they anticipate and answer the questions a critical reader will ask when reading the piece of writing.

Writers make sure that the *form* is appropriate to the subject and the audience. Form, or genre, is the vehicle which carries meaning to the reader, but form cannot be selected until the writer has adequate information to discover its significance and an audience which needs or wants that meaning.

Once writers are sure the form is appropriate, they must then look at the *structure*, the order of what they have written. Good writing is built on a solid framework of logic, argument, narrative, or motivation which runs through the entire piece of writing and holds it together. This is the time when many writers find it most effective to outline as a way of visualizing the hidden spine by which the piece of writing is supported.

The element on which writers may spend a majority of their time is *development*. Each section of a piece of writing must be adequately developed. It must give readers enough information so that they are satisfied. How much information is enough? That's as difficult as asking how much garlic belongs in a salad. It must be done to taste, but most beginning writers underdevelop, underestimating the reader's hunger for information.

As writers solve development problems, they often have to consider questions of *dimension*. There must be a pleasing and effective proportion among all the parts of the piece of writing. There is a continual process of subtracting and adding to keep the piece of writing in balance.

20   Finally, writers have to listen to their own voices. *Voice* is the force which drives a piece of writing forward. It is an expression of the writer's authority and concern. It is what is between the words on the page, what glues the piece

of writing together. A good piece of writing is always marked by a consistent, individual voice.

As writers read and reread, write and rewrite, they move closer and closer to the page until they are doing line-by-line editing. Writers read their own pages with infinite care. Each sentence, each line, each clause, each phrase, each word, each mark of punctuation, each section of white space between the type has to contribute to the clarification of meaning.

Slowly the writer moves from word to word, looking through language to see the subject. As a word is changed, cut, or added, as a construction is rearranged, all the words used before that moment and all those that follow that moment must be considered and reconsidered.

Writers often read aloud at this stage of the editing process, muttering or whispering to themselves, calling on the ear's experience with language. Does this sound right—or that? Writers edit, shifting back and forth from eye to page to ear to page. I find I must do this careful editing in short runs, no more than fifteen or twenty minutes at a stretch, or I become too kind with myself. I begin to see what I hope is on the page, not what actually is on the page.

This sounds tedious if you haven't done it, but actually it is fun. Making something right is immensely satisfying, for writers begin to learn what they are writing about by writing. Language leads them to meaning, and there is the joy of discovery, of understanding, of making meaning clear as the writer employs the technical skills of language.

25   Words have double meanings, even triple and quadruple meanings. Each word has its own potential for connotation and denotation. And when writers rub one word against the other, they are often rewarded with a sudden insight, an unexpected clarification.

The maker's eye moves back and forth from word to phrase to sentence to paragraph to sentence to phrase to word. The maker's eye sees the need for variety and balance, for a firmer structure, for a more appropriate form. It peers into the interior of the paragraph, looking for coherence, unity, and emphasis, which make meaning clear.

I learned something about this process when my first bifocals were prescribed. I had ordered a large section of the reading portion of the glass because of my work, but even so, I could not contain my eyes within this new limit of vision. And I still find myself taking off my glasses and bending my nose towards the page, for my eyes unconsciously flick back and forth across the page, back to another page, forward to still another, as I try to see each evolving line in relation to every other line.

When does this process end? Most writers agree with the great Russian writer Tolstoy, who said, "I scarcely ever reread my published writings, if by chance I come across a page, it always strikes me: all this must be rewritten; this is how I should have written it."

The maker's eye is never satisfied, for each word has the potential to ignite new meaning. This article has been twice written all the way through the writing process, and it was published four years ago. Now it is to be republished in a book. The editors make a few small suggestions, and then I read it with my maker's eye. Now it has been re-edited, re-vised, re-read, re-re-edited, for each piece of writing to the writer is full of potential and alternatives.

30   A piece of writing is never finished. It is delivered to a deadline, torn out of the typewriter on demand, sent off with a sense of accomplishment and shame and pride and frustration. If only there were a couple more days, time for just another run at it, perhaps then . . .

Critical Reading Questions

1. Reflect on your own experiences with writing and revision. Do you agree with the author, Donald M. Murray, that "when a draft is completed, the job of writing can begin"? Explain why or why not.

2. According to Murray, effective writing requires "a special kind of reading skill" because "the words on the page are never finished." Identify some of the things you look for when doing "special reading" to review your own writing.

3. Murray identifies elements for writers to examine when critically reading their drafts: information, audience, form, structure, development, dimension, and voice. Reread the essay you revised for the Thinking-Writing Activity on page 134, paying special attention to each of these elements. Make whatever new revision you think will help express your meaning more successfully.

4. As a final stage, reread this same essay aloud to yourself and see if your "ear's experience with language" suggests any additional changes.

How to Say Nothing in Five Hundred Words

BY PAUL ROBERTS

It's Friday afternoon, and you have almost survived another week of classes. You are just looking forward dreamily to the weekend when the English instructor says: "For Monday you will turn in a five-hundred-word composition on college football."

Well, that puts a good big hole in the weekend. You don't have any strong views on college football one way or the other. You get rather excited during the season and go to all the home games and find it rather more fun than not. On the other hand, the class has been reading Robert Hutchins in the anthology and perhaps Shaw's "Eighty-Yard Run," and from the class discussion you have got the idea that the instructor thinks college football is for the birds. You are no fool. You can figure out what side to take.

You might as well get it over with and enjoy Saturday and Sunday. Five hundred words is about two double-spaced pages with normal margins. You put in a sheet of paper, think up a title, and you're off:

Why College Football Should Be Abolished

College football should be abolished because it's bad for the school and also bad for the players. The players are so busy practicing that they don't have any time for their studies.

This, you feel, is a mighty good start. The only trouble is that it's only thirty-two words. You still have four hundred and sixty-eight to go, and you've pretty well exhausted the subject. It comes to you that you do your best thinking in the morning, so you put away the typewriter and go to the movies. But the next morning you have to do your washing and some math problems, and in the afternoon you go to the game. The English instructor turns up too, and you wonder if you've taken the right side after all. Saturday night you have a date, and Sunday morning you have to go to church. (You can't let English assignments interfere with your religion.) What with one thing and another, it's ten o'clock Sunday night before you get out the typewriter again. You make a pot of coffee and start to fill out your views on college football. Put a little meat on the bones.

Why College Football Should Be Abolished

In my opinion, it seems to me that college football should be abolished. The reason why I think this is to be true is because I feel that football is bad for the colleges in nearly every aspect. As Robert Hutchins says in his article in our anthology in which he discusses college football, it would be better if the colleges had race horses and had races with one another, because then the horses would not have to attend classes. I firmly agree with Mr. Hutchins on this point, and I am sure that many other students would agree too.

One reason why it seems to me that college football is bad is that it has become too commercial. In the olden times when people played football just for the fun of it, maybe college football was all right, but they do not play football just for the fun of it now as they used to in the old days. Nowadays college football is what you might call a big business. Maybe this is not true at all schools, and I don't think it is especially true here at State, but certainly this is the case at most colleges and universities in America nowadays, as Mr. Hutchins points out in his very interesting article. Actually the coaches and alumni go around to the high schools and offer the high school stars large salaries to come to their colleges and play football for them. There was one case where a high school star was offered a convertible if he would play football for a certain college.

Another reason for abolishing college football is that it is bad for the players. They do not have time to get a college education, because they are so busy playing football. A football player has to practice every afternoon from three to six and then he is so tired that he can't concentrate on his studies. He just feels like dropping off to sleep after dinner, and then the next day he goes to his classes without having studied and maybe he fails the test.

(Good ripe stuff, so far, but you're still a hundred and fifty-one words from home. One more push.)

Also I think college football is bad for the colleges and the universities because not very many students get to participate in it. Out of a college of ten thousand males only seventy-five or a hundred play football, if that many. Football is what you might call a spectator sport. That means that most people go to watch it but do not play it themselves.

(Four hundred and fifteen. Well, you still have the conclusion, and when you retype it, you can make the margins a little wider.)

These are the reasons why I agree with Mr. Hutchins that college football should be abolished in American colleges and universities.

5   On Monday you turn it in, moderately hopeful, and on Friday it comes back marked "weak in content" and sporting a big "D."

This essay is exaggerated a little, not much. The English instructor will recognize it as reasonably typical of what an assignment on college football will bring in. He knows that nearly half of the class will contrive in five hundred words to say that college football is too commercial and bad for the players. Most of the other half will inform him that college football builds character and prepares one for life and brings prestige to the school. As he reads paper after paper all saying the same things in almost the same words, all bloodless, five hundred words dripping out of nothing, he wonders how he allowed himself to get trapped into teaching English when he might have had a happy and interesting life as an electrician or a confidence man.

Well, you may ask, what can you do about it? The subject is one on which you have few convictions and little information. Can you be expected to make a dull subject interesting? As a matter of fact, that is precisely what you are expected to do. This is the writer's essential task. All subjects, except sex, are dull until somebody makes them interesting. The writer's job is to find the argument, the approach, the angle, the wording that will take the reader with him. This is seldom easy, and it is particularly hard in subjects that have been much discussed: College Football, Fraternities, Popular Music, Is Chivalry Dead?, and the like. You will feel that there is nothing you can do with such subjects except repeat the old bromides. But there are some things you can do which will make your papers, if not throbbingly alive, at least less insufferably tedious than they might otherwise be.

Avoid the Obvious Content

Say the assignment is college football. Say that you've decided to be against it. Begin by putting down the arguments that come to your mind: It is too commercial, it takes the students' minds off their studies, it is hard on the players, it makes the university a kind of circus instead of an intellectual center, for most schools it is financially ruinous. Can you think of any more arguments, just off hand? All right. Now when you write your paper, *make sure that you don't use any of the material on this list.* If these are the points that leap to your mind they will leap to everyone else's too, and whether you get a "C" or a "D" may depend on whether the instructor reads your paper early when he is fresh and tolerant or late, when the sentence "In my opinion, college football has become too commercial," inexorably repeated, has brought him to the brink of lunacy.

Be against college football for some reason or reasons of your own. If they are keen and perceptive ones, that's splendid. But even if they are trivial or foolish or indefensible, you are still ahead so long as they are not everybody else's reasons too. Be against it because the colleges don't spend enough money on it to make it worthwhile, because it is bad for the characters of the spectators, because the players are forced to attend classes, because the football stars hog all the beautiful women, because it competes with baseball and is therefore un-American and possibly Communist inspired. There are lots of more or less unused reasons for being against college football.

10   Sometimes it is a good idea to sum up and dispose of the trite and conventional points before going on to your own. This has the advantage of indicating to the reader that you are going to be neither trite nor conventional. Something like this:

We are often told that college football should be abolished because it has become too commercial or because it is bad for the players. These arguments are no doubt very cogent, but they don't go to the heart of the matter.

Then you go to the heart of the matter.

Take the Less Usual Side

One rather simple way of getting into your paper is to take the side of the argument that most of the citizens will want to avoid. If the assignment is an essay on dogs, you can, if you choose, explain that dogs are faithful and lovable companions, intelligent, useful as guardians of the house and protectors of children, indispensable in police work—in short, when all is said and done, man's best friends. Or you can suggest that those big brown eyes conceal, more often than not, a vacuity of mind and an inconstancy of purpose; that the dogs you have known most intimately have been mangy, ill-tempered brutes, incapable of instruction; and that only your nobility of mind and fear of arrest prevent you from kicking the flea-ridden animals when you pass them on the street.

Naturally personal convictions will sometimes dictate your approach. If the assigned subject is "Is Methodism Rewarding to the Individual?" and you are a pious Methodist, you have really no choice. But few assigned subjects, if any, will fall into this category. Most of them will lie in broad areas of discussion with much to be said on both sides. They are intellectual exercises, and it is legitimate to argue now one way and now another, as debaters do in similar circumstances. Always take the side that looks to you hardest, least defensible. It will almost always turn out to be easier to write interestingly on that side.

15   This general advice applies where you have a choice of subjects. If you are to choose among "The Value of Fraternities" and "My Favorite High School Teacher" and "What I Think About Beetles," by all means plump for the beetles. By the time the instructor gets to your paper, he will be up to his ears in tedious tales about the French teacher at Bloombury High and assertions about how fraternities build character and prepare one for life. Your views on beetles, whatever they are, are bound to be a refreshing change.

Don't worry too much about figuring out what the instructor thinks about the subject so that you can cuddle up with him. Chances are his views are no stronger than yours. If he does have convictions and you oppose him, his problem is to keep from grading you higher than you deserve in order to show he is not biased. This doesn't mean that you should always cantankerously dissent from what the instructor says; that gets tiresome too. And if the subject assigned is "My Pet Peeve," do not begin, "My pet peeve is the English instructor who assigns papers on 'my pet peeve.'" This was still funny during the War of 1812, but it has sort of lost its edge since then. It is in general good manners to avoid personalities.

Slip Out of Abstraction

If you will study the essay on college football [near the beginning of this essay], you will perceive that one reason for its appalling dullness is that it never gets down to particulars. It is just a series of not very glittering generalities: "Football is bad for the colleges," "it has become too commercial," "football is a big business," "it is bad for the players," and so on. Such round phrases thudding against the reader's brain are unlikely to convince him, though they may well render him unconscious.

If you want the reader to believe that college football is bad for the players, you have to do more than say so. You have to display the evil. Take your roommate, Alfred Simkins, the second-string center. Picture poor old Alfy coming home from football practice every evening, bruised and aching, agonizingly tired, scarcely able to shovel the mashed potatoes into his mouth. Let us see him staggering up to the room, getting out his econ textbook, peering desperately at it with his good eye, falling asleep and failing the test in the morning. Let us share his unbearable tension as Saturday draws near. Will he fail, be demoted, lose his monthly allowance, be forced to return to the coal mines? And if he succeeds, what will be his reward? Perhaps a slight ripple of applause when the third-string center replaces him, a moment of elation in the locker room if the team wins, of despair if it loses. What will he look back on when he graduates from college? Toil and torn ligaments. And what will be his future? He is not good enough for pro football, and he is too obscure and weak in econ to succeed in stocks and bonds. College football is tearing the heart from Alfy Simkins and, when it finishes with him, will callously toss aside the shattered hulk.

This is no doubt a weak enough argument for the abolition of college football, but it is a sight better than saying, in three or four variations, that college football (in your opinion) is bad for players.

20   Look at the work of any professional writer and notice how constantly he is moving from the generality, the abstract statement, to the concrete example, the facts and figures, the illustration. If he is writing on juvenile delinquency, he does not just tell you that juveniles are (it seems to him) delinquent and that (in his opinion) something should be done about it. He shows you juveniles being delinquent, tearing up movie theaters in Buffalo, stabbing high school principals in Dallas, smoking marijuana in Palo Alto. And more than likely he is moving toward some specific remedy, not just a general wringing of the hands.

It is no doubt possible to be *too* concrete, too illustrative or anecdotal, but few inexperienced writers err this way. For most the soundest advice is to be seeking always for the picture, to be always turning general remarks into see-able examples. Don't say, "Sororities teach girls the social graces." Say, "Sorority life teaches a girl how to carry on a conversation while pouring tea, without sloshing the tea into the saucer." Don't say, "I like certain kinds of popular music very much." Say, "Whenever I hear Gerber Sprinklittle play 'Mississippi Man' on the trombone, my socks creep up my ankles."

Get Rid of Obvious Padding

The student toiling away at his weekly English theme is too often tormented by a figure: five hundred words. How, he asks himself, is he to achieve this staggering total? Obviously by never using one word when he can somehow work in ten.

He is therefore seldom content with a plain statement like "Fast driving is dangerous." This has only four words in it. He takes thought, and the sentence becomes:

In my opinion, fast driving is dangerous.

Better, but he can do better still:

In my opinion, fast driving would seem to be rather dangerous.

If he is really adept, it may come out:

In my humble opinion, though I do not claim to be an expert on this complicated subject, fast driving, in most circumstances, would seem to be rather dangerous in many aspects, or at least so it would seem to me.

Thus four words have turned into forty, and not an iota of content has been added.

25   Now this is a way to go about reaching five hundred words, and if you are content with a "D" grade, it is as good a way as any. But if you aim higher, you must work differently. Instead of stuffing your sentences with straw, you must

try steadily to get rid of the padding, to make your sentences lean and tough. If you are really working at it, your first draft will greatly exceed the required total, and then you will work it down, thus:

> It is thought in some quarters that fraternities do not contribute as much as might be expected to campus life.

> Some people think that fraternities contribute little to campus life.

> The average doctor who practices in small towns or in the country must toil night and day to heal the sick.

> Most country doctors work long hours.

> When I was a little girl, I suffered from shyness and embarrassment in the presence of others.

> I was a shy little girl.

> It is absolutely necessary for the person employed as a marine fireman to give the matter of steam pressure his undivided attention at all times.

> The fireman has to keep his eye on the steam gauge.

You may ask how you can arrive at five hundred words at this rate. Simple. You dig up more real content. Instead of taking a couple of obvious points off the surface of the topic and then circling warily around them for six paragraphs, you work in and explore, figure out the details. You illustrate. You say that fast driving is dangerous, and then you prove it. How long does it take to stop a car at forty and eighty? How far can you see at night? What happens when a tire blows? What happens in a head-on collision at fifty miles an hour? Pretty soon your paper will be full of broken glass and blood and headless torsos, and reaching five hundred words will not really be a problem.

Call a Fool a Fool

Some of the padding in freshman themes is to be blamed not on anxiety about the word minimum but on excessive timidity. The student writes, "In my opinion, the principal of my high school acted in ways that I believe every unbiased person would have to call foolish." This isn't exactly what he means. What he means is, "My high school principal was a fool." If he was a fool, call him a fool. Hedging the thing about with "in-my-opinion's" and "it-seems-to-me's" and "as-I-see-it's" and "at-least-from-my-point-of-view's" gains you nothing. Delete these phrases whenever they creep into your paper.

The student's tendency to hedge stems from a modesty that in other circumstances would be commendable. He is, he realizes, young and inexperienced, and he half suspects that he is dopey and fuzzy-minded beyond the average. Probably only too true. But it doesn't help to announce your incompetence six times in every paragraph. Decide what you want to say and say it as vigorously as possible, without apology and in plain words.

Linguistic diffidence can take various forms. One is what we call *euphemism*. This is the tendency to call a spade "a certain garden implement" or women's underwear "unmentionables." It is stronger in some eras than others and in some people than others but it always operates more or less in subjects that are touchy or taboo: death, sex, madness, and so on. Thus we shrink from saying "He died last night" but say instead "passed away," "left us," "joined his Maker," "went to his reward." Or we try to take off the tension with a lighter cliché: "kicked the bucket," "cashed in his chips," "handed in his dinner pail." We have found all sorts of ways to avoid saying *mad:* "mentally ill," "touched," "not quite right upstairs," "off his trolley," "not in his right mind." Even such a now plain word as *insane* began as a euphemism with the meaning "not healthy."

30   Modern science, particularly psychology, contributes many polysyllables in which we can wrap our thoughts and blunt their force. To many writers there is no such thing as a bad schoolboy. Schoolboys are maladjusted or unoriented or misunderstood or in the need of guidance or lacking in continued success toward satisfactory integration of the personality as a social unit, but they are never bad. Psychology, no doubt, makes us better men and women, more sympathetic and tolerant, but it doesn't make writing any easier. Had Shakespeare been confronted with psychology, "To be or not to be" might have come out, "To continue as a social unit or not to do so. That is the personality problem. Whether 'tis a better sign of integration at the conscious level to display a psychic tolerance toward the maladjustments and repressions induced by one's lack of orientation in one's environment or—" But Hamlet would never have finished the soliloquy.

Writing in the modern world, you cannot altogether avoid modern jargon. Nor, in an effort to get away from euphemism, should you salt your paper with four-letter words. But you can do much if you will mount guard against those roundabout phrases, those echoing polysyllables that tend to slip into your writing to rob it of its crispness and force.

Beware of Pat Expressions

Other things being equal, avoid phrases like "other things being equal." Those sentences that come to you whole, or in two or three doughy lumps, are sure to be bad sentences. They are no creation of yours but pieces of common thought floating in the community soup.

Pat expressions are hard, often impossible, to avoid, because they come too easily to be noticed and seem too necessary to be dispensed with. No writer avoids them altogether, but good writers avoid them more often than poor writers.

By "pat expressions" we mean such tags as "to all practical intents and purposes," "the pure and simple truth," "from where I sit," "the time of his life," "to the ends of the earth," "in the twinkling of an eye," "as sure as you're born," "over my dead body," "under cover of darkness," "took the easy way out," "when all is said and done," "told him time and time again," "parted the best of friends," "stand up and be counted," "gave him the best years of her life," "worked her fingers to the bone." Like other clichés, these expressions were once forceful. Now we should use them only when we can't possibly think of anything else.

35   Some pat expressions stand like a wall between the writer and thought. Such a one is "the American way of life." Many student writers feel that when they have said that something accords with the American way of life or does not, they have exhausted the subject. Actually, they have stopped at the highest level of abstraction. The American way of life is the complicated set of bonds between a hundred and eighty million ways. All of us know this when we think about it, but the tag phrase too often keeps us from thinking about it.

So with many another phrase dear to the politician: "this great land of ours," "the man in the street," "our national heritage." These may prove our patriotism or give a clue to our political beliefs, but otherwise they add nothing to the paper except words.

Colorful Words

The writer builds with words, and no builder uses a raw material more slippery and elusive and treacherous. A writer's work is a constant struggle to get the right word in the right place, to find that particular word that will convey his meaning exactly, that will persuade the reader or soothe him or startle or amuse him. He never succeeds altogether—sometimes he feels that he scarcely succeeds at all—but such successes as he has are what make the thing worth doing.

There is no book of rules for this game. One progresses through everlasting experiment on the basis of ever-widening experience. There are few useful generalizations that one can make about words as words, but there are perhaps a few.

Some words are what we call "colorful." By this we mean that they are calculated to produce a picture or induce an emotion. They are dressy instead of plain, specific instead of general, loud instead of soft. Thus, in place of "Her heart beat," we may write, "Her heart *pounded, throbbed, fluttered, danced.*" Instead of "He sat in his chair," we may say, "He *lounged, sprawled, coiled.*" Instead of "It was hot," we may say, "It was *blistering, sultry, muggy, suffocating, steamy, wilting.*"

40   However, it should not be supposed that the fancy word is always better. Often it is as well to write "Her heart beat" or "It was hot" if that is all it did or all it was. Ages differ in how they like their prose. The nineteenth century liked it rich and smoky. The twentieth has usually preferred it lean and cool. The twentieth century writer, like all writers, is forever seeking the exact word, but he is wary of sounding feverish. He tends to pitch it low, to understate it, to throw it away. He knows that if he gets too colorful, the audience is likely to giggle.

See how this strikes you: "As the rich, golden glow of the sunset died away along the eternal western hills, Angela's limpid blue eyes looked softly and trustingly into Montague's flashing brown ones, and her heart pounded like a drum in time with the joyous song surging in her soul." Some people like that sort of thing, but most modern readers would say, "Good grief," and turn on the television.

Colored Words

Some words we call not so much colorful as colored—that is, loaded with associations, good or bad. All words—except perhaps structure words—have associations of some sort. We have said that the meaning of a word is the sum of the contexts in which it occurs. When we hear a word, we hear with it an echo of all the situations in which we have heard it before.

In some words, these echoes are obvious and discussible. The word *mother*, for example, has for most people, agreeable associations. When you hear *mother* you probably think of home, safety, love, food, and various other pleasant things. If one writes, "She was like a mother to me," he gets an effect which he would not get in "She was like an aunt to me." The advertiser makes use of the associations of *mother* by working it in when he talks about his product. The politician works it in when he talks about himself.

So also with such words as *home, liberty, fireside, contentment, patriot, tenderness, sacrifice, childlike, manly, bluff, limpid*. All of these words are loaded with associations that would be rather hard to indicate in a straightforward definition. There is more than a literal difference between "They sat around the fireside" and "They sat around the stove." They might have been equally warm and happy around the stove, but *fireside* suggests leisure, grace, quiet tradition, congenial company, and *stove* does not.

45   Conversely, some words have bad associations. *Mother* suggests pleasant things, but *mother-in-law* does not. Many mothers-in-law are heroically lovable and some mothers drink gin all day and beat their children insensible, but these facts of life are beside the point. The point is that *mother* sounds good and *mother-in-law* does not.

Or consider the word *intellectual*. This would seem to be a complimentary term, but in point of fact it is not, for it has picked up associations of impracticality and ineffectuality and general dopiness. So also such words as *liberal, reactionary, Communist, Socialist, capitalist, radical, schoolteacher, truck driver, undertaker, operator, salesman, huckster, speculator*. These convey meaning on the literal level, but beyond that—sometimes, in some places—they convey contempt on the part of the speaker.

The question of whether to use loaded words or not depends on what is being written. The scientist, the scholar, try to avoid them; for the poet, the advertising writer, the public speaker, they are standard equipment. But every writer should take care that they do not substitute for thought. If you write, "Anyone who thinks that is nothing but a Socialist (or Communist or capitalist)," you have said nothing except that you don't like people who think that, and such remarks are effective only with the most naive readers. It is always a bad mistake to think your readers more naive than they really are.

Colorless Words

But probably most student writers come to grief not with words that are colorful or those that are colored but with those that have no color at all. A pet example is *nice*, a word we would find it hard to dispense with in casual conversation but which is no longer capable of adding much to a description. Colorless words are those of such general meaning that in a particular sentence they mean nothing. Slang adjectives like *cool* ("That's real cool") tend to explode all over the language. They are applied to everything, lose their original force, and quickly die.

Beware also of nouns of very general meaning, like *circumstances, cases, instances, aspects, factors, relationships, attitudes, eventualities,* etc. In most circumstances you will find that those cases of writing which contain too many instances of words like these will in this and other aspects have factors leading to unsatisfactory relationships with the reader resulting in unfavorable attitudes on his part and perhaps other eventualities, like a grade of "D." Notice also what "etc." means. It means "I'd like to make this list longer, but I can't think of any more examples."

Critical Reading Questions

1. Describe the last time you can remember writing a five-hundred-word essay that you were concerned about because it said (almost) nothing. What was your topic? Why did you have trouble composing a more substantive paper?

2. According to Paul Roberts, "All subjects, except sex, are dull until somebody makes them interesting." If you were to revise the essay you identified in question 1, how would you make it more interesting?

3. Roberts discusses a number of points to remember when you are writing and revising:

   • Avoid the obvious content

   • Take the less usual side

   • Slip out of abstraction

   • Get rid of obvious padding

   • Call a fool a fool

   • Beware of pat expressions

   • Be aware of colorful words, colored words, and colorless words

   Do you think that the author "practices what he preaches"? Identify one example of each point to "show" what you mean.

4. Again review the essay you revised for the Thinking-Writing Activity on page 134, paying special attention to each of these points. Make whatever new revision you think will help express your meaning more successfully.

Thinking ↔ Writing Activity

Analyzing Writers' Ideas About Writing

This chapter examines three approaches to revising: the step-by-step method by this book's authors on pages 132–134, the strategies Donald Murray discusses on pages 134–138, and the points Paul Roberts explores in this last essay. These different approaches are not in conflict: They work together to help you refine your writing. Identify at least ten of the strategies from these three sources that you believe will be most helpful for improving your writing and include them in a Personal Revision Guide that you can keep for handy reference. For each strategy, provide an example.

Writing Project: Analyzing a Decision to Be Made

This chapter includes both readings and Thinking-Writing Activities that encourage you to reflect on decision making and revision. Be sure to reread what you wrote for those activities; you may be able to use your responses to complete this project.

Write an essay in which you analyze a decision you must make now or in the near future. Be sure to select a decision for which you already have considerable information or want to obtain more. Include all five steps of the decision-making method. After you have drafted your essay, revise it as best you can. Follow your instructor's directions for length, format, and so on.

THE WRITING SITUATION

Begin by considering the key elements in the Thinking-Writing Model.

Purpose You have a variety of purposes here. First, you can use this opportunity to work through an important real-life decision to obtain the best possible outcome. If others will be involved in or affected by this decision, your paper can show them your best thinking about it, making them more likely to agree with your decision. Also, in writing this paper, you can practice the creative and critical thinking involved in the five-step decision-making method. You can hone your revision skills both by carefully working through the revision questions on pages 132–134 and by using ideas about revision from Chapter 1 as well as ideas from this chapter.

Audience As in the Writing Project for Chapter 3, you have a range of readers for your audience. You yourself are an important audience, for by working through the possible choices, you may find yourself actually making the decision you face. If the decision involves other people in your life, they would make an excellent audience for both early drafts and final copy because they could provide ideas about the choices, suggest choices you haven't thought of, and offer reactions to your decision. Your classmates can be valuable peer reviewers of a draft, reacting as intelligent readers who are not involved in the decision and therefore able to be objective about both the clarity of your writing and the logic of your decision. Your instructor remains an audience who will judge how well you have planned, drafted, and revised. As a writing teacher, your instructor cares about a clear focus, logical organization, specific examples, and correctness; keep these requirements in mind as you revise, edit, and proofread. In the future, the audience for your writing will likely include business colleagues, various organizations, and, if your work is published, the world at large.

Subject Decisions can be challenging to think about and difficult to make. Sometimes we haven't enough information to make an intelligent choice; sometimes we *think* we know what the right decision is yet are reluctant to actually make it. Therefore, we often tend to put off decision making for as long as possible. Keep in mind that not making a decision is, in a way, making a decision to do nothing. For this assignment, try to identify a decision which will have significant consequences. It may be what area to major in, whether to get a part-time job, whether to participate in a sport or other extracurricular activity, or whether to get a dog. The more significant the decision, the more helpful this assignment will be to you.

Writer You approach this Writing Project as the expert on the subject since you are analyzing one of your own decisions. If you have done the projects in Chapter 2 or Chapter 3, you may have felt the confidence that such expertise brings and the satisfaction of sharing your experiences with the audience to whom you have directed your writing. One challenge here is to distinguish between your own expertise about the decision-making situation and your audience's needs for enough background and information. Another challenge is to focus on the material provided earlier in this chapter because this assignment moves away from recollecting experience and asks you to apply the decision-making process to a decision you need to make soon.

THE WRITING PROCESS

The following sections will guide you through the stages of generating, planning, drafting, and revising as you work on an essay about making a decision. Try to be particularly conscious of both the creative and the critical thinking you do while making your decision and of the critical thinking and decision-making you do as you revise.

Generating Ideas   Refer back to the list you made in the Thinking-Writing Activity on page 130 for possible subject choices. You may want to develop the writing you did for that assignment, or you may feel that another decision would work better for this project.

- Think about when each of the decisions must be made. Is there one you must make in the near future? If so, this is a good opportunity for you to accomplish two things at once: writing your paper and making your decision.
- Think about how much additional information you would need to evaluate possible choices for each of the decisions on your list. Do you have time to locate and absorb all of it?
- Think about which decision you are most interested in making or which worries you most.
- Decide on a tentative topic: that is, which decision you will work on.
- Describe the decision-making situation and your goals as clearly as you can.
- Brainstorm as many possible choices as you can. Ask others involved in the decision to help.
- Eliminate choices that you know are impractical or undesirable.
- Determine what information you must find for each choice. Locate that information.
- Write each choice on a separate sheet of paper. Then divide the paper into two columns: pros and cons. Write as much as you can in each column.
- For each, freewrite for five minutes on what would happen and how you would feel if you selected that choice.
- Freewrite for five minutes on how you would know if any given choice were the right one.

Defining a Focus   Write a tentative thesis statement which signals your audience that you are going to explore a decision-making situation. You might write something like "After thinking about the situation carefully, I realize that I have only two possible choices." Or you might "blueprint" your paper by naming the possible choices: "My choices for housing next year come down to these three: living with my aunt, sharing an apartment with my friend, or looking for a live-in job situation." You may even decide to announce your decision in your thesis statement: "After carefully weighing my options, I have decided to major in business administration." Or you may find a more creative way to state your thesis.

Organizing Ideas The five-step method for making decisions fits well with essay structure. Your description of the decision-making situation might be the beginning of an introduction, to be completed by your thesis statement. You could include your goals in the introduction or state them in a separate paragraph. Each of the possible choices, explained in as much detail as possible along with the pros and cons of that choice, could serve as a body paragraph. Your decision of the best choice and your plan for monitoring it could be be the essay's conclusion.

Drafting Begin with the easiest part to draft. Your description of the decision-making situation could begin the introduction, but consider what, if any, additional information your audience might need in order to understand the situation. The introduction can end with your tentative thesis statement.

A clear way to begin each body paragraph is with a topic sentence that names the possible choice being discussed. Then provide the audience with sufficient information to help them understand what selecting that choice would mean. Use the sheets you prepared on the advantages and disadvantages of each choice for help.

Once you have drafted your body paragraphs, you will be ready to decide on the best order for them. Try arranging them in different orders until you discover the one most likely to help your audience.

In your conclusion or thesis statement, name the choice you have selected. You may want to explain why if you think your reason may not be obvious to your audience. Remember to explain how you will monitor the results of your decision.

 Revising One of the best revision strategies is to get an audience's reactions to your draft. Your classmates, or peers, can help you see where your draft is already successful and where it needs more or less information. Your peers can also help you see if your draft needs reorganization. If your instructor allows class time for peer review (see pages 65–66 and 105–107), be sure to have a draft ready so that you can benefit from this activity. Here are some questions to ask your peers about this assignment:

- What questions do you have about my decision-making situation and my goals?
- What questions do you have about the alternative choices I described? What else do you need to know about them? Can you suggest any others?
- Do you understand why I am making this decision?

- What could I add to clarify why this choice is best for me?

Armed with the information from peer review, you are now ready to begin revising by using the revision method presented on page 132 of this chapter (and included on the inside back cover). If possible, use the following directions for revising with a word processor as you work through the revision process.

Revising Strategy: Using Word Processing to Revise Use the revision method by creating a series of files, one for each time you revise using your word processor. This system will give you a complete record of your work so that you can track how each draft changes.

- Call your first draft Decision 1 and print and save it.
- Later, create a new file called Decision 2 by copying and pasting Decision 1. Then make changes to the draft as a whole, being guided by your answers from the peer review and your answers to the Think Big questions on page 132. Print and save this draft.
- Now, consider the Think Medium questions to evaluate your individual paragraphs. Create a new file called Decision 3 by copying and pasting Decision 2. Then make whatever changes are suggested by your answers to the Think Medium questions on page 132. Print and save this draft.
- Next, consider the Think Small questions. Create a new file called Decision 4 by copying and pasting Decision 3. Then make whatever changes at the sentence level which are suggested by your answers to the Think Small questions on page 133. Print and save this draft.
- Finally, consider the Think "Picky" questions. Create a new file called Decision 5 by copying and pasting Decision 4. Then make whatever changes are suggested by your answers to the Think "Picky" questions on page 133. Run the spelling and grammar checking features of your word processing program, and use your judgment about which suggested changes to make. Print and save this draft. Decision 5 should present your very best work. It is now ready to be submitted to your instructor and any other audience you select.

Revised Paragraph Notice how a student revised a draft of a paragraph after a class discussion of topic sentences and unity, followed by peer review examining those components. How did she change her paragraph?

Draft (a paragraph using comparison to make a point)

Although Sweden and the United States are in two different parts of the world, their cultures have a lot of similarities. Two of the things I value most in life are freedom and equality of opportunity between women and men, and both countries are doing big improvements on those fields. People in both countries eat way too much junk food and are always in a hurry. Both nationalities value family, health and happiness very much and unfortunately they also seem to think that money is the answer to all problems in the universe.

Revision

Although Sweden and the United States are in two different parts of the world, the residents in both countries have a tendency to eat too much junk food. I believe that many people in both countries are living hectic lives, and that really influences the food culture. I have noticed that it is easy to skip lunch or just eat a sandwich during the busy weekdays in the United States, and it is just the same in Sweden. Then, back home after a hard day's work, hardly anybody is looking forward to cooking, so many families are thankful for McDonald's or pizza delivery. This is true in both countries. I am sad to say that it is because I do not believe that this is a healthy lifestyle.

Editing and Proofreading After you have prepared a final draft, check for standard grammar and punctuation usage. Proofread carefully for omitted words and punctuation marks. Run your spelling checker program, but be aware of its limitations. Proofread again for the kinds of errors the computer can't catch.

Your essay should now have been completed to the best of your ability, and, of course, you will need to submit it to your instructor by the due date. But also consider other possible audiences for this essay. Do you want to share your ideas with other people involved in your decision-making situation? Would members of your family or your close friends benefit by reading it? If your paper is about a decision that others must also make, such as selecting a major, perhaps your student newspaper would be interested in publishing it as a model of good decision-making which others could emulate.

The following essays show how two students responded to this assignment.

STUDENT WRITING

Deciding What to Do About My Hearing Problem
BY BAO-TOAN LE

I work in the Computer Writing Center at my college. Every day I listen and reply to many students' questions. But six months ago, when students asked me questions, I noticed that I could not hear them very clearly. I had to ask them to repeat three or four times. From that day forward, my hearing kept getting worse. I realized that I had to do something about it. I thought I had two alternative solutions to consider and choose from: using the traditional Chinese treatments or following the advice of my otolaryngologists. Fortunately, I discovered that there was a third alternative, which combined the best features of the other two.

The first alternate solution was to use the traditional treatments, such as the therapy of point acupuncture and Chinese medicinal herbs. Point acupuncture is a very effective method to cure various kinds of diseases, especially earache, by massaging the thumb and index fingers right on the fourteen pressure points of the head. Chinese medical herbs, which are refined from roots, stalks, and leaves of many different trees, are also good medicines. The advantage of this solution was that I could restore my hearing and gain more confidence. For instance, massaging eight particular vital points around my head and neck with my thumb, I could alleviate the headache which accompanies my deafness in just a few minutes. Therefore, I would not be scared of getting sick anymore. Another advantage was that I would not have to pay anything for this treatment because my uncle who is a traditional pharmacist would teach me at no charge. Nevertheless, these remedies require much time and precision. I would have to spend at least three months to memorize the pressure points, and of course I would stay "deaf" for five or six months more. Also, I would have to find the right kinds of herbs and to prepare the combination of these herbs. For instance, first I would need to find three different herbs: A, B, and C. Then I would have to blend 25 percent of the A leaves, 30 percent of the B radicles, 45 percent of the stalks of the vegetable C herbs, and salt, and then pour in the water and boil until the water equals one-third of the original amount. Another minor disadvantage is that most of the Chinese herbs are very bitter and have unpleasant smells.

Another alternative was to follow the advice of my otolaryngologists: have some tests done, take medicine, and have surgery if necessary. The doctors carefully did the tests, including graphing tests, beeping tests, listening and speaking tests, and examining the throat, the nose and both ears. Therefore, their opinions were reliable, and the remedy would be quick and effective. After the tests, they told me that my eardrums did not have enough air flow into them. They decided to give me medicine. If the medicine did not cure me, they would do surgery to rearrange the ear bones. The surgery would stop the problem forever. And because I have health insurance, the fees for the doctors were not expensive: only ten dollars per visit. But there were some disadvantages to their treatments: suffering from lack of appetite and sleeplessness from the medication as well as suffering from the ringing in my ears which I thought it caused. The operation, if I needed it, might hurt and leave a scar on my face.

After considering the advantages and disadvantages of each solution, I decided to use the point acupuncture therapy and to ask the otolaryngologists to give me a lighter dose of the medicine to reduce the side effects. I also stopped taking the Chinese herbs with my medicine, and this helped with the ear ringing. After three weeks of taking the lighter drugs and massaging the fourteen vital points, my hearing now is much better than it was before. My decision was the right one, and I am very happy with my progress.

STUDENT WRITING

A Space Problem

BY JON COHEN

My rock and roll band, "The Love Machine," needed a place to practice. We had practiced at my parents' spacious home in Bethesda, which had worked out very well. We had made noise until 10:00 P.M. without any problems, we had practiced in a location central to the members of the band, we had easy parking, we had not caused any tension in a user-lender relationship as my parents were supportive of us, our practice space had been comfortable, and we had been able to store our equipment with confidence that it would be safe. Unfortunately, my parents sold their home and moved into a condominium where loud noise was not allowed. We had to find a different place to practice; we didn't have many choices, and deciding what to do wasn't easy.

One place I was interested in was a large apartment in Georgetown. In this apartment were people I did not know who had their own rock band that practiced in a loft located in the apartment. They wanted someone else to use their practice space at an arranged time for a small fee. I actually looked at the place. The tenants claimed we could make noise because they were located in the business district of Georgetown where noise was allowed in the evenings. The location was close to all of us. The fee was small, at less than $200 a month, and the tenants said we could store equipment in the space.

There were problems with this apartment, however. Parking in Georgetown was very difficult. Also, the practice space, although big, could only be reached by way of a ladder and that I felt was an uncomfortable prospect. Finally, we did not know the people who were renting the space at all, and I was a little nervous about leaving our equipment with them.

Another place in which I was interested was a group house in Arlington, Virginia. The people who were living in the group house I knew a little bit as they had seen "The Love Machine" perform. The people in the group house were planning to have a space in their basement available for music. They were going to use it for their own projects but felt we could use it also. Their location in Arlington was close to everyone in the band. The rent they asked was very low at less than $100 a month. Parking was readily available in front of the house, and I felt that the band's relationship with these people would be strengthened by our association because they truly believed in the band.

There were some problems with the house in Virginia. The houses in the residential neighborhood were very close together, and there was a possibility that the neighbors would be bothered by the noise and would not tolerate it. Also, there was sometimes flooding in the basement where the practice space was. The people in the house wanted to build a stage over the space to protect it from water; also, they wanted to insulate the space so that sound would not escape.

Another choice I had was to pass these places up and keep waiting. My band and I were looking for opportunities and people were aware that we had a problem. However, while waiting, the band would not be practicing. When a band does not stay active, band members start to set aside their time for other things. Getting the band started again might have been impossible.

The decision we made was to practice at the group house in Virginia. Our equipment did stay safe, and our relationship with the people in the house became better. However, we were still a little uncomfortable using the place of people we did not know really well. Also, the neighbors did start to complain about the noise.

Fortunately, my drummer recently moved into a house in Washington, D.C., that happened to have space for a band to practice. We are practicing there now, and we will see how it goes.

ALTERNATIVE WRITING PROJECT: ANALYZING A GROUP DECISION TO BE MADE

Write an essay in which you analyze a decision which must be made soon by some group to which you belong: for example, your religious group, your college, or your town. Select a decision for which you and your group already have considerable information or one for which you would like more information. Include all five steps in the decision-making method. Think carefully about purpose, audience, subject, and writer as you move through the steps of generating ideas, defining a focus, organizing ideas, drafting, revision, and proofreading. Follow your instructor's directions for length, format, and so on.

"Only where there is language is there world." —Adrienne Rich

5

Understanding Language

Writing Precisely

Critical Thinking Focus: Language as a system

Writing Focus: Using language to clarify thinking

Reading Theme: Using language effectively

Writing Project: The impact of language on your life

Every time we use language, we send a message about our thinking. When we speak or write, we are not simply making sounds or writing symbols; we are conveying ideas, sharing feelings, and describing experiences. At the same time, language itself shapes and influences thinking. When language use is sloppy—vague, general, indistinct, imprecise, foolish, inaccurate—it leads to the same sort of thinking. The reverse is also true: clear, precise language leads to clear, precise thinking, speaking, and writing.

Thus, it is vital to use language with clarity and precision if other people are to understand the thoughts we are trying to communicate. And to use language effectively, we need to view language as a system, one with agreed-upon sets of rules and expectations.

To comprehend this essential tool more fully and use it more powerfully, we will begin by considering both the development of languages and the symbolic nature of language. We will then examine strategies for using language effectively and for using language to clarify thinking. Finally, we will consider the social uses of language: how it is used in different social contexts and how it can be used to influence thinking and behavior.

The chapter ends with a Writing Project which asks you to write about your own experience with language and to connect that experience to the concepts in this chapter. The project places special emphasis on thinking and writing with precision: clearly conceptualizing what you want to say and discovering the best use of language to say it.

Thinking ↔ Writing Activity

A World Without Language

Imagine a world without language. Imagine that you have suddenly lost your ability to speak, to write, to read. Imagine that your only means of expression is grunts, shrieks, and gestures. And finally, imagine that you soon discover that everyone else in the world has also lost the ability to use language. Write a one-page description of what such a world would be like. Be prepared to share your response with the class.

The Development of Language

Language forms the bedrock of human relations. Sharing thoughts, feelings, and experiences through writing and speaking draws people together and leads to forming relationships.

Consider the social groups in your school, neighborhood, or community. Have you ever thought about how language plays a central role in drawing people into groups and then maintaining them? A loss of language would both limit the complexity of individual relationships and drastically affect the way people live within society.

Speculation about the origin of language has excited the human imagination for ages. Today we know that no single language is the root of all others.

Rather, like people, languages belong to families. Languages in the same family share some characteristics with other members but also have individual characteristics. We know that languages, like the human beings of whom they are a natural part, live, change, and die. For example, Latin is no longer a living language; neither is the ancient Indian language Sanskrit.

English—like Spanish, French, Chinese, Urdu, or any other spoken language—is a living language, and it has changed over hundreds of years. The English language has undergone four major evolutionary stages: Old English (A.D. 460–1050), Middle English (A.D. 1050–1450), Early Modern English (A.D. 1450–1700), and Modern English (A.D. 1700 to the present). Because languages are systems based on sound, these stages of English reflect differences in how the language has sounded. It is difficult to represent accurately the sounds for older periods because recording devices did not exist. For example, the following versions of the Lord's Prayer, sacred to Christians, present written symbols that are only approximations based on the consensus of linguistic scholars.

As you read these versions of the Lord's Prayer, think about the variations in sounds, words, and sentences. Then, with the other members of your class, discuss variations in the language(s) you speak.

The Lord's Prayer

Old English

Faeder ure
Thu the eart on heofonum,
Si thin name gehalgod.
Tobecume thin rice.
Gewurthe thin willa on eorthan swa swa on heofonum.
Urne gedaeghwamlican hlaf syle you to daeg.
And forgyf you urne gyltas, swa swa you forgyfath urum gyltendum.
And ne gelaed thu you on costnunge, ac alys you of yfele. Sothlice.

Middle English

Oure fadur
that art in hauenes
halewid be thi name;
thi kyngdoom come to;
be thi wile don in erthe as in heuene;
zyue to vs this dai oure breed ouer othir substaunce;
and forzyue to vs oure dettis, as you forzyuen to oure dettouris;
and lede vs not in to temptacioun,
but delyuere vs from yeul. Amen.

Early Modern English

Our Father
which art in heaven,
hallowed be thy name.
Thy kingdom come.
Thy will be done, in earth, as it is in heaven.
Give us this day our daily bread.
And forgive us our debts, as we forgive our debtors.
And lead us not into temptation,
but deliver us from evil:
for Thine is the kingdome, and the power, and the glory for ever. Amen.

Modern English

Our Father in heaven
may your name be held holy.
Your kingdom come,
your will be done, on earth as in heaven.
Give us today our daily bread.
And forgive us our debts as we have forgiven those who are in debt to us.
And do not put us to the test,
but save us from evil.

The Symbolic Nature of Language

As human beings, we are able to share our thoughts and feelings with one another because of our ability to *symbolize*, to let one thing represent another. Words are the most common symbols we use in our daily life. Although words are only sounds or written marks that have no meaning in and of themselves, they stand for objects, ideas, and other aspects of human experience. For example, the word *sailboat* is a symbol that represents a watergoing vessel with sails that is propelled by the wind. When you speak or write *sailboat*, you are able to communicate what you are thinking about. Of course, if other people are to understand what you are referring to when you use this symbol, they must first agree that it does in fact represent a wind-propelled vessel that floats on water. Of course, you could always take others to the object and point to it, but using a symbol is much more convenient.

Language symbols (or words) can take two forms: spoken sounds or written markings. The symbol *sailboat* can either be written or spoken. Either way, it communicates the same idea. Since language use is so natural to us, we rarely stop to realize that our **language** is really a system of spoken sounds and written markings that we use to represent various aspects of our experience.

SOUNDS

In certain respects, language is like a set of symbolic building blocks. The basic blocks are **sounds,** which may be symbolized by letters—such as A T C Q Y N. Sounds form the phonetic foundation of a language, and this explains why different languages have such distinctly different sounds. Members of the class should speak a few sentences in other languages they know. Listen to how the overall sound of each language differs from that of the others.

When human beings are infants, they possess the ability to make all the sounds of all languages. However, as they are continually exposed to the specific group of sounds of their own society's language, they gradually concentrate on making only those sounds, discarding or never developing others.

WORDS

Sounds combine to form larger sets of blocks called **words**. Words are used to represent the various aspects of experience—they symbolize objects, thoughts, feelings, actions, and concepts. When you read, hear, or think about a word, it usually calls to mind a variety of ideas and feelings. Describe, for instance, your responses to the following words: *college education, happiness, freedom, creativity, love.*

The combination of all the ideas and feelings that a word arouses is the "meaning" that word has for you. The responses that you just described reflect the meaning that each of those words has for you as an individual. And although these meanings are probably similar to the meanings the words have for other people, there are likely also many differences. Consider the different meanings those same words have for the two people in the following dialogue:

A: For me, a *college education* represents the most direct path to my dreams. It's the only way I can develop the knowledge and abilities required for my career.

B: I can't agree with you. I pursued a *college education* for a while, but it didn't work out. I found that most of my courses consisted of large classes with professors lecturing about subjects that had little relation to my life. The value of a college education is overblown. I know many people with college degrees who have not been able to find rewarding careers.

A: Don't you see? An important part of achieving *happiness* is learning about things you aren't familiar with, expanding your horizons about the world, developing new interests. That's what college can give you.

B: I have enough interests. As far as I'm concerned, *happiness* consists of having the opportunity to do the things that I enjoy doing with the people I enjoy doing them with. For me, happiness is *freedom*!

A: Freedom to do what? *Freedom* is meaningful only when you have worthwhile options and the wisdom to select the right ones. A college education can help provide both!

B: That sounds very idealistic, but it's also naive. Many of the college graduates I have met are neither wise nor happy. In order to be truly happy, you have to be involved in *creative* activities. Every day should be a surprise, something different to look forward to. Many careers pay well, but they don't provide creative opportunities.

A: Being *creative* means doing things you love. When you really love something you're doing, you are naturally creative. For example, I love to draw and paint, and this provides a creative outlet for me. I don't need to be creative at work—I have enough creative opportunities outside work.

B: You're wrong! *Creativity* doesn't mean simply being artistic. We should strive to be creative in every part of our lives and keep looking for new possibilities and unique experiences. And I think that you are misusing the word love. You can really *love* only things that are alive, like people and pets.

A: That's a very weird idea of love you have. As far as I'm concerned, *love* is a word that expresses a strong caring emotion that can be directed toward objects ("I love my car"), activities ("I love to dance"), or people. I don't see what's so complicated about that.

B: To be able to *love* in any meaningful sense, the object of your love has to be able to respond to you so that the two of you can develop a relationship together. When was the last time that your car responded to your love for it?

A: Very funny. I guess that we just have different ideas about the word love—as well as the words happiness, freedom, and creativity.

As this dialogue suggests, words are not simple entities with one clear meaning that everyone agrees on. Instead, most words are complex, multidimensional carriers of meaning; their exact meaning often varies from person to person. These differences in meaning can lead to disagreements and confusion, as the previous dialogue illustrates. To understand how words function in your own language and thinking, you have to examine the way that words serve as vehicles to express meaning.

Words arouse a variety of ideas, feelings, and experiences in each person. Taken together, these responses express the total meaning of the words for each individual. Linguists believe that this total meaning is actually composed of four different types of meaning:

- semantic meaning
- perceptual meaning
- syntactic meaning
- pragmatic meaning

Let us examine each of them in turn.

SEMANTIC MEANING (DENOTATION)

The **semantic meaning** of a word expresses the relationship between a **linguistic event** (speaking or writing) and a **nonlinguistic event** (an object, idea, or feeling). For example, saying "chair" relates to an object you sit in while saying "college education" relates to the experience of earning an academic degree through postsecondary study. What events (ideas, feelings, objects) relate to happiness? to freedom? to creativity? to love?

The semantic meaning of a word, also referred to as its **denotative meaning,** expresses the general properties of the word, and these properties determine how the word is used within its language system. How do you discover the general properties that determine word usage? Besides examining your own knowledge of the meaning and use of words, you can check dictionary definitions. They tend to focus on the general properties that determine word usage. For example, a dictionary definition of *chair* might be "a piece of furniture consisting of a seat, legs, and back, and often arms, designed to accommodate one person."

However, to understand a word's semantic meaning fully, you often need to go beyond defining its general properties to identifying examples that embody those properties. If you are sitting in a chair or can see one from where you are, examine its design. Does it embody all the properties identified in the definition? (Sometimes unusual examples embody most, but not all, the properties of a word's dictionary definition—for example, a beanbag chair lacks legs and arms.) If you are trying to communicate the semantic meaning of a word to someone, it is generally useful to provide both the word's general properties and examples that illustrate them. Try identifying general properties and examples for these words: *happiness, freedom, creativity, love.*

PERCEPTUAL MEANING (CONNOTATION)

The total meaning of a word also includes its **perceptual meaning,** which expresses the relationship between a linguistic event and an individual's consciousness. For each of us, words elicit unique and personal thoughts and feelings based on previous experiences and past associations. A person might relate saying "chair" to his favorite chair in his living room or the small chair that he built for his daughter. Perceptual meaning also includes an individual's positive and negative responses to the word. When you read or hear the word *book,* what positive or negative feelings does it arouse? What about *textbook? mystery book? comic book? cookbook?* In each case, the word probably elicits distinct feelings, and these contribute to the meaning each word has for you. For this reason, perceptual meaning is also sometimes called **connotative meaning,** the literal or basic meaning of a word plus all it suggests or connotes to you.

Think about your earlier responses to these words and describe what perceptions, experiences, associations, and feelings they called to mind: *college education, happiness, freedom, creativity, love.*

SYNTACTIC MEANING

A third component of a word's total meaning is its **syntactic meaning,** which defines its relation to other words in a sentence. The syntactic meaning defines three relationships among words:

- *Content:* words that express the major message of the sentence
- *Description:* words that elaborate or modify the major message of the sentence
- *Connection:* words that join the major message of the sentence

For example, in the sentence "The two novice hikers crossed the ledge cautiously," *hikers* and *crossed* represent the content, or major message, of the sentence. *Two* and *novice* describe *hikers,* and *cautiously* elaborates on *crossed.*

At first, you may think that this sort of relationship among words involves nothing more than semantic meaning. The following sentence, however, clearly demonstrates the importance of syntactic meaning in language: "Invisible fog rumbles in on lizard legs." Although *fog* does not *rumble,* and it is not *invisible,* and the notion of moving on *lizard legs* seems incompatible with *rumbling,* the sentence does "make sense" at some level of meaning—namely, at the syntactic level. One reason it does is that there are three basic content words—*fog, rumbles,* and *legs*—and two descriptive words—*invisible* and *lizard.*

The third major syntactic relationship is connection. Connective words join ideas, thoughts, or feelings being expressed. For example, you could connect content meaning to either of the two sentences in the following ways:

The two novice hikers crossed the ledge cautiously *after* one of them slipped.

Invisible fog rumbles in on lizard legs, *but* acid rain doesn't.

When you add the content words *one slipped* and *rain doesn't,* you join the ideas, thoughts, and feelings they represent to the ideas, thoughts, or feelings expressed earlier (*hikers crossed* and *fog rumbles*) by using the connective words *after* and *but.*

The second reason that "Invisible fog rumbles in on lizard legs" makes sense at the syntactic level of meaning is that the words of that sentence obey the syntax, or order, of English. Most English speakers would have trouble making sense of "Invisible rumbles legs lizard on fog in"—or of "Barks big endlessly dog brown the," for that matter. Because of syntactic meaning, each word in the sentence derives part of its total meaning from the ways in which it is combined with the other words in that sentence. Look at the following sentences and explain the difference in meaning between the two in each pair.

1. a. The process of obtaining an *education at college* changes a person's future possibilities.
   b. The process of obtaining a *college education* changes a person's future possibilities.

2.   a. She felt *happiness* for her long-lost brother.
     b. She felt the *happiness* of her long-lost brother.

3.   a. The most important thing to me is *freedom from* the things that restrict my choices.
     b. The most important thing to me is *freedom to* make my choices without restrictions.

4.   a. Michelangelo's painting of the Sistine Chapel ceiling represents his *creative* genius.
     b. The Sistine Chapel ceiling represents the *creative* genius of Michelangelo's greatest painting.

5.   a. I *love* the person I have been involved with for the past year.
     b. I am *in love* with the person I have been involved with for the past year.

PRAGMATIC MEANING

The fourth element that contributes to the total meaning of a word is its **pragmatic meaning**. The pragmatic meaning of a word involves the person who is speaking and the situation in which the word is spoken. For example, the statement "That student likes to borrow books from the library" allows a number of pragmatic interpretations:

1. Was the speaker outside looking at *that student* carrying books out of the library?
2. Did the speaker have this information because he or she is a classmate of *that student* but did not actually see the student carrying books?
3. Was the speaker in the library watching *that student* check the books out?

The correct interpretation or meaning of the sentence depends on what was actually taking place in the situation—in other words, its pragmatic meaning, which is also called its **situational meaning.** For each of the following sentences, try describing a pragmatic context that identifies the person speaking and the situation in which it is being spoken.

1. A *college education* is currently necessary for many careers that formerly only required high school preparation.
2. The utilitarian ethical system is based on the principle that the right course of action is that which brings the greatest *happiness* to the greatest number of people.

3. The laws of this country attempt to balance the *freedom* of the individual with the rights of society as a whole.

4. "You are all part of things, you are all part of *creation*, all kings, all poets, all musicians, you have only to open up, to discover what is already there."—Henry Miller

5. "If music be the food of *love*, play on."—Shakespeare

After completing the activity, compare your answers with those of your classmates. In what ways are the answers similar or different? Analyze the ways in which different pragmatic contexts (persons speaking and situations) affect the meanings of the italicized words.

The four types of meanings you just examined—semantic, perceptual, syntactic, and pragmatic—create the total meaning of a word. That is, all the dimensions of a word—all the relationships that connect linguistic events with nonlinguistic events, with your consciousness, with other linguistic events, and with situations in the world—make up the meaning you assign to the word. Chapter 9, Forming Concepts—Writing to Classify and Define, will build on the ideas of this section.

Recognizing Effective Use of Language

To develop your ability to use language effectively in communicating your thoughts, feelings, and experiences, you have to understand how language functions when it is used well. One effective way to improve your writing is to read widely. By reading as much good writing as possible, you can get a "feel" for how language can be used well. You can get more specific ideas by analyzing the work of highly regarded writers who use word meanings accurately. They also often use many action verbs, concrete nouns, and vivid adjectives to communicate effectively. And, of course, another way to become a better writer is by writing and by seeking feedback from readers. In this section, you will be using all these strategies. The following passage by Malcolm X chronicles his discovery of the power of language while he was serving time in prison. Frustrated by not being able to communicate his ideas in writing, he commited himself to mastering the use of words by copying the dictionary. This is a sound lesson for all people who want to improve their writing, speaking, and reading. Communicating your ideas effectively involves using the full range of words to express yourself. Writing is like painting a "word picture" of your thoughts: you need to use the full range of colors, not just a few basic ones. As you read, pay special attention to the way Malcolm X uses language to share his experiences with us. Do you find his personal quest inspiring? Why?

FROM

The Autobiography of Malcolm X

BY MALCOLM X, WITH ALEX HALEY

I became increasingly frustrated at not being able to express what I wanted to convey in letters that I wrote, especially those to Mr. Elijah Muhammad. In the street, I had been the most articulate hustler out there—I had commanded attention when I said something. But now, trying to write simple English, I not only wasn't articulate, I wasn't even functional. How would I sound writing in slang, the way I would *say* it, something such as, "Look, daddy, let me pull your coat about a cat, Elijah Muhammad—"

Many who today hear me somewhere in person, or on television, or those who read something I've said, will think I went to school far beyond the eighth grade. This impression is due entirely to my prison studies.

It had really begun back in the Charlestown Prison, when Bimbi first made me feel envy of his stock of knowledge. Bimbi had always taken charge of any conversation he was in, and I had tried to emulate him. But every book I picked up had few sentences which didn't contain anywhere from one to nearly all of the words that might as well have been in Chinese. When I just skipped those words, of course, I really ended up with little idea of what the book said. So I had come to the Norfolk Prison Colony still going through only book-reading motions. Pretty soon, I would have quit even these motions, unless I had received the motivation that I did.

I saw that the best thing I could do was get hold of a dictionary—to study, to learn some words. I was lucky enough to reason also that I should try to improve my penmanship. It was sad. I couldn't even write in a straight line. It was both ideas together that moved me to request a dictionary along with some tablets and pencils from the Norfolk Prison Colony school.

5   I spent two days just riffling uncertainly through the dictionary's pages. I'd never realized so many words existed! I didn't know *which* words I needed to learn. Finally, just to start some kind of action, I began copying.

In my slow, painstaking, ragged handwriting, I copied into my tablet everything printed on that first page, down to the punctuation marks.

I believe it took me a day. Then, aloud, I read back, to myself, everything I'd written on the tablet. Over and over, aloud, to myself, I read my own handwriting.

I woke up the next morning, thinking about those words—immensely proud to realize that not only had I written so much at one time, but I'd written words that I never knew were in the world. Moreover, with a little effort, I also could remember what many of these words meant. I reviewed the words whose meaning I didn't remember. Funny thing, from the dictionary's first page right now, that "aardvark" springs to my mind. The dictionary had a picture of it, a long-tailed, long-eared, burrowing African mammal, which lives off termites caught by sticking out its tongue as an anteater does for ants.

I was so fascinated that I went on—I copied the dictionary's next page. And the same experience came when I studied that. With every succeeding page, I also learned of people and places and events from history. Actually the dictionary is like a miniature encyclopedia. Finally the dictionary's A section had filled a whole tablet—and I went on into the B's. That was the way I started copying what eventually became the entire dictionary. It went a lot faster after so much practice helped me to pick up handwriting speed. Between what I wrote in my tablet, and writing letters, during the rest of my time in prison I would guess I wrote a million words.

10   I suppose it was inevitable that as my word-base broadened, I could for the first time pick up a book and read and now begin to understand what the book was saying. Anyone who has read a great deal can imagine the new world that opened. Let me tell you something: from then until I left the prison, in every free moment I had, if I was not reading in the library, I was reading on my bunk. You couldn't have gotten me out of books with a wedge. Between Mr. Muhammad's teachings, my correspondence, my visitors—usually Ella and Reginald—and my reading of books, months passed without my even thinking about being imprisoned. In fact, up to then, I never had been so truly free in my life.

The Norfolk Prison Colony's library was in the school building. A variety of classes was taught there by instructors who came from such places as Harvard and Boston universities. The weekly debates between inmate teams were also held in the school building. You would be astonished to know how worked up convict debaters and audiences would get over subjects like "Should Babies Be Fed Milk?"

Available on the prison library's shelves were books on just about every general subject. Much of the big private collection that Parkhurst had willed to the prison was still in crates and boxes in the back of the library—thousands of old books. Some of them looked ancient: covers faded, old-time parchment-looking binding. Parkhurst, I've mentioned, seemed to have been principally interested in history and religion. He had the money and the special interest to have a lot of books that you wouldn't have in general circulation. Any college library would have been lucky to get that collection.

As you can imagine, especially in a prison where there was heavy emphasis on rehabilitation, an inmate was smiled upon if he demonstrated an unusually intense interest in books. There was a sizable number of well-read inmates, especially the popular debaters. Some were said by many to be practically walking encyclopedias. They were almost celebrities. No university would ask any student to devour literature as I did when this new world opened to me, of being able to read and *understand*.

I read more in my room than in the library itself. An inmate who was known to read a lot could check out more than the permitted maximum number of books. I preferred reading in the total isolation of my own room.

15   When I had progressed to really serious reading, every night at about ten (P.M.) I would be outraged with the "lights out." It always seemed to catch me right in the middle of something engrossing.

Fortunately, right outside my door was a corridor light that cast a glow into my room. The glow was enough to read by, once my eyes adjusted to it. So when "lights out" came, I would sit on the floor where I could continue reading in that glow.

At one-hour intervals the night guards paced past every room. Each time I heard the approaching footsteps, I jumped into bed and feigned sleep. And as soon as the guard passed, I got back out of bed onto the floor area of that light-glow, where I would read for another fifty-eight minutes—until the guard approached again. That went on until three or four every morning. Three or four hours of sleep a night was enough for me. Often in the years in the streets I had slept less than that.

Critical Reading Questions

1. Malcolm X states that, although he was an articulate "street hustler," this ability was of little help in expressing his ideas in writing. Explain the differences between expressing your ideas orally and in writing, including the advantages and disadvantages of each form of language expression.

2. Malcolm X envied one of the other inmates, Bimbi, because his stock of knowledge enabled him to take charge of any conversation he was in. Explain why knowledge—and our ability to use it—leads to power in our dealings with others. Describe a situation from your own experience in which having expert knowledge about a subject enabled you, through writing, to influence the thinking of other people.

3. About pursuing his mastery of language and exploring books, Malcolm X states, "Up to then, I never had been so truly free in my life." Explain what you think he means by this statement. Then describe a time in your life when you felt "truly free."

The following selection is from *Blue Highways,* a book written by a man of Native American heritage. After losing his university teaching job and separating from his wife, he decided to explore America. He outfitted his van (named Ghost Dancing) and drove around the country using back roads (represented on maps by blue lines) rather than superhighways. During his travels, he saw fascinating sights, met intriguing people, and developed some significant insights about himself. Read the passage carefully; then respond to the Critical Reading Questions and complete the Thinking-Writing Activity that follows.

FROM

Blue Highways
BY WILLIAM LEAST HEAT-MOON

Back at Ghost Dancing, I saw a camper had pulled up. On the rear end, by the strapped-on aluminum chairs, was something like "The Wandering Watkins." Time to go. I kneeled to check a tire. A smelly furry white thing darted from behind the wheel, and I flinched. Because of it, the journey would change.

"Harmless as a stuffed toy." The voice came from the other end of the leash the dog was on. "He's nearly blind and can't hear much better. Down just to the nose now." The man, with polished cowboy boots and a part measured out in the white hair, had a face so gullied even the Soil Conservation Commission couldn't have reclaimed it. But his eyes seemed lighted from within.

"Are you Mr. Watkins?" I asked.

"What's left of him. The pup's what's left of Bill. He's a Pekingese. Chinese dog. In dog years, he's even older than I am, and I respect him for that. We're two old men. What's your name?"

5 "Same as the dog's."

"I wanted to give him a Chinese name, but old what's-her-face over there in the camper wouldn't have it. Claimed she couldn't pronounce Chinese names. I says, 'You can't say Lee?' She says, 'You going to name a dog Lee?' 'No,' I says, 'but what do you think about White Fong?' Now, she's not a reader unless it's a beauty parlor magazine with a Kennedy or Hepburn woman on the cover, so she never understood the name. You've read your Jack London, I hope. She says, 'When I was a girl we had a horse called William, but that name's too big for that itty-bitty dog. Just call him Bill.' That was that. She's a woman of German descent and a decided person. But when old Bill and I are out on our own, I call him White Fong."

Watkins had worked in a sawmill for thirty years, then retired to Redding; now he spent time in his camper, sometimes in the company of Mrs. Watkins.

"I'd stay on the road, but what's-her-face won't have it."

As we talked, Mrs. What's-her-face periodically thrust her head from the camper to call instructions to Watkins or White Fong. A finger-wagging woman, full of injunctions for man and beast. Whenever she called, I watched her, Watkins watched me, and the dog watched him. Each time he would say, "Well, boys, there you have it. Straight from the back of the horse."

10 "You mind if I swear?" I said I didn't. "The old biddy's in there with her Morning Special—sugar doughnut, boysenberry jam, and a shot of Canadian Club in her coffee. In this beauty she sits inside with her letters."

"What kind of work you in?" he asked.

That question again. "I'm out of work," I said to simplify.

"A man's never out of work if he's worth a damn. It's just sometimes he doesn't get paid. I've gone unpaid my share and I've pulled my share of pay. But that's got nothing to do with working. A man's work is doing what he's supposed to do, and that's why he needs a catastrophe now and again to show him a bad turn isn't the end, because a bad stroke never stops a good man's work. Let me show you my philosophy of life." From his pressed Levi's he took a billfold and handed me a limp business card. "Easy. It's very old."

The card advertised a cafe in Merced when telephone numbers were four digits. In quotation marks was a motto: "Good Home Cooked Meals."

15 "'Good Home Cooked Meals' is your philosophy?"

"Turn it over, peckerwood."

Imprinted on the back in tiny, faded letters was this:

I've been bawled out, balled up, held up, held down, hung up, bulldozed, blackjacked, walked on, cheated, squeezed and mooched; stuck for war tax, excess profits tax, sales tax, dog tax, and syntax, Liberty Bonds, baby bonds, and the bonds of matrimony, Red Cross, Blue Cross, and the double cross; I've worked like hell, worked others like hell, have got drunk and got others drunk, lost all I had, and now because I won't spend or lend what little I earn, beg, borrow or steal, I've been cussed, discussed, boycotted, talked to, talked about, lied to, lied about, worked over, pushed under, robbed, and damned near ruined. The only reason I'm sticking around now is to see WHAT THE HELL IS NEXT.

"I like it," I said.

"Any man's true work is to get his boots on each morning. Curiosity gets it done about as well as anything else."

Critical Reading Questions

1. After reading the passage from *Blue Highways,* analyze Least Heat Moon's use of language. Make three columns on a page. Use these headings: Action Verbs, Concrete Nouns, and Vivid Adjectives. List at least six examples of each from the reading.

2. Describe how the author uses dialogue and analogies to introduce us to Mr. Watkins.

3. According to Mr. Watkins, "A man's never out of work if he's worth a damn. It's just sometimes he doesn't get paid. . . . Any man's true work is to get his boots on each morning. Curiosity gets it done about as well as anything else." What do you think he's trying to say about the challenges posed by life to both men and women?

Thinking ↔ Writing Activity

Practicing the Effective Use of Language

Create your own description of an experience you have had while traveling. Use language as effectively as possible to communicate the thoughts, feelings, and impressions you wish to share. Be conscious of your use of action verbs, concrete nouns, and vivid adjectives. Ask other students to read your description and identify examples of these words. Then ask for feedback on ways to improve your description.

Using Language to Clarify Thinking

Language reflects thinking, and thinking is shaped by language. Previous sections of this chapter examine the creature we call *language,* which is composed of small cells, or units, pieces of sound that combine to form larger units called *words.* When words are combined into groups according to the rules of a language to form sentences, the creature grows by leaps and bounds. Various types of sentence structure not only provide multiple ways of expressing the same ideas, thoughts, and feelings but also help to structure those thoughts, weaving into them nuances of focus. In turn, patterns of thinking breathe life into language, giving both processes power.

The relationship between thinking and language is *interactive;* both processes are continually influencing each other in many ways. This is particularly true in the case of language, as George Orwell points out in the following passage from his classic essay "Politics and the English Language":

> A man may take a drink because he feels himself to be a failure, and then fail all the more completely because he drinks. It is rather the same thing that is happening to the English language. It becomes ugly and inaccurate because our thoughts are foolish, but the slovenliness of our language makes it easier for us to have foolish thoughts. The point is that the process is reversible. Modern English, especially written English, is full of bad habits which spread by imitation and which can be avoided if one is willing to take the necessary trouble. If one gets rid of these habits, one can think more clearly.

Just as a drinker can fall into a cycle that keeps getting worse, so too can language and thinking. When language use is sloppy—vague, general, indistinct, imprecise, foolish, inaccurate, and so on—it leads to the same sort of thinking. And the reverse is also true. Clear and precise language leads to clear and precise thinking, as shown in Figure 5.1.

The opposite of clear, effective language is language that fails to help the reader picture or understand what the writer means because it is vague or ambiguous. Most of us are guilty of using such ineffective language in speech ("It was a great party!"), but for college and work writing, we need to be as precise as possible. And our writing can

Figure 5.1 Clear Language and Clear Thinking

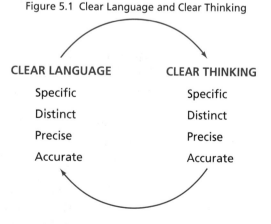

CLEAR LANGUAGE	CLEAR THINKING
Specific	Specific
Distinct	Distinct
Precise	Precise
Accurate	Accurate

gain clarity and power if we use our creative thinking skills to develop fresh, striking figures of speech to illuminate our ideas.

IMPROVING VAGUE LANGUAGE

Although our ability to name and identify gives us the power to describe the world in a precise way, we often tend to describe it in words that are imprecise and general. Such nonspecific words are termed *vague* words. Consider the following sentences:

- I had a *nice* time yesterday.
- That is an *interesting* book.
- She is an *old* person.

In each of these cases, the italicized word does not provide a precise description of the thought, feeling, or experience that the writer or speaker is trying to communicate. Vagueness occurs whenever a word is used to represent an area of experience without clearly defining it. A **vague word** is one that lacks a clear and distinct meaning.

Most words of general measurement—*short, tall, big, small, heavy, light,* and so on—are vague. The exact meanings of these words depend on the specific situation in which they are used and on the particular perspective of the person using them. For example, give specific definitions for the following italicized words by filling in the blanks. Then compare your responses with those of your classmates. Can you account for the differences in meaning?

1. A *middle-aged* person is one who is _____ years old.
2. A *tall* person is one who is over _____ feet _____ inches tall.
3. It's *cold* when the temperature is _____ degrees.
4. A person is *wealthy* when he or she is worth _____ dollars.

Although the vagueness of general measurement terms can lead to confusion, other forms of vagueness are more widespread and often more problematic. Terms such as *good* and *enjoyable,* for example, are imprecise and unclear. Vagueness of this sort permeates every level of human discourse, undermines clear thinking, and is extremely difficult to combat. To use language clearly and precisely, you must develop an understanding of the way language functions and commit yourself to breaking the entrenched habit of using vague expression.

For example, read the following opinion of a movie and circle all the vague, general words that do not express a clear meaning.

Pulp Fiction is a really funny movie about some really unusual characters in California. The movie consists of several different stories that connect at different points. Some of the stories are nerve-wracking and others are hilarious, but all of them are very well done. The plots are very interesting, and the main characters are excellent. I liked this movie a lot.

Because of the vague language in this passage, it expresses only general approval—it does not explain in exact or precise terms what the experience of seeing the movie was like. Thus, the writer of the passage has not successfully communicated the experience.

Most people use vague language extensively in day-to-day conversations. In many cases, it's natural that your immediate reaction to an experience would be fairly general ("That's nice," "She's interesting"). If you are truly concerned about sharp thinking and meaningful communication, however, you should follow up these initial reactions by more precisely clarifying what you really mean.

I think that she is a nice person *because* . . .

I think that he is a good teacher *because* . . .

I think that this is an interesting class *because* . . .

Vagueness is always a matter of degree. In fact, you can think of your descriptive/informative use of language as falling somewhere on a scale between extreme generality and extreme specificity. The following statements move from the general to the specific.

General

She is really smart.

She does well in school.

She gets straight As.

She earned an A+ in physics.

Specific

Although different situations require various degrees of specificity, you should work to become increasingly more precise in your use of language. For example, examine the following response to the assignment "Describe what you think about the school you are attending." Circle the vague words.

I really like it a lot. It's a very good school. The people are nice, and the teachers are interesting. There are a lot of different things to do, and students have a good time doing them. Some of the courses are pretty hard, but if you study enough, you should do all right.

Notice how general the passage is. The writer says, for example, that "the people are nice" but gives no concrete or specific descriptions to show why he thinks they are nice. The writer could have been more specific if he had used statements such as these:

Everyone says "hello."

The students introduced themselves to me in class.

I always feel welcome in the student lounge.

The teachers take a special interest in each student.

Although these statements are more precise than saying, "The people are nice," they could also be more specific. To illustrate this, create more specific descriptions for each of the previous statements.

Using language imprecisely can lead to miscommunication, sometimes with disastrous results. For example, on January 29, 1990, an Avianca Airlines flight from Colombia, South America, to New York City crashed, killing seventy-three people. After circling Kennedy Airport for forty-five minutes, the plane ran out of fuel before it could land, apparently because of imprecise communication between the pilot and the air traffic controllers. Read the following excerpts from the *New York Times* January 30, 1990, account of the incident; then answer the questions that follow.

FROM

An Account of Avianca Flight 52

NEW YORK TIMES

The Federal Aviation Administration today defended the controllers who guided a Colombian jetliner toward Kennedy International Airport, releasing the first verbatim transcripts of communication in the hour before the jet crashed. The officials suggested that the plane's pilot should have used more precise language, such as the word "emergency," in telling controllers how seriously they were short of fuel. They made the statements a day after Federal investigators said that regional controllers never told local controllers the plane was short of fuel and had asked for priority clearance to land.

The transcripts show that the crew of Avianca Flight 52 told regional controllers about 45 minutes before the plane crashed that "we would run out of fuel" if the plane was redirected to Boston instead of being given priority to land at Kennedy. The crew said it would be willing to continue in its holding pattern 40 miles south of Kennedy for "about five minutes—that's all we can do" before the plane would have to move onward to Kennedy. But the regional controllers who gave that message to the local controllers who were to guide the plane on its final descent to Kennedy did not tell them that there was a problem with fuel supplies on the jet or that the plane had requested priority handling, the transcripts recorded by the FAA confirmed.

Taken by itself, the information that the plane could circle for just five more minutes would not make the immediate danger of the plane clear to the local controllers. Without being told that the plane did not have enough fuel to reach Boston or that its crew had asked for priority clearance, the local controllers might have assumed that it had reached a point where it could still land with adequate reserves of fuel still on board.

Despite the apparent lapse in communications among controllers, an FAA spokesman said they acted properly because the plane's crew had not explicitly declared a fuel emergency. An emergency would require immediate clearance to land.

R. Steve Bell, president of the National Air Traffic Controllers Association, called the safety board's statement during its inquiry "highly misleading and premature." Mr. Bell, in a statement issued today, said the pilots of the plane should have made known to controllers the extent of their problem in order to obtain immediate clearance to land the plane. "The Avianca pilot never declared a 'fuel emergency' or 'minimum fuel,' both of which would have triggered an emergency response by controllers," he said. "Stating that you are low on fuel does not imply an immediate problem. In addition, this information would not necessarily be transmitted when one controller hands off to another."

Chronology of final minutes of Flight 52:

8:00 P.M.: Forty miles south of Kennedy, Avianca Flight 52 is delayed for 46 minutes, after earlier delays of 16 minutes over Norfolk, Va., and 27 minutes farther north.

8:46 P.M.: The plane's crew tells regional air controllers in Islip, L.I., that they have a "low-fuel problem." Regional controllers immediately release the plane from its holding pattern, passing it to local controllers in Garden City, L.I.

9:24 P.M.: First landing attempt at Kennedy is aborted and jet circles. Pilot twice tells Kennedy tower that he is "low on fuel."

9:32 P.M.: Pilot tells tower while circling: "Two engines lost"; he also says that he is "very short on fuel."

9:35 P.M.: The plane crashes.

Critical Reading Questions

1. If the pilot of the airplane were alive (all crew died in the crash), how do you think he would analyze the cause of the crash?

2. How did the air traffic controllers and the FAA analyze the cause of the crash?

3. What do you consider the cause of the crash? What are your reasons for your conclusion?

4. Describe a situation in which you were involved or that you heard about which resulted in a serious misunderstanding due to imprecise use of language.

Using Figurative Language

Thus far in this section, we have been concerned with saying and writing exactly what we mean as precisely as possible. However, there is another way to use language to express thinking: to say something we do not literally mean. When we do this effectively, our readers or listeners understand that we are not speaking literally but rather that we are speaking *figuratively*, using a *figure of speech*. There are many different figures of speech; some literary experts have identified as many as 250. Here, though, we will focus on two which may already be familiar: *simile* and *metaphor*.

Both simile and metaphor are based on a special kind of comparative thinking called an **analogy** which is a limited comparison of two essentially unlike things for the purpose of illuminating or enriching our understanding. Analogies differ from the more common comparisons that examine the similarities and differences of two items in the same general category, such as two items on a menu or two methods of birth control. Similes and metaphors focus on unexpected likenesses between items from different categories. Thus, when we compare a baby's skin to velvet, we may be calling attention to the skin's color or softness, but we are not suggesting that it has pile or can be dyed different shades.

Consider the following example:

Life's but a walking shadow, a poor player
That struts and frets his hour upon the stage,
And then is heard no more. . . .

—Shakespeare, *Macbeth*

In this famous metaphor, Shakespeare is comparing two things that at first seem to have nothing in common: life and an actor. Yet a closer look reveals that even though they are dissimilar in many ways, they share some undeniable similarities.

People often create and use similes and metaphors to make a point. Using them appropriately can help you communicate better. That is particularly important when you are having trouble finding the right words to represent your experiences. Powerful or complex emotions can make you speechless or make you say things like "Words cannot describe what I feel." Imagine that you're trying to describe your feelings of love for someone. You might compare your emotions to "the first rose of spring," noting the following similarities:

Like the first rose, this is the first great love of my life.

Like the fragile yet supple petals of the rose, my feelings are tender and sensitive.

Remember, however, that you are dealing with a limited comparison. You would not want anyone to think, "Like the rose, this love will die after a week"! Readers who are familiar with similes and metaphors will not make that mistake.

Another favorite subject for similes and metaphors is the meaning or purpose of life, which the simple use of the word *life* does not communicate. You have just read Shakespeare's comparison of life to an actor. Shakespeare also said: "[Life] is a tale/Told by an idiot, full of sound and fury,/Signifying nothing." Here are some other popular metaphors involving life. In what ways are they similar?

> Life is just a bowl of cherries.
>
> Life is a football game.
>
> Life is a box of chocolates.

Create a metaphor for life that represents your feelings and explain the points of similarity.

DISTINGUISHING SIMILES AND METAPHORS

From the examples discussed so far, you can see that these figures of speech have two parts: an original subject and a compared subject. In comparing your love to the first rose of spring, the *original subject* is your feelings of love for someone; the *compared subject* is what you are likening those feelings to in order to describe them—the first rose of spring.

The connection between the original subject and the compared subject can be either obvious (explicit) or implied (implicit). For example, you can echo the lament of the great pool hustler Minnesota Fats and say, "A pool player in a tuxedo is like a hotdog with whipped cream on it." This is a simile because it explicitly notes the connection between the original subject (man in tuxedo) and the compared subject (hotdog with whipped cream) by using the comparative word *like*. You can also use other words indicating obvious comparison such as *is similar to, reminds me of, makes me think of,* or *as*. (To the goalie, Mia Hamm's shot appeared as a photon of light.) Thus, a **simile** is an *explicit* comparison between basically dissimilar things.

You could also make an *implicit* comparison by saying, "A pool player in a tuxedo *is* a hotdog with whipped cream on it." In this case, you are creating a metaphor because you have not included any words indicating that you are making a comparison. Instead, you state that the original subject *is* the compared subject. (Most people will understand that you are making a limited comparison between two different things, not describing a biological transformation.) Thus, a **metaphor** is an *implied* comparison between basically dissimilar things.

Thinking ↔ Writing Activity

Creating Similes and Metaphors

1. Use your creative thinking skills to create a simile for a subject of your own choosing, noting at least two points of comparison.

2. Now use your creative thinking skills to create a metaphor (implied analogy) for a subject of your own choosing, noting at least two points of comparison.

A final point about figurative language is that it does need to be fresh. "He runs like a deer" and "I slept like a baby" were wonderful similes the first time they were used, but they have become old and tired: clichés. Use your creative thinking skills to write original, striking figures of speech.

Very skillful speakers and writers are able to weave similes and metaphors together into a striking tapestry. Read the following selection by Martin Luther King Jr. Then respond to the Critical Reading questions that follow.

I Have a Dream

BY MARTIN LUTHER KING, JR.

Five score years ago, a great American, in whose symbolic shadow we stand, signed the Emancipation Proclamation. This momentous decree came as a great beacon light of hope to millions of Negro slaves who had been seared in the flames of withering injustice. It came as a joyous daybreak to end the long night of captivity.

But one hundred years later, we must face the tragic fact that the Negro is still not free. One hundred years later, the life of the Negro is still sadly crippled by the manacles of segregation and the chains of discrimination. One hundred years later, the Negro lives on a lonely island of poverty in the midst of a vast ocean of material prosperity. One hundred years later, the Negro is still languishing in the corners of American society and finds himself an exile in his own land. So we have come here today to dramatize an appalling condition.

In a sense we have come to our nation's capital to cash a check. When the architects in our republic wrote the magnificent words of the Constitution and the Declaration of Independence, they were signing a promissory note to which every American was to fall heir. This note was a promise that all men would be guaranteed the unalienable rights of life, liberty, and the pursuit of happiness.

It is obvious today that America has defaulted on this promissory note insofar as her citizens of color are concerned. Instead of honoring this sacred obligation, America has given the Negro people a bad check; a check which has come back marked "insufficient funds." But we refuse to believe that the bank of justice is bankrupt. We refuse to believe that there are insufficient funds in the great vaults of opportunity of this nation. So we have come to cash this check—a check that will give us upon demand the riches of freedom and the security of justice. We have also come to this hallowed spot to remind America of the fierce urgency of *now*. This is no time to engage in the luxury of cooling off or to take the tranquilizing drugs of gradualism. *Now* is the time to make real the promises of Democracy. *Now* is the time to rise from the dark and desolate valley of segregation to the sunlit path of racial justice. *Now* is the time to open the doors of opportunity to all of God's children. *Now* is the time to lift our nation from the quicksands of racial injustice to the solid rock of brotherhood.

5   It would be fatal for the nation to overlook the urgency of the moment and to underestimate the determination of the Negro. This sweltering summer of the Negro's legitimate discontent will not pass until there is an invigorating autumn of freedom and equality. 1963 is not an end, but a beginning. Those who hope that the Negro needed to blow off steam and will now be content will have a rude awakening if the nation returns to business as usual. There will be neither rest nor tranquillity in America until the Negro is granted his citizenship rights. The whirlwinds of revolt will continue to shake the foundations of our nation until the bright day of justice emerges.

But there is something that I must say to my people who stand on the warm threshold which leads into the palace of justice. In the process of gaining our rightful place we must not be guilty of wrongful deeds. Let us not seek to satisfy our thirst for freedom by drinking from the cup of bitterness and hatred. We must forever conduct our struggle on the high plane of dignity and discipline. We must not allow our creative protest to degenerate into physical violence. Again and again we must rise to the majestic heights of meeting physical force with soul force. The marvelous new militancy which has engulfed the Negro community must not lead us to a distrust of all white people, for many of our white brothers, as evidenced by their presence here today, have come to realize that their destiny is tied up with our destiny and their freedom is inextricably bound to our freedom. We cannot walk alone.

And as we walk, we must make the pledge that we shall march ahead. We cannot turn back. There are those who are asking the devotees of civil rights, "When will you be satisfied?" We can never be satisfied as long as the Negro is the victim of the unspeakable horrors of police brutality. We can never be satisfied as long as our bodies, heavy with the fatigue of travel, cannot gain lodging in the motels of the highways and the hotels of the cities. We cannot be satisfied as long as the Negro's basic mobility is from a smaller ghetto to a larger one. We can never be satisfied as long as a Negro in Mississippi cannot vote and a Negro in New York believes he has nothing for which to vote. No, no, we are not satisfied, and we will not be satisfied until justice rolls down like waters and righteousness like a mighty stream.

I am not unmindful that some of you have come here out of great trials and tribulations. Some of you have come fresh from narrow jail cells. Some of you have come from areas where your quest for freedom left you battered by the storms of persecution and staggered by the winds of police brutality. You have been the veterans of creative suffering. Continue to work with the faith that unearned suffering is redemptive.

Go back to Mississippi, go back to Alabama, go back to South Carolina, go back to Georgia, go back to Louisiana, go back to the slums and ghettos of our northern cities, knowing that somehow this situation can and will be changed. Let us not wallow in the valley of despair.

10   I say to you today, my friends, that in spite of the difficulties and frustrations of the moment I still have a dream. It is a dream deeply rooted in the American dream.

I have a dream that one day this nation will rise up and live out the true meaning of its creed: "We hold these truths to be self-evident; that all men are created equal."

I have a dream that one day on the red hills of Georgia the sons of former slaves and the sons of former slaveowners will be able to sit down together at the table of brotherhood.

I have a dream that one day even the state of Mississippi, a desert state sweltering with the heat of injustice and oppression, will be transformed into an oasis of freedom and justice.

I have a dream that my four little children will one day live in a nation where they will not be judged by the color of their skin but by the content of their character.

15   I have a dream today.

I have a dream that one day the state of Alabama, whose governor's lips are presently dripping with the words of interposition and nullification, will be transformed into a situation where little black boys and black girls will be able to join hands with little white boys and white girls and walk together as sisters and brothers.

I have a dream today.

I have a dream that one day every valley shall be exalted, every hill and mountain shall be made low, the rough places will be made plain, and the crooked places will be made straight, and the glory of the Lord shall be revealed, and all flesh shall see it together.

This is our hope. This is the faith with which I return to the South. With this faith we will be able to hew out of the mountain of despair a stone of hope. With this faith we will be able to transform the jangling discords of our nation into a beautiful symphony of brotherhood. With this faith we will be able to work together, to pray together, to struggle together, to go to jail together, to stand up for freedom together, knowing that we will be free one day.

20   This will be the day when all of God's children will be able to sing with new meaning:

My country, 'tis of thee, Sweet land of liberty, Of thee I sing: Land where my fathers died, Land of the pilgrims' pride, From every mountain-side Let freedom ring.

And if America is to be a great nation, this must become true. So let freedom ring from the prodigious hilltops of New Hampshire. Let freedom ring from the mighty mountains of New York. Let freedom ring from the heightening Alleghenies of Pennsylvania!

Let freedom ring from the snowcapped Rockies of Colorado!

Let freedom ring from the curvaceous peaks of California!

25 But not only that; let freedom ring from Stone Mountain of Georgia!

Let freedom ring from Lookout Mountain of Tennessee!

Let freedom ring from every hill and molehill of Mississippi. From every mountainside, let freedom ring.

When we let freedom ring, when we let it ring from every village and every hamlet, from every state and every city, we will be able to speed up that day when all of God's children, black men and white men, Jews and Gentiles, Protestants and Catholics, will be able to join hands and sing in the words of the old Negro spiritual, "Free at last! free at last! thank God almighty, we are free at last!"

Critical Reading Questions

1. List at least four different similes or metaphors that King uses.

2. Pick one of these similes or metaphors and trace it throughout the speech (list each time it occurs).

3. Why do you think King uses these figures of speech? What effect do they have on you? Do you think they had the same effect on his listeners?

Choosing Language for Different Audiences

LANGUAGE STYLES

Language is always used in a context. We always speak or write with an audience, a person, or a group of people in mind. The audience may only be oneself; the group may be made up of friends, coworkers, or strangers. Moreover, we always use language in a particular situation. We converse with friends, meet with the boss, or carry out a business transaction at the bank or supermarket. In each situation, we use the appropriate language style. For example, describe how you usually greet the following people when you see them?

A professor

A parent

An employer

A good friend

A waiter/waitress

When greeting a friend, you probably say something like "Hey, Richard, how's it going?" or "Hi, Sue, good to see ya." When greeting your employer, however, or even a coworker, something more like "Good morning, Mrs. Jones" or "Hello, Dan; how are you this morning?" is in order. The two different contexts, personal friendship and the workplace, call for different language responses. In a working environment, no matter how frequently you interact with coworkers or employers, your language style is likely to be more formal than it is with personal friends. Conversely, the more familiar you are with someone, the better you know the person, the more abbreviated your style of language will be in that context, for you share a variety of ideas, opinions, and experiences with her or him. The **language style** identifies this shared thinking and consequently restricts the group of people who can communicate within this context.

All of us belong to social groups in which we use styles that separate "insiders" from "outsiders." When you use an abbreviated style of language with a friend, you are identifying that person as a friend and sending a social message that says, "I know you very well; I can assume that we share many common perspectives." When you speak to a coworker in a more elaborate language style, you send a different social message: "I know you within a particular context (this workplace); therefore, I can assume only certain common perspectives between us."

In this way we use language to identify the social context and to define the relationship of the people communicating. Language styles vary from **informal,** in which we abbreviate not only sentence structure but also the sounds that form words—as in *ya*—to increasingly **formal,** in which we use more complex sentence structure as well as complete words in terms of sound patterns.

Standard American English   The language style used in most academic and workplace writing is called **Standard American English (SAE).** SAE follows the rules and conventions given in handbooks and taught in school. The ability to use SAE marks a person as part of an educated group who understands how and when to use it.

Unless otherwise specified, you should use SAE for college speaking and writing assignments, and your vocabulary should be appropriate for the intended audience. For example, social science students and instructors would immediately understand what *bell curve* means, but other audiences might need an explanation of this term. Again, if your literature teacher is the sole intended audience for your paper, you don't need to define a *literary symbol*. But if the assignment asks you to write for a fourth-grade audience to encourage them to enjoy poetry, then you would want to define literary terms.

Depending on your intended audience and purpose, you may or may not wish to employ slang, jargon, or dialect, but you should understand these forms of language.

Slang **Slang** is the unconventional, very informal language of particular subgroups in our culture.

Thinking ↔ Writing Activity

Translating Slang

Read the following dialogue; then rewrite it in your own style and also in SAE. How would you describe the style of the original dialogue? How would you describe the style of your version of it?

Girl 1: "Hey, did you see that new guy? He's a dime. I mean, really diesel."

Girl 2: "All the guys in my class are busted. They are tore up from the floor up. Punks and lowlifes. Let's exit. There's a jam tonight that is going to be the bomb, really fierce. I've got to hit the books so that I'll still have time to chill."

The linguist Shoshana Hoose writes:

As any teen will tell you, keeping up with the latest slang takes a lot of work. New phrases sweep into town faster than greased lightning, and they are gone just as quickly. Last year's "hoser" is this year's "dweeb" (both meaning somewhat of a "nerd"). Some slang consists of everyday words that have taken a new, hip meaning. "Mega" for instance, was used mainly by astronomers and mathematicians until teens adopted it as a way of describing anything great, cool, and unbelievable. Others are words such as "gag" that seem to have naturally evolved from one meaning (to throw up) to another (a person or thing that is gross to the point of making one want to throw up). And then there are words that come from movies, popular music, and the media. "Rambo," the macho movie character who singlehandedly defeats whole armies, has come to mean a muscular, tough, adventurous boy who wears combat boots and fatigues.

As linguists have long known, cultures create the most words for things that preoccupy them the most. For example, Eskimos have been reported to have more than seventy-six words for *ice* and *snow*, and Hawaiians can choose from scores of variations of the word *water*. Most teenage slang falls into one or two categories: words meaning "cool" and words meaning "out of it." Persons considered really out of it have been described as *nerds, goobers, geeks, fades,* or *pinheads,* to name just a few.

Thinking ↔ Writing Activity

Analyzing Slang

For each term, list a slang word that you use, or have heard, to mean the same thing.

Word(s)	Your Word:	Meaning:
dime, buff, diesel, hot	_____	good-looking (guy)
phat, shorty, fly, all that	_____	good-looking (girl)
busted	_____	gross, disgusting
punk, loser	_____	an unsuccessful person
hip, fierce, cool	_____	awesome
the bomb	_____	really cool
trifling	_____	showoff
played	_____	out-of-date
exit, be out, step off, bounce, jet	_____	leave

If your meanings did not match those in the meanings list, or if you did not recognize some of the words in the list on the left, explain why.

Slang, while creative and entertaining, is a restrictive style of language because its use is limited to a particular audience. As Hoose points out, age is usually the determining factor in using slang. But there are special forms of slang that are not determined by age; rather, they are determined by profession or interest group.

Jargon **Jargon** is made up of words, expressions, and technical terms that are intelligible to professional circles or interest groups but not to the general public. Consider the following exchanges:

1. A: Breaker 1–9. Com'on, Little Frog.

   B: Roger and back to you, Charley.

A: You got to back down; you got a Smokey ahead.

B: I can't afford to feed the bears this week. Better stay at 5–5 now.

A: That's a big 10–4.

B: I'm gonna cut the coax now.

2. OK, Al, number six takes two eggs; wreck 'em, with a whiskey down and an Adam and Eve on a raft. Don't forget the Jack Tommy, express to California.

3. Please take further notice, that pursuant to and in accordance with Article II, Paragraphs Second and Fifteenth of the aforesaid Proprietary Lease Agreement, you are obligated to reimburse Lessor for any expense Lessor incurs including legal fees in instituting any action or proceeding due to a default of your obligations as contained in the Proprietary Lease Agreement.

Can you identify the groups who would understand the meaning of each of the previous examples?

Dialects Within the boundaries of geographical regions and among ethnic groups, the form of a language used may differ so from the usual (or standard) in terms of sound patterns, vocabulary, and sentence structure that it cannot be understood by people outside the specific regional or ethnic group. Here, we are no longer referring to variations in language style; we are referring to distinct dialects. Consider these sentences from two different dialects of English:

Dialect A: Dats allabunch of byoks at de license bureau. He fell out de rig and broke his leg boon.

Dialect B: I went out to the garden to pick the last of them Kentucky Wonder pole beans of mine, and do you know, there on the grass was just a little mite of frost.

Though you can recognize these sentences as English, you may not recognize all the words, sentence structures, and sound patterns that the speakers use. **Dialects** differ from language styles not only in being restricted to geographical or ethnic groups but also in varying from the standard language to a greater degree than language styles do. Dialects vary not only in words but also in sound patterns and in syntax. In the previous two examples of dialect, how do the sound patterns, vocabulary, and sentence structure differ from that of Standard English? Can you interpret the meaning conveyed by each example? What words or syntactic forms contributed to any difficulty you may have had in interpreting the meaning?

If you speak a dialect, write one or two sentences in that dialect and share them with your classmates. How does your dialect vary from Standard English in terms of words and syntactic forms?

Of course, many people are not limited to using only one form of English. They are **bilingual** in that they can switch from using a dialect fluently to using Standard English fluently. Such speakers often report, in fact, that their ability to use several forms of the language gives them great pleasure and an enhanced perspective on experience.

So far, we have noted that most of us have different language styles that we employ for different audiences and that some of us even have a variety of dialects which we use in our speech and writing. It is important to consider that the language you use and the way you use it serve as important clues to your social identity. For example, dialect identifies your geographical area or group, slang marks your age group and subculture, and jargon often identifies your occupation or other areas of interest.

The connection between language and thought, in both speech and writing, turns language into a powerful social force that separates us as well as binds us together. The social dimensions of language are important influences in shaping our responses to others. Sometimes the social dimensions of language can trigger stereotypes we hold about a person's interests, social class, intelligence, personal attributes, and so on. When we fall into stereotyping, we are not thinking critically. The ability to think critically gives us the insight and intellectual ability to distinguish people's language use from their individual qualities, to correct inaccurate beliefs about people, and to avoid stereotypical responses.

Thinking ↔ Writing Activity

Language Styles and Dialects

Write responses to the following questions.

1. Describe examples from your personal experience of each of the following: dialect, jargon, and slang.

2. Describe your immediate responses to the examples you just provided. For example, what is your immediate response to someone speaking in each of the dialects on page 187 to someone with a British accent? to someone speaking "computerese"? to someone speaking in slang that you don't understand?

3. Analyze the responses you just described. How were they formed? Does each represent an accurate understanding of a person or a stereotyped belief?

4. Identify strategies for overcoming inaccurate and inappropriate responses to others based on their language usage.

GENDER DIFFERENCES IN LANGUAGE

Recently gender differences in language use have reached the forefront of social research, even though variation in language use between the sexes has been noted for centuries. Proverbs such as "A woman's tongue wags like a lamb's tail" historically attest to supposed differences—usually alleged inferiorities—in women's speech and, by implication, in their thinking, as compared with men's. Vocabulary, swearing and taboo language, pronunciation, and verbosity have all been indicated as contexts that illustrate gender differences in language. Only within the last two decades, however, have scholars of the social use of language paid serious attention to the variation between men's and women's language and to social factors that contribute to these differences. The following excerpt from the work of Deborah Tannen reflects current interest in sociolinguistic variations between women and men. After reading the selection, answer the Critical Reading questions that follow.

FROM *Sex, Lies and Conversation*

Why Is It So Hard for Men and Women to Talk to Each Other?
BY DEBORAH TANNEN

I was addressing a small gathering in a suburban Virginia living room—a women's group that had invited men to join them. Throughout the evening, one man had been particularly talkative, frequently offering ideas and anecdotes, while his wife sat silently beside him on the couch. Toward the end of the evening, I commented that women frequently complain that their husbands don't talk to them. This man quickly concurred. He gestured toward his wife and said, "She's the talker in our family." The room burst into laughter; the man looked puzzled and hurt. "It's true," he explained. "When I come home from work I have nothing to say. If she didn't keep the conversation going, we'd spend the whole evening in silence."

This episode crystallizes the irony that although American men tend to talk more than women in public situations, they often talk less at home. And this pattern is wreaking havoc with marriage.

The pattern was observed by political scientist Andrew Hacker in the late '70s. Sociologist Catherine Kohler Riessman reports in her new book *Divorce Talk* that most of the women she interviewed—but only a few of the men—gave lack of communication as the reason for their divorces. Given the current divorce rate of nearly 50 percent, that amounts to millions of cases in the United States every year—a virtual epidemic of failed conversation.

In my own research, complaints from women about their husbands most often focused not on tangible inequities such as having given up the chance for a career to accompany a husband to his, or doing far more than their share of daily life-support work like cleaning, cooking, social arrangements and errands. Instead, they focused on communication: "He doesn't listen to me," "He doesn't talk to me." I found, as Hacker observed years before, that most wives want their husbands to be, first and foremost, conversational partners, but few husbands share this expectation of their wives.

5   In short, the image that best represents the current crisis is the stereotypical cartoon scene of a man sitting at the breakfast table with a newspaper held up in front of his face, while a woman glares at the back of it, wanting to talk.

Linguistic Battle of Sexes

How can women and men have such different impressions of communication in marriage? Why the widespread imbalance in their interests and expectations?

    In the April issue of *American Psychologist,* Stanford University's Eleanor Maccoby reports the results of her own and others' research showing that children's development is most influenced by the social structure of peer interactions. Boys and girls tend to play with children of their own gender, and their sex-separate groups have different organizational structures and interactive norms.

    I believe these systematic differences in childhood socialization make talk between women and men like cross-cultural communication, heir to all the attraction and pitfalls of that enticing but difficult enterprise. My research on men's and women's conversations uncovered patterns similar to those described for children's groups.

    For women, as for girls, intimacy is the fabric of relationships, and talk is the thread from which it is woven. Little girls create and maintain friendships by exchanging secrets; similarly, women regard conversation as the cornerstone of friendship. So a woman expects her husband to be a new and improved version of a best friend. What is important is not the individual subjects that are discussed but the sense of closeness, a life shared, that emerges when people tell their thoughts, feelings, and impressions.

10   Bonds between boys can be as intense as girls', but they are based less on talking, more on doing things together. Since they don't assume talk is the cement that binds a relationship, men don't know what kind of talk women want, and they don't miss it when it isn't there.

    Boys' groups are larger, more inclusive, and more hierarchical, so boys must struggle to avoid the subordinate position in the group. This may play a role in women's complaints that men don't listen to them. Some men really don't like to listen, because being the listener makes them feel one-down, like a child listening to adults or an employee to a boss.

    But often when women tell men, "You aren't listening," and the men protest, "I am," the men are right. The impression of not listening results from misalignments in the mechanics of conversation. The misalignment begins as soon as a man and a woman take physical positions. This became clear when I studied videotapes made by psychologist Bruce Dorval of children and adults talking to their same-sex best friends. I found that at every age, the girls and women faced each other directly, their eyes anchored on each other's faces. At every age, the boys and men sat at angles to each other and looked elsewhere in the room, periodically glancing at each other. They were obviously attuned to each other, often mirroring each other's movements. But the tendency of men to face away can give women the impression they aren't listening even when they are. A young woman in college was frustrated: Whenever she told her boyfriend she wanted to talk to him, he would lie down on the floor, close his eyes, and put his arm over his face. This signaled to her, "He's taking a nap." But he insisted he was listening extra hard. Normally, he looks around the room, so he is easily distracted. Lying down and covering his eyes helped him concentrate on what she was saying.

Analogous to the physical alignment that women and men take in conversation is their topical alignment. The girls in my study tended to talk at length about one topic, but the boys tended to jump from topic to topic. Girls exchanged stories about people they knew. The second-grade boys teased, told jokes, noticed things in the room and talked about finding games to play. The sixth-grade girls talked about problems with a mutual friend. The sixth-grade boys talked about 55 different topics, none of which extended over more than a few turns.

Listening to Body Language

Switching topics is another habit that gives women the impression men aren't listening, especially if they switch to a topic about themselves. But the evidence of the 10th-grade boys in my study indicates otherwise. The 10th-grade boys sprawled across their chairs with bodies parallel and eyes straight ahead, rarely looking at each other. They looked as if they were riding in a car, staring out the windshield. But they were talking about their feelings. One boy was upset because a girl had told him he had a drinking problem, and the other was feeling alienated from all his friends.

15   Now, when a girl told a friend about a problem, the friend responded by asking probing questions and expressing agreement and understanding. But the boys dismissed each other's problems. Todd assured Richard that his drinking was "no big problem" because "sometimes you're funny when you're off your butt." And when Todd said he felt left out, Richard responded, "Why should you? You know more people than me."

Women perceive such responses as belittling and unsupportive. But the boys seemed satisfied with them. Whereas women reassure each other by implying, "You shouldn't feel bad because I've had similar experiences," men do so by implying, "You shouldn't feel bad because your problems aren't so bad."

There are even simpler reasons for women's impression that men don't listen. Linguist Lynette Hirschman found that women make more listener-noise, such as "mhm," "uhuh," and "yeah," to show "I'm with you." Men, she found, more often give silent attention. Women who expect a stream of listener-noise interpret silent attention as no attention at all.

Women's conversational habits are as frustrating to men as men's are to women. Men who expect silent attention interpret a stream of listener-noise as overreaction or impatience. Also, when women talk to each other in a close, comfortable setting, they often overlap, finish each other's sentences and anticipate what the other is about to say. This practice, which I call "participatory listenership," is often perceived by men as interruption, intrusion and lack of attention.

A parallel difference caused a man to complain about his wife, "She just wants to talk about her own point of view. If I show her another view, she gets mad at me." When most women talk to each other, they assume a conversationalist's job is to express agreement and support. But many men see their conversational duty as pointing out the other side of an argument. This is heard as disloyalty by women, and refusal to offer the requisite support. It is not that women don't want to see other points of view, but that they prefer them phrased as suggestions and inquiries rather than as direct challenges.

20   In his book *Fighting for Life,* Walter Ong points out that men use "agonistic," or warlike, oppositional formats to do almost anything; thus discussion becomes debate, and conversation a competitive sport. In contrast, women see conversation as a ritual means of establishing rapport. If Jane tells a problem and June says she has a similar one, they walk away feeling closer to each other. But this attempt at establishing rapport can backfire when used with men. Men take too literally women's ritual "trouble talk," just as women mistake men's ritual challenges for real attack.

The Sounds of Silence

These differences begin to clarify why women and men have such different expectations about communication in marriage. For women, talk creates intimacy. Marriage is an orgy of closeness: you can tell your feelings and thoughts, and still be loved. Their greatest fear is being pushed away. But men live in a hierarchical world, where talk maintains independence and status.They are on guard to protect themselves from being put down and pushed around.

This explains the paradox of the talkative man who said of his silent wife, "She's the talker." In the public setting of a guest lecture, he felt challenged to show his intelligence and display his understanding of the lecture. But at home, where he has nothing to prove and no one to defend against, he is free to remain silent. For his wife, being home means she is free from the worry that something she says might offend someone, or spark disagreement, or appear to be showing off; at home she is free to talk.

The communication problems that endanger marriage can't be fixed by mechanical engineering. They require a new conceptual framework about the role of talk in human relationships. Many of the psychological explanations that have become second nature may not be helpful, because they tend to blame either women (for not being assertive enough) or men (for not being in touch with their feelings). A sociolinguistic approach by which male-female conversation is seen as cross-cultural communication allows us to understand the problem and forge solutions without blaming either party.

Once the problem is understood, improvement comes naturally, as it did to the young woman and her boyfriend who seemed to go to sleep when she wanted to talk. Previously, she had accused him of not listening, and he had refused to change his behavior, since that would be admitting fault. But then she learned about and explained to him the differences in women's and men's habitual ways of aligning themselves in conversation. The next time she told him she wanted to talk, he began, as usual, by lying down and covering his eyes. When the familiar negative reaction bubbled up, she reassured herself that he really was listening. But then he sat up and looked at her. Thrilled, she asked why. He said, "You like me to look at you when you talk, so I'll try to do it." Once he saw their differences as cross-cultural rather than right and wrong, he independently altered his behavior.

25   Women who feel abandoned and deprived when their husbands won't listen to or report daily news may be happy to discover their husbands trying to adapt once they understand the place of small talk in women's relationships. But if their husbands don't adapt, the women may still be comforted that for men, this is not a failure of intimacy. Accepting the difference, the wives may look to their friends or family for that kind of talk. And husbands who can't provide it shouldn't feel their wives have made unreasonable demands. Some couples will still decide to divorce, but at least their decisions will be based on realistic expectations.

In these times of resurgent ethnic conflicts, the world desperately needs cross-cultural understanding. Like charity, successful cross-cultural communication should begin at home.

Critical Reading Questions

1. Identify the distinctive differences between the communication styles of men and women as described by Deborah Tannen and explain how these differences can lead to miscommunication and misunderstanding. (Note that Tannen is describing general patterns of communication to which there are many exceptions, individually and culturally.)
2. On the basis of your own experience, explain whether or not you believe Tannen's analysis of these different communication styles is accurate. Provide specific examples to support your viewpoint.
3. Describe a situation in which you have a miscommunication with a person of the opposite sex. Analyze this situation in terms of points made in the Tannen article.
4. Identify strategies that both men and women can use to avoid miscommunication that can result from their contrasting communication styles.

Using Language to Influence

Because of the intimate relationship between language and thinking, people naturally use language to influence the thinking of others. We noted earlier that within the boundaries of social groups, people use a given language style or dialect to emphasize shared information and experience. The expression "Now you're speaking my language" illustrates this point.

Some people make a profession of using language to influence others' thinking. They are interested in influencing—and sometimes in controlling—your thoughts, feelings, and behavior. To avoid being unconsciously manipulated by these efforts, you need to be aware of how language functions. This knowledge will help you to distinguish actual arguments, information, and reasons from techniques of persuasion that others use to get you to accept their views without thinking critically. Two types of language often used to promote the uncritical acceptance of views are euphemistic language and emotive language.

EUPHEMISTIC LANGUAGE

The term *euphemism* is derived from a Greek word meaning "to speak with good words." Using a **euphemism** involves substituting a more pleasant, less objectionable expression for a blunt or more direct one. For example, an entire collection of euphemisms exists to disguise the unpleasantness of death: *passed away, went to her reward, departed this life,* and *blew out the candle.*

Why do people use euphemisms? Probably to help smooth out the "rough edges" of life, to make the unbearable bearable and the offensive inoffensive. Sometimes people use them to make their occupations sound more dignified (a garbage collector, for instance, might be called a "sanitation engineer"). Sometimes euphemisms can be humorous, as are the following "New Euphemisms for Bad Stuff at School."

Course failure	Unrequested course reregistration
Incomplete course grade	An unrequited educational encounter
Suspension	Mandatory discontinued attendance
Absence	A non-school learning experience

Euphemisms can become dangerous, though, when they are used to evade or to create misperceptions of serious issues. An alcoholic may describe herself as a "social drinker," thus denying her problem and need for help. A politician may indicate that one of his statements was "somewhat at variance with the truth"—meaning that he lied. Another example would be to describe rotting slums as "substandard housing," making deplorable conditions appear reasonable and the need for action less urgent. One of the most devastating examples of the destructive power of euphemisms was Nazi Germany's characterizing the slaughter of millions of men, women, and children as "the final solution" and "the purification of the race." The "ethnic cleansing" in Bosnia in the 1990s is a similar example.

In the following passage from his classic essay "Politics and the English Language," George Orwell describes how governments often employ euphemisms to disguise and justify wrongful policies.

In our time, political speech and writing are largely the defense of the indefensible. Things like the continuance of British rule in India, the Russian purges and deportations, the dropping of the atom bombs on Japan, can indeed be defended, but only by arguments which are too brutal for most people to face, and which do not square with the professed aims of political parties. Thus political language has to consist largely of euphemism, question-begging and sheer cloudy vagueness. Defenseless villages are bombarded from the air, the inhabitants driven out into the countryside, the cattle machine-gunned, the huts set on fire with incendiary bullets: this is called pacification. Millions of peasants are robbed of their farms and sent trudging along the roads with no more than they can carry: this is called transfer of population or rectification of frontiers. People are imprisoned for years without trial, or shot in the back of the neck or sent to die of scurvy in Arctic lumber camps: this is called elimination of unreliable elements. Such phraseology is needed if one wants to name things without calling up mental pictures of them.

Thinking ↔ Writing Activity

Thinking Critically About Euphemisms

Read the following passage by *New York Times* columnist Bob Herbert, which deals with euphemisms for "getting fired." Then answer the following questions in your journal.

1. Why do you think these bureaucratic euphemisms are so prevalent?

2. Select an important social problem such as drug use, crime, poverty, juvenile delinquency, support for wars in other countries, racism, unethical or illegal behavior in government. List several euphemisms commonly used to describe the problem; then explain how these euphemisms can lead to dangerous misperceptions and serious consequences.

FROM

Separation Anxiety
BY BOB HERBERT

The euphemism of choice for the corporate chopping block is downsizing, but variations abound. John Thomas, a 59-year-old AT&T employee, was told on

Tuesday that his job was "not going forward." One thinks of a car with transmission trouble, or the New York Jets offense, not the demise of a lengthy career.

Other workers are discontinued, involuntarily severed, surplussed. There are men and women at AT&T who actually talk about living in a "surplus universe."

There are special leaves, separations, rebalances, bumpings and, one of my favorites, cascade bumpings. A cascade bumping actually sounds like a joyful experience.

In the old days some snarling ogre would call you into the office and say, "Jack, you're fired." It would be better if they still did it that way because that might make the downsized, discontinued, surplussed or severed employee mad as hell. And if enough employees got mad they might get together and decide to do something about the ever-increasing waves of corporate greed and irresponsibility that have capsized their lives and will soon overwhelm many more.

5   Instead, with the niceties scrupulously observed, and with employment alternatives in extremely short supply, the fired workers remain fearful, frustrated, confused, intimidated and far too docile. . . . The staggering job losses, even at companies that are thriving, are rationalized as necessary sacrifices to the great gods of international competition. Little is said about the corrosive effect of rampant corporate greed, and even less about peculiar notions like corporate responsibility and accountability—not just to stockholders, but to employees and their families, to the local community, to the social and economic well-being of the country as a whole.

New York Times, January 19, 1996

EMOTIVE LANGUAGE

What is your immediate reaction to each of the following words?

| *tyrant* | *peaceful* | *disgusting* | *God* | *filthy* |
| *mouthwatering* | *bloodthirsty* | *freedom* | *Nazi* | |

Most of these words probably arouse strong feelings in you. In fact, this ability to evoke feelings accounts for the extraordinary power of language.

Certain words (like those just listed) are used to stand for the emotive areas of your experience. These emotive words symbolize the whole range of human feelings, from powerful emotions ("I detest you!") to the subtlest of feelings, as revealed in this passage spoken by Chief Seattle in 1855, as he responded to a U.S. government proposal to buy his tribe's land and place the tribe on a reservation:

> Every part of this soil is sacred in the estimation of my people. Every hillside, every valley, every plain and grove, has been hallowed by some sad or happy event in days long vanished. . . . The very dust upon which you now stand responds more lovingly to their footsteps than to yours, because it is rich with the blood of our ancestors and our bare feet are conscious of the sympathetic touch. . . . And when the last red man shall have perished, and the memory of my tribe shall have become a myth among the white men, these shores will swarm with the invisible dead of my tribe. . . . At night when the streets of your cities and villages are silent and you think them deserted, they will throng with the returning hosts that once filled and still love this beautiful land. The white man will never be alone. Let him be just and deal kindly with my people, for the dead are not powerless. Dead, did I say? There is no death, only a change of worlds.

Emotive language often plays a double role: it not only symbolizes and expresses our feelings but also arouses or *evokes* feelings in others. When you tell someone, "You're my best friend," you usually are not simply expressing your feelings for the person; you also hope to inspire that person to have similar feelings for you. Even when communicating factual information, we make use of the emotive influence of language to interest other people in what we are saying. For example, compare the *New York Times* account (page 249) of Malcolm X's assassination with the *Life* magazine account (page 249). Which account do you find more emotive? Which seems more objective? Which do you find more engaging? Why?

Although an emotive word may be an accurate description of feelings, it is not the same as a factual statement because it is true only for the speaker—not for others. For instance, even though you may feel that a movie is "tasteless" and "repulsive," someone else may find it "exciting" and "hilarious." By describing your feelings about the movie, you are giving your personal evaluation, which often may differ from the personal evaluations of others (it is not unusual to see conflicting reviews of the same movie). A factual statement, on the other hand, is a statement with which all rational people will agree, providing that suitable evidence to verify it is available (for example, the fact that mass transit uses less energy than automobiles).

In some ways, symbolizing emotions is more difficult than representing factual information about the world. For example, expressing your feelings about a person often is more challenging than stating facts about him or her.

When emotive words are used in larger groups (such as sentences, paragraphs, compositions, poems, plays, or novels), they become even more powerful.

The pamphlets of Thomas Paine helped to inspire American patriots in the Revolutionary War, and Abraham Lincoln's Gettysburg Address has endured as an expression of Americans' most cherished values. In horrifying contrast were the vehement speeches of Adolf Hitler that influenced German people before and during World War II.

One way to think about the meaning and power of emotive words is to see them on a scale or continuum, from mild to strong. For example:

overweight   fat   obese

The thinker Bertrand Russell used this continuum to illustrate how we perceive the same trait in various people:

- I am *firm*.

- You are *stubborn*.

- He/she is *pigheaded*.

We usually tend to perceive ourselves favorably ("I am firm"). I am speaking to you face to face, so I view you only somewhat less favorably ("You are stubborn"). But since a third person is not present, I can use stronger emotive language ("He/she is pigheaded"). Try this technique with two other emotive words:

1. I am . . .   You are . . .   He/she is . . .

2. I am . . .   You are . . .   He/she is . . .

Finally, emotive words can be used to confuse opinions with facts, a situation that commonly occurs when we combine emotive uses of language with informative uses. Although people may appear to be giving factual information, they actually may be adding personal evaluations that are not factual. These opinions are often emotional, biased, unfounded, or inflammatory. Consider the following statement: "New York City is the filthiest and most dangerous city; only idiots would want to live there." Although the speaker at first appears to be giving factual information, he or she is really using emotive language to advance an opinion. Yet emotive uses of language are not always negative. The statement "She's the most generous, wise, honest, and warm friend anyone could have" also illustrates the potential confusion of the emotive and the informative uses of language, except that in this case the feelings are positive.

Emotive words usually signal that a personal opinion or evaluation, rather than a fact, is being stated. Speakers occasionally do identify their opinions as opinions, using phrases like "In my opinion" or "I feel that." Often, however, speakers do not identify their opinions as such because they want you to treat their judgments as facts. In these cases, the combination of the informative use and the emotive use of language can be misleading and even dangerous.

Thinking ↔ Writing Activity

Evaluating Emotive Language

Identify examples of emotive language in the following passages and explain how the writer is using it to influence people's thoughts and feelings.

I draw the line in the dust and toss the gauntlet before the heel of tyranny, and I say segregation now, segregation tomorrow, segregation forever. —Governor George C. Wallace, 1963

We dare not forget today that we are heirs of that first revolution. Let the word go forth from this time and place, to friend and foe alike, that the torch has been passed to a new generation of Americans—born in this century, tempered by war, disciplined by a hard and bitter peace, proud of our ancient heritage—and unwilling to witness or permit the slow undoing of those human rights to which this nation has always been committed, and to which we are committed today at home and around the world. —President John F. Kennedy, Inaugural Address, 1961

Every criminal, every gambler, every thug, every libertine, every girl ruiner, every home wrecker, every wife beater, every dope peddler, every moonshiner, every crooked politician, every pagan Papist priest, every shyster lawyer, every white slaver, every brothel madam, every Rome-controlled newspaper, every black spider—is fighting the Klan. Think it over. Which side are you on? —From a Ku Klux Klan circular

Now consider the following hand-edited draft of one of the most famous speeches in American history and respond to the Critical Reading Questions which follow it.

Proposed Message to Congress ("Day of Infamy" speech)
FRANKLIN DELANO ROOSEVELT

DRAFT No. 1   December 7, 1941.

PROPOSED MESSAGE TO THE CONGRESS

Yesterday, December 7, 1941, a date which will live in ~~world history~~ *infamy*,

the United States of America was ~~simultaneously~~ *suddenly* and deliberately attacked

by naval and air forces of the Empire of Japan,

The United States was *at the moment at peace with that nation and was*

~~continuing the~~ *still* conversations with its Government and its Emperor looking

toward the maintenance of peace in the Pacific. Indeed, one hour after,

Japanese air squadrons had commenced bombing in *Oahu* ~~the and the Philippines~~

the Japanese Ambassador to the United States and his colleague delivered

to the Secretary of State a formal reply to a ~~former~~ *recent* message, ~~from the~~

~~secretary.~~ This reply ~~contained a statement~~ *stated* that diplomatic negotiations

~~must be considered at an end,~~ *it* contained no threat ~~and no~~ *or* hint of ~~an~~ *war or*

armed attack.

It will be recorded that the distance ~~of~~ of

Hawaii, from Japan make*s* it obvious that the attack *was* ~~was~~ deliberate~~ly~~

planned many days *or even weeks* ago. During the intervening time the Japanese Govern-

ment has deliberately sought to deceive the United States by false

statements and expressions of hope for continued peace.

DRAFT NO. 1

-2-

The attack ~~yesterday~~ on ~~Manila and on the Island of Oahu have~~ *the Hawaiian Islands* *has*

caused severe damage to American naval and military forces. Very

many American lives have been lost. In addition American ~~████~~ ships

have been torpedoed on the high seas between San Francisco and

Honolulu.

Yesterday the Japanese Government also launched an attack

against Malaya.

¶ Last night Japanese forces attacked Guam.

¶ Japan has, "therefore", undertaken a "surprise offensive extending *the Philippine Islands*

throughout the Pacific area. The facts of yesterday speak for

themselves. The people of the United States have already formed

their opinions and well understand the implications ~~through attacks~~

~~bear on~~ *to very* the safety of our nation.

As Commander-in-Chief of the Army and Navy I have, ~~of course,~~

directed that all measures be taken for our defense.

Long will we remember the character of the onslaught against

us.

Ⓐ *No matter how long it may take us to overcome this premeditated invasion, the American people will in their righteous might win through to absolute victory.*

DRAFT NO. 1   —3—

I speak the will of the Congress and of the people ~~of this~~ ~~country~~ when I assert that we will not only defend ourselves to the uttermost but will see to it that this form of treachery shall never endanger us again. Hostilities exist. There is no mincing the fact that our people, our territory and our interests are in grave danger.

I, therefore, ask that the Congress declare that since the unprovoked and dastardly attack by Japan on Sunday, December seventh, a state of war exists between the United Statew and the Japanese Empire.

Critical Reading Questions

1. Which changes in the speech appear to be for factual purposes?
2. Which changes appear to be for emotive purposes?
3. How do President Roosevelt's changes make his language more effective?

Writing Project: The Impact of Language on Your Life

This chapter explores the essential role of language in developing sophisticated thinking abilities. The goal of clear, effective thinking and communication is accomplished through the joint efforts of thought and language. Learning to use the appropriate language style, which depends on the social context in which you are operating, requires both critical judgment and flexible expertise with various language forms. Critically evaluating the pervasive attempts of advertisers and others to bypass your critical faculties and influence your thinking involves insight into the way language and thought create and express meaning. We will be examining these relationships between language and thought further in upcoming chapters, especially in Chapter 12, Constructing Arguments—Writing to Persuade.

The following Writing Project provides an opportunity for you to apply what you have learned in this chapter to your own writing.

> Write a paper in which you discuss some specific aspect of your experience with language. Analyze some way or ways in which words have affected you. You could write about a favorite poem or song lyric, about how the language of a religious ceremony or political statement influenced you, or about advertisements that made you desire or reject a product. You might tell of the impact of statements made by your parents, grandparents, teachers, or friends. You could recount one event or several situations, positive or negative effects. Whenever possible, connect your experience to concepts explained in this chapter. Follow your instructor's directions for topic limitations, length, format, and so on.

Because this paper may either focus on one experience or pull several situations together, the principles you need to consider are those involved in writing any paper that connects your personal experience with a complex issue.

1. Present your experience vividly and use specific details.

2. Clearly state your point or thesis about the effect(s) the experience had on you. Think about the best place in your paper to do this.

3. Be explicit about the connections you see between your experience and the concepts about language that they illustrate. You may want to quote from the chapter. If you do, cite material as directed by your instructor.

4. Consider using some of the language techniques explored in this chapter (such as figurative language).

THE WRITING SITUATION

Begin by considering the key elements in the Thinking-Writing Model (illustrated in Chapter 1, page 31).

Purpose You have several purposes for this piece of writing. One is to connect abstract ideas about language with real-life experiences so that you and your readers can understand the concepts better. Another is to meet the challenge of connecting ideas, a thinking activity that is central to your college studies. As with any writing project, a major purpose is to make your points clear and convincing to your audience.

Audience As always, consider who could benefit from reading your paper. Perhaps your ideas would appeal to a national audience, in which case you could submit your writing for publication, possibly in the "My Turn" column in *Newsweek* or in some other magazine or newspaper.

Your classmates are an important audience since they are also participating in this reading and writing experience and should enjoy learning from your paper. They are a particularly good audience for your drafts. If your instructor encourages or requires peer review sessions, be sure to take advantage of this opportunity to work with knowledgeable readers.

Your instructor is the audience who will judge how well you have planned, drafted, and revised. As a writing teacher, he or she cares about a clear focus, logical organization, sound evidence, and correct usage in finished versions. Your instructor will also want to see how you connect your ideas to those in this chapter.

Subject Because language is such a large subject, one involving fairly simple as well as very complex ideas, writing about a real-life experience can clarify—and test—the ideas you choose to write about. And remember that the reader of this paper will be especially conscious of your use of language.

Writer Because this project draws on your own experience, you are in a position of authority. However, the project asks you to focus on an aspect of your experience that you might not have thought about before, and it requires an analytical approach rather than a narrative one, even though you may decide to tell of an event. Therefore, you will need a sort of double consciousness as a writer: you first want to recall your experience as directly as you can, but then you will have to distance yourself as you analyze the effect of language on the experience.

THE WRITING PROCESS

The following sections will guide you through the stages of generating, planning, drafting, and revising as you work on this writing assignment.

Generating Ideas

1. Before you start, review what you wrote for Thinking-Writing Activities in this chapter, especially when answering the questions related to the Tannen reading on page 189.

2. Think of times when something you heard, read, or even said had an impact on you. Did someone use harsh language that upset you or comforting language that soothed you? Did you say something funny, helpful, embarrassing, or astute? Has a particular phrase ever made you want to do or try something? Why?

3. Do you find any common denominator among several experiences, or does one experience stand out and ask to be told as a single story?

4. Have your significant language experiences involved spoken words more often than written ones?

5. Have any of your experiences involved more than one language or more than one dialect or level of usage?

6. Freewrite for five minutes about the ideas that have come to you. Do any of them seem to be developing into a possible essay topic?

7. Look at the questions for generating ideas on pages 75–77 in Chapter 3. Can any of them help you with this project?

Defining a Focus   What do you want your audience to understand about the way the experience has affected you? If you are going to recount several experiences, is it important to make that clear in your thesis? Draft a thesis statement that makes a point about your experience(s).

Share your tentative thesis with classmates. Do they consider your idea worthwhile? Next, list things you might say to develop your thesis. How do your peers respond?

Organizing Ideas   The organization of this paper will depend on whether you are discussing one or two events or a number of experiences. However you approach it, you will need to consider what arrangement will best help your audience understand the effects of your experience. If you are using specific concepts from the chapter, you will have to think about how and where to present them so that their relevance is clear. Using a mind map or a web may help you organize your ideas. Here is one possible format:

First experience	Second experience	Why the two experiences are related
Circumstances	Circumstances	_____
What was said	What was said	_____
How it affected you	How it affected you	_____

Drafting Start with the part that will be easiest to write. Look at your freewriting, your possible thesis statement, and your list or map of ideas. Now, work those early-stage writings into a coherent draft. Remember that shaping ideas is your biggest concern at this stage. Trust yourself to speak about your own experiences and to explain what they mean to you.

After you have drafted enough material, give attention to paragraphs. Where does your material cluster into divisions? Which paragraphs need topic sentences? Where in the paragraphs should topic sentences be placed?

Draft an opening paragraph and a conclusion. What connections exist between them? Will they create an effective beginning and a good ending for your essay?

Revising One of the best revision strategies is to get an audience's reactions to your draft. Your classmates, or peers, can help you see where your draft is already successful and where it needs improvement. If your instructor allows class time for peer review, be sure to have a draft ready so that you can benefit from this activity (see pages 65–66 and 105–107). After peer review, you can revise.

1. **Think big.** Look at your draft as a whole.
   - Does your thesis make clear that the experience(s) affected you because of the way language was involved?
   - How could you state the thesis more clearly?
   - What parts of the draft, if any, do not relate to the thesis?
   - How could you reorganize the draft to make it easier for your audience to follow?
   - What evidence could you add to accomplish your purpose?
   - How could you make the flow between paragraphs smoother?
   - Is your point of view consistent throughout?
   - Is your own use of language effective throughout, as the language was in the readings in this chapter?

2. **Think medium.** Look at your draft paragraph by paragraph. First consider your *introduction*.
   - How could you rewrite your lead to make your audience more interested in reading about your experience(s)? (See the suggestions for being creative with introductions on pages 80–81 of Chapter 3.)
   - How could you make your introduction more appropriate for the rest of your draft—that is, how could you make the tone of the introduction match the tone of the rest of the draft?
   - If you are working with a "visible structure," how could you state your focus more clearly?
   - If you are working with an "invisible structure," how could you imply your focus more clearly?

Then look at each of your body paragraphs.

- Do they present the experience(s) and the impact on you clearly and specifically?
- Does each support the thesis?
- Does each present relevant, specific evidence not presented elsewhere?
- Which, if any, body paragraphs should be combined or eliminated?
- Which body paragraphs use topic sentences effectively?
- Which body paragraphs do not have topic sentences? Do they need them?
- Where could transitions be used to improve the flow within a body paragraph?
- Where could transitions be used to improve the flow between body paragraphs?

Now look at your conclusion. It is your last chance to accomplish your purpose with your intended audience.

- How could you make your conclusion more effective? (See the suggestions for being creative with conclusions on pages 80–81 of Chapter 3.)
- Does the conclusion provide a satisfying ending by making clear how the experience(s) has/have affected you?
- Is the tone of the conclusion appropriate?

3. **Think small.** Look at your draft sentence by sentence.
   - Since this is a paper about language, have you been especially careful in your own use of language? Are there any places where the language could be improved?
   - Have you used emotive language? Figurative language? Should you?
   - Which sentences are difficult to understand? How could you reword them?
   - Which, if any, sentences are so long that your audience could get lost in them? How could you shorten or divide them?
   - Are there any short, choppy sentences that could be combined?
   - Which sentences seem vague? How could you clarify them?
   - Which, if any, sentences have errors in Standard English grammar or usage? How could you correct them?

4. **Think "picky."** Look at your draft as the fussiest critic might.
   - Which words are unclear or not quite right for your meaning? What words could you use instead?
   - Are any words misspelled? (Run the spelling checker on your computer, but don't rely on it alone.)

- Are the pages numbered consecutively?
- Does your draft make a good impression by being neat?
- Is there anything else you can do to improve your draft?

Editing and Proofreading   After you prepare a final draft, check again for correct grammar and punctuation usage. Proofread carefully to detect omitted words or punctuation marks. Run your spelling checker program, but be aware of its limitations. Proofread again for the kinds of errors the computer can't catch.

The following essay shows how one student responded to this assignment. It is followed by a poem by Roberto Obregon.

STUDENT WRITING

The Power of Language
BY JESSIE LANGE

Language is indeed one of the most powerful things we possess. It is how we communicate our ideas, how we put our abstract feelings for others into words, and it is what we use to describe and evaluate our human experience. Being a "good speaker" in public is something we value highly as we do effective communication in our personal lives. One of the most incredible things about language is the power that just a phrase or even a single word can have. In fact, just a few words often have more of an impact than long speeches and rambling sentences. How does it happen that a small combination of letters can have such a tremendous effect on us?

In the play *Kiss of the Spider Woman* by Manuel Puig, one of the characters, Molina, comments on the power of language. Molina, a gentle soul and an expert storyteller, is desperately in love with the man with whom he is sharing a prison cell. "How does it happen that sometimes someone says something and wins someone else over forever?" he wonders. If only he knew, he could win the love of his cell-mate, Valentin. What Molina is acknowledging is that it doesn't take an infinite number of words to say something powerful. It can be a phrase or even a single word that has the most profound impact on others. In this case, it is the "one thing" uttered that causes another to fall in love with you. In the everyday, there are particular words and phrases that stay with us, that we roll over in our minds, repeating them to ourselves again and again. There are certain words that have such an impact that they stay with us eternally longer than the time it took to utter them. I recently had a personal experience with the effects of this.

After my first four months of college, I returned home for the winter break. After four months of reading inspirational writers, attending the lectures of powerful speakers, learning about language itself in my linguistics course, speaking French, and having discussions with intelligent professors who are at the top of their field, I returned home to be more affected by one word uttered by my twelve-year-old brother than I had been by any of the speaking or listening I'd engaged in first semester. My brother and I have always been extremely close. We do not have the "sibling rivalry" I so often hear about from others. And so being apart had been a struggle. The fact that we had been apart so long and the impending separation just a few weeks away were probably much of the reason his words had such an effect on me. We were saying goodnight one night and my brother who, in many ways, is a miniature me, was holding my hand. I'd just finished assuring him that he was the "bomb" and he was smiling at me. Somewhere out of his slim twelve-year-old frame a thought emerged in the form of speech: "I wish I could take you with me," he said. "Where?" I asked, thoroughly confused. His smile broadened. "Everywhere," he said matter-of-factly. Such a simple word but, to me, so profoundly meaningful, causing a complete overflow of emotion. I had visions of never letting go of his hand. Of bringing him to college with me, of going to school with him, of bringing him all through my life and never missing a day or a second of his getting older. Just one word: *Everywhere.*

If I've learned anything about language, it's that the cliché "quality, not quantity" definitely applies. It took one utterance from my brother to almost bring me to tears. With one word, I could imagine myself holding his fingers in mine wherever I went, wherever we went.

Equal to a Pebble

BY ROBERTO OBREGON

TRANSLATED BY ZOE ANGLESEY

Words, when exposed to air
grow like calves.
Over the years they mature and increase in value
or they may be stillborn.
Either one.

The word reveals to us
what constitutes the spirit.
It's a very delicate thing.

In the mouth of a liar
it exposes to the bone
a thankless soul.

The word, equal to nuclear power
in good hands can save lives
if not, it amounts to doomsday
in a darkened conscience.

By impact of a word alone
a Hollywood star can fall from grace.
Tyrants fear it
and the guilty prefer not to use it.

Like coins we drop words
into the mind of a child
so that with time
the thinking will be a storehouse of riches.

The word is the most precious of gems
we give to our loved ones
so they believe and confide in us.
If love falls apart it's proof we lie.

A moist word, vital like earth
whispers in the hush of silence
and true it can soothe, be lusty
or instrumental to a plan that urges on a nation.

Sure. People live not by bread alone.
The word also offers sustenance
being what it is:
product of my hands, and yours.
And no such things!

Thinking and Writing to Shape Our World

All of us actively shape, as well as discover, the world of our experience in which we live. Our world does not exist as a finished product waiting for us to perceive it, think about it, and describe it with words and pictures. Instead, we are active participants in composing our world—selecting, organizing, and interpreting sensations into a coherent whole. Many times, our shaping of this world will reflect basic thinking patterns that we rely on constantly whenever we think, act, speak, or write.

Part Two explores four basic ways of relating and organizing: relationships in space and time, relationships of comparison, relationships of cause, and relationships of classification and definition. The Writing Projects at the end of each chapter ask you to integrate ideas from one, two, or three other sources into your essays as you explore these relationships, and the thinking/organizing patterns that develop from them.

6

Exploring Perceptions

Writing to Describe and Narrate

"The real voyage of discovery consists not in seeking new landscapes, but in having new eyes." —Marcel Proust

Critical Thinking Focus: Understanding perceptions

Writing Focus: Detail and order in chronologies

Reading Theme: Narratives and process descriptions

Writing Project: Narrative showing the effect of a perception

The way we make sense of the world is through thinking, but our first experiences of the world come to us through our senses: sight, hearing, smell, touch, and taste. These senses are our bridges to the world, making us aware of what occurs outside us. The process of becoming aware of the world through our senses is known as *perceiving*.

This chapter and Chapter 7 will explore the way the perceiving process operates and how it relates to the ability to think, read, and write effectively. In particular, these chapters examine the way each of us shapes personal experience by actively selecting from, organizing, and interpreting the information provided by our senses. In a way, we each view the world through a pair of individual "contact lenses" that reflect our past experiences and our unique personalities. As critical thinkers, we want to become aware of the nature of our own lenses in order to offset any bias or distortion they may be causing. We also want to become aware of the lenses of others so that we can better understand why they view things the way that they do.

Developing insight into the nature of people's lenses—our own and others'—is essential to becoming an effective writer. When we write, it's helpful to understand our own point of view, to be aware of our own biases. That doesn't mean that we should strive to be completely "objective." In fact, such absolute objectivity is not possible because we can never completely remove our personal lenses. However, understanding our lenses helps us achieve our goals as writers. For example, if we want to present our ideas objectively, then we can work to compensate for our inherent bias. On the other hand, if our intention is to persuade others, we may choose to enhance and strengthen our point of view.

Analogously, we need to understand our audience's lenses if we are to communicate our thoughts and feelings effectively through our writing. This involves appreciating their point of view and understanding their biases. We can then use this knowledge to craft our writing, shape our language, and utilize the appropriate terminology and logic.

Once again, we can see the essential union of writing and thinking, communicating and knowing. This chapter will provide you with a foundation for understanding how you develop your beliefs and knowledge about the world and how you can communicate your ideas through clear, expressive, and compelling writing. Let's begin by exploring our main source of information—the perceiving process. Some of the most basic patterns of thinking and of presenting ideas draw directly on perceptions. This chapter will focus on three such patterns: description, process, and narrative.

Thinking Critically About Perceptions

BECOMING AWARE OF YOUR OWN PERCEPTIONS

At almost every waking moment of life, our senses are being bombarded by a tremendous number of stimuli: images to see, noises to hear, odors to smell, textures to feel, and flavors to taste. Experiencing all such sensations at once could create what the nineteenth-century American philosopher William James called "a bloomin' buzzin' confusion." Yet to us, the world usually seems much more orderly and understandable. Why is this so?

In the first place, our sense equipment can receive sensations only within certain limited ranges. For example, there are many sounds and smells that animals can detect but we cannot; animals' sense organs have broader ranges in these areas than ours do. A second reason we can handle sensory bombardment is that from the stimulation available, we select only a small amount on which to focus our attention. To demonstrate this, complete the following Thinking-Writing Activity.

Thinking ↔ Writing Activity

What Do You Sense Right Now?

Respond to the following questions in writing, using a spontaneous, free-flowing style. In other words, record your sensations as you experience them rather than first taking time to reflect and deliberate. Concentrate on what you can see, ignoring your other senses for the moment. Focus on sensations that you were not previously aware of; then answer the first question. Follow the same procedure for the rest of the questions.

1. What can you *see?* (for example, the shape of the letters on the page, the design of the clothing on your arm)
2. What can you *hear?* (for example, the hum of the air circulator, the rustling of a page)
3. What can you *feel?* (for example, the pressure of the clothes against your skin, the texture of the page on your fingers)
4. What can you *smell?* (for example, the perfume someone is wearing, the odor of stale cigarette smoke)
5. What can you *taste?* (for example, the aftertastes of your last meal)

Compare your responses with those of your classmates. Did they perceive sensations different from the ones you perceived? If so, how do you explain these differences?

This simple exercise demonstrates that for every sensation on which you focus, there are countless others which you are simply ignoring. If you were aware of everything that was happening at every moment, you would be completely overwhelmed. By selecting particular sensations, you are able to make sense of your world in a relatively orderly way. That is, you are **perceiving,** a process by which you actively select, organize, and interpret what is experienced by the senses.

It is tempting to think that our senses simply record what is happening out in the world, as if we were human camcorders. We are not, however, passive receivers of information, containers into which sense experience is poured. Instead, we are active participants who are always trying to understand the sensations we are encountering. As we perceive the world, our experiences are the result of combining the sensations we receive with our understanding of these sensations. For instance, examine the collection of markings in Figure 6.1. What do you see? If all you see is a collection of black spots, try turning the illustration sideways; you will probably perceive a familiar animal.

Figure 6.1 Recognizing a Pattern

From this example you can grasp how, when you perceive the world, you are doing more than simply recording what your senses experience; instead, you are actively making sense of these sensations. The collection of blue spots suddenly became the figure of an animal because your mind was able to actively organize the spots into a pattern you recognized. Or think about times when you looked up at white, billowy clouds and saw different figures and designs. The figures you were perceiving were not actually in the clouds but were the result of your giving meaningful form to shapes you were experiencing.

The same is true for virtually everything we experience. Our perceptions of the world result from combining information provided by our senses with the way we actively make sense of this information. And since making sense of information is what we are doing when we are thinking, perceiving the world involves using our minds in an active way. Of course, we are usually not aware that we are using our minds to interpret sensations we are experiencing. We simply see the animal or the figures in the clouds as if they were really there.

ACTIVELY SELECTING, ORGANIZING, AND INTERPRETING SENSATIONS

When we actively perceive the sensations we are experiencing, we are usually engaged in three distinct activities:

- *Selecting* certain sensations to pay attention to
- *Organizing* these sensations into a design or pattern
- *Interpreting* what this design or pattern means

In the case of Figure 6.1, you were able to perceive an animal because you selected certain markings to concentrate on, organized these markings into a pattern, and interpreted this pattern as representing a dog.

Of course, when we perceive, the three operations of selecting, organizing, and interpreting are usually performed quickly, automatically, and often simultaneously. Also, because they are so rapid and automatic, we are not normally aware of performing these operations.

Take a few moments to explore more examples that illustrate how you actively select, organize, and interpret your perceptions of the world. Carefully examine Figure 6.2. Do you see both the young woman and the old woman? If you do, try switching back and forth between the two images. As you do so, notice how for each image, you are doing the following things:

Figure 6.2 Young Woman/Old Woman

- *Selecting* certain lines, shapes, and shadings on which to focus your attention
- *Organizing* these lines, shapes, and shadings into different patterns
- *Interpreting* these patterns as representing things you can recognize—a hat, a nose, a chin

Another way to become aware of your active participation in perceiving your world is to consider how you perceive objects and their relationships. Examine Figure 6.3. Do you perceive different-sized people or same-sized people at different distances?

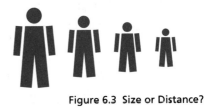

Figure 6.3 Size or Distance?

When we see someone who is far away, we usually do not perceive a tiny person. Instead, we see a normal-sized person who is far away. Our experience in the world has enabled us to discover that the farther away things are, the smaller they look. The moon in the night sky appears to be about the size of a quarter, yet we perceive it as considerably larger. As we look down a long stretch of railroad tracks or gaze up at a tall building, the boundary lines seem to come together. Even though these images are what our eyes "see," we do not usually perceive the tracks meeting or the building coming to a point. Instead, our minds actively organize and interpret a world composed of constant shapes and sizes, even though the images seen usually vary, depending on how far away they are and the angle from which we perceive them.

So far, we have been exploring how the mind actively participates in the ways we perceive the world. By combining the sensations we are receiving with the way our minds select, organize, and interpret these sensations, we perceive a world that is stable and familiar. Thus, each of us develops a perspective on the world, one that usually makes sense to us.

The process of perceiving takes place on various levels. At the most basic level, *perceiving* refers to the selection, organization, and interpretation of sensations: for example, being able to perceive various objects such as a basketball. However, we also perceive larger patterns of meaning at more complex levels, as in watching the action of a group of people engaged in a basketball game. Although these are very different contexts, both engage us in the process of perceiving.

NOTING DIFFERENCES IN PEOPLE'S PERCEPTIONS

As we have noted, we are not usually aware of our active participation in perceiving the world. We normally assume that what we are perceiving is what is actually taking place. Only when we find that our perception of an event differs from others' perceptions of it are we forced to examine the manner in which we are selecting, organizing, and interpreting the event.

Thinking ↔ Writing Activity

Comparing Your Perceptions with Others'

Carefully examine the picture presented in Figure 6.4 and then explore your reactions. What do you think is happening in this picture? Explain by answering the following questions.

1. Describe as specifically as possible what you perceive as taking place in the picture.

2. Describe what you think will take place next.

3. Identify which details of the picture inform your perceptions.

4. Compare your perceptions with those of your classmates.

List several perceptions that differ from yours.

Figure 6.4 A Scene to Interpret

In most cases, people in a group will have a variety of perceptions about what is taking place in Figure 6.4. Some will see the person as frustrated because the work is too difficult. Others will see him concentrating on what has to be done. Still others may see him as annoyed because he is being forced to do something he doesn't want to do. In each case, the perception depends on how the viewer is actively using his or her mind to organize and interpret what is taking place.

Writing Thoughtfully About Perceptions

Although the verb *describe* can be used to mean the giving of any detailed account, it more precisely indicates the reporting of sensory impressions: what you see, hear, feel, smell, or taste—your perceptions. Look back at the questions on page 214 to note how your five senses responded; also, reflect on what you have been reading about selecting, organizing, and interpreting sensations. This material should help you understand the two types of descriptions that you will be writing about in the Thinking-Writing Activity on page 223, descriptions that you might also write in other college courses or in work situations.

WRITING OBJECTIVELY AND SUBJECTIVELY

Descriptions can be broadly divided into two categories: *objective*, involving as little judgment as possible, or *subjective*, involving whatever personal judgment is appropriate to a writer's purpose. Objective descriptions are often expected in scientific, medical, engineering, and law enforcement writing. The purpose of an objective description is to help the audience sense an object or situation as it is. Later, judgments and implications can be drawn from objective descriptions, but the cleanest possible rendering is needed as a starting point. Of course, the selection and presentation of *any* ideas or information involve conscious and unconscious judgments. However, when objectivity is the purpose, you should try to perceive with as little bias as you can and to describe in language that is as neutral as possible.

In other writing situations, descriptions are intended to be more subjective. Then the explicit purpose is to shape the audience's opinion of the object under scrutiny. Subjective descriptions occur in literary texts of all kinds: stories, poems, personal essays, and biographies; in argumentative pieces; and in personal writing such as letters to friends and journal entries. Think of how a novelist describes characters or settings; think of how an attorney might reword the police report's objective description of a victim in order to influence a jury; think of how you would describe your new special person to a close friend! When writing a subjective description, you will be selecting details purposefully and using language that creates the effect that you want your audience to experience.

Objective Language	Subjective Language
A German shepherd	A vicious, snarling dog
A lake at night	A shimmering mirror of moonlight
Drove at 85 mph	Recklessly tore down the road
A six-foot five-inch man	A towering man
Quit my job	Told them to take their job and shove it
Filed for divorce	Got revenge on the lowlife
Won the election	Stole victory from the real winner

CONTRASTING OBJECTIVE AND SUBJECTIVE WRITING

Analyze the following articles in terms of the objectivity and subjectivity of their language. Though the articles may seem unrelated, consider the kinds of woodworking joints needed in the construction of caskets!

Woodworking Joints

BY JOHN CHAFFEE

At the heart of woodworking is a question: How do you join two pieces of wood together? In fact, this is the reason why cabinetmaking was traditionally known as the art of "joinery."

The easiest way to attach two pieces of wood is simply to nail or screw the edge of one board to another. This is known as a *butt joint,* from the word *abut.* Though this is a simple joint, it is not a very strong joint because it depends entirely on the nail or screw to hold the two pieces together.

The *miter joint,* used in most picture frames, is like a butt joint except that the two edges which are to be joined are cut at an angle (usually 45 degrees) and together form a 90-degree corner.

Although it sounds like a cartoon character, the *dado joint* is in reality a strong, effective joint found in many bookshelves. It is formed by cutting a channel across one of the pieces to be joined, into which the other board fits snugly.

5   To understand the *tongue and groove joint,* imagine sticking your tongue into a small opening—and then having it glued in place! Because of its unusual strength, this joint is used extensively in the construction of furniture (particularly chairs) that will receive considerable active use over its lifetime.

The *dovetail joint,* cut in the shape of a dove's tail, is formed by fitting together two interlocking sets of "tails" in the same way that you interlock your fingers together. It is one of the strongest edge joints and is used in making desk and bureau drawers because of the constant pulling and pushing these joints will receive.

In summary, joining two pieces of wood is not simply a matter of nailing them together—it is an art that has been developed over the last seven thousand years. In each case, the particular wood joint selected should reflect the specific purposes for which the joint will be used.

FROM

At Your Disposal:
The Funeral Industry
Prepares for Boom Times

BY JUDITH NEWMAN

"Now, here's what you do if you've tied their mouths too tight, or they have no lips and the family's not happy," says Dina Ousley, placing a stencil over the mouth of an audience volunteer. Using an airbrush, she gently sprays on a full, lush pout in vermilion. "And these lips stay on, even when people are kissing their loved ones good-bye!" Ousley, the president of Dinair Airbrush Makeup Systems of Beverly Hills, California, is a makeup artist for Hollywood stars, but occasionally she takes clients who are, well, less fussy. She is here, at the 115th annual convention of the National Funeral Directors Association (NFDA) in Cincinnati, to sell her system of airbrushed makeup for glamorizing the deceased.

"Hmm, sort of like detailing a car," murmurs a man behind me, as Ousley, a cheerful, birdlike blonde, demonstrates how easy it is to cover bruises and restore a "natural" glow to skin. At the end of Ousley's demonstration comes the piece de resistance: airbrushing, compared with the application of conventional cosmetics, makes it much easier to beautify the client who suffered from jaundice; apparently, when a jaundiced corpse is embalmed, the chemicals can turn it green. Grabbing another volunteer from the audience, Ousley first airbrushes him the color of Herman Munster, then attempts to restore him to his natural hue by spraying him white, as a primer, and applying an alabaster foundation. When I finally fled the room, the volunteer was the shade of a buttercup. He would have looked perfectly natural had he been not a human but a suburban kitchen circa 1950. Ousley did not look happy.

Here's the thing about death that's hard to grasp: It's going to happen to you. Whether you are embalmed and entombed or your ashes are shot out of a duck blind, your loved ones will be spending a small portion of the $7 billion that every year is poured into the U.S. funeral industry. Since the average funeral costs about $4,600—not including the expense of the cemetery or mausoleum, which can add thousands more—disposing of their dead is, for many families, one of the most expensive purchases they will ever make, right behind a house or a car. . . .

As expensive as funerals may seem, when adjusted for inflation, the price of an average funeral has risen only a few percentage points in the last twenty-five years. It's the creative introduction of all sorts of new services and accoutrements, says Berkeley professor Dwayne Banks, that has increased the range of prices.

5   I got a little taste for all those delicious extras during a tour of the exhibitor's floor at the NFDA. First I spotted the mahogany casket my grandfather had unfortunately test-driven into eternity a few years earlier.

At the time, the funeral director was keen on selling my family a model with a special seal to "protect" the body from wildlife; I seem to recall a speech that featured a Hitchcockian vision of marauding gophers. The memory made me a little nauseous: I had recently discovered that, far from protecting the body, the expensive protective seal is the best way to guarantee that anaerobic bacteria will turn the body into goo in record time.

Moving on, I strolled through row upon row of caskets, burial vaults, embalming chemicals to plump up dehydrated tissues (my favorite: a disinfectant called Mort-O-Cide), and restorative waxes to fill in those pesky irregularities left by, say, feeding tubes or gunshot wounds. Burial clothing consists of loose-fitting pastel nightgowns for ladies and pinstripe suits for the gents; apparently, in the afterlife, all women are napping and all men are taking meetings. The dominatrix in me almost sprang for an "extremities positioner," a rope gadget for the proper positioning of the arms over the chest. The Cincinnati College of Mortuary Science was trolling for students, proudly exhibiting a life-size model of Uncle Sam in restorative wax ("Careful, his limbs come off easily!") and the American Funeral Service Museum in Houston exhibited Victorian mourning jewelry made from the hair of the deceased and memorial cards of the rich and famous (some jokester had placed Bobby Kennedy's next to Marilyn Monroe's).

These days, you can buy blowup digital "memory pictures" of the deceased to leave at the graveside and solar-powered memorial lights to keep those pictures backlit into eternity. For the pious, the NFDA exhibitors offered urns with portraits of Jesus and Mary; for the sportsman, there were urns shaped like deer, cowboy boots, and golfclub bags; and for Zsa Zsa Gabor impersonators, an Aurora, Illinois, mortician has created a line of cremation jewelry—gold-and-diamond hearts, teardrops, and cylinders (from $1,995 to $10,000) that can hold a few precious motes of Mom and Dad.

Batesville Casket Company, the largest manufacturer in the United States, was introducing a coffin with a special "memory drawer" for personal keepsakes. Marsellus Casket Company featured "the Rolls Royce of caskets," a handpolished model of solid African mahogany lined with velvet (retail: about $10,000) that had been the final resting place for such stiff luminaries as Richard Nixon, Harry Truman, and John Kennedy. "And don't forget Jackie O.," said the salesman excitedly. Marsellus may have had presidential cachet, but The York Group was drawing crowds with a new casket model it calls "Expressions": the light, ash-wood exterior is treated with a veneer that allows the casket to be scrawled on in Magic Marker. . . .

10   Companies whose primary source of business is in more lively industries were scavenging for scraps of the death market as well. GeneLink, a Margate, New Jersey, company that deals in DNA testing and storage, was offering the bereaved an opportunity to save a bit more of a loved one than mere dust. The mouth of the dead is swabbed for a cell sample, which is sent to GeneLink's lab in Forth Worth, Texas, where the DNA is extracted and stored for twenty-five years. A kit costs about $100, and funeral directors will be charging about $295 for collecting a sample. I must admit, I never quite understood why anyone

would want this service; after all, if you fear you are at increased risk for some genetically linked problem such as Alzheimer's, you could always test yourself.

Here's an idea that does make sense to me: cybergrieving. Jack Martin, president of Simplex Knowledge, an Internet production company in White Plains, New York, has come up with an idea that's bound to appeal to boomers too busy to hop halfway across the continent to weep over Aunt Martha's grave. Mourners will be issued a Website password; a camera will be set up at the funeral, and pictures of the service will be broadcast on the Internet every thirty seconds or so. "The family and funeral director can choose what will be highlighted," says Martin. "The grieving family, the body, the minister, whatever." About half of the funeral directors who have learned about Martin's concept see it as a valuable marketing tool, a service they could offer families gratis. The other half see it strictly as profitable: fees could be collected not only from the families (about $200) but also from the mourners. "They imagined that someone, say, in New Jersey without Internet access could drop by their funeral home and witness a service going on in California," says Martin. "And then the funeral director could charge each mourner ten or twenty bucks. But frankly, I don't think this concept will go over too well. Making people pay to mourn isn't such great publicity for the industry."

Of course, it's possible to bypass the traditional burial altogether. You might want to be put on ice until medical science figures out a cure for what ails you (the first cryonically frozen man, James H. Bedford, just celebrated his thirtieth anniversary of "de-animation," as cryonics enthusiasts call it). Then again, you might want to have yourself mummified. On its Web page, Summum, a New Age, quasi-religious organization in Salt Lake City that practices modern mummification, offers this sales pitch: "Unlike the mummification techniques used by ancient Egyptians, which left the dead shriveled, discolored, and ugly, Summum's method is designed to keep you looking healthy and robust for millennia. The appeal may be to anyone who has labored to stay in shape. Why spend thousands of dollars in healthclub fees while you're alive, then let everything go to pot just because you've died?"

Why, indeed.

Critical Reading Questions

1. Which of the two previous selections is more objective? Is it completely so? Identify some objective sentences; identify others that seem subjective.

2. Can you picture the joints discussed in the first selection without seeing illustrations of them? If so, what wording in the description helps you see? If not, rewrite one paragraph by using more graphic language. What effect does your experience with carpentry (if you have any) have on your understanding of this piece?

3. Which of these selections is more subjective? Identify some words and sentences that you believe the author is using to influence your thinking. What impressions do you get from these words and sentences?

4. In each selection, identify one or two sentences that you think contribute well to the description. Which senses are involved? What details are effective?

Thinking ↔ Writing Activity

Creating Objective and Subjective Descriptions

Write two separate paragraphs in which you describe the same person or object in two different ways. Make one paragraph as objective as possible; make the other primarily subjective in order to create a particular impression for your readers. Each paragraph should have about six to eight sentences.

Which of these paragraphs will have a strong topic sentence? Why? Which may not have a topic sentence or may have one that makes no claim? Why?

Chronological Relationships

Chronological forms of writing organize events or ideas in a time sequence. The focus in chronological writing is on describing growth, development, or change—from a person's life story to the steps in creating a favorite dish. The **chronological pattern** organizes a topic into a series of events in the time sequence in which they occurred. Many chronologies are narratives or stories. For example, when you relate a personal experience by telling what happened first, next, and so on, you are presenting it chronologically. The process mode of thinking organizes an activity into a series of steps necessary for reaching a certain end. Here the focus is on describing aspects of growth, development, or change, as you might do when explaining how to prepare a favorite dish or perform a new dance.

NARRATIVES

Perhaps the oldest and most universal form of chronological expression is the *narrative,* a story about real or fictional experiences. Many people who study communication believe that narrative is the starting point for other patterns of presentation because we often process our perceptions in storylike ways.

Every human culture has used narratives to pass on values and traditions from one generation to the next, as exemplified by such enduring works as the *Odyssey*, the Bible, and the Koran. One of America's great storytellers, Mark Twain, once said that a good story has to accomplish something and arrive somewhere. In other words, if a story is to be effective in engaging the interest of the audience, it has to have a purpose. The purpose may be to provide more information on a subject, to illustrate an idea, to lead the audience to a particular way of thinking, or to entertain. An effective narrative does not merely record the complex, random, and often unrelated events of life. Instead, it has focus, an ordered structure, and a meaningful point of view.

Back, But Not Home

BY MARIA MUNIZ

With all the talk about resuming diplomatic relations with Cuba, and with the increasing number of Cuban exiles returning to visit friends and relatives, I am constantly being asked, "Would you ever go back?" In turn, I have asked myself, "Is there any reason for me to go?" I have had to think long and hard before finding my answer. *Yes.*

I came to the United States with my parents when I was almost five years old. We left behind grandparents, aunts, uncles and several cousins. I grew up in a very middle-class neighborhood in Brooklyn. With one exception, all my friends were Americans. Outside of my family, I do not know many Cubans. I often feel awkward visiting relatives in Miami because it is such a different world. The way of life in Cuban Miami seems very strange to me and I am accused of being too "Americanized." Yet, although I am now an American citizen, whenever anyone has asked me my nationality, I have always and unhesitatingly replied, "Cuban."

Outside American, inside Cuban.

I recently had a conversation with a man who generally sympathizes with the Castro regime. We talked of Cuban politics and although the discussion was very casual, I felt an old anger welling inside. After 16 years of living an "American" life, I am still unable to view the revolution with detachment or objectivity. I cannot interpret its results in social, political or economic terms. Too many memories stand in my way.

5   And as I listened to this man talk of the Cuban situation, I began to remember how as a little girl I would wake up crying because I had dreamed of my aunts and grandmothers and I missed them. I remembered my mother's trembling voice and the sad look on her face whenever she spoke to her mother over

the phone. I thought of the many letters and photographs that somehow were always lost in transit. And as the conversation continued, I began to remember how difficult it often was to grow up Latina in an American world.

It meant going to kindergarten knowing little English. I'd been in this country only a few months and although I understood a good deal of what was said to me, I could not express myself very well. On the first day of school I remember one little girl's saying to the teacher: "But how can we play with her? She's so stupid she can't even talk!" I felt so helpless because inside I was crying, "Don't you know I can understand everything you're saying?" But I did not have words for my thoughts and my inability to communicate terrified me.

As I grew a little older, Latina meant being automatically relegated to the slowest reading classes in school. By now my English was fluent, but the teachers would always assume I was somewhat illiterate or slow. I recall one teacher's amazement at discovering I could read and write just as well as her American pupils. Her incredulity astounded me. As a child, I began to realize that being Latina would always mean proving I was as good as the others. As I grew older, it became a matter of pride to prove I was better than the others.

As an adult I have come to terms with these memories and they don't hurt as much. I don't look or sound very Cuban. I don't speak with an accent and my English is far better than my Spanish. I am beginning my career and look forward to the many possibilities ahead of me.

But a persistent little voice is constantly saying, "There's something missing. It's not enough." And this is why when I am now asked, "Do you want to go back?" I say "yes" with conviction.

10   I do not say to Cubans, "It is time to lay aside the hurt and forgive and forget." It is impossible to forget an event that has altered and scarred all our lives so profoundly.

But I find I am beginning to care less and less about politics. And I am beginning to remember and care more about the child (and how many others like her) who left her grandma behind. I have to return to Cuba one day because I want to know that little girl better.

When I try to review my life during the past 16 years, I almost feel as if I've walked into a theater right in the middle of a movie. And I'm afraid I won't fully understand or enjoy the rest of the movie unless I can see and understand the beginning. And for me, the beginning is Cuba. I don't want to go "home" again; the life and home we all left behind are long gone. My home is here and I am happy. But I need to talk to my family still in Cuba.

Like all immigrants, my family and I have had to build a new life from almost nothing. It was often difficult, but I believe the struggle made us strong. Most of my memories are good ones.

But I want to preserve and renew my cultural heritage. I want to keep "la Cubana" within me alive. I want to return because the journey back will also mean a journey within. Only then will I see the missing piece.

1. What point is Muniz making with her narrative? Where does she state it? Are her statements well placed? Why?

2. Which sections of this passage are in chronological order? Which are not? Why do you think the author organized the piece in this way?

3. If you or other members of your family have recently come to the United States, draft a similar narrative. What point do you want to make? If your family has been here for generations, draft a fictional narrative in the voice of one of your family's first arrivals. What point do you want to make?

PROCESS DESCRIPTIONS

A second type of time-ordered thinking pattern is the *process relationship*, which describes events or experiences in terms of their growth and development. From birth, we are involved with processes in every facet of life. They can be classified in various ways: *natural* (such as growing physically), *mechanical* (such as assembling a bicycle), *physical* (such as learning a sport), *mental* (such as developing a way of thinking), and *creative* (such as writing a poem).

Writing a process description involves two basic tasks. The first is to divide the process being analyzed into parts or stages. The second is to explain the movement of the process through these parts or stages from beginning to end. The stages identified should be separate and distinct and should involve no repetition or significant omissions.

A process description attempts to achieve one of two purposes. One purpose is to give step-by-step instruction on how to perform an activity, such as taking a photograph or changing a tire. The intended audience would be people who want or need to perform the process but don't know how to do it. The other purpose is to explain a process, not to teach someone how to perform it. For example, a biology teacher would explain the process of photosynthesis to help students understand how green plants function, not to teach them how to transform sunlight into chlorophyll. Instructions may use the pronoun *you;* explanations do not. (This is a good time to ask your instructor about when to use *you* in college writing—and when not to use it.)

EXAMPLES OF PROCESS WRITING

Read the following two examples of process writing. What is the purpose of each paragraph? How can you tell? What are some words in each paragraph that indicate sequence?

Jacketing was a sleight-of-hand I watched with wonder each time, and I have discovered that my father was admired among sheepmen up and down the valley for his skill at it: He was just pretty catty at that, the way he could get that ewe to take on a new lamb every time. Put simply, jacketing was a ruse played on a ewe whose lamb had died. A substitute lamb quickly would be singled out, most likely from a set of twins. Sizing up the tottering newcomer, Dad would skin the dead lamb, and into the tiny pelt carefully snip four leg holes and a head hole. Then the stand-in lamb would have the skin fitted onto it like a snug jacket on a poodle. The next step of disguise was to cut out the dead lamb's liver and smear it several times across the jacket of pelt. In its borrowed and bedaubed skin, the new baby lamb then was presented to the ewe. She would sniff the baby impostor endlessly, distrustful but pulled by the blood-smell of her own. When in a few days she made up her dim sheep's mind to accept the lamb, Dad snipped away the jacket and recited his victory: Mother him like hell now, don't ye? See what a hellava dandy lamb I got for ye, old sister? Who says I couldn't jacket day onto night if I wanted to, now-I-ask-ye? —Ivan Doig, *This House of Sky*

◆

If you are inexperienced in relaxation techniques, begin by sitting in a comfortable chair with your feet on the floor and your hands resting easily in your lap. Close your eyes and breathe evenly, deeply, and gently. As you exhale each breath let your body become more relaxed. Starting with one hand direct your attention to one part of your body at a time. Close your fist and tighten the muscles of your forearm. Feel the sensation of tension in your muscles. Relax your hand and let your forearm and hand become completely limp. Direct all your attention to the sensation of relaxation as you continue to let all tension leave your hand and arm. Continue this practice once or several times each day, relaxing your other hand and arm, your legs, back, abdomen, chest, neck, face, and scalp. When you have this mastered and can relax completely, turn your thoughts to scenes of natural tranquillity from your past. Stay with your inner self as long as you wish, whether thinking of nothing or visualizing only the loveliest of images. Often you will become completely unaware of your surroundings. When you open your eyes you will find yourself refreshed in mind and body. —Laurence J. Peter, *The Peter Prescription*

Thinking ↔ Writing Activity

Writing Process Descriptions

Write two substantive paragraphs about two processes that you understand very well. In one, give instructions to a specific audience who would benefit from learning how to perform this activity. In the other, explain a process—but do not give instructions.

Although we often think of process descriptions in terms of more finite, daily events and activities like those previously described, we also apply these concepts to the larger and more profound processes of living, such as the life passages each person goes through from birth to death. The following article describes the work of Elisabeth Kübler-Ross, who has devoted her life to exploring the process of dying and to helping people navigate this final life passage.

We Are Breaking the Silence About Death

BY DANIEL GOLEMAN

Psychiatrist Elisabeth Kübler-Ross and I were to meet and fly together to Colorado Springs, where she was to give a workshop for nurses, doctors and volunteers who work with dying patients. Our flight was soon to board, but there was no sign of Kübler-Ross. Then she appeared, bustling down the corridor, a small, wiry woman carrying two huge shoulder-bags. After the briefest exchange of amenities, she explained that she was concerned that one of her patients might be late *for* the flight. The patient was to be one of 12 dying people at the seminar. They would teach those who work with the dying by sharing their private fears and hopes.

At the last minute her patient, an emaciated but smiling woman, showed up at the gate. Kübler-Ross and I had planned to talk on the plane, but instead she spent the entire flight giving her patient emergency oxygen. Later I learned that Kübler-Ross had met her patient the week before. She saw that the woman had only a few more weeks or months to live, and learned that she had never traveled far from her hometown. So, on the spur of the moment, Kübler-Ross invited her to come along as her guest. She should, the doctor felt, live her remaining days fully.

Kübler-Ross began her work with the dying in the mid '60s when she decided to interview a dying patient for a medical-school seminar she was teaching. She searched the school's 600-bed hospital, asking the staff on each ward if there were any dying patients. On every ward she got the same answer: No. Yet on any given day in a hospital that size, many patients are near death. When she then went back and asked about specific patients, their doctors reluctantly admitted that they were terminally ill.

Medical schools in those days avoided the topic of death and dying. Medical staffs treated the physical problems of their dying patients but, more often than not, ignored the fact of approaching death. Virtually no one, the doctor included, was comfortable with the fact of death. It was taboo, best kept out of sight and out of mind.

5   Once a patient died, he vanished. One of Kübler-Ross's students realized that in all her months as a hospital resident she could hardly recall seeing a dead person. In part she chose to avoid them, but there was also "the remarkable disappearing act that occurs as the body is cleverly whisked out of sight . . ."

In the decade since Kübler-Ross first gave her seminar on dying, the taboo has weakened. Death is in vogue as a topic of books, seminars, scholarly articles, and classes at every level from college down to elementary school. There are two professional journals devoted to the study of death, dozens of volunteer groups working with the dying, and one or two medical facilities geared solely to helping people die with dignity.

There is no single cause for this change, but Elisabeth Kübler-Ross has done more to further it than any other person. Through her 1969 best seller *On Death and Dying*, her seminars for physicians, clergy, and others who work with dying people, and her public talks, Kübler-Ross has alerted us to a new way of handling dying.

Kübler-Ross is Chairman of the National Advisory Council to Hospice in New Haven, Connecticut, which leads the way in humane care of the dying. Modeled on a similar center in London, New Haven Hospice puts Kübler-Ross's advice into practice with a team on call around-the-clock to help people die in their own homes rather than in a strange hospital. Hospice has plans for building a center for dying patients. In contrast to policy at most hospitals, family members will be encouraged to join the medical staff in caring for their dying relatives. Visiting hours will be unlimited, and patients, children and even pets will be free to visit.

Kübler-Ross's natural openness toward the dying reflects her experience as a child in rural Switzerland. In her community, she saw death confronted with honesty and dignity. She also has the authority of one whose medical practice has been limited for the last decade to dying patients and their families; lately, her practice has been restricted to dying children. Her public life as an author and a lecturer allows her a rare luxury in her medical work; she charges no one for her services.

10   Kübler-Ross's career has been unusually humanitarian from the start. Before entering medical school in Switzerland, she worked at the close of the Second World War in eastern Europe, helping the survivors of bombed-out cities and death camps. After becoming a psychiatrist, she gravitated to treating chronic schizophrenics, and then to work with retarded children, whose mental slowness was compounded by being deaf, dumb or blind.

From the thousands of hours she has spent with patients facing death, Kübler-Ross has charted the psychological stages people typically go through once they know they are soon to die. Though any single person need not go through the entire progression, most everyone facing death experiences at least one of these stages. The usual progression is from denial of death through rage, bargaining, depression, and finally, acceptance.

These reactions are not restricted to dying, but can occur with a loss of any kind. We all experience them to some degree in the ordinary course of life changes. Every change is a loss, every beginning an end. In the words of the Tibetan poet Milarepa, "All worldly pursuits end in sorrow, acquisition in dispersion, buildings in destruction, meetings in separation, birth in death."

A person's first reaction to the news that he has a terminal disease is most often denial. The refusal to accept the fact that one is soon to die cushions death's impact. It gives a person time to come to grips with the loss of everything that has mattered to him.

Psychoanalysts recognize that at the unconscious level, a person does not believe he will die. From this refusal to believe in one's own death springs the hope that, despite a life-threatening illness, one will not die. This hope can take many forms: that the diagnosis is wrong, that the illness is curable, that a miracle treatment will turn up. As denial fades into a partial acceptance, the person's concern shifts from the hope of longer life to the wish that his or her family will be well and his affairs taken care of after his death.

15   Denial too often typifies the hospital staff's reaction to a patient who faces death. Doctors and nurses see themselves as healers; a dying patient threatens this role. Further, a person who cannot contemplate his own death, even if he is a physician, feels discomfort with someone who is dying. For this reason hospital staff often enclose the dying patient in a cocoon of medical details that keeps death under wraps.

Sociologists Barney Glaser and Anselm Strauss studied the mutual pretense that often exists when patient and staff know the patient is dying. A staff member and a terminal patient might safely talk about his disease, they found, so long as they skirt its fatal significance. But they were most comfortable when they stuck to safe topics like movies and fashions—anything, in short, that signifies life going on as usual.

This is a fragile pretense, but not one that either party can easily break. Glaser and Strauss found that a patient would sometimes send cues to the staff that he wanted to talk about dying, but the nurses and doctors would decide not to talk openly with him because they feared he would go to pieces. The patient would openly make a remark acknowledging his death, but the doctor or nurse would ignore him. Then, out of tact or empathy for the embarrassment or distress he caused, the patient would resume his silence. In this case, it is the staff's uneasiness that maintains the pretense, not the patient's.

In the reverse instance, a doctor may give the patient an opening to talk about dying, and have the patient ignore it. Kübler-Ross urges hospital staff members to let the patient know that they are available to talk about dying, but not to force the subject on the patient. When he no longer needs to deny his death, the patient will seek out a staff member and open the topic.

When the family knows a patient is dying and keeps the secret from him, they create a barrier that prevents both patient and family from preparing for the death. The dying patient usually sees through a make-believe, smiling mask. Genuine emotions are much easier on the patient, allowing relatives to share his feelings. When his family can be open about the seriousness of the illness, there is time to talk and cry together and to take care of important matters under less emotional pressure.

20   A student nurse hospitalized for a fatal illness wrote to her professional colleagues in a nursing journal: "You slip in and out of my room, give me medications and check my blood pressure. Is it because I am a student nurse myself that

I sense your fright? If only we could be honest, both admit our fears, touch one another. Then it might not be so hard to die—in a hospital—with friends close by."

Denial becomes increasingly hard as the patient's health deteriorates. Although mutual pretense avoids embarrassment and emotional strains, it sacrifices valuable time in which the dying patient and his family could take care of unfinished emotional and practical matters, like unsettled arguments or unwritten wills, that death will forestall forever.

Kübler-Ross feels that a period of denial is useful if it gives the patient and his family time to find a way to deal with the stark truth of death. But when denial persists until the person dies, the survivors' grief is needlessly prolonged by the guilt and regrets. Often patients near death say they wished they had been told they were dying sooner so that they could have prepared themselves and their families.

A few rare patients, though, need to cling to denial because the reality is too much to bear. When those closest to the person offer no love or comfort, as when children of the dying patient blame the parent for deserting them, the patient may deny the inevitable to the very end. But this is rare; of 500 patients, Kübler-Ross found only four who refused to the last to admit that they were dying.

Once a dying patient accepts the invitation to talk about his death, Kübler-Ross tries to help him recognize any unfinished business that needs his attention. Straightforward truth helps the dying person fully live the time left. She tries to elicit their hidden hopes and needs, then find someone who can fulfill these needs.

25 Physical pain sometimes prevents a dying patient from making the best use of his remaining days. When his pain is overwhelming, he either becomes preoccupied with it or dependent on painkillers that leave him groggy. Kübler-Ross controls pain with Brompton's mixture. This old-time formula of morphine, cocaine, alcohol, syrup, and chloroform water dulls the patient's pain without dimming his alertness.

When a patient stops denying his impending death, the feelings that most often well up are rage and anger. The question, "Why me?" is asked with bitterness. The patient aims his resentment at whoever is handy, be it staff, friends or family. Healthy people remind the patient that he will die while they live. The unfairness of it all arouses his rage. He may be rude, uncooperative, or downright hostile. For example, when a nurse was late with his pain medication, the patient snapped "Why are you late? You don't care if I suffer. Your coffee break is more important to you than my pain."

As the rage abates the patient may start to bargain with God or fate, trying to arrange a temporary truce. The question switches from "Why me?" to "Why now?" He hopes for more time to finish things, to put his house in order, to arrange for his family's future needs, to make a will. The bargain with God takes the form of the patient promising to be good or to do something in exchange for another week, month, or year of life.

With full acceptance of his approaching death, a person often becomes depressed. Dying brings him a sense of hopelessness, helplessness and isolation. He mourns past losses, and regrets things left undone or wrongs he's committed. One of Kübler-Ross's patients, for example, regretted that when his daughter was small and needed him, he was on the road making money to provide a good home. Now that he was dying, he wanted to spend every moment he could with her, but she was grown and had her own friends. He felt it was too late. At this stage the dying person starts to mourn his own death, the loss of all the people and things he has found meaningful, the plans and hopes never to be fulfilled. Kübler-Ross calls this kind of depression a "preparatory grief." It allows a person to get ready for his death by letting go of his attachments to life.

During this preparatory grief, the patient may stop seeing family and friends, and become withdrawn and silent. His outer detachment matches the inner renunciation of what once mattered to him. Family members sometimes misinterpret his detachment as a rejection. Kübler-Ross helps them to see that the patient is beginning to accept his death. Hence, he needs much less contact with family and friends.

30   After this preparatory mourning, the dying person can reach a peaceful acceptance. He is no longer concerned with the prolongation of his life. He has made peace with those he loves, settled his affairs, relinquished his unfinished dreams. He may feel an inner calm, and become mellow in outlook. He can take things as they come, including the progress of his illness. People bring him pleasure, but he no longer speaks of plans for the future. His focus becomes the simple joys of everyday life; he enjoys today without waiting for tomorrow. At this stage, the person is ready to live his remaining days fully and die well. The story of a modern Zen master's death shows this frame of mind. As the master lay dying, one of his students brought him a special cake, of which he had always been fond. With a wan smile the master slowly ate a piece of the cake. As he grew weaker still, his students leaned close and asked if he had any final words for them. "Yes," he said, as they leaned forward eagerly. "My, but this cake is delicious."

What the dying teach us, says Kübler-Ross, is how to live. In summing up what she has learned from her dying patients, she likes to recite a poem by Richard Allen that goes:

. . . as you face your death, it is only the love you have given and received which will count. . . . if you have loved well then it will have been worth it . . . but if you have not death will always come too soon and be too terrible to face.

Critical Reading Questions

1. What process is described in this essay? Where in this essay is the process explained? Identify the steps that are given.

2. Obviously, the process discussed in this piece is not a mechanical one but rather a complex emotional and psychological sequence. Think of another such human process, perhaps one that you have experienced. What is it, and what are its stages?

3. Write your personal reaction to the ideas in this essay. If someone close to you has died recently, you may have strong reactions. If you

have not experienced a loved one's death, you might respond with less emotion. Do you want to share this writing? Why or why not?

4. This article was first published in 1976. Are its concepts still relevant? What connections do you see with current questions about the "right to die"?

Writing Project: A Narrative Showing the Effect of a Perception

The readings and Thinking-Writing Activities in this chapter encourage you to become more aware of your perceptions and to use perceptions in writing descriptions and time sequences. Be sure to reread what you wrote for previous activities because you may be able to use some of it to complete this project.

Write a narrative essay telling about an experience that you had in which another person's perception had an effect on you. The perception should be about a social issue such as concerns about ethnicity, gender, age, education, or job status. You may have been treated in a certain way because of the person's perception about this issue and your connection to it. What impact did this treatment have on you? Do you understand why the other person has (or had) this perception? Describe and tell about the perception and its effects as clearly as you can.

As part of your preparation for writing your essay, find a magazine or newspaper article dealing with the perception and quote from it at least once in your essay. Document the quoted material according to your instructor's directions. If an academic documentation format such as that of the Modern Language Association (MLA) or American Psychological Association (APA) is required, be sure that your entry conforms exactly to the models in a writing handbook. After drafting your essay, revise it to the best of your ability. Follow your instructor's directions for topic limitations, length, format, and so on.

Principles for Writing Narratives

The following principles for writing narratives are not fixed rules; you may have good reasons for not following some of them. In general, though, they should help you to write an effective essay.

1. Identify the relevant issue fully so that the narrative has a meaningful context.

2. State your thesis well; place it effectively in your paper.

3. Use description to introduce your readers to the people involved and to let them visualize the place. Consider whether subjective or objective description, or a combination of the two, will best serve your purpose.

4. Tell the story as fully as seems appropriate for your intended audience, without either rambling excessively or leaving out important details or events.

5. Be sure to begin and end effectively. The conclusion is likely to be especially important in this essay since you may want to reiterate your main point there.

THE WRITING SITUATION

Begin by considering the key elements in the Thinking-Writing Model.

Purpose You have a variety of purposes here. You have the opportunity to recall and relate a significant experience. You also can think about an issue that concerns you and learn more about it by finding the required article. In addition, you will be improving your ability to connect what you read with your own ideas, something you must do regularly as a college student. Most important, you can inform your classmates, your instructor, and your other readers about a social issue that concerns you and about the impact of another person's perception of that same issue.

Audience As always, you are a member of your own audience and perhaps the person who will enjoy the narrative most since it is connected with your life. Your classmates will be a good audience, both to learn from your narrative and to share your experience. In addition, they are valuable as peer reviewers of your draft, reacting as intelligent readers who are also immersed in the assignment. Of course, anyone else who has had a similar experience would also benefit from reading your essay. Perhaps your campus newspaper would be interested. Finally, your instructor remains the audience who will judge how well you have planned, drafted, and revised. As a writing teacher, he or she cares about a clear focus, logical organization, specific details, and correctness. Keep these aspects in mind as you revise, edit, and proofread.

Subject Although you and your readers are probably concerned about many perceptual issues, both you and they may need to be reminded of how an issue and a person's perceptions of it can affect someone else. People do at times forget how connected they may be to situations presented in the media. To what extent does your narrative illuminate a widespread situation in society?

Writer You are in a dual position here. You are, of course, the expert on your own story. This is both an advantage and a disadvantage: no one can argue with you about your story, but you still need to remember that your audience was not there. You must provide them with sufficient background and description to make them feel as if they did share your experience, but you don't want to overwhelm them with details. Therefore, you will need to be selective as you decide what to include and what to omit. Also, remember that you are not the expert on the article from which you plan to quote, so do think carefully about what it says and where to use it in your own work.

THE WRITING PROCESS

The following sections will guide you through the stages of generating, planning, drafting, and revising as you work on a descriptive and illustrative narrative.

Generating Ideas

1. You may immediately recall a meaningful experience that you want to narrate. If not, think about past events that were worrisome, frightening, amusing, or exciting and then think again about the context of the event.

2. You may be deeply involved in dealing with others' perceptions of social issues because of who you are, where you live, or which organizations you support. If so, you should have no problem identifying a concern you want to address. If not, look around, talk with friends and family members, read newspapers and magazines, and watch the news.

3. Think locally. Look at issues in your community or those connected with your college or job. Then try to recall any experiences in which another person's perceptions had an impact on you.

4. Think of how a perceptual stereotype may be part of a national or a worldwide one. Here, you will need to consult and acknowledge sources if you have not had direct experience with such situations.

Defining a Focus
Draft a thesis statement that connects your experience with the perception you plan to write about. You may want to emphasize the directness of the connection, or you may need to show that what is not obvious is indeed related. Perhaps you may wish to emphasize a time element: "I didn't understand at the time, but now I see that . . ." or "I knew at that moment that . . ." You may want to focus on the impact this perception has had on your life.

Organizing Ideas
You could tell the story first and then connect it with the perceptual stereotype. Or you might make statements about the perception regularly throughout the narration as different events illustrate various aspects of the situation. In either case, your use of chronological order will help your audience follow the events of your story. Therefore, unless you see some serious reason not to do so, give background information first and then guide your audience through the time sequence of the events. You need to consider what arrangements will best help your audience see their connection to the issue. Be

sure to select and place carefully the material quoted from your source and to incorporate it smoothly into your writing by introducing and commenting on it.

Drafting Begin with the easiest part to write, possibly the experience itself. Tell it fully; then plan to increase its effectiveness by including sharp details and a tight sequence of events at the revision stage. The paragraphs within the narrative may or may not have topic sentences. This is one of the differences between narration and exposition. Since your purpose is to connect the experience with others' perceptions, you may want to have topic sentences for the paragraphs which do that.

After you have drafted the narrative, draft the paragraphs that state the thesis and make the connection between the experience and the issue. Then establish and write any necessary transitions.

Revising One of the best revision strategies is to get an audience's reactions to your draft. If you are writing about an experience in which others were involved, you could ask them to read and comment on your draft.

If your instructor allows class time for peer review (shown on pages 65–66 and 105–107) be sure to have a draft ready so that you can benefit from this activity. Use your classmates' questions to improve your draft before next working through these revision questions. If you did not work with classmates, let these questions guide you in revising.

1. **Think big.** Look at your draft as a whole.

   - Does it tell about a time when someone's perception affected you? Is it clear what the effect on you was? Does it include relevant quoted material from a magazine or newpaper? Does it follow your instructor's requirements for length and format?

   - How could the connection between the person's perception and its effect on you be stated more clearly? What parts of the draft, if any, do not relate to the thesis?

   - How could the draft be reorganized to make it more logical? How could the flow between paragraphs be made smoother? Could you add transitions to indicate chronological order?

   - Could the quoted material be placed more effectively?

   - Is your point of view consistent throughout?

2. **Think medium.** Look at your draft paragraph by paragraph.

   - How could you rewrite your introduction to make your audience more interested in reading about the way you were perceived?

   - Do all body paragraphs support this thesis? Do they use topic sentences effectively? Does each present relevant, specific information not presented elsewhere in your essay? Can any paragraphs be combined or eliminated?

   - Where could transitions be used to improve the flow within a body paragraph?

- Does the conclusion provide a satisfying ending by showing how the perception affected you? Or is it effective in some other way? (See the suggestions for being creative with conclusions on pages 80–81 of Chapter 3.)
- Is the conclusion appropriate in tone?

3. **Think small.** Look at your draft sentence by sentence.

   - Which sentences are difficult to understand? How could you reword them?
   - Are you using objective or subjective language? Do you want to make any changes to your language?
   - Should some sentences be shortened or combined?
   - Which sentences seem vague? How could you clarify them?
   - Which, if any, sentences have errors in standard English grammar or usage? How could you correct them?

4. **Think "picky."** Look at your draft as the fussiest critic might.

   - Which words are not clear or not quite right for your meaning? What words could you use instead?
   - Are any words spelled incorrectly? (Run the spell checker on your computer, but don't rely on it alone.)
   - Is your documentation correct? Double-check your handbook for format and punctuation in documentation.
   - Are the pages numbered consecutively?
   - Does your draft make a good impression by being neat?
   - Is there anything else you can do to improve your draft?

Editing and Proofreading After you prepare a final draft, check once again for standard grammar and punctuation usage. Proofread carefully to detect omitted words or punctuation marks. Make sure your quotations from the article begin and end with quotation marks. Run your spelling checker program, but be aware of its limitations. Proofread carefully for the kinds of errors the computer can't catch.

The following essay shows how one student responded to this assignment.

STUDENT WRITING

Unfair Expectations

BY ANGELICA WILLEY

The most influential people in a child's world are her or his parents. Parents, therefore, should try to be aware of their biases based on traditions inherited from their upbringings that are not appropriate for a younger generation. If they are not careful, parents can limit the potential of their children by not recognizing that some preconceived notions that they carry over from their childhoods are not helpful to their children. This situation happened in my life when my father couldn't reconcile his generation's version of gender roles with a more modern version for the raising of his children.

My father is a born and bred southern gentleman. Being raised on the eastern shore (across the Bay), he connects with the old southern way of doing things. He plants Crepe Myrtles, refuses to walk ahead of a lady through a doorway, and speaks with a slight accent if you catch him off guard. However, he also has a tendency towards admiring "southern" ladies who carry parasols to shield the sun and act out an overplayed shyness to attract "gentleman callers." Somehow he envisioned me as fitting into that mold, and he took it upon himself to make sure that I lived up to those standards which he admired.

The earliest incident which I can recall of my father's acting on these notions occurred when my best childhood friend from across the road took off his shirt to relieve the heat of a summer day. Watching this, through my five-year-old eyes, I decided to also cool down by removing my shirt. Upon seeing this, my father flew out of the house and herded me inside, all the while trying to explain why I could not do the same thing as a boy. These tendencies became most apparent after the birth of my brother.

Though I was five years his senior, my brother was treated as if, solely due to his gender, he was entitled to special privileges in some areas. For example, he was allowed to get his driver's license at the minimum age of sixteen because he had to take girls out on dates. I was told that I would not be allowed to have my license until I turned eighteen because it was not a necessity—my dates could pick me up. Never mind that I had a job, internship, and a school career to maintain. While I'm sure that he sent my brother back to wash his face when we were going out, his nudges at me to go back and put on some make-up and change to a dress had a negative effect on my attitude and my self-esteem.

Today I know that my father was not trying to inhibit me. He was simply acting on the way he was raised. He probably wanted me to become the kind of woman that one article calls "The Princess, the most desirable woman in patriarchal culture and fantasy," a woman who "waits for a man to make her life meaningful" (Gilbert and Webster 47). However, I don't want to be a helpless, flirtatious "princess." I want to be an independent, capable person who has good relationships with men, and with women. I like to look nice, but I don't want to worry very much about make-up and dresses. Most of my fellow female students feel the same way that I do.

I suppose that there will always be generation gaps. However, parents need to think about their hand-me-down ideals and try to have fair expectations that fit with their children's generation's ideas.

Work Cited

Gilbert, Lucy, and Paula Webster. "The Dangers of Femininity." In *The Gender Reader.* Edited by Evelyn Ashton Jones and Gary Olson. Boston: Allyn and Bacon, 1991.

7

Exploring Perspectives

"Nothing that God ever made is the same thing to more than one person."
—Zora Neale Hurston

Writing to Compare

Critical Thinking Focus: Critically evaluating perceptions and perspectives

Writing Focus: Using comparative thinking

Reading Theme: Differing perspectives from history

Writing Project: Comparing perspectives on an issue or an event

Chapter 6 introduced the concept of perceptions and showed how writers use their perceptions when they describe, narrate, and explain processes. As critical thinkers and thoughtful writers, however, we need to go beyond simply recognizing that people have different perceptions. We have to think carefully about perceptions. In addition, we need to see how *perceptions*—messages from the senses—are connected to *perspectives*—points of view that develop from and also influence perceptions.

This chapter emphasizes critical evaluation of perceptions and perspectives. It will help you think about the differing points of view that people bring to what they say and write. Perspectives often conflict with one another, so you then must try to determine which one makes the most sense. You need to be able to analyze the differences and similarities that you find.

Because so many life situations and college assignments involve comparing and contrasting perspectives in an organized way, this chapter presents strategies for using comparative analysis in thinking and writing. The Writing Project asks you to analyze different perspectives on one event or issue.

Perceptions and Perspectives

Perspectives, or points of view, are what people express when they speak and write and also the vantage points from which they perceive events or issues. So a complex interaction exists between perceptions and perspectives. People's perspectives are formed by beliefs, interests, needs, age, gender, nationality, ethnicity, health, education—the multiple factors of life. These factors of perspective influence perceptions; at the same time, perceptions continuously influence perspectives.

To understand how various people can be exposed to the same stimuli or events and yet have different perceptions, it helps to imagine that each of us views the world through personal "contact lenses," an analogy from the previous chapter. (You might think of the factors that go into forming perspectives as the prescription for the lenses!)

We aren't usually aware that we are wearing these lenses. Instead, without our realizing it, our lenses act as filters that select and shape what we perceive. When members of your class had different perceptions of the person pictured at the desk in the Thinking-Writing Activity on page 217, they were caused by the different lenses through which each of you views the world.

To understand how people perceive the world, we have to understand their individual lenses, which influence how they actively select, organize, and interpret the events in their experience. A diagram of the process might look like Figure 7.1.

Examine the following pairs of statements. In each pair, two people are being exposed to the same basic stimulus or event, yet the perception of one differs greatly from that of the other. Explain how the various perceptions might have developed.

Figure 7.1 Differing Perceptions of an Event

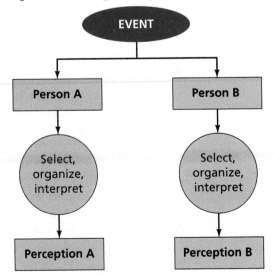

1. a. That chili was much too spicy to eat.

   Explanation: _____

   b. That chili needed more hot peppers and chili powder to spice it up a little.

   Explanation: _____

2. a. People who wear lots of makeup and jewelry are very sophisticated.

   Explanation: _____

   b. People who wear lots of makeup and jewelry are ostentatious and overdressed.

   Explanation: _____

3. a. The music young people enjoy listening to is a highly creative cultural expression.

   Explanation: _____

   b. The music young people enjoy listening to is obnoxious noise.

   Explanation: _____

4. a. I really enjoy how stimulating and intellectually challenging this English class is.

   Explanation: _____

   b. This English class is too much work. All the teacher wants to do is make us think, think, think. It makes my head hurt.

   Explanation: _____

Effective critical thinkers are aware of the lenses that they—and others—are wearing. People unaware of the nature of their own lenses can often mistake their own perceptions for objective truth, not having examined either the facts or others' perceptions of a given issue.

In the cartoon "The Investigation," each witness is giving what he or she (or it!) believes is an accurate description of the man in the center, and all are unaware that their descriptions are being influenced by who they are and the way that they perceive things.

SELECTING PERCEPTIONS: WHY DO WE NOTICE THE THINGS WE NOTICE?

We tend to select perceptions about subjects that have been called to our attention. For instance, at the age of three, one author's child suddenly became aware of beards. On entering a subway car, she would ask in a penetrating voice, "Any beards here?" and proceed to count them out loud. In so doing, she naturally focused her parents' attention—as well as that of other passengers—on beards.

Another aspect of our perceiving lenses is our tendency to notice what we need, desire, or otherwise find interesting. When we go shopping, we focus on whatever items we are looking for. Walking down the street, we tend to notice certain kinds of people or events while completely ignoring others. Even while watching a movie or reading a book, we tend to concentrate on and remember the elements most meaningful to us. Another person can perform *exactly* the same actions—shop at the same store, walk down the same street, read the same book, or go to the same movie—and yet notice and remember entirely different things.

THE INVESTIGATION

HE WAS A REAL TALL GUY DRESSED NORMALLY, WITH LIGHT, DRY HAIR.

HE WAS A HEALTHY, GOOD LOOKING YOUNG KID... BUT DRESSED RATHER SHABBILY.

HE WAS REAL BIG AND REAL OLD.

HE WAS A WELL-DRESSED SORT, A LITTLE OVERWEIGHT AND WITH A LOT OF HAIR.

I REMEMBER HE HAD A LARGE HEAD AND HE SMELLED FUNNY.

HE WAS SURELY A WESTERNER.

HE WAS A SCRAWNY LITTLE SHORT-HAIRED TWERP FROM BACK EAST.

HE HAD DARK HAIR AND A CUTE NOSE. A REAL DOLL.

HE WAS A ROUGH, FURRY GUY WITH LITTLE BEADY EYES PROBABLY INEDIBLE

Although we tend to focus on what is familiar, normally we are not aware of doing so. In fact, we often take for granted what is familiar to us—the taste of chili or eggs, the street that we live on, our family or friends—and normally don't think about how we perceive it. When something happens that makes the familiar seem strange and unfamiliar, though, we do become aware of our perceptions and start to evaluate them.

To sum up, we actively select our perceptions on the basis of

- What has been called to our attention
- What our needs or interests are
- What our moods or feelings are
- What seems familiar or unfamiliar
- What our backgrounds are

The way in which we select perceptions is a paramount factor in shaping the lenses through which we view the world and it influences our writing to a great extent. Our writing is based on the points we choose to make, the details we select to include. Even when different people are writing about the same subject, the results are often very different because their lenses and their perspectives lead them to make different selections.

ORGANIZING PERCEPTIONS

Not only do you actively select certain perceptions; you also actively organize them into meaningful relationships and patterns. Carefully examine Figure 6.2 from page 216, Chapter 6. Do you see both the young woman and the old woman? If you do, try switching your perspective back and forth between the two images. As you do so, notice how for each image, you are doing the following things:

- *Selecting* certain lines, shapes, and shadings on which to focus your attention
- *Organizing* these lines, shapes, and shadings into different patterns
- *Interpreting* these patterns as representing things you can recognize—a hat, a nose, a chin

We naturally try to order and organize what we are experiencing into patterns and relationships that make sense to us. When we succeed in doing so, the completed whole means more than the sum of the individual parts. We are continually organizing the world in this way during virtually every waking moment. We do not live in a world of isolated sounds, patches of color, random odors, and individual textures. Instead, we live in a world of objects and people, language and music—a world in which all these individual stimuli are woven together. We are able to perceive this world of complex experiences because we can organize the individual stimuli we are receiving into relationships that have meaning for us.

This organizing process is integral to the writing process. When you write an essay, compose a letter, or create a story, you are actively organizing the ideas you selected to include into various relationships. Instead of simply stringing together words, you are developing a coherent structure through which to communicate thoughts and feelings.

INTERPRETING PERCEPTIONS

Besides selecting and organizing perceptions, we also actively interpret what we perceive: we are figuring out what something means. One of the elements that influences interpretations is the *context*, or overall situation, within which the perception is occurring. For example, imagine that you see a man running down the street. Your interpretation of his action will depend on the specific context. For example, is there a bus waiting at the corner? Is a police officer running behind him? Is the man wearing a jogging suit?

We are continually trying to interpret what we perceive, whether it is a design, someone else's behavior, or a social situation. As in the example of someone running down the street, many perceptions can be interpreted in more than one way. When a situation has more than one possible interpretation, it is ambiguous. The more ambiguous a situation is, the greater its possible meanings or interpretations.

Feelings often influence our interpretations of experience. When we feel happy and optimistic, the world often seems friendly and the future full of possibilities, so we interpret problems as challenges to be overcome. When we are depressed or unhappy, we may perceive the world entirely differently. The future can appear filled with problems that are trying to overwhelm us. In both cases the outer circumstances may be very similar; it is our own interpretations of the world through our lenses that vary so completely.

Perceptions of the world are also influenced by the perspectives that come from training and education. Consider two people watching a football game. One of them, who has very little understanding of football, sees merely a bunch of grown men hitting each other for no apparent reason. The other person, who loves football, sees complex play patterns, daring coaching strategies, effective blocking and tackling techniques, and zone defenses with seams that the receivers are trying to split. Both spectators have their eyes focused on the same event, but they are perceiving two entirely different situations. Their perceptions differ because each person is actively selecting, organizing, and interpreting the available stimuli in different ways.

The same is true of any situation in which we are perceiving something about which we have special knowledge or expertise. The following are examples.

- A builder examining the construction of a new house
- A musician attending a concert
- A naturalist experiencing the outdoors
- A chef tasting a dish just prepared
- A lawyer examining a contract

Naturally, your knowledge (or lack thereof) influences your writing in significant ways. When you are very familiar with a subject, your writing expresses an informed perspective, a knowledgeable point of view.

Thinking ↔ Writing Activity

How Knowledge Influences Perceptions

1. Think about one of your special areas of interest or expertise and about how your perceptions in that area might differ from those of people who don't share your knowledge. List some specific things that you would notice that others might not. Note how your knowledge influences what you see, hear, or otherwise perceive.

2. Write a paragraph telling of what you've noticed. Share it with classmates and see what they think about what you've said.

3. Respond to classmates' paragraphs. How do you perceive things in their areas of expertise?

4. Does this activity help you to understand perspectives?

Understanding Different Perspectives

The perceptions of a knowledgeable person usually differ substantially from those of a person who lacks such specialized knowledge. The following reading illuminates this point.

Two Ways of Viewing the River
BY MARK TWAIN

Now when I had mastered the language of this water and had come to know every trifling feature that bordered the great river as familiarly as I knew the letters of the alphabet, I had made a valuable acquisition. But I had lost something, too. I had lost something which could never be restored to me while I lived. All the grace, the beauty, the poetry, had gone out of the majestic river! I still kept in mind a certain wonderful sunset which I witnessed when steamboating was new to me. A broad expanse of the river was turned to blood; in the middle distance the red hue brightened into gold, through which a solitary log came floating, black and conspicuous; in one place a long, slanting mark lay sparkling upon the water; in another the surface was broken by boiling, tumbling rings that were as many-tinted as an opal; where the ruddy flush was faintest, was a smooth spot that was covered with graceful circles and radiating lines, ever so delicately traced; the shore on our left was densely wooded and the somber shadow that fell from this forest was broken in one place by a long, ruffled trail that shone like silver; and high above the forest wall a clean-stemmed dead tree waved a single leafy bough that glowed like a flame in the unobstructed splendor that was flowing from the sun. There were graceful curves, reflected images, woody heights, soft distances, and over the whole scene, far and near, the dissolving lights drifted steadily, enriching it every passing moment with new marvels of coloring.

I stood like one bewitched. I drank it in, in a speechless rapture. The world was new to me and I had never seen anything like this at home. But as I have said, a day came when I began to cease from noting the glories and the charms which the moon and the sun and the twilight wrought upon the river's face; another day came when I ceased altogether to note them. Then, if that sunset scene had been repeated, I should have looked upon it without rapture, and should have commented upon it inwardly after this fashion: "This sun means that we are going to have wind tomorrow; that floating log means that the river is rising, small thanks to it; that slanting mark on the water refers to a bluff reef which is going to kill somebody's steamboat one of these nights, if it keeps on stretching out like that; those tumbling 'boils' show a dissolving bar and a changing channel there; the lines and circles in the slick water over yonder are a warning that the troublesome place is shoaling up dangerously; that silver streak in the shadow of the forest is the 'break' from a new snag and he has located himself in the very best place he could have found to fish for steamboats; that tall dead tree, with a single living branch, is not going to last long, and then how is a body ever going to get through this blind place at night without the friendly old landmark?"

No, the romance and beauty were all gone from the river. All the value any feature of it had for me now was the amount of usefulness it could furnish toward compassing the safe piloting of a steamboat. Since those days, I have pitied doctors from my heart. What does the lovely flush in a beauty's cheek mean to a doctor but a "break" that ripples above some deadly disease? Are not all her visible charms sown thick with what are to him the signs and symbols of hidden decay? Does he ever see her beauty at all, or doesn't he simply view her professionally and comment upon her unwholesome condition all to himself? And doesn't he sometimes wonder whether he has gained most or lost most by learning his trade?

Critical Reading Questions

1. In this passage Twain provides a compelling description of the way developing a knowledgeable perspective as a river pilot influenced his perceptions of the river. How did his perceptions change? Why did he feel that his shift of perspective caused him to both gain and lose in his experience of the river?

2. Describe how your perception of something changed because you had learned more about it. Did you, like Twain, both lose and gain? Explain why or why not.

Acquired Knowledge

ANONYMOUS

When news of the Acquired Immune Deficiency Syndrome first began to spread, it was just another one of those issues on the news that I felt did not really concern me. Along with cancer, leukemia, and kidney failure, I knew these diseases ran rampant across the country, but they didn't affect me.

Once the AIDS crisis became a prevalent problem in society, I began to take a little notice of it, but my interest only extended as far as taking precautions to insure that I would not contract the disease. Sure, I felt sorry for all the people who were dying from it, but again, it was not my problem.

My father was an intravenous drug user for as long as I can remember. This was a fact of life when I was growing up. I knew that what he was doing was wrong, and that eventually he would die from it, but I also knew that he would never change.

On July 27th, my father died. An autopsy showed his cause of death as pneumonia and tuberculosis, seemingly natural causes. However, I was later informed that these were two very common symptoms related to carriers of the HIV virus. My father's years of drug abuse had finally caught up with him. He had died from AIDS.

My father's death changed my life. Prior to that, I had always felt that as long as a situation did not directly affect me, it was really no concern of mine. I felt that somewhere, someone would take care of it. Having a crisis strike so close to me made me wake up to reality. Suddenly I became acutely aware of all the things that are wrong in the world. I began to see the problems of AIDS, famine, homelessness, unemployment, and others from a personal point of view, and I began to feel that I had an obligation to join the crusade to do something about these problems.

I organized a youth coalition called UPLIFT INC. In this group, we meet and talk about the problems in society, as well as the everyday problems that any of our members may have in their lives. We organize shows (talent shows, fashion shows) and give a large portion of our proceeds to the American Foundation for AIDS Research, the Coalition for the Homeless, and many other worthy organizations.

Now I feel that I am doing my duty as a human being by trying to help those who are less fortunate than myself. My father's death gave me insight into my own mortality. Now I know that life is too short not only to try to enjoy it, but to really achieve something worthwhile out of it. Material gains matter only if you are willing to take your good fortune and spread it around to those who could use it.

Critical Reading Questions

1. Explain how the author's perception of AIDS changed after experiencing her father's death. How did this change of perception influence other areas of her life?

2. Describe an example in your own life in which your perceptions changed as a result of a   significant event.

Thinking ↔ Writing Activity

Looking at Car Ads

Carefully examine the advertisements for cars below.

1. What different perceptions about cars do these ads seem to want readers to adopt? List as many as you can. Do you think that these differences are related to the purposes of the ads?

2. Do you find any similarities in some of the ideas presented in the two ads? List any that you find. How did you respond to them?

3. Share your lists and comments with classmates. See if you have differing perceptions of the ads.

Get A Little Extra Mileage From Your Used Car

Since 1880, The Salvation Army has helped many people in lots of different ways because of your donations. So, when you get ready to donate that used car, think of us...your used car can help men in the area win the battle against drug/alcohol addiction and give them hope for a better life.

CALL TODAY
In Washington/Suburban MD-800-538-2438
In Northern Virginia-703-642-9270

Your donation is tax deductible, and towing is free.

TRUSTED FOR 120 YEARS!

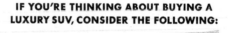

IF YOU'RE THINKING ABOUT BUYING A LUXURY SUV, CONSIDER THE FOLLOWING:

Have UN relief workers ever driven it into a war zone?

Has it ever discovered a lost city in the Arabian desert?

Has anyone ever written a song about it?

Has the Royal Geographical Society ever trekked across Afghanistan in it?

And can it breathe new life into your cul-de-sac?

With references like these, there's no question that a Land Rover is unlike any other vehicle on earth. Hardly surprising, considering its robust V8 engine (nicknamed 'Thor' by our engineers) and state-of-the-art, permanent four-wheel-drive system. Yes, the Discovery Series II SD has seen a lot, and thanks to a command driving position and Alpine windows, you can, too. Which leaves but one question unanswered: how much?

Thinking ↔ Writing Activity

Five Accounts of the Assassination of Malcolm X, 1965

Let's examine a situation in which a number of different people had differing perceptions about an event they were describing. Chapter 5 of this book contains a passage by Malcolm X (pages 168–170), written when he was just beginning his life's work. A few years later, this work came to a tragic end with his assassination at a meeting in Harlem. As you read through the various accounts, pay particular attention to the perceptions each presents. After reading the accounts, analyze some of the differences in these perceptions by writing answers to the questions that follow. Your instructor may decide to limit your analysis to two or three of the accounts.

1. What details of the events has each writer selected to focus on?

2. How has each writer organized the selected details? Remember that most newspapers give what they consider the most important information first.

3. How does each writer depict Malcolm X, his followers, the gunmen, and the significance of the assassination?

The *New York Times* (February 22, 1965)

Malcolm X, the 39-year-old leader of a militant Black Nationalist movement, was shot to death yesterday afternoon at a rally of his followers in a ballroom in Washington Heights. The bearded Negro extremist had said only a few words of greeting when a fusillade rang out. The bullets knocked him over backwards.

A 22-year-old Negro, Thomas Hagan, was charged with the killing. The police rescued him from the ballroom crowd after he had been shot and beaten.

Pandemonium broke out among the 400 Negroes in the Audubon Ballroom at 160th Street and Broadway. As men, women and children ducked under tables and flattened themselves on the floor, more shots were fired. The police said seven bullets struck Malcolm. Three other Negroes were shot. Witnesses reported that as many as 30 shots had been fired. About two hours later the police said the shooting had apparently been a result of a feud between followers of Malcolm and members of the extremist group he broke with last year, the Black Muslims. . . .

Life (March 5, 1965)

His life oozing out through a half dozen or more gunshot wounds in his chest, Malcolm X, once the shrillest voice of black supremacy, lay dying on the stage of a Manhattan auditorium. Moments before, he had stepped up to the lectern and 400 of the faithful had settled down expectantly to hear the sort of speech for which he was famous—flaying the hated white man. Then a scuffle broke out in the hall and Malcolm's bodyguards bolted from his side to break it up—only to discover that they had been faked out. At least two men with pistols rose from the audience and pumped bullets into the speaker, while a third cut loose at close range with both barrels of a sawed-off shotgun. In the confusion the pistol man got away. The shotgunner lunged through the crowd and out the door, but not before the guards came to their wits and shot him in the leg. Outside he was swiftly overtaken by other supporters of Malcolm and very likely would have been stomped to death if the police hadn't saved him. Most shocking of all to the residents of Harlem was the fact that Malcolm had been killed not by "whitey" but by members of his own race.

The *New York Post* (February 22, 1965)

They came early to the Audubon Ballroom, perhaps drawn by the expectation that Malcolm X would name the men who firebombed his home last Sunday. . . . I sat at the left in the 12th row and, as we waited, the man next to me spoke of Malcolm and his followers: "Malcolm is our only hope. You can depend on him to tell it like it is and to give Whitey hell."

There was a prolonged ovation as Malcolm walked to the rostrum. Malcolm looked up and said "A salaam aleikum (Peace be unto you)" and the audience replied "We aleikum salaam (And unto you, peace)."

Bespectacled and dapper in a dark suit, sandy hair glinting in the light, Malcolm said: "Brothers and sisters . . ." He was interrupted by two men in the center of the ballroom, who rose and, arguing with each other, moved forward. Then there was a scuffle at the back of the room. I heard Malcolm X say his last words: "Now, brothers, break it up," he said softly. "Be cool, be calm."

Then all hell broke loose. There was a muffled sound of shots and Malcolm, blood on his face and chest, fell limply back over the chairs behind him. The two men who had approached him ran to the exit on my side of the room, shooting wildly behind them as they ran. I heard people screaming, "Don't let them kill him." "Kill those bastards." At an exit I saw some of Malcolm's men beating with all their strength on two men. I saw a half dozen of Malcolm's followers bending over his inert body on the stage. Their clothes stained with their leader's blood.

Four policemen took the stretcher and carried Malcolm through the crowd and some of the women came out of their shock and one said: "I hope he doesn't die, but I don't think he's going to make it."

Associated Press (February 22, 1965)

A week after being bombed out of his Queens home, Black Nationalist leader Malcolm X was shot to death shortly after 3 (P.M.) yesterday at a Washington Heights rally of 400 of his devoted followers. Early today, police brass ordered a homicide charge placed against a 22-year-old man they rescued from a savage beating by Malcolm X supporters after the shooting. The suspect, Thomas Hagan, had been shot in the left leg by one of Malcolm's bodyguards as, police said, Hagan and another assassin fled when pandemonium erupted. Two other men were wounded in the wild burst of firing from at least three weapons. The firearms were a .38, a .45 automatic and a sawed-off shotgun. Hagan allegedly shot Malcolm X with the shotgun, a double-barrelled sawed-off weapon on which the stock also had been shortened, possibly to facilitate concealment. Cops charged Reuben Frances, of 871 E. 179th St., Bronx, with felonious assault in the shooting of Hagan, and with Sullivan Law violation—possession of the .45. Police recovered the shotgun and the .45.

The *Amsterdam News* (February 27, 1965)

"We interrupt this program to bring you a special newscast . . .," the announcer said as the Sunday afternoon movie on the TV set was halted temporarily. "Malcolm X was shot four times while addressing a crowd at the Audubon Ballroom on 166th Street." "Oh no!" That was my first reaction to the shocking event that followed one week after the slender, articulate leader of the Afro-American Unity was routed from his East Elmhurst home by a bomb explosion. Minutes later we alighted from a cab at the corner of Broadway and 166th St. just a short 15 blocks from where I live on Broadway. About 200 men and women, neatly dressed, were milling around, some with expressions of awe and disbelief. Others were in small clusters talking loudly and with deep emotion in their voices. Mostly they were screaming for vengeance. One woman, small, dressed in a light gray coat and her eyes flaming with indignation, argued with a cop at the St. Nicholas corner of the block. "This is not the end of it. What they were going to do to the Statue of Liberty will be small in comparison. We black people are tired of being shoved around." Standing across the street near the memorial park one of Malcolm's close associates commented: "It's a shame." Later he added that "if it's war they want, they'll get it." He would not say whether Elijah Muhammed's followers had anything to do with the assassination. About 3:30 P.M. Malcolm X's wife, Betty, was escorted by three men and a woman from the Columbia Presbyterian Hospital. Tears streamed down her face. She was screaming, "They killed him!" Malcolm X had no last words. . . . The bombing and burning of the No. 7 Mosque early Tuesday morning was the first blow by those who are seeking revenge for the cold-blooded murder of a man who at 39 might have grown to the stature of respectable leadership.

Thinking ↔ Writing Activity

Seven Accounts of Events at Tiananmen Square, 1989

In the spring of 1989, a vigorous pro-democracy movement erupted in Beijing, the capital of China. Protesting the authoritarian control of the Communist regime, thousands of students staged demonstrations, engaged in hunger strikes, and organized marches involving hundreds of thousands of people. The geographical heart of these activities was the historic Tiananmen Square, taken over by the demonstrators who had erected a symbolic "Statue of Liberty." On June 4, 1989, the fledgling pro-democracy movement came to a bloody end when the Chinese army entered Tiananmen Square and seized control of it. The following are various accounts of this event from different sources. After analyzing these accounts, construct your own version of what you believe took place on that day. Use the following questions to guide your analysis of the varying accounts.

- Does the account provide a convincing description of what took place?
- What reasons and evidence support the account?
- How reliable does the source seem to be? What are the author's perceiving lenses, which might influence his or her account?

The *New York Times* (June 4, 1989)

Tens of thousands of Chinese troops retook the center of the capital from pro-democracy protesters early this morning, killing scores of students and workers and wounding hundreds more as they fired submachine guns at crowds of people who tried to resist. Troops marched along the main roads surrounding central Tiananmen Square, sometimes firing in the air and sometimes firing directly at crowds who refused to move. Reports on the number of dead were sketchy. Students said, however, that at least 500 people may have been killed in the

Days before their violent confrontation, demonstrating students surround policemen near Tiananmen Square, calling for freedom and democracy. What is your perception of what is taking place? © Associated Press.

crackdown. Most of the dead had been shot, but some had been run over by personnel carriers that forced their way through the protesters' barricades.

A report on the state-run radio put the death toll in the thousands and denounced the Government for the violence, the Associated Press reported. But the station later changed announcers and broadcast another report supporting the governing Communist party. The official news programs this morning reported that the People's Liberation Army had crushed a "counter-revolutionary rebellion." They said that more than 1,000 police officers and troops had been injured and some killed, and that civilians had been killed, but did not give details.

Deng Xiaoping, Chairman of the Central Military Commission, as reported in *Beijing Review* (July 10–16, 1989)

The main difficulty in handling this matter lay in that we had never experienced such a situation before, in which a small minority of bad people mixed with so many young students and onlookers. Actually, what we faced was not just some ordinary people who were misguided, but also a rebellious clique and a large number of the dregs of society. The key point is that they wanted to overthrow our state and the Party. They had two main slogans: to overthrow the Communist Party and topple the socialist system. Their goal was to establish a bourgeois republic entirely dependent on the West.

During the course of quelling the rebellion, many comrades of ours were injured or even sacrificed their lives. Some of their weapons were also taken

Aftermath of the bloody clash between a pro-democracy student movement and the Chinese army on June 4, 1989. Based on this photograph, what is your perception of what took place? Why? © Patrick Durand/SYGMA

from them by the rioters. Why? Because bad people mingled with the good, which made it difficult for us to take the firm measures that were necessary. Handling this matter amounted to a severe political test for our army, and what happened shows that our People's Liberation Army passed muster. If tanks were used to roll over people, this would have created a confusion between right and wrong among the people nationwide. That is why I have to thank the PLA officers and men for using this approach to handle the rebellion. The PLA losses were great, but this enabled us to win the support of the people and made those who can't tell right from wrong change their viewpoint. They can see what kind of people the PLA are, whether there was bloodshed at Tiananmen, and who were those that shed blood.

This shows that the people's army is truly a Great Wall of iron and steel of the Party and country. This shows that no matter how heavy the losses we suffer and no matter how generations change, this army of ours is forever an army under the leadership of the Party, forever the defender of the country, forever the defender of socialism, forever the defender of the public interest, and they are the most beloved of the people. At the same time, we should never forget how cruel our enemies are. For them we should not have an iota of forgiveness.

Additional Chinese Government Accounts

"Comrades, thanks for your hard work. We hope you will continue with your fine efforts to safeguard security in the capital."
—Prime Minister Li Peng (addressing a group of soldiers after the Tiananmen Square event)

"It never happened that soldiers fired directly at the people."
—General Li Zhiyun

"Not a single student was killed in Tiananmen Square."
—Chinese army commander

"The People's Liberation Army crushed a counter-revolutionary rebellion. More than 1,000 police officers and troops were injured and killed, and some civilians were killed."
—Official Chinese news program

"At most 300 people were killed in the operation, many of them soldiers."
—Yuan Mu, official government spokesman

"My government has stated that a mob led by a small number of people prevented the normal conduct of the affairs of state. There was, I regret to say, loss of life on both sides. I wonder whether any other government confronting such an unprecedented challenge would have handled the situation any better than mine did."
—Han Xu, Chinese ambassador to the United States

Reporter (*eyewitness account*), reported in the *New York Times*
(June 4, 1989)

Changan Avenue, or the Avenue of Eternal Peace, Beijing's main east-west thoroughfare, echoed with screams this morning as young people carried the bodies of their friends away from the front lines. The dead or seriously wounded were heaped on the backs of bicycles or tricycle rickshaws and supported by friends who rushed through the crowds, sometimes sobbing as they ran.

The avenue was lit by the glow of several trucks and two armed personnel carriers that students and workers set afire, and bullets swooshed overhead or glanced off buildings. The air crackled almost constantly with gunfire and tear gas grenades.

Students and workers tried to resist the crackdown, and destroyed at least sixteen trucks and two armored personnel carriers. Scores of students and workers ran alongside the personnel carriers, hurling concrete blocks and wooden staves into the treads until they ground to a halt. They then threw firebombs at one until it caught fire, and set the other alight after first covering it with blankets soaked in gasoline. The drivers escaped the flames, but were beaten by students. A young American man, who could not be immediately identified, was also beaten by the crowd after he tried to intervene and protect one of the drivers.

Clutching iron pipes and stones, groups of students periodically advanced toward the soldiers. Some threw bricks and firebombs at the lines of soldiers, apparently wounding many of them. Many of those killed were throwing bricks at the soldiers, but others were simply watching passively or standing at barricades when soldiers fired directly at them.

It was unclear whether the violence would mark the extinction of the seven-week-old democracy movement, or would prompt a new phase in the uprising, like a general strike. The violence in the capital ended a period of remarkable restraint by both sides, and seemed certain to arouse new bitterness and antagonism among both ordinary people and Communist Party officials for the Government of Prime Minister Li Peng.

"Our Government is already done with," said a young worker who held a rock in his hand, as he gazed at the army forces across Tiananmen Square. "Nothing can show more clearly that it does not represent the people." Another young man, an art student, was nearly incoherent with grief and anger as he watched the body of a student being carted away, his head blown away by bullets. "Maybe we'll fail today," he said. "Maybe we'll fail tomorrow. But someday we'll succeed. It's a historical inevitability."

The *New York Times* (June 5, 1989)

It was clear that at least 300 people had been killed since the troops first opened fire shortly after midnight on Sunday morning but the toll may be much higher. Word-of-mouth estimates continued to soar, some reaching far into the thousands. . . . The student organization that coordinated the long protests continued to function and announced today that 2,600 students were believed to have been killed. Several doctors said that, based on their discussions with ambulance drivers and colleagues who had been on Tiananmen Square, they estimated that at least 2,000 had died. Soldiers also beat and bayoneted students and workers after daybreak on Sunday, witnesses said, usually after some provocation but sometimes entirely at random. "I saw a young woman tell the soldiers that they are the people's army, and that they mustn't hurt the people," a young doctor said after returning from one clash Sunday. "Then the soldier shot her, and ran up and bayoneted her."

Xiao Bin (*eyewitness account immediately after the event*)

Tanks and armored personnel carriers rolled over students, squashing them into jam, and the soldiers shot at them and hit them with clubs. When students fainted, the troops killed them. After they died, the troops fired one more bullet into them. They also used bayonets. They were too cruel. I never saw such things before.

Xiao Bin (*account after being taken into custody by Chinese authorities*)

I never saw anything. I apologize for bringing great harm to the party and the country.

Thinking ↔ Writing Activity

Analyzing Multiple Perspectives in the News

Locate three different newspaper or magazine accounts of a significant event—a court decision, a compromise between heads of state, or a political demonstration are possible topics. Identify two specific differences in each account.

Analyze each account's perceptual "lenses" by using some of the questions in the Thinking-Writing Activities on pages 249 and 252.

CHANGES IN PERCEPTIONS AND PERSPECTIVES

Just as Mark Twain's perceptions of the river were changed by his perspective of increased knowledge, your ways of viewing the world will develop and change through the experiences you have, the knowledge you acquire, and your reflections on your experiences and knowledge. As you think critically about perceptions, you will learn more about how you make sense of the world. This understanding may strengthen your perceptions, or it may change them.

Obtaining More Accurate Perceptions: Adjusting the Lenses

So far, we have emphasized the great extent to which, by selecting, organizing, and interpreting, we directly affect our perceptions. We have suggested that each of us views the world through his or her own unique lenses, that no two of us perceive the world in exactly the same way.

Because we actively participate in selecting, organizing, and interpreting the sensations we experience, however, our perceptions are often incomplete, inaccurate, or subjective. To complicate the situation further, our own limitations in perceiving are not the only factors that can cause us problems. Other people often purposefully create perceptions and misperceptions. An advertiser who wants to sell a product may try to create the impression that our lives will be changed if we use it. Or a person who wants to discredit someone else may spread untrue rumors about her.

DEVELOP AWARENESS

The only way to correct the mistakes, distortions, and incompleteness of our perceptions is to become aware of the ordinarily unconscious process by which we perceive and make sense of the world. By doing so, we will be able to think critically about what is going on and to correct our mistakes and distortions. In other words, we can use our critical thinking abilities to create a clearer and more informed idea of what is taking place. We cannot rely on the validity of our perceptions alone. If we remain unaware of how our process of perceiving operates and of our active role in it, we will be unable to control it. We will be convinced that the way we see the world is the way the world is, even when our perceptions are mistaken, distorted, or incomplete.

Besides asking questions, we have to become aware of the personal perspectives that we bring to our perceptions. Each of us brings to every situation a whole collection of expectations, interests, fears, and hopes that can influence what we are perceiving.

Consider the following situations:

- You've been fishing all day without a nibble. Suddenly you get a strike! You reel the fish in, but just as you're about to pull it into the boat, it frees itself from the hook and swims away. When you get home later, your friends ask you, "How large was the fish that got away?"

- Your teacher asks you to evaluate the performance of a classmate who is giving a report to the class. You don't like this other student because he acts as if he's superior to everyone else in the class. How do you evaluate his report?

- You are asked to estimate the size of an audience attending an event that your organization has sponsored. How many people are there?

In each of these cases, your perceptions might be influenced by whatever hopes, fears, or prejudices you brought to the situation, causing your observations to be distorted or inaccurate. Although you usually cannot eliminate the personal feelings that influence your perceptions, you can become aware of these feelings and try to control them.

GET INPUT FROM OTHERS

The first step in critically examining your perceptions is to be willing to ask questions about them. As long as you believe that the way you see things is the only way to see them, you will not be able to recognize when your perceptions are distorted or inaccurate.

For instance, if you believe that your interpretation of the person shown at the computer in the Thinking-Writing Activity on page 217 is the only correct one, you will probably not consider other interpretations. But if you are willing to entertain other possible interpretations, you will open the way to more fully developing your perception of what is taking place.

As noted in Chapter 2, critical thinkers strive to see things from different perspectives. One of the best ways to do so is by communicating with others. This means exchanging and critically examining ideas in an open and organized way. Engaging in dialogue is one of the main ways to check your perceptions—by asking others what their perceptions are and comparing and contrasting them with yours.

This is exactly what you did when you discussed the various possible interpretations of the sketch of the person at the computer. By comparing your perceptions with those of your classmates, you developed a more complete sense of how differently events can be viewed as well as an appreciation of the reasons supporting the different perspectives.

FIND EVIDENCE

Also, you should try to discover independent proof or evidence regarding your perceptions. You can evaluate the accuracy of your perceptions when evidence is available in the form of records, photographs, videotapes, or the results of experiments. What independent forms of evidence could verify your perceptions about the person at the computer?

KEEP AN OPEN MIND

Thinking critically about perceptions means trying to avoid developing impulsive or superficial ones that you are unwilling to change. As explained in Chapter 2, a critical thinker is *thoughtful* in approaching the world and open to modifying his or her views in light of new information or better insights. Consider the following perceptions:

- Women are very emotional.
- Politicians are corrupt.
- Teenagers are wild and irresponsible.
- People who are good athletes are usually poor students.
- Men are thoughtless and insensitive.

These types of general perceptions are known as *stereotypes* because they express a belief about an entire group of people without recognizing the individual differences among members of the group.

For instance, it is probably accurate to say that there are some politicians who are corrupt, but this is not the same as saying that all, or even most, politicians are corrupt. Stereotypes affect our perceptions of the world because they encourage us to form inaccurate and superficial ideas about a whole group of

What is your perception of mosh pits, tattoos, and body piercings? Why do you think people often make negative judgments when confronted with things that seem strange or unfamiliar? © Ederfield/Liaison.

people ("Teenagers are reckless drivers"). When we meet someone who falls into this group, we automatically perceive that person as possessing a stereotyped quality ("This person is a teenager, so he is a reckless driver"). Even if we find that the person does not fit our stereotyped perception ("This teenager is not a reckless driver"), this sort of superficial and thoughtless labeling does not encourage us to change our perceptions of the group as a whole. Instead, it encourages us to overlook the conflicting information in favor of our stereotyped perceptions ("All teenagers are reckless drivers—except this one"). In contrast, when we are perceiving in a thoughtful fashion, we try to see what a person is like as an individual instead of trying to fit him or her into a pre-existing category.

Sometimes stereotypes are so built into a culture that it is difficult for a person to be aware of them until they are brought to his or her attention. The perspective, or view of the world, that the culture presents may not even acknowledge the possibility of other perspectives, so it can be very difficult for an individual to become aware of them and then to "switch lenses" to try to see a situation from those viewpoints.

True critical thinkers can and do switch lenses, and in their writing they help others to do so as well. The following two readings present varying perspectives on Native Americans. One was written by a famous eighteenth-century American; the other was written in the early twentieth century by a member of the Sioux nation. As you read these accounts, think about what factors probably contributed to the writers' perspectives.

Remarks Concerning the Savages of North America
BY BENJAMIN FRANKLIN

Savages we call them, because their Manners differ from ours, which we think the Perfection of Civility; they think the same of theirs.

Perhaps, if we could examine the Manners of different Nations with Impartiality, we should find no People so rude, as to be without any Rules of Politeness; nor any so polite, as not to have some Remains of Rudeness.

The Indian Men, when young, are Hunters and Warriors; when old, Counsellors; for all their Government is by Counsel of the Sages; there is no Force, there are no Prisons, no Officers to compel Obedience, or inflict Punishment. Hence they generally study Oratory, the best Speaker having the most Influence. The Indian Women till the Ground, dress the Food, nurse and bring up the Children, and preserve and hand down to Posterity the Memory of public Transactions. These Employments of Men and Women are accounted natural and honourable. Having few artificial Wants, they have abundance of Leisure for Improvement by Conversation. Our laborious Manner of Life, compared with theirs, they esteem slavish and base; and the Learning, on which we value ourselves, they regard as frivolous and useless. An Instance of this occurred at the

Treaty of Lancaster, in Pennsylvania, *anno* 1744, between the Government of Virginia and the Six Nations. After the principal Business was settled, the Commissioners from Virginia acquainted the Indians by a Speech, that there was at Williamsburg a College, with a Fund for Educating Indian youth; and that, if the Six Nations would send down half a dozen of their young Lads to that College, the Government would take care that they should be well provided for, and instructed in all the Learning of the White People. It is one of the Indian Rules of Politeness not to answer a public Proposition the same day that it is made; they think it would be treating it as a light matter, and that they show it Respect by taking time to consider it, as of a Matter important. They therefore deferr'd their Answer till the Day following; when their Speaker began, by expressing their deep Sense of the kindness of the Virginia Government, in making them that Offer; "for we know," says he, "that you highly esteem the kind of Learning taught in those Colleges, and that the Maintenance of our young Men, while with you, would be very expensive to you. We are convinc'd, therefore, that you mean to do us Good by your Proposal; and we thank you heartily. But you, who are wise, must know that different Nations have different Conceptions of things; and you will therefore not take it amiss, if our Ideas of this kind of Education happen not to be the same with yours. We have had some Experience of it; Several of our young People were formerly brought up at the Colleges of the Northern Provinces; they were instructed in all your Sciences; but, when they came back to us, they were bad Runners, ignorant of every means of living in the Woods, unable to bear either Cold or Hunger, knew neither how to build a Cabin, take a Deer, or kill an Enemy, spoke our Language imperfectly, were therefore neither fit for Hunters, Warriors, nor Counsellors; they were totally good for nothing. We are however not the less oblig'd by your kind Offer, tho' we decline accepting it; and, to show our grateful Sense of it, if the Gentlemen of Virginia will send us a Dozen of their Sons, we will take great Care of their Education, instruct them in all we know, and make *Men* of them."

Having frequent Occasions to hold public Councils, they have acquired great Order and Decency in conducting them. The old Men sit in the foremost Ranks, the Warriors in the next, and the Women and Children in the hindmost. The Business of the Women is to take exact Notice of what passes, imprint it in their Memories (for they have no Writing), and communicate it to their Children. They are the Records of the Council, and they preserve Traditions of the Stipulations in Treaties 100 Years back; which, when we compare with our Writings, we always find exact. He that would speak, rises. The rest observe a profound Silence. When he has finish'd and sits down, they leave him 5 to 6 Minutes to recollect, that, if he has omitted anything he intended to say, or has anything to add, he may rise again and deliver it. To interrupt another, even in common Conversation, is reckon'd highly indecent. How different this is from the conduct of a polite British House of Commons, where scarce a day passes without some Confusion, that makes the Speaker hoarse in calling *to Order;* and how different from the Mode of Conversation in many polite Companies of Europe, where, if you do not deliver your Sentence with great Rapidity, you are cut off in the middle of it by the Impatient Loquacity of those you converse with, and never suffer'd to finish it!

The Politeness of these Savages in Conversation is indeed carried to Excess, since it does not permit them to contradict or deny the Truth of what is asserted in their Presence. By this means they indeed avoid Disputes; but then it becomes difficult to know their Minds, or what Impression you make upon them. The Missionaries who have attempted to convert them to Christianity, all complain of this as one of the great Difficulties of their Mission. The Indians hear with Patience the Truths of the Gospel explain'd to them, and give their usual Tokens of Assent and Approbation; you would think they were convinc'd. No such matter. It is mere Civility.

5   A Swedish Minister, having assembled the chiefs of the Susquehanah Indians, made a Sermon to them, acquainting them with the principal historical Facts on which our Religion is founded; such as the Fall of our first Parents by eating an Apple, the coming of Christ to repair the Mischief, his Miracles and Suffering, &c. When he had finished, an Indian Orator stood up to thank him. "What you have told us," says he, "is all very good. It is indeed bad to eat Apples. It is better to make them all into Cyder. We are much oblig'd by your kindness in coming so far, to tell us these Things which you have heard from your Mothers. In return, I will tell you some of those we had heard from ours. In the Beginning, our Fathers had only the Flesh of Animals to subsist on; and if their Hunting was unsuccessful, they were starving. Two of our young Hunters, having kill'd a Deer, made a Fire in the Woods to broil some Part of it. When they were about to satisfy their Hunger, they beheld a beautiful young Woman descend from the Clouds, and seat herself on that Hill, which you see yonder among the blue Mountains. They said to each other, it is a Spirit that has smelt our broiling Venison, and wishes to eat of it; let us offer some to her. They presented her with the Tongue; she was pleas'd with the Taste of it, and said, 'Your kindness shall be rewarded; come to this Place after thirteen Moons, and you shall find something that will be of great Benefit in nourishing you and your Children to the latest Generations.' They did so, and, to their Surprise, found Plants they had never seen before; but which, from that ancient time, have been constantly cultivated among us, to our great Advantage. Where her right Hand had touched the Ground, they found Maize; where her left hand had touch'd it, they found Kidney-Beans; and where her Backside had sat on it, they found Tobacco." The good Missionary, disgusted with this idle Tale, said, "What I delivered to you were sacred Truths; but what you tell me is mere Fable, Fiction, and Falshood." The Indian, offended, reply'd, "My brother, it seems your Friends have not done you Justice in your Education; they have not well instructed you in the Rules of common Civility. You saw that we, who understand and practise those Rules, believ'd all your stories; why do you refuse to believe ours?"

When any of them come into our Towns, our People are apt to crowd round them, gaze upon them, and incommode them, where they desire to be private; this they esteem great Rudeness, and the Effect of the Want of Instruction in the

Rules of Civility and good Manners. "We have," say they, "as much Curiosity as you, and when you come into our Towns, we wish for Opportunities of looking at you; but for this purpose we hide ourselves behind Bushes, where you are to pass, and never intrude ourselves into your Company."

Their Manner of entering one another's village has likewise its Rules. It is reckon'd uncivil in travelling Strangers to enter a Village abruptly, without giving Notice of their Approach. Therefore, as soon as they arrive within hearing, they stop and hollow, remaining there till invited to enter. Two old Men usually come out to them, and lead them in. There is in every Village a vacant Dwelling, called *the Strangers' House.* Here they are plac'd, while the old Men go round from Hut to Hut, acquainting the Inhabitants, that Strangers are arriv'd, who are probably hungry and weary; and every one sends them what he can spare of Victuals, and Skins to repose on. When the Strangers are refresh'd, Pipes and Tobacco are brought; and then, but not before, Conversation begins, with Enquiries who they are, whither bound, what News, &c.; and it usually ends with offers of Service, if the Strangers have occasion of Guides, or any Necessaries for continuing their Journey; and nothing is exacted for the Entertainment.

The same Hospitality, esteem'd among them as a principal Virtue, is practis'd by private Persons; of which Conrad Weiser, our Interpreter, gave me the following Instance. He had been naturaliz'd among the Six Nations, and spoke well the Mohock Language. In going thro' the Indian Country, to carry a Message from our Governor to the Council at Onondaga, he call'd at the Habitation of Canassatego, an old Acquaintance, who embrac'd him, spread Furs for him to sit on, plac'd before him some boil'd Beans and Venison, and mix'd some Rum and Water for his Drink. When he was well refresh'd, and had lit his Pipe, Canassatego began to converse with him; ask'd how he had far'd the many Years since they had seen each other; whence he then came; what occasion'd the Journey, &c. Conrad answered all his Questions; and when the Discourse began to flag, the Indian, to continue it, said, "Conrad, you have lived long among the white People, and know something of their Customs; I have been sometimes at Albany, and have observed, that once in Seven Days they shut up their Shops, and assemble all in the great House; tell me what it is for? What do they do there?" "They meet there," says Conrad, "to hear and learn *good Things.*" "I do not doubt," says the Indian, "that they tell you so; they have told me the same; but I doubt the Truth of what they say, and I will tell you my Reasons. I went lately to Albany to sell my Skins and buy Blankets, Knives, Powder, Rum, &c. You know I us'd generally to deal with Hans Hanson; but I was a little inclin'd this time to try some other Merchant. However, I call'd first upon Hans, and asked him what he would give for Beaver. He said he could not give any more than four Shillings a Pound; 'but,' says he, 'I cannot talk on Business now; this is the Day when we meet together to learn *Good Things,* and I am going to the Meeting.' So I thought to myself, 'Since we cannot do any Business to-day, I may as well go to the meeting too,' and I went with him. There stood up a Man in Black, and began to talk to the People very angrily. I did not understand what he said; but, perceiving that he look'd much at me and at Hanson, I imagin'd he was angry at seeing me there; so I went out, sat down near the House, struck Fire, and lit my Pipe, waiting till the Meeting should break up. I thought too, that the Man had mention'd something of Beaver, and I suspected it might be the Subject of their Meeting. So, when they came out, I accosted my Merchant. 'Well, Hans,' says I, 'I hope you have agreed to give more than four Shillings a Pound.' 'No,' says he, 'I cannot give so much; I cannot give more than three shillings and sixpence.' I then spoke to several other Dealers, but they all sung the same song,—Three and sixpence,—Three and sixpence. This made it clear to me, that my Suspicion was right; and, that whatever they pretended of meeting to learn *good Things,* the real purpose was to consult how to cheat Indians in the Price of Beaver. Consider but little, Conrad, and you must be of my Opinion. If they met so often to learn *good Things,* they would certainly have learnt some before this time. But they are still ignorant. You know our Practice. If a white Man, in travelling thro' our Country, enters one of our Cabins, we all treat him as I treat you; we dry him if he is wet, we warm him if he is cold, we give him Meat and Drink, that he may allay his Thirst and Hunger; and we spread soft Furs for him to rest and sleep on; we demand nothing in return. But, if I go into a white Man's House at Albany, and ask for Victuals and Drink, they say, 'Where is your Money?' and if I have none, they say, 'Get out, you Indian Dog.' You see they have not yet learned those little *Good Things,* that we need no Meetings to be instructed in, because our Mothers taught them to us when we were Children; and therefore it is impossible their Meetings should be, as they say, for any such purpose, or have any such Effect; they are only to contrive *the Cheating of Indians in the Price of Beaver."*

FROM

The Soul of the Indian

BY CHARLES ALEXANDER EASTMAN (SIOUX)

The original attitude of the American Indian toward the Eternal, the "Great Mystery" that surrounds and embraces us, was as simple as it was exalted. To him it was the supreme conception, bringing with it the fullest measure of joy and satisfaction possible in this life.

The worship of the "Great Mystery" was silent, solitary, free from all self-seeking. It was silent, because all speech is of necessity feeble and imperfect; therefore the souls of my ancestors ascended to God in wordless adoration. It was solitary, because they believed that He is nearer to us in solitude, and there were no priests authorized to come between a man and his Maker. None might exhort or confess or in any way meddle with the religious experience of another. Among us all men were created sons of God and stood erect, as conscious of their divinity. Our faith might not be formulated in creeds, nor forced upon any who were unwilling to receive it; hence there was no preaching, proselyting, nor persecution, neither were there any scoffers or atheists.

There were no temples or shrines among us save those of nature. Being a natural man, the Indian was intensely poetical. He would deem it sacrilege to build a house for Him who may be met face to face in the mysterious, shadowy aisles of the primeval forest, or on the sunlit bosom of virgin prairies, upon dizzy spires and pinnacles of naked rock, and yonder in the jeweled vault of the night sky! He who enrobes Himself in filmy veils of cloud, there on the rim of the visible world where our Great-Grandfather Sun kindles his evening camp-fire, He who rides upon the rigorous wind of the north, or breathes forth His spirit upon aromatic southern airs, whose warcanoe is launched upon majestic rivers and inland seas—He needs no lesser cathedral!

That solitary communion with the Unseen which was the highest expression of our religious life is partly described in the word *hambeday*, literally "mysterious feeling," which has been variously translated "fasting" and "dreaming." It may better be interpreted as "consciousness of the divine."

5

The first *hambeday*, or religious retreat, marked an epoch in the life of the youth, which may be compared to that of confirmation or conversion in Christian experience. Having first prepared himself by means of the purifying vapor-bath, and cast off as far as possible all human or fleshly influences, the young man sought out the noblest height, the most commanding summit in all the surrounding region. Knowing that God sets no value upon material things, he took with him no offerings or sacrifices other than symbolic objects, such as paints and tobacco. Wishing to appear before Him in all humility, he wore no clothing save his moccasins and breech-clout. At the solemn hour of sunrise or sunset he took up his position, overlooking the glories of earth and facing the "Great Mystery," and there he remained, naked, erect, silent, and motionless, exposed to the elements and forces of His arming, for a night and a day to two days and nights, but rarely longer. Sometimes he would chant a hymn without words, or offer the ceremonial "filled pipe." In this holy trance or ecstasy the Indian mystic found his highest happiness and the motive power of his existence.

When he returned to the camp, he must remain at a distance until he had again entered the vapor-bath and prepared himself for intercourse with his fellows. Of the vision or sign vouchsafed to him he did not speak, unless it had included some commission which must be publicly fulfilled. Sometimes an old man, standing upon the brink of eternity, might reveal to a chosen few the oracle of his long-past youth.

The native American has been generally despised by his white conquerors for his poverty and simplicity. They forget, perhaps, that his religion forbade the accumulation of wealth and the enjoyment of luxury. To him, as to other single-minded men in every age and race, from Diogenes to the brothers of Saint Francis, from the Montanists to the Shakers, the love of possessions has appeared a snare, and the burdens of a complex society a source of needless peril and temptation. Furthermore, it was the rule of his life to share the fruits of his skill and success with his less fortunate brothers. Thus he kept his spirit free from the clog of pride, cupidity, and envy, and carried out, as he believed, the divine decree—a matter profoundly important to him.

It was not, then, wholly from ignorance or improvidence that he failed to establish permanent towns and to develop a material civilization. To the untutored sage, the concentration of population was the prolific mother of all evils, moral no less than physical. He argued that food is good, while surfeit kills; that love is good, but lust destroys; and not less dreaded than the pestilence following upon crowded and unsanitary dwellings was the loss of spiritual power inseparable from too close contact with one's fellow-men. All who have lived much out of doors know that there is a magnetic and nervous force that accumulates in solitude and that is quickly dissipated by life in a crowd; and even his enemies have recognized the fact that for a certain innate power and self-poise, wholly independent of circumstances, the American Indian is unsurpassed among men.

The red man divided mind into two parts—the spiritual mind and the physical mind. The first is pure spirit, concerned only with the essence of things, and it was this he sought to strengthen by spiritual prayer, during which the body is subdued by fasting and hardship. In this type of prayer there was no beseeching of favor or help. All matters of personal or selfish concern, as success in hunting or warfare, relief from sickness, or the sparing of a beloved life, were definitely relegated to the plane of the lower or material mind, and all ceremonies, charms, or incantations designed to secure a benefit or to avert a danger, were recognized as emanating from the physical self.

10   The rites of this physical worship, again, were wholly symbolic, and the Indian no more worshiped the Sun than the Christian adores the Cross. The Sun and the Earth, by an obvious parable, holding scarcely more of poetic metaphor than of scientific truth, were in his view the parents of all organic life. From the Sun, as the universal father, proceeds the quickening principle in nature, and in the patient and fruitful womb of our mother, the Earth, are hidden embryos of plants and men. Therefore our reverence and love for them was really an imaginative extension of our love for our immediate parents, and with this sentiment of filial piety was joined a willingness to appeal to them, as to a father, for such good gifts as we may desire. This is the material or physical prayer.

The elements and majestic forces in nature, Lightning, Wind, Water, Fire, and Frost, were regarded with awe as spiritual powers, but always secondary and intermediate in character. We believed that the spirit pervades all creation and that every creature possesses a soul in some degree, though not necessarily a soul conscious of itself. The tree, the waterfall, the grizzly bear, each is an embodied Force, and as such an object of reverence.

The Indian loved to come into sympathy and spiritual communion with his brothers of the animal kingdom, whose inarticulate souls had for him something of the sinless purity that we attribute to the innocent and irresponsible child. He had faith in their instincts, as in a mysterious wisdom given from above; and while he humbly accepted the supposedly voluntary sacrifice of their bodies to preserve his own, he paid homage to their spirits in prescribed prayers and offerings.

In every religion there is an element of the supernatural, varying with the influence of pure reason over its devotees. The Indian was a logical and clear thinker upon matters within the scope of his understanding, but he had not yet charted the vast field of nature or expressed her wonders in terms of science. With his limited knowledge of cause and effect, he saw miracles on every hand,—the miracle of life in seed and egg, the miracle of death in lightning flash and in the swelling deep! Nothing of the marvelous could astonish him; as that a beast should speak, or the sun stand still. The virgin birth would appear scarcely more miraculous than is the birth of every child that comes into the world, or the miracle of the loaves and fishes excite more wonder than the harvest that springs from a single ear of corn.

Who may condemn his superstition? Surely not the devout Catholic, or even Protestant missionary, who teaches Bible miracles as literal fact! The logical man must either deny all miracles or none, and our American Indian myths and hero stories are perhaps, in themselves, quite as credible as those of the Hebrews of old. If we are of the modern type of mind, that sees in natural law a majesty and grandeur far more impressive than any solitary infraction of it could possibly be, let us not forget that, after all, science has not explained everything. We have still to face the ultimate miracle,—the origin and principle of life! Here is the supreme mystery that is the essence of worship, without which there can be no religion, and in the presence of this mystery our attitude cannot be very unlike that of the natural philosopher, who beholds with awe the Divine in all creation.

15   It is simple truth that the Indian did not, so long as his native philosophy held sway over his mind, either envy or desire to imitate the splendid achievements of the white man. In his own thought he rose superior to them! He scorned them, even as a lofty spirit absorbed in its stern task rejects the soft beds, the luxurious food, the pleasure-worshiping dalliance of a rich neighbor. It was clear to him that virtue and happiness are independent of these things, if not incompatible with them.

There was undoubtedly much in primitive Christianity to appeal to this man, and Jesus' hard sayings to the rich and about the rich would have been entirely comprehensible to him. Yet the religion that is preached in our churches and practiced by our congregations, with its element of display and self-aggrandizement, its active proselytism, and its open contempt of all religions but its own, was for a long time extremely repellent. To his simple mind, the professionalism of the pulpit, the paid exhorter, the moneyed church, was an unspiritual and unedifying thing, and it was not until his spirit was broken and his moral and physical constitution undermined by trade, conquest, and strong drink, that Christian missionaries obtained any real hold upon him. Strange as it may seem, it is true that the proud pagan in his secret soul despised the good men who came to convert and to enlighten him!

Nor were its publicity and its Phariseeism the only elements in the alien religion that offended the red man. To him, it appeared shocking and almost incredible that there were among this people who claimed superiority many irreligious, who did not even pretend to profess the national faith. Not only did they not profess it, but they stooped so low as to insult their God with profane and sacrilegious speech! In our own tongue His name was not spoken aloud, even with utmost reverence, much less lightly or irreverently.

More than this, even in those white men who professed religion we found much inconsistency of conduct. They spoke much of spiritual things, while seeking only the material. They bought and sold everything: time, labor, personal independence, the love of woman, and even the ministrations of their holy faith! The lust for money, power, and conquest so characteristic of the Anglo-Saxon race did not escape moral condemnation at the hands of his untutored judge, nor did he fail to contrast this conspicuous trait of the dominant race with the spirit of the meek and lowly Jesus.

He might in time come to recognize that the drunkards and licentious among white men, with whom he too frequently came in contact, were condemned by the white man's religion as well, and must not be held to discredit it. But it was not so easy to overlook or to excuse national bad faith. When distinguished emissaries from the Father at Washington, some of them ministers of the gospel and even bishops, came to the Indian nations, and pledged to them in solemn treaty the national honor, with prayer and mention of their God; and when such treaties, so made, were promptly and shamelessly broken, is it strange that the action should arouse not only anger, but contempt? The historians of the white race admit that the Indian was never the first to repudiate his oath.

20   It is my personal belief, after thirty-five years' experience of it, that there is no such thing as "Christian civilization." I believe that Christianity and modern civilization are opposed and irreconcilable, and that the spirit of Christianity and of our ancient religion is essentially the same.

Critical Reading Questions

1. In describing the Native Americans, both Franklin and Eastman are making efforts to transcend the biased lenses of their cultures. What does Franklin mean when he says, "Perhaps, if we could examine the Manners of different Nations with Impartiality, we should find no People so rude, as to be without any Rules of Politeness; nor any so polite, as not to have some Remains of Rudeness"?

2. What does Franklin consider to be the main virtues of the Native Americans? Which of their virtues does Eastman focus on? How do their two perspectives compare?

3. What does the Native American speaker mean when he says, "If the Gentlemen of Virginia will send us a Dozen of their Sons, we will take great Care of their Education, instruct them in all we know, and make *Men* of them"?

4. How does Eastman describe the role of the "Great Mystery" in Native American culture?

5. How do the portrayals of Native Americans in these two articles compare with the descriptions you were given in your earlier schooling?

Writing Thoughtfully About Perspectives

COMPARISON AND CONTRAST

Whenever we place two or more perspectives, or two or more other things, together and examine them for similarities and differences, we are engaging in the powerful thinking pattern called **comparison and contrast.** To be precise, when we *compare,* we are focusing on likenesses or areas of agreement; when we *contrast,* we are focusing on differences or areas of disagreement. Generally, the items examined are from the same category. We will discuss writing about items from the same category in the next section, Thinking in Comparisons. Sometimes, in order to make a point or to explain something, we may compare items from different categories. We will discuss these unusual comparisons in the Analogy section (pages 272–273).

THINKING IN COMPARISONS

We use comparison and contrast informally in our daily lives when we make decisions such as what food to buy or which TV programs to watch. When we use comparison and contrast in a formal way by following certain established principles, we are using it to think critically to arrive at a significant conclusion. That is, we use it not only to list areas of similarity or difference but also to help achieve a clearer understanding or new insight. When we use comparison and contrast to examine different perspectives, we do so in order to understand each perspective, to see if one is superior to another, to see if we ourselves have yet another perspective, and so on.

The principles for using comparison and contrast to think critically are straightforward.

1. *Compare or contrast two or more things that have something essential in common (that is, items from the same category).* Thus, it makes sense to compare two accounts of the same event or two essays on affirmative action.

2. *Establish important bases or points for comparison and contrast.* In everyday situations, it is fairly easy to determine which points are important. In deciding between two cars, the important points may be price, model, and safety features; exterior color or exact trunk capacity may

be lesser concerns. But when you are working with written texts, finding points for comparison and contrast and deciding which of them are important require careful thought. When comparing or contrasting two accounts of the same event, important points might include the actual presence of the writers at the event or the writers' reliance on the accounts of others, the language the writers use to describe the participants or actions, and which details the writers have included or omitted. The writer's gender or the length of an account might or might not be significant.

3. *Develop or locate relevant, specific evidence for each point.* Opinions valued by critical thinkers are those supported by evidence. In everyday situations, evidence usually means facts: the prices of two different cars, the presence or absence of air bags, and so on. With written texts, the evidence comes from the texts themselves, either in the form of accurate paraphrases or direct quotations.

4. *Determine the significance of the comparison and contrast: What can be learned from it?* What should be done as a result? In everyday situations, this significance is often a determination: one car is superior to another and is therefore the one to purchase. When you are working with written texts, the significance may be that the texts disagree on important points; therefore, you may decide that one is more persuasive than the other.

Guidelines for Using Comparisons in Writing

When you are ready to present the results of your critical thinking in writing for others to read and consider, you need to present your thinking in such a way that readers will be able to follow it and, hopefully, agree with your conclusion. Therefore, for writing, you should also follow these principles:

1. *Early and accurately, introduce the things to be compared and contrasted.* When you work with written texts, this means identifying what the texts are (personal essays, poems, newspaper accounts, excerpts from books, and so on) and naming the titles and authors, probably in the introductory paragraph.

2. *Develop a thesis which states that you will examine likenesses and/or differences.* Because you will be discussing two or more things and introducing points about each, the audience will be confronting a difficult reading task. A clear statement of what is to come can offer them a framework to follow.

3. *Organize the comparison or contrast in the way that will be easiest for the audience to follow.* Basically, there are three ways to organize a comparison and contrast: block, point-by-point, or a careful combination of the two.

- *Block* means that after the introduction, you first present all the material about the first subject; then, you present all the material about the second. The selection by Mark Twain on pages 245–246 uses block organization.

- *Point-by-point* means that for each key point or basis of comparison, you first give information about one of the things being compared and contrasted, then give information about the other. In this way, you can move back and forth between the two things being compared and contrasted. The selection by Benjamin Franklin on pages 260–264 uses point-by-point organization.

- You can also use a *combination* of these two patterns when there are some items of similarity or difference that you can present in blocks, followed by points that you may want to address separately. Topic sentences and transitions are very important in a combination method!

4. *Bring up the same bases or points of comparison or contrast for each subject, and in the same order.* An incomplete comparison results when, for instance, the language used in one text is addressed but the language used in another is not discussed. If an important detail appears in one text but not in the other, it is reasonable to simply tell the audience this: "No mention is made of a doctor in this account."

5. *Assist the audience by using words, phrases, or sentences that show relationships and shifts.* Logical connections that exist in your mind may not necessarily be apparent to your audience, but you can point them out by using appropriate expressions.

Comparison words and phrases	Contrast words and phrases
Same	Different, differ from, difference
Similar, similarly	In contrast
Like, alike	Unlike
Reminds me of	On the other hand
Resembles	Conversely
Shows connections with	
Both	Is separate from
(Can you think of more examples?)	(Can you think of more examples?)

6. *State the significance of your comparison and contrast at the place in the essay where it will be most effective.* Sometimes writers use the significance as the opening lead, sometimes they incorporate it into the thesis statement, and sometimes they save it for the conclusion. In deciding where to place it, ask yourself where it will have the greatest impact on your audience.

ANALOGY

We noted earlier that comparative relationships involve examining the similarities and differences of two items in the same general category, such as two perspectives, two items on a menu, or two methods of birth control. There is another kind of comparison, however, one that does not focus on things in the same category. Such comparisons are known as *analogies,* and their goal is to clarify or illuminate a concept from one category by saying that in some ways, it resembles a concept from a very different category.

The purpose of an analogy is not the same as the purpose of the comparison we have been discussing. We noted that the goal of comparing similar things is often to make a choice and that the process of comparing can provide us with information on which we can base an intelligent decision. The main goal of analogies, however, is not to choose or decide; it is to illuminate our understanding. Identifying similarities between very different things can often stimulate us to see these things in a new light or from a different perspective.

We often create and use analogies to put a point across. Used appropriately, an analogy can help to illustrate what we are trying to communicate. This device is particularly useful when we have difficulty finding the right words to represent our experiences. Similes and metaphors, two figures of speech based on analogy that help us to "say things for which we have not words," are discussed on pages 179–180 of Chapter 5.

In addition to communicating experiences that resist simple characterization, analogies are useful when a writer is explaining a complicated concept. For instance, we might compare the eye to a camera lens or compare the body's immune system to the National Guard (corpuscles are called to active duty and rush to the scene of danger when undesirable elements threaten the well-being of the organism).

Analogies are often used to describe shape or size. They help our readers to visualize size if we describe an object as "about the size of a dollar bill" or a piece of property as "roughly the size of two football fields."

Analogies enliven human discourse by evoking images that illuminate the points of comparison. Consider the following analogies and explain the points of comparison.

> "Laws are like cobwebs, which may catch small flies, but let wasps and hornets break through." —Jonathan Swift

> "Like as the waves make towards the pebbled shore, so do our minutes hasten to their end." —William Shakespeare

> "Some books are to be tasted, others to be swallowed, and some few to be chewed and digested." —Francis Bacon

> "He has all the qualities of a dog, except its devotion." —Gore Vidal

In addition to *simple analogies* like the preceding ones that are designed to make one or two penetrating points, *extended analogies* have a more ambitious purpose. They attempt to illuminate a more complex subject by identifying a number of points of comparison. For example, we might seek to explain the theory of causal determinism by drawing an analogy between the universe and a watch or by analogizing the chemical interaction of molecules to a choreographed dance.

A word of caution about using analogies is in order here. Since they are based on items from different categories and have only limited points of similarity, be very careful when writing or reading arguments based on analogies. The failed U.S. military policy in Vietnam was partially based on the "domino theory," which held that since the countries in Southeast Asia had common borders, if one country became Communist, the other countries would also "fall" to Communism, just as a row of dominoes would all fall if one were knocked down. However, the countries were separate entities, places with people, history, cultures, and policies of their own. They were not small game pieces like dominoes, so the theory proved false. Analogies do have value for describing and explaining, but by their very nature, they have limited value in an argument.

Thinking ↔ Writing Activity

Examining Extended Analogies

1. Identify the items being compared in the following paragraphs and note the points of similarity. How does the analogy help to illuminate the subject being discussed?

2. Where does each analogy fall apart, or, in other words, where do categorical differences in the items cause the analogy to be interesting but not really accurate?

3. Try writing a paragraph-length analogy of your own.

The mountain guide, like the true teacher, has a quiet authority. He or she engenders trust and confidence so that one is willing to join the endeavor. The guide accepts his leadership role, yet recognizes that success (measured by the heights that are scaled) depends upon the close cooperation and active participation of each member of the group. He has crossed the terrain before and is familiar with the landmarks, but each trip is new and generates its own anxiety and excitement. Essential skills must be mastered; if they are lacking, disaster looms. The situation demands keen focus and rapt attention; slackness, misjudgment, or laziness can abort the venture. The teacher is not a pleader, not a performer, not a huckster, but a confident, exuberant guide on expeditions of shared responsibility into the most exciting and least-understood terrain on earth—the mind itself. —Nancy K. Hill, *Scaling the Heights: The Teacher as Mountaineer*

Life's but a walking shadow, a poor player,
That struts and frets his hour upon the stage,
And then is heard no more. It is a tale
Told by an idiot, full of sound and fury,
Signifying nothing. —William Shakespeare, *Macbeth*, V.v

The following extended analogies were written by students in a college composition class.

Love in a good marriage is like an exponential function; it will grow until infinity. As time passes, love increases. It doesn't grow in the shape of a linear function; it grows faster. As I say every day to my husband, I love him more today than yesterday and less than tomorrow. And that is the exponential way.

Becoming a wise shopper is like becoming a smart chef in a fancy restaurant. Everywhere the chef turns in the kitchen, he finds an exotic treat. But he can't taste everything, much less consume it all. A chef who tastes too much will get a stomach ache. A shopper who buys too much will spend a lot of money and then suffer the pain of paying off those credit card bills. A wise shopper can resist the sweet temptations of the shopping life like the smart cook can resist the delicious temptations in the kitchen.

Phone conversations with my stepmother and writing assignments are both difficult for me in similar ways. Finding topics for them is often hard. After I tell my stepmother that I'm fine and ask about her and my father, I sometimes don't know what else to say. When I have an assignment to write about whatever I want, I sometimes can't think of a topic. Also, I must worry about my vocabulary in both situations. My stepmother doesn't know the new "in" words, and my English papers have to be written correctly. I only increase my difficulty with both of these obligations by putting them off. I wait until Sunday night to call my father's house and then, after the phone call, work on my English paper for Monday morning.

Writing Project: Comparing Perspectives on an Issue or Event

This chapter has included both readings and Thinking-Writing Activities that encourage you to reflect on the nature of perception and on comparing and contrasting different perspectives. Be sure to reread what you wrote for those activities; you may be able to use the material when completing this project.

> Write an essay comparing and contrasting two or more written texts that present different perspectives on the same event or issue. Your primary purpose is to present some significant insights about the perspectives and the texts. Follow your instructor's directions for choosing texts and for the paper's length and format.

Begin by considering the key elements in the Thinking-Writing Model on page 31.

THE WRITING SITUATION

Purpose Along with presenting significant insights about the texts and their subject, you will better understand how to use the thinking patterns of comparison and contrast. Also, you will think more about the implications of different perspectives presented in various accounts. And, since comparative papers invite logical organization, your planning abilities should improve. Finally, you will be sharing your insights about the texts with your audience.

Audience One audience for this paper would be anyone interested in the subject discussed in your choice of texts. This audience might be outside of your college since most events or issues that are written about have community, national, or international significance. If you can, identify such an audience and see if you can share your paper with them by publishing it in a newspaper or newsletter or by otherwise distributing it. If the texts pertain to history, sociology, psychology, or some other academic subject, perhaps people studying those subjects would want to read your essay.

You should consider whether or not your audience has read the texts that you are analyzing. If they have, you will not need to include much summary of content or explanation of context. If your readers have not read the texts, you will have to include a brief summary and perhaps an explanation of why the texts were written.

To communicate with your audience, you will need to include enough evidence from the texts to demonstrate your points. You should not merely *tell* your audience that a likeness or difference exists; you must *show* them the evidence so they can see it for themselves.

Your classmates will be a good audience since they are working on the same assignment. Your instructor remains the audience who will judge how well you have established your contrasts, your comparisons, and their significance. Everyone in your audience cares about a clear focus, logical organization, specific examples, and good presentation.

Subject If your instructor specifies which texts you should compare and contrast, consider why he or she may have chosen them. A question to ask yourself is what those texts have in common. If your instructor has left the choice to you, remember that you must use texts that have something essential in common. It helps a great deal to pick texts that genuinely interest you, either because of their subject matter or because of their style. Or you may decide to select an issue or event that interests you and use your research skills to locate texts about the topic. In that case, it may be necessary to provide copies of the texts for your audience.

Writer   This project asks you to bring your critical reading and thinking skills to other writers' works and to analyze their perspectives. Your position of authority and your comfort level may depend on how much you know about the subject. However, neither your personal opinions nor your experiences are the focus of this project. You must be as objective as possible as you write and as thoughtful as possible as you establish the significance of your analysis.

THE WRITING PROCESS

The following sections will guide you through the stages of generating, planning, drafting, and revising as you work on your essay. Try to be particularly conscious of applying the principles discussed in this chapter and of the critical thinking you do when you revise.

Generating Ideas   Once you have decided which texts you will use, reread each of them several times. Likenesses and differences may not be immediately apparent, nor may any significance strike you at the start. Doing some preliminary writing may help.

- Make a list of the ideas in each text.
- Make a list of what you notice about each text. Are you struck by the opening, the choice of words, the author's bias or objectivity, the presence or absence of specific details, or any other elements or characteristics?
- After you have made these lists, begin to look for bases or points of likeness or difference. Doing this requires abstract thinking on your part, but patience will yield results.
- Collaboration can be productive. Talk with others about the texts.
- Read the student papers at the end of this chapter. They may help you to see what needs to be done.
- Carefully read any other models your instructor provides.
- Try freewriting for five minutes on what the texts have in common, then for five minutes on how they differ.
- Once you have established some bases for comparison or contrast, go back to the texts themselves and look for passages you could quote to illustrate your points.
- If you own the publication(s) in which the texts appear, use a highlighting pen to mark areas you may wish to quote. If you don't own them, copy the quotations or make photocopies to highlight.
- Now begin to think about significance. What are you beginning to observe about the texts? What are you beginning to feel about them?

- Try freewriting for five minutes on any or all of these questions:

  Does one text do a better job than the other? If so, in what way or ways?

  Do you agree with either or both texts? If not, what *is* your perspective?

  Have the texts caused you to re-evaluate or change your own ideas or perspectives?

  Do the texts have different styles or vocabularies?

Defining a Focus Write a thesis statement that will clearly inform your audience that you are going to explore similarities, differences, or both. You might decide to write something like "After studying both of these accounts carefully, I saw two distinct differences." Or you might decide to name the areas of likeness or difference: "The authors are similar in their recognition of the need for more education and their determination in pursuing that education." You may even decide to announce the personal significance of your comparisons in your thesis statement: "Seeing the biased way in which one of the texts presented this event made me wary of accepting any printed reports at face value."

Organizing Ideas This assignment fits well with what you have already learned about essay structure but requires you to move a few steps beyond what you have accomplished previously. Your description of the issue or event and of the texts that describe it can give you an introduction that will end with your thesis statement. The actual discussion of likenesses and/or differences will take place in the body paragraphs, and the significance of your analysis can be introduced or expanded upon in the conclusion. The major decision you will have to make is whether to use block or point-by-point organization or some combination of the two.

Drafting Begin with the easiest paragraph to draft. If you are using point-by-point, remember to begin each body paragraph with a topic sentence indicating that this point will be discussed for both (or all) texts: for example, "Both accounts agree on the cause of the contamination." Then provide the audience with as much information as is needed to help them see what you mean. Use the quotations you highlighted to support your points and let the audience see that the texts really do say very similar—or very different—things. You will, of course, have to decide on the most logical order for the body paragraphs: which point to present first, which second, and so on.

Generally, readers have an easier time following point-by-point organization, but some writing situations call for block. Fortunately, word processors make it easy to move material around, so try it both ways to see which will be easier for your audience.

In your conclusion, name or expand upon the significance of your analysis, but be careful not to make too broad a statement. Consideration of two or three texts does not prove, for instance, that all texts are racist or sexist, but discovering racism or sexism in some texts should encourage you and your readers to be aware that these perspectives may be present in others.

Revising Reactions to your draft are helpful. Your classmates, or peers, can see where your draft is successful and where it needs work. If your instructor schedules peer review, be sure to have a draft ready. Use one of the methods on pages 65–66 or 105–107. (Change the questions to fit this assignment.) Think about your classmates' reactions and use them to improve your draft. Then work through the following revision questions.

If you did not have a chance for classmates' reactions, put your draft aside for a while, and then use these questions to guide you in finishing your comparison well.

1. **Think big.** Look at your draft as a whole.

   - Does it fulfill the assignment? Does it compare two or more written reports?
   - Do you state clearly the *significance* of the comparisons and contrasts that you are making?
   - Where do you state this significance—in the beginning? in the conclusion? in more than one place? Is this placement effective?
   - Can your draft be better organized?
   - Have you quoted examples for every point that you make about the texts?
   - Are there effective transitions between paragraphs?

2. **Think medium.** Look at your draft paragraph by paragraph.

   - Does your first paragraph make clear that you are comparing two or more written accounts? If not, does this paragraph provide another good approach to the assignment?
   - Which paragraphs have topic sentences? Do the topic sentences point out comparisons and contrasts? Does any paragraph that lacks a topic sentence need one?
   - How does the concluding paragraph bring your essay to a close? Does it discuss differing perspectives and differing accounts?

3. **Think small.** Look at your draft sentence by sentence.

   - Are any sentences difficult to understand? How can you make them clearer?
   - Are any sentences too long? How can you shorten them? Are any too short? How can you expand them?
   - Have you blended quoted material well into your sentences? Be sure that each quotation is integrated into the syntax of a sentence.

- • Do any sentences contain errors in Standard English grammar? How can you correct them?

4. **Think "picky."** Look at your draft as your fussiest critic might.

- • Which words are not specific enough? What words could you use instead?

- • Have you used comparing and contrasting words (*similar, like, in the same sense, different, on the other hand,* and so on) well?

- • Have you quoted accurately? Do you use both beginning and ending quotation marks?

- • Have you used ellipsis points (dots) if you have edited words or sentences out of a quoted passage? Have you used them correctly?

- • Are any words misspelled? Run your spell checker, but remember that it cannot identify all mistakes that produce a real word.

- • Are the pages numbered? Is your name on all pages?

- • Will your finished paper make a good impression by being nicely presented in the format that your instructor requires?

- • Is there anything else you could do to improve your draft?

Develop alternatives based on your answers to these questions, decide which will improve your draft, and revise your draft to produce a good essay.

Editing and Proofreading After you prepare a final draft, check again for correct grammar and punctuation usage. Proofread carefully to detect omitted words or punctuation marks. Also proofread for the kinds of errors the spell checker can't catch.

The following essays show how two students responded to this assignment. The first is organized by the block method, and the second is presented point-by-point.

STUDENT WRITING

Opposing Stories
BY JESSE CHEN

I can never forget what happened to my people at Tiananmen Square in Beijing, China, on the morning of June 4, 1989. My parents and I stayed up all night in our home in Hong Kong watching the news on television. It was broadcasting the quelling of the demonstrators in Tiananmen Square, and it was abhorrent and unbelievable. The Chinese Army entered Tiananmen Square and shot the students who were protesting for the pro-democracy movement. It came to a bloody end in that many innocent students were killed on that blood red morning. I remember that my parents were both crying when they saw their own people being killed by the "People's Army." When I read the accounts in my textbook from the *New York Times* (June 4, 1989) and the Official Chinese Government Accounts which include quotations from six Chinese persons, I found it incredible that they turned out to be two completely different stories even though they were about the same event. The *New York Times* tends to focus on reporting the facts of the slaughter while the Official Chinese Government Accounts tend to glorify the People's Liberation Army and the sacrifices made by its members. Because of different backgrounds and perspectives, the *New York Times* and the Official Chinese Government Accounts have come to two different stories about the slaughter; therefore, we need to think critically and analyze carefully before we can recognize a reliable source.

As a public medium, the *New York Times* plays a neutral role which only reports the fact of the slaughter without adding any biased opinion. It describes the students as "students," a factual title. Moreover, when describing the scene of the slaughter, it reports that the troops "fired submachine guns at the crowd of people who tried to resist." It states, "Troops marched along the roads surrounding central Tiananmen Square, sometimes firing in the air and sometimes firing directly at crowds who refused to move." It reports, "Most of the dead had been shot, but some had been run over by personnel carriers that forced their way through the protestors' barricades." Those descriptions of the scene are very close to the news which I saw and heard broadcast on TV, so the reliability is high. Moreover, in reporting the death toll, the *Times* does not give a very accurate number because it is impossible to be estimated or proved. Therefore, it merely gives a sketchy death toll: "Students said, however, that at least 500 people may have been killed in the crackdown." Furthermore, the *Times* does not render a judgment; it neither praises nor criticizes one side or the other since its responsibility is to report the facts only.

On the contrary, the Official Chinese Government Accounts give a different report, mainly glorifying the People's Liberation Army and sympathizing with the sacrifices made by its soldiers. Unlike the *Times,* these accounts do not name the students as "students." Han Xu, the Chinese ambassador to the United States, criticized them as "a mob led by a small number of people" who were trying to prevent "the normal conduct of the affairs of state." Also, General Lie Zgiyun said, "It never happened that soldiers fired directly at the people." Moreover, the Official Accounts even deny the death of the students: "Not a single student was killed at Tiananmen Square," said a Chinese army commander. However, the Official Chinese news program reported, "More than 1,000 police officers and troops were injured and killed, and some civilians were killed." Yuan Mu, an official government spokesman, said, "At most 300 people were killed in the operation, many of them soldiers." Finally, Prime Minister Li Peng offered his appreciation to the army: "Comrades, thanks for your hard work. We hope you will continue your fine efforts to safeguard security in the capital."

In conclusion, people's perspectives vary according to their backgrounds and status. Because of the differences in the backgrounds and status, the *Times* and the Chinese Government came to two opposed stories. We can measure their reliability by analyzing their backgrounds and status. Being a public medium, the *Times* tends to be neutral, not biased toward either side. However, in order to evade responsibility and cover up the faults, the Official Chinese Government Accounts tend to by-pass the sacrifices of the students and glorify the "hard work" of the army. Even until now, the Chinese Government still denies that they killed any students. Therefore, before we can trust or believe a source, we need to think critically about its perspective before we accept its reliability.

STUDENT WRITING

The Tiananmen Square Event: An Analysis of Several Different Accounts
BY RISSA MILLER

To depict an event truthfully is a task reporters hold sacred in this country, but to report a story free of bias and perception is almost an impossibility. As Americans we accept this and realize as long as uncovering truth is the ultimate goal, sifting through bias is up to the reader. However, through bias a story may take a politically or personally moti-vated angle, and without several different views, there is no way for a reader to deci-pher this perception. This is seen in seven accounts given in our textbook of the Tiananmen Square event.

In an eye-witness account published in the *New York Times* on June 4, 1989, the opening scene was set on a main road in Beijing which "echoed with screams . . . as young people carried the bodies of their friends . . . sobbing . . ." The depiction of vio-lence was detailed, and took up over half the article. The students were said to be fight-ing with iron pipes, stones, and other crude and ineffective objects against the army's more advanced weapons. "Many of those killed were throwing bricks at the soldiers . . . students and workers ran alongside the personnel carriers, hurling concrete blocks and wooden staves into the treads. . . ." Any description of action taken by the People's Lib-eration Army was entirely left out. The best sense the reader gets of it is from a student who says, "Nothing can show more clearly that it does not represent the people." The stu-dents' political stand was described as a "democracy movement" and an "uprising."

Another article in the *New York Times,* published on June 5, 1989, focused on the number of student deaths. It began, ". . . 300 people had been killed since the troops first opened fire. . . ." The report continued to state that, through word of mouth, estimates were between 2,000 and 2,600 casualties. Also, its only depictions of soldiers were of beating and bayoneting students, workers, and young women, ". . . after daybreak . . . sometimes entirely at random." This article is absent of any explanation of the political motivation on the students' part or that of the army. The language used was extremely neutral. "The student organization" was how the protesters were named, as opposed to calling them "rebels" or "democrats."

According to Deng Xiaoping as reported in the *Bejing Review,* the protesters were ". . . bad people mixed with students and onlookers . . . a rebellious clique and the dregs of society." They were not described as part of a movement or uprising but as wanting to "overthrow our state. . . ." Their stated goal was to establish a system dependent on the Western world. The only statement that addressed any student death was, "*If* tanks were used to roll over people. . . ." The soldiers, however, were named ". . . comrades [who] were injured or even sacrificed their lives." Xiaoping alluded to the army's victimization when they ". . . had their weapons taken by the rioters." How-ever, their strength overcame and they were congratulated as ". . . truly a Great Wall of iron and steel." This article finished with exclamations of the army as forever the defender of socialism, public interest, and the country, with a quick and final reminder of the cruelty of the "enemies."

The first two articles were written for a pro-Democracy public that had been intensely steered against Communism in the previous decade. Knowing this, it seems fitting that no motivation on the soldiers' part was taken into account. Also that the student death tolls and the violence against them was of great importance, rather than the underlying causes and effects of the incident. However, trying to attain a factual account was the main goal in the American articles. This is shown best by the quoting of protesters and eyewitnesses, as well as the impartial language found in the second *Times* article. We see the blatant opposition to this approach in the third article, and can assume some effects it might have on an unenlightened audience. It is possible to conclude that the American articles give a more accurate account. However, we must remember that no writer is free from bias and personal perspective. He/she will inevitably state, or just as importantly not state, things that will leave the reader lacking a complete perspective.

ALTERNATIVE WRITING PROJECT: COMPARING TWO REVIEWS

Find a recent review of a movie that you have seen or of a restaurant at which you have eaten. Compare the review with your experience. Do you agree with the reviewer? Identify specific examples of points you agree with and explain why. Do you disagree with the reviewer? Identify specific examples of these, too. Write an essay presenting your analysis of the review as it relates to your experience with the movie or at the restaurant.

8

Exploring Causal Relationships

"Our whole life consists of despairing of an answer and seeking an answer."
—Dorothee Solle

Writing to Speculate

Critical Thinking Focus: Causal reasoning

Writing Focus: Presenting causal reasoning

Reading Theme: Ecological relationships

Writing Project: Exploring causes of a recent event

The last two chapters have examined thinking and writing patterns that help us to understand our perceptions as we make sense of the world. As we perceive and make sense of the world, we experience the human tendency to ask why things are as they are: Why do some marriages endure for years and others end in divorce? Why does a northern area of the country have relatively mild winters for several years, then experience a record-breaking blizzard? Why do certain political ideas take hold during particular periods of history?

When we contemplate such questions, we are asking about (1) **causes,** factors that contribute to events and bring them about, and (2) **effects,** events that result directly or indirectly from causes or from other events. Much thinking about causes and effects occurs in an impromptu way as we attempt to guess why things happened the way they did. For example, about a divorce, we might say, "I think the marriage failed because of money problems." Though that might in fact be the reason, other factors are probably also involved. Determining causes is a complicated business since

- an event can have more than one cause
- an event can have various types of causes
- determining causes with certainty is often impossible

Nevertheless, because we want to "know why," and because it may be important to know why, we do try to determine causes and effects. When we think about causal relationships in an organized way, ever conscious of the difficulty and uncertainty of the task, we are taking part in the important critical thinking pattern called **causal analysis.**

The Writing Project in this chapter asks you to find information about some causes of a recent event and then to write a paper in which you present this information. The chapter should help you to write effectively about causal relationships.

Kinds of Causal Relationships

Causal patterns of thinking involve relating events in terms of the influence or effect they have on one another. Of course, when you make (or think) causal statements, you do not always use the word *cause*. For example, the following statements are all causal statements. In each case, underline the cause and circle the effect.

- Since I was the last to leave, I turned off the lights.
- Taking plenty of vitamin C really cured that terrible cold I had.
- I accidentally toasted my hand along with the marshmallows by getting too near the campfire.

In these statements, the words *since, turned off, cured,* and *getting too near* all point to the fact that something has caused something else to take place. Our language contains thousands of these causal "cousins." Try composing three statements of your own that express a causal relationship without using the word *cause*.

You are probably realizing that you make causal statements all the time and that you are constantly thinking in terms of causal relationships. In fact, the goal of much of your thinking is to figure out why something happened or how something came about, since if you can figure out how and why things occur, you may be able to predict what will happen in the future.

Predictions of anticipated results form the basis of many of your decisions. For example, the experience of toasting your hand along with the marshmallows might lead you to choose a longer stick for future toasting—simply because you are able to figure out the causal relationships involved and make predictions based on your understanding (namely, that a longer stick will keep your hand further away from the fire).

Consider the following activities which you likely performed today. Each activity assumes the existence of certain causal relationships which influenced your decision to perform it. Explain one such causal relationship for each activity.

- Brushing your teeth
  Causal relationship:

- Locking the door
  Causal relationship:

- Studying for an exam
  Causal relationship:

CAUSAL CHAIN

Although you may think of causes and effects in isolation—A caused B—in reality, causes and effects rarely appear by themselves. There is not just one cause of the resulting effect; there is a whole string of causes, as illustrated by the structures in Figure 8.1. They generally appear as parts of more complex patterns, including three that we will examine next: *causal chains, contributory causes,* and *interactive causes.* Consider the following scenario:

Your paper on the topic "life after death" is due on Monday morning. You have reserved the whole weekend to work on it and are just getting started when the phone rings. A favorite childhood friend is in town and wants to stay with you for the weekend. You say *yes*. By Sunday night, you've had a great weekend but have made little progress on your paper. You brew a pot of coffee and get started. At 3:00 A.M. you are too exhausted to continue. Deciding to get a few hours' sleep, you set the alarm clock for 6:00 A.M., giving yourself plenty of time to finish up. When you wake up, it's nine o'clock; the alarm failed to go off. Your class starts in forty minutes. You have no chance of getting the paper done on time. On your way to class, you mentally review the causes of this disaster. No longer concerned about life after death, you are very worried about life after this class!

- What causes in this situation are responsible for your paper's being late?
- What do you think is the single most important cause?
- What do you think your instructor will identify as the most important cause? Why?

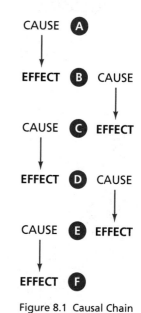

Figure 8.1 Causal Chain

A **causal chain,** as you have gathered from the preceding example, is a situation in which one thing leads to another, which then leads to another, and so on. There is not just one cause of the resulting effect; there is a whole string of causes. Which cause in the string is the "real" cause? Your answer will depend on your perspective on the situation. You might see the cause of the unfinished paper as a defective alarm clock. Your instructor, though, might see the cause of the problem as overall lack of planning. Proper planning, he or she might say, does not involve leaving assignments until the last minute, when unexpected problems can prevent a person from reaching a goal. You can illustrate this causal structure with Figure 8.1.

Thinking ↔ Writing Activity

Creating a Causal Chain

1. Create a similar scenario, detailing a chain of causes that results in your being late for class, meeting the "right" person, saving someone's life, or an effect of your own choosing.

2. Review the scenario you have just created. Explain how the "real" cause of the final effect could vary, depending on your perspective on the situation.

CONTRIBUTORY CAUSES

In addition to operating in causal chains over a period of time (A leads to B, which leads to C, which leads to D, and so on), causes can also serve simultaneously to produce an effect. When this happens (as it often does), you have a situation in which a number of different **contributory causes** are instrumental in bringing something about. Instead of working in isolation, each cause contributes to bringing about the final effect. When this situation occurs, each cause serves to support and reinforce the action of the other causes, a condition illustrated in Figure 8.2.

Consider the following situation:

It is the end of the term, and you have been working incredibly hard at school—writing papers, preparing for exams, finishing up course projects. You haven't been getting enough sleep, and you haven't been eating regular, well-balanced meals. To make matters worse,

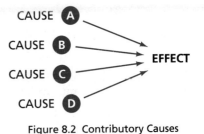

Figure 8.2 Contributory Causes

you have been under intense pressure in your personal life, having serious arguments with the person you have been dating, and this is constantly on your mind. It is the middle of the flu season, and many people you know have been sick with various respiratory infections. Walking home one evening, you get soaked by an unexpected downpour. By the time you get home, you are shivering. You soon find yourself in bed with a thermometer in your mouth—you are sick!

What was the "cause" of your illness? In this situation, you can see that evidently, a combination of factors led to your physical breakdown: low resistance, getting wet and chilled, being exposed to various germs and viruses, physical exhaustion, lack of proper eating, and so on. Taken by itself, no one factor might have been enough to cause your illness. Together, they all contributed to the final outcome.

Thinking ↔ Writing Activity

Creating a Contributory-Cause Scenario

Create a similar scenario, detailing the contributory causes that led to your asking someone for a date, choosing a major, losing or winning a game, or an effect of your own choosing.

INTERACTIVE CAUSES

Our examination of causal relationships has revealed that causes rarely operate in isolation but instead often influence (and are influenced by) other factors. Imagine that you are scheduled to give a speech to a large group of people. As your moment in the spotlight approaches, you become anxious, which results in a dry mouth and throat, making your voice sound more like a croak. The prospect of sounding like a bullfrog increases your anxiety, which in turn dries your mouth and constricts your throat further, reducing your croak to something much worse—silence.

This common scenario reveals the way different factors can relate to each other through reciprocal influences that flow back and forth from one to the other. Understanding this type of **interactive causal relationship** is an extremely important way of organizing and making sense of your experiences. For instance, to comprehend social relationships, such as families, teams, groups of friends, and so on, you have to understand the complex ways in which each individual influences—and is influenced by—all the other members of the group. Understanding biological systems and other systems is similar to understanding social systems. To comprehend and explain how an organ such as the heart, liver, or

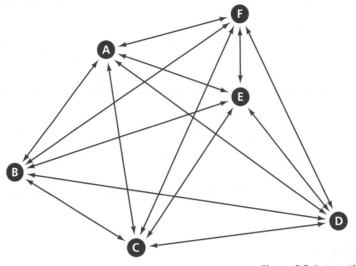

Figure 8.3 Interactive Causes

brain functions, you have to describe its complex, interactive relationships with all the other parts of the biological system. Figure 8.3 illustrates these dynamic causal relationships.

Thinking ↔ Writing Activity

Identifying Causal Patterns

Read the following passages which illustrate causal patterns of thinking. For each passage, identify the kind of causal relationship (chain, contributory, or interactive), and explain how the causes are related to one another.

Nothing posed a more serious threat to the bald eagle's survival than a modern chemical compound called DDT. Around 1940, a retired Canadian banker named Charles L. Broley began keeping track of eagles nesting in Florida. Each breeding season, he climbed into more than 50 nests, counted the eaglets and put metal bands on their legs. In the late 1940's, a sudden drop-off in the number of young produced led him to conclude that 80 percent of his birds were sterile. Broley blamed DDT. Scientists later discovered that DDE, a breakdown product of DDT, causes not sterility, but a fatal thinning of eggshell among birds of prey. Applied on cropland all over the United States, the pesticide was running off into waterways where it concentrated in fish. The bald eagles ate the fish and the DDT impaired their ability to reproduce. They were not alone, of course. Ospreys and pelicans suffered similar setbacks. —Jim Doherty, "The Bald Eagle and DDT"

It is popularly accepted that Hitler was the major cause of World War II, but the ultimate causes go much deeper than one personality. First, there were long-standing German grievances against reparations levied on the nation following its defeat in World War I. Second, there were severe economic strains that caused resentment among the German people. Third, there were French and English reluctance to work out a sound disarmament policy and American non-involvement in the matter. Finally, there was the European fear that communism was a much greater danger than National Socialism. These factors contributed to the outbreak of World War II. —Gilbert Muller, *The American College Handbook*

You crunch and chew your way through vast quantities of snacks and confectioneries and relieve your thirst with multicolored, flavored soft drinks, with and without calories, for two basic reasons. The first is simple; the food tastes good, and you enjoy the sensation of eating it. Second, you associate these foods, often without being aware of it, with the highly pleasurable experiences depicted in the advertisements used to promote their sale. Current television advertisements demonstrate this point: people turn from grumpiness to euphoria after crunching a corn chip. Others water ski into the sunset with their loved ones while drinking a popular soft drink. People entertain on the patio with friends, cook over campfires without mosquitoes, or go to carnivals with granddad munching away at the latest candy or snack food. The people portrayed in these scenarios are all healthy, vigorous, and good looking; one wonders how popular the food they convince you to eat would be if they would crunch or drink away while complaining about low back pain or clogged sinuses. —Judith Wurtman, *Eating Your Way Through Life*

Ways of Testing Causes

NECESSARY CONDITION AND SUFFICIENT CONDITION

In addition to the three patterns of causality we have just examined, we need to consider necessary and sufficient conditions. A **necessary condition** is a factor that is required to bring about a certain result: for example, an intact light bulb is required for a lamp's illumination. However, by itself, an intact light bulb is not sufficient to provide illumination: you also need electricity, which is another necessary condition. Most of us have experienced that moment of bewilderment when we flip on a light during a power failure—and nothing happens!

A **sufficient condition** is a factor that of itself is always sufficient for bringing about a certain result. For example, a pinch on the arm is a sufficient cause for discomfort. Of course, even with a sufficient condition, there may be an additional necessary condition, or several necessary conditions, for a result to occur. Having healthy nerves in the arm and being conscious are two necessary conditions for someone's feeling a sensation when pinched on the arm.

IMMEDIATE CAUSE AND REMOTE CAUSE

Yet another way to think critically about causes is to classify them by how close in time the cause is to its result. Something that happens just before an event that it causes is called an **immediate cause.** A factor that also helped to bring about this same event but that occurred further back in time is called a **remote cause.** For example, a last-minute touchdown could be the immediate cause of a football championship, but wise trades made for key players before the season began might be remote causes.

To give a more personal example, getting an A on a college history exam is a happy outcome that may result from the following different types of causes and conditions. The immediate cause could be the fact that you spent an entire weekend studying, carefully reviewing your notes and rehearsing answers to possible questions. More remote causes could include your faithful class attendance throughout the semester and your having asked questions in class to clear up any areas of misunderstanding. An even more remote cause might be a grade-school trip to a museum, which sparked your interest in history. Necessary conditions for your success could include having sufficient intelligence to understand the material and being in good health on the day of the exam.

Thinking ↔ Writing Activity

Seeing Causal Relationships

1. Study the picture on the next page of young people at a bar and see how many causal relationships are being suggested. What are your perceptions of why they are there and why some of them have the expressions that they do? See what perceptions your classmates have and notice how they differ.

2. Carefully examine the Budweiser ad in the background. What do you think are the causal relationships among advertisements for alcoholic drinks, these young peoples' apparent moods, and the drinking behaviors of college students whom you know.

3. What are the causes of your attitudes toward drinking alcohol? Have your attitudes changed since attending college? If you wish, share your analysis of your perspectives with your classmates.

© B. Stitzer/PhotoEdit.

Debates over important environmental issues, ranging from global warming to pollution of our water, are dominated by discussions of causes and effects. The following four articles are about water, its availability, and its quality.

FROM

The Last Days of Florida Bay

BY CARL HIAASEN

On a gum-gray June afternoon, between thundershowers, my son and I are running a 17-foot skiff through the backcountry of Florida Bay. The wind has lain down, the water is silk. Suddenly, a glorious eruption: bottle-nosed dolphins, an acre of them, in a spree of feeding, play and rambunctious lust. From a hundred yards we can hear the slap of flukes and the hiss of blowholes. We can see the misty geysers, the slash of black dorsals, the occasional detonation as a luckless bait fish gets gobbled.

No matter how often I witness the sight, I'm always dazzled. A stranger to these waters could only assume he was traveling in authentic wilderness, pure and thriving. If only it were so.

It's easy, when surrounded by dolphins, to forget that the bay is fatefully situated downstream from the ulcerous sprawl of Florida's Gold Coast. Four-and-a-half million people live only a morning's drive away.

The river that feeds the backcountry is the Everglades, sometimes parched and sometimes flooded. Water that once ran untainted and bountiful is now intercepted and pumped extravagantly to sugarcane fields, swimming pools, golf courses, city reservoirs—and even the Atlantic. What's left is dispensed toward the bay in a criminally negligent fraction of its natural flow. The water isn't as clean as it once was, and it doesn't always arrive in the right season.

5   That the bay is sick is hardly a surprise. The wonder is that it has survived so long and the dolphins haven't fled to sea forever. . . .

That's why it is imperative that a natural flow be restored as soon as possible, while the political will and funds exist to do it. The engineering isn't as daunting as the politics. Powerful special-interest groups are demanding a say in where the lifeblood of the Everglades goes, how much they get to keep and what they're allowed to dump in the water on its way downstream.

The battle begins up at Lake Okeechobee, where Big Sugar finally (and reluctantly) has agreed to filter phosphates from the runoff of the cane fields. Farther south, the cities siphon heavily from the diked "conservation areas"— cheap, accessible reservoirs that help fuel the breakneck westward growth in Palm Beach, Broward and Dade counties. Even below Miami, on Florida's still rural southern tip, water policy is disproportionately influenced by private interests. In the dry months what would otherwise trickle through the glades to the bay is diverted instead to a small cluster of tomato and avocado farms. Conversely, in the wet season the surplus water is pumped off the fields to protect the crops. The canal network was absurdly designed to flush millions of gallons not into the Everglades (which were made to absorb them) but into Manatee Bay and Barnes Sound, which are saltwater bodies. The effect of such a copious, sudden injection of freshwater is an overdose—lethal on an impressive scale to fish, corals and other marine life.

But it's all for a good cause. Upstream the avocados are plump and safe.

Critical Reading Questions

1. List the causes Hiaasen identifies as having brought about the present condition of the bay.
2. What is the immediate cause?
3. Do any of these causes make up a causal chain?
4. Are any of the causes contributory?
5. Are any of the causes interactive? If so, how?

The following editorial appeared in the *Washington Post* five years after Hiaasen's article (July 7, 2000).

Replumbing Florida

WASHINGTON POST

One of the largest public works projects of modern times has been the draining of the southern third of Florida. A vast swamp was converted into land fit for urban development and agriculture; Florida has become the fourth most populous state. But the price was loss of an environmental treasure house—perhaps the world's preeminent wetland, the Everglades—and degradation of Florida Bay.

Now the pendulum has swung. The government and its agent in these matters, the Corps of Engineers, having done great environmental damage, propose to reverse it. Without particular fanfare, the Senate Environment and Public Works Committee reported out, 16 to 1, the other day, a bill authorizing the first 10 of 68 planned projects meant not quite to restore the Everglades and bay—that will never happen—but to revive and allow them to flourish once again.

Some other steps have already been taken in that direction. The southern third of Florida was anciently covered by a sheet of water moving slowly south from Lake Okeechobee, from which it overflowed. The lake is fed by the Kissimmee River. To dry out land for development, the Corps reduced and channeled the flow, diverting vast amounts of water east and west, to the Atlantic Ocean and Gulf of Mexico. The new game is to restore as much as possible of the natural flow—and the wildlife it sustains—without producing flooding. Among much else, that requires creating or re-creating water storage areas for the state's dry season.

5   The Corps years ago had spent enormous sums to straighten out the winding Kissimmee, thus reclaiming land on either bank. Now it's putting the kinks back in. Filtration marshes are being created south of the sugar and other agricultural lands just below the lake as a means of diluting runoff and reducing pollution. Now the Corps will begin to reconstruct some of the plumbing—storage areas, canals and levees—farther south.

Some Senate committee members objected to the cost of the project—the estimate of $8 billion over 30-odd years is almost certainly low—and the share to be paid by the federal government as opposed to the state. But this is not the usual Corps project. It is, in a way, the reverse of the massive reclamation projects in the western states, in which desert has been turned into arable and habitable land. The draining of Florida was mainly a federal undertaking that went too far. The correction of it deserves to be mainly a federal undertaking as well. It won't happen otherwise, and that would be a terrible result.

Critical Reading Questions

1. What do you think are the causes of this proposed reversal of environmental policy?

2. What would be the "terrible result" referred to in the last sentence? Is your answer influenced by your reading of the Hiaasen article?

Holy Water

BY JOAN DIDION

Some of us who live in arid parts of the world think about water with a reverence others might find excessive. The water I will draw tomorrow from my tap in Malibu is today crossing the Mojave Desert from the Colorado River, and I like to think about exactly where that water is. The water I will drink tonight in a restaurant in Hollywood is by now well down the Los Angeles Aqueduct from the Owens River, and I also think about exactly where that water is: I particularly like to imagine it as it cascades down the 45-degree stone steps that aerate Owens water after its airless passage through the mountain pipes and siphons. As it happens my own reverence for water has always taken the form of this constant meditation upon where the water is, of an obsessive interest not in the politics of water but in the waterworks themselves, in the movement of water through aqueducts and siphons and pumps and forebays and afterbays and weirs and drains, in plumbing on the grand scale. I know the data on water projects I will never see. I know the difficulty Kaiser had closing the last two sluiceway gates on the Guri Dam in Venezuela. I keep watch on evaporation behind the Aswan in Egypt. I can put myself to sleep imagining the water dropping a thousand feet into the turbines at Churchill Falls in Labrador. If the Churchill Falls Project fails to materialize, I fall back on waterworks closer at hand—the tailrace at Hoover on the Colorado, the surge tank in the Tehachapi Mountains that receives California Aqueduct water pumped higher than water has ever been pumped before— and finally I replay a morning when I was seventeen years old and caught, in a military-surplus life raft, in the construction of the Nimbus Afterbay Dam on the American River near Sacramento. I remember that at the moment it happened I was trying to open a tin of anchovies with capers. I recall the raft spinning into the narrow chute through which the river had been temporarily diverted. I recall being deliriously happy.

I suppose it was partly the memory of that delirium that led me to visit, one summer morning in Sacramento, the Operations Control Center for the California State Water Project. Actually so much water is moved around California by so many different agencies that maybe only the movers themselves know on any given day whose water is where, but to get a general picture it is necessary only to remember that Los Angeles moves some of it, San Francisco moves some of it, the Bureau of Reclamation's Central Valley Project moves some of it and the California State Water Project moves most of the rest of it, moves a vast amount of it, moves more water farther than has ever been moved anywhere. They collect this water up in the granite keeps of the Sierra Nevada and they store roughly a trillion gallons of it behind the Oroville Dam and every morning, down at the Project's headquarters in Sacramento, they decide how much of their water they want to move the next day. They make this morning decision according to supply and demand, which is simple in theory but rather more complicated in practice. In theory each of the Project's five field divisions—the

Oroville, the Delta, the San Luis, the San Joaquin and the Southern divisions—places a call to headquarters before nine A.M. and tells the dispatchers how much water is needed by its local water contractors, who have in turn based their morning estimates on orders from growers and other big users. A schedule is made. The gates open and close according to schedule. The water flows south and the deliveries are made.

In practice this requires prodigious coordination, precision, and the best efforts of several human minds and that of a Univac 418. In practice it might be necessary to hold large flows of water for power production, or to flush out encroaching salinity in the Sacramento–San Joaquin Delta, the most ecologically sensitive point on the system. In practice a sudden rain might obviate the need for a delivery when that delivery is already on its way. In practice what is being delivered here is an enormous volume of water, not quarts of milk or spools of thread, and it takes two days to move such a delivery down through Oroville into the Delta, which is the great pooling place for California water and has been for some years alive with electronic sensors and telemetering equipment and men blocking channels and diverting flows and shoveling fish away from the pumps. It takes perhaps another six days to move this same water down the California Aqueduct from the Delta to the Tehachapi and put it over the hill to Southern California. "Putting some over the hill" is what they say around the Project Operations Control Center when they want to indicate that they are pumping Aqueduct water from the floor of the San Joaquin Valley up and over the Tehachapi Mountains. "Pulling it down" is what they say when they want to indicate that they are lowering a water level somewhere in the system. They can put some over the hill by remote control from this room in Sacramento with its Univac and its big board and its flashing lights. They can pull down a pool in the San Joaquin by remote control from this room in Sacramento with its locked doors and its ringing alarms and its constant print-outs of data from sensors out there in the water itself. From this room in Sacramento the whole system takes on the aspect of a perfect three-billion-dollar hydraulic toy, and in certain ways it is. "LET'S START DRAINING QUAIL AT 12:00" was the 10:51 A.M. entry on the electronically recorded communications log the day I visited the Operations Control Center. "Quail" is a reservoir in Los Angeles County with a gross capacity of 1,636,018,000 gallons. "OK" was the response recorded in the log. I knew at that moment that I had missed the only vocation for which I had any instinctive affinity: I wanted to drain Quail myself.

Not many people I know carry their end of the conversation when I want to talk about water deliveries, even when I stress that these deliveries affect their lives, indirectly, every day. "Indirectly" is not quite enough for most people I know. This morning, however, several people I know were affected not "indirectly" but "directly" by the way the water moves. They had been in New Mexico shooting a picture, one sequence of which required a river deep enough to sink a truck, the kind with a cab and a trailer and fifty or sixty wheels. It so happened that no river near the New Mexico location was running that deep this year. The production was therefore moved today to Needles, California, where the Colorado River normally runs, depending upon releases from Davis Dam, eighteen to twenty-five feet deep. Now. Follow this closely: yesterday we had a freak tropical storm in Southern California, two inches of rain in a normally dry month, and because this rain flooded the fields and provided more irrigation than any grower could possibly want for several days, no water was ordered from Davis Dam.

5   No order, no releases.

Supply and demand.

As a result the Colorado was running only seven feet deep past Needles today, Sam Peckinpah's desire for eighteen feet of water in which to sink a truck not being the kind of demand anyone at Davis Dam is geared to meet. The production closed down for the weekend. Shooting will resume Tuesday, providing some grower orders water and the agencies controlling the Colorado release it. Meanwhile many gaffers, best boys, cameramen, assistant directors, script supervisors, stunt drivers and maybe even Sam Peckinpah are waiting out the weekend in Needles, where it is often 110 degrees at five P.M. and hard to get dinner after eight. This is a California parable, but a true one.

I have always wanted a swimming pool, and never had one. When it became generally known a year or so ago that California was suffering severe drought, many people in water-rich parts of the country seemed obscurely gratified, and made frequent reference to Californians having to brick up their swimming pools. In fact a swimming pool requires, once it has been filled and the filter has begun its process of cleaning and recirculating the water, virtually no water, but the symbolic content of swimming pools has always been interesting: a pool is misapprehended as a trapping of affluence, real or pretended, and of a kind of hedonistic attention to the body. Actually a pool is, for many of us in the West, a symbol not of affluence but of order, of control over the uncontrollable. A pool is water, made available and useful, and is, as such, infinitely soothing to the western eye.

It is easy to forget that the only natural force over which we have any control out here is water, and that only recently. In my memory California summers were characterized by the coughing in the pipes that meant the well was dry, and California winters by all-night watches on rivers about to crest, by sandbagging, by dynamite on the levees and flooding on the first floor. Even now the place is not all that hospitable to extensive settlement. As I write a fire has been burning out of control for two weeks in the ranges behind the Big Sur coast. Flash floods last night wiped out all major roads into Imperial County. I noticed this morning a hairline crack in a living-room tile from last week's earthquake, a 4.4 I never felt. In the part of California where I now live aridity is the single most prominent feature of the climate, and I am not pleased to see, this year, cactus spreading wild to the sea. There will be days this winter when the humidity will drop to ten, seven, four. Tumbleweed will blow against my house and the sound of the rattlesnake will be duplicated a hundred times a day by dried bougainvillea drifting in my driveway. The apparent ease of California life is an illusion, and those who believe the illusion real live here in only the most temporary way. I know as well as the next person that there is considerable transcendent value in a river running wild and undammed, a river running free over granite, but I have also lived beneath such a river when it was running in flood, and gone without showers when it was running dry.

10   "The West begins," Bernard DeVoto wrote, "where the average annual rainfall drops below twenty inches." This is maybe the best definition of the West I have ever read, and it goes a long way toward explaining my own passion for seeing the water under control, but many people I know persist in looking for psychoanalytical implications in this passion. As a matter of fact I have explored, in an amateur way, the more obvious of these implications, and come up with nothing interesting. A certain external reality remains, and resists interpretation. The West begins where the average annual rainfall drops below twenty inches. Water is important to people who do not have it, and the same is true of control. Some fifteen years ago I tore a poem by Karl Shapiro from a magazine and pinned it on my kitchen wall. This fragment of paper is now on the wall of a sixth kitchen, and crumbles a little whenever I touch it, but I keep it there for the last stanza, which has for me the power of a prayer:

> It is raining in California, a straight rain
> Cleaning the heavy oranges on the bush,
> Filling the gardens till the gardens flow,
> Shining the olives, tiling the gleaming tile,
> Waxing the dark camellia leaves more green,
> Flooding the daylong valleys like the Nile.

I thought of those lines almost constantly on the morning in Sacramento when I went to visit the California State Water Project Operations Control Center. If I had wanted to drain Quail at 10:51 that morning, I wanted, by early afternoon, to do a great deal more. I wanted to open and close the Clifton Court Forebay intake gate. I wanted to produce some power down at the San Luis Dam. I wanted to pick a pool at random on the Aqueduct and pull it down and then refill it, watching for the hydraulic jump. I wanted to put some water over the hill and I wanted to shut down all flow from the Aqueduct into the Bureau of Reclamation's Cross Valley Canal, just to see how long it would take somebody over at Reclamation to call up and complain. I stayed as long as I could and watched the system work on the big board with the lighted checkpoints. The Delta salinity report was coming in on one of the teletypes behind me. The Delta tidal report was coming in on another. The earthquake board, which has been desensitized to sound its alarm (a beeping tone for Southern California, a high-pitched one for the north) only for those earthquakes which register at least 3.0 on the Richter Scale, was silent. I had no further business in this room and yet I wanted to stay the day. I wanted to be the one, that day, who was shining the olives, filling the gardens, and flooding the daylong valleys like the Nile. I want it still.

Critical Reading Questions

1. Why does Didion think so much about water?

2. Why do you think that the people she knows do not want to talk much about water delivery?

3. Identify the causes that led to Sam Peckinpah's film company's having to wait out the weekend idly in Needles.

4. What do you think that Didion means when she says, "The apparent ease of California life is an illusion. . . . "? What are some causes of this illusion?

5. What insight does this essay provide into causal connections between water delivery and social or political issues?

Competition Grows in China Over Dwindling Water Resources

BY TED PLAFKER

Anqiu, China—Mud up to his thighs and naked as the day he was born, Yong Peixing emerged from the Mushan Reservoir clutching a burlap bag full of clams in one hand and a tangle of leafy lake weeks in the other. After hawking two dozen clams on the spot to a passerby for the equivalent of 75 cents, he prepared to take the soggy weeds home and feed them to his ducks.

Yong used to rely on one of the reservoir's runoff streams to irrigate his nearby plot of corn and vegetables. But since July, when local authorities here in eastern Shandong province moved to block the flow of those streams, Yong has had to find other ways to make a living.

He is not alone. Whether it is blamed on global warming, drought, a massive waste of precious resources, a population boom or desertification, China is facing a serious water shortage that experts say could hinder development and spark an environmental and political crisis in years to come.

This is true not only here in Shandong—a province about 200 miles south of Beijing, where the amount of rainfall this spring is 84 percent below that of last year—but all across the northern part of the country. Millions of people are struggling, like Yong, to do more with less water, and millions more, like his angry fellow villagers, are feuding over dwindling supplies.

5   On July 6, they revolted when government workers were sent to the reservoir to block the streams, confronting them with shovels and farm tools. Police moved in, and in the ensuing chaos one officer was killed and scores of policemen and villagers were injured, according to Yong and other local witnesses.

"It's getting drier here all the time, and people depend on that water for drinking and for farming, so of course their reaction was very extreme," said Yong, 54, adding that he did not participate in the violence.

The consequences are being felt in nearly 100 Chinese cities, where some form of water rationing has been imposed on industrial and residential users, and in the countryside, where officials blame drought for this year's 9.3 percent decline in the summer grain yield. Even in the Yangtze River city of Chongqing in south-central China, which most summers faces danger from flooding, navigation is hampered by water levels that have dropped to their lowest levels in 40 years.

According to Ma Jun, the Beijing-based author of a new book called "China's Water Crisis," the nation has been mismanaging its water resources for centuries, and has inflicted the greatest damage in the 50 years of development since the start of Communist rule.

Shanghai, China's heavily built-up commercial center with a population of 13 million, has drawn so heavily on its water table over the years that the ground beneath it is sinking. Experts say the rate of subsidence peaked at four inches per year in the 1960s but has been reduced to less than a half-inch annually.

10   Hardest hit has been the Yellow River, which snakes for 3,000 miles through the northern heartland before reaching—sometimes, anyway—the spot on Shandong's shore where it flows into the Bo Hai, an arm of the Yellow Sea. For generations, Chinese tried to control the Yellow River by building ever higher embankments, but these often failed, resulting in devastating floods. In recent decades, the government has built a series of dams to keep the river in check.

"For 50 years they have succeeded in avoiding any major destructive breach, and that's a miracle that they deserve some credit for," Ma said. "But in the process of taming the Yellow River, they have killed it. It is no longer a natural river."

Indeed, the river has run dry and failed to reach the sea for part of nearly every year since 1972. The dry spells have grown steadily longer, reaching a peak from 1996 to 1998 of an average of 106 days per year.

Officials take credit for the fact that the Yellow River has not yet dried out this year, citing improved water conservation efforts and more efficient management of reservoirs. But as the work going on at the Mushan Reservoir illustrates, any effort to save water in one place can mean taking it from someplace else.

According to a senior engineer at the Mushan project, the reservoir's retaining wall was crumbling and needed repair. He denied that officials meant to deprive villagers of the runoff water they had come to rely on but acknowledged that local residents had been affected.

15   After the July riot, officials started digging a new channel to restore water for the people here, sacrificing some of the gains they had hoped to attain for the reservoir. Throughout China, similar compromises are being made, as authorities shift and divert valuable water resources in search of a balance between those who have political influence, those whose needs are greatest, and those whose protests are loudest.

City dwellers and factories compete with farmers for water, and far-flung regions of China compete with each other. And it is the Yellow River, together with other northern Chinese watersheds, that are in the greatest demand.

When the city of Qingdao—also in Shandong but far to the east of the Yellow River delta—began growing rapidly in the 1980s, the government built a channel to provide it with extra water from the Yellow River. The capital, Beijing, ran into water problems even earlier, and in the 1970s began diverting water from the Hai River, which used to serve the nearby port city of Tianjin. But Tianjin has been growing too, and in August city officials announced a plan to commandeer 400 million tons of Shandong's Yellow River water through a 300-mile diversion channel.

Experts agree that China's longstanding cheap water policy has encouraged wasteful consumption, and China is now embarked on a program to raise water prices throughout the country. But the government is also wary of angering people who have grown used to cheap water. Prices are rising slowly, and will likely remain below cost for several years.

Critical Reading Questions

1. What causes does Plafker's *Washington Post* article give for this water shortage in China? Can you identify any interactions between various causes?

2. What effects are reported? What would be some effects if water were rationed where you live?

3. Compare this article with the excerpt from Didion's "Holy Water." What similarities or differences do you see between what is said in these two readings about management of water? What do they say about the influence of water and power over human lives?

Identifying Causal Fallacies

Because causality plays such a dominant role in the way we make sense of the world, it is not surprising that people make many mistakes and many errors in judgment in trying to determine causal relationships. These mistakes and errors can lead to unsound arguments, or **fallacies.** The following are some of the most common fallacies associated with causality.

- Questionable cause
- Misidentification of the cause
- *Post hoc ergo propter hoc*
- Slippery slope

QUESTIONABLE CAUSE

The fallacy of *questionable cause* occurs when someone presents a causal relationship for which no real evidence exists. Superstitious beliefs such as "If you break a mirror, you will have seven years of bad luck" usually fall into this category. Some people feel that astrology, a system of beliefs tying one's personality and fortunes in life to the position of the planets at the moment of birth, also falls into this category.

Consider the following passage from the *Confessions* of St. Augustine. Does it seem to support the causal assertions of astrology or deny them? Why?

> Firminus had heard from his father that when his mother had been pregnant with him, a slave belonging to a friend of his father's was also about to bear. It happened that since the two women had their babies at the same instant, the men were forced to cast exactly the same horoscope for each newborn child down to the last detail, one for his son, the other for the little slave. Yet Firminus, born to wealth in his parents' house, had one of the more illustrious careers in life whereas the slave had no alleviation of his life's burden.

Other examples of this fallacy include explanations like those given by fourteenth-century sufferers of the bubonic plague who claimed that the Jews were poisoning the Christians' wells. This charge was nonsensical. An equal percentage of Jews were dying of the plague. No evidence supported the allegation.

MISIDENTIFICATION OF THE CAUSE

In causal situations we are not always certain about what is causing what—in other words, about what is the cause and what is the effect. For example, in the following pairs of items, which is the cause, and which is the effect? Why?

- Headaches and tension
- Failure in school and personal problems
- Shyness and lack of confidence
- Substance abuse and emotional difficulties

Sometimes a third factor is responsible for two effects that we are examining. Headaches and tension may both be the result of a third element—such as some new medication a person is taking. When we fail to recognize the third element, we commit the fallacy of *ignoring a common cause*. There also exists the fallacy of *assuming a common cause*—such as assuming that a person's sore toe and earache both stem from the same cause.

POST HOC ERGO PROPTER HOC

The translation of the Latin phrase *post hoc ergo propter hoc* is "After that, therefore because of that." It refers to situations in which, because two things occur closely together in time, we assume that one has caused the other. Suppose your team wins the game each time you wear your favorite shirt; you just may be tempted to conclude that the one event (wearing your favorite shirt) has some influence on the other event (winning the game). As a result, you may continue to wear this shirt "for good luck." It is easy to see how this sort of mistaken thinking can lead to all sorts of superstitious beliefs. Consider the following causal conclusion arrived at by Mark Twain's fictional character Huckleberry Finn in the following passage. How would you analyze his conclusion?

> I've always reckoned that looking at the new moon over your left shoulder is one of the carelessest and foolishest things a body can do. Old Hank Bunker done it once, and bragged about it; and in less than two years he got drunk and fell off a shot tower and spread himself out so that he was just a kind of layer. . . . But anyway, it all came of looking at the moon that way, like a fool.

Can you identify any of your own superstitious beliefs or practices that may have resulted from *post hoc* thinking?

SLIPPERY SLOPE

The causal fallacy of *slippery slope* is illustrated in the following advice:

Don't miss that first deadline, because if you do, it won't be long before you're missing all your deadlines. This will spread to the rest of your life, as you will be late for every appointment. This terminal procrastination will ruin your career, and friends and relatives will abandon you. You will end up a lonely failure who is unable to ever do anything on time.

Slippery slope thinking asserts that one undesirable action will inevitably lead to a worse action, which will necessarily lead to still a worse one, all the way down the "slippery slope" to some terrible disaster at the bottom. Although this progression may indeed occur, there certainly is no causal guarantee that it will. Create slippery slope scenarios for one of the following warnings:

- If you get behind on one credit card payment . . .
- If you fail that first test . . .
- If you eat that first fudge square . . .

Summary: Causal Fallacies	
Questionable Cause:	Presenting a causal relationship for which no real evidence exists
Misidentification of Cause:	Uncertainty about what is the cause and what is the effect: ignoring a common cause, assuming a false common cause
Post Hoc Ego Propter Hoc:	Assuming a causal relationship between situations occurring closely together in time
Slippery Slope:	Asserting that one undesirable action will lead to a worse action, which will lead to still a worse one—down, down the slippery slope

Thinking ↔ Writing Activity

Diagnosing Causal Fallacies

Review the four causal fallacies just described; then identify and explain the reasoning pitfalls illustrated in the following examples.

1. The person who won the lottery says she dreamed the winning numbers. I'm going to start writing down the numbers that I dream about.

2. Yesterday I forgot to take my vitamins, and I immediately got sick. That mistake won't occur again!

3. I'm warning you: if you miss a class, it won't be long before you flunk out of school and ruin your future.

4. I always take the first seat in the bus. Today I took another seat, and the bus broke down.

5. I think the reason I'm not doing well in school is that I simply don't have enough time to study, and my classes aren't interesting, either.

Detecting Causal Claims

Sometimes people use causal reasoning because they want us to see cause-and-effect relationships that they believe exist. When they do this, we say they are making **causal claims.** Consider the following examples.

1. Politicians assure us that a vote for them will result in better schools and lower taxes.

2. Advertisers tell us that using a detergent will leave our wash "cleaner than clean, whiter than white."

3. Doctors tell us that eating a balanced diet will result in better health.

4. Educators tell us that a college degree is worth an average of $830,000 additional income over an individual's lifetime.

5. Utility companies inform us that using nuclear energy will result in less pollution.

In each of these examples, certain causal claims are being made about how the world operates in an effort to persuade us to adopt a certain point of view. As critical thinkers, it is our duty to evaluate these various causal claims to determine whether they are valid or questionable.

Thinking ↔ Writing Activity

Evaluating Causal Claims

Explain how you might go about evaluating the causal claims previously listed.

- *Example:* Electing politicians and claims about getting better schools and lower taxes.
- *Evaluation:* Speak to teachers and principals about school needs. Understand what a politician in a specific office can and cannot do about education. Learn about budgets for school systems. Remember your own school experiences and think about why they were good or bad. Learn about taxes and schools in your area.

Writing Thoughtfully About Causal Relationships

Clearly, because of the complexity of determining cause and effect, writing a causal analysis requires special care. Causal analyses range all the way from rigorous scientific studies that can establish causes with some degree of certainty to theorizing about events in our personal lives. The causal analysis assignments you will encounter in college are likely to be of two types: those for which you conduct some kind of study to determine causality and then report your results, and those for which you research what others have said about the causes of an event and report their findings.

For the first type, you are likely to be given a format, such as for a lab report or an experimental design. It will be important for you to follow directions as you plan and conduct your study, and important for you to observe the conventions of the discipline in which you are writing as you prepare your report. Models are extremely helpful, so study them carefully if your professor provides them. If not, ask a librarian for guidance.

The second type, in which you report what others have said about the causes of an event, can be structured in the traditional essay format. Though you may worry that a paper for which research is required will be more difficult to write, you may be pleasantly surprised to discover that the sources you discover in research became "assistant writers." The authors of the sources help you complete the paper by providing information for you to include. Of course, the information from sources must be properly documented.

Principles for Analyzing Causes

The principles for presenting causal analysis in writing are not firm rules; at times, you may have good reason for varying or adapting them. In general, though, it makes sense to follow them.

1. Be cautious. Causal relationships are difficult to prove. You may have to use wording such as *possible cause* or *may have affected.*

2. Name the event and perhaps describe it and/or people's reactions to it in your introduction.

3. In your thesis statement, indicate that you will be analyzing the causes of this event or that you will be reporting what others have said about its causes.

4. Discuss each cause in a separate section (at least one body paragraph for each cause).

5. Amplify how or why each cause brought about the event. Simply naming the cause is not enough.

6. Whenever possible, focus on immediate rather than remote causes.

7. Use the labels in this chapter (contributory, causal chain, interactive, sufficient, and so on) to identify causal relationships if they are suitable for the style of your paper.

8. Represent accurately any sources that you use and document them honestly and correctly.

9. Avoid logical fallacies such as *post hoc ergo propter hoc.*

10. In your conclusion, name the causes and discuss the level of certainty for each of them. You may, of course, wish to do more than this in your conclusion.

Writing Project: Exploring Some Causes of a Recent Event

This chapter has included both readings and Thinking-Writing Activities that encourage you to think about causal relationships in your own life and in the environment. Be sure to reread what you wrote for those activities; you may be able to use some of the material when completing this project.

Write an essay in which you report and discuss some of the causes of a specific local or national event that occurred within the last three years. You might want to choose an event that had an environmental impact, or, depending on your interests or your instructor's assignment, you might want to write about something else that has affected the lives of many people (such as recent Supreme Court decisions or a current international crisis). Include material from two to four sources.

After you have drafted your essay, revise it to the best of your ability. Follow your instructor's directions for topic choices, length, format, documentation style, and so on.

Begin by considering the key elements in the Thinking-Writing Model.

THE WRITING SITUATION

Purpose You have a variety of purposes here. You can satisfy your own curiosity about why an event occurred and explain the causes to others. You can improve your ability to think critically about causal relationships. You can hone your revision skills by working through the revision questions that follow.

Audience You have a range of readers within your audience. *You* are an important audience, for in researching and analyzing causes, you can become a better thinker and possibly a more concerned citizen. Your classmates can be a valuable audience for review of a draft, reacting as intelligent readers who are not as knowledgeable as you about the causes of this event. Others interested in the event may find your paper enlightening. Finally, your instructor remains the audience who will judge how well you have planned, drafted, and revised. As a writing teacher, he or she cares about a clear focus, logical organization, specific details and examples, accurate documentation of sources, and correctness. Your classmates and your instructor will be interested in how you have applied this chapter's ideas.

Subject You should think seriously about the event in terms of its causes and effects on the community or the nation. For example, if you decide to write about an event affecting the environment, consider that all of us need to be concerned about both positive and negative environmental changes. Not only our future, but our children's and their children's futures depend on our careful stewardship of the earth. At the same time, there are competing economic and political pressures that can act against a strict conservationist view. By researching and analyzing even one specific event, we can add to our own knowledge and that of our audience, thereby preparing all for responsible future action.

Writer You will be using sources for this essay, but you should not feel intimidated by them; rather, you should consider them your "assistant writers." Or think of yourself as a talk show host with your sources as the guests. Others will speak, but you will be in control, so your paper should be written in your own voice (it should sound like you). You will report and document the published writers' words and ideas and comment upon them as you think appropriate. If you find disagreement among your sources, don't discard any of them: the lack of agreement gives you a variety of views to report.

The Writing Process

The following sections will guide you through the stages of generating, planning, drafting, and revising as you work on your essay. Try to be particularly conscious of both the critical thinking you find in your sources and the critical thinking you do as you examine them.

Generating Ideas

- Within your instructor's parameters for the assignment, begin by finding an event that interests you. If one comes to mind immediately, you can begin to research it. If not, begin by brainstorming a list of all the local and national events you can remember from the last few years. Other good sources for events are encyclopedia yearbooks and December ("The Year in Review") issues of magazines. Then make a tentative choice.

- After you have selected an event, you should use your college library and your own Internet access programs to find articles about it. Consult Chapter 13 and your handbook about locating sources. Most important, go to your college library and learn how to find material there. If you are an expert Internet user, you can probably locate sources with your own computer. Look for full texts of articles from reputable publications. Check titles for words like *causes, factors, results in, reasons,* or *underlie.*

- Locate or print the sources that you identify and read them carefully. First, check to see that they do indeed discuss the causes of the event, not just the event itself. Then see what causes they identify and how they label them (contributory, interactive, and so on). If they do not label them, try to do that yourself. Also, look for language that indicates the source's level of certainty about these causes ("has been definitely identified as a cause," or "may be partially responsible").

- Highlight sections of the source that you will include (if you own the source or have photocopied it). If you are required to do so, make note cards based on the marked sections.

- Think about how much information you have. Do you need more? If so, continue researching, reading, and marking until you have enough to answer the question "Why did this event take place?"

Defining a Focus Write a thesis statement that will make clear to your audience that you are going to analyze *why* the event occurred. There are at least two possible ways to frame this type of thesis.

The first is simply to report what your sources say. If your sources agree and present some degree of certainty, you can simply state this. If your sources disagree, you can state that as your thesis. If your sources are less than certain about the causes, you can indicate that.

A second type of thesis involves one more level of thinking on your part: if you want or are required to take a position on the causal relationships involved, you should include this position in your thesis statement. For example, you could say, "Having read four sources dealing with the causes of this event, I agree with three of them but reject a theory proposed in the fourth." Your instructor should be able to offer you additional advice about what focus to take.

Organizing Ideas If you made note cards, read through them two or three times. Then spread them all out on a table or desk so that you can see them all at once. Begin to group them into stacks: one to describe the event and one for each cause mentioned. Ideally, doing this will help you to integrate material from your different sources into various parts of your essay. You may decide not to use a few note cards; this often happens and indicates that you have done a good job of finding sufficient information. If you discover that you don't have enough information, you can do more research.

If you didn't make note cards, spread your marked sources out and try to plan how you will use information from each.

Review the principles for writing an essay of causal analysis on page 305 of this chapter. In addition, you will need to determine the order of your body paragraphs. For a causal chain, you will probably want chronological order. For contributory causes, you may want to use climactic (least to most important) order. For interactive causes, you may want to try different orders until you discover which will make the interaction of the causes easiest for your audience to understand.

Drafting If you have note cards in stacks, you can draft one section from each stack. A highly specific description of the event could become the introduction. Quotations from eyewitnesses or participants in the event can help to interest your audience. The introduction can conclude with the tentative thesis statement you have written.

Clearly introduce each cause. If you have several causes and are devoting one paragraph to each, begin each body paragraph with a topic sentence that names the possible or verifiable cause being discussed. Then provide the audience with as much information as necessary to help them understand how that cause actually could or did bring about the event.

Be sure to note the author or title and page where any information from a source comes from. Do not trust yourself to add documentation as you revise your paper. It's easy to lose track and therefore to plagiarize accidentally.

In your conclusion, you can summarize the causes and discuss the level of certainty, or uncertainty, about them. If you found considerable disagreement among your sources, you can comment on that. If research is still ongoing about the causes, you can say so. You can, of course, do more than this in your conclusion, depending on your content. A well-chosen quotation from a source is often an effective last sentence.

On a separate page, draft a Works Cited list, using the format specified by your instructor.

 Revising One of the best revision strategies is to get an audience's reactions to your draft. Your classmates, or peers, can help you see where your draft is already successful and where it needs more or less information. Your peers can also help you see if your draft needs reorganization. If your instructor allows class time for peer review (see pages 65–66 and 105–107), be sure to have a draft ready so that you can benefit from this activity.

1. **Think big.** Look at your draft as a whole.

   - Does it fulfill the assignment in terms of topic and length? Does it actually explain some causes of a recent event? Is the event important enough so that people will want to read about it?

   - Does it let your audience know that you will be discussing different probable causes?

   - How could you state the thesis more clearly? Do any parts of the draft not relate to the thesis?

   - How could you reorganize the draft to make it more logical? Should you change the order in which you present the causes? Can you make the flow between paragraphs smoother?

   - Is your point of view consistent throughout?

2. **Think medium.** Look at your draft paragraph by paragraph.

   - How could you rewrite your first paragraph to interest your audience in reading on?

- Does each body paragraph deal with a cause or a specific aspect of a cause? Does each present relevant, specific information? Which, if any, paragraphs should be expanded, combined, or eliminated?
- Which paragraphs use topic sentences effectively? Which do not have topic sentences? Do they need them?
- Where could transitions be used to improve the flow within a paragraph? Where could transitions be used to improve the flow between paragraphs?
- Now look at your conclusion. It is your last chance to accomplish your purpose with your intended audience. Does it provide a satisfying ending by saying something important about the event and its causes? How could you make your conclusion more effective?

3. **Think small.** Look at your draft sentence by sentence.

- Which sentences are difficult to understand? How could you reword them?
- Which, if any, sentences are so long that your audience could get lost in them? How could you shorten or divide them?
- Are there choppy sentences that can be combined?
- Which sentences seem vague? How could you clarify them or make them more specific?
- Which, if any, sentences have errors in Standard English grammar or usage? How can you correct them?

4. **Think "picky."** Look at your draft as your fussiest critic might.

- Which words are not clear or not quite right for your meaning? What words could you use instead? Have you used appropriate vocabulary about causes?
- Are any words spelled incorrectly? (Run your spell checker program, but don't expect it to detect all errors.)
- Do you cite sources in the required format? Is your Works Cited list correct? Check the models in your handbook.
- Will your final draft be in the format expected by your instructor? Are the pages numbered consecutively?
- Is there anything else you could do to improve your draft?

Decide which revision strategies will improve your draft and make changes before handing in your best version.

Editing and Proofreading After you have prepared a final draft, check again for correct grammar and punctuation usage. Proofread carefully to detect omitted words or punctuation marks. Also proofread for the kinds of errors the spell checker can't catch.

Check your Works Cited list against your model once more, paying particular attention to indentation, use of underlining and quotation marks for titles, and special use of punctuation.

The following essays show how two students responded to this assignment.

Crows at the Mall

BY LY TRUC HOANG

I am a newcomer to the United States. Amazingly, a bird which I saw on my first day in this country was a crow. I wondered if in America crows are common birds. Now I know that there are thousands of crows which live around my city. Recently, some of these crows have caused concern because they have moved into the trees at White Flint Mall, a large, upscale shopping center.

In the *Washington Post,* an article by reporter Alona Wartofsky has a photo of crows with this caption: "Ruling the roost: Crows are making their presence known and felt at White Flint Mall" (D1). Because people are upset about too many crows at the mall, Wartofsky reports the people tend "to use words like 'eradicate' and 'terminate'" (D8). Why have the crows appeared at White Flint Mall? After reading some articles, I think I can answer this question. Missing the trees in Rockville, seeking spaces to live, and looking for food are some causes that many experts discuss about the crows' taking up residence in the mall parking lot.

First of all, missing the trees in Rockville is a cause for the crows to immigrate to White Flint. Wartofsky believes, "As many as 200,000 crows spent fall and winter around the intersection of Montrose Road and East Jefferson Drive in Rockville. But last November, developers cut down many of the trees there, and most of the birds have moved on" (D1). This is consistent with a national trend. Crows "[have] suffered huge losses in recent decades from disease, predation, logging, and development" (Kelly 107). Since the traditional habitats of crows are being destroyed by development, the birds are increasingly finding new homes. Moreover, Miller observes that "they must rapidly search for new habitat and shelter when critical habitats are disturbed" (32).

Thus, seeking a new place to live is a cause for the crows' coming to White Flint. In "Birds Need Open Space," Miller indicates, "Birds have tried to adapt and seek new shelters and places . . . as our human encroachment continues to grow" (32). They choose places that provide an appropriate habitat for nesting and for spending the winter. Some species, such as crows, prefer to spend the winter in large colonies. "Colonial roosts afford individual crows several advantages, primarily greater awareness of predators, such as owls and hawks" (Wartofsky D8). The same article quotes Audubon Naturalist Society's Mark Garland, who told Wartofsky that "many birds packed together can actually raise the ambient temperature of a particular area" (D8). In the case of White Flint, the displaced crows did not have to go far from their old location; White Flint was only a few blocks away from their old trees.

A good food supply was another cause for the crows' choice of White Flint. Many experts agree that birds' movements are typically motivated by food. In *National Wildlife*, Les Line states, "Migration is the avian solution to the problem of a disappearing food supply" (54). Crows are among the most intelligent and adaptable of birds. "The crow is a flexible omnivore," says Pete Budo, a reporter for the *New York Times* (8:9). Therefore, their food includes garbage as well as eggs and nestlings, small animals, vegetables, and carrion. And, like parking lots in malls all across the country, the lot at White Flint has food dropped by shoppers, trash receptacles, and the small animal life which trash attracts.

For all these reasons, thousands of crows enjoy spending the winter in the White Flint parking lot; that has become a serious problem for this mall. The crows are noisy, and their droppings fall on cars, sidewalks, bushes, benches, and sometimes shoppers.

Human beings intervene in natural environments, perhaps only slightly and with good intentions. However, the results are unforeseen and unwanted effects, like the crows at the mall.

Works Cited

Bodo, Pete. "The Cunning, Resourceful Crow Doesn't Deserve Its Bad Rap." *New York Times* 21 Jan. 1996: 8: 9.

Kelly, Mary Sidney. "A Crow's Last Stand." *Audubon* Sept. 1996: 107.

Line, Les. "Staying the Winter." *National Wildlife* Feb. 1995: 52–59.

Miller, David. "Birds Need Open Space." *New York State Conservationist* Aug. 1996: 32.

Wartofsky, Alona. "Caws for Concern at White Flint." *Washington Post* 2 Apr. 1997: D1+.

STUDENT WRITING

What Caused the Flood at Yosemite National Park?

BY ELMON L. BURTON IV

"Heavy snowpack in the high Sierras was melted on New Year's Eve by the arrival of the 'Pineapple Express,' a warm moist storm that blew onto the mountains from Hawaii, dropping rain and raising temperatures above 37 degrees at 10,000 feet" (Booth A1). The result: a record breaking flood which swept through Yosemite National Park destroying everything in its path. Newspaper accounts say that park officials had no choice but to close access to most of the park for several months (Brooke 5:3). When all was done, "the New Year's flood caused an estimated $178 million in damage" (Booth A1). The amount of snowfall that was present at Yosemite and the arrival of the Pineapple Express are the two contributory causes of this flood that I will discuss.

The first contributory cause of the flood was the massive amount of snow which laid upon the mountains within Yosemite National Park. This is nothing out of the ordinary, however. The book *Floods* says that each year the western mountain regions receive over 60 inches of precipitation in the form of snow, and sometimes snowfall accumulates to over 200 inches (Hoyt and Langbein 28). In fact, says *Floods*, each spring the Merced River rises above its average height as a result of the enormous amount of snowmelt; and ". . . many northern and high mountainous areas have deep snow every year without floods because the thaw begins slowly with the onset of spring, and snow cover is fairly depleted before high temperatures occur" (Hoyt and Langbein 28). However, the 1997 flood took place January 1, at the early part of winter. This was obviously a rare occurrence, leaving the residents in a complete state of bewilderment. According to William G. Hoyt and Walter B. Langbein, the authors of *Floods:*

> It's important to note that snowmelt is only a contributor to winter floods, . . . which are primarily caused by heavy rains. Snow sets the stage, but seldom causes serious floods by itself. Even the most rapid rate of snowmelt is only equal to a moderate rain. (29)

Also, scientists point out that the amount of snow and the rate at which it melts are important factors contributing to the severity of snowmelt floods (Ward 28). Further, when rain is added to the equation, it magnifies the rate of snowmelt which could increase the river by ten times its usual size (Flood 236). The result: total devastation to everything in its path. Such was the case when the Merced River, within Yosemite National Park, flooded.

The Pineapple Express, the second contributory cause of the flood, was a warm tropical storm when it originated off the Pacific Ocean, hundreds of miles away near the Hawaiian Islands. The *Washington Post* reported that the storm followed the atmosphere's jet stream, which carried it east towards the coast of California. Then, upon the storm's arrival, California experienced a period of heavy rains and extremely mild temperatures. Although the Yosemite region was not hit directly by this unusual storm, it definitely felt the effects. The result was an incredible rate of snowmelt along the Sierra mountain range. The most cataclysmic results took place near and along the rising Merced River within Yosemite. Park officials are calling it "the cruelest winter on record" (Booth A1).

The abundant amount of snowfall in the high Sierras, the heavy amount of rain that fell, and the extended period of mild temperatures supported and reinforced the actions of one another, creating a synergistic effect. While no one contributor would have caused such a devastating outcome, when working in conjunction with each other they created a force greater than the sum of their individual effects, thus creating a rare, yet horrific natural disaster.

Works Cited

Booth, William. "Floods Brought Yosemite the Break of the Century." *Washington Post* 7 Mar. 1997: A1+.

Brooke, James. "Flood Damage Closes Much of Yosemite Valley." *New York Times* 2 Feb. 1997: sec. 5: 3.

"Flood." *World Book Encyclopedia,* 1992.

Hoyt, William G., and Walter B. Langbein. *Floods.* Princeton: Princeton University Press, 1955.

Ward, Roy. *Floods: A Geographical Perspective.* New York: Roy Ward, 1978.

9

Forming Concepts

"Our life is what our thoughts make it."
—Marcus Aurelius

Writing to Classify and Define

Critical Thinking Focus: The conceptualizing process

Writing Focus: Defining and applying concepts

Reading Theme: Gender issues

Writing Project: Defining an important concept

Internet, *beauty, hip-hop culture, channel surfing, truth, bungee jumping, attitude,* and *thinking* are only a few examples of concepts in a world filled with them. As you speak and write, you refer to concepts you have formed. Your academic study involves learning new concepts as well, and being successful in college and in your career requires understanding the conceptualizing process.

When you read textbooks or listen to lectures and take notes, you have to grasp key concepts and follow them as they are developed and supported. Many course examinations involve applying the key concepts you have learned to new sets of circumstances. When you write papers, you are usually expected to focus on certain concepts, develop a thesis around them, present the thesis (itself a concept), and back it up with specific evidence.

Your college writing will often require the defining of terms or concepts. Chapter 5 discussed the fact that words are complex carriers of meaning—with meanings varying from person to person. This chapter will explore further implications of this vital communication issue.

The Writing Project in the chapter asks you to write a full definition of a concept that is important to your life. As you write this paper, you will see that definition usually involves using all the patterns of thinking that the previous chapters in Part Two have discussed.

Definition is a very important thinking and writing pattern. The analytical activity of classifying, which underlies defining, also is essential to good thinking. Defining and classifying rely on comparative relationships in order to establish categories by means of similarities and in order to distinguish among concepts within categories by identifying differences. Definitions usually include descriptions and sometimes employ causal, chronological, or process analyses to make distinctions or to show the development of a concept. Understanding the thinking patterns that you have already worked with and being able to use them effectively can ease the difficult task of defining concepts.

To help you define significant concepts, this chapter will explain the conceptualizing process, present readings that involve definitions, and give you opportunities to define some terms that are significant in various aspects of your life.

What Are Concepts?

Concepts are general ideas that you use to organize your experience and, in so doing, bring order to your life. In the same way that words are the vocabulary of language, concepts are the vocabulary of thought. As organizers of your experience, concepts work in conjunction with language to identify, describe, distinguish, and relate all the various aspects of your world.

To become a sophisticated thinker and writer, you must develop expertise in the conceptualizing process, thereby improving your ability to form, apply, and relate concepts. This complex conceptualizing process is going on all the time in your mind, enabling you to think in a distinctly human way. When you form opinions or make judgments, you are applying and relating concepts. And when you write, you are expressing your thinking with the help of concepts.

How do you use concepts to organize and make sense of experience? Think back to the first day of the semester. For most students, this is a time to evaluate their courses by trying to determine which concepts apply.

- Will this course be interesting? useful? challenging?
- Is the instructor stimulating? demanding? understanding?
- Are the other students friendly? intelligent? conscientious?

Each of these descriptive words or phrases represents a concept you are attempting to apply so that you can understand what is occurring at the moment and also anticipate what will occur. As the course progresses, you gather more information from experiences in class. This information may support your initial concepts, or it may conflict with them. If it supports them, you tend to maintain them ("Yes, I can see that this is going to be a difficult course"). When the information you receive conflicts with your initial concepts, you tend to find new concepts to explain the situation ("No, I can see that I was wrong—this course isn't going to be as difficult as I first thought"). A diagram of this process might look something like the one in Figure 9.1.

Throughout this thinking process you are making judgments that establish classifications of kinds or types: What *kind* of course—difficult? easy? What *kind* of teacher? What *kind* of reading? What *kind* of student am I in relation to this course? And you are consciously or unconsciously using definitions that you have formulated: When I say "difficult course," I mean one that . . . When I say "demanding teacher," I mean one who . . . And so on.

Figure 9.1 Experience Leads to Action

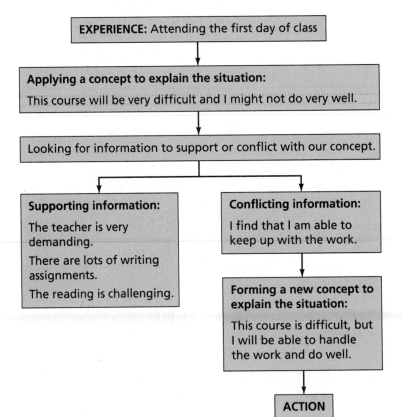

For another example, imagine that you are a physician, and one of your patients comes to you complaining of shortness of breath and occasional pain in his left arm. After he describes his symptoms, you ask a number of questions, examine him, and perhaps order some tests. Your ability to diagnose the underlying problem depends on your knowledge of various human diseases. Each disease is identified and described by a different concept. Identifying these various diseases means that you can distinguish among different concepts and that you know in which situations to apply a given concept correctly. In addition, when the patient asks, "What's wrong with me, doctor?" you are able to describe the overall concept (for example, heart disease) and explain how it is revealed by his symptoms. Fortunately, modern medicine has developed remarkably precise concepts to describe and explain diseases. In the patient's case, you may conclude that the problem is heart disease. Of course, there are different kinds of heart disease, represented by different concepts, and your success in treating the patient will depend on figuring out exactly which type is involved.

Thinking ↔ Writing Activity

Changing Your Concepts

Identify an initial concept you had about an event in your life (a new job, attending college, getting married, and so on). After identifying your initial concept, describe the experiences that led you to change or modify the concept; then explain the new concept you formed to explain the situation. Your response should include the following elements.

- The initial concept
- New information provided by additional experiences
- The new concept formed to explain the situation

THE IMPORTANCE OF CONCEPTS

Learning to understand and write about concepts will help you in every area of your life: academic, career, and personal. In college study, each academic discipline or subject is composed of many different concepts that are used to organize experience, give explanations, and solve problems. Here is a sampling of college-level concepts: *entropy, subtext, Gemeinschaft, cell, metaphysics, relativity, parallel processing, prehistory, unconscious, aesthetic, minor key, interface, health, quantum mechanics, schizophrenia.* To make sense of how disciplines function, you need to understand what the concepts of that discipline mean, how to define them, how to apply them, and how they relate to other concepts.

The previous sentence describes the content of many of the papers that you will write in your college classes. You will regularly present your understanding of definitions, of applications, and of relationships among concepts in your written work. You will also need to learn the methods of investigation, patterns of thought, and forms of reasoning that various disciplines use to form larger conceptual theories and methods. Successful completion of writing assignments in the courses that you will take will depend on your understanding of the key concepts that form the core of each discipline.

Regardless of their specific knowledge content, all careers require conceptual abilities, whether you are trying to apply a legal principle, develop a promotional theme, or devise a new computer program. Similarly, expertise in forming and applying concepts helps you to make sense of your personal life, understand others, and make informed decisions. The Greek philosopher Aristotle said that the intelligent person is a "master of concepts."

THE STRUCTURE OF CONCEPTS

Concepts, in addition to being general ideas that you use to identify and organize your experience, are useful for distinguishing and connecting one thing to another. Concepts allow you to organize your world into patterns that make sense to you.

In their role of organizers of experience, concepts act to group aspects of your experience on the basis of their similarity. Consider the object that you usually write with: a pen. The concept *pen* represents an instrument that you use for writing. Now look around the classroom at other instruments people are using to write. You use the concept *pen* to identify these as well, even though they may look quite different from yours. Thus, the concept *pen* not only helps you to make distinctions in your experience by indicating how pens differ from pencils, crayons, or markers; it also helps you to determine which items are similar enough to all be called pens. When you put items into a group with a single description—such as *pen*—you are focusing on their similarities:

- They use ink.
- They are used for writing.
- Each is held in one hand.

Being able to see and name the similarities among certain things in your experience is the way you form concepts and is crucial for making sense of your world. If you were not able to do this, everything in the world would appear to be different, with its own individual name.

THE PROCESS OF CLASSIFYING

The process by which you group things on the basis of their similarities is known as **classifying**. Classifying is a natural human activity that goes on all the time. In most cases, however, you are not conscious of classifying something in a particular sort of way; you do so automatically. The process of classifying is one of the main ways that you order, organize, and make sense of your world. Because no two things or experiences are exactly alike, your ability to classify things into various groups is what enables you to recognize things in your experience. When you perceive a pen, you recognize it as a *kind* of object you have seen before. Even though you may not have seen this particular pen, you recognize that it belongs to a category of things that is familiar.

The best way to understand the structure of concepts is to visualize them by means of a model. Examine Figure 9.2. The **sign** is the word or symbol used to name or designate the concept; for example, the word *triangle* is a sign. The **referents** represent all the various examples of the concept; the three-sided figure we are using as our model is an example of the concept *triangle*. The **properties** of the concept are the features that all things named by the word or sign share in common; all examples of the concept *triangle* share the characteristics of being a polygon and having three sides. These are the properties that we refer to when we define concepts; thus, "A triangle is a three-sided polygon."

Let's take another example. Suppose you wanted to explore the structure of the concept *automobile*. The sign that names the concept is the word *automobile* or the symbol 🚗 . Referents of the concept include the 1954 MG "TF" currently residing in the garage as well as the Ford Explorer parked in front of the house. The properties that all things named by the sign *automobile* include are wheels, a chassis, an engine, seats, and so on. Figure 9.3 shows a conceptual model of the concept *automobile*.

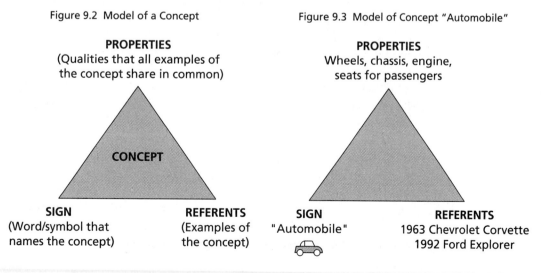

Figure 9.2 Model of a Concept

PROPERTIES
(Qualities that all examples of
the concept share in common)

CONCEPT

SIGN
(Word/symbol that
names the concept)

REFERENTS
(Examples of
the concept)

Figure 9.3 Model of Concept "Automobile"

PROPERTIES
Wheels, chassis, engine,
seats for passengers

SIGN
"Automobile"
🚗

REFERENTS
1963 Chevrolet Corvette
1992 Ford Explorer

Thinking ↔ Writing Activity

Diagramming Concepts

Using the model we have developed, diagram the structure of three of the following concepts as well as those of two concepts of your own choice: *dance, success, student, religion, music, friend.*

Forming Concepts

You form—and apply—concepts to organize your experience, make sense of what is happening, and anticipate what may happen in the future. You form concepts by the interactive processes of **generalizing** (focusing on the common properties shared by a group of things) and **interpreting** (finding examples of the concept). The common properties form the necessary requirements that must be met in order for you to be able to apply the concept to your experience. If you examine the diagrams of concepts in the last section, you can see that the process of forming concepts involves moving back and forth between the referents (examples) of the concept and the properties (common features) shared by all examples of the concept. Let's further explore the way this interactive process of forming concepts operates.

Consider the following conversation between two people trying to form and clarify the concept *philosophy.*

A: What is your idea of what philosophy *means*?

B: Well, I think philosophy involves expressing important beliefs that you have—like discussing the meaning of life, assuming that there is a meaning.

A: Is explaining my belief about who's going to win the Super Bowl engaging in philosophy? After all, this is a belief that is very important to me—I've got a lot of money riding on the outcome!

B: I don't think so. A philosophical belief is usually a belief about something that is important to everyone—like what standards we should use to guide our moral choices.

A: What about the message that was in my fortune cookie last night: "Eat, drink, and be merry, for tomorrow we diet!"? This is certainly a belief that most people can relate to, especially during a holiday season! Is this philosophy?

B: I think that's what my grandmother used to call "foolosophy"! Philosophical beliefs are usually deeply felt views to which we have given a great deal of thought—not something plucked out of a cookie.

A: What about my belief in the golden rule: "Do unto others as you would have them do unto you" because "What goes around comes around"? Doesn't that have the qualities that you mentioned?

B: Now you've got it!

As we review this dialogue, we can see that forming the concept *philosophical belief* works hand in hand with applying the concept to different examples. When two or more things work together in this way, we say that they *interact*. In this case, there are two parts of this interactive process.

We form concepts by generalizing, by focusing on the similar features among different things. In the previous dialogue, the things about which generalizations are being made are types of beliefs—beliefs about the meaning of life or about standards we use to guide our moral choices. By focusing on the similar features of these beliefs, the dialogue's two participants develop a list of properties philosophical beliefs share, including (1) beliefs dealing with important issues in life about which everyone is concerned and (2) beliefs reflecting deeply felt views—views to which people have given much thought. These common properties act as the requirements a viewpoint must meet to be considered a philosophical belief.

We apply concepts by interpreting, by looking for different examples of a concept and seeing if they meet the requirements of the concept we are developing. In the preceding dialogue, one participant attempts to apply the concept *philosophical belief* to the following examples:

a belief about the outcome of the Super Bowl

a fortune cookie message: "Eat, drink, and be merry, for tomorrow we diet."

Each of these proposed examples suggests the development of new requirements for the concept to help clarify how the concept can be applied. Applying a concept to different possible examples thus becomes the way we develop and gradually sharpen our idea of it.

Even when a proposed example turns out not to be a valid one, we have often clarified our understanding of that concept. For instance, although the proposed example of a belief about the outcome of the Super Bowl turned out not to be an example of the concept *philosophical belief*, examining it helped to clarify the concept and suggest other examples.

The process of developing concepts involves a constant back-and-forth movement between generalizing and interpreting. As the back-and-forth movement progresses, we gradually develop a list of specific requirements for an example of the concept; at the same time, we gain a clearer sense of how the concept is defined. We are also developing a collection of examples that embody the qualities of the concept and demonstrate situations in which the concept applies. This interactive process is illustrated in Figure 9.4.

Figure 9.4 Movement from General Concept to Well-Defined Concept

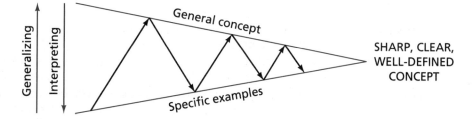

Thinking ↔ Writing Activity

Forming a Concept

Select a type of music with which you are familiar (e.g., jazz, alternative, hip-hop, rock, heavy metal, and so on) and write a dialogue similar to the one just examined. In the course of the dialogue, be sure to include the following:

1. Examples from which you are generalizing (such as specific bands).
2. General properties shared by various types of this music (e.g., "Jazz is a uniquely American form of music which uses complex rhythms and improvisation.").
3. Examples to which you are trying to apply the developing concept (such as the music of Marian McPartland, Miles Davis, or Thelonius Monk).

Forming concepts involves performing the operations of generalizing and interpreting together for two reasons.

1. You cannot form a concept unless you know how it might apply. If you have absolutely no idea what *jazz* or *philosophy* might exemplify, you cannot begin to form the concept, even in vague or general terms.
2. You cannot gather examples of the concept unless you know what they might be examples of. Until you begin to develop some idea of what the concepts *jazz* or *philosophy* might be (based on certain similarities among various things), you won't know where to look for examples of the concept (or how to evaluate them).

This interactive process is the way that you usually form all concepts, particularly the complicated ones. In school, much of your education is focused on carefully forming and exploring key concepts such as *democracy, dynamic equilibrium,* and *personality.* This book, too, has focused on key concepts such as *thinking critically, writing effectively, making decisions, revising drafts, perceiving, thinking creatively,* and *language.*

Applying Concepts

Making sense of our experience means finding the right concept to explain what is going on. To determine whether the concept we have selected fits a situation, we have to determine whether the requirements that form the concept are being met. For example, episodes of the original radio series "Superman" used to begin with the words "Faster than a speeding bullet—more powerful than a locomotive. Look—up in the sky! It's a bird! It's a plane! It's Superman!"

To figure out which concept applies to the situation, we must do the following.

1. Be aware of the properties that form the boundaries of the concept.

2. Determine whether the experience meets those requirements, for only if it does can we apply the concept to it.

In the opening lines from "Superman," what are some of the requirements for using the concepts being identified?

- Bird:

- Plane:

- Superman:

If we have the requirements of the concept clearly in mind, we can proceed to figure out which of these requirements are met by the experience—whether it is a bird, a plane, or the "man of steel" himself. This is how we apply concepts, which is one of the most important ways we have for figuring out what is taking place in our experience.

DETERMINING THE REQUIREMENTS OF A CONCEPT

In determining exactly what the requirements of a concept are, we can ask ourselves: *Would something still be an example of this concept if that thing did not meet this requirement?* If the answer to this question is *no*—that something would not be an example of this concept if it did not meet this requirement—we can say the requirement is a necessary part of the concept.

Consider the concept *dog*. Which of the following descriptions are requirements that must be met by an example of this concept?

1. Is an animal

2. Normally has four legs and a tail

3. Bites the mail carrier

It is clear that descriptions 1 and 2 are requirements that must be met to apply the concept *dog* because if we apply our test question—"Would something be an example of this concept if that thing did not meet this requirement?"—we can say that the thing would not be an example of the concept *dog* if it did not fit the first two descriptions: if it was not an animal and did not normally have four legs and a tail.

This does not seem to be the case, however, with description 3. If we ask ourselves the same test question, we can see that the thing might still be an example of the concept *dog* even if it did not bite the mail carrier. Even though some dogs do in fact bite mail carriers, this is not a requirement for being a dog.

Of course, there may be other things that meet these requirements but are not dogs. For example, a cat is an animal (description 1) that normally has four legs and a tail (description 2). What this means is that the requirements of a concept tell us only what attributes something must have to be an example of the concept. As a result, we often have to identify additional requirements that will define the concept more sharply. This point is clearly illustrated by observing how children form concepts. Not identifying a sufficient number of the concept's requirements leads to such misconceptions as "All four-legged animals are doggies" or "All yellow colored metal is gold."

This is why it is so important to have a very clear idea of the greatest possible number of specific requirements of each concept. These requirements determine when the concept can be applied and indicate those things that qualify as examples of it. When we are able to identify all the requirements of the concept, we say these requirements are both necessary and sufficient for applying the concept.

ANALYZING COMPLEX CONCEPTS

Although dealing with concepts like *dog* and *cat* may seem simple, matters become somewhat confusing when you start analyzing the more complex concepts you will encounter in your academic study. For example, consider the concepts of *masculinity* and *femininity*, two of the more emotionally charged and politically contentious concepts in our culture. There are many different perspectives on what these concepts mean, what they should mean, or whether we should be using them at all. See if you can identify properties and examples of these two concepts by completing the following Thinking-Writing Activity.

Thinking ↔ Writing Activity

Exploring the Concepts of *Masculine* and *Feminine*

Identify what you consider the essential properties (specific requirements that must be met to apply the concept) for each of these concepts as well as examples of people or behavior that illustrates these properties. For example, you might identify physical risk taking as a property of the concept *masculinity* and identify Bruce Willis as a person who illustrates this quality. Or you might identify intuition as a property of the concept *femininity*, illustrating this with the behavior "knowing without the conscious use of rational processes."

General Properties   Specific Examples

FEMININITY

1. _____   1. _____

2. _____   2. _____

3. _____   3. _____

MASCULINITY

1. _____   1. _____

2. _____   2. _____

3. _____   3. _____

Compare your list with those of your classmates. What similarities and differences do you notice? What factors might account for these similarities and differences? Look back at your responses after you have read the following selections.

Discussions of gender often call for definitions. What does it mean to be a woman or a man? What are femininity and masculinity? Do males and females tend to think differently about friendship? The following five readings suggest definitions of some concepts connected with sensitive issues in the United States.

Read the following passage and then answer the questions which follow. Share your written responses with classmates and see where you agree.

FROM

Femininity

BY SUSAN BROWNMILLER

We had a game in our house called "setting the table" and I was Mother's helper. Forks to the left of the plate, knives and spoons to the right. Placing the cutlery neatly, as I recall, was one of my first duties, and the event was alive with meaning. When a knife or a fork dropped on the floor, that meant a man was unexpectedly coming to dinner. A falling spoon announced the surprise arrival of a female guest. No matter that these visitors never arrived on cue, I had learned a rule of gender identification. Men were straight-edged, sharply pronged and formidable; women were softly curved and held the food in a rounded well. It made perfect sense, like the division of pink and blue that I saw in babies, an orderly way of viewing the world. Daddy, who was gone all day at work and who loved to putter at home with his pipe, tobacco and tool chest was knife and fork. Mommy and Grandma, with their ample proportions and pots and pans, were grownup soup spoons, large and capacious. And I was a teaspoon, small and slender, easy to hold and just right for pudding, my favorite dessert.

Being good at what was expected of me was one of my earliest projects, for not only was I rewarded, as most children are, for doing things right, but excellence gave pride and stability to my childhood existence. Girls were different from boys, and the expression of that difference seemed mine to make clear. Did my loving, anxious mother, who dressed me in white organdy pinafores and Mary Janes and who cried hot tears when I got them dirty, give me my first instruction? Of course. Did my doting aunts and uncles with their gifts of pretty dolls and miniature tea sets add to my education? Of course. But even without the appropriate toys and clothes, lessons in the art of being feminine lay all around me and I absorbed them all: the fairy tales that were read to me at night, the brightly colored advertisements I pored over in magazines before I learned to decipher the words, the movies I saw, the comic books I hoarded, the radio soap operas I happily followed whenever I had to stay in bed with a cold. I loved being a little girl, or rather I loved being a fairy princess, for that was who I thought I was.

As I passed through a stormy adolescence to a stormy maturity, femininity increasingly became an exasperation, a brilliant, subtle esthetic that was bafflingly inconsistent at the same time that it was minutely, demandingly concrete, a rigid code of appearance and behavior defined by do's and don't-do's that went against my rebellious grain. Femininity was a challenge thrown down to the female sex, a challenge no proud, self-respecting young woman could afford to ignore, particularly one with enormous ambition that she nursed in secret, alternately feeding or starving its inchoate life in tremendous confusion.

"Don't lose your femininity" and "Isn't it remarkable how she manages to retain her femininity?" had terrifying implications. They spoke of a bottom-line failure so irreversible that nothing else mattered. The pinball machine had registered "tilt," the game had been called. Disqualification was marked on the forehead of a woman whose femininity was lost. No records would be entered in her name, for she had destroyed her birthright in her wretched, ungainly effort to imitate a man. She walked in limbo, this hapless creature, and it occurred to me that one day I might see her when I looked in the mirror. If the danger was so palpable that warning notices were freely posted, wasn't it possible that the small bundle of resentments I carried around in secret might spill out and place the mark on my own forehead? Whatever quarrels with femininity I had I kept to myself; whatever handicaps femininity imposed, they were mine to deal with alone, for there was no women's movement to ask the tough questions, or to brazenly disregard the rules.

5   Femininity, in essence, is a romantic sentiment, a nostalgic tradition of imposed limitations. Even as it hurries forward in the 1980s, putting on lipstick and high heels to appear well dressed, it trips on the ruffled petticoats and hoopskirts of an era gone by. Invariably and necessarily, femininity is something that women had more of in the past, not only in the historic past of prior generations, but in each woman's personal past as well—in the virginal innocence that is replaced by knowledge, in the dewy cheek that is coarsened by age, in the "inherent nature" that a woman seems to misplace so forgetfully whenever she

steps out of bounds. Why should this be so? The XX chromosomal message has not been scrambled, the estrogen-dominated hormonal balance is generally as biology intended, the reproductive organs, whatever use one has made of them, are usually in place, the breasts of whatever size are most often where they should be. But clearly, biological femaleness is not enough.

Femininity always demands more. It must constantly reassure its audience by a willing demonstration of difference, even when one does not exist in nature, or it must seize and embrace a natural variation and compose a rhapsodic symphony upon the notes. Suppose one doesn't care to, has other things on her mind, is clumsy or tone-deaf despite the best instruction and training? To fail at the feminine difference is to appear not to care about men, and to risk the loss of their attention and approval. To be insufficiently feminine is viewed as a failure in core sexual identity, or as a failure to care sufficiently about oneself, for a woman found wanting will be appraised (and will appraise herself) as mannish or neutered or simply unattractive, as men have defined these terms.

We are talking, admittedly, about an exquisite esthetic. Enormous pleasure can be extracted from feminine pursuits as a creative outlet or purely as relaxation; indeed, indulgence for the sake of fun, or art, or attention, is among femininity's great joys. But the chief attraction (and the central paradox, as well) is the competitive edge that femininity seems to promise in the unending struggle to survive, and perhaps to triumph. The world smiles favorably on the feminine woman: it extends little courtesies and minor privilege. Yet the nature of this competitive edge is ironic, at best, for one works at femininity by accepting restrictions, by limiting one's sights, by choosing an indirect route, by scattering concentration and not giving one's all as a man would to his own, certifiably masculine, interests. It does not require a great leap of imagination for a woman to understand the feminine principle as a grand collection of compromises, large and small, that she simply must make in order to render herself a successful woman. If she has difficulty in satisfying femininity's demands, if its illusions go against her grain, or if she is criticized for her shortcomings and imperfections, the more she will see femininity as a desperate strategy of appeasement, a strategy she may not have the wish or the courage to abandon, for failure looms in either direction.

It is fashionable in some quarters to describe the feminine and masculine principles as polar ends of the human continuum, and to sagely profess that both polarities exist in all people. Sun and moon, yin and yang, soft and hard, active and passive, etcetera, may indeed be opposites, but a linear continuum does not illuminate the problem. (Femininity, in all its contrivances, is a very active endeavor.) What, then, is the basic distinction? The masculine principle is better understood as a driving ethos of superiority designed to inspire straightforward, confident success, while the feminine principle is composed of vulnerability, the need for protection, the formalities of compliance and the avoidance of conflict—in short, an appeal of dependence and good will that gives the masculine principle its romantic validity and its admiring applause.

Femininity pleases men because it makes them appear more masculine by contrast; and, in truth, conferring an extra portion of unearned gender distinction on men, an unchallenged space in which to breathe freely and feel stronger, wiser, more competent, is femininity's special gift. One could say that masculinity is often an effort to please women, but masculinity is known to please by displays of mastery and competence while femininity pleases by suggesting that these concerns, except in small matters, are beyond its intent. Whimsy, unpredictability and patterns of thinking and behavior that are dominated by emotion, such as tearful expressions of sentiment and fear, are thought to be feminine precisely because they lie outside the established route to success.

10   If in the beginnings of history the feminine woman was defined by her physical dependency, her inability for reasons of reproductive biology to triumph over the forces of nature that were the tests of masculine strength and power, today she reflects both an economic and emotional dependency that is still considered "natural," romantic and attractive. After an unsettling fifteen years in which many basic assumptions about the sexes were challenged, the economic disparity did not disappear. Large numbers of women—those with small children, those left high and dry after a mid-life divorce—need financial support. But even those who earn their own living share a universal need for connectedness (call it love, if you wish). As unprecedented numbers of men abandon their sexual interest in women, others, sensing opportunity, choose to demonstrate their interest through variety and a change in partners. A sociological fact of the 1980s is that female competition for two scarce resources—men and jobs—is especially fierce.

So it is not surprising that we are currently witnessing a renewed interest in femininity and an unabashed indulgence in feminine pursuits. Femininity serves to reassure men that women need them and care about them enormously. By incorporating the decorative and the frivolous into its definition of style, femininity functions as an effective antidote to the unrelieved seriousness, the pressure of making one's way in a harsh, difficult world. In its mandate to avoid direct confrontation and to smooth over the fissures of conflict, femininity operates as a value system of niceness, a code of thoughtfulness and sensitivity that in modern society is sadly in short supply.

There is no reason to deny that indulgence in the art of feminine illusion can be reassuring to a woman, if she happens to be good at it. As sexuality undergoes some dizzying revisions, evidence that one is a woman "at heart" (the inquisitor's question) is not without worth. Since an answer of sorts may be furnished by piling on additional documentation, affirmation can arise from such identifiable but trivial feminine activities as buying a new eyeliner, experimenting with the latest shade of nail color, or bursting into tears at the outcome of a popular romance novel. Is there anything destructive in this? Time and cost factors, a deflection of energy and an absorption in fakery spring quickly to mind, and they need to be balanced, as in a ledger book, against the affirming advantage.

Critical Reading Questions

1. According to Brownmiller, what are some of the properties of the concept of *femininity*? What are some examples that she gives of the properties that she identifies?

2. Do you agree with the conceptual properties that Brownmiller has identified? Explain why or why not. Do you think that she has defined *femininity*? Explain how she has achieved a definition or failed to do so.

3. How would you define your own concept of *femininity*? Why?

 Read the following passage and answer the questions that follow. Share your written responses with classmates and see where you agree.

Standing His Ground

BY MICHAEL NORMAN

I have bruised a knuckle and bloodied another man's nose, but I am not, by most measures, a fighter. The last time I broke the peace was more than a decade ago in a small restaurant on the west slope of the Rocky Mountains in Colorado. My stepfather had encountered an old nemesis. Words were exchanged and the distance between the two narrowed. I stepped in to play the peacemaker and ended up throwing the first punch. For the record, my target, a towering 230-pound horseman, easily absorbed the blow and then dispatched the gnat in front of him.

The years since have been filled with discretion—I preach it, embrace it and hide behind it. I am now the careful watchman who keeps his eye on the red line and reroutes pressure before it has a chance to blow. Sometimes, I backslide and turn a domestic misdemeanor into a capital case or toss the cat out of the house without bothering to see where he lands. But I do not punch holes in the plaster or call my antagonists to the woodshed. The Furies may gather, but the storm always stays safely out to sea. And yet, lately, I have been struggling with this forced equanimity. The messenger of reason, the advocate of accord, once again has the urge to throw the first punch—in spirit at least.

All of this began rather quietly, a deep stirring that would come and go and never take form, an old instinct, perhaps, trying to reassert itself. I was angry, restless, combative, but I could not say why. It was a mystery of sorts. I was what I was expected to be, the very model of a modern man, a partner instead of a husband, a proponent of peace over action, thin-skinned rather than thick, a willow instead of a stone. And yet there was something about this posture that did not fit my frame. Then, an acquaintance, a gentle man who spent his Peace Corps days among the villagers of Nepal, suddenly acted out of character. He got into an argument with a local brute in a neighborhood tavern and instead of walking away from trouble, stood his ground. It was, he said, a senseless confrontation, but he had no regrets, and it made me think of Joey.

Joey, the bully of the sixth grade, used to roam the hallways picking victims at random and slugging them on the arm. When he rounded a corner, we scattered or practiced a crude form of mysticism and tried to think ourselves invisible in the face of the beast. Since I was slow and an inept mystic, my mother kept on hand an adequate supply of Ben Gay to ease the bruises and swelling.

5 One day, a boy named Tony told the marauder that he had had enough and an epic duel was scheduled in the playground after school. Tony had been taking boxing lessons on the sly. He had developed a stinging left jab and when the appointed hour arrived, he delivered it in the name of every bruised shoulder in the school.

The meek pack of which Tony was once a part took courage from his example and several weeks later when a boy at my bus stop sent me sprawling, I returned the favor.

There were only a few challenges after that. On the way up, a Joey would occasionally round the corner. But in the circles I traveled, he was the exception rather than the rule. In the Marine Corps in Vietnam, we were consumed by a much larger kind of warfare. In college, faculty infighting and bullying aside, violence was considered anti-intellectual. And in the newsrooms where I have practiced my trade, reporters generally have been satisfied with pounding a keyboard instead of their editors.

And then came Colorado and the battle of the west slope. For years, I was embarrassed by the affair. I could have walked away and dragged my stepfather with me. As it was, we almost ended up in jail. I had provoked a common brawl, a pointless, self-destructive exercise. The rationalist had committed the most irrational of acts. It was not a matter of family or honor, hollow excuses. I had simply succumbed to instinct, and I deeply regretted it. But not any longer. Now I see virtue in that vulgar display of macho. It disqualifies me from the most popular male club—the brotherhood of nurturers, fraternity sensitivus.

From analyst's couch to tavern booth, their message is the same: The male animus is out of fashion. The man of the hour is supposed to be gentle, thoughtful, endearing and compassionate, a wife to his woman, a mother to his son, an androgynous figure with the self-knowledge of a hermaphrodite. He takes his lumps on the psyche, not the chin, and bleeds with emotion. Yes, in the morning, he still puts on a three-piece suit, but his foulard, the finishing touch, is a crying towel.

10 He is so ridden with guilt, so pained about the sexist sins of his kind, he bites at his own flanks. Not only does he say that he dislikes being a man, but broadly proclaims that the whole idea of manhood in America is pitiful.

He wants to free himself from the social conditioning of the past, to cast off the yoke of traditional male roles and rise above the banality of rituals learned at boot camp or on the practice field. If science could provide it, he would swallow an antidote of testosterone, something to stop all this antediluvian thumping and bashing.

And he has gone too far. Yes, the male code needs reform. Our rules and our proscriptions have trapped us in a kind of perpetual adolescence. Why else would a full-grown rationalist think he could get even with Joey by taking a poke at another bully 25 years later in a bar in Colorado? No doubt there is something pitiful about that.

But the fashion for reform, the drive to emasculate macho, has produced a kind of numbing androgyny and has so blurred the lines of gender that I often find myself wanting to emulate some of the women I know—bold, aggressive, vigorous role models.

It sometimes seems that the only exclusively male trait left is the impulse to throw a punch, the last male watermark, so to speak, that is clear and readable. Perhaps that is why the former Peace Corps volunteer jumped into a brawl and why I suspect that the new man—the model of sensitivity, the nurturer—goes quietly through the day with a clenched fist behind his back.

Critical Reading Questions

1. According to Norman, what are the properties of the concept *masculinity*? What are some examples he gives of the properties that he has identified?

2. Do you agree with the properties that Norman has identified? Explain why or why not. Does Norman achieve a definition of *masculinity*, or a partial definition? What thinking-writing patterns has he used?

3. Some people believe that the concepts of *masculinity* and *femininity* were formed by earlier cultures, are outdated in our current culture, and should be revised. Other people believe that these concepts reflect essential qualities of the human species and should not be excessively tampered with. Where do you stand on this issue?

4. Do you see connections among the concepts *feminism/feminist* and *masculism/masculinist* and the concepts of *femininity* and *masculinity*? What are some differences among these related concepts? Where does *macho* fit in?

 Read the following speech by Sojourner Truth and then answer the questions that follow. Discuss your written responses with classmates and see where you agree.

Ain't I a Woman?

BY SOJOURNER TRUTH

Well, children, where there is so much racket there must be something out of kilter. I think that 'twixt the negroes of the South and the women at the North, all talking about rights, the white men will be in a fix pretty soon. But what's all this here talking about?

That man over there says that women need to be helped into carriages, and lifted over ditches, and to have the best place everywhere. Nobody ever helps me into carriages, or over mud-puddles, or gives me any best place! And ain't I a woman? Look at me! Look at my arm! I have ploughed and planted, and gathered into barns, and no man could head me! And ain't I a woman? I could work as much and eat as much as a man—when I could get it—and bear the lash as well! And ain't I a woman? I have borne thirteen children, and seen them most all sold off to slavery, and when I cried out with my mother's grief, none but Jesus heard me! And ain't I a woman?

Then they talk about this thing in the head: what's this they call it? [Intellect, someone whispers.] That's it, honey. What's that got to do with women's rights or negro's rights? If my cup won't hold but a pint, and yours holds a quart, wouldn't you be mean not to let me have my little half-measure full?

Then that little man in black there, he says women can't have as much rights as men, 'cause Christ wasn't a woman! Where did your Christ come from? Where did your Christ come from? From God and a woman! Man had nothing to do with Him.

If the first woman God ever made was strong enough to turn the world upside down all alone, these women together ought to be able to turn it back, and get it right side up again! And now they is asking to do it, the men better let them.

Obliged to you for hearing me, and now old Sojourner ain't got nothing more to say.

Critical Reading Questions

1. Understanding that Sojourner Truth was a famous black speaker in the nineteenth-century abolitionist and women's suffrage movements, can you identify passages in her speech that pertain to those political issues?

2. Some people claim that many of the concerns addressed by present-day gender studies are middle-class issues and are not relevant to less affluent groups. Can you connect Sojourner Truth's speech to this view? Can you identify some gender questions that seem specific to social classes?

Read the following essay and then answer the questions that follow. Discuss your written answers with classmates and see where you agree.

Men and Their Hidden Feelings

BY RICHARD COHEN

My friends have no friends. They are men. They think they have friends, and if you ask them whether they have friends they will say yes, but they don't really. They think, for instance, that I'm their friend, but I'm not. It's OK. They're not my friends either.

The reason for that is that we are all men—and men, I have come to believe, cannot or will not have real friends. They have something else—companions, buddies, pals, chums, someone to drink with and someone to wench with and someone to lunch with, but no one when it comes to saying how they feel—especially how they hurt.

Women know this. They talk about it among themselves. I heard one woman describe men as the true Third World people—still not yet emerged. To women, this inability of men to say what they feel is a source of amazement and then anguish and then, finally, betrayal. Women will tell you all the time that they don't know the men they live with. They talk of long silences and drifting off and of keeping feelings hidden and never letting on that they are troubled or bothered or whatever.

If it's any comfort to women, they should know that it's nothing personal. Men treat other men the same way.

5   For instance, I know men who have suffered brutal professional setbacks and never mentioned it to their friends. I know of a guy who never told his best friend that his own son had a rare childhood disease. And I know others who never have sex with their wives, but talk to their friends as though they're living in the Playboy Mansion, either pretending otherwise or saying nothing.

This is something men learn early. It is something I learned from my father, who taught me, the way fathers teach sons, to keep my emotions to myself. I watched him and learned from him. One day we went to the baseball game, cheered and ate and drank, and the next day he was taken to the hospital with yet another ulcer attack. He had several of them. My mother said he worried a lot, but I saw none of this.

Legend has it that men talk a lot about sex. They don't. They talk about it only in the sense that it is treated like sports. They joke about it and rate women from 1 to 10. But they almost never talk about it in a way that matters—the quality of it. They almost never talk in real terms, in terms other than a cartoon, in terms that apply to them and the woman or women with whom they have a relationship.

Women do talk that way. Women talk about fulfillment, and they admit—maybe complain is the better word—to nonexistent sex lives. No man would admit to having virtually no sex life, yet there are plenty who do.

When I was a kid, I believed that it was men who had real friendships and women who did not. This seemed to be the universal belief, and boys would talk about this. We wondered about girls, about what made them so catty that they could not have friendships, and we really thought we were lucky to be men and have real friends.

10   We thought our friendships would last forever; we talked about them in some sort of Three Musketeer fashion—all for one and one for all. If one of us needed help, all of us would come running. We are still good friends, some of us, anyway, and I still feel that I will fight for them, but I don't think I could confide in them. No—not that.

Sometimes I think that men are walking relics—outmoded and outdated, programmed for some other age. We have all the essential qualities for survival in the wild and for success in battle, but we run like hell from talking about our feelings. We are, as the poet said in a different context, truly a thing of wonder.

Some women say that they have always had this ability to confide in one another—to talk freely. Others say that this is something relatively new—yet another benefit of the women's movement. I don't know. All I know is that they have it, and most men don't, and even the men who do—the ones who can talk about how they feel—talk to women. Have we been raised to think of feelings and sentiment as feminine? Can a man talk intimately with another man and not wonder about his masculinity? I don't know. I do know it sometimes makes the other men feel uncomfortable.

I know this is a subject that concerns me, and yet I find myself bottling it all up—keeping it all in. I've been on automatic pilot for years now.

It would be nice to break out of it. It would be nice to join the rest of the human race, connect with others in a way that makes sense, in a way that's meaningful—in a way that's more than a dirty joke and a slap on the back. I wonder whether it can be done.

15   If it can, it will happen because women will insist on it, because they themselves have shown the way, come out of the closet as women, talked about it, organized, defined an agenda, set their goals and admitted that as women—just as women—they have problems in common. So do men. It's time to talk about them.

Critical Reading Questions

1. According to Cohen, what are the properties of men's relationships? Why does he think that these properties do not fit a definition of *friendship*?

2. Do you believe that talking about feelings is a good idea? If so, talking

with whom? under what circumstances? How important is such talk to friendship?

Read the following essay; then answer the questions that follow. Share your written answers with classmates and see where you agree.

How Friendship Was "Feminized"
BY CAROL TAVRIS

Once upon a time and not so very long ago, everyone thought that men had the great and true-blue friendships. The cultural references stretched through time and art: Damon and Pythias, Hamlet and Horatio, Butch Cassidy and the Sundance Kid. The Lone Ranger never rode off with anyone but Tonto, and Laurel never once abandoned Hardy in whatever fine mess he got them into.

Male friendships were said to grow from the deep roots of shared experience and faithful camaraderie, whereas women's friendships were portrayed as shallow, trivial and competitive, like Scarlett O'Hara's with her sisters. Women, it was commonly claimed, would sell each other out for the right guy, and even for a good time with the wrong one.

Some social scientists told us that this difference was hard wired, a result of our evolutionary history. In the early 1970's, for example, the anthropologist Lionel Tiger argued in "Men in Groups" that "male bonding" originated in prehistoric male hunting groups and was carried on today in equivalent pack-like activities: sports, politics, business and war.

Apparently, women's evolutionary task of rummaging around in the garden to gather the odd yam or kumquat was a solo effort, so females do not bond in the same way. Women prattle on about their feelings, went the stereotype, but men act.

5   My, how times have changed. Today, we are deluged in the wave of best-selling books that celebrate female friendships—"Girlfriends," "Sisters," "Mothers and Daughters" and its clever clone, "Daughters and Mothers." The success of this genre is partly because the book market is so oriented to female readers these days.

But it is also a likely result of two trends that began in the 1970's and 1980's: Female scholars began to dispel the men-are-better stereotype in all domains and women became the majority of psychotherapists. The result was a positive reassessment of the qualities associated with women, including a "feminizing" of definitions of intimacy and friendship.

Accordingly, female friendships are now celebrated as the deep and abiding ones, based as they are on shared feelings and confidences. Male friendships are scorned as superficial, based as they are on shared interests in, say, the Mets and Michelle Pfeiffer.

In our psychologized culture, "intimacy" is defined as what many women like to do with their friends: talk, express feelings and disclose worries. Psychologists, most of whom are good talkers, validate this definition as the true measure of intimacy. For example, in a study of "intimacy maturity" in marriage, published in the *Journal of Personality and Social Psychology*, researchers equated "most mature" with "most verbally expressive." As a woman, I naturally think this is a perfectly sensible equation, but I also know it is an incomplete one. To label people mature or immature, you also have to know how they actually behave toward others.

What about all the men and women who support their families, put the wishes of other family members ahead of their own or act in moral and considerate ways when conflicts arise? They are surely mature, even if they are inarticulate or do not express their feelings easily. Indeed, what about all the men and women who define intimacy in terms of deeds rather than words: sharing activities, helping one another or enjoying companionable silence? Too bad for them. That's a "male" definition, and out of favor in these talky times.

10   Years ago, my husband had to have some worrisome medical tests, and the night before he was to go to the hospital we went to dinner with one of his best friends who was visiting from England. I watched, fascinated, as male stoicism combined with English reserve produced a decidedly unfemale-like encounter. They laughed, they told stories, they argued about movies, they reminisced. Neither mentioned the hospital, their worries or their affection for each other. They didn't need to.

It is true that women's style of intimacy has many benefits. A large body of research in health psychology and social psychology finds that women's greater willingness to talk about feelings improves their mental and physical health and makes it easier to ask for help.

But as psychologists like Susan Nolen-Hoeksema of Stanford University have shown, women's fondness for ruminating about feelings can also prolong depression, anxiety and anger. And it can keep women stuck in bad jobs or relationships, instead of getting out of them or doing what is necessary to make them better.

Books and movies that validate women's friendships are overdue, and welcome as long as they don't simply invert the stereotype. Playing the women-are-better game is fun, but it blinds us to the universal need for intimacy and the many forms that friendship takes. Maybe men could learn a thing or two about friendship from women. But who is to say that women couldn't learn a thing or two from them in exchange?

Critical Reading Questions

1. What perspectives does Tavris present that are different from those of Cohen? What ideas in her essay are similar to those in his?

2. How do you respond to reading these two essays together? Do you see connections with concepts discussed in Chapter 7?

3. How do Cohen's and Tavris's essays relate to your definition of *friendship*?

Using Concepts to Classify

When you apply a concept to an object, idea, or experience, you are in effect classifying it by placing it in a group of things that are defined by the properties or requirements of the concept. In fact, the same things can often be classified in many different ways. For example, if someone handed you a tomato and asked, "Which category does this tomato belong in, fruit or vegetable?" how would you respond? The fact is that a tomato can be classified as both a fruit and a vegetable because its botanical definition does not seem consistent with its uses as a food.

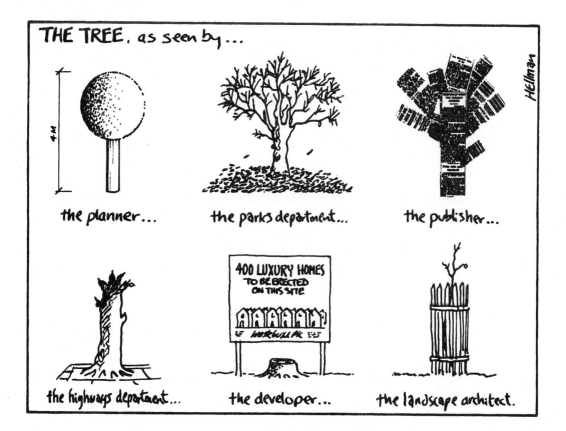

Let's consider another example. Imagine that you are walking on undeveloped land with some other people when you come across an area of soggy ground with long grass and rotting trees. One person in your group surveys the parcel and announces, "That's a smelly marsh. All it does is breed mosquitoes. It ought to be covered with landfill and built on so that we can use it productively." Another member of your group disagrees with the classification "smelly marsh," stating, "This is a wetland of great ecological value. There are many plants and animals that need this area and other areas like it to survive. Wetland areas also help to prevent the rivers from flooding, by absorbing excess water during heavy rains." Which person is right? Should the wet area be classified as a "smelly marsh" or as a "valuable wetland"? Actually, the wet area can be classified both ways. The classification that you select depends on your needs and your interests.

These examples illustrate how the way you classify reflects and influences the way you see the world, the way you think about the world, and the way you behave in the world. You classify many of the things in your experience differently than others do because of your individual needs, interests, and values. For instance, smoking marijuana might be classified by some as "use of a dangerous drug" and by others as a "harmless good time." Some view SUVs as "gas guzzlers"; others see the same cars as "safer, more comfortable vehicles." Some people categorize body piercing as "perverse abuse" while others think of it as "creative fashion." The way you classify aspects of your experience reflects the kind of individual you are and the way you think and feel about the world.

CLASSIFYING PEOPLE AND THEIR ACTIONS

You also place people in various categories. The specific categories you select depend on who you are and how you see the world. Similarly, each of us is placed in a variety of classifications by other people. Here, for instance, are some of the categories in which certain people have placed one of this book's authors:

Classification	People Who Classify Him
First-born son	His parents
Taxpayer	Internal Revenue Service
Tickler	His son/daughter
Bagel with cream cheese	Restaurant where he picks up his breakfast

List some of the different ways that you can be classified and identify the people who would classify you that way.

Not only do you continually classify things and people and place them in various groups on the basis of common properties you choose to focus on; you also classify ideas, feelings, actions, and experiences. Explain, for instance, why the killing of another person might be classified in different ways, depending on the circumstances.

Classification	Circumstance	Example
1. Manslaughter	Killing someone accidentally	Driving while intoxicated
2. Self-defense	_____	_____
3. Premeditated murder	_____	_____
4. Mercy killing	_____	_____
5. Diminished capacity	_____	_____

Each of these classifications represents a separate legal concept, one with its own properties and referents (examples). Of course, even when you clearly understand what the concept means, the complexity of the circumstances often makes it difficult to determine which concept applies. Court cases raise complex and disturbing issues. During a trial, trying first to identify the appropriate concept of the crime and then to determine which of the related concepts—*guilty* or *not guilty*—also applies is a challenging process. This is also true of many of life's other complex situations: you must work hard at identifying appropriate concepts to apply to the circumstances you are trying to make sense of, then be prepared to change or modify these concepts on the basis of new information or better insights.

WRITING AND CLASSIFYING

The intellectual act of classifying is an essential part of writing in three ways.

First, writings themselves are classified into many different forms. You know this already, of course. Novels, poems, essays, news stories, letters, emails, lab reports—the list is almost endless. And each of these forms of writing has subclassifications: science fiction, historical novels, romance novels, and so forth. Different classifications of writing have different purposes and styles. You are aware of this as a reader. As a college writer, you must become more aware of using styles and formats appropriate to the kind of writing that you are doing for your classes.

Second, almost any piece of writing is organized by classifying material into sections, chapters, or paragraphs in which the content is sorted out and arranged in logical ways. Usually, writers put similar material together so that readers can think about related items that have been assembled for their easy comprehension. You—and other writers—do this when you revise drafts to create good paragraphs that each focus on one idea. You do this when you are sorting your research notes into topics (or categories) in order to organize a paper, report, or speech.

Third, much writing concentrates on presenting *kinds, categories, types,* or *classifications* of concepts. The readings by Cohen and Tavris in this chapter discuss different classifications of friendship. "What Is Religion?" is organized around different kinds of questions to ask about conceptions of religion. This book itself is divided into different categories of approaches to thinking and writing.

Thinking ↔ Writing Activity

Identifying Classifications

1. Think of any reading selection in this book that you recall as being well organized. Turn to it and see how the writer classified or sorted the material into logical arrangements. Note the classifications of information. Perhaps topic sentences of paragraphs will show you what the writer has done.

2. Share your observations with classmates. See if they agree.

3. How did analyzing this piece of writing provide ideas about organizing your own work?

Defining Concepts

When you define a concept, you usually identify the necessary properties or requirements that determine when the concept can be applied. In fact, the word *definition* is derived from a Latin word meaning "boundary." A definition provides the boundaries of whatever territory in your experience can be described by the concept.

Definitions also use examples of the concept being defined. Consider the following:

Oxymoron   A rhetorical figure in which incongruous or contradictory terms are combined as in *a deafening silence* and *a mournful optimist.*

        —The American Heritage Dictionary of the English Language

An edible	Good to eat and wholesome to digest, as a worm to a toad, a toad to a snake, a snake to a pig, a pig to a man, and a man to a worm.

—Ambrose Bierce

Facts, theories	Facts and theories are different things, not rungs in a hierarchy of increasing certainty. Facts are the world's data. Theories are structures of ideas that explain and interpret facts. Facts do not go away when scientists debate rival theories to explain them. Einstein's theory of gravitation replaced Newton's, but apples did not suspend themselves in mid-air pending the outcome.

—Stephen Jay Gould

Contrast these definitions with the one illustrated in the following passage from Charles Dickens's *Hard Times:*

"Bitzer," said Thomas Gradgrind. "Your definition of a horse." "Quadruped. Graminivorous. Forty teeth, namely twenty-four grinders, four eye teeth, and twelve incisive. Sheds coat in the spring; in marshy countries sheds hoofs, too. Hoofs hard, but requiring to be shod with iron. Age known by marks in mouth." That (and much more) Bitzer. "Now girl number twenty," said Mr. Gradgrind, "you know what a horse is."

Although Bitzer has certainly done an admirable job of listing some of the necessary properties or requirements of the concept *horse*, it is unlikely that "girl number twenty" has any better idea of what a horse is than she had before since Bitzer's definition relies exclusively on a technical listing of the properties characterizing the concept *horse* without giving any examples that might illustrate the concept more completely. Definitions like this which rely exclusively on a technical description of the concept's properties are not very helpful unless you already know what the concept means. A more concrete way of communicating the concept *horse* would be to point out various animals that qualify as horses and other animals that do not. You could also explain why they do not. (For example, "That can't be a horse because it has two humps and its legs are far too long.")

Although examples do not take the place of a clearly understood definition, they are often very useful in clarifying, supplementing, and expanding such a definition. If someone asked you, "What is a horse?" and you replied by giving examples of different kinds of horses (thoroughbred racing horses, plow horses for farming, quarter horses for cowhands, circus horses), you certainly would be communicating a good portion of the meaning of *horse*. Giving examples of a concept complements and clarifies the necessary requirements for the correct use of that concept.

Giving an effective definition of a concept requires

- Identifying the general qualities of the concept, which determine when it can be correctly applied
- Classifying it, which means identifying its category, type, or "family"
- Using appropriate examples that embody its general qualities
- Differentiating it from other items in its classification

The process of providing definitions of concepts is basically the same process that you use to develop concepts.

Thinking ↔ Writing Activity

Trying to Define a Concept

Before you read the next selections, try to write a short definition of one of the concepts that they discuss. One reading is about *religion,* and the other is about *poverty.*

1. Identify and list the general qualities or properties of *religion* or of *poverty.*
2. Classify it. In what category of human activity does it belong? Write the classification. (Is religion an expression of belief or a system? Is poverty an economic state or an insufficiency of any kind?)
3. Write down an example or two.
4. Now try to write a definition in one, two, or three sentences. You might want to begin your definition with the classification or category that you have decided upon.
5. Then read the selection about the concept you have defined. What did you write that is similar to what you read? What was different?

There are few concepts more complex and emotionally charged than that of *religion.* The following passage is taken from the book *Ways of Being Religious* and presents a thoughtful introduction to the concepts of *religion* and *religious experience.*

What Is Religion?
BY FREDERICK J. STRONG, CHARLES L. LLOYD, AND JAY T. ALLEN

An African proverb, from the Ganda tribe in central Uganda, states, "He who never visits thinks his mother is the only cook." As with most proverbs, its meaning is larger than the explicit subjects referred to—in this case food and visiting.

It suggests that a person is much the poorer for not having had exposure to and acquaintance with the ways of other people.

All of us have had some acquaintance with religious people, just as we have tasted our mother's food. But do we really understand very well what it means to be religious? The "Father of the Scientific Study of Religion," Max Mueller, once said: "He who knows one religion understands none." That is perhaps too extreme a statement as it stands, and yet it says about the study of religion what the African proverb says about the knowledge of life in general—that we sacrifice much if we confine ourselves to the familiar.

If a visit is to be fruitful, the "traveler" must do more than just move from place to place. He must respond to what he sees. But what is it that shapes the way we respond to new experiences? Our perception of things is often colored by our previous attitudes toward them. In this case, what do you, the reader, expect from an exposure to various expressions of religion? What sorts of things do you expect to see? How do you think you will respond to them? If you were asked to define, illustrate, or to characterize religious behavior, how would you do so? The answers to these questions, of course, reflect your pre-conceptions. To become conscious of your pre-conceptions, ask yourself the following four questions:

Does your definition *reduce* religion to what you happen to be acquainted with by accident of birth and socialization? Perhaps that goes without saying. It may be true of anyone's "off-the-cuff" definition of religion. However, we ask this question to encourage you to consider whether your definition has sufficient *scope*. Is it broad enough to include the religious activities of human beings throughout the world? In surveying university students we have commonly gotten responses to the question, "What is religion?" as follows: "Being Christian, I would define it [religion] as [a] personal relationship with Christ." "Religion [is]: God, Christ, and Holy Ghost and their meaning to each individual." Other students think of worship rather than belief. In this vein, one edition of Webster's dictionary, in the first of its definitions, describes religion as "the service and adoration of God or a god as expressed in forms of worship." If we were to accept any of the above definitions, many people in the world would be excluded—people who regard some of their most important activities as religious, but who do not focus upon a deity. That is to say, not all religions are theistic. It remains to be seen, of course, whether and to what extent this is true. But let us all be warned of taking our habits or our dictionary as the sole resource for defining religion. In some areas, the main lines of significant understanding are already well established. Therefore we have no serious quarrel with Webster's definition of food as "nutritive material taken into an organism for growth, work, or repair and for maintaining the vital processes." But in religion, interpretive concepts are more problematical. Therefore we are suspicious of the adequacy of the dictionary's definition of religion.

5

Another common way to define religion is to regard it as "morality plus stories," or "morality plus emotion." These are ways of asserting that religion has to do mainly with ethics, or that its myths merely support the particular views of a people. There are, of course, persons for whom religion has been reduced to ethics, as when Thomas Paine stated (in *The Rights of Man*): "My country is the world, and my religion is to do good." But we should be cautious in assuming that this testimony would do for all religious people.

A final example of a definition that begins with personal experience is one that claims: "Religion is a feeling of security"; or, as one student put it: "Religion is an aid in coping with that part of life which man does not understand, or in some cases a philosophy of life enabling man to live more deeply." In locating the basis of religion in man's need for a sense of security, this approach suggests that the deepest study of religion is through psychology. It has been dramatically expressed by the psychiatrist and writer C. G. Jung when he wrote: "Religion is a relationship to the highest or strongest value . . . the value by which you are possessed unconsciously. That psychological fact which is the greatest power in your system is the god, since it is always the overwhelming psychic factor which is called 'god.'" Although this understanding of religion expresses a very important point, many theologians and religious philosophers point out that an interpretation that reduces all of religious experience to psychological, biological, or social factors omits the central reality exposed in that experience—the Sacred or Ultimate Reality. Thus, a student of religion should keep open the question of whether a familiar interpretation of religious life that fits into a conventional, social science perspective of man is adequate for interpreting the data.

Does your definition reflect a *bias* on your part—positive or negative—toward religion as a whole, or toward a particular religion? There are many examples of biased definitions that could be cited. Some equate religion with superstition, thus reflecting a negative evaluation. One man defined religion as "the sum of the scruples which impede the free exercise of the human faculties." Another hostile view of religion is to see religion as a device of priests to keep the masses in subjection and themselves in comfort. Similarly, Karl Marx, while not actually attempting to define religion, called it "the opiate of the people," again reflecting a bias against (all) religion.

Still others, in defining religion, are stating their concept of *true* religion as opposed to what they regard as false or pagan faiths. Henry Fielding, in his novel *Tom Jones,* has the provincial parson Mr. Thwackum saying, "When I mention religion I mean the Christian religion; and not only the Christian religion, but the Protestant religion; and not only the Protestant religion; but the Church of England." Some Christians assume that their personal conviction comprises a definition of religion, so the religion is regarded as "the worship of God through his Son Jesus Christ," or "a personal relationship with Christ." A Muslim can point out that the essence of religion is to make peace with God through complete submission to God's will, a submission that he will insist is brought to fulfillment in Islam. (In Arabic the word "Islam" means "submission," "peace," "safety," and "salvation.")

Therefore the student interested in reflecting on religious experience that includes more than a single institutional or cultural expression should remember the distinction between descriptive (neutral) and evaluative definitions. A descriptive definition attempts to be as inclusive as possible about a class of items, such as religious forms. An evaluative definition, on the other hand, reflects one's own criteria for truth or falsity, for reality or illusion. In "visiting" religious people, we suggest that you delay making an evaluation until you have understood why their expressions and processes have profound meaning for them—however strange those expressions may seem to you. In the final analysis, each person must evaluate different religious alternatives; but one of our goals in bringing together the material in this volume is to provide you with a variety of options—a variety that is reduced if you limit religion to any single historical expression.

10   Obviously the believer who advocates one religion to the exclusion of all others differs sharply from one who rejects all. Nevertheless, if either accepts his own convictions about what is best or worst in religion as a description of what religion in fact is everywhere and for everyone, he exhibits a common indifference to unfamiliar, and therefore potentially surprising, religious patterns. As a believer (or skeptic), you have a right to declare your own understanding of what is most important, most real, in religion. This declaration is, in fact, essential, for it guides you in your quest for whatever is most real in life. As a student, on the other hand, you have an obligation to carry your studies as far as necessary to include relevant data. In this role, your obligation is not only to your own perception of value but also to a common world of understanding in which men of many religious persuasions can converse with each other.

Does your definition *limit* religion to what it has been in the past, and nothing else, or does your definition make it possible to speak of emerging forms of religion? In asking this question, we should observe two striking facts of the history of religion: there was a time when some present religions did not exist, and some of the religions which once emerged no longer exist (for example, the Egyptian and Babylonian religions). Human history, then, has witnessed the emergence and abandonment of several religions.

Even religious traditions that have maintained a sense of continuity over vast stretches of time (Hinduism, Buddhism, Judaism, Christianity, for example) have undergone important changes. Is it really as obvious as we tend to think that they are essentially the same now as they were at their origins? Do the terms naming these traditions even today point to a single entity, however complex? You are familiar with at least some instances of religious warfare *within* the Christian tradition. Roman Catholics have persecuted and killed Lutherans; Lutherans have persecuted and killed Calvinists; Calvinists, Anglicans; Anglicans, Quakers; and most have returned the act with interest. Are all of these groups expressions of "the one true church"? Are some more Christian than others? Is there only one form of Christianity? Are new movements violations of the tradition? Or is the one who speaks to his own time the one who is most faithful to the genius of his tradition? These questions can be asked of all religious traditions. All have experienced change and diversity. Furthermore, it seems likely that this will continue, and that new religious traditions will emerge.

Therefore, the conventions of the past cannot be regarded as the limits of future religious forms.

In part because history has witnessed the emergence and internal changes of many religions, anthropologists and cultural historians commonly suggest that religion (and human culture in general) has attained only its adolescence. Likewise, philosophers and religious thinkers in both East and West point to the anxiety and tensions today that are expressed in political, social, economic, and intellectual upheaval. They raise a question of whether or not man's moral, psychic, and evaluative resources can catch up with his self-destructive potential seen in technologically advanced weapons and psychological-chemical techniques for social control. The most hopeful of these philosophers perceive the present turmoil as a lack of "maturity" in human consciousness, and express the hope that it is not too late (quite) to change the direction of man from self-destruction to self-fulfillment.

From this perspective most of mankind's experience is still in the future. The history of religious life to the present is only a beginning. But the basis of these projections is the recognition that man's survival requires him to recognize religious dynamics and processes for evaluations as major forces in human life. Should not a definition of religion aid us in looking at contemporary phenomena to see if any new ways of being religious are emerging? At least it should not inhibit persons with an interest in this matter, and we think an introduction to religion should encourage such reflection.

15   **Does your definition have sufficient *precision*?** Are there any limits to the scope of religion, or are the limits so vague that they fail to mark out an object of study? In an attempt to be as broadminded as possible, many definitions are like a student's statement that religion is "the means man has of coping with his world." Or they are similar to the claim that religion is "believing in a way of life which involves understanding and caring for others," or "religion is love." Such definitions tell us a good deal, but without some qualification they might refer to many other expressions of human life than specifically religious ones. In order to find a focus and a set of limitations at the outer circumference of that focus, we need to designate what are those essential elements of religion that will expose the *religious* meaning of the evidence we look at.

When one has "visited" (seen) a wide range of religious life, from all parts of the world and throughout human history, it becomes apparent that religion is a way of life that involves many processes—all of which, in different ways, are directed toward a common end. The goal is to reach a state of being that is conceived to be the highest possible state or condition. Religion is the general term for the various ways by which people seek to become changed into that highest state. We understand *religion as a means toward ultimate transformation*. By this we are not claiming that every activity you think of as religious will in fact transform you ultimately. It might, but that is not our point. We mean that *any* reasonably specific means that *any* person adopts with the serious hope and intention of moving toward ultimate transformation should be termed "religious." We think it possible to speak of all religious activity (Eastern and Western, past, present, and emerging) without reducing religion to what is merely familiar to us and without putting a value judgment on one or more religions.

Critical Reading Questions

1. Where in this excerpt is the definition of *religion* given? Do you find that placement effective? If so, why?

2. What do you find helpful about the questions at the beginning of many of the paragraphs?

3. Apply one of those questions to a different concept and write a paragraph modeled on the one following the question, substituting this other concept for *religion*.

Poverty might seem easy to define, particularly if you think only in terms of money. The following essay takes a physical approach to defining what could be classified as an economic problem.

What Is Poverty?

BY JO GOODWIN PARKER

You ask me what is poverty? Listen to me. Here I am, dirty, smelly, and with no "proper" underwear on and with the stench of my rotting teeth near you. I will tell you. Listen to me. Listen without pity. I cannot use your pity. Listen with understanding. Put yourself in my dirty, worn out, ill-fitting shoes, and hear me.

Poverty is getting up every morning from a dirt- and illness-stained mattress. The sheets have long since been used for diapers. Poverty is living in a smell that never leaves. This is a smell of urine, sour milk, and spoiling food sometimes joined with the strong smell of long-cooked onions. Onions are cheap. If you have smelled this smell, you did not know how it came. It is the smell of the outdoor privy. It is the smell of young children who cannot walk the long dark way in the night. It is the smell of the mattresses where years of "accidents" have happened. It is the smell of the milk which has gone sour because the refrigerator long has not worked, and it costs money to get it fixed. It is the smell of rotting garbage. I could bury it, but where is the shovel? Shovels cost money.

Poverty is being tired. I have always been tired. They told me at the hospital when the last baby came that I had chronic anemia caused from poor diet, a bad case of worms, and that I needed a corrective operation. I listened politely—the poor are always polite. The poor always listen. They don't say that there is no money for iron pills, or better food, or worm medicine. The idea of an operation is frightening and costs so much that, if I had dared, I would have laughed. Who takes care of my children? Recovery from an operation takes a long time. I have three children. When I left them with "Granny" the last time I had a job, I came home to find the baby covered with fly specks, and a diaper that had not been changed since I left. When the dried diaper came off, bits of my baby's flesh came with it. My other child was playing with a sharp bit of broken glass, and my oldest was playing alone at the edge of a lake. I made twenty-two dollars a week, and a good nursery school costs twenty dollars a week for three children. I quit my job.

Poverty is dirt. You say in your clean clothes coming from your clean house, "Anybody can be clean." Let me explain about housekeeping with no money. For breakfast I give my children grits with no oleo or cornbread without eggs and oleo. This does not use up many dishes. What dishes there are, I wash in cold water and with no soap. Even the cheapest soap has to be saved for the baby's diapers. Look at my hands, so cracked and red. Once I saved for two months to buy a jar of Vaseline for my hands and the baby's diaper rash. When I had saved enough, I went to buy it and the price had gone up two cents. The baby and I suffered on. I have to decide every day if I can bear to put my cracked, sore hands into the cold water and strong soap. But you ask, why not hot water? Fuel costs money. If you have a wood fire it costs money. If you burn electricity, it costs money. Hot water is a luxury. I do not have luxuries. I know you will be surprised when I tell you how young I am. I look so much older. My back has been bent over the wash tubs every day for so long. I cannot remember when I ever did anything else. Every night I wash every stitch my school-age child has on and just hope her clothes will be dry by morning.

5   Poverty is staying up all night on cold nights to watch the fire, knowing one spark on the newspaper covering the walls means your sleeping children die in flames. In summer, poverty is watching gnats and flies devour your baby's tears when he cries. The screens are torn and you pay so little rent you know they will never be fixed. Poverty means insects in your food, in your nose, in your eyes, and crawling over you when you sleep. Poverty is hoping it never rains because diapers won't dry when it rains and soon you are using newspapers. Poverty is seeing your children forever with runny noses. Paper handkerchiefs cost money and all your rags you need for other things. Even more costly are antihistamines. Poverty is cooking without food and cleaning without soap.

Poverty is asking for help. Have you ever had to ask for help, knowing your children will suffer unless you get it? Think about asking for a loan from a relative, if this is the only way you can imagine asking for help. I will tell you how it feels. You find out where the office is that you are supposed to visit. You circle that block four or five times. Thinking of your children, you go in. Everyone is very busy. Finally, someone comes out and you tell her that you need help. That never is the person you need to see. You go see another person, and after spilling the whole shame of your poverty all over the desk between you, you find that this isn't the right office after all—you must repeat the whole process, and it never is any easier at the next place.

You have asked for help, and after all it has a cost. You are again told to wait. You are told why, but you don't really hear because of the red cloud of shame and the rising black cloud of despair.

Poverty is remembering. It is remembering quitting school in junior high because "nice" children had been so cruel about my clothes and my smell. The attendance officer came. My mother told him I was pregnant. I wasn't, but she thought that I could get a job and help out. I had jobs off and on, but never long enough to learn anything. Mostly I remember being married. I was so young then. I am still young. For a time, we had all the things you have. There was a little house in another town, with hot water and everything. Then my husband lost his job. There was unemployment insurance for a while and what few jobs I could get. Soon, all our nice things were repossessed and we moved back here. I was pregnant then. This house didn't look so bad when we first moved in. Every week it gets worse. Nothing is ever fixed. We now had no money. There were a few odd jobs for my husband, but everything went for food then, as it does now. I don't know how we lived through three years and three babies, but we did. I'll tell you something, after the last baby I destroyed my marriage. It had been a good one, but could you keep on bringing children in this dirt? Did you ever think how much it costs for any kind of birth control? I knew my husband was leaving the day he left, but there were no goodbys between us. I hope he has been able to climb out of this mess somewhere. He never could hope with us to drag him down.

That's when I asked for help. When I got it, you know how much it was? It was, and is, seventy-eight dollars a month for the four of us; that is all I ever can get. Now you know why there is no soap, no needles and thread, no hot water, no aspirin, no worm medicine, no hand cream, no shampoo. None of these things forever and ever and ever. So that you can see clearly, I pay twenty dollars a month rent, and most of the rest goes for food. For grits and cornmeal, and rice and milk and beans. I try my best to use only the minimum electricity. If I use more, there is that much less for food.

10 Poverty is looking into a black future. Your children won't play with my boys. They will turn to other boys who steal to get what they want. I can already see them behind the bars of their prison instead of behind the bars of my poverty. Or they will turn to the freedom of alcohol or drugs, and find themselves enslaved. And my daughter? At best, there is for her a life like mine.

But you say to me, there are schools. Yes, there are schools. My children have no extra books, no magazines, no extra pencils, or crayons, or paper and the most important of all, they do not have health. They have worms, they have infections, they have pink-eye all summer. They do not sleep well on the floor, or with me in my one bed. They do not suffer from hunger, my seventy-eight dollars keeps us alive, but they do suffer from malnutrition. Oh yes, I do remember what I was taught about health in school. It doesn't do much good. In some places there is a surplus commodities program. Not here. The county said it cost too much. There is a school lunch program. But I have two children who will already be damaged by the time they get to school.

But, you say to me, there are health clinics. Yes, there are health clinics and they are in the towns. I live out here eight miles from town. I can walk that far (even if it is sixteen miles both ways), but can my little children? My neighbor will take me when he goes; but he expects to get paid, *one way or another.* I bet you know my neighbor. He is that large man who spends his time at the gas station, the barbershop, and the corner store complaining about the government spending money on the immoral mothers of illegitimate children.

Poverty is an acid that drips on pride until all pride is worn away. Poverty is a chisel that chips on honor until honor is worn away. Some of you say that you would do *something* in my situation, and maybe you would, for the first week or the first month, but for year after year after year?

Even the poor can dream. A dream of a time when there is money. Money for the right kinds of food, for worm medicine, for iron pills, for toothbrushes, for hand cream, for a hammer and nails and a bit of screening, for a shovel, for a bit of paint, for some sheeting, for needles and thread. Money to pay *in money* for a trip to town. And, oh, money for hot water and money for soap. A dream of when asking for help does not eat away the last bit of pride. When the office you visit is as nice as the offices of other governmental agencies, when there are enough workers to help you quickly, when workers do not quit in defeat and despair. When you have to tell your story to only one person, and that person can send you for other help and you don't have to prove your poverty over and over and over again.

15   I have come out of my despair to tell you this. Remember I did not come from another place or another time. Others like me are all around you. Look at us with an angry heart, anger that will help you help me. Anger that will let you tell of me. The poor are always silent. Can you be silent too?

Critical Reading Questions

1. How do you respond to Parker's technique of defining by using analogies? Is there one that you find particularly effective?

2. Identify a paragraph in which Parker gives strong, specific physical examples. What effect do these specifics have? Rewrite one sentence, using more general language. Does it seem more, or less, effective than Parker's sentence?

3. Do you think a man might speak or write differently about poverty? What might a father in a similar situation say?

Writing Thoughtfully to Define Concepts

Writing a full definition, often called an *extended definition,* is among the most important and most difficult of writing activities. Defining terms is a necessary part of college-level writing and speaking. For productive discussions about complex issues, all involved must agree on the meanings of significant terms, so clear definitions are often required. Difficulties arise because significant terms related to complex issues are usually abstract concepts, with possibilities of different definitions for different people. For example, the common political terms *conservative* and *liberal* often have varied meanings, even to people who identify themselves as one or the other.

No one has much trouble agreeing on definitions of physical objects. A table, a tree, a television set—not many arguments arise about what these objects are. But like *liberal* and *conservative*, concepts such as *religion, love, democracy, femininity,* and *masculinity* can be defined in different ways. If people discussing ideas like these do not establish definitions, their discussions will not be productive. Worse, these discussions sometimes lead to disagreements, arguments, and even wars. The readings and Thinking-Writing Activities in this chapter have been selected and planned to demonstrate the importance of definitions.

Notice how with both simple objects and complex concepts, defining is somewhat easier as long as a single word is being examined. As soon as modifying and classifying ideas are added, defining becomes more challenging and more significant to critical thinking. A *beautiful* table, a *good* tree to plant in a *small* yard, the *best* television set to buy for *your family room*—now these objects call for fuller definitions. The *kind* of democracy that can work in a country with a *history of despotism,* the *kind* of love that a *parent* might have for an *adult child*—these are the types of concepts that people must define in order to present arguments, to make decisions, to solve problems. These are the kinds of terms that you might want to define in the Writing Project in this chapter because they are the kinds that involve judgments; they are important to our lives because they influence our actions.

Clear, satisfying definitions can be as extended as book chapters, articles, or entire books; however, a definition often will be developed in a paragraph or two as a vital part of a paper or report. In the Writing Project for this chapter, you will write an essay that defines; you will see the need for using a variety of thinking/organizing patterns as you develop it. The guidelines for writing definitions are not fixed rules; there may be times when you would have good reasons for varying or adapting some of them. Try to use them, though, unless you have good reason not to.

Guidelines for Writing Definitions

1. Establish the need for a definition. Why is it needed? Do people disagree on the meaning of the concept? Are there multiple meanings? Are earlier definitions no longer satisfactory? Is this a new concept or new terminology?

2. Choose carefully the word or words in which you state the concept. Definitions provide precision, so you need to be sure that you have presented the concept in the words that are most indicative.

3. Incorporate two kinds of dictionary definitions: the short one that

gives meaning, as in a regular college dictionary, and a longer one giving the history of the word's usage, which can be found in the *Oxford English Dictionary.* Word origins and past meanings can often illuminate the meaning that you want to present.

4. Be sure that you identify the category into which the concept fits.

5. Show comparative thinking. Point out similar concepts, but then make clear how your concept is distinct. Think of analogies that can illuminate the meaning of the concept.

6. Provide specific examples to show what the concept means. Illustrative anecdotes are often effective.

7. Include the meaning of the concept in the thesis statement. Give careful thought to where you state the thesis.

8. Throughout your definition, emphasize that you are establishing the meaning you believe the concept has within the context that you have identified.

9. Address the foregoing principles in separate paragraphs or sections of the definition. Provide each paragraph with a clear topic sentence whenever appropriate.

10. Document any sources that you use. Introduce source material into your definition, explain and comment on it, and cite it correctly.

Writing Project: Defining an Important Concept

This chapter has included readings, questions, and Thinking-Writing Activities that encourage you to define concepts that affect your life. Be sure to reread what you wrote for the activities; you may be able to use some of that material in completing this project.

Write an essay in which you define a concept that is important to your life now or to your future life. Include explanations of why this concept is significant for you and why it needs defining or redefining. You may want to think of a concept that is expressed in a phrase rather than in a single word. Include material from two sources in addition to any dictionaries that you consult. Integrate your sources into your essay and document them as your instructor advises. After you have drafted your essay, revise it to the best of your ability. Follow your instructor's directions for topic limits, length, format, and so on.

Begin by considering the key elements in the Thinking-Writing Model.

THE WRITING SITUATION

Purpose You have several purposes here. You want to think about and formulate a definition that will be significant as you continue your college studies, decide on your profession, or enter a new phase in your personal life. Indeed, all of us need to be able to define the complex terms that are foundations for our thinking, our decisions, and our actions in life. In addition, you can improve your ability to present a full definition in order to clarify your own thinking and to increase your audience's understanding.

Audience You have a multilevel audience. *You* are an important audience, for in facing the challenge of defining a complex concept, you can think more clearly about some aspect of your life. Your classmates can learn from your definition and also can be a valuable audience in peer reviews of a draft, reacting as intelligent readers who are not as knowledgeable as you about the concept that pertains to your life. Of course, your instructor remains the audience who will judge how well you have developed your definition. As a writing teacher, your instructor cares about clear focus, logical organization, solid evidence, accurate documentation of sources, and correctness. Keep these aspects in mind as you revise, edit, and proofread. In addition, you should think about and identify people outside your class who might enjoy or profit from reading your definition. Is there somewhere you could publish the paper so that others can read it and provide feedback?

Subject All of us need to be able to define abstract, complex terms that are foundations for our thinking, our decisions, and our actions in life. College courses, family life, spiritual concerns, and romantic relationships all involve concepts that need to be well defined. Clear definitions help us understand what we mean when we speak and write, understand what others mean when they communicate with us, and—most important—avoid confusion and conflict. For this assignment, try to identify an important concept that is central to how you see yourself and your future. Concepts like *creative expression, enlightened free choice, authentic person, fulfillment, achieving potential, meaningful empathy, social responsibility, critical thinker,* and (of course) *thoughtful writer* are all examples with broad implications in a person's life.

Writer This project provides you with the opportunity to participate in the "conversation of ideas" that is the lifeblood of thoughtful, reflective people in a society. By defining a complex concept, you are explaining how the concept you have selected has personal meaning for you. You are also suggesting to others—your audience—how they might think about your analysis of the concept. The definition you propose may help them understand something in their experience more clearly, or it may provide an added meaning they have not previously considered. The outside sources integrated into your analysis ensure that your definition is grounded in a common understanding that goes beyond your own experience.

THE WRITING PROCESS

The following sections will guide you through the recursive stages of generating, planning, drafting, and revising as you work on an essay in which you define a significant concept. Try to be particularly conscious of both the critical thinking you do as you articulate your definition and the critical thinking and decision making you do as you revise.

Generating Ideas

- Refer back to the responses you wrote for the Thinking-Writing Activities for the readings on gender issues and the essays on defining religion and poverty. These concepts are important in many people's lives, so perhaps you will write about one of them—or perhaps what you read and wrote will lead you to another concept to define.

- Think about the activities or concerns that are central to your life. Some of these are probably rather serious, as are the subjects discussed in this chapter, but some parts are surely more lighthearted, like sports you play or watch, television comedies, thriller movies, or parties.

- Next, think of concepts inherent in some of your activities, such as a satisfying relationship or what it means to be a good athlete, college student, or practitioner of your religion.

- Now, list the properties of two or three concepts that you have identified. Include specific examples. How should each example be classified?

- Think about why any of these concepts need to be defined or redefined. Do people agree on the meaning? Have you formulated a meaning that is more precise and accurate?

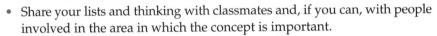

- Share your lists and thinking with classmates and, if you can, with people involved in the area in which the concept is important.

- Use as many thinking patterns as you can to discover ideas about your concept. What is it different from? similar to? analogous to? Describe it; think about what causes it; think about what effects it has.

- Look up the concept's key words in a good college-level dictionary and also in the *Oxford English Dictionary*. Ask your instructor or one of your college librarians to explain the OED to you. See if you can use any of your concept's word history in your definition.

- Freewrite for at least five minutes about why the concept is important to your life, why it needs to be defined, and what information needs to be in your definition.

Defining a Focus

- Look at your freewriting and lists to see what main idea you are moving toward in your definition. Write this idea in any way that you can.

- Now draft a thesis statement that gives the key ideas in your definition. Recently a student defining *freedom of religion* had this as her thesis sentence: "To me, freedom of religion means more than simply being able to practice our religions as we believe that we should; it also means that we must understand and respect other people's religions." Another student, working on a definition of today's *superwoman*, wrote, "The main properties of a superwoman are being capable, tenacious, and independent."

- Be sure that your thesis statement emphasizes the meaning of the concept that you are defining.

Organizing Ideas Essays emphasizing definition are not easy to organize because there are so many approaches to a clear definition of a complex concept. Because the thesis—the essence of the definition—needs to be placed in a context and explained in a number of ways, the question of where to state the thesis is especially crucial. This is the kind of essay in which it might come at the end. (Reread "What Is Religion?" on pages 342–347 to see how this organizing technique is used.) When you state the thesis at the end, you need to lead up to it or preview it throughout the essay. However, you will want to think of stating the thesis provisionally near the beginning and referring to it elsewhere in the paper as you establish your definition.

Identify the approaches that you have used in your generative writing and early drafts. Where have you used contrast, comparison, analogy, narration, and so on? The material developed by each of these approaches is likely to form a paragraph. The definitions that you have found in your dictionary and in the OED will need a paragraph or two to connect them with the definition that you are developing. As always, give careful thought to paragraphing. Try your drafted paragraphs in different orders to discover which will best help your readers understand your definition.

Because it is important that your readers understand the need for a definition, explaining that need is an effective way to begin. Explaining the significance of this concept in your life might be part of the beginning or conclusion.

Drafting Be sure to set your word-processing program to double- or triple-space as you draft. Then you will have room to make changes as you revise and edit. Or if you are writing by hand, use alternate lines.

Be sure to identify source material as you include it in your draft. Remember to use quotation marks with quoted material. Sometimes students think that they can give proper attribution in the final copy, but it's easy to forget if attribution is not made in every draft—even the roughest.

Begin with the easiest paragraph to draft. Explaining the concept's significance in your life is likely to be easy since you are writing about your thoughts and feelings; showing the need for a definition should not be difficult because you are writing about one of your convictions. Therefore, you may want to draft these personal paragraphs first. Then you might feel more comfortable explaining the connection of the word history to your concept and also may find it easier to give classifying, comparative, and contrastive explanations. As you draft, be sure that each paragraph contains real-life examples that pertain to the meaning of the concept—unless for some good reason a specific paragraph does not need examples.

After you draft your paragraphs, make every effort to write topic sentences that focus on how the material in each paragraph helps to establish the meaning of your concept.

As you draft the conclusion, be sure that it provides a satisfying ending with some reference to the thesis and emphasis on the meaning of the concept.

Revising One of the best revision strategies is to get an audience's reactions to your draft. If your instructor allows class time for peer review, be sure to have a draft ready so that you can participate and gain valuable feedback. Likewise, be ready to help your classmates. Peer review guidelines are located on pages 65–66 and 105–107. After thinking about your classmates' questions and using them to improve your draft, you will be ready to work through the following revision concerns.

If you did not have a chance to work with classmates, let your draft sit for a day or two and then look at it with the following questions in mind.

1. **Think big.** Look at your draft as a whole.

   - Does it fulfill the assignment? Does it present a definition of a concept that is important to your life?

   - Is your definition stated clearly in an effective place?

   - How does your thesis deal with your definition?

   - Have you explained why a definition is needed?

   - In what ways are your specific examples effective?

   - How can you connect the paragraphs more smoothly?

   - Could you introduce your sources more effectively?

2. **Think medium.** Look at your draft paragraph by paragraph.

   - Do you need to rewrite your first paragraph to explain why you want to define this concept?

   - How have you used topic sentences to make clear what each paragraph is about?

- Does any paragraph that does not have a topic sentence need one to be more effective?

- Is the paragraph that presents your definition well written?

- Is your concluding paragraph effective? Does it wrap up your definition?

- Where could you use transitions to improve the flow within paragraphs?

3. **Think small.** Look at your draft sentence by sentence.

- Which sentences present the concept in your definition? Can these concepts be stated more clearly?

- How can you shorten or divide sentences that seem too long?

- How can you combine or expand sentences that seem choppy or too short?

- Do any sentences contain errors in Standard English grammar? How can you correct them?

4. **Think "picky."** Look at your draft as the fussiest critic might.

- Which words are not quite right for what you are trying to say? What words could you use instead?

- Are any words misspelled? Run your spell checker, but remember that it won't identify all errors.

- Is your documentation correct? Check your handbook for the required format.

- Are the pages numbered? Is your name on all pages?

- Will your finished paper make a good impression by being nicely presented in the format that your instructor expects?

- Is there anything else that you can do to improve your draft?

Editing and Proofreading   After you have prepared a final draft, check again for correct grammar and punctuation usage. Proofread carefully to detect omitted words or punctuation marks. Also proofread for the kinds of errors the spell checker can't catch.

The following essays show how two students responded to this assignment.

STUDENT WRITING

True Friendship

BY JEFF JOHN

When asked if they have friends, people will almost always say yes. Friendship is the most universal relationship we have and probably a necessity for everyone. Friendship is something that people love to say they have, but I think that it is often misunderstood. Many people are quick to call anyone a friend even if it's someone they just met. However, there are other words to use for companions, buddies, or acquaintances who may not truly be friends.

There are certain questions you have to ask to find out if someone is really a friend. Do you trust this person? Are you open with this person? Is he or she supportive? These are three characteristics of a true friendship.

Trust is probably the most important characteristic of friendship. You must have trust in a friendship. You need someone to be honest about all aspects of life. You need someone who will not mislead you. You need someone you can rely on. For example, in "Why My Sister's My Best Friend," a young woman named Angela says, "Who else can you rely on to tell you whether your new boyfriend's a major dork or how your butt really looks in that dress?" (Fisher 150). You need friends who will not hide things from you and will give you an honest opinion. If you trust someone, you do not fear telling him or her a secret. When you trust someone, you have strong faith in him or her.

Another characteristic in friendship is the opportunity to be open. You know that a person is your friend if you are capable of expressing your thoughts and feelings to him or her. If you are able to do so, then you know you will not be ridiculed or criticized about your feelings. In "Men and Their Hidden Feelings," Richard Cohen states, "Can a man talk intimately with another man and not wonder about his masculinity?" (342). If someone is truly a friend, you should be able to communicate intimately with him or her. Differences in gender are never a fear if you can be open with someone. When you feel open with someone, you feel comfortable around him or her no matter how you appear. For example, in "Why My Sister's My Best Friend," a young woman named Michelle says, "My sister has seen me skinny, pudgy, drunk, hung over, pregnant, laughing until I peed my pants, and crying uncontrollably" (Fisher 150). Michelle is obviously very open with her sister. She has no fear of being herself around her. Having a friend you can open up to feels great, because you feel there is not much that you have to hide. In "Men and Their Hidden Feelings," Cohen says, "For instance, I know men who have suffered brutal professional setbacks and never mentioned it to their friends" (341). If you feel open to a friend, you would never feel like you have to hide something. You would never have a problem with being honest with him or her.

Tough times come a lot in life, and then you need someone's support. My sister is getting ready to give birth, and she needs more support now than ever. She needs support from friends, and also from her family. If you're a good friend to someone, you are always supportive. You help in times of need. You share your time and energy. A friend doesn't let friends go through rough times alone.

Friendship is the most common relationship to have with someone, but it can be misunderstood. There are certain characteristics a friend must have to be called a friend.

Webster's Seventh New Collegiate Dictionary defines *friend* as "one attached to another by affection or esteem" (335). Therefore, by definition you cannot call everyone a friend. You have to have some form of affection or esteem for that person. If you have affection or esteem for someone, you are more likely to trust him or her, be open with him or her, and be supported by him or her. As nice as it is to have a million companions or buddies, we need to acknowledge who our true friends are.

Works Cited

Cohen, Richard. "Men and Their Hidden Feelings." *Critical Thinking, Thoughtful Writing.* By John Chaffee, with Christine McMahon and Barbara Stout. Boston: Houghton Mifflin, 1999. 341–342.

Fisher, Deirdre. "Why My Sister's My Best Friend." *Cosmopolitan,* Oct. 1999: 150.

STUDENT WRITING

Genius

BY TZE WING CHAN

Have you ever been called "genius"? I hope you have. When we know someone who has outstanding ability, we say that this person must be a genius. Even though the word *genius* is used frequently, everybody might not agree on the exact meaning of the word. We might wonder sometimes what a real genius is and why we cannot all be geniuses. Since the meaning of the word *genius* seems questionable, I did some research in order to learn about it.

The word *genius* has changed meaning through history. According to one definition in the *Oxford English Dictionary*, genius means:

> A native intellectual power of an exalted type, such as is attributed to those who are esteemed greatest in any department of art, speculation, or practice; instinctive and extraordinary capacity for imaginative creation, original thought, invention, or discovery.

Perhaps this modern definition is accepted by almost everybody, but it was derived from different meanings as time went by. The very beginning sources are Latin and Greek words that mean "to be born." The ancient Romans considered genius as the spirit that protected one's household (Sternberg 483). Greigson and Gibbs-Smith discussed the origin of the word in *Ideas* and said that the term came "to personify one's wishes" and to mean "the guardian angel"; then later on, by the seventeenth century, it meant talent and innate ability (159). After a long time, the word *genius* acquired the meaning that we know nowadays. According to the *Oxford English Dictionary*, in 1749 in the book *Tom Jones*, the modern meaning is used in the phrase "By the wonderful force of genius only, without the least assistance of learning."

After thinking about these meanings, I decided that childhood life experiences and good fortune are factors that can cause one to develop his or her innate ability. Some of the sources that I found discussed these ideas. Sternberg said that some geniuses, such as some of the Nobel prize winners in literature, suffered from their family situations (486). These geniuses might have had no parents or been discriminated against, which might make them feel and think differently. On the other hand, some geniuses come from families which offered them opportunities to work with their interests from the time that they were children. For example, Mozart and Beethoven came from musical families.

A cause that I found very interesting, discussed in the *Encyclopedia of Human Intelligence* is good fortune. As the author Sternberg stated:

> The difference between being outstandingly able and being considered a genius
> is akin to the distinction between being one of the numerous soldiers who act
> bravely in a battle and one of the few who are awarded a medal for heroism
> (484).

So to be considered as a genius, it is essential that one should have an innate ability in a certain area, but also luck. For instance, a poet who has unbelievable skill for writing poems might never be recognized as a genius if no one around him or her knows how to appreciate the poems. Therefore, a genius is the product of the ability combined with fortune.

Geniuses have existed at all times. Even though we can see some of the factors that cause someone to be a genius, we might still not be exactly sure why it happens. If God created all of us equal, how can one have some powers that others cannot have? Some people might consider this an injustice. However, I think that we need geniuses. How would we communicate if Alexander Graham Bell had not invented the telephone? Geniuses and their creations benefit us all, even if we all do not have "a native intellectual power of an exalted type."

Works Cited

"Genius." *The Encyclopedia Dictionary of Psychology.* 3rd ed. 1986.

Griegson, Geoffrey, and Charles H. Gibbs-Smith. "Genius." *Ideas.* 2nd ed. 1957.

Sternberg, Robert J. "Genius." *Encyclopedia of Human Intelligence.* 1994.

PART THREE

Thinking and Writing to Explore Issues and Take Positions

As you have become more aware of your own thinking and writing abilities, and more confident about using them, you may also have developed more respect for the thinking and writing of others. You have probably observed how academic work and even democracy itself depend on understanding sources of beliefs and various perspectives. You have been learning how to evaluate information and how to express your own perspectives clearly.

Part One of this book helped you focus on yourself as a thinker and a writer, and you wrote from your experiences and observations. Part Two asked you to explore important thinking patterns and to incorporate some ideas from others into your writing. Here in Part Three assignments will lead to the presentation of your ideas and those from sources in well-reasoned writing.

The Writing Projects at the end of each chapter in Part Three ask you to integrate material from several sources into your written work. As you do so, you will learn effective, responsible ways of introducing, commenting on, and documenting ideas from others. You will consider the principles that underlie research and citation, and you will use appropriate academic formats.

10

Believing and Knowing

Writing to Analyze

"A belief is not merely an idea the mind possesses, it is an idea that possesses the mind." —Robert Bolton

Critical Thinking Focus: Analyzing beliefs and their accuracy

Writing Focus: Evaluating evidence and presenting beliefs

Reading Theme: How the media shape our thinking

Writing Project: Analyzing influences on beliefs about a social or academic issue

Writers write about what they believe, and their purposes often include explaining their beliefs and persuading others to adopt them. Yet what exactly are beliefs, and how are they constructed? When should they be kept, when should they be modified, and when should they be discarded? What are the differences between believing and knowing, and how do writers handle these differences? How do writers present beliefs they hold with varying degrees of certainty?

In this information age, we are flooded with data, stories, and pictures from television, radio, newspapers, magazines, books, and computers. Much of this information is accurate, but much is not. We are aware of the "spin doctors" who seek to influence the way we interpret information, trying to persuade us to accept their construction of events. Thus, critical thinkers and thoughtful writers face a continuing challenge to evaluate information they receive and to redefine their beliefs accordingly.

Chapter 2 examined the sources of beliefs, especially those related to personal life. This chapter continues that discussion by further examining the structure of beliefs, by presenting guidelines for evaluating beliefs, and by drawing distinctions between believing and knowing and between knowledge and truth. This chapter presents some of the ways in which beliefs take shape and some of the ways in which they are presented. The concepts of *interpretation, evaluation, conclusion, prediction, report, inference,* and *judgment* will provide a vocabulary to help you think about your beliefs and those of others.

The Writing Project at the end of the chapter asks you to analyze some influences on your beliefs about a social or an academic issue.

Ways of Forming Beliefs

Throughout our lives, we form beliefs about the world around us to explain why things happen as they do, to predict how things will happen, and to govern the way we decide to act. Consider, for example, the extent to which you believe the following statements.

1. Human beings need to eat in order to stay alive.

2. Smoking marijuana is a harmful activity.

3. Every human life is valuable.

4. Developing your mind is as important as taking care of your body.

5. People should care about other people, not just about themselves.

Your responses to these statements reflect certain beliefs you have, beliefs not all people share.

So what exactly are "beliefs"? We can define a **belief** as an interpretation, evaluation, conclusion, or prediction that a person believes to be true. You may not have considered these different representations of beliefs before, but, if you think about it, you might see that most of your beliefs fit into one of these categories. Sometimes it might be important as you consider a belief to see which type it is. For example, *interpretation* suggests that other explanations are possible, and *prediction* makes clear that an event has not yet happened. Such understandings help when thinking critically about your beliefs.

The statement "I believe that the U.S. Constitution's guarantee of 'the right of the people to keep and bear arms' does not prohibit all governmental regulation of firearms" represents an interpretation of the Second Amendment. To say, "I believe that watching soap operas is unhealthy because they focus almost exclusively on the seamy side of human life" expresses an *evaluation* of soap operas. The statement "I believe that one of the main reasons two out of three people in the world go to bed hungry each night is that industrially advanced nations like the United States have not done a satisfactory job of sharing their knowledge" expresses a *conclusion* about the problem of world hunger. To say, "I believe that if drastic environmental measures are not undertaken to slow the global warming trend, the polar icecaps will melt and the earth will be flooded" is to make a prediction about events that will occur in the future.

Besides expressing an interpretation, evaluation, conclusion, or prediction about the world, a belief also expresses the speaker's *endorsement* of its accuracy—an indication that the belief is held to be true. This endorsement by the speaker is a necessary dimension of a belief. For example, the statement "Astrological predictions are meaningless because there is no persuasive evidence that the position of the planets has any effect on human affairs" expresses a belief even though it doesn't specifically include the words *I believe.*

In addition, it is necessary to recognize that beliefs are not static—at least not if we apply a critical approach. We continually form and re-form our beliefs throughout much of our lives. This process often follows the following sequence:

1. We *form* beliefs in order to explain what is taking place. (These initial beliefs are often based on our past experiences.)

2. We *test* these beliefs by acting on the basis of them.

3. We *revise* (or "re-form") these beliefs if our actions do not achieve our goals.

4. We *retest* these revised beliefs by again using them as a basis for action.

As we actively participate in this ongoing process of forming and re-forming beliefs, we are using our critical thinking abilities to identify and critically examine our beliefs by, in effect, asking the following questions.

- How effectively do these beliefs explain what is taking place?

- To what extent are the beliefs consistent with other beliefs about the world?

- How effectively do the beliefs help us to predict what will happen in the future?

- To what extent are these beliefs supported by sound reasons and compelling evidence derived from reliable sources?

This process of critical exploration enables us to develop more understanding of various situations and to exert more control over them.

Thinking ↔ Writing Activity

Identifying Beliefs

State in a sentence or two one of your beliefs for each of these four categories: interpretation, evaluation, conclusion, and prediction. At least some of your statements should be ones that not everyone would agree with.

1. *Interpretation:* I believe that "X means this."
2. *Evaluation:* I believe that "X is good/bad, harmful/beneficial because . . ."
3. *Conclusion:* I believe that "X is what exists/should exist."
4. *Prediction:* I believe that "X will happen."

BELIEFS BASED ON PERSONAL EXPERIENCE

The introductory discussion of beliefs in Chapter 2 identified four sources of beliefs: people of authority, recorded references, observed evidence, and personal experience. The last two involve direct experience. Yet how we interpret and understand direct experience—what conclusions we draw from what we perceive—depends to some extent on what we already believe. In offering evidence to support their beliefs, people generally choose those perceptions and experiences that fit with their previous beliefs; contradictory experiences may be ignored or downplayed.

In the following pair of readings, two writers offer differing beliefs about the situation of the homeless in the United States, based on their perceptions of direct experience. L. Christopher Awalt's essay appeared as a "My Turn" column in *Newsweek*. Following that is "The Allesandros," a chapter from a book about homelessness by Jonathan Kozol, a long-time advocate for the politically and socially disenfranchised.

Before you begin to read, write down two or three of your beliefs about homelessness and the homeless. After you have read both pieces, write a few sentences about how your beliefs were affected by your reading these articles. If possible, share your statements with your classmates.

Brother, Don't Spare a Dime

BY L. CHRISTOPHER AWALT

Homeless people are everywhere—on the street, in public buildings, on the evening news and at the corner parking lot. You can hardly step out of your house these days without meeting some haggard character who asks you for a cigarette or begs for "a little change." The homeless are not just constant symbols of wasted lives and failed social programs—they have become a danger to public safety.

What's the root of the homeless problem? Everyone seems to have a scapegoat: Advocates of the homeless blame government policy; politicians blame the legal system; the courts blame the bureaucratic infrastructure; the Democrats blame the Republicans; the Republicans, the Democrats. The public blames the economy, drugs, the "poverty cycle," and "the breakdown of society." With all this finger-pointing, the group most responsible for the homeless being the way they are receives the least blame. That group is the homeless themselves.

How can I say this? For the past two years I have worked with the homeless, volunteering at the Salvation Army and at a soup kitchen in Austin, Texas. I have led a weekly chapel service, served food, listened, counseled, given time and money, and shared in their struggles. I have seen their response to troubles, and though I'd rather report otherwise, many of them seem to have chosen the lifestyles they lead. They are unwilling to do the things necessary to overcome their circumstances. They must bear the greater part of the blame for their manifold troubles.

Let me qualify what I just said. Not everyone who finds himself out of a job and in the street is there because he wants to be. Some are victims of tragic circumstances. I met many dignified, capable people during my time working with Austin's homeless: the single father struggling to earn his high-school equivalency and to be a role model for his children; the woman who fled a good job in another city to escape an abusive husband; the well-educated young man who had his world turned upside down by divorce and a layoff. These people deserve every effort to help them back on their feet.

5　　But they're not the real problem. They are usually off the streets and resuming normal lives within a period of weeks or months. Even while "down on their luck," they are responsible citizens, working in the shelters and applying for jobs. They are homeless, true, but only temporarily, because they are eager to reorganize their lives.

For every person temporarily homeless, though, there are many who are chronically so. Whether because of mental illness, alcoholism, poor education, drug addiction, or simple laziness, these homeless are content to remain as they are. In many cases they choose the streets. They enjoy the freedom and consider begging a minor inconvenience. They know they can always get a job for a day or two for food, cigarettes, and alcohol. The sophisticated among them have learned to use the system for what it's worth and figure that a trip through the welfare line is less trouble than a steady job. In a society that has mastered dodging responsibility, these homeless prefer a life of no responsibility at all.

◆

Waste of time. One person I worked with is a good example. He is an older man who has been on the streets for about 10 years. The story of his decline from respectability to alcoholism sounded believable and I wanted to help. After buying him toiletries and giving him clothes, I drove him one night to a Veterans Administration hospital, an hour and a half away, and put him into a detoxification program. I wrote him monthly to check on his progress and attempted to line up a job for him when he got out. Four months into his program, he was thinking and speaking clearly and talking about plans he wanted to make. At five months, he expressed concern over the life he was about to lead. During the sixth month, I called and was told that he had checked himself out and returned home. A month later I found him drunk again, back on the streets.

Was "society" to blame for this man? Hardly. It had provided free medical care, counseling, and honest effort. Was it the fault of the economy? No. This man never gave the economy a chance to solve his problems. The only person who can be blamed for his failure to get off the streets is the man himself. To argue otherwise is a waste of time and compassion.

Those who disagree will claim that my experience is merely anecdotal and that one case does not a policy make. Please don't take my word for it. The next time you see someone advertising that he'll work for food, take him up on it. Offer him a hard day's work for an honest wage, and see if he accepts. If he does, tell him you'll pay weekly, so that he will have to work for an entire week before he sees any money. If he still accepts, offer a permanent job, with taxes withheld and the whole shebang. If he accepts again, hire him. You'll have a fine employee and society will have one less homeless person. My guess is that you won't find many takers. The truly homeless won't stay around past the second question.

10   So what are the solutions? I will not pretend to give ultimate answers. But whatever policy we decide upon must include some notion of self-reliance and individual responsibility. Simply giving over our parks, our airports, and our streets to those who cannot and will not take care of themselves is nothing but a retreat from the problem and allows the public property that we designate for their "use" to fall into disarray. Education, drug, and alcohol rehabilitation, treatment for the mentally ill, and job training programs are all worthwhile projects, but without requiring some effort and accountability on the part of the homeless for whom these programs are implemented, all these efforts do is break the taxpayer. Unless the homeless are willing to help themselves, there is nothing anyone else can do. Not you. Not me. Not the government. Not anyone.

The Allesandros

BY JONATHAN KOZOL

Far from any zone of safety lives a man named Mr. Allesandro. He's six feet tall and weighs 120 pounds—down 20 pounds from late September. When he came to the hotel a year ago he weighed 165. I first met him in the ballroom before Christmas when I handed him an apple. One bright apple. One week later he does not forget and, when he sees me in the lobby, asks me if I have some time to talk.

His two daughters are asleep. Christopher, his nine-year-old, is lying on the top bunk, fully dressed and wrapped beneath a pile of blankets, but he is awake and vigilant and almost belligerently alert. It's a cold night and the room appears to be unheated. Mr. Allesandro shows me a cracked pane of glass that he has covered over with a sheet of garbage plastic and Scotch tape. The two coils of the hot plate offer a symbolic reassurance ("heat exists") but they do not provide much warmth. He's wearing a coat and woolen hat. His mother, who is seventy-three, lives with them; for some reason, she's not here.

There aren't many men as heads of households in this building; this fact, I think, adds to his feeling of humiliation. His story, quickly told, remains less vivid for me later on than certain details like his trembling hands, the freezing room, the strange sight of his watchful boy, unsleeping on the bed. The boy reminds me of a rabbit staring from a thicket or caught in the headlights of a car.

These, as Mr. Allesandro tells me, are the facts: He was one of several maintenance workers in a high-rise building in Manhattan owned by one of the well-known developers. It was early autumn and his wife, for reasons I don't learn until much later, just picked up one day and disappeared. He tried to keep his job and home by rising early, feeding the children, bringing them to school, then rushing to his job. But his shift required him to be on duty very early. He was reprimanded and, when he explained his problem, was permitted to stay on but cut back to a half-time job. Half-time work was not enough to pay the rent. He was evicted. In the subsequent emergency he had to take leave from his job.

5   "My mother went with me to the EAU. We asked them if we could be placed together. That way, she could get the kids to school and I could keep my job." Instead, they put him in a barracks shelter with the children but would not allow his mother to go with them. As best he understands, this is because she drew a Social Security check and was on a different budget from his own. Eligibility rules are difficult to fathom; but, even where the consequences are calamitous and costly, they are faithfully observed.

"So I'm alone there in this place with about 200 cots packed side by side. Men and women, children," he says, "all together. No dividers. There's no curtains and no screens. I have to dress my kids with people watching. When my girls go to the toilet I can't take them and they're scared to go alone. A lot of women there are frantic. So I stand and wait outside the door."

He went back to the EAU and begged once more. "In my line of work," he says, "you don't earn much of your money from the salary. The people in the building get to know you and you do them favors and they give you money in return. Christmas is a time you get your tips. They'll hand you an envelope. Twenty dollars. Fifty dollars. Some give you a hundred. These are very wealthy people . . ." So his disappointment was intensified by recognition of the fact that he could not get back his job in time to benefit from the expected generosity of people whom he'd known: "Some of those people knew me well. They liked me." He seems desperate to be assured that he was liked, remembered, missed, by people who had frequently befriended him.

The use of barracks shelters as deterrence to the homeless is not absolute.

Assignments are made "on an ad hoc basis," as one social worker states it. But nothing that Mr. Allesandro said could bring the EAU to place his mother with him. His former boss, he says, had told him he would take him back if he could start the day at 5:00 A.M. "There's no way that I could do it. Would you leave your kids alone within a place like that at 5:00 A.M.? I couldn't do it."

The upshot is this: He loses the chance to go back to his job a few weeks before Christmas. Although he's worked for many years, he hasn't been on *this* job long enough to have accumulated pension benefits. Dispossession from his home has left him unemployed; unemployment now will render permanent his homelessness.

10   Having finally lost everything he had, he returns a few weeks later to the EAU. This time having undergone "deterrence" and still being homeless, he is granted "temporary" placement at the Martinique. His mother can join him now. But he is no longer a wage earner; he's an AFDC father, broken in spirit, mourning for those lost tips which he will obsessively recall each time we talk. His job has been assigned to someone else. He loses self-control. He thanks God for his mother. This strikes me as a gruesome and enormously expensive instance of municipal assault upon a man's work ethic and familial integrity at the same time.

How does he feel not working?

"It's a nightmare, I'm Italian. You know—I don't mean this to sound prejudiced"—all of the white people here, I notice, are extremely careful and apologetic on this score—"my people work. My father and grandfather worked. My mother worked. I can do construction, carpentry. I can repair things. I'm somebody who's mechanically inclined. I would make beds, I would clean toilets. I'd do anything if I could have a decent job."

He searches the ads, walks the pavement, rides the subway; but he cannot find a job that pays enough to rent a home and feed three children. His rent allowance is $281. He's seen apartments for $350 and $400. If he takes an apartment over his rent limit he will have to make the difference up by cutting back on food and clothes. His mother's pension is too small to offer them a safety margin. "I wouldn't risk it. I'm afraid to take a chance. Even if I got a job, what if I lost it? I'd be back there with the children in the barracks."

So, like everybody else, he's drowning in the squalor of the Martinique Hotel but dreads the thought of being forced to leave.

15   "My mother helps to make it like a home. She tries. We got the kids a kitten, which is something that is not allowed. I don't like to break the rules, but you have got to give them something to remember that they're children."

Thinking of his hunger, I ask how he feeds the cat.

"We don't need to. We have never bought one can. She eats better than we do—on the mice and rats."

Around midnight I notice that Christopher is wide awake and watching from the bed: blue eyes, pale skin, blondish hair. Mrs. Allesandro cuts the children's hair.

Where is Mrs. Allesandro?

20   Mr. Allesandro calls her "grandma" and he speaks of her as if she were *his* grandmother as well. Grandma fell in the stairwell Friday afternoon. There had been a fire and the stairs were still slick from the water left there by the fire hoses. She's in the hospital for an examination of her hip. He tells me that she has a heart condition. "If anything happens to her [pauses] . . . I'd be dead. She's the one that's holding us together."

    Other people in this building speak of Mrs. Allesandro in almost identical words. They count on her perhaps even a little more than on the nurse or on the other people in the crisis center. Unlike the crisis workers she is here around the clock. As short of food and money as the Allesandros are, I am told that she is often in the hallways bringing food to neighbors, to a pregnant woman, a sick child living somewhere on the floor. A man who knows her but does not live on this floor speaks of Mrs. Allesandro in these words: "Here she is, an old Italian lady. Here are all these women. Most of them are Puerto Rican, black . . . You will see them holding onto her, crying to her as if she was their mother."

    Mrs. Allesandro, however, is not here tonight. Her son is on his own—a skeleton of hunger, disappointment, fear. I look at him, at the two girls, asleep, and at the boy—awake, alert. The boy's persistent gaze unsettles me. I ask him: "Are you sleepy?" He just shakes his head. His father is too proud to tell me that the boy is hungry. I feel embarrassed that it's taken me so long to ask. At my request he opens the refrigerator door. There is one packaged dinner, smuggled out of the lunch program. "There was something wrong with it," he says. It has a rancid smell. "It's spoiled." There's a gallon tin of peanut butter, two part-empty jars of applesauce, some hardened bread. That's it.

    Mr. Allesandro takes the $20 that I hand him to the corner store. Christopher sits up halfway and talks with me. He lists for me the ten largest cities of America. I ask him whether he likes school. He does not give the usual perfunctory affirmative response. "I hate it," Christopher says. I ask him what he does for fun. He plays ball on the sidewalk at the corner of the street across from the hotel.

    "Is there room to play ball on the sidewalk?"

25   He explains: "We play against the building of the bank—against the wall."

    He falls asleep after I think of giving him a candy bar. His father returns in twenty minutes with a box of Kellogg's Special K, a gallon of juice, half-gallon of milk, a loaf of bread, a dozen eggs, a package of sausages, a roll of toilet paper. He wakes his son. The boy has a bowl of cereal with milk. His father stands before the counter where he placed the food. He looks like a man who has been admitted to an elegant buffet.

    Is Mr. Allesandro laden with anxiety? Is Christopher depleted, sick, exhausted? Yes, I suppose both statements are correct. Are they candidates for psychiatric care? Perhaps they are, but I should think a more important observation is that they are starving.

    A few months after my evening with the Allesandros, President Reagan meets a group of high school students from New York. Between government help and private charity, he says, "I don't believe there is anyone that is going hungry in America simply by reason of denial. . . ." The president says there is a problem of "people not knowing where or how to get this help." This is what he also says of those who can't find space in public housing that he has stopped building.

His former counselor and now attorney general, Edwin Meese, concedes that people have been turning to soup kitchens but refuses to accept that they are in real need. They go to soup kitchens "because the food is free," he says, and adds, "that's easier than paying for it."

30   Marian Wright Edelman of the Children's Defense Fund makes this interesting calculation: If Defense Secretary Caspar Weinberger were to give up just a single Pentagon budget item, that which pays for him to have a private dining room, one million low-income school children could get back their morning snack—a snack denied them by administration cuts.

Hundreds of miles from Christopher's bedroom in the Martinique, a reporter describes an underground limestone cave near Kansas City: the largest surplus-food repository in the nation. In this cave and in some other large facilities, in the winter of 1986, the government was storing some 2 billion pounds of surplus food. To a child like Christopher, the vision of millions of pounds of milk and cheese and butter secreted in limestone caves might seem beyond belief. Storage of this surplus food costs taxpayers $1 million a day.

Getting surplus food from limestone caves to children's tables calls for modest but essential transportation costs. In an extraordinary action, termed illegal by the General Accounting Office, the president deferred funds allocated by the Congress for transporting food to homeless people. The sum involved, $28 million, is a small amount beside the $365 million spent to store this food in limestone caves and other warehouse areas. The withholding of such funds may possibly make sense to an economist. I do not know whether it would make much sense to Christopher.

◆

November 1986: I'm in New York and visit with the Allesandros. Grandma's back. She says her health is good. But Christopher looks frighteningly thin. Food was scarce before. The situation's worsened since I was here last. Families in the homeless shelters of New York have been cut back on their food-stamp allocations. The White House has decided to consider money paid for rental to the hotel owners as a part of family income. By this standard, families in the Martinique are very rich. "Tightening of eligibility requirements" has an abstract sound in Washington. On the twelfth floor of the Martinique what does it mean?

I study the computerized receipts that Mr. Allesandro has received. In June, his food-stamp allocation was $145. In August, the first stage in government reductions lowered this to $65. In October: $50. As of December it will be $33.

35   Mrs. Allesandro does not speak in ambiguities about the lives of her grandchildren. I ask her what the cuts will mean. "They mean," she says, "that we aren't going to eat." New York announces it will help make up the difference but, at the time I visit, no supplemental restaurant allowances have been received.

Critical Reading Questions

1. Awalt and Kozol have formed different beliefs based on their direct experiences working with the homeless. Awalt states his beliefs directly; Kozol is less direct, but his beliefs are nonetheless clear. Summarize their differing beliefs.

2. Why do you think the experiences the two men describe are so different? Do you think that the nature of the experiences that each writer presents is primarily responsible for his beliefs—or do previously held beliefs seem to have contributed to either writer's perception of direct experience?

3. Identify passages in each of the readings that express interpretations, evaluations, conclusions, and predictions.

4. Are any of your beliefs about homelessness based on direct experience? If so, whose experiences are closer to yours, Awalt's or Kozol's? How did your own beliefs affect your response to each essay?

5. Are Awalt's and Kozol's experiences with the homeless equally effective as evidence for each writer's beliefs? Do you feel as though you have enough evidence in general to form your own beliefs about homelessness? Why or why not?

BELIEFS BASED ON INDIRECT EXPERIENCE

No matter how much we have experienced in our lives, the fact is, of course, that no one person's direct experiences are enough to establish an adequate set of accurate beliefs. We all depend on the experience of others to provide us with beliefs and also to serve as foundations for those beliefs. For example, does Antarctica exist? How do we know? Have we ever been there and seen it with our own eyes? Probably not; nevertheless, we believe in the existence of Antarctica and its ice and penguins. Of all the beliefs each of us has, few are actually based on our direct personal experience. Instead, other people have in some way or form communicated to us virtually all these beliefs and the evidence for them. As we reach beyond our personal experiences to form and revise our beliefs, we find that information is provided by two sources: people of authority and recorded references.

As we have seen in the essays about homelessness by Awalt and Kozol, the beliefs of others cannot be accepted without question. Each of us views the world through individual lenses which shape and influence the way we select and present information. Comparing different sources helps to make these lenses explicit and highlights the different interests and purposes involved. In fact, examining sources may lead us to recognize that there are a variety of competing viewpoints, some fairly similar, some quite contradictory. In critically reviewing the beliefs of others, it is essential for us to pursue the same goals of accuracy and completeness that we set when examining beliefs based on personal experience. As a result, we focus on the reasons or evidence that support the information others are presenting.

Thinking ↔ Writing Activity

The Origin of a Belief

Select one of the beliefs that you identified in the Thinking-Writing Activity at the beginning of this chapter (page 365). What indirect sources helped shape it: your family, friends, teachers, religious leaders, television, radio, the Internet? What direct personal experiences or observations have had an impact on it? Note specifically how some of these influences shaped your belief.

Evaluating Sources and Information

When we depend on information that others provide, we need to ask key questions. The most crucial part of determining the reliability of a source's information is determining the reliability of the source itself.

HOW RELIABLE IS THE SOURCE?

We know that some sources—such as advertising—can be very unreliable whereas other sources, such as *Consumer Reports,* are generally considered reliable. Sometimes, however, the reliability of a source of information is not immediately clear. In those cases, we have to use a variety of standards or criteria to evaluate a source's reliability, whether the source is written or audible.

HOW KNOWLEDGEABLE OR EXPERIENCED IS THE SOURCE?

When seeking information from indirect sources, we want to locate people of authority or recorded references that can offer a special understanding of a subject. When a car begins making strange noises, we search for someone who knows cars. When we want to learn more about a social issue such as homelessness, we turn to articles and books written by people who have studied the problem.

In seeking information from sources, it is important to distinguish between nonexpert sources and expert sources who have training, education, and experience in a particular area. Also, any expert source's credentials should be up-to-date. A book about careers in the computer industry published twenty years ago is not likely to be reliable.

Sports and entertainment figures often endorse products in TV commercials, but their testimony is not very convincing if those products have nothing to do with sports or entertainment (and if these "experts" have been paid large sums of money and told exactly what to say). Finally, we should not accept expert opinion without question or critical examination, even if the experts meet all of our criteria.

WAS THE SOURCE ABLE TO MAKE ACCURATE OBSERVATIONS?

You may have heard about an experiment in which an angry student enters a classroom, argues with the professor, then pulls out a gun and apparently shoots the professor before running out. Students in the class are then quickly informed that the situation has been staged to test their powers of observation and asked to record what happened in as much detail as they can remember. Invariably many witnesses are quite mistaken about much of what they remember while others can recall many fine details exactly. The same is true in any kind of eyewitness account: some people have quite sharp memories while others may "remember" many imagined details. In addition, a person's vantage point as a witness may color the reliability of the testimony. The amount of light, obstructions to vision, and other matters can make his or her perceptions less than wholly reliable.

The reliability of an indirect source also depends on the personal viewpoints and beliefs the source brings to a situation. These feelings, expectations, and interests often influence what a witness perceives without his or her full awareness of the process. For example, a group that sponsored an anti-racism rally on a campus might claim a crowd of more than five hundred while campus security issues a report estimating rally attendance at about two hundred. We have seen that two different writers can draw very different conclusions after spending time working in a homeless shelter. What further questions could be asked, and how might additional sources be located to evaluate the reliability of such differing sources?

HOW REPUTABLE IS THE SOURCE?

When evaluating the reliability of sources, it is useful to consider how accurate and reliable their information has been in the past. If someone has consistently given sound information over a period of time, we gradually develop confidence in the accuracy of that person's reports. Police officers and newspaper reporters must continually evaluate the reliability of information sources. Of course, this works the other way as well. When people consistently give inaccurate or incomplete information, others lose confidence in their reliability. Nevertheless, few people provide information that is either completely reliable or completely unreliable. You probably realize that your own reliability tends to vary, depending on the situation, the type of information you are providing, and the person to whom you are giving it. Thus, in trying to evaluate information offered by others, you have to explore the following factors before arriving at a provisional conclusion, which you may have to revise later in light of additional information.

WHAT ARE THE SOURCE'S PURPOSES AND INTERESTS?

Evaluating information means thinking critically about the perceiving lenses through which the source of the information views the situation. Is this source presenting an argument or giving information? Are you looking at a report, an inference, or a judgment (see pages 393–394)? In other words, what is the rhetorical purpose of the piece? How is the purpose reflected in the selection of details and in wording and tone?

You also need to think about the piece's audience. Who is the intended audience? Is it friendly, neutral, or hostile? Is it informed or new to the subject? Writers or speakers can focus on specific audiences without being dishonorable, but sometimes they can emphasize one point of view or tap emotions in manipulative ways. Can you detect any slanting, or does this source's material seem balanced?

HOW VALUABLE IS INFORMATION FROM THIS SOURCE?

Of course, you also need to assess the credibility of the information itself by asking these questions: What are the main ideas being presented? What evidence is provided? Does the information seem accurate? Is it up-to-date? Does anything seem false? Does anything seem to have been left out?

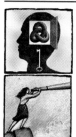

Thinking ↔ Writing Activity

Evaluating a Source of a Belief

Select one of the beliefs that you discussed in the Thinking-Writing Activity on page 365 that is based on sources such as people of authority or recorded references. Now, based on the criteria just discussed, evaluate the reliability of one source of your belief.

Believing and Knowing

Developing beliefs that are as accurate as possible is important to us as critical thinkers because the more accurate our beliefs are, the better we are able to understand the world around us and to make predictions about the future. As the preceding discussion has suggested, however, the accuracy of the beliefs we form can vary tremendously.

We use the word *knowing* to distinguish beliefs supported by strong reasons or evidence (such as the belief that life exists on earth) from beliefs for which there is less support (such as the belief that life exists on other planets) or from beliefs disproved by reasons or evidence to the contrary. This saying expresses another way to understand the difference between believing and knowing:

"You can believe what is not so, but you cannot know what is not so."

In the following essay, an astrophysicist considers a question that would seem to have an obvious answer. In doing so, he analyzes the difference between believing and knowing.

Is the Earth Round or Flat?

BY ALAN LIGHTMAN

I propose that there are few of you who have personally verified that the Earth is round. The suggestive globe in the den or the Apollo photographs don't count. These are secondhand pieces of evidence that might be thrown out entirely in court. When you think about it, most of you simply believe what you hear. Round or flat, whatever. It's not a life-or-death matter, unless you happen to live near the edge.

A few years ago I suddenly realized, to my dismay, that I didn't know with certainty if the Earth were round or flat. I have scientific colleagues, geodesists they are called, whose sole business is determining the detailed shape of the Earth by fitting mathematical formulae to someone else's measurements of the precise locations of test stations on the Earth's surface. And I don't think those people really know either.

Aristotle is the first person in recorded history to have given proof that the Earth is round. He used several different arguments, most likely because he wanted to convince others as well as himself. A lot of people believed everything Aristotle said for 19 centuries.

His first proof was that the shadow of the Earth during a lunar eclipse is always curved, a segment of a circle. If the Earth were any shape but spherical, the shadow it casts, in some orientations, would not be circular. (That the normal phases of the moon are crescent-shaped reveals the moon is round.) I find this argument wonderfully appealing. It is simple and direct. What's more, an inquisitive and untrusting person can knock off the experiment alone, without special equipment. From any given spot on the Earth, a lunar eclipse can be seen about once a year. You simply have to look up on the right night and carefully observe what's happening. I've never done it.

5   Aristotle's second proof was that stars rise and set sooner for people in the East than in the West. If the Earth were flat from east to west, stars would rise as soon for Occidentals as for Orientals. With a little scribbling on a piece of paper, you can see that these observations imply a round Earth, regardless of whether it is the Earth that spins around or the stars that revolve around the Earth. Finally, northbound travelers observe previously invisible stars appearing above the northern horizon, showing the Earth is curved from north to south. Of course, you do have to accept the reports of a number of friends in different places or be willing to do some traveling. Aristotle's last argument was purely theoretical and even philosophical. If the Earth had been formed from smaller pieces at some time in the past (or *could* have been so formed), its pieces would fall toward a common center, thus making a sphere. Furthermore, a sphere is clearly the most perfect solid shape. Interestingly, Aristotle placed as much emphasis on this last argument as on the first two. Those days, before the modern "scientific method," observational check wasn't required for investigating reality. Assuming for the moment that the Earth is round, the first person who measured its circumference accurately was another Greek, Eratosthenes (276–195 B.C.). Eratosthenes noted that on the first day of summer, sunlight struck the bottom of a vertical well in Syene, Egypt, indicating the sun was directly overhead. At the same time in Alexandria, 5,000 stadia distant, the sun made an angle with the vertical equal to 1/50 of a circle. (A stadium equaled about a tenth of a mile.) Since the sun is so far away, its rays arrive almost in parallel. If you draw a circle with two radii extending from the center outward through the perimeter (where they become local verticals), you'll see that a sun ray coming in parallel to one of the radii (at Syene) makes an angle with the other (at Alexandria) equal to the angle between the two radii. Therefore, Eratosthenes concluded that the full circumference of the Earth is 50 x 5,000 stadia, or about 25,000 miles. This calculation is within one percent of the best modern value.

For at least 600 years educated people have believed the Earth is round. At nearly any medieval university, the quadrivium was standard fare, consisting of arithmetic, geometry, music, and astronomy. The astronomy portion was based on the *Tractatus de Sphaera,* a popular textbook first published at Ferrara, Italy, in 1472 and written by a 13th century, Oxford-educated astronomer and mathematician, Johannes de Sacrobosco. The *Sphaera* proves its astronomical assertions, in part, by a set of diagrams with movable parts, a graphical demonstration of Aristotle's second method of proof. The round Earth, being the obvious center of the universe, provides a fixed pivot for the assembly. The cutout figures of the sun, the moon, and the stars revolve about the Earth.

By the year 1500, 24 editions of the *Sphaera* had appeared. There is no question that many people *believed* the Earth was round. I wonder how many *knew* this. You would think that Columbus and Magellan might have wanted to ascertain the facts for themselves before waving good-bye. To protect my honor as a scientist, someone who is supposed to take nothing for granted, I set out with my wife on a sailing voyage in the Greek islands. I reasoned that at sea I would be able to calmly observe landmasses disappear over the curve of the Earth and thus convince myself, firsthand, that the Earth is round.

Greece seemed a particularly satisfying place to conduct my experiment. I could sense those great ancient thinkers looking on approvingly, and the layout of the place is perfect. Hydra rises about 2,000 feet above sea level. If the Earth has a radius of 4,000 miles, as they say, then Hydra should sink down to the horizon at a distance of about 50 miles, somewhat less than the distance you were to sail from Hydra to Kea. The theory was sound and comfortable. At the very least, I thought, you would have a pleasant vacation.

As it turned out, that was all you got. Every single day was hazy. Islands faded from view at a distance of only eight miles, when the land was still a couple of degrees above the horizon. I learned how much water vapor was in the air but nothing about the curvature of the Earth.

10   I suspect that there are quite a few items you take on faith, even important things, even things you could verify without much trouble. Is the gas you exhale the same as the gas you inhale? (Do you indeed burn oxygen in your metabolism, as they say?) What is your blood made of? (Does it indeed have red and white "cells"?) These questions could be answered with a balloon, a candle, and a microscope.

When you finally do the experiment, you relish the knowledge. At one time or another, you have all learned something for yourselves, from the ground floor up, taking no one's word for it. There is a special satisfaction and joy in being able to tell somebody something you have pieced together from scratch, something you really know. I think that exhilaration is a big reason why people do science.

Someday soon, I'm going to catch the Earth's shadow in a lunar eclipse, or go to sea in clear air, and find out for sure if the Earth is round or flat. Actually, the Earth is reported to flatten at the poles, because it rotates. But that's another story.

Critical Reading Questions

1. Why does the author, a scientist, state: "A few years ago I suddenly realized, to my dismay, that I didn't know with certainty if the Earth were round or flat?"

2. Describe one conclusive "proof" for the roundness of the Earth that the author identifies and explain the reasons why it is a valid proof.

3. Explain the difference between *believing* that the Earth is round and *knowing* that the Earth is round.

4. Lightman states, "I suspect that there are quite a few items you take

on faith. . . . When you finally do the experiment, you relish the knowledge." Describe one thing that you *believed* to be true that you were finally able to *know* was true by proving it to your satisfaction.

Thinking ↔ Writing Activity

Weighing Your Beliefs and Knowledge

Look again at the beliefs you have written about for previous activities. Could you say about any of them "I know this" rather than merely "I believe this"? Why? Write answers to these questions.

KNOWLEDGE AND TRUTH

Authorities often disagree about the true nature of a given situation or the best course of action. It is common, for example, for doctors to disagree about a diagnosis, for economists to differ on the state of the economy, or for psychiatrists to disagree on whether a convicted felon is a menace to society or a victim of social forces.

What do we do when experts disagree? As critical thinkers, we must analyze and evaluate all the available information, develop our own well-reasoned beliefs, and recognize when we lack sufficient information to arrive at well-reasoned beliefs. We must realize, too, that such beliefs may evolve over time as we obtain more information or improve our insight.

Although there are compelling reasons to view knowledge and truth as evolving, some people resist doing so. Either they take refuge in a belief in the absolute, unchanging nature of knowledge and truth as presented by the appropriate authorities, or they conclude that there is no such thing as knowledge or truth and that trying to seek either is futile.

UNDERSTANDING RELATIVISM

In this latter view of the world, known as *relativism,* all beliefs are considered "relative" to the person or context in which they arise. For the relativist, all opinions are equal in validity to all others; no one is ever in a position to say with confidence that one view is right and another one wrong. Although a relativistic view is appropriate in some areas of experience—for example, in matters of taste such as fashion—in many other areas it is not. Knowledge, in the form of well supported beliefs, does exist. Some beliefs are better than others, not because an authority has proclaimed them so but because they can be analyzed in terms of the criteria discussed earlier in this chapter.

UNDERSTANDING FALSIFIABLE BELIEFS

Another important criterion for evaluating certain beliefs is that the beliefs be *falsifiable*. This means that it is possible to state conditions—tests—under which the beliefs could be disproved, and that the beliefs then pass those tests. For example, if you believe that you can create ice cubes by placing water-filled trays in a freezer, you can conduct an experiment to determine whether your belief is accurate. If no ice cubes form after you put the trays in the freezer, your theory is disproved. If, however, you believe that your destiny is related to the positions of the planets and stars (as astrologers do), it is not clear how you can conduct an experiment to determine whether your belief is accurate. Since a belief that is not falsifiable can never be proved, such a belief is questionable.

Thinking ↔ Writing Activity

Constructing Knowledge: Four Accounts of the Battle of Lexington

Read the following passages, which purport to give factual reports about the events that were observed at the Battle of Lexington during the American Revolution.* After analyzing these accounts, develop your own version of what you believe took place on that day. Include such information as the size of the two forces, the sequence of events (for example, who fired the first shot?), and the manner in which the two groups conducted themselves (were they honorable? brave?). In rating the reliability of each source, consider the following information.

Account 1 is drawn from a mainstream American history textbook.

Account 2 is taken from a British history book written by a former prime minister of England.

Account 3 comes from a colonist who participated in this event with the colonial forces. He gave the account thirty years after the battle in order to qualify for a military pension.

Account 4 comes from a British soldier who participated in the event. He gave the account in a deposition while he was a prisoner of war of the colonial forces.

*This exercise was developed by Kevin O'Reilly, creator of the Critical Thinking in History Project.

In April 1775, General Gage, the military governor of Massachusetts, sent out a body of troops to take possession of military stores at Concord, a short distance from Boston. At Lexington, a handful of "embattled farmers," who had been tipped off by Paul Revere, barred the way. The "rebels" were ordered to disperse. They stood their ground. The English fired a volley of shots that killed eight patriots. It was not long before the swift-riding Paul Revere spread the news of this new atrocity to the neighboring colonies. The patriots of all of New England, although still a handful, were now ready to fight the English. Even in faraway North Carolina, patriots organized to resist them. —Samuel Steinberg, *The United States: Story of a Free People*

At five o'clock in the morning the local militia of Lexington, seventy strong, formed up on the village green. As the sun rose the head of the British column, with three officers riding in front, came into view. The leading officer, brandishing his sword, shouted, "Disperse, you rebels, immediately!" The militia commander ordered his men to disperse. The colonial committees were very anxious not to fire the first shot, and there were strict orders not to provoke open conflict with the British regulars. But in the confusion someone fired. A volley was returned. The ranks of the militia were thinned and there was a general melee. Brushing aside the survivors, the British column marched on to Concord. —Winston Churchill, *History of the English-speaking Peoples*

The British troops approached you rapidly in platoons, with a General officer on horse-back at their head. The officer came up to within about two rods of the centre of the company, where I stood—the first platoon being about three rods distant. They there halted. The officer then swung his sword, and said, "Lay down your arms, you damn'd rebels, or you are all dead men—fire." Some guns were fired by the British at you from the first platoon, but no person was killed or hurt, being probably charged only with powder. Just at this time, Captain Parker ordered every man to take care of himself. The company immediately dispersed; and while the company was dispersing and leaping over the wall, the second platoon of the British fired, and killed some of your men. There was not a gun fired by any of Captain Parker's company within my knowledge. —Sylvanus Wood, *Deposition*

I, John Bateman, belonging to the Fifty-Second Regiment, commanded by Colonel Jones, on Wednesday morning on the nineteenth day of April instant, was in the party marching to Concord, being at Lexington, in the County of Middlesex; being nigh the meeting-house in said Lexington, there was a small party of men gathered together in that place when your Troops marched by, and I testify and declare, that I heard the word of command given to the Troops to fire, and some of said Troops did fire, and I saw one of said small party lay dead on the ground nigh said meeting-house, and I testify that I never heard any of the inhabitants so much as fire one gun on said Troops. —John Bateman, *Testimony*

THE MEDIA AND TRUTH

We are all aware in a general way that the media can shape our beliefs by the information they provide and the interpretations they give to that information. We may not be aware, however, of some of the subtle ways in which this is done or of the profound influences that result. As you read the following essays, consider how your beliefs might be shaped by the sources that these writers discuss.

The following article originally appeared in *Newsweek*. It reports on studies conducted by a University of Pennsylvania professor, concerning the influence of television on people's beliefs.

Life According to TV

BY HARRY WATERS

The late Paddy Chayefsky, who created Howard Beale, would have loved George Gerbner. In "Network," Chayefsky marshaled a scathing, fictional assault on the values and methods of the people who control the world's most potent communications instrument. In real life, Gerbner, perhaps the nation's foremost authority on the social impact of television, is quietly using the disciplines of behavioral research to construct an equally devastating indictment of the medium's images and messages. More than any spokesman for a pressure group, Gerbner has become the man that television watches. From his cramped, book-lined office at the University of Pennsylvania springs a steady flow of studies that are raising executive blood pressures at the networks' sleek Manhattan command posts.

George Gerbner's work is uniquely important because it transports the scientific examination of television far beyond familiar children-and-violence arguments. Rather than simply studying the link between violence on the tube and crime in the streets, Gerbner is exploring wider and deeper terrain. He has turned his lens on TV's hidden victims—women, the elderly, blacks, blue-collar workers and other groups—to document the ways in which video-entertainment portrayals subliminally condition how we perceive ourselves and how we view those around us. Gerbner's subjects are not merely the impressionable young; they include all the rest of us. And it is his ominous conclusion that heavy watchers of the prime-time mirror are receiving a grossly distorted picture of the real world that they tend to accept more readily than reality itself.

The 63-year-old Gerbner, who is dean of Penn's Annenberg School of Communications, employs a methodology that meshes scholarly observation with mundane legwork. Over the past 15 years, he and a tireless trio of assistants (Larry Gross, Nancy Signorielli and Michael Morgan) videotaped and exhaustively analyzed 1,600 prime-time programs involving more than 15,000 characters. They then drew up multiple-choice questionnaires that offered correct answers about the world at large along with answers that reflected what Gerbner perceived to be the misrepresentations and biases of the world according to TV. Finally, these questions were posed to large samples of citizens from all socio-economic strata. In every survey, the Annenberg team discovered that heavy viewers of television (those watching more than four hours a day), who account for more than 30 percent of the population, almost invariably chose the TV-influenced answers, while light viewers (less than two hours a day) selected the answers corresponding more closely to actual life. Some of the dimensions of television's reality warp:

Sex

Male prime-time characters outnumber females by 3 to 1 and, with a few star-turn exceptions, women are portrayed as weak, passive satellites to powerful, effective men. TV's male population also plays a vast variety of roles, while females generally get typecast as either lovers or mothers. Less than 20 percent of TV's married women with children work outside the home—as compared with more than 50 percent in real life. The tube's distorted depictions of women, concludes Gerbner, reinforce stereotypical attitudes and increase sexism. In one Annenberg survey, heavy viewers were far more likely than light ones to agree with the proposition: "Women should take care of running their homes and leave running the country to men."

Age

5   People over 65, too, are grossly underrepresented on television. Correspond-ingly, heavy-viewing Annenberg respondents believe that the elderly are a van-ishing breed, that they make up a smaller proportion of the population today than they did 20 years ago. In fact, they form the nation's most rapidly expand-ing age group. Heavy viewers also believe that old people are less healthy today than they were two decades ago, when quite the opposite is true. As with women, the portrayals of old people transmit negative impressions. In general, they are cast as silly, stubborn, sexually inactive and eccentric. "They're often shown as feeble grandparents bearing cookies," says Gerbner. "You never see the power that real old people often have. The best and possibly only time to learn about growing old with decency and grace is in youth. And young peo-ple are the most susceptible to TV's messages."

Race

The problem with the medium's treatment of blacks is more one of image than of visibility. Though a tiny percentage of black characters come across as "unre-alistically romanticized," reports Gerbner, the overwhelming majority of them are employed in subservient, supporting roles—such as the white hero's comic sidekick. "When a black child looks at prime time," he says, "most of the peo-ple he sees doing interesting and important things are white." That imbalance, he goes on, tends to teach young blacks to accept minority status as naturally inevitable and even deserved. To assess the impact of such portrayals on the general audience, the Annenberg survey forms included questions like "Should white people have the right to keep blacks out of their neighborhoods?" and "Should there be laws against marriages between blacks and whites?" The more that viewers watched, the more they answered "yes" to each question.

Work

Heavy viewers greatly overestimated the proportion of Americans employed as physicians, lawyers, athletes and entertainers, all of whom inhabit prime-time in hordes. A mere 6 to 10 percent of television characters hold blue-collar or service jobs vs. about 60 percent in the real work force. Gerbner sees two dangers in TV's skewed division of labor. On the one hand, the tube so overrepresents and glamorizes the elite occupations that it sets up unrealistic expectations among those who must deal with them in actuality. At the same time, TV largely neglects portraying the occupations that most youngsters will have to enter. "You almost never see the farmer, the factory worker or the small businessman," he notes. "Thus not only do lawyers and other professionals find they cannot measure up to the image TV projects of them, but children's occupational aspirations are channeled in unrealistic directions." The Gerbner team feels this emphasis on high-powered jobs poses problems for adolescent girls, who are also presented with views of women as homebodies. The two conflicting views, Gerbner says, add to the frustration over choices they have to make as adults.

Health

Although video characters exist almost entirely on junk food and quaff alcohol 15 times more often than water, they manage to remain slim, healthy and beautiful. Frequent TV watchers, the Annenberg investigators found, eat more, drink more, exercise less and possess an almost mystical faith in the curative powers of medical science. Concludes Gerbner: "Television may well be the single most pervasive source of health information. And its overidealized images of medical people, coupled with its complacency about unhealthy life-styles, leaves both patients and doctors vulnerable to disappointment, frustration and even litigation."

Crime

On the small screen, crime rages about 10 times more often than in real life. But while other researchers concentrate on the propensity of TV mayhem to incite aggression, the Annenberg team has studied the hidden side of its imprint: fear of victimization. On television, 55 percent of prime-time characters are involved in violent confrontations once a week; in reality, the figure is less than 1 percent. In all demographic groups in every class of neighborhood, heavy viewers overestimated the statistical chance of violence in their own lives and harbored an exaggerated mistrust of strangers—creating what Gerbner calls a "mean-world syndrome." Forty-six percent of heavy viewers who live in cities rated their fear of crime "very serious" as opposed to 26 percent for light viewers. Such paranoia is especially acute among TV entertainment's most common victims: women, the elderly, nonwhites, foreigners and lower-class citizens.

10   Video violence, proposes Gerbner, is primarily responsible for imparting lessons in social power: it demonstrates who can do what to whom and get away with it. "Television is saying that those at the bottom of the power scale cannot get away with the same things that a white, middle-class American male can," he says. "It potentially conditions people to think of themselves as victims."

At a quick glance, Gerbner's findings seem to contain a cause-and-effect, chicken-or-the-egg question. Does television make heavy viewers view the world the way they do or do heavy viewers come from the poorer, less experienced segment of the populace that regards the world that way to begin with? In other words, does the tube create or simply confirm the unenlightened attitudes of its most loyal audience? Gerbner, however, was savvy enough to construct a methodology largely immune to such criticism. His samples of heavy viewers cut across all ages, incomes, education levels and ethnic backgrounds—and every category displayed the same tube-induced misconceptions of the world outside.

Needless to say, the networks accept all this as enthusiastically as they would a list of news-coverage complaints from the Ayatollah Khomeini. Even so, their responses tend to be tinged with a singular respect for Gerbner's personal and professional credentials. The man is no ivory-tower recluse. During World War II, the Budapest-born Gerbner parachuted into the mountains of Yugoslavia to join the partisans fighting the Germans. After the war, he hunted down and personally arrested scores of high Nazi officials. Nor is Gerbner some videophobic vigilante. A Ph.D. in communications, he readily acknowledges TV's beneficial effects, noting that it has abolished parochialism, reduced isolation and loneliness and provided the poorest members of society with cheap, plug-in exposure to experiences they otherwise would not have. Funding for his research is supported by such prestigious bodies as the National Institute of Mental Health, the surgeon general's office and the American Medical Association, and he is called to testify before congressional committees nearly as often as David Stockman.

Mass Entertainment

When challenging Gerbner, network officials focus less on his findings and methods than on what they regard as his own misconceptions of their industry's function. "He's looking at television from the perspective of a social scientist rather than considering what is mass entertainment," says Alfred Schneider, vice president of standards and practices at ABC. "We strive to balance TV's social effects with what will capture an audience's interests. If you showed strong men being victimized as much as women or the elderly, what would comprise the dramatic conflict? If you did a show truly representative of society's total reality, and nobody watched because it wasn't interesting, what have you achieved?"

CBS senior vice president Gene Mater also believes that Gerbner is implicitly asking for the theoretically impossible. "TV is unique in its problems," says

Mater. "Everyone wants a piece of the action. Everyone feels that their racial or ethnic group is underrepresented or should be portrayed as they would like the world to perceive them. No popular entertainment form, including this one, can or should be an accurate reflection of society."

15 On that point, at least, Gerbner is first to agree; he hardly expects television entertainment to serve as a mirror image of absolute truth. But what fascinates him about this communications medium is its marked difference from all others. In other media, customers carefully choose what they want to hear or read: a movie, a magazine, a best seller. In television, notes Gerbner, viewers rarely tune in for a particular program. Instead, most just habitually turn on the set—and watch by the clock rather than for a specific show. "Television viewing fulfills the criteria of a ritual," he says. "It is the only medium that can bring to people things they otherwise would not select." With such unique power, believes Gerbner, comes unique responsibility: "No other medium reaches into every home or has a comparable, cradle-to-grave influence over what a society learns about itself."

Critical Reading Questions

1. According to Waters, George Gerbner believes that "heavy watchers of the prime-time mirror are receiving a grossly distorted picture of the real world that they tend to accept more readily than reality itself." How well does the evidence offered in Waters's article support this belief?

2. This article was written in 1982. Do you think television has changed in the years since then? Do you have any reason to believe that the "prime-time mirror" is a more accurate reflection of reality today? Keep in mind that many of the "realities" the article describes—the growth in the population over sixty-five, the proportion of various professions in the work force, and so on—have changed very little.

3. Can you think of any of your own specific beliefs that have much of their basis in your television viewing? To what extent do you think Gerbner's claims may be exaggerated? Do you know anyone whom you would consider a "heavy watcher"? If so, how realistic are that person's beliefs about the world?

4. Discuss your responses with other students in the class.

Cynthia Crossen is a *Wall Street Journal* reporter. Her book *Tainted Truth: The Manipulation of Fact in America* reports on the many "scientific, objective" studies published under the guise of objectivity that actually are conducted to reflect their sponsors' intentions. The following chapter from that book focuses on studies designed to influence beliefs about public policy issues.

False Truth and the Future of the World

BY CYNTHIA CROSSEN

Common sense, common knowledge and the gospels of environmentalism held that disposable diapers were bad for the earth. Yet a study, published to great fanfare in the spring of 1990, found that disposable diapers were actually no worse for the environment than reusable cotton ones.

This was good news for many parents. Cotton diapers may have been ecologically correct, but they were also less efficient and less convenient. Some who bought disposable diapers were guilt-ridden, embarrassed to be seen toting a 26-pack around the neighborhood. Now research exonerated them of a crime against nature. They could love the earth *and* throw away a dozen plastic-and-chemical-gel diapers a day.

The study's sponsor? Procter & Gamble, one of the biggest buyers of research in the United States and, of course, the country's largest maker of disposable diapers. The company controls about half the $3.5-billion-a-year U.S. market with its Pampers and Luvs brands. For several years, it had been fighting a public relations battle against environmentalists and the cloth diaper industry. Although the disposable diaper industry, born in the 1960s, was thriving, the Earth Day mentality had made inroads. Between 1988 and 1990, customers for cloth diapers almost doubled. Even more ominous for the disposable makers, more than a dozen state legislatures were considering various bans, taxes and warning labels on disposable diapers.

A few studies later, the campaign against disposables was all but dead. Researchers paid by the disposable diaper industry had produced a new, improved truth about disposable diapers. Disposables, symbol of the throwaway society, were environmentally correct. In fact, they would no longer even be called disposable; henceforth they would be known as "single-use." The media disseminated the studies' contrarian findings widely. "People Claiming Cloth Diapers Are Clearly Superior May Be All Wet," said the *Louisville* (Kentucky) *Courier-Journal*. "Grass Isn't Greener on Green Side, Environmentally Conscious Choices May Be Doing More Harm," said the *Cincinnati Enquirer*. In statehouses around the country, diaper legislation withered away. By early 1992, Gerber Products, the largest supplier of cloth diapers in the country, said it would close three cloth-weaving operations and lay off 900 workers. "In the past year," Alfred A. Piergallini, Gerber's chairman and chief executive, said at the time, "there was a dramatic change in the cloth diaper market caused by reduced environmental concerns about disposable diapers."

5   Procter & Gamble's diaper study was a landmark example of the public policy study, a form of research that increasingly shapes people's beliefs and decisions on social, political, economic and environmental questions. Political debates of the 1980s and 1990s on issues from homelessness to garbage to the spotted owl have been driven by research. The industry that generates this research has developed an unspoken but almost inviolable rule: Its numbers

will anoint the ideology of whoever commissioned the research. The sponsor is rarely surprised or betrayed.

Studies done for public policy debates rank second only to research done for advertising in their disdain for objectivity and fact. While in other arenas researchers would be embarrassed to admit their study was partisan, in public policy they are not. "Who says it has to be neutral?" challenged an aide to U.S. Representative Fortney H. Stark about a distorted cable television questionnaire his office had sent out. Commenting on the same study, the aide later said, "We're proud that it was biased. Our viewpoint is that cable TV should be re-regulated."

The researchers themselves are not evil. They are devoted to their profession, and they genuinely seek to improve its methods. Yet they have let their ethical habits slip to a level more often seen among lobbyists and public relations executives. A Washington economist, who asked not to be named because his former employer is still a member of the House of Representatives, described two studies he did on a hydroelectric dam project planned for the home district. "My boss says, 'Write me the best justification for this project that you can.' So I did this cost-benefit analysis that made the project look like a gold mine. About a month later, he calls me in and says, 'Give me the most objective, independent, comprehensive analysis of this project you can.' I came back to him and said, 'This project is a dog.' He knew how to use me and that's fine. Researchers are for hire."

Exaggeration, hyperbole, creative projections, wild assumptions and hand-waving are the building blocks of public policy research, where people fight for the ear of the people and the good of the world. Anything goes. Most public policy wars are fought on huge plains, where people are counted in the millions, economic impacts in the billions and the very survival of mankind and the earth may be at stake—the very places it is most tempting to justify means with ends. Public policy studies are seldom challenged by either the press or public because they address mammoth and complex questions about which most people have little if any personal experience or knowledge. Nor has the press, by and large, learned to accord research studies the routine skepticism that reporters bring to more obviously self-serving news releases.

The creative manipulation of public policy studies crosses all political, gender, racial, religious and age lines. Whatever your beliefs and politics, your team does it. Organizations from Procter & Gamble, the country's largest advertiser, to the smallest and poorest social action groups sponsor advocacy research. No result is too absurd or self-evident to be peddled to the press.

10

- "Rental Housing for Poor Still a Problem, Study Says," announced a newspaper headline about a study sponsored by two nonprofit advocacy groups for the poor.

- "Americans Want to Live to 100 Years, Survey Says; Bar Nursing Homes, Losing Independence," reported the nonprofit Alliance for Aging Research, which advocates more investment in scientific research about aging.

- "Life on Streets Dangerous for Homeless Youth," concluded a study sponsored by the Chicago Coalition for the Homeless.

Public interest groups are masters of the tactical study. Their motives for their creative numbers are less commercial than industry's, but they can be just as self-centered. Public interest groups thrive on attention from the press because that is how they recruit new members. While business may understate hazards, public interest groups tend to exaggerate them. "Each group convinces itself that its worthy goals justify oversimplification to an 'ignorant' public," wrote Daniel E. Koshland, Jr.

Among life-and-death issues, researchers are not quite so fastidious about creating perfectly neutral questions for their surveys. A mail survey for the environmental guerrilla group Greenpeace asked people's attitudes on several issues. Among the leading questions was this: "Depletion of Earth's protective ozone layer leads to skin cancers and numerous other health and environmental problems. Do you support Greenpeace's demand that DuPont, the world's largest producer of ozone-destroying chemicals, stop making unneeded ozone-destroying chemicals immediately?"

But from industry: "Do you favor setting up an additional Consumer Protection Agency over all the others, or do you favor doing what is necessary to make the agencies we now have more effective in protecting the consumer's interests?" asked a survey commissioned by the Business Roundtable, which was opposing the creation of a federal consumer protection agency. Seventy-five percent of those surveyed said they opposed creating such an agency. The survey was released during the height of congressional debate on the subject.

And from a Connecticut representative to Congress, a body that has become addicted to questionnaires: "Would you support universal health care if it would mean the loss of thousands of jobs, particularly in Connecticut?"

15   Legislators know most studies prepared for policy debates are sponsored by a self-interested industry or lobby. What they may not realize is that such research nevertheless influences the course of events. Occasionally a piece of research has a decisive influence on the outcome of the debate—Procter & Gamble's diaper study, for example. But more often, contradictory studies simply paralyze the decision-making process, shelving the resolution of immediate problems. "Someone will produce a study that statistically demonstrates X or Y," said Ray Sentes, a Canadian political science professor who has studied the effects of asbestos on human health. "So the workers have to rush out and get an epidemiologist to do a study for them. And so it goes. For ten years we flash studies at each other. If the practical outcome of a scientific study ends up being delayed of any activity, shouldn't the scientist say, 'You don't need this study'?" For issues like the health effects of asbestos, Sentes noted, it would take several studies of thousands of people over dozens of years to come up with meaningful results. "They don't have the time or the money or the data," he said. "So they do these slash-and-burn studies that get plonked into the middle of the public policy process."

Strategic research has dominated modern debates over abortion, gun control, family leave, recycling, school choice and the speed limit, just to name a few. Each issue has its dueling polls. The timber industry has its polls showing most people wouldn't sacrifice a single job to protect an endangered species; and nature groups have their poll showing that most people support the Endangered Species Act. Proponents of school choice have surveys showing that people want it, and opponents have their surveys showing people do not. Gun control activists have surveys showing that many people want increased regulation of guns; the National Rifle Association has surveys showing the opposite.

The battle over abortion rights has produced hundreds of surveys showing contrary results. In June 1991, the abortion warrriors—Planned Parenthood and the National Right to Life Committee—each produced survey results showing people's opinions of a recent Supreme Court ruling that the government could prohibit the discussion of abortion in family planning clinics that received federal funding. Planned Parenthood's survey asked this question: "Do you favor or oppose that Supreme Court decision preventing clinic doctors and medical personnel from discussing abortion . . . ?" Sixty-five percent said they opposed the ruling.

The other survey first asked people if they favored or opposed the Supreme Court ruling. The survey described the ruling as "the federal government is not required to use taxpayer funds for family planning programs to perform, counsel or refer for abortion as a method of family planning." The Supreme Court, of course, had said no such thing: the question was whether the government should be permitted, not required, to finance family planning programs where abortion was discussed. No one was talking about abortion as a method of family planning. And the Supreme Court was ruling on whether such clinics could discuss, not perform, abortions. Even so, only 48 percent said they favored the court's decision. Then the survey asked, "If you knew that any government funds not used for family-planning programs that provide abortion will be given to other family-planning programs that provide contraception and other preventive methods of family-planning, would you then favor or oppose the Supreme Court's ruling?" Here the group got the mandate it was seeking, the one they pitched to the press: 69 percent said they favored the decision. In hearings before the House of Representatives, which was considering an amendment that would prevent the regulation from being enforced, the National Right to Life poll was cited. The amendment was defeated.

Since bigger numbers almost always mean bigger allocations or more attention, most of the numbers flying around policy debates exaggerate on the high side. The National Association for Prenatal Addiction Research and Education says as many as 375,000 babies who may have been affected by drugs are born every year; that is, 375,000 babies whose mothers ingested either alcohol or a drug at one point in their pregnancy. In the late 1970s, the American Cancer Society predicted that cancer would claim the lives of at least 8.5 million Americans in the 1980s. In fact, between 1980 and 1990, 4.5 million Americans died of cancer. And while it costs only $3,205 to provide disposable cups, forks, plates, etc., for one school for one year, it costs a staggering $12,413 for reusable material—or so argued a Tennessee school district fighting the mandated use of reusable materials. The disposable figure included the price of buying the materials, the labor of handling them and their waste disposal; the figure for reusables included the cost of the materials, the labor to wash them, the cost of the washing equipment and the water. It did not compare the cost of making the reusables and disposables, nor did it take into account environmental costs. Furthermore, if it is so economical to use disposables, why have they not replaced glass, china and stainless steel in every home in America?

20   "Even if congressmen discount for biases in the material they are given," wrote James Payne, "this does not solve the problem. When you cut a 50-fold exaggeration in half, you are still left believing a 25-fold exaggeration."

The size of the homeless population has been the subject of several studies whose estimates range from 230,000 to 3 million. Homeless advocates have estimated 2 million to 3 million people have been homeless at some time during the previous year. (On any particular night, advocates say, the number of homeless may be closer to half a million to one million.) The advocates' number was derived from estimating the percentage of the population that was homeless—1 percent—and building in a huge margin of error. Martha Burt of the Urban Institute said that the last time 1 percent of the population was homeless was in the heart of the Depression. "Nineteen thirty-three is what 1 percent homeless looks like," she said.

In 1984, the Department of Housing and Urban Development estimated there were between 250,000 and 300,000 homeless. That figure was developed from sixty local experts estimating how many homeless they had in their cities. Their answers were added together and then projected to the nation. In 1987, the Urban Institute estimated 500,000 to 1,000,000 homeless. That number was derived from sampling homeless shelters and soup kitchens in cities with populations of more than 100,000 and then doing elaborate adjustments.

In March 1990, the Census Bureau sent 15,000 census takers out one night—S night, it was called, for streets and shelters—to count the homeless. They found 230,000. Homeless advocates quickly disputed the figure, saying that with a few exceptions the census takers did not go to any city with a population of less than 50,000: they did not count any homeless people they saw in alleyways or streets; and they, like other homeless researchers, had no way of counting the people sleeping on the couch or floor of someone's house who might be looking for shelter the following night. Research built on shelter data is inherently skewed because a huge part of the homeless population—single people who are highly impaired and chronically homeless—tend not to use shelters.

In November 1993, another count of the homeless in two big cities—New York and Philadelphia—was released. This study counted the homeless using computer records of Social Security numbers at city shelters. The study found that 3.3 percent of New York's population had stayed in a shelter sometime over the past five years. The stay could be as short as one day. Should one one-day stay sometime in the past five years define a person as homeless?

25   It is not possible to count the homeless population precisely; they are transient, wary of authority and sometimes mentally ill or addicted to drugs. Sadly, the issue of counting the homeless long ago overwhelmed the moral debate on what to do about people living in the street, as though without agreeing on the numbers there could be no agreement that homelessness is a problem. A decade after the plight of the homeless appeared on the national agenda, there is still a sizable homeless population. Statistical formulas do not solve our problems any faster or better, and they cannot eliminate politics, as the political scientist Kenneth Prewitt points out. They simply push politics back one stop, to disputes about methods: "Arguments about numerical quotas, availability pools and demographic imbalance become a substitute for democratic discussion of the principles of equity and justice."

In public policy debates and deliberations, words like decency, right and wrong, peace, fairness, trust and hope have lost their force. Numbers, which can offer so much illumination and guidance if used professionally and ethically, have become the tools of advocacy. Even if their cause is worthy, people who massage data undermine the power and purity of statistics that may be crucial to future decisions. There are numbers we will never know, and we should admit it. It is essential to understand the homeless before making policy about them. But in this case, as in so many others in public policy, understanding is not the same as counting.

Critical Reading Questions

1. In the introduction to her book, Crossen states that her own survey found that while 76 percent of her respondents agreed that "you can find a scientific study to prove just about anything you want to prove," 86 percent said that "references to scientific research in a story increased its credibility." Why are scientific studies used so extensively by the media? Do you think such studies increase a news story's credibility?

2. Crossen gives several examples demonstrating that the way a survey question is worded influences the kinds of responses people make to it. Do you think a survey can be conducted in a completely objective way? Why or why not?

3. Crossen suggests that competing, contradictory studies effectively serve to prevent any progress toward solving serious social problems such as homelessness. Is it also true that competing beliefs among politicians and others in power tend to stymie real solutions? Can you imagine any way that such competing beliefs could be combined to discover something closer to the "truth"? Discuss your ideas with classmates, analyzing differences in your perspectives.

Ways of Presenting Beliefs

When you write, you are presenting your beliefs. No matter what its form—letters, college papers, business documents, even stories and poems—your written expression states what you believe. When you write, you present your beliefs in three ways: reports, inferences, and judgments. Your choice of words establishes which of the three you are using:

- Report: My bus was late today.
- Inference: My bus will probably be late tomorrow.
- Judgment: The bus system is unreliable.

Now try to identify which of the three is being used in these statements:

1. Each modern nuclear warhead has over one hundred times the explosive power of the bomb dropped on Hiroshima.
2. With all the billions of planets in the universe, the odds are that there are other forms of life in the cosmos.
3. In the long run, the energy needs of the world will best be met by solar energy technology rather than nuclear energy or fossil fuels.

As you examine these various statements, you can see that they provide readers with different types of information. For example, the first statement in each list reports aspects of the world that can be verified—that is, checked for accuracy. Appropriate investigation can determine whether the bus was actually late today and whether modern nuclear warheads really have the power attributed to them. When you describe the world in ways that can be verified through investigation, you are **reporting factual information**.

Looking at the second statement in each list, you can see that each provides a different sort of information than the first one does. These statements cannot be verified. There is no way to investigate and determine with certainty whether the bus will indeed be late tomorrow or whether there is life on other planets. Although these conclusions may be based on facts, they go beyond them. When you describe the world in ways based on factual information yet go beyond it to make statements about what is not currently known, you are **inferring** conclusions about the world.

Finally, as you examine the third statement in each list, it is apparent that these statements differ from both factual reports and inferences. In each the speaker is applying certain standards (criteria) to deem the bus service as unreliable and solar energy as more promising than nuclear energy or fossil fuels. You are **judging** when you describe the world in ways that evaluate it on the basis of certain criteria.

You continually use these ways of describing and organizing your world—reporting, inferring, and judging—to make sense of your experience. In most instances, you are not aware that you are actually performing these activities, nor are you usually aware of the differences among them. Yet these three activities work together to help you see the world as a complete picture.

Thinking ↔ Writing Activity

Identifying Reports, Inferences, and Judgments

1. Write three statements that you believe—one as a report, one as an inference, and one as a judgment.
2. Locate a short article from a newspaper or magazine and identify the reports, inferences, and judgments it contains.
3. Share your statements and your findings with classmates.

REPORTING FACTUAL INFORMATION

Statements written as reports express the most accurate beliefs you have about the world. Factual beliefs have earned this distinction because they are verifiable, usually by using one or more of your senses. For example, consider the following factual statement: "That young woman is wearing a brown hat in the rain." This statement about an event in the world is considered factual because you can verify it immediately with sensual experience—what you can (in principle or in theory) see, hear, touch, taste, or smell. It is important to say *in principle or in theory* because often you do not use all of your senses to check out what you are experiencing. Look again at the factual statement: you would normally be satisfied to see this event without insisting on touching the hat or giving the person a physical examination. If necessary, however, you could perform these additional actions.

You use the same reasoning when you believe other people's factual statements that you are not in a position to check immediately. For instance:

- The Great Wall of China is more than fifteen hundred miles long.
- There are large mountains and craters on the moon.
- Your skin is covered with germs.

You consider these factual statements because even though you cannot verify them with your senses at the moment, you could in principle or in theory do so *if* you were flown to China, *if* you were rocketed to the moon, or *if* you were to examine your skin with a powerful microscope. The process of verifying factual statements involves identifying the sources of information on which they are based and evaluating the reliability of these sources.

You communicate factual information to others by means of reports. A

report is a description of something that has been experienced, then communicated in as accurate and complete a way as possible. Through reports you share your sense experiences with other people, and this mutual sharing enables you to learn much more about the world than if you were confined to knowing only what you experience. The recording (making records) of factual reports has also made it possible to accumulate the knowledge acquired by previous generations.

Because factual reports play such an important role in the exchange and accumulation of information about the world, it is important that they be as accurate and complete as possible. This brings us to a problem. We have already seen in previous chapters that our perceptions and observations often are not accurate or complete. This means that sometimes when we think we are making true factual reports, they actually are inaccurate or incomplete. For instance, consider our earlier factual statement: "That young woman is wearing a brown hat in the rain." Here are questions you could ask concerning the accuracy of the statement:

- Is the woman really young, or does she merely look young?
- Is the person really a woman, or a man disguised as a woman?
- Is that really a hat the woman is wearing, or is it something else (such as a helmet or a paper bag)?

Of course, there are methods you could use to answer these questions. Can you describe some of them?

Besides difficulties with observations, the "facts" that you see in the world actually depend on more *general beliefs* that you have about how the world operates. Consider this question: "Why did the man's body fall from the top of the building to the sidewalk?" Having had some general science courses, you might respond, "The body was simply obeying the law of gravity" and consider that a factual statement. But how did people account for this sort of event before Newton formulated the law of gravity? Some popular responses might have included the following:

- Things always fall down, not up.
- The spirit in the body wanted to join with the spirit of the earth.

In the past, when people made statements like these—such as "Humans can't fly"—they thought they were stating facts. Increased knowledge and understanding have since shown these "factual beliefs" to be inaccurate, so they have been replaced by "better" beliefs. These better beliefs explain the world in a way that is more accurate and predictable. Will many of the beliefs now considered to be factually accurate also be replaced by more precise and predictable beliefs? If history is any indication, this will most certainly happen. Newton's formulations have already been replaced by Einstein's, based on the latter's theory of relativity. Einstein's have been refined and modified as well and may someday be replaced.

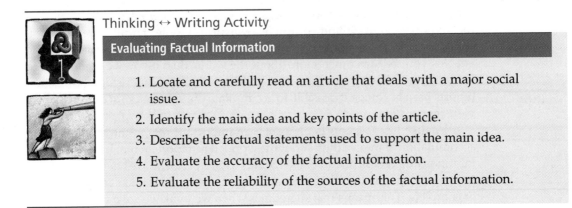

Thinking ↔ Writing Activity

Evaluating Factual Information

1. Locate and carefully read an article that deals with a major social issue.
2. Identify the main idea and key points of the article.
3. Describe the factual statements used to support the main idea.
4. Evaluate the accuracy of the factual information.
5. Evaluate the reliability of the sources of the factual information.

INFERRING FROM EVIDENCE OR PREMISES

Imagine yourself in the following situations.

1. It is 2:00 A.M. and your roommate comes crashing into the room. He staggers to his bed and falls across it, dropping (and breaking) a nearly empty whiskey bottle. Startled, you gasp, "What's the matter?" With alcohol fumes blasting from his mouth, he mumbles: "I jus' wanna hadda widdel drink!" What do you conclude?

2. Your roommate has just learned that she passed a math exam for which she had done absolutely no studying. Humming the refrain "I did it my way," she comes dancing over to you with a huge grin on her face and says, "Let me buy you dinner to celebrate!" What do you conclude about how she is feeling?

3. It is midnight and the library is about to close. As you head for the door, you spy your roommate shuffling along in an awkward waddle. His coat bulges out in front as if he's pregnant. When you ask, "What's going on?" he gives you a glare and hisses, "Shhh!" Just before he reaches the door, a pile of books slides from under his coat and crashes to the floor. What do you conclude?

In these examples, it would be reasonable to make the following conclusions.

1. Your roommate is drunk.
2. Your roommate is happy.
3. Your roommate is stealing library books.

Although these conclusions are reasonable, they are not factual reports; they are inferences. You have not directly experienced your roommate's "drunkenness," "happiness," or "stealing." Instead, you have inferred it on the basis of your roommate's behavior and the circumstances. What clues in these situations might lead to these conclusions? One way of understanding the inferential nature of these views is to ask yourself the following questions.

1. Have you ever pretended to be drunk when you weren't? Could other people tell?
2. Have you ever pretended to be happy when you weren't? Could other people tell?
3. Have you ever been accused of stealing something when you were perfectly innocent? How did this happen?

From these examples you can see that whereas factual beliefs can in principle be verified by direct observation, *inferential beliefs* go beyond what can be directly observed. For instance, in the previous examples, your observation of some of your roommate's actions led you to infer things that you were not observing directly—"He's drunk," "She's happy," "He's stealing books."

Making such simple inferences is something you do all the time. It is so automatic that usually you are not even aware that you are going beyond your immediate observations or that you may be having trouble distinguishing between what you *observe* and what you *infer*. Making such inferences enables you to see the world as a complete picture, to fill in the blanks and to supplement the fragmentary sensations being presented to your senses. Presenting your inferences along with your beliefs in writing paints a complete picture for your readers.

Your writing may also include *predictions* of what will occur in the near future. Predictions and expectations are also inferences because you attempt to determine what is currently unknown from what is already known.

It is possible that your inferences may be wrong; in fact, they frequently are. You may infer that the woman sitting next to you is wearing two earrings and then discover that she has only one. You may expect the class to end at noon but find that the teacher lets you out early—or late. In the last section, we concluded that not even factual beliefs are ever absolutely certain. Comparatively speaking, inferential beliefs are much more uncertain than factual beliefs, so it is important to distinguish between the two.

The distinction between what is observed and what is inferred is given particular attention in courtroom settings, where defense lawyers usually want witnesses to describe only what they observed—not what they inferred as they observed. When a witness includes an inference such as "I saw him steal it," the lawyer may object that the statement represents a "conclusion of the witness" and move to have the observation struck from the record. For example, imagine that you are a defense attorney listening to the following testimony. At what points would you object by saying, "This is a conclusion of the witness"?

I saw Harvey running down the street, right after he knocked the old lady down. He had her purse in his hand and was trying to escape as fast as he could. He was really scared. I wasn't surprised because Harvey has always taken advantage of others. It's not the first time that he's stolen, either; I can tell you that. Just last summer he robbed the poor box at St. Anthony's. He was bragging about it for weeks.

Finally, keep in mind that even though in *theory* facts and inferences can be distinguished, in *practice* it is almost impossible to communicate with others in speech or writing by sticking only to factual observations. A reasonable approach is to state your inference along with the observable evidence on which the inference is based (e.g., John seemed happy because . . .). Our language has an entire collection of terms (*seems, appears, is likely,* and so on) that signal when we are making an inference and not expressing an observable fact. Thoughtful writers use these words carefully and deliberately.

Many of the predictions that you make are inferences based on your past experiences and information that you presently have. Even when there appear to be sound reasons supporting them, these inferences are often wrong due to incomplete information or unanticipated events. The fact that even people whom society considers "experts" regularly make inaccurate predictions should encourage you to exercise caution when presenting your beliefs as inferences. Here are some examples:

> "So many centuries after the Creation, it is unlikely that anyone could find hitherto unknown lands of any value." —The Advisory Committee to King Ferdinand and Queen Isabella of Spain, before Columbus's voyage in 1492

> "What will the soldiers and sailors, what will the common people say to 'George Washington, President of the United States'? They will despise him to all eternity." —John Adams, 1789

> "What use could the company make of an electrical toy?" —Western Union's rejection of the telephone in 1878

> "The actual building of roads devoted to motor cars is not for the near future in spite of many rumors to that effect." —a 1902 article in *Harper's Weekly*

> "You ain't goin' nowhere, son. You ought to go back to driving a truck." —Jim Denny, Grand Ole Opry manager, firing Elvis Presley after one performance, 1954

Examine the following list of statements, noting which are *factual beliefs* (based on observations) and which are *inferential beliefs* (conclusions that go beyond observations). For each factual statement, describe how you might go about verifying the information. For each inferential statement, describe a factual observation on which the inference could be based. (*Note:* Some statements may contain both factual beliefs and inferential beliefs.)

- When my leg starts to ache, that means snow is on the way.
- The grass is wet—it must have rained last night.
- I think that it's pretty clear from the length of the skid marks that the accident was caused by that person's driving too fast.
- Fifty men lost their lives in the construction of the Queensboro Bridge.
- Nancy said she wasn't feeling well yesterday—I'll bet that she's out sick today.

Now consider the following situations. What inferences might you be inclined to make on the basis of what you are observing? How could you investigate the accuracy of an inference?

- A student in your class is consistently late for class.
- You see a friend driving a new car.
- An instructor asks the same student to stay after class several times.
- You don't receive any birthday cards.

So far, we have been exploring relatively simple inferences. Many of the inferences people make, however, are much more complicated. In fact, much of our knowledge of the world rests on our ability to make complicated inferences in a systematic and logical way. However, just because an inference is more complicated does not mean that it is more accurate; in fact, the opposite is often the case. One of the masters of inference is the legendary Sherlock Holmes. In the following passage, Holmes makes an astonishing number of inferences upon meeting Dr. Watson. Study Holmes's conclusions carefully. Are they reasonable? Can you explain how he reaches them?

> "You appeared to be surprised when I told you, on our first meeting, that you had come from Afghanistan."
>
> "You were told, no doubt."
>
> "Nothing of the sort. I knew you came from Afghanistan. From long habit the train of thoughts ran so swiftly through my mind that I arrived at the conclusion without being conscious of intermediate steps. There were such steps, however. The train of reasoning ran, 'Here is a gentleman of a medical type, but with the air of a military man. Clearly an army doctor, then. He is just come from the tropics, for his face is dark, and that is not the natural tint of his skin, for his wrists are fair. He has undergone hardship and sickness, as his haggard face says clearly. His left arm has been injured. He holds it in a stiff and unnatural manner. Where in the tropics could an English army doctor have seen much hardship and got his arm wounded? Clearly in Afghanistan.' The whole train of thought did not occupy a second. I then remarked that you came from Afghanistan, and you were astonished." —Sir Arthur Conan Doyle, *A Study in Scarlet*

Thinking ↔ Writing Activity

Analyzing an Incorrect Inference

Describe an experience in which you made an incorrect inference. For example, it might have been a situation in which you mistakenly accused someone, an accident based on a miscalculation, a poor decision based on an inaccurate prediction, or some other event. Analyze that experience by answering the following questions:

1. What was (were) your mistaken inference(s)?

2. What was the factual evidence on which you based your inference(s)?

3. Looking back, what could you have done to avoid making the erroneous inference(s)?

The following essay was written by a geology professor at Harvard University who also writes widely on scientific themes for nonscientific audiences. This essay illustrates the ongoing process by which natural scientists use inferences to discover factual information and to construct theories explaining the information.

Evolution as Fact and Theory
BY STEPHEN JAY GOULD

Kirtley Mather, who died last year at age 89, was a pillar of both science and the Christian religion in America and one of my dearest friends. The difference of half a century in our ages evaporated before our common interests. The most curious thing we shared was a battle we each fought at the same age. For Kirtley had gone to Tennessee with Clarence Darrow to testify for evolution at the Scopes trial of 1925. When I think that we are enmeshed again in the same struggle for one of the best documented, most compelling and exciting concepts in all of science, I don't know whether to laugh or cry.

According to idealized principles of scientific discourse, the arousal of dormant issues should reflect fresh data that give renewed life to abandoned notions. Those outside the current debate may therefore be excused for suspecting that creationists have come up with something new, or that evolutionists have generated some serious internal trouble. But nothing has changed; the creationists have not a single new fact or argument. Darrow and Bryan were at least more entertaining than we lesser antagonists today. The rise of creationism is politics, pure and simple; it represents one issue (and by no means the major concern) of the resurgent evangelical right. Arguments that seemed kooky just a decade ago have re-entered the mainstream.

Creationism Is Not Science

The basic attack of the creationists falls apart on two general counts before we even reach the supposed factual details of their complaints against evolution. First, they play upon a vernacular misunderstanding of the word "theory" to convey the false impression that we evolutionists are covering up the rotten core of our edifice. Second, they misuse a popular philosophy of science to argue that they are behaving scientifically in attacking evolution. Yet the same philosophy demonstrates that their own belief is not science, and that "scientific creationism" is therefore meaningless and self-contradictory, a superb example of what Orwell called "newspeak."

In the American vernacular, "theory" often means "imperfect fact"—part of a hierarchy of confidence running downhill from fact to theory to hypothesis to guess. Thus the power of the creationist argument: evolution is "only" a theory, and intense debate now rages about many aspects of the theory. If evolution is less than a fact, and scientists can't even make up their minds about the theory, then what confidence can we have in it? Indeed, President Reagan echoed this argument before an evangelical group in Dallas when he said (in what I devoutly hope was campaign rhetoric): "Well, it is a theory. It is a scientific theory only, and it has in recent years been challenged in the world of science—that is, not believed in the scientific community to be as infallible as it once was."

5   Well, evolution *is* a theory. It is also a fact. And facts and theories are different things, not rungs in a hierarchy of increasing certainty. Facts are the world's data. Theories are structures of ideas that explain and interpret facts. Facts do not go away when scientists debate rival theories to explain them. Einstein's theory of gravitation replaced Newton's, but apples did not suspend themselves in mid-air pending the outcome. And human beings evolved from apelike ancestors whether they did so by Darwin's proposed mechanism or by some other, yet to be discovered.

Moreover, "fact" does not mean "absolute certainty." The final proofs of logic and mathematics flow deductively from stated premises and achieve certainty only because they are *not* about the empirical world. Evolutionists make no claim for perpetual truth, though creationists often do (and then attack us for a style of argument that they themselves favor). In science, "fact" can only mean "confirmed to such a degree that it would be perverse to withhold provisional assent." I suppose that apples might start to rise tomorrow, but possibility does not merit equal time in physics classrooms.

Evolutionists have been clear about this distinction between fact and theory from the very beginning, if only because we have always acknowledged how far we are from completely understanding the mechanisms (theory) by which evolution (fact) occurred. Darwin continually emphasized the difference between his two great and separate accomplishments: establishing the fact of evolution, and proposing a theory—natural selection—to explain the mechanism of evolution. He wrote in *The Descent of Man:* "I had two distinct objects in view; firstly, to show that species had not been separately created, and secondly, that natural selection had been the chief agent of change. . . . Hence if I have erred in . . . having exaggerated its [natural selection's] power . . . I have at least, as I hope, done good service in aiding to overthrow the dogma of separate creations."

Thus Darwin acknowledged the provisional nature of natural selection while affirming the fact of evolution. The fruitful theoretical debate that Darwin initiated has never ceased. From the 1940s through the 1960s, Darwin's own theory of natural selection did achieve a temporary hegemony that it never enjoyed in his lifetime. But renewed debate characterizes our decade, and while no biologist questions the importance of natural selection, many now doubt its ubiquity. In particular, many evolutionists argue that substantial amounts of genetic change may not be subject to natural selection and may spread through populations at random. Others are challenging Darwin's linking of natural selection with gradual, imperceptible change through all intermediary degrees; they are arguing that most evolutionary events may occur far more rapidly than Darwin envisioned.

Scientists regard debates on fundamental issues of theory as a sign of intellectual health and a source of excitement. Science is—and how else can I say it?—most fun when it plays with interesting ideas, examines their implications, and recognizes that old information may be explained in surprisingly new ways. Evolutionary theory is now enjoying this uncommon vigor. Yet amidst all this turmoil no biologist has been led to doubt the fact that evolution occurred; we are debating *how* it happened. We are all trying to explain the same thing: the tree of evolutionary descent linking all organisms by ties of genealogy. Creationists pervert and caricature this debate by conveniently neglecting the common conviction that underlies it, and by falsely suggesting that we now doubt the very phenomenon we are struggling to understand.

10   Using another invalid argument, creationists claim that "the dogma of separate creations," as Darwin characterized it a century ago, is a scientific theory meriting equal time with evolution in high school biology curricula. But a prevailing viewpoint among philosophers of science belies this creationist argument. Philosopher Karl Popper has argued for decades that the primary criterion of science is the falsifiability of its theories. We can never prove absolutely, but we can falsify. A set of ideas that cannot, in principle, be falsified is not science.

The entire creationist argument involves little more than a rhetorical attempt to falsify evolution by presenting supposed contradictions among its supporters. Their brand of creationism, they claim, is "scientific" because it follows the Popperian model in trying to demolish evolution. Yet Popper's argument must apply in both directions. One does not become a scientist by the simple act of trying to falsify another scientific system; one has to present an alternative system that also meets Popper's criterion—it too must be falsifiable in principle.

"Scientific creationism" is a self-contradictory, nonsense phrase precisely because it cannot be falsified. I can envision observations and experiments that would disprove any evolutionary theory I know, but I cannot imagine what potential data could lead creationists to abandon their beliefs. Unbeatable systems are dogma, not science. Lest I seem harsh or rhetorical, I quote creationism's leading intellectual, Duane Gish, Ph.D., from his recent (1978) book *Evolution? The Fossils Say No!* "By creation we mean the bringing into being by a supernatural Creator of the basic kinds of plants and animals by the process of sudden, or flat, creation. We do not know how the Creator created, what processes He used, *for He used processes which are not now operating anywhere in the natural universe* [Gish's italics]. This is why we refer to creation as special creation. We cannot discover by scientific investigations anything about the creative processes used by the Creator." Pray tell, Dr. Gish, in the light of your last sentence, what then is "scientific" creationism?

The Fact of Evolution

Our confidence that evolution occurred centers upon three general arguments. First, we have abundant, direct, observational evidence of evolution in action, from both the field and the laboratory. It ranges from countless experiments on change in nearly everything about fruit flies subjected to artificial selection in the laboratory to the famous British moths that turned black when industrial soot darkened the trees upon which they rest. (The moths gain protection from sharp-sighted bird predators by blending into the background.) Creationists do not deny these observations; how could they? Creationists have tightened their act. They now argue that God only created "basic kinds," and allowed for limited evolutionary meandering within them. Thus toy poodles and Great Danes come from the dog kind and moths can change color, but nature cannot convert a dog to a cat or a monkey to a man.

The second and third arguments for evolution—the case for major changes—do not involve direct observation of evolution in action. They rest upon inference, but are no less secure for that reason. Major evolutionary change requires too much time for direct observation on the scale of recorded human history. All historical sciences rest upon inference, and evolution is no different from geology, cosmology, or human history in this respect. In principle, we cannot observe processes that operated in the past. We must infer them from results that still survive: living and fossil organisms for evolution, documents and artifacts for human history, strata and topography for geology.

15   The second argument—that the imperfection of nature reveals evolution—strikes many people as ironic, for they feel that evolution should be most elegantly displayed in the nearly perfect adaptation expressed by some organisms—the camber of a gull's wing, or butterflies that cannot be seen in ground litter because they mimic leaves so precisely. But perfection could be imposed by a wise creator or evolved by natural selection. Perfection covers the tracks of past history. And past history—the evidence of descent—is our mark of evolution.

Evolution lies exposed in the *imperfections* that record a history of descent. Why should a rat run, a bat fly, or porpoise swim, and I type this essay with structures built of the same bones unless we all inherited them from a common ancestor? An engineer, starting from scratch, could design better limbs in each case. Why should all the large native mammals of Australia be marsupials, unless they descended from a common ancestor isolated on this island continent? Marsupials are not "better," or ideally suited for Australia; many have been wiped out by placental mammals imported by man from other continents. This principle of imperfection extends to all historical sciences. When we recognize the etymology of September, October, November, and December (seventh, eighth, ninth, and tenth, from the Latin), we know that two additional items (January and February) must have been added to an original calendar of ten months.

The third argument is more direct: transitions are often found in the fossil record. Preserved transitions are not common—and should not be, according to our understanding of evolution . . . —but they are not entirely wanting, as creationists often claim. The lower jaw of reptiles contains several bones, that of mammals only one. The nonmammalian jawbones are reduced, step by step, in mammalian ancestors until they become tiny nubbins located at the back of the jaw. The "hammer" and the "anvil" bones of the mammalian ear are descendants of these nubbins. How could such a transition be accomplished?, the creationists ask. Surely a bone is either entirely in the jaw or in the ear. Yet paleontologists have discovered two transitional lineages of therapsids (the so-called mammal-like reptiles) with a double jaw joint—one composed of the old quadrate and articular bones (soon to become the hammer and anvil), the other of the squamosal and dentary bones (as in modern mammals). For that matter, what better transitional form could we desire than the oldest human, *Australopithecus afarensis*, with its apelike palate, its human upright stance, and a cranial capacity larger than any ape's of the same body size but a full 1,000 cubic centimeters below ours? If God made each of the half dozen human species discovered in ancient rocks, why did he create an unbroken temporal sequence of progressively more modern features—increasing cranial capacity, reduced face and teeth, larger body size? Did he create a mimic evolution and test our faith thereby?

Conclusion

I am both angry at and amused by the creationists; but mostly I am deeply sad. Sad for many reasons. Sad because so many people who respond to creationist appeals are troubled for the right reason, but venting their anger at the wrong target. It is true that scientists have often been dogmatic and elitist. It is true that we have often allowed the white-coated, advertising image to represent us— "Scientists say that Brand X cures bunions ten times faster than . . . " We have not fought it adequately because we derive benefits from appearing as a new priesthood. It is also true that faceless bureaucratic state power intrudes more and more into our lives and removes choices that should belong to individuals and communities. I can understand that requiring that evolution be taught in the schools might be seen as one more insult on all these grounds. But the culprit is not, and cannot be, evolution or any other fact of the natural world. Identify and fight your legitimate enemies by all means, but we are not among them.

I am sad because the practical result of this brouhaha will not be expanded coverage to include creationism (that would also make me sad), but the reduction or excision of evolution from high school curricula. Evolution is one of the half dozen "great ideas" developed by science. It speaks to the profound issues of genealogy that fascinate all of us—the "roots" phenomenon writ large. Where did we come from? Where did life arise? How did it develop? How are organisms related? It forces us to think, ponder, and wonder. Shall we deprive millions of this knowledge and once again teach biology as a set of dull and unconnected facts, without the thread that weaves diverse material into a supple unity?

20   But most of all I am saddened by a trend I am just beginning to discern among my colleagues. I sense that some now wish to mute the healthy debate about theory that has brought new life to evolutionary biology. It provides grist for creationist mills, they say, even if only by distortion. Perhaps we should lie low and rally around the flag of strict Darwinism, at least for the moment—a kind of old-time religion on our part.

But we should borrow another metaphor and recognize that we too have to tread a straight and narrow path, surrounded by roads to perdition. For if we ever begin to suppress our search to understand nature, to quench our own intellectual excitement in a misguided effort to present a united front where it does not and should not exist, then we are truly lost.

Critical Reading Questions

1. According to Gould, evolution is both a scientific "fact" and a scientific "theory" asserting that all life forms are the result of a process of gradual development and differentiation over time, much like the progressive growth of tree branches from the central trunk. In contrast, creationism asserts that all basic forms of life were brought into being in a sudden act by a supernatural creator. From your reading of the article, explain what you understand about the theory of evolution and about creationism. Compare your views with those of your classmates.

2. Gould defines *facts* as the "world's data" and refers to observing an apple fall from the tree as Isaac Newton is alleged to have done. Identify some of the facts Gould presents in his writing as evidence to support the theory of evolution.

3. Gould defines *theories* as "structures of ideas that explain and interpret facts," such as Newton's theory of gravitation which was introduced to explain facts like falling apples. In addition to facts, Gould states, the theory of evolution is supported by reasonable inferences. Identify the inferences he cites as evidence.

The comic strip below was probably intended to be funny, but it reflects what Gould says about theories as "structures of ideas that explain and interpret facts." Historical facts are interpreted differently at different times; theories about history change. School textbooks about United States history of fifty years ago usually focused on the Founding Fathers, pioneers moving westward, and military actions. Books published now usually include material on Native Americans, women, slaves, and daily life. You might want to discuss this change with your grandparents or older friends.

JUDGING BY APPLYING CRITERIA

Identify and write a description of a friend, a course you have taken, or the college you attend. Be sure your descriptions are specific and include what you think about the friend, the course, and the college.

1. _____ is a friend I have. He/she is . . .

2. _____ is a course I have taken. It was . . .

3. _____ is the college I attend. It is . . .

Now review your writing. Does it include factual descriptions? Note any facts that can be verified. Your writing may also contain inferences based on factual information. Can you identify any? In addition, your writing may include judgments about the person, the course, and the school—descriptions that express your evaluation based on certain criteria. Facts and inferences help you figure out what is actually happening (or will happen); the purpose of judgments is to express your evaluation about what is happening (or will happen). For example:

- My new car has broken down three times in the first six months. (Factual report)
- My new car will probably continue to have difficulties. (Inference)
- My new car is a lemon. (Judgment)

When you label your new car a "lemon," you are making a judgment based on certain criteria. For instance, a lemon is usually a newly purchased item—often an automobile—with which you have repeated problems. For another example of judging, consider the following statements:

- Carla always does her work thoroughly and completes it on time. (Factual report)
- Carla will probably continue to do her work in this fashion. (Inference)
- Carla is a very responsible person. (Judgment)

By judging Carla to be responsible, you are evaluating her on the basis of the criteria or standards that you believe indicate a responsible person. One such criterion is completing assigned work on time. Can you identify additional criteria for judging someone as being responsible?

Review your previous description of a friend, a course, or your college. Can you identify any judgments in your description? For each judgment you have listed, identify the criteria on which you based the judgment.

Many of our disagreements with others focus on differences in judgments. To write thoughtfully, you need to approach such differences intelligently by following these guidelines:

- Make explicit the criteria or standards used as a basis for the judgment.
- Try to establish the reasons that justify these criteria.

For instance, if you write "Professor Andrews is an excellent teacher," you are basing your judgment on certain criteria of teaching excellence. Once these standards are made explicit, they can be discussed to see whether they make sense and what justifies them. Of course, your idea of what makes an excellent teacher may be different from someone else's, so you can test your conclusion by comparing your criteria with those of your classmates. When disagreements occur, use these two steps for resolution.

In short, not all judgments are equally good or equally poor. The credibility of a judgment depends on the criteria used to make the judgment and on the evidence or reasons that support these criteria. For example, there may be legitimate disagreements about judgments on the following points:

- Who was the greatest United States president?
- Which movie deserves the Oscar this year?
- Which is the best baseball team this year?

However, in these and countless other cases, the quality of judgments depends on presenting the criteria used for the competing judgments and then demonstrating that your candidate best meets the agreed-upon criteria by providing supporting evidence and reasons. With this approach, you can often engage in intelligent discussion and establish which judgments are best supported by the evidence.

Thinking ↔ Writing Activity

Analyzing Judgments

Review the following passages, which illustrate various judgments. For each passage, do the following:

1. Identify the evaluative criteria on which the judgments are based.
2. Describe the reasons or evidence the author uses to support the criteria.
3. Explain whether you agree or disagree with the judgments and give your rationale.

One widely held misconception concerning pizza should be laid to rest. Although it may be characterized as fast food, pizza is not junk food. Especially when it is made with fresh ingredients, pizza fulfills our basic nutritional requirements. The crust provides carbohydrates; from the cheese and meat or fish comes protein; and the tomatoes, herbs, onions, and garlic supply vitamins and minerals. —Louis Philip Salamone, "Pizza: Fast Food, Not Junk Food"

Let us return to the question of food. Responsible agronomists report that before the end of the year millions of people if unaided might starve to death. Half a billion deaths by starvation is not an uncommon estimate. Even though the United States has done more than any other nation to feed the hungry, our relative affluence makes us morally vulnerable in the eyes of other nations and in our own eyes. Garrett Hardin, who has argued for a "lifeboat" ethic of survival (if you take all the passengers aboard, everybody drowns), admits that the decision not to feed all the hungry requires of us "a very hard psychological adjustment." Indeed it would. It has been estimated that the 3.5 million tons of fertilizer spread on American golf courses and lawns could provide up to 30 million tons of food in overseas agricultural production. The nightmarish thought intrudes itself. If we as a nation allow people to starve while we could, through some sacrifice, make more food available to them, what hope can any person have for the future of international relations? If we cannot agree on this most basic of values—feed the hungry—what hopes for the future can we entertain? —James R. Kelly, "The Limits of Reason"

DISTINGUISHING AMONG REPORTS, INFERENCES, AND JUDGMENTS

Although the activities of reporting, inferring, and judging tend to be woven together in your experiences and in your writing, it is important to be able to distinguish these activities. Each plays a different role in helping you make sense of the world for yourself and for your readers, and you should be careful not to confuse these roles. For instance, although writers may appear to be reporting factual information, they may actually be expressing personal evaluations, which are not factual. Consider the statement "Los Angeles is a smog-ridden city drowning in automobiles." Although seeming to be reporting factual information, the writer really is expressing his or her personal judgment. Of course, writers can identify their judgments with such phrases as "in my opinion," "my evaluation is," and so forth.

Sometimes, however, writers do not identify their judgments. In some cases they do not do so because the context within which they are writing (such as a newspaper editorial) makes it clear that the information is judgment rather than fact. In other cases, however, they want their judgments to be treated as factual information. Confusing the activities of reporting, inferring, and judging, whether accidental or deliberate, can be misleading and even dangerous.

Confusing factual information with judgments can be personally damaging as well. For example, there is a big difference between these two statements:

- I failed my exam today. (Factual report)
- I am a failure. (Judgment)

Stating the fact "I failed my exam today" describes your situation in a concrete way, enabling you to evaluate (judge) it as a problem you can hope to solve through reflection and hard work. If, however, the situation causes you to make the judgment "I am a failure," this sort of general evaluation will not encourage you to explore solutions to the problem or improve your situation.

Finally, another main reason for distinguishing among the activities of reporting, inferring, and judging concerns the accuracy of statements. We noted, for instance, that factual statements tend to be reasonably accurate because they are by nature verifiable whereas inferences are usually much less certain. As a result, it is crucial to be aware of whether you are presenting a belief as a report, an inference, or a judgment. If you write the superintendent of your apartment building a note saying "My thermostat is broken," an inference on your part based on the fact that you feel uncomfortably hot, you will feel foolish if you later discover that you have a fever and that the thermostat is functioning well.

Presenting Beliefs in Your Writing

Understanding and evaluating beliefs pertains in three particular ways to your college papers as well as to the writing you will do in other settings. First, as you are better able to distinguish among reports, inferences, and judgments, you will be able to present different types of beliefs more accurately. Although you may not often use the terms *report, inference,* or *judgment,* you will word your beliefs in precise ways that indicate the level of speculation behind your statements.

Second, a strong relationship exists between the thesis of a paper and your beliefs about the topic. The thesis, most of all, expresses what you believe is the main point of your paper. As you work to clarify your thesis statement, you also clarify your beliefs about the issue you are addressing. And when you state the thesis clearly in your paper, you are making your beliefs clear to your readers.

Third, as a college writer and quite possibly as a working professional, you will regularly use source material in your papers. The techniques for evaluating beliefs will help you evaluate sources of information. Then, as you present in your researched writing what others have said, you can comment on their beliefs as you integrate the material into your papers. (See Chapter 13 on research.)

Writing Project: Analyzing Influences on Your Beliefs About a Social or Academic Issue

This chapter has included both readings and Thinking-Writing Activities that encourage you to think about the sources of your beliefs. Be sure to reread what you wrote for the activities as you may be able to use some of it in completing this project.

Write an essay in which you consider some influences on the development of your beliefs about a social issue or an idea related to an academic field. As much as possible, apply the concepts discussed in this chapter.

As a college student, you receive much of your information about social or academic issues from print and electronic sources. Therefore, you should analyze at least two media sources such as newspaper, magazine, or journal articles; material from a web site; a film or a video; a book or book chapter. In addition, think about what your teachers and other people have told you and, perhaps, about personal experiences.

If you completed the Writing Project in Chapter 2, you may want to think about some differences between personal experiences and media sources as influences on your beliefs. Consider the limitations and impacts of different influences. If you completed the Writing Project in Chapter 7, you may want to see how the comparative techniques used there can apply to this project.

Follow your instructor's directions for topic limitations, length, format, citation methods, and so on.

Begin by considering the key elements of the Thinking-Writing Model.

THE WRITING SITUATION

Purpose Your primary purpose here is to further your own development as a capable college student. You will be exploring some of the ways in which you come to accept concepts. In addition, you will be sharing your insights with your audience, which always provides another purpose: to write an effective paper.

On a technical level, you are required to take different kinds of information and pull them together. Such *synthesis* is the central purpose of many kinds of academic and professional writing. Most research papers, case studies, field reports, project summaries, product proposals, and business plans use information which must be analyzed and synthesized.

You also have an intellectual purpose. You will look closely at your own ways of defining what you believe and what you consider true as well as what you do not believe and what you consider false.

Audience As usual, your classmates are a good audience for this paper, both in draft and finished versions, since they are doing the same assignment and will want to see how you handle it. In addition, people interested in the social issue or academic field will naturally be potential readers. If you are taking a class pertaining to your subject, you could share your paper with those students. If you are writing about a social issue relevant to your community, you could share your work in a newsletter or on a web site.

Of course, your instructor remains the audience who will judge how well you have articulated your beliefs, how you have selected the influences on your beliefs, how you have handled the sources, and how you have planned, drafted, revised, and edited your essay.

Subject Examining the sources of beliefs and evaluating evidence are among the most challenging of activities. If you are just beginning to learn about the issue on which you are writing, you may not have enough background to be very inquisitive or judgmental. However, you should be aware of criteria that any thoughtful student can detect: specific support for a claim, whether information is current, appropriateness of examples and authorities, and responsible attribution. Also, you have some understanding of reports, inferences, predictions, and judgments to apply to your analysis.

Writer For this Writing Project, you should be as open as possible to new ways of thinking about your beliefs. After such critical analysis, some writers find that their beliefs have been strengthened; others may realize that some of their beliefs were based on unreliable information and need to be reevaluated.

As with the Writing Projects in Part One, you are in a position of authority here when you are writing about your own reactions and realizations. At the same time, since you are writing about a social issue or an academic field instead of about your personal life, you are a writer who is dealing with other people's beliefs in addition to your own. After writing the paper, you may want to consider whether you are a more accepting or more skeptical person.

THE WRITING PROCESS

The following sections will guide you through the stages of planning, drafting, and revising your essay analyzing the sources of your beliefs.

Generating Ideas

- Identify some ideas in the Thinking-Writing Activities that you may be able to use. Then write informally about them.
- Think about teachers, books, films, articles, the Internet, and other sources of information in your field that have provided you with information that you believe. Why have they had this effect?
- Think about any sources that you are reluctant to trust or believe. Why have they had this effect?
- What concepts in this field do you believe most firmly?
- Are there some that you question?
- Freewrite for five minutes about your ideas for this project.
- Look at the list of questions for exploring topics in Chapter 3. Which of them can help you generate ideas for this project?

Defining a Focus

- The Writing Project itself provides a wide-angle focus, but you must sharpen it in order to produce an understandable paper.
- Notice if your issue or idea has several components. For example, the issue of high-stakes testing in public schools raises questions about the kind of tests used, the effects on students' passing to the next level, the effects on school funding or ratings, and the effects on curriculum. You may want to focus only on one aspect. Perhaps your beliefs about evolution in biology or parallel processing in computer science are really beliefs about several components of the general idea.
- Write down your belief to be sure that you can state it well. If you haven't decided on one belief, write several. Are they interpretations, evaluations, conclusions, or predictions in your statement? Do these terms help you find a focus?
- Consider your level of belief. Are you strongly convinced that your belief is plausible? Do you have questions about it? Why?
- Focus on differences. Does a popular press, TV, or web site account differ from what a book says or what a professor has taught you?
- Draft a thesis statement that gives direction to the essay.
- Create a map, web, or rough outline so that you can see how ideas might cluster or separate.

Organizing Ideas If you created a map or rough outline while you were looking for a focus, review it and try to be more specific about how to arrange the ideas for your paper.

- Have you drafted a tentative thesis that states your belief, one that says something about the sources of the belief, or one that includes both? What kind would be most effective?

- If you have several sources for your belief, does each one deserve a paragraph?

- If your beliefs have changed, have you discussed this in an effective place?

- If you are contrasting two differing perspectives, have you structured the contrast logically?

- If you are presenting similar perspectives, have you structured the comparison logically?

- Have you planned a conclusion? Does it refer to the influences on your beliefs?

- Remember that you may modify your plan or outline as you draft.

Drafting

- Begin with the part easiest to draft. Is it writing about your teachers or dealing with your print or electronic sources?

- Perhaps you should then shift to a part that is hard to draft and at least make some notes or write questions.

- Draft a new outline or map, if necessary, as you rethink what you want to say. Look at the preliminary thesis statement that you drafted. Do you need to rework it now, or should you wait until you have drafted more?

- Shape the paragraphs that will make up the body of your essay. Draft clear topic sentences; think about where the topic sentence should be placed in each paragraph.

- Draft an opening paragraph and a concluding paragraph, understanding that you may want to revise them substantially later.

Revising One of the best revision strategies is to get an audience's reactions to your draft. Your classmates, or peers, can help you see where your draft is already fulfilling your purposes and where it needs improvement. If your instructor allows class time for peer review, be sure to have a draft ready. Also be prepared to help your classmates.

Follow your instructor's directions or use one of the systems presented on pages 65–66 and 105–107. After your classmates have made suggestions, work through the following revision questions.

If you do not have an opportunity to participate in a peer review, put your draft aside for a day or two and then work through these revision questions.

1. **Think big.** Look at your draft as a whole.

   - Does it fulfill the assignment by discussing influences on your beliefs about a social or academic issue?
   - Can you state your thesis more effectively?
   - Can you make the organization more logical? Are your discussions of influences arranged in a good sequence?
   - How can you improve the transitions between paragraphs?
   - Did you include enough specific examples of exactly what influenced you?
   - How can you make your draft more concise if it seems too long? How can you provide more substance if it seems too short?

2. **Think medium.** Look at your draft paragraph by paragraph.

   - Can the first paragraph do a better job of introducing your belief? Does it provide a background for it?
   - Can the first paragraph do a better job of explaining your belief?
   - Should you reorganize any paragraphs? Do they present the influences on your belief in a logical way?
   - Can you write more effective topic sentences? Is there any paragraph without a topic sentence that needs one?
   - Can you make any paragraph more unified? Can you improve the transition words and phrases?
   - Does any paragraph need another specific example?
   - Does the concluding paragraph need improvement? Does it do a good job of wrapping things up?

3. **Think small.** Look at your draft sentence by sentence.

   - Be sure that sentences that contain material from sources include a good introduction of each source.
   - Be sure that material from sources fits smoothly into the syntax of a sentence. Read such sentences out loud to be sure that they sound natural.
   - Find any sentences that are so long that they are confusing. Can they be divided or better punctuated?
   - Find any sentences that seem too short. Should they be expanded or combined with other sentences?
   - Do any sentences need to be corrected for Standard English grammar and usage?

4. **Think "picky."** Look at your draft as your fussiest critic might.

- If you are using an academic format to cite sources, check your handbook to be sure that everything conforms with its models.
- If you are citing your material informally, as Jessie Lange did in her paper, be sure that you clarify what the source is and what material came from it.
- Is quoted material placed within quotation marks?
- Are any words misspelled?
- Are there any punctuation errors?
- Can your draft be finished into a neatly presented paper?
- Is there anything else you could do to improve your draft?

Editing and Proofreading After you have prepared the final draft, edit and proofread it carefully. Run your spell checker, but don't rely on it to detect all errors. If you can, ask a friend who is a good detail person to review your paper to spot any errors.

Here is how one student responded to an assignment for a criminal justice course. Her professor asked the students to show how media treatments of a current issue helped them to develop beliefs about that issue.

STUDENT WRITING

Dealing with Sex Offenders
BY JESSIE LANGE

In the past few years we have heard much about Megan's Law, which states that people should be made aware of charged sex offenders in their community. While I wholeheartedly believe that people, for the protection of themselves and their children, have the right to know, there is another twist on the issue I hadn't thought about until I heard a story recently on "60 Minutes." The story involved Stephanie's Law—a new law in place in some states under which sex offenders are kept *after* they have served their time to go through a therapy program in an attempt to "cure" them. The question that this provoked in me was not whether the state should have the right to hold sexual criminals beyond their sentence, but whether they can be cured at all. If not, should they ever be released back into a world where they are likely to do more damage, destroy more lives?

A recent *New York Times* article described a rehabilitation program in Texas whereby prisoners are immersed in religion—taking classes, having discussions, and owning up to their "sins." Interestingly, while there are 79 men convicted of "robbery, drug possession, and murder" participating, those convicted of sexual crimes are not accepted into the program. This is partly because they are "looked down on by other prisoners" and partly because, according to criminologists, "sexual criminals are the most difficult to rehabilitate."

In fact, there is a question as to whether this rehabilitation is even possible. Sexual criminals in particular seem to be under the influence of urges which are out of their control. The "60 Minutes" report said that, while many may have good intentions in being treated through therapy and returning to society, it may be out of their hands. They may say they understand their wrongs, they may feel cured, but if they are released it seems impossible for even the offenders to know if they will be able to control their impulses. If there is such a question, do they deserve a chance at freedom when it means potentially committing another crime?

There is no question in my mind that, while many sex offenders do not repent for what they have done and have no real interest in being cured, there are also many for whom their crimes are almost out of their hands—as disgusting to them as to anyone else. The *New York Times* ran an article entitled "Sex Offender Agrees To Be Castrated." In Illinois, a convicted child sex offender is having himself castrated "in an effort to win a lighter sentence." The offender, in fact, "volunteered to be castrated even before he was convicted" previously of an attack on a young girl. It seems as though the man is making an attempt to control his urges but, according to the article, "experts disagree on whether castration helps" in controlling these urges.

Both the *New York Times* and "60 Minutes" have good reputations as reliable media sources. I read this paper and watch this show regularly. (I'm pleased that my parents introduced me to them.) I think that these reports are as reliable as the popular press can be. If I decide to do research on this subject and write a substantial paper, I will have to use criminal justice and sociology journals and try to interview one or two experts, as well.

I have not had any personal experience with sex offenders, but I have read and heard enough to know that their crimes destroy not only the lives of victims but also the lives of families and friends of the victims and that their crimes can so haunt victims that these fears are never resolved. In addition, victims of sexual crimes may grow up to inflict these crimes on others, continuing the cycle. In my opinion, the damage done by sex offenders and the risk of untreatable urges to commit these crimes, a risk illustrated by the high percentage of repeat offenders, is too great to justify their release. At least not until there is a proven "cure," a sure-fire way to *know* that they are treatable, have been treated, and will not continue to make victims of others.

Through the media, I have come to understand that many may be operating on urges not within their control, but this does not justify their release. At some point the blame has to fall on the individual. If they were to learn that their rehabilitation was an impossibility, I think that those who are truly disgusted by their crimes might even agree that they are too dangerous to be returned to a society where they have already done so much damage.

Works Cited

60 Minutes, January 11, 1998

The *New York Times*, June 24, 1997

ALTERNATIVE WRITING PROJECT: EVOLVING BELIEFS IN AN ACADEMIC FIELD

Locate a college or high school science, history, or literature textbook from forty or fifty years ago. Compare several specific points made in the decades-old book with points made in one of your textbooks in the same field.

In order to establish a context for what you observe, ask your instructor or a librarian to guide you to sources that discuss changes in theories in the field that your material is about. For example, in history, you could examine material about multicultural or gender-based approaches; in literature, material about "the canon"; in science, material about a specific discovery in genetics or physics.

Write an essay presenting the differences and similarities that you have found and comment on what beliefs they seem to reflect. Follow your instructor's directions for topic limitation, length, format, and citation methods.

11

Solving Problems

Writing to Propose Solutions

"Problems call forth our courage and our wisdom. . . . It is only because of problems that we grow mentally and spiritually."
—M. Scott Peck

Critical Thinking Focus: The problem-solving model
Writing Focus: Applying the problem-solving model
Reading Theme: Solving a social problem
Writing Project: Proposing a solution to a problem

P roblem solving is one of the most powerful thinking patterns we possess, and writing is the main vehicle we use to analyze challenging problems and propose solutions. On a personal level, you have probably written a letter or email about a problem you were dealing with. You may have been trying to sustain a romantic relationship with someone while geographically separated, helping a friend resolve a personal crisis, or writing to family members to coordinate a holiday reunion. To address civic problems, you or family members may have written letters to newspapers or petitioned your local government. Writing memos and position papers to solve problems is an integral part of most careers, from finance to filmmaking.

Although proposing solutions is a common form of writing, it is a very challenging one. In order to compose an insightful document, you need to do the following.

- *Define the problem clearly.* Your audience needs to understand that there *is* a problem and know exactly what it is.

- *Analyze the problem systematically.* Complex problems are often a confusing tangle of needs, ideas, frustrations, goals, and pieces of information. You need to disentangle the issues so that your audience can understand the core of the problem and what alternatives are possible.

- *Propose a well-reasoned solution.* After presenting a lucid analysis of the problem, along with feasible alternatives, you need to reach a conclusion that you support with thoughtful reasoning and solid evidence. As part of your proposed solution, you should explain why other alternative solutions are less desirable than yours. You should also address anticipated objections to your solution and explain how these difficulties can be overcome.

You will notice that the problem-solving method is similar to the decision-making method discussed in Chapter 4. However, this chapter presents the process in more detail; the focus is on problems instead of on decisions, and you will be considering social issues as well as personal ones. The chapter readings address societal problems. This chapter asks you to work with a powerful problem-solving method, and the Writing Project involves analyzing a social or personal problem that needs a solution.

Problems in Personal and Civic Life

Throughout your life, you will continually be solving problems. As a student, for example, you have to deal with a steady stream of academic assignments—quizzes, exams, papers, homework projects, and oral presentations. In order to solve these academic problems effectively—how to do well on an exam, for example—you need to define the problem (what areas will the exam cover, and what will be its format?), identify and evaluate various alternatives (what are possible study approaches?), and then combine all these factors to reach a solution (what will be your study plan and schedule?). Relatively simple problems like preparing for an exam do not require a systematic or complex analysis. You can solve them with a little effort and concentration. However, the difficult and complicated problems in your personal life, such as choosing a college major or ending a relationship, may be a different story. Because these are such crucial situations, you will need to to solve such problems in the best possible way by using all your creative and critical thinking skills.

The problems that exist in society also need the very best thinking of all citizens. Violent crime is far too common, parents feel stressed about their children's safety, drugs and alcohol continue to destroy lives, and both racism and sexism create conflicts. These problems may seem overwhelming, and it is true that you cannot control them in the same way that you can control your own life situations. Still, by thinking creatively and critically about them, and by gathering information, you can at least develop your own views about contending with them. Then you will be in a position to act on such problems and to vote for candidates whose positions are similar to yours.

Basics of the Problem-Solving Method

Consider the following problem:

My best friend is addicted to drugs, but he won't admit it. Jack always liked to drink, but I never thought too much about it. After all, a lot of people like to drink socially, get relaxed, and have a good time. But over the last few years, he's started using other drugs as well as alcohol, and it's ruining his life. He's stopped taking classes at the college and will soon lose his job if he doesn't change. Last week I told him that I was really worried about him, but he told me that he has no drug problem and that in any case it really isn't any of my business. I don't know what to do. I've known Jack since we were in elementary school together, and he's a wonderful person. It's as if he's in the grip of some terrible force and I'm powerless to help him.

In working through this problem, the writer of this description could only think of one possible course of action to try. But if he or she chose instead to approach the problem as a critical thinker, the writer would have to think carefully and systematically in order to reach a solution.

In order to think effectively in situations like this, we usually ask ourselves a series of questions, although we may not be aware of this mental process. These are the questions to ask in a five-step problem-solving method:

1. What is the *problem*?
2. What are the *alternatives*?
3. What are the *advantages* and/or *disadvantages* of each alternative?
4. What is the *solution*?
5. How well is the solution *working*?

Put yourself in the position of the student whose friend seems to have a serious addiction and apply the questions to that problem.

1. WHAT IS THE PROBLEM?

There are a variety of ways to define the problem. For instance, you might define it simply as "Jack has a drug dependency." You might view the problem as "Jack has a drug dependency, but he won't admit it." You might even define the problem as "Jack has a drug dependency, but he won't admit it—and I want to help him solve this problem." Notice that each redefinition of the problem results in a more specific definition, which in turn helps you better understand the essence of the problem and your responsibility with respect to it.

2. WHAT ARE THE ALTERNATIVES?

In dealing with this problem, you can consider a wide variety of possible actions before selecting the best ones. Identify some of the alternatives.

1. Speak to my friend in a candid and forceful way to convince him that he has a serious drug dependency.

2. _____

3. _____

3. WHAT ARE THE ADVANTAGES AND DISADVANTAGES OF EACH ALTERNATIVE?

Evaluate the strengths and weaknesses of each alternative you have identified so that you can weigh your choices and determine the best course of action.

1. Speak to my friend in a candid and forceful way to convince him that he has a serious problem.

   Advantage: He may respond to my direct emotional appeal, acknowledge that he has a problem, and seek help.

   Disadvantage: He may react angrily, further alienating me from him and making it more difficult for me to have any influence on him.

2. _____

   Advantage: _____

   Disadvantage: _____

3. _____

   Advantage: _____

   Disadvantage: _____

4. WHAT IS THE SOLUTION?

After evaluating the various alternatives, select the one you think would be most effective for solving the problem and describe the sequence of steps you would take to act on that alternative.

Alternative: _____

Steps:

    1. _____

    2. _____

5. HOW WELL IS THE SOLUTION WORKING?

The final step in the process comes after you have begun to implement your choice of action. You review the solution and decide whether it is working well. If it is not, you must modify your solution or perhaps try an alternate solution you disregarded earlier. In this situation, trying to figure out the best way to help your friend recognize his dependency and seek treatment leads to a series of decisions. This is what the thinking process is all about—trying to make sense of what is going on in the world and acting appropriately in response. When we solve problems effectively, our thinking process exhibits a coherent organization, following the general approach just outlined.

If we can understand the way the mind operates when we are thinking effectively, we can apply this understanding to improve our thinking in new, challenging situations. In the remainder of this chapter, we will explore a more sophisticated version of this problem-solving approach and apply it to a variety of complex, difficult problems.

Thinking ↔ Writing Activity

Analyzing a Problem Solved Previously

1. Write a description of a problem you have recently solved.
2. Explain how you went about solving the problem. What were the steps, strategies, and approaches you used to understand the problem and to make an informed decision?
3. Analyze your thinking process by applying the five-step problem-solving method we have been exploring.
4. Share your problem with classmates and have them try to analyze and solve it. Then explain the solution you arrived at.

The Problem-Solving Method in Detail

Imagine yourself in the following situation. What would be your next move, and what are your reasons for deciding on it?

You are about to begin your second year of college, following a very successful first year. Until now, you have financed your education through a combination of savings, financial aid, and a part-time job (sixteen hours a week) at a local store. However, you just received a letter from your college telling that your financial aid package has been reduced by half due to budgetary problems. The letter concludes, "We hope this aid reduction will not prove to be too great an inconvenience." From your perspective, the loss of aid isn't an inconvenience—it's a disaster! Your budget last year was already tight, and with your job, you barely had enough time to study, participate in a few college activities, and have a modest (but essential) social life. To make matters worse, your mother has been ill, reducing her income and creating financial problems at home. You're panicking—what in the world are you going to do?

As noted earlier, at first a difficult problem often seems like a confused tangle of information, feelings, alternatives, opinions, considerations, and risks. The problem just described is a complicated situation that does not seem to have a single simple solution. Without applying a systematic approach, your thoughts might wander through the tangle of issues in this manner:

I want to stay in school, . . . but I'm not going to have enough money. . . . I could work more hours at my job, . . . but I might not have enough time to study and get top grades . . . and if all I'm doing is working and studying, what about my social life? . . . and what about Mom and the kids? They might need my help. . . . I could drop out of school for a while, . . . but if I don't stay in school, what kind of future do I have?

Very often, when faced with difficult problems like this one, you simply may not know where to begin to try to solve them. Every issue is connected to many others. Frustrated by not knowing where to take the first step, you may give up trying to understand the problem. Or you may behave in one of the following ways:

1. Act impulsively without thought or consideration (e.g., "I'll just quit school").

2. Follow someone else's advice without seriously evaluating the suggestion (e.g., "Tell me what I should do—I'm tired of thinking about this").

3. Do nothing as you wait for events to make the decision for you (e.g., "I'll just wait and see what happens").

None of these approaches is likely to succeed in the long run, and each can gradually reduce your confidence in dealing with complex problems. An alternative to these reactions is to *think critically* about the problem, analyzing it with an organized approach based on the following five-step method.

Detailed Method for Solving Problems

Step 1: What is the problem?

    a. What do I know about the situation?

    b. What results am I seeking in this situation?

    c. How can I define the problem?

Step 2: What are the alternatives?

    a. What are the boundaries of the problem situation?

    b. What alternatives are possible within these boundaries?

Step 3: What are the advantages and disadvantages of each alternative?

    a. What are the advantages?

    b. What are the disadvantages?

    c. What additional information do I need in order to evaluate this alternative?

Step 4: What is the solution?

    a. Which alternative(s) will I pursue?

    b. What steps can I take to act on this/these alternative(s)?

Step 5: How well is the solution working?

    a. What is my evaluation?

    b. What adjustments are necessary?

Even when we are using an organized method for working through difficult problems and arriving at thoughtful conclusions, our minds may not always work in a logical, step-by-step fashion. Effective problem solvers typically pass through all the steps we will be examining, but not always in sequence.

Instead, the best problem solvers take a flexible approach to the process, one in which they utilize a repertoire of problem-solving strategies as needed. Sometimes, exploring the various alternatives helps them to go back and redefine the original problem. Similarly, seeking to implement the solution can often suggest a new alternative or alternatives that combine the best points of previous ones. This approach is shown in Figure 11.1

The key point is that although the problem-solving steps are presented in a

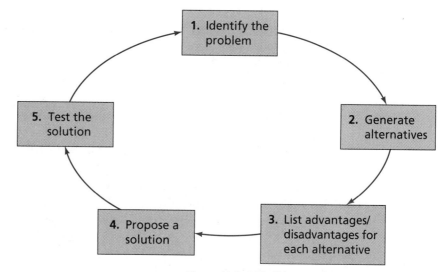

Figure 11.1 A Flexible Approach to Problem Solving

logical sequence here, you need not follow them in a mechanical and unimaginative fashion. At the same time, in learning a problem-solving method like this, it is generally not wise to skip steps because each one deals with an important aspect of the problem. As you become more proficient in using the method, you will find that you can apply its concepts and strategies to problem solving in an increasingly flexible and natural fashion, just as learning the basics of an activity like driving a car gradually results in a more integrated performance of the skills involved.

BEFORE YOU BEGIN: ACCEPTING THE PROBLEM

To solve a problem, you must first be willing to *accept* the problem by acknowledging that it exists and committing yourself to trying to solve it. Sometimes you may have difficulty recognizing there is a problem unless it is pointed out to you. At other times, you may actively resist acknowledging a problem, even when it is pointed out to you. The person who confidently states, "I don't really have any problems," sometimes has very serious problems—but is simply unwilling to acknowledge them.

However, mere acknowledgment is not enough to solve a problem. Once you have identified a problem, you must commit yourself to solving it. Successful problem solvers are highly motivated and willing to persevere through the many challenges and frustrations of the problem-solving process. How do you find this motivation and commitment? There are not simple answers, but the following strategies may help:

- *List the benefits.* Making a detailed list of the benefits you will derive from successfully dealing with the problem is a good place to begin. Such a process helps you clarify why you might want to tackle the problem, motivates you to get started, and serves as a source of encouragement when you encounter difficulties or lose momentum.

- *Formalize your acceptance.* You can formalize your acceptance of a problem by "going on record," either by preparing a signed declaration or by signing a "contract" with someone else. This formal commitment can serve as an explicit statement of original intentions to which you can refer if your resolve weakens.

- *Accept responsibility for your life.* Former U.S. Attorney General Robert F. Kennedy, who was assassinated in 1968, once said, "Some people see things as they are, and ask, 'Why?' I see things as they could be, and ask, 'Why not?'" You have the potential to control the direction of your own life, but to do so, you must accept your freedom to choose and the responsibility that goes with it.

- *Create a "worst case" scenario.* Some problems persist because people are able to ignore their possible implications. When you create a worst-case scenario, you remind yourself, as graphically as possible, of the potentially disastrous consequences of your actions. For example, looking at vivid color photographs and research conclusions can remind a person that excessive smoking, drinking, or eating can lead to myriad health problems and social and psychological difficulties as well as death.

- *Identify the constraints.* If you are having trouble accepting a problem, it is usually because something is holding you back. For example, you might be concerned about the amount of time and effort involved, you might be reluctant to confront the underlying issues the problem represents, you might be worried about finding out unpleasant things about yourself or others, or you might be inhibited by other problems in your life, such as a tendency to procrastinate. Whatever the constraints, using this strategy involves identifying and describing all the factors that are preventing you from attacking the problem and then addressing them one at a time.

STEP 1: WHAT IS THE PROBLEM?

The problem-solving process begins by determining exactly what the central issues of the problem are. Otherwise, your chances of solving it are considerably reduced. You may even spend time trying to solve the wrong problem. For instance, consider the different formulations of the following problems. How might they lead a person in different directions when trying to solve it?

"School is boring" versus "I am bored in accounting class."

"I'm unloveable" versus "I was just turned down for a date."

In each of these cases, a very general conclusion (first formulation) has been replaced by a more specific characterization of the problem (second formulation).

The general conclusions ("I'm a failure") do not suggest productive ways of resolving the difficulties. They are too absolute, too all-encompassing. On the other hand, the more specific descriptions of the problem situation ("I just failed an exam") do permit you to attack problems with useful strategies. In short, the way you define a problem determines not only how you will go about solving it, but whether you feel that the problem can be solved at all. Correct identification of a problem is essential if you are going to be able to successfully analyze it and reach an appropriate conclusion. Incorrectly identifying the problem can lead to pursuing an unproductive, even destructive, course of action.

Consider the problem of the college student whose financial aid package was cut in half (page 423) and analyze it using this problem-solving method. Ask:

1. What do I know about the situation?
2. What results am I aiming for in this situation?
3. How can I define the problem?

Step 1A: What do I know about the situation? Solving a problem begins with determining what you *know* to be the case and what you *think* may be the case. To explore the problem successfully, you need to have a clear idea of the details of your beginning circumstances. Sometimes a situation may appear to be a problem when it really isn't, simply because your information isn't accurate. Suppose you are convinced that someone you are attracted to doesn't reciprocate your interest. If this belief is inaccurate, your "problem" doesn't really exist.

You can identify and organize what you know about the problem situation by posing key questions. By asking—and trying to answer—questions of fact, you are establishing a sound foundation for exploring your problem. Imagine that you are the student described earlier who is facing a reduction in financial aid. Answer the following questions of fact—who? what? where? when? how? why?—about your problem.

- *Who* are the people involved in this situation?
  Who will benefit from my solving this problem?
  Who can help me solve this problem?

- *What* are the various parts or dimensions of the problem?
  What are my strengths and resources for solving this problem?

- *When* did the problem begin?
  When should the problem be resolved?

- *How* did the problem arise or develop?

- *Why* is solving this problem important to me?

  Why is this problem difficult to solve?

- Additional questions: _____

Step 1B: What results am I aiming for in this situation? The second part of answering the question "What is the problem?" consists of identifying the specific results or objectives you are trying to achieve. The results will eliminate the problem if you are able to achieve them. Whereas the first part of step 1 oriented you in terms of the history of the problem and the current situation, this part encourages you to look to the future. To identify results, you need to ask yourself the question "What are the objectives that, once achieved, will solve this problem?" For instance, one of the results or objectives in the sample problem might be having enough money to pay for college. Describe additional results you might be trying to achieve in this situation.

1. Having enough money to pay for college.

2. _____

3. _____

4. _____

Step 1C: How can I define the problem? After exploring what you know about the problem and the results you want to achieve, you need to conclude step 1 by defining the problem as clearly and specifically as possible. This is a crucial task in the problem-solving process because this definition will determine the direction of your analysis. To define the problem, you need to identify its central issue(s). Sometimes defining the problem is relatively straightforward, such as "trying to find enough time to exercise."

Often, however, identifying the central issue of a problem is a much more complex process. For example, the statement "My problem is relating to other people" suggests a complicated situation with many interacting variables that resists simple definition. In fact, you may not even begin to develop a clear idea of the problem until you engage in the process of trying to solve it. Or you might begin by believing that your problem is, say, not having the ability to succeed but end by concluding that the problem is really a fear of success.

As you will see, the same insights also apply to societal problems. For example, the problem of high school dropouts might initially be defined in terms of problems in the school system whereas later formulations might identify drug use or social pressure as the core of the problem.

Although there are no simple formulas for defining challenging problems, you can try several strategies to identify the central issue most effectively:

- *View the problem from different perspectives.* As you saw in Chapters 2, 6, and 7, perspective taking is a key ingredient of thinking critically; it can also help you to zero in on many problems. When you describe how various individuals might view a given problem—such as the high school dropout rate—the essential ingredients of the problems begin to emerge. In the student financial-aid problem, how would you describe the student's perspective? the college's perspective? the student's mother's perspective?

- *Identify component problems.* Larger problems are often composed of component problems. To define a larger problem, it is often necessary to identify and describe the subproblems that comprise it. A student's poor school performance, for instance, might result from a number of factors like ineffective study habits, inefficient time management, and preoccupation with a personal problem. Defining, and dealing effectively with, a larger problem means defining and dealing with the subproblems first. Can you identify two possible subproblems in the financial-aid problem?

- *State the problem clearly and specifically.* A third defining strategy is to state the problem as clearly and specifically as possible as you examine your objectives for solving it. Stating this sort of precise description of the problem is an important step toward solving it. If you state the problem in very general terms, you won't have a clear idea of how best to proceed in dealing with it. However, if you can describe it in specific terms, your description will begin to suggest actions you can take to solve the problem. Examine the differences between the statements of the following problem:

    General: "My problem is money."

    More specific: "My problem is needing to budget my money so that I won't always run out of it near the end of the month."

    Most specific: "My problem is my need to develop the habits and discipline to budget my money so that I won't always run out of it near the end of the month."

Review your analysis of the student's financial-aid problem; then state the problem in writing as clearly and specifically as you can.

STEP 2: WHAT ARE THE ALTERNATIVES?

Once you have identified a problem clearly and specifically, your next move is to examine each possible action that might help you to solve it. Before you list the alternatives, however, it makes sense to explore the situation's boundaries to determine which actions are possible and which are not.

Step 2A: What are the boundaries of the problem situation? Boundaries are limits that you simply cannot change. They are part of the problem, and they must be accepted and dealt with. For example, in the case involving the loss of financial aid, the fact that a day has only twenty-four hours must be accepted as part of the problem situation. There is no point in developing alternatives that ignore this fact. At the same time, you must be careful not to identify as boundaries circumstances that *can* be changed. For instance, again imagining yourself as the student with the financial-aid problem, you might assume that your problem must be solved in your current location, without realizing that transferring to a less expensive college is one of your options. Identify additional boundaries that might be part of this sample situation and list some of the questions you should answer about these boundaries.

Step 2B: What alternatives are possible within these boundaries? After you have established a general notion of the boundaries of the problem situation, you can proceed to identify the possible courses of action that can occur within them. Of course, identifying all the possible alternatives is not always easy; in fact, that may be part of your problem. Often we cannot see a way out of a problem because our thinking is set in certain ruts, fixed in certain perspectives. We may be blind to other approaches, either because we reject them without seriously considering them ("That will never work!") or because they simply do not occur to us. You can use several strategies to overcome these obstacles:

- *Discuss the problem with other people.* Discussing possible alternatives with others uses a number of the aspects of critical thinking we explored in Chapter 2. Thinking critically involves being open to seeing situations from different viewpoints and discussing ideas with others in an organized way. Both of these abilities are important in solving problems. As critical thinkers we live—and solve problems—in a community, not simply by ourselves. Other people can often suggest alternatives we haven't thought of since they are outside the situation and thus have a more objective perspective, and since they naturally view the world differently than we do because of their past experiences and their personalities. In addition, discussions are often creative experiences that generate ideas participants would not have come up with on their own. The dynamics of these interactions lead to products that are greater than the individual "sum" of the ideas of those involved.

- *Brainstorm ideas.* Group brainstorming, a method introduced by Alex Osborn, builds on the strengths of working with other people to generate ideas and solve problems. In a typical brainstorming session, a group of people work together to propose as many ideas as possible in a specific time period. As ideas are produced, they are not judged or evaluated, as this tends to inhibit the free flow of ideas and discourage people from making suggestions. Evaluation is deferred until a later stage. People are encouraged to build on the ideas of others since the most creative ideas are often generated through the constructive interplay of various minds.

- *Change your location.* Your perspectives on a problem are often tied to the circumstances in which the problem exists. For example, a problem you may be having in school is connected with your daily experiences and your habitual reactions to them. Sometimes you need a fresh perspective, which you can gain by getting away from the problem situation so that you can view it more clearly in a different light. Perhaps spending a day or two out of town will help, or even taking a long walk in a different neighborhood.

Using these strategies, as well as your own reflections, identify as many alternatives to help solve the financial-aid problem that you can think of.

1. Attend school part-time

2. _____

3. _____

4. _____

STEP 3: WHAT ARE THE ADVANTAGES AND DISADVANTAGES OF EACH ALTERNATIVE?

Once you have identified the various alternatives, your next step is to evaluate them. Each possible course of action offers certain advantages in the sense that if you were to select that alternative, there would be some positive results. At the same time, each possible course of action probably also has disadvantages in the sense that if you were to select that alternative, you may incur a cost or risk some negative results. Determine how helpful each course of action would or would not be in solving the problem.

Step 3A: What are the advantages of each alternative? The alternative we listed in step 2 for the sample problem ("Attend college part-time") might include the following advantages.

Alternative	Advantages
Attend college part-time	1. Doing this would remove some of the immediate time and money pressures I am experiencing while still allowing me to prepare for the future.
	2. I would have more time to focus on the courses that I would be taking and to work additional hours.

Identify the advantages of each of the alternatives that you listed in step 2. Be sure that your responses are thoughtful and specific. For example, how many additional hours could you work? How much additional income would doing that generate?

Step 3B: What are the disadvantages of each alternative?   The alternative we listed in step 2 for the sample problem might include the following disadvantages.

Alternative	Disadvantages
Attend college part-time	1. It would take me much longer to complete my schooling, thus delaying my progress toward my goals. 2. I might lose motivation and drop out before completing school because the process would be taking so long. 3. Being a part-time student might threaten my eligibility for financial aid.

Now identify the disadvantages of each of the alternatives that you listed for step 2. Make sure that your responses are thoughtful and specific. For example, how much longer would it take you to get your degree?

Step 3C: What additional information do I need to evaluate each alternative? The next part of step 3 consists of determining what you must know (information needed) to best evaluate and compare the alternatives. For each alternative there are questions that you must answer in order to establish which alternatives make sense and which do not. In addition, you need to figure out where to get this information (sources).

The information—and the sources of it—that must be located for the first alternative in the sample problem might include the following.

Information Needed

1. How long will it take me to complete my schooling?
2. How long can I continue in school without losing interest and dropping out?
3. Will I threaten my eligibility for financial aid if I become a part-time student?

   Sources: Myself, other part-time students, school counselors, financial aid office

Identify the information needed and the sources of this information for each of the alternatives that you identified on pages 430–431. Be sure that your responses are thoughtful and specific.

STEP 4: WHAT IS THE SOLUTION?

The purpose of steps 1 through 3 is to analyze your problem in a systematic and detailed fashion—to work through the problem in order to become thoroughly familiar with it and with possible solutions. After breaking down the problem in this way, your final step should be to try to put the pieces back together—that is, to decide on a thoughtful course of action based on your increased understanding. Even though conducting this sort of problem analysis does not guarantee finding a specific solution to the problem, it should deepen your understanding of exactly what the problem is. And in locating and evaluating the alternatives, it should give you some very good ideas about the general direction in which you should move and the immediate steps you should take.

Step 4A: Which alternative(s) will I pursue? There is no simple formula or recipe to tell you which alternatives to select. As you work through the different courses of action that are possible, you may find that you can immediately rule some out. In the sample problem, for example, you may know with certainty that you do not want to attend college part-time (alternative 1) because you will forfeit your remaining financial aid. However, it may not be as simple to select which of the other alternatives you wish to pursue. How do you decide?

The decisions we make usually depend on what we believe is most important to us. These beliefs are known as **values.** Our values are the starting points of our actions and strongly influence our decisions. For example, if we value staying alive (as most of us do), we will make many decisions each day that express this value—eating proper meals, not walking in front of moving traffic, and so on.

Our values help us set priorities in life—that is, decide what aspects of our lives are most important to us. We might decide that for the present, going to school is more important than having an active social life. In this case, going to school has higher priority than having an active social life. Unfortunately, our values are not always consistent with each other—we may have to choose either going to school or having an active social life. Both activities may be important to us; they are simply not compatible with each other. Very often the *conflicts* between our values constitute the problem. Let's examine some strategies for selecting alternatives that might help to solve the sample problem.

- *Evaluate and compare alternatives.* Although each alternative may have certain advantages and disadvantages, not all advantages are equally desirable or potentially effective. For example, giving up college entirely would certainly solve some aspects of the sample problem, but its obvious disadvantages would rule out this solution for most people. Thus, it makes sense to try to evaluate and rank the various alternatives on the basis of how effective they are likely to be and how they match up with your value system. A good place to begin is at the "Results" stage, step 1B. Examine each of your alternatives and evaluate how well it will contribute to achieving the results you are aiming for in the situation. You may want to rank the alternatives or develop your own rating system to assess their relative effectiveness.

After evaluating the alternatives in terms of their anticipated *effectiveness*, the next step is to evaluate them in terms of their *desirability* relative to your needs, interests, and value system. Again, you can use either a ranking or a rating system to assess their relative desirability. After completing these two separate evaluations, you can select whatever alternatives seem most appropriate. Review the alternatives you identified in the sample problem; then rank or rate them according to their potential effectiveness and desirability.

- *Synthesize a new alternative.* After reviewing and evaluating the alternatives you have generated, you may develop a new alternative that combines the best qualities of several options while avoiding the disadvantages some of them would have if implemented exclusively. In the sample problem, you might combine attending college part-time during the academic year with attending school during summer session so that progress toward your degree wouldn't be impeded. Examine the alternatives you identified and develop a new option that combines the best elements of several of them.

- *Try out each alternative—in your imagination.* Focus on each alternative and try to imagine, as concretely as possible, what it would be like if you actually selected it. Visualize what impact your choice would have on your problem and what the implications would be for your life as a whole. By trying out the alternative in your imagination, you can sometimes avoid unpleasant results or unexpected consequences. As a variation of this strategy, you can sometimes test alternatives on a very limited basis in a practice situation. Suppose you are trying to overcome your fear of speaking out in groups. You can practice various speaking techniques with your friends or family until you find an approach that works for you.

Step 4B: What steps can I take to act on the alternative(s) chosen? Once you have decided on an alternative to pursue, your next move is to plan what steps to take in acting on it. Planning the specific steps you will take is extremely important. Although thinking carefully about your problem is necessary, it is not enough if you hope to solve the problem. You have to take action. In the sample problem, for example, imagine that one of the alternatives you have selected is "find additional sources of income that will enable me to work part-time and attend school full-time." The specific steps you would take might include these:

- Contact the financial aid office to learn what other forms of monetary aid are available and how to apply for them.

- Contact some local banks to find out what sort of student loans they offer.
- Look for a higher-paying job to earn more money without working additional hours.
- Discuss your problem with students in similar circumstances in order to generate new ideas.

Identify the steps you would have to take to pursue the alternative(s) you identified on pages 430–431.

Plans, of course, do not implement themselves. Once you know what actions are needed, you have to make a commitment to taking the necessary steps. This is where many people stumble in the problem-solving process; they remain paralyzed by inertia or fear. To overcome such blocks and inhibitions, you sometimes need to re-examine your original acceptance of the problem, perhaps making use of some of the strategies you explored on page 426. Once you get started, the rewards of actively attacking your problem are often enough incentive to keep you focused and motivated.

STEP 5: HOW WELL IS THE SOLUTION WORKING?

As you work toward reaching a reasonable and informed conclusion, be wary of falling into the trap of thinking that there is only one "right" solution and that if you don't figure out what it is and implement it, all is lost. You should remind yourself that any analysis of problem situations, no matter how careful and systematic, is ultimately limited. You simply cannot anticipate or predict everything that will happen in the future. Consequently, every decision you make is provisional in the sense that your ongoing experience will inform you whether it is working out or needs to be modified.

Maintaining this perspective is precisely the attitude of the critical thinker—someone who is receptive to new ideas and experiences and flexible enough to change or modify beliefs on the basis of new information. Critical thinking is not a compulsion to find the "right" answer or make the "correct" decision; it is a continuing process of exploration and discovery.

Step 5A: What is my evaluation?   In many cases the relative effectiveness of your efforts will be apparent. In other cases you will find it helpful to pursue a more systematic evaluation along the lines suggested in the following strategies.

- *Compare the results with the goals.* The essence of evaluation is comparing the results of your efforts with your initial goals. For example, the goals of the sample problem are embodied in the results you specified on page 428. Compare the anticipated results of the alternative(s) you selected.

To what extent will your choice(s) meet these goals? Are any goals not likely to be met by your alternative(s)? If so, which ones? Could they be addressed by other alternatives? Asking these questions and others will help you to assess the success of your efforts and will provide a foundation for future decisions.

- *Get other perspectives.* As you have seen throughout the problem-solving process, getting the opinions of others is a productive strategy at virtually every stage, and this is certainly true of evaluation. Other people often can provide perspectives that are both different and more objective than your own. Naturally, the evaluations of others are not always better or more accurate than yours, but even when they are not, reflecting on these different views usually deepens your understanding of the situation. It is not always easy to accept the evaluations of others, but keeping an open mind about outside opinions is a very valuable attitude to cultivate, because it will stimulate and guide you to produce your best efforts.

  To receive specific, practical feedback, you need to ask specific, practical questions that will elicit such information. General questions ("What do you think of this?") typically receive overly general, unhelpful answers ("It sounds okay to me"). Be focused when soliciting feedback and remember that you do have the right to ask people for *constructive* comments—that is, to provide suggestions for improvement rather than just to tell you what they think is wrong. For example, you could say, "What do you know about me that you think will help me maintain my motivation to stay in school—even if it takes two years longer than I had planned?" Or you can ask, "Do you have any ideas about how I can cut my expenses by 10 percent each month?"

Step 5B: What adjustments are necessary?   As a result of your review, you may discover that the alternative you selected is not feasible or is not producing satisfactory results. Suppose that in the sample problem, you cannot find additional sources of income that will allow you to work part-time instead of full-time. In that case, you simply have to go back and review the other alternatives to identify another possible course of action. At other times, you may find that the alternative you selected is succeeding fairly well but requires some adjustments as you continue to work toward your goals. In fact, this is a typical situation that you should expect to occur. Even when things initially appear to be working reasonably well, an active thinker continues to ask questions such as "What might I have overlooked?" and "How could I have done this differently?" Of course, asking—and trying to answer—questions like this is even more essential if solutions are hard to come by (as they usually are in real-world problems) and if you are to retain the flexibility and optimism you will need to tackle a new option.

"As soon as one problem is solved, another rears its ugly head."

Thinking ↔ Writing Activity

Analyzing a Problem in Your Life

This Thinking-Writing Activity provides you with the opportunity to apply the problem-solving method to an important *un*solved problem in your own life. First, select from your own life a problem that you are currently grappling with and have not been able to solve. Next, strengthen your acceptance of the problem by using several strategies described on page 426. Finally, work your way through each of the problem-solving steps outlined on page 424. Write out responses to the questions in each step, and be sure to discuss your problem with other class members to generate fresh perspectives and unusual alternatives that might not have occurred to you. Your ultimate goal is to decide on a provisional solution to your problem and establish a plan of action that will help you move in the right direction.

The following are some common problems other students have described. Your instructor may have you work in a group with other class members to analyze one of these problems as a way of preparing you to analyze one of your own.

Problem 1: Taking Tests. One of my problems is that I have trouble taking tests. It's not that I don't study. What happens is that when I get the test, I panic and forget what I have studied. For example, in my social science class, the teacher told the class on Tuesday that there would be a test on Thursday. That afternoon I went home and began studying for the test. By Thursday I knew most of the material, but when the test was handed out, I got nervous and my mind went blank. For a long time I just stared at the test, and I ended up failing it.

Problem 2: Smoking. My problem is tobacco use. I have been smoking cigarettes for over five years. At first I did it because I liked the image, and most of my friends were also smoking. Gradually, I got hooked. It's such a part of my life now that I don't know if I can quit. Having a cup of coffee, studying, talking to people—it just also seems natural to have a cigarette in my hand. I know there are a lot of good reasons for me to stop. I've even tried a few times, but I always end up bumming cigarettes from friends and then giving up on quitting. I don't want my health to go up in smoke, but I don't know what to do.

Problem 3: Learning English. One of the serious problems in my life is learning English. It is not easy to learn a new language, especially when you live in an environment where only your native language is spoken. When I came to this country three years ago, I could speak almost no English. I have learned a lot, but my lack of fluency is causing problems with my studies and my social relationships.

Solving Social Problems

The problems we have analyzed up to this point are "personal" problems in the sense that they represent individual challenges we encounter as we live our lives. Problems are not only of a personal nature, however. We also face problems as members of a community, the larger society, and the world.

As with personal problems, we need to approach these kinds of problems in an organized and thoughtful way in order to explore the issues, develop a clear understanding, and decide on an informed plan of action. For example, racism and prejudice directed toward African Americans, Hispanics, Asians, Jews, homosexuals, and other groups seems to be on the rise at many college campuses. There has been an increase of overt racist incidents at colleges and universities during the past several years, which is particularly disturbing given the lofty egalitarian ideals of higher education. Experts from different fields have offered a variety of explanations to account for this behavior. Think about why you believe these racial and ethnic incidents are occurring.

Making sense of this kind of complex, challenging situation is not a simple process. Although the problem-solving method we have been using in this chapter is a powerful approach, its successful application depends on having sufficient information about the situation to be solved. Therefore, it is often necessary for us to find articles and other sources of information to develop informed opinions about the problem we are investigating.

The famous newspaperman H. L. Mencken once said, "To every complex question there is a simple answer—and it's wrong!" In this chapter we have seen that complex problems do not have simple solutions, whether they are personal problems or larger social problems like racial prejudice or world hunger. We have also learned that by working through these complex problems thoughtfully and systematically, we can achieve a deeper understanding of their many interacting elements as well as develop and implement strategies for solving them.

A thoughtful problem solver employs all the critical thinking abilities we have examined in this book. And although we might agree with Mencken's evaluation of simple answers to complex questions, we would expand upon it: "To many complex questions there are complex answers—and these are well worth pursuing."

The following reading selections deal with significant social problems. The information that they present provides a framework for thoughtful analysis and productive solutions. The *Washington Post* article "Public Backs Uniform U.S. Voting Rules" tells of solutions suggested by the general public in a poll addressing the problem of varied voting procedures. "Young Hate" examines the insidious problem of intolerance on college campuses while "When Is It Rape?" explores the issues related to the problem of "date rape."

Thinking ↔ Writing Activity

Analyzing a Social Problem

Work with one of the following articles. After reading the article carefully, identify and analyze the problem being discussed by using the problem-solving method explained in this chapter.

FROM

Public Backs Uniform U.S. Voting Rules

Poll Finds Wide Support for Guidelines on Ballots, Closing Times, Recounts
Washington Post, December 18, 2000
BY RICHARD MORIN AND CLAUDIA DEANE

Overwhelming majorities of Americans support a major overhaul of election rules and procedures, including a uniform poll-closing time across the nation, a standard ballot design and consistent rules for conducting recounts, according to a *Washington Post*–ABC News poll.*

The survey also found that most Americans want to strip authority for setting election rules from local and state officials and give the federal government the task of imposing order on election laws and practices that currently vary widely from state to state and county to county.

---

*This *Washington Post*–ABC News poll is based on telephone interviews with 807 randomly selected adults nationwide, conducted December 14–15. The margin of error for overall results is plus or minus 3.5 percentage points. Sampling error is only one of many potential sources of error in this or any other public opinion poll. Interviewing was conducted by TNS Intersearch of Horsham, PA.

On question after question, the survey suggests that the public, sharply divided at virtually every bizarre twist and turn of the [2000] post-election drama, has finally found common ground: Nearly everyone agrees that America must change the way it elects its president.

Some reform-minded voters were startled by the variety and the vagaries of voting procedures revealed since Election Day. "I just always assumed it was standardized. Wasn't that stupid of me?" laughed Karin Cabell, 36, a customer service representative who lives in Hazleton, PA, and voted to elect Texas Gov[ernor] George W. Bush. "I thought everyone voted in the same manner everywhere. It just blew my mind."

5   Despite the broad call to change the way Americans vote, the *Post*–ABC News poll found the post-election struggle has done little immediate damage to public confidence in the political system or major political institutions, including the U.S. Supreme Court, the Congress and the presidency. Nine in 10 Americans still remain confident that, despite all its problems, this country still has "the best system of government in the world." . . .

But most voters agreed that the election revealed problems. . . . Fifty-three percent of those interviewed said the post-election controversies have revealed "serious problems in this country's system of electing the president"—up 21 percentage points from a *Post*–ABC News poll conducted five days after the Nov[ember] 7 election.

Most voters agree it's a mess, and 61 percent said they want the federal government to clean it up. Barely a third said they wanted to allow local and state governments to continue to set election law.

"I think they need to get a system that everybody votes the same in the United States," said Nancy Jackson, 74, a retiree living in Detroit who voted for Gore. "It partially made me sick, it was so unfair. I'm African American. There are so many young black people we got out to vote, and then their vote wasn't counted."

Nine in 10 said they want a federal law that requires the same design and layout for all presidential election ballots, retiring forever Palm Beach County's confusing "butterfly ballot."

10   About two in three say they want the federal government to outlaw punch-card ballots, ending the possibility of future debates over whether to count or ignore dimpled, pregnant or hanging chads.

Nearly nine in 10 want a federal rule that requires all jurisdictions in the country to use one kind of voting machine, effectively eliminating current claims that some voters, including many African Americans and other minorities, were discriminated against because they live in areas that use older, more error-prone voting machines.

And a similar percentage—86 percent—said they want standard rules for how and when recounts are done, issues that were at the heart of the vote-counting controversy in South Florida that ultimately was decided by the U.S. Supreme Court.

Two in three support a single poll-closing time across the country, which would eliminate the possibility that news reports of election results from states in the East would affect voter turnout in the West.

"I don't have a chance to get to the voting booth until 6 or 6:30 at night, and I'm intending to vote for Bush, and they're telling me Gore already won," said Rachel Glidden, 44, an operating room technician from La Luz, NM. "That's not fair. I haven't even had a chance to voice my say, and I already know what the result is."

15   Overall, the survey suggests Americans want uniformity and simplicity in their election laws as well as in the way people vote.

"I never thought we still used punch machines," said Yvonne Martin, 55, a retiree who voted for Gore and lives in Rome, NY. "That's primitive."

Martin said it's critical that the federal government and not the states or counties establish the rules and decide which type of voting machine is used—with no exceptions granted. "One state can really mess it up if they don't do it right," she said. "I mean, Mickey Mouse could have done a better job than the election officials in Florida."

About six in 10 Americans say they want to amend the U.S. Constitution to select the president by direct popular vote and do away with the electoral college. If this system had been in place this year, Gore would have won because he received approximately 300,000 more votes nationwide than Bush.

"The electoral college is completely outdated," said Ed Evans, 29, a computer analyst in Beaverton, OR, who voted for Gore. "It may have made sense 120 years ago. But we have the technology now that we can get an accurate popular vote. This is the country that invented democracy. Al Gore won the popular vote. It was the will of the people to elect him as president, but because of the electoral college, George Bush will be the president."

20   But most political observers say lawmakers and residents of less-populated states fear that presidential candidates would ignore them in favor of the larger states, and would effectively block any constitutional amendment.

That argument clearly resonates with the public, the *Post*–ABC News poll found. When those who supported direct election of a president were asked, "What if it meant presidential candidates paid less attention to the smaller states," the proportion favoring direct election dropped from 62 percent to 42 percent.

"I have mixed feelings," Martin said. "I realize that some of the states are smaller and they're helped [by the electoral college]. But in many ways, the public really feels the vote has been taken out of our hands in this election. It needs to be looked at but maybe not changed."

Critical Reading Questions

1. Think back or research the 2000 presidential election between Al Gore and George W. Bush and describe what you consider to have been the three biggest problems responsible for the post-election confusion.

2. Imagine that you have been appointed U.S. Commissioner of Election

Reform. What steps would you take to solve the three problems that you have identified?

Young Hate

BY DAVID SHENK

Death to gays. Here is the relevant sequence of events: On Monday night Jerry Mattioli leads a candlelight vigil for lesbian and gay rights. *Gays are trash.* On Tuesday his name is in the school paper and he can hear whispers and feel more, colder stares than usual. On Wednesday morning a walking bridge in the middle of the Michigan State campus is found to be covered with violent epithets warning campus homosexuals to *be afraid, very afraid,* promising to *abolish faggots from existence,* and including messages specifically directed at Mattioli. Beginning Friday morning fifteen of the perpetrators, all known to Mattioli by name and face, are rounded up and quietly disciplined by the university. *Go home faggots.* On Friday afternoon Mattioli is asked by university officials to leave campus for the weekend, for his own safety. He does, and a few hours later receives a phone call from a friend who tells him that his dormitory room has been torched. MSU's second annual "Cross-Cultural Week" is over.

"Everything was ruined," Mattioli says. "What wasn't burned was ruined by smoke and heat and by the water. On Saturday I sat with the fire investigator all day, and we went through the room, literally ash by ash. . . . The answering machine had melted. The receiver of the telephone on the wall had stretched to about three feet long. That's how intense the heat was."

"Good news!" says Peter Jennings. A recent *Washington Post*–ABC News poll shows that integration is up and racial tension is down in America, as compared with eight years ago. Of course, in any trend there are fluctuations, exceptions. At the University of Massachusetts at Amherst, an estimated two thousand whites chase twenty blacks in a clash after a 1986 World Series game, race riots break out in Miami in 1988 and in Virginia Beach in 1989; and on college campuses across the country, our nation's young elite experience an entire decade's aberration from the poll's findings: incidents of ethnic, religious, and gender-related harassment surge throughout the eighties.

Greatest hits include Randy Bowman, a black student at the University of Texas, having to respectfully decline a request by two young men wearing Ronald Reagan masks and wielding a pistol to exit his eighth-floor dorm room through the window; homemade T-shirts, *Thank God for AIDS* and *Aryan by the Grace of God,* among others, worn proudly on campus; Jewish student centers shot at, stoned, and defaced at Memphis State, University of Kansas, Rutgers (*Six million, why not*), and elsewhere; the black chairperson of United Minorities Council at U Penn getting a dose of hi-tech hate via answering machine: *We're going to lynch you, nigger shit. We are going to lynch you.*

What is the best way to deal with people espousing racist views? How can we best encourage such people to develop more open-minded ideas? © John S. Zeedick/Liaison.

What do you think motivates people to join an organization like the KKK? What is the source of their ideas regarding other races? © Corbis Sygma.

5   The big picture is less graphic, but just as dreadful: reports of campus harassment have increased as much as 400 percent since 1985. Dropout rates for black students in predominantly white colleges are as much as five times higher than white dropout rates at the same schools and black dropout rates at black schools. The Anti-Defamation League reports a sixfold increase in anti-Semitic episodes on campuses between 1985 and 1988. Meanwhile, Howard J. Ehrlich of the National Institute Against Prejudice and Violence reminds us that "up to 80 percent of harassed students don't report the harassment." Clearly, the barrage of news reports reveals only the tip of a thoroughly sour iceberg.

Colleges have responded to incidents of intolerance—and the subsequent demands of minority rights groups—with the mandatory ethnic culture classes and restrictions on verbal harassment. But what price tranquility? Libertarian and conservative student groups, faculty, and political advisors lash out over limitations on free speech and the improper embrace of liberal political agendas. "Progressive academic administrations," writes University of Pennsylvania professor Alan Charles Kors in the *Wall Street Journal*, "are determined to enlighten their morally benighted students and protect the community from political sin."

Kors and kind bristle at the language of compromise being attached to official university policy. The preamble to the University of Michigan's new policy on discriminatory behavior reads, in part, "Because there is tension between freedom of speech, the right of individuals to be free from injury caused by discrimination, and the University's duty to protect the educational process . . . it may be necessary to have varying standards depending on the locus of regulated conduct." The policy tried to "strike a balance" by applying different sets of restrictions to academic centers, open areas, and living quarters, but in so doing, hit a wall. Before the policy could go into effect, it was struck down in a Michigan court as being too vague. At least a dozen schools in the process of formulating their own policies scurried in retreat as buoyant free-speech advocates went on the offensive. Tufts University president Jean Mayer voluntarily dismissed his school's "Freedom of Speech versus Freedom from Harassment" policy after a particularly inventive demonstration by late-night protesters who used chalk, tape, and poster board to divide the campus into designated free speech, limited speech, and non-free speech zones. "We're not working for a right to offensive speech," says admitted chalker Andrew Zappia, co-editor of the conservative campus paper, *The Primary Source*. "This is about protecting free speech, in general, and allowing the community to set its own standards about what is appropriate. . . .

"The purpose of the Tufts policy was to prosecute people for what the university described as 'gray area'—meaning unintentional—harassment." Zappia gives a hypothetical example: "I'm a Catholic living in a dorm, and I put up a poster in my room [consistent with my faith] saying that homosexuality is bad. If I have a gay roommate or one who doesn't agree with me, he could have me prosecuted, not because I hung it there to offend him, but because it's gray area harassment. . . . The policy was well intended, but it was dangerously vague. They used words like *stigmatizing, offensive, harassing*—words that are very difficult to define."

Detroit lawyer Walter B. Connolly, Jr., disagrees. He insists that it's quite proper for schools to act to protect the victims of discrimination as long as the restrictions stay out of the classroom. "Defamation, child pornography, fighting words, inappropriate comments on the radio—there are all sorts of areas where the First Amendment isn't the preeminent burning omnipotence in the sky. . . . Whenever you have competing interests of a federal statute [and] the Constitution, you end up balancing."

10   If you want to see a liberal who follows this issue flinch, whisper into his or her ear the name Shelby Steele. Liberals don't like Steele, an (African American) English professor at California's San Jose State; they try to dismiss him as having no professional experience in the study of racial discrimination. But he's heavily into the subject, and his analyses are both lucid and disturbing. Steele doesn't favor restrictions on speech, largely because they don't deal with what he sees as the problem. "You don't gain very much by trying to legislate the problem away, curtailing everyone's rights in the process," he says. In a forum in which almost everyone roars against a shadowy, usually nameless contingent of racist thugs, Steele deviates, choosing instead to accuse the accusers. He blames not the racists, but the weak-kneed liberal administrators and power-hungry victims' advocates for the mess on campuses today.

"Racial tension on campus is the result more of racial equality than inequality," says Steele. "On campuses today, as throughout society, blacks enjoy equality under the law—a profound social advancement. . . . What has emerged in recent years . . . in a sense as a result of progress . . . is *a politics of difference*, a troubling, volatile politics in which each group justifies itself, its sense of worth and its pursuit of power, through difference alone." On nearly every campus, says Steele, groups representing blacks, Hispanics, Asians, gays, women, Jews, and any combinations therein solicit special resources. Asked for—often demanded, in intense demonstrations—are funds for African-American (Hispanic . . .) cultural centers, separate (face it, segregated) housing, ethnic studies programs, and even individual academic incentives—at Penn State, minority students are given $275 per semester if they earn a C average, twice that if they do better than 2.75.

These entitlements, however, do not just appear *deus ex machina*. Part two of Steele's thesis addresses what he calls the "capitulation" of campus presidents. To avoid feelings of guilt stemming from past discrimination against minority groups, Steele says, "[campus administrators have] tended to go along with whatever blacks put on the table, rather than work with them to assess their real needs. . . . Administrators would never give white students a theme house where they could be 'more comfortable with people of their own kind,' yet more and more universities are doing this for black students." Steele sees white frustration as the inevitable result.

"White students are not invited to the negotiating table from which they see blacks and others walk away with concessions," he says. "The presumption is that they do not deserve to be there, because they are white. So they can only be defensive, and the less mature among them will be aggressive."

Course, some folks see it another way. The students fighting for minority rights aren't wicked political corrupters, but champions of a cause far too long suppressed by the white male hegemony. Responsive administrators are engaged not in capitulation, but in progress. And one shouldn't look for the cause of this mess on any campus, because he doesn't live on one. His address used to be the White House, but then he moved to 666 St. Cloud Road. Ronald Reagan, come on down.

15   *Dr. Manning Marble, University of Colorado:* "The shattering assault against the economic, social, and political status of the black American community as a whole [is symbolized by] the Reagan Administration in the 1980s. The Civil Rights Commission was gutted; affirmative action became a 'dead letter'; social welfare, health care, employment training, and educational loans were all severely reduced. This had a disproportionately more negative impact upon black youth."

The "perception is already widespread that the society at large is more permissive toward discriminatory attitudes and behaviors, and less committed to equal opportunity and affirmative action," concluded a 1988 conference at Northern Illinois University. John Wiener, writing in *The Nation*, attacks long-standing institutions of bigotry, asserting, for example, that "racism is endemic to the fraternity subculture," and praises the efforts of some schools to double the number of minority faculty and increase minority fellowships. On behalf of progressives across the land, Wiener writes off Shelby Steele as someone who is content to "blame the victim."

So the machine has melted, the phone has stretched to where it is useless. This is how intense the heat is. Liberals, who largely control the administration, faculty, and students' rights groups of leading academic institutions, have, with virtually no intensive intellectual debate, inculcated schools with their answers to the problem of bigotry. Conservatives, with a long history of insensitivity to minority concerns, have been all but shut out of the debate, and now want back in. Their intensive pursuit of the true nature of bigotry and the proper response to it—working to assess the "real needs" of campuses rather than simply bowing to pressure—deserves to be embraced by all concerned parties, and probably would have been by now but for two small items: (a) Reagan, their fearless leader, clearly *was* insensitive to ethnic/feminist concerns (even Steele agrees with this); and (b) some of the more coherent conservative pundits *still* show a blatant apathy to the problems of bigotry in this country. This has been sufficient ammunition for liberals who are continually looking for an excuse to keep conservatives out of the dialogue. So now we have clashes rather than debates: on how much one can say, on how much one should have to hear. Two negatives: one side wants to crack down on expression, the other on awareness. The machine has melted, and it's going to take some consensus to build a new one. Intellectual provincialism will have to end before young hate ever will.

A Month in the Life of Campus Bigotry

April 1 Vandals spray-paint "Jewhaters will pay" and other slogans on the office walls of *The Michigan Daily* (University of Michigan) in response to editorials condemning Israel for policies regarding the Palestinians. Pro-Israeli and pro-Palestinian shanties defaced; one is burned.

U of M: Fliers circulated over the weekend announce "White Pride Month." Southern Connecticut State University reportedly suspends five fraternity officers after racial brawl.

April 2 Several gay men of the University of Connecticut are taunted by two students, who yell "faggot" at them.

20 **April 3** The University of Michigan faculty meet to discuss a proposal to require students to take a course on ethnicity and racism.

April 4 Students at the University of California at Santa Barbara suspend hunger strike after university agrees to negotiate on demands for minority faculty hiring and the changed status of certain required courses.

April 5 The NCAA releases results of survey on black student athletes, reporting that 51 percent of black football and basketball players at predominantly white schools express feelings of being different; 51 percent report feelings of racial isolation; 33 percent report having experienced at least six incidents of individual racial discrimination.

The *New York Times* prints three op-ed pieces by students on the subject of racial tension on campus.

Charges filed against a former student of Penn State for racial harassment of a black woman.

April 6 University of Michigan: Hundreds of law students wear arm bands, boycott classes to protest lack of women and minority professors.

Michigan State University announces broad plan for increasing the number of minority students, faculty, and staff; the appointment of a senior advisor for minority affairs; and the expansion of multicultural conferences. "It's not our responsibility just to mirror society or respond to mandates," President John DiBioggio tells reporters, "but to set the tone."

April 7 Wayne State University (Detroit, Michigan) student newspaper runs retraction of cartoon considered offensive following protest earlier in the week.

Controversy develops at the State University of New York at Stony Brook, where a white woman charges a popular black basketball player with rape. Player denies charges. Charges are dismissed. Protests of racial and sexual assault commence.

25 **April 12** Twelve-day sit-in begins at Wayne State University (Michigan) over conditions for black students on campus.

April 14 Racial brawl at Arizona State.

April 20 Demonstrations at several universities across the country (Harvard, Duke, Wayne State, Wooster College, Penn State, etc.) for improvements in black student life.

Separate escort service for blacks started at Penn State out of distrust of the regular service.

April 21 200-student sit-in ends at Arizona State University when administrators agree to all thirteen demands.

April 24 Proposed tuition increase at City Universities of New York turns into racial controversy.

30 **April 25** After eighteen months in office, Robert Collin, Florida Atlantic University's first black dean, reveals he has filed a federal discrimination complaint against the school.

Two leaders of Columbia University's Gay and Lesbian Alliance receive death threat. "Dear Jeff, I will kill you butt fucking faggots. Death to COLA!"

April 26 A black Smith College (Massachusetts) student finds note slipped under door, ". . . African monkey do you want some bananas? Go back to the jungle. . . ."

"I don't think we should have to constantly relive our ancestors' mistakes," a white student at the University of North Carolina at Greensboro tells a reporter. "I didn't oppress anybody. Blacks are now equal. You don't see any racial problems anymore."

White Student Union is reported to have been formed at Temple University in Philadelphia, "City of Brotherly Love."

April 28 Note found in Brown University (Rhode Island) dorm. "Once upon a time, Brown was a place where a white man could go to class without having to look at little black faces, or little yellow faces or little brown faces, except when he went to take his meals. Things have been going downhill since the kitchen help moved into the classroom. Keep white supremecy [sic] alive!!! Join the Brown chapter of the KKK today." Note is part of series that began in the middle of the month with "Die Homos." University officials beef up security, hold forum.

April 29 Controversy reported over proposed ban on verbal harassment at Arizona State.

April 30 Anti-apartheid shanty at University of Maryland, Baltimore County, is defaced. Signs read "Apartheid now," and "Trump Plaza."

University of California at Berkeley: Resolution is passed requiring an ethnic studies course for all students.

University of Connecticut: Code is revised to provide specific penalties for acts of racial intolerance.

Critical Reading Questions

1. Discuss with classmates the problems related to diversity on your own campus. Have you witnessed or heard about incidents of bigotry directed at people because of their race, sexual orientation, or some other distinguishing quality? If so, describe one such incident and analyze

why you think it occurred. If not, explain why your campus doesn't seem to suffer from problems related to intolerance and discrimination.

2. Have you ever been the victim of prejudice or discrimination? If so, describe one such experience and explain how the incident made you feel about yourself and the people victimizing you.

3. Using the problem-solving method from this chapter, analyze the problem of bigotry—on your campus, if you think it exists there—and develop some practical solutions for dealing with this troubling issue.

When Is It Rape?

BY NANCY GIBBS

Be careful of strangers and hurry home, says a mother to her daughter, knowing that the world is a frightful place but not wishing to swaddle a child in fear. Girls grow up scarred by caution and enter adulthood eager to shake free of their parents' worst nightmares. They still know to be wary of strangers. What they don't know is whether they have more to fear from their friends.

Most women who get raped are raped by people they already know—like the boy in biology class, or the guy in the office down the hall, or their friend's brother. The familiarity is enough to make them let down their guard, sometimes even enough to make them wonder afterward whether they were "really raped." What people think of as "real rape"—the assault by a monstrous stranger in the shadows—accounts for only one out of five attacks.

So the phrase "acquaintance rape" was coined to describe the rest, all the cases of forced sex between people who already knew each other, however casually. But that was too clinical for headline writers, and so the popular term is the narrower "date rape," which suggests an ugly ending to a raucous night on the town.

These are not idle distinctions. Behind the search for labels is the central mythology about rape; that rapists are always strangers, and victims are women who ask for it. The mythology is hard to dispel because the crime is so rarely exposed. The experts guess—that's all they can do under the circumstances—that while one in four women will be raped in her lifetime, less than 10 percent will report the assault, and less than 5 percent of the rapists will go to jail.

Women charge that date rape is the hidden crime; men complain it is hard to prevent a crime they can't define. Women say it isn't taken seriously; men say it is a concept invented by women who like to tease but not take the consequences. Women say the date-rape debate is the first time the nation has talked frankly about sex; men say it is women's unconscious reaction to the excesses of the sexual revolution. Meanwhile, men and women argue among themselves about the "gray area" that surrounds the whole murky arena of sexual relations, and there is no consensus in sight.

5   In court, on campus, in conversation, the issue turns on the elasticity of the word *rape*, one of the few words in the language with the power to summon a shared image of a horrible crime.

At one extreme are those who argue that for the word to retain its impact, it must be strictly defined as forced sexual intercourse: a gang of thugs jumping a jogger in Central Park, a psychopath preying on old women in a housing complex, a man with an ice pick in a side street. To stretch the definition of the word risks stripping away its power. In this view, if it happened on a date, it wasn't rape. A romantic encounter is a context in which sex *could* occur, and so what omniscient judge will decide whether there was genuine mutual consent?

Others are willing to concede that date rape sometimes occurs, that sometimes a man goes too far on a date without a woman's consent. But this infraction, they say, is not as ghastly a crime as street rape, and it should not be taken as seriously. The New York *Post*, alarmed by the Willy Smith case, wrote in a recent editorial, "if the sexual encounter, *forced or not*, has been preceded by a series of consensual activities—drinking, a trip to the man's home, a walk on a deserted beach at three in the morning—the charge that's leveled against the alleged offender should, it seems to us, be different than the one filed against, say, the youths who raped and beat the jogger."

This attitude sparks rage among women who carry scars received at the hands of men they knew. It makes no difference if the victim shared a drink or a moonlit walk or even a passionate kiss, they protest, if the encounter ended with her being thrown to the ground and forcibly violated. Date rape is not about a misunderstanding, they say. It is not a communications problem. It is not about a woman's having regrets in the morning for a decision she made the night before. It is not about a "decision" at all. Rape is rape, and any form of forced sex—even between neighbors, coworkers, classmates and casual friends—is a crime.

A more extreme form of that view comes from activists who see rape as a metaphor, its definition swelling to cover any kind of oppression of women. Rape, seen in this light, can occur not only on a date but also in a marriage, not only by violent assault but also by psychological pressure. A Swarthmore College training pamphlet once explained that acquaintance rape "spans a spectrum of incidents and behaviors, ranging from crimes legally defined as rape to verbal harassment and inappropriate innuendo." No wonder, then, that the battles become so heated. When innuendo qualifies as rape, the definitions have become so slippery that the entire subject sinks into a political swamp. The only way to capture the hard reality is to tell the story.

10   A 32-year-old woman was on business in Tampa last year for the Florida supreme court. Stranded at the courthouse, she accepted a lift from a lawyer involved in her project. As they chatted on the ride home, she recalls, "he was saying all the right things, so I started to trust him." She agreed to have dinner, and afterward, at her hotel door, he convinced her to let him come in to talk. "I went through the whole thing about being old-fashioned," she says. "I was a virgin until I was twenty-one. So I told him talk was all we were going to do."

But as they sat on the couch, she found herself falling asleep. "By now, I'm comfortable with him, and I put my head on his shoulder. He's not tried anything all evening, after all." Which is when the rape came. "I woke up to find him on top of me, forcing himself on me. I didn't scream or run. All I could think about was my business contacts and what if they saw me run out of my room screaming rape.

"I thought it was my fault. I felt so filthy, I washed myself over and over in hot water. Did he rape me? I kept asking myself. I didn't consent. But who's gonna believe me? I had a man in my hotel room after midnight." More than a year later, she still can't tell the story without a visible struggle to maintain her composure. Police referred the case to the state attorney's office in Tampa, but without more evidence it decided not to prosecute. Although her attacker has admitted that he heard her say no, maintains the woman, "he says he didn't know that I meant no. He didn't feel he'd raped me, and he wanted to see me again."

Her story is typical in many ways. The victim herself may not be sure right away that she has been raped, that she had said no and been physically forced into having sex anyway. And the rapist commonly hears but does not heed the protest. "A date rapist will follow through no matter what the woman wants because his agenda is to get laid," says Claire Walsh, a Florida-based consultant on sexual assaults. "First comes the dinner, then a dance, then a drink, then the coercion begins." Gentle persuasion gives way to physical intimidation with alcohol as the ubiquitous lubricant. "When that fails, force is used," she says. "Real men don't take no for an answer."

The Palm Beach case serves to remind women that if they go ahead and press charges, they can expect to go on trial along with their attacker, if not in a courtroom then in the court of public opinion. The New York *Times* caused an uproar on its own staff not only for publishing the victim's name but also for laying out in detail her background, her high-school grades, her driving record, along with an unattributed quote from a school official about her "little wild streak." A freshman at Carleton College in Minnesota, who says she was repeatedly raped for four hours by a fellow student, claims that she was asked at an administrative hearing if she performed oral sex on dates. In 1989 a man charged with raping at knife point a woman he knew was acquitted in Florida because his victim had been wearing lace shorts and no underwear.

15   From a purely legal point of view, if she wants to put her attacker in jail, the survivor had better be beaten as well as raped, since bruises become a badge of credibility. She had better have reported the crime right away, before taking the hours-long shower that she craves, before burning her clothes, before curling up with the blinds down. And she would do well to be a woman of shining character. Otherwise the strict constructionist definitions of rape will prevail in court. "Juries don't have a great deal of sympathy for the victim if she's a willing participant up to the nonconsensual sexual intercourse," says Norman Kinne, a prosecutor in Dallas. "They feel that many times the victim has placed herself in the situation." Absent eyewitnesses or broken bones, a case comes

down to her word against his, and the mythology of rape rarely lends her the benefit of the doubt.

She should also hope for an all-male jury, preferably composed of fathers with daughters. Prosecutors have found that women tend to be harsh judges of one another—perhaps because to find a defendant guilty is to entertain two grim realities: that anyone might be a rapist, and that every woman could find herself a victim. It may be easier to believe, the experts muse, that at some level the victim asked for it. "But just because a woman makes a bad judgment, does that give the guy a moral right to rape her?" asks Dean Kilpatrick, director of the Crime Victim Research and Treatment Center at the Medical University of South Carolina. "The bottom line is, Why does a woman's having a drink give a man the right to rape her?"

Last week the Supreme Court waded into the debate with a 7-to-2 ruling that protects victims from being harassed on the witness stand with questions about their sexual history. The Justices, in their first decision on "rape shield laws," said an accused rapist could not present evidence about a previous sexual relationship with the victim unless he notified the court ahead of time. In her decision, Justice Sandra Day O'Connor wrote that "rape victims deserve heightened protection against surprise, harassment, and unnecessary invasions of privacy."

That was welcome news to prosecutors who understand the reluctance of victims to come forward. But there are other impediments to justice as well. An internal investigation of the Oakland police department found that officers ignored a quarter of all reports of sexual assaults or attempts, though 90 percent actually warranted investigation. Departments are getting better at educating officers in handling rape cases, but the courts remain behind. A New York City task force on women in the courts charged that judges and lawyers were routinely less inclined to believe a woman's testimony than a man's.

The present debate over degrees of rape is nothing new; all through history, rapes have been divided between those that mattered and those that did not. For the first few thousand years, the only rape that was punished was the defiling of a virgin, and that was viewed as a property crime. A girl's virtue was a marketable asset, and so a rapist was often ordered to pay the victim's father the equivalent of her price on the marriage market. In early Babylonian and Hebrew societies, a married woman who was raped suffered the same fate as an adulteress—death by stoning or drowning. Under William the Conqueror, the penalty for raping a virgin was castration and loss of both eyes—unless the violated woman agreed to marry her attacker, as she was often pressured to do. "Stealing an heiress" became a perfectly conventional means of taking—literally—a wife.

20

It may be easier to prove a rape case now, but not much. Until the 1960s it was virtually impossible without an eyewitness; judges were often required to instruct jurors that "rape is a charge easily made and hard to defend against; so examine the testimony of this witness with caution." But sometimes a rape was taken very seriously, particularly if it involved a black man attacking a white woman—a crime for which black men were often executed or lynched.

Susan Estrich, author of *Real Rape*, considers herself a lucky victim. This is not just because she survived an attack 17 years ago by a stranger with an ice pick, one day before her graduation from Wellesley. It's because police, and her friends, believed her. "The first thing the Boston police asked was whether it was a black guy," recalls Estrich, now a University of Southern California law professor. When she said yes and gave the details of the attack, their reaction was, "So you were really raped." It was an instructive lesson, she says, in understanding how racism and sexism are factored into perceptions of the crime.

A new twist in society's perception came in 1975, when Susan Brownmiller published her book *Against Our Will: Men, Women and Rape.* In it she attacked the concept that rape was a sex crime, arguing instead that it was a crime of violence and power over women. Throughout history, she wrote, rape has played a critical function. "It is nothing more or less than a conscious process of intimidation, by which *all men* keep *all women* in a state of fear."

Out of this contention was born a set of arguments that have become politically correct wisdom on campus and in academic circles. This view holds that rape is a symbol of women's vulnerability to male institutions and attitudes. "It's sociopolitical," insists Gina Rayfield, a New Jersey psychologist. "In our culture men hold the power, politically, economically. They're socialized not to see women as equals."

This line of reasoning has led some women, especially radicalized victims, to justify flinging around the term *rape* as a political weapon, referring to everything from violent sexual assaults to inappropriate innuendoes. Ginny, a college senior who was really raped when she was sixteen, suggests that false accusations of rape can serve a useful purpose. "Penetration is not the only form of violation," she explains. In her view, *rape* is a subjective term, one that women must use to draw attention to other, nonviolent, even nonsexual forms of oppression. "If a woman did falsely accuse a man of rape, she may have had reasons to," Ginny says. "Maybe she wasn't raped, but he clearly violated her in some way."

25   Catherine Comins, assistant dean of student life at Vassar, also sees some value in this loose use of "rape." She says angry victims of various forms of sexual intimidation cry rape to regain their sense of power. "To use the word carefully would be to be careful for the sake of the violator, and the survivors don't care a hoot about him." Comins argues that men who are unjustly accused can sometimes gain from the experience. "They have a lot of pain, but it is not a pain that I would necessarily have spared them. I think it ideally initiates a process of self-exploration. 'How do I see women?' 'If I didn't violate her, could I have?' 'Do I have the potential to do to her what they say I did?' Those are good questions."

Taken to extremes, there is an ugly element of vengeance at work here. Rape is an abuse of power. But so are false accusations of rape, and to suggest that men whose reputations are destroyed might benefit because it will make them more sensitive is an attitude that is sure to backfire on women who are seeking justice for all victims. On campuses where the issue is most inflamed, male students are outraged that their names can be scrawled on a bathroom-wall list of rapists and they have no chance to tell their side of the story.

"Rape is what you read about in the New York *Post* about seventeen little boys raping a jogger in Central Park," says a male freshman at a liberal-arts college, who learned that he had been branded a rapist after a one-night stand with a friend. He acknowledges that they were both very drunk when she started kissing him at a party and ended up back in his room. Even through his haze, he had some qualms about sleeping with her: "I'm fighting against my hormonal instincts, and my moral instincts are saying, 'This is my friend and if I were sober, I wouldn't be doing this.'" But he went ahead anyway. "When you're drunk, and there are all sorts of ambiguity, and the woman says 'Please, please' and then she says no sometime later, even in the middle of the act, there still may very well be some kind of violation, but it's not the same thing. It's not rape. If you don't hear her say no, if she doesn't say it, if she's playing around with you—oh, I could get squashed for saying it—there is an element of say no, mean yes."

The morning after their encounter, he recalls, both students woke up hung over and eager to put the memory behind them. Only months later did he learn that she had told a friend that he had torn her clothing and raped her. At this point in the story, the accused man starts using the language of rape. "I felt violated," he says, "I felt like she was taking advantage of me when she was very drunk. I never heard her say 'No!,' 'Stop!,' anything." He is angry and hurt at the charges, worried that they will get around, shatter his reputation and force him to leave the small campus.

So here, of course, is the heart of the debate. If rape is sex without consent, how exactly should consent be defined and communicated, when and by whom? Those who view rape through a political lens tend to place all responsibility on men to make sure that their partners are consenting at every point of a sexual encounter. At the extreme, sexual relations come to resemble major surgery, requiring a signed consent form. Clinical psychologist Mary P. Koss of the University of Arizona in Tucson, who is a leading scholar on the issue, puts it rather bluntly: "It's the man's penis that is doing the raping, and ultimately he's responsible for where he puts it."

30   Historically, of course, this has never been the case, and there are some who argue that it shouldn't be—that women too must take responsibility for their behavior, and that the whole realm of intimate encounters defies regulation from on high. Anthropologist Lionel Tiger has little patience for trendy sexual politics that make no reference to biology. Since the dawn of time, he argues, men and women have always gone to bed with different goals. In the effort to keep one's genes in the gene pool, "it is to the male advantage to fertilize as many females as possible, as quickly as possible and as efficiently as possible." For the female, however, who looks at the large investment she will have to make in the offspring, the opposite is true. Her concern is to "select" who "will provide the best set-up for their offspring." So, in general, "the pressure is on the male to be aggressive and on the female to be coy."

No one defends the use of physical force, but when the coercion involved is purely psychological, it becomes hard to assign blame after the fact. Journalist Stephanie Gutmann is an ardent foe of what she calls the date-rape dogmatists. "How can you make sex completely politically correct and completely safe?" she asks. "What a horribly bland, unerotic thing that would be! Sex is, by nature, a risky endeavor, emotionally. And desire is a violent emotion. These people in the date-rape movement have erected so many rules and regulations that I don't know how people can have erotic or desire-driven sex."

Nonsense, retorts Cornell professor Andrea Parrot, co-author of *Acquaintance Rape: The Hidden Crime.* Seduction should not be about lies, manipulation, game playing or coercion of any kind, she says. "Too bad that people think that the only way you can have passion and excitement and sex is if there are miscommunications, and one person is forced to do something he or she doesn't want to do." The very pleasures of sexual encounters should lie in the fact of mutual comfort and consent: "You can hang from the ceiling, you can use fruit, you can go crazy and have really wonderful sensual erotic sex, if both parties are consenting."

It would be easy to accuse feminists of being too quick to classify sex as rape, but feminists are to be found on all sides of the debate, and many protest the idea that all the onus is on the man. It demeans women to suggest that they are so vulnerable to coercion or emotional manipulation that they must always be escorted by the strong arm of the law. "You can't solve society's ills by making everything a crime," says Albuquerque attorney Nancy Hollander. "That comes out of the sense of overprotection of women, and in the long run that is going to be harmful to us."

What is lost in the ideological debate over date rape is the fact that men and women, especially when they are young, and drunk, and aroused, are not very good at communicating. "In many cases," says Estrich, "the man thought it was sex, and the woman thought it was rape, and they are both telling the truth." The man may envision a celluloid seduction, in which he is being commanding, she is being coy. A woman may experience the same event as a degrading violation of her will. That some men do not believe a woman's protests is scarcely surprising in a society so drenched with messages that women have rape fantasies and a desire to be overpowered.

35   By the time they reach college, men and women are loaded with cultural baggage, drawn from movies, television, music videos and "bodice ripper" romance novels. Over the years they have watched Rhett sweep Scarlett up the stairs in *Gone With the Wind;* or Errol Flynn, who was charged twice with statutory rape, overpower a protesting heroine who then melts in his arms; or Stanley rape his sister-in-law Blanche du Bois while his wife is in the hospital giving birth to a child in *A Streetcar Named Desire.* Higher up the cultural food chain, young people can read of date rape in Homer or Jane Austen, watch it in *Don Giovanni* or *Rigoletto.*

The messages come early and often, and nothing in the feminist revolution has been able to counter them. A recent survey of sixth- to ninth-graders in Rhode Island found that a fourth of the boys and a sixth of the girls said it was acceptable for a man to force a woman to kiss him or have sex if he has spent money on her. A third of the children said it would not be wrong for a man to rape a woman who had had previous sexual experiences.

Certainly cases like Palm Beach, movies like *The Accused* and novels like

Avery Corman's *Prized Possessions* may force young people to reexamine assumptions they have inherited. The use of new terms, like *acquaintance rape* and *date rape*, while controversial, has given men and women the vocabulary they need to express their experiences with both force and precision. This dialogue would be useful if it helps strip away some of the dogmas, old and new, surrounding the issue. Those who hope to raise society's sensitivity to the problem of date rape would do well to concede that it is not precisely the same sort of crime as street rape, that there may be very murky issues of intent and degree involved.

On the other hand, those who downplay the problem should come to realize that date rape is a crime of uniquely intimate cruelty. While the body is violated, the spirit is maimed. How long will it take, once the wounds have healed, before it is possible to share a walk on a beach, a drive home from work or an evening's conversation without always listening for a quiet alarm to start ringing deep in the back of the memory of a terrible crime?

Critical Reading Questions

1. If rape is "sex without consent," as the author of this article suggests, how would you define *date rape*? Provide an example to illustrate your definition.

2. Do you know someone who has been involved in a date rape situation? If so, describe this person's experience (without divulging his or her identity).

3. Some people explain date rape as a breakdown of communication; others see it as the result of the sex roles in our culture. Explain why you believe date rape occurs.

4. Some feminists contend that even false accusations of rape serve a useful purpose. How can society protect the rights of both the accused and the accuser in an effort to ensure that justice is served?

5. Imagine that you were the Dean of Students at your college. Describe what actions you would take to address this problem and explain your reasons for taking these actions. Discuss your ideas with other class members.

Taking a Problem-Solving Approach to Writing

Problem solving provides you with a framework that you can use in much of your writing. A problem-solving approach can assist you in generating ideas and organizing information for most subjects. For example, you can look at a writing assignment as a problem and use a modification of the five-step method as a way to work on it:

1. What exactly is the assignment?

2. What are some alternative ways to complete it?

3. What are the advantages and disadvantages of the alternatives?

4. What is the best way for me to complete this assignment?

5. After some drafting ask: How is my solution to the problem of the assignment working out?

Then, as you write any paper, you can use modifications of the problem-solving steps at any stage. Look at the thesis as a problem and ask the preceding questions about it. Look at any part of the paper and ask the questions. Actually, effective writers do this to some extent—perhaps less systematically—as they draft, plan, and revise. As you recall, Chapter 4 sets forth a similar pattern for approaching revision.

Also, research projects are often seen and approached as problems. Just as you can apply a problem-solving approach to any writing assignment, so can you apply it to most research projects (see Chapter 13).

When you are asked to write a proposal or a paper about solving a problem, as this chapter's Writing Project does, you can use the problem-solving method as a system of organization. The following principles for writing about problem-solving may not apply to every instance, but they should help you convert answers to the questions in the problem-solving model into an effective essay.

1. Be aware of the needs of your audience. You may have lived with the problem for so long, or researched it so thoroughly, that you almost cannot remember a time when the details were not familiar to you. However, your readers need specific details about background, history, special circumstances, and so forth, and they need to have this information presented in an order that they can understand. So unless you have some pressing reason not to do so, begin by presenting this information in the clearest order you can devise. As you write your essay, continually ask yourself, "Does my audience have all the information necessary to understand the point I am trying to make?"

2. Present all the information your audience needs in order to understand the problem before you begin to discuss alternative solutions.

3. Include a thesis statement indicating that you are going to discuss alternative solutions. You may also want to mention your proposed solution.

4. Discuss each alternative solution by explaining what it would involve and by presenting its advantages and disadvantages. Provide enough specific information to allow your audience to see these advantages and disadvantages. Don't just say, "A program could be developed to help students see how to avoid date rape." Instead, begin a paragraph by saying: "Respected student leaders from honor societies and athletic teams could participate in a forum explaining how excessive

drinking, certain drugs, and certain behaviors can lead to situations in which date rape might occur."

5. Present the alternative solutions in the order that will most help your audience comprehend them and understand why you would select the one you did.

6. Conclude your essay by stating one solution, or some combination of solutions, and explain clearly why you chose it. If you have had time to implement the solution, tell whether or not it is working. If you have not yet implemented it, explain how you will determine whether or not it is working.

Writing Project: Proposing a Solution to a Problem

This chapter includes both readings and Thinking-Writing Activities that encourage you to familiarize yourself with the problem-solving model and the steps required for implementing it. Be sure to reread what you wrote for those activities, as you may be able to use some of that material when completing this project.

> Write an essay in which you apply the five-step problem-solving method to a local, national, or international problem or to a personal problem. If you are analyzing a social problem, you will have to do some research and locate several articles that provide background information about and discussion of the problem. If you are analyzing a personal problem, you will enrich your paper by consulting some sources that pertain to it. Be sure to document all sources honestly and correctly in the format required by your instructor.
>
> After you have drafted your essay, revise it to the best of your ability. Follow your instructor's directions about focus, length, scope, format, and so on.

Begin by considering the key elements in the Thinking-Writing Model.

THE WRITING SITUATION

Purpose   You have a variety of purposes here. You can use this opportunity to learn about a major problem in order to arrive at the best possible solution—and thus become a better-informed citizen. You might be able to help solve the problem if you are involved in the situation. Also, you will be practicing the creative and critical thinking involved in the problem-solving model.

Audience   As usual, you will have several audiences for your paper. While working through the problem-solving model, you will be your own audience since in describing the problem and working through the alternative solutions, you will be determining the solution to the problem. As you begin to shape the answers to the model's questions into an essay, your audience will include readers other than yourself, so their needs should now occupy your attention.

Your classmates can be a valuable audience for peer review of a draft. They can react as intelligent readers who are not as knowledgeable as you are about the problem and its possible solutions but who can become interested as they read your description of it and your evaluation of the possible solutions. Finally, your instructor remains the audience who will judge how well you have analyzed the problem. As a writing teacher, he or she cares about a clear focus, logical organization, relevant details and examples, and accepted usage. Keep these factors in mind as you revise, edit, and proofread.

Subject   Problems are problems precisely because they are difficult to think about and to solve. Often this is true because we don't have enough accurate information to arrive at an intelligent solution. Working on this paper will encourage you to find good information and to think about viable alternative solutions. Since you will be deeply involved in the subject, select a problem that you care about, one that is challenging—but compelling—to write about.

Writer   This assignment provides you an opportunity to learn more about a problem that you care about but perhaps do not know enough about to propose a solid solution. You will have the chance to use the Internet or your library's holdings to find articles that will increase your knowledge of the problem and give you the pleasure of having additional expertise about something significant. If your instructor asks or allows you to write about a personal problem, you might not have to do as much research, but you will have the opportunity to work out something that is of immediate concern. Equipped with the problem-solving model and the direction it provides, you should work as a confident writer as you complete this assignment.

THE WRITING PROCESS

The following sections will guide you through the stages of generating, planning, drafting, and revising as you work on an essay about solving an important problem. Try to be particularly conscious of both the critical thinking you do while working through the problem-solving model and the critical thinking and decision making you do as you revise.

Generating Ideas   You may find yourself in one of three situations:

1. If your instructor's directions specify that you must write about a particular local, national, or international problem, you must begin there. You might start by working through the problem-solving model and answering each question on the basis of your current knowledge. Then you will be able to see what additional information you need to know and thus will be aware of what to look for as you research the problem.

2. If your instructor's directions allow you to choose any important local, national, or international problem, you might begin by brainstorming a list of each of these types of problems. Then you can select the one that seems most important, the one that interests you most, or the one about which you are most informed.

3. If your instructor's directions allow you to write about a personal problem, you might begin by brainstorming a list of problems you now face. It might help to make three columns: school problems, work problems, and personal problems. Then you can pick one, preferably one that you have to solve soon and for which you would need to gather information to write about.

Whichever situation describes yours, once you have worked through the problem-solving model, you will almost certainly spot gaps in your information. Think about how much additional information you will need in order to evaluate each of the alternative solutions. Then locate that information, asking a librarian for assistance if necessary.

Once you have filled in all the gaps and selected a solution—and a means to determine whether it is working—you are ready to turn your attention to presenting your information to your audience.

Defining a Focus   Write a thesis statement that will make clear to your audience that you are going to explore a problem-solving situation. You might decide to write something like "After thinking about the problem carefully, I realize that I have only two possible choices." Or you might decide to name the possible choices: "Newton's possible solutions to its budget problem include raising more revenue, cutting the budget, or some combination of the two." You may even decide to announce your chosen solution in your thesis statement: "After carefully weighing the alternatives, raising more revenue while continuing to cut the budget appears to be the best choice."

Organizing Ideas   The five-step method for solving problems fits well with essay structure. Your description of the problem together with its necessary history and other background information will give you a working introduction which can end with your thesis statement. Each of the alternative solutions, explained in as much detail as possible, along with its advantages and disadvantages, will provide one section of the body (one or more paragraphs). Your determination of the best solution and how it could be monitored will provide a conclusion.

Drafting Begin with the easiest paragraph to draft. Keep your written answers to each part of the problem-solving model in front of you.

Remember to begin each section of the body with a topic sentence that names the alternative solution being discussed. If you are discussing advantages or disadvantages in separate paragraphs, draft topic sentences that prepare your readers for that information—such as "Unfortunately, cutting the budget further will create serious disadvantages for many citizens." Then provide specific information.

You will, of course, have to determine the best order in which to arrange the sections. Experiment until you find the one that seems most helpful to your audience. Switch the sections around on your word processor. You could even cut up a printout and tape the sections together in different arrangements until you discover one that seems smooth and logical.

Be sure to indicate the sources of your information. You do not have to use the correct citation format in a draft, but you do have to remind yourself exactly where you obtained the material so that you won't forget to cite it as you finish the paper.

In your conclusion, name the solution you have chosen. You may want to explain why you selected it if you think that will not be obvious to your audience. Remember to explain how you will evaluate the effectiveness of your solution.

Revising One of the best revision strategies is to get an audience's reactions to your draft. Your classmates, or peers, can help you see where your draft is already successful and where it needs improvement. If your instructor allows class time for peer review, be sure to have a draft ready so that you can participate. (Your instructor may ask you to use the Peer Review activity located on pages 65–66 and 105–107). Be ready to help your classmates and to be helped.

After thinking about your classmates' questions and using them to improve your draft, you will be ready to work through the following revision concerns. If you did not have a chance to work with classmates, let your draft sit for a day or two and then examine it with these questions in mind.

1. **Think big.** Look at your draft as a whole.

   - Does it focus on a problem and on alternative solutions for it?

   - Have you addressed the problem in your thesis?

   - Could you state the thesis in a more effective place (or places)?

   - Where do you explain the solution(s) that you recommend?

   - Have you followed the problem-solving method in your organization?

- Could the paragraphs be connected more effectively?
- Have you documented all sources?
- Does the draft fulfill the assignment in terms of focus and length?

2. **Think medium.** Look at your draft paragraph by paragraph.

- Does the introduction talk about or lead up to the problem?
- Can you make the paragraph that states the thesis more effective?
- Have you presented each alternative solution in a separate paragraph?
- Does every paragraph have a specific example pertaining to the problem or to a possible solution?
- Could you make the concluding paragraph more effective? Does it present the solution that you propose? If not, should it?

3. **Think small.** Look at your draft sentence by sentence.

- Could you word the sentences that state the problem better?
- Could you word the sentences that state the alternatives better?
- Are any sentences difficult to understand?
- Are any sentences too long? Are any too short and choppy?
- How could you rewrite such sentences to make them smoother?
- How could you make any vague sentences more specific?
- Do you need to correct any sentences for Standard English grammar and usage?

4. **Think "picky."** Look at your draft as your fussiest critic might.

- Which words might not be clear or appropriate?
- Are any words misspelled?
- Are there any punctuation errors?
- Are all citation formats correct? Check your handbook again.
- Are all the pages numbered?
- Can your draft be revised into a neatly formatted paper?
- Is there anything else that you can do to improve your draft?

Editing and Proofreading After you have prepared a final draft, check it for any grammar or punctuation mistakes. Run the spell checker program, but don't rely on it to detect all errors. If you can, ask a friend who is a good editor to read your paper for a final check.

The following essays show how two students responded to this assignment—one student writing about a personal problem and citing informally, the other writing about a social problem and citing according to Modern Language Association (MLA) format.

STUDENT WRITING

Problem Solving Made Easy

BY JANA RIGGLE

Life is full of problems; some are easier to solve than others, and some never get solved. I have had a problem for the last two years that, so far, I have not been able to solve. My problem is that my mother and my boyfriend do not get along. This problem has always seemed too overwhelming to deal with. I didn't know where to start until I read *Critical Thinking, Thoughtful Writing*. This book shows its readers how to break their problems into steps in order to reach solutions. It gave me a place to start, and I will now try to solve my problem by using the book's five-step problem solving process.

Critical Thinking, Thoughtful Writing says, "The first step in solving problems is to determine exactly what the central issues of the problems are." In my problem the central issue is that my mother, due to her dislike of my boyfriend, refuses to acknowledge him, which in turn hurts me. I want my mother to not mind being in the same room with my boyfriend for more than five minutes. Most of all, I want my mother to stop fighting with him.

The second step to solving a problem according to this book is to "examine each of the possible actions that might help solve the problem." It also helps, the book says, to determine the actions which are impossible or the boundaries of the problem. The boundary of my problem is that I will not leave my boyfriend in order for my mother to stop fighting with him. This leaves me with the alternatives of going on with the situation as it is, having my mother and my boyfriend sit down and try to talk out their differences, or not having my boyfriend around my house.

The third step is to determine the advantages and disadvantages of each alternative. The first alternative—letting the problem continue and hoping it will solve itself—presents me with the disadvantage that I have to continue to put up with the problem and it may never be solved. The advantage is that maybe, just maybe, it will solve itself without any interference from me. My second alternative of having my boyfriend and my mother sit down and try to talk out their differences has the disadvantage that she may decide she dislikes him more. The advantage is that she may start to see in him what I do and start to get along with him. The last alternative of not having him near my house has the advantage of not having to listen to her put him down but the disadvantage that the problem will not really be solved.

The fourth step, the book says, is to find a solution by pursuing an alternative and acting on it. The alternative that looks best to me is to try to have my mother and my boyfriend sit down and have a civil conversation. I think they will agree to it if I tell them how much it means to me, that I love them both, and that I just want her to learn to tolerate him.

The fifth step of this process is to determine how well the solution is working and what adjustments to the original solution might have to be made. Since I have not yet tried out my solution, I cannot evaluate it.

I believe that these five steps really work and that they can simplify even the most confusing problems. The steps offer specific ways to move towards solving a problem, which can turn an overwhelming problem into something that a person can deal with.

Critical Thinking About Uncritical Drinking

BY JOSHUA BARTLETT

There is widespread agreement that excessive student drinking is a serious problem on many college campuses. However, there are different views on the causes of this problem and on the best solutions for it. In this paper I will present some perspectives on the problem of student drinking and conclude with suggestions on how to deal with this serious threat to student health and success.

Why do college students drink to excess? According to many experts, it is mainly due to the influence of the people around them. When most students enter college, they do not have a drinking problem. However, although few realize it, they are entering a culture in which alcohol is often the drug of choice, one that can easily destroy their lives. According to some estimates, 80 to 90 percent of the students on many campuses drink alcohol, and many of them are heavy drinkers (Engs 543). One study found that nearly 30 percent of university students consume more than 15 alcoholic drinks a week (Gerson A43). An additional study found that among those who drink at least once a week, 92 percent of the men and 82 percent of the women consume at least five drinks in a row, and half said they wanted to get drunk (Rosenberg 81).

The results of all this drinking are predictably deadly. Virtually all college administrators agree that alcohol is the most widely used drug among college students and that its abuse is directly related to emotional problems and violent behavior, ranging from date rape to death (Dodge, "Campus Crime" A33+; Leatherman A33). For example, at one university, a 20-year-old woman became drunk at a fraternity party and fell to her death from the third floor ("Clemson" A3). At another university, two students were killed in a drunk-driving accident after drinking alcohol at an off-campus fraternity house; the families of both students have filed lawsuits against the fraternity (Dodge, "Beer Kegs Banned" A28). When students enter a college or university, they often become socialized into the alcohol-sodden culture of "higher education," at both formal and informal parties. The influence of peer pressure is enormous. Students often find it difficult to resist the pressures from their friends and fellow students to drink.

However, some observers of young people believe that, although peer pressure is certainly a factor in excessive college drinking, it is only one of a number of factors. They point out that the misuse of alcohol is a problem for all youth in our society, not just college students. For example, a recent study by the surgeon general's office shows that 1 in 3 teenagers consumes alcohol every week. This abuse leads to traffic deaths, academic difficulties, and acts of violence (Elson 64). Another study based on a large, nationally representative sample indicates that although college students are more likely to use alcohol, they tend to drink less per drinking day than nonstudents of the same age (Crowley 14); in other words, most college students who drink are more social drinkers than problem drinkers. One survey of undergraduate students found that college drinking is not as widespread as many people think (O'Hare 540). The conclusion from this data is that even though drinking certainly takes place on college campuses, it is no greater a problem than in the population at large.

Whatever the extent, the misuse of alcohol by college students is a serious situation with a number of probable causes. Certainly the influence of friends, whether in college or out, plays a role, as I've already discussed. But it is not the only factor. To begin with, there is evidence that family history is related to alcohol abuse. For example, one survey of college students found more problem drinking among students whose parents or grandparents had been diagnosed with alcoholism (Perkins and Berkowitz 237–240). Another study found that college students who come from families with high degrees of conflict display a greater potential for alcoholism (Pardeck 342–343).

Another important factor to consider in the misuse of alcohol by young people is advertising. A recent article entitled "It Isn't Miller Time Yet, and This Bud's Not for You" underscores the influence advertisers exert on the behavior of youth (Siler 52). By portraying beer drinkers as healthy, fun-loving, attractive young people, they create role models that many youths imitate. In the same way that cigarette advertisers used to encourage smoking among our youth—without regard for the health hazards—so alcohol advertisers try to sell as much booze as they can to whoever will buy it—no matter what the consequences.

A final factor in the abuse of alcohol is the people themselves. Although young people are subject to a huge number of influences, in the final analysis, they are free to choose what they want to do. They don't have to drink, no matter what the social pressure. In fact, many students resist these pressures and choose not to drink excessively or at all. In short, some students choose to think critically, while others choose to drink uncritically.

In order to encourage good judgment by more students and to minimize the causes of excessive drinking, I think that the following strategies could help solve the college alcohol problem. Only the last one has any disadvantages to be considered.

1. Colleges should have orientation and educational programs aimed at preventing alcohol abuse, and colleges should give top priority to campaigns against underage and excessive drinking.

2. Advertising and promotion of alcoholic beverages on college campuses and in college publications should be banned. Liquor distributors should not sponsor campus events. In addition, alcoholic beverage companies should be petitioned not to target young people in their ads.

3. Depending on the campus culture, colleges should ban or restrict alcohol use on campus and include stiff penalties for students who violate the rules.

4. Students at residential colleges should be able to live in substance-free housing, offering them a voluntary haven from alcohol, other drugs, tobacco, and peer pressure.

5. Colleges should create attractive alcohol-free clubs or pubs.

6. Colleges should ban the use of beer kegs, a symbol of cheap and easy availability of alcohol.

7. Fraternities should eliminate all alcohol-based contests or hazing torments.

8. Where possible, the on-campus drinking age should be reduced to 18, so that students won't be forced to move parties off-campus. At off-campus parties,

there is no college control, and as a result, students tend to drink greater quantities and more dangerous concoctions.

Of course, this suggestion has the disadvantages of being in conflict with laws in many states or counties and also of seeming to encourage drinking by connecting it even more extensively with social events. But it has the advantages of control and of eliminating the attraction of what's forbidden.

In conclusion, alcohol abuse on college campuses is an extremely serious problem that is threatening the health and college careers of many students. As challenging as this problem is, I believe that it can be solved if students, teachers, and college officials work together in harmony and with determination to implement the suggestions made in this paper.

Works Cited

"Clemson Issues Ban on Parties Using Alcohol." Chronicle of Higher Education 31 Jan. 1990: A3.

Crowley, Joan E. "Educational Status and Drinking Patterns: How Representative Are College Students?" Journal of Studies on Alcohol 52.1 (1991) : 10–16.

Dodge, Susan. "Campus Crime Linked to Students' Use of Drugs and Alcohol." Chronicle of Higher Education 17 Jan. 1990 : A33+.

––– ."Use of Beer Kegs Banned by Some Colleges and National Fraternities." Chronicle of Higher Education 12 June 1991 : A27–28.

Elson, John. "Drink Until You Finally Drop." Time 16 Dec. 1991 : 64.

Engs, Ruth C. "Family Background of Alcohol Abuse and Its Relationship to Alcohol Consumption among College Students: An Unexpected Finding." Journal of Studies on Alcohol 51.6 (1990) : 542–547.

Gerson, Mark. "30 Pct. of Ontario's Students Called 'Heavy Drinkers.'" Chronicle of Higher Education 12 April 1989 : A43.

Leatherman, Courtney. "College Officials Are Split on Alcohol Policies; Some Seek to End Underage Drinking; Others Try to Encourage 'Responsible' Use." Chronicle of Higher Education 31 Jan. 1990 : A33–35.

O'Hare, Thomas M. "Drinking in College: Consumption Patterns, Problems, Sex Differences and Legal Drinking Age." Journal of Studies on Alcohol 51.6 (1990) : 536–541.

Pardeck, John T. "A Multiple Regression Analysis of Family Factors Affecting the Potential for Alcoholism in College Students." Adolescence 26.102 (1991) : 341–347.

Perkins, H. Wesley, and Alan D. Berkowitz. "Collegiate COAs and Alcohol Abuse: Problem Drinking in Relation to Assessment of Parent and Grandparent Alcoholism." Journal of Counseling and Development 69.3 (1991) : 237–240.

Rosenberg, Debra. "Bad Times at Hangover U." Newsweek 19 Nov. 1990 : 81.

Siler, Julie Flynn. "It Isn't Miller Time Yet, and This Bud's Not For You." Business Week 24 June 1991 : 52.

12

Constructing Arguments

Writing to Persuade

"Give me the liberty to know, to utter, and to argue freely according to conscience, above all liberties." —John Milton

Critical Thinking Focus: Using reasons, evidence, and logic

Writing Focus: Convincing an audience

Reading Theme: Arguments about important issues

Writing Project: Arguing a position on a significant issue

Principles of Argument

People who study communication, argument, and rhetoric believe that much of what we say and write can be defined as argument because most statements seek listeners' or readers' agreement with the ideas being presented. Unless someone is just saying "Hmmmm" or "Hello" or is asking a question only to obtain information, the purpose of his or her statement usually is to make a point, to convince the audience of its validity, and often to bring about change or action. Essays, letters, stories, poems, movies, web sites—and even paintings and clothes—can be considered arguments or have argumentative purposes.

This chapter is devoted to argument, even though most of your previous writing has had argumentative characteristics. Some writing is supposed to be predominantly argumentative, and you need to know how to produce it and how to analyze it. Arguing effectively is essential to academic and professional success. In addition, since both politicians and advertisers use argumentative techniques, you need to understand both valid and fallacious arguments in order to evaluate claims that people want you to accept.

Thinking ↔ Writing Activity

Analyzing Argumentative Writing

1. Select an essay that you have written for this course that you believe has an argumentative purpose. What is your thesis or claim? What specific evidence do you present? Who are your audiences? Does the paper advocate for any change or action? What is it?

2. Select a reading from a previous chapter that you consider argumentative. What is its claim? What evidence does it present? Who are its audiences? What change or action does it seek?

This chapter will introduce concepts related to argument, provide readings and Thinking-Writing Activities to help you grasp them, and conclude with a Writing Project that asks you to write a logical, well-organized argument for a position that is important to you. The chapter will also explore ways to construct effective arguments and to evaluate arguments.

CLASSICAL CONCEPTS

The concepts that guide logical argument are central to Western culture. Articulated by the philosophers and rhetoricians of ancient Greece and Rome, they have been studied and applied for more than two thousand years. Even though emotions, gut reactions, and intuition cannot be brushed aside—because they are so human—logical thinking and the resulting structured arguments are expected in business, government, and scholarship. Therefore, as a college composition student, you have both practical and historical reasons for giving attention to principles of argument or rhetoric.

The Greek philosopher Aristotle, in his famous work the *Rhetoric* and in other writings on logic, is the source of many concepts basic to our ideas of argument. But even Aristotle, more than three hundred years B.C.E., was responding to earlier works on rhetoric; and to this day, those who have followed him have modified and redefined his ideas and those of other classical rhetoricians. Those concepts include *ethos,* the character of the speaker or writer; *pathos,* the effect on the audience; and *logos,* the logic and substance of an argument. Some other centuries-old concepts are the techniques for generation or discovery of ideas, the arrangement of sections of an argument, the thinking methods of deduction and induction, techniques for refutation, and moral concerns about the use of rhetorical power for honorable ends.

Links to the Thinking-Writing Model   The classical rhetoricians were concerned with speech; literacy for all, print, and electronics were yet to come. Speech is, of course, still essential to communication, both face to face and via electronic media. This book concentrates on writing, but the ancient concepts have never gone out of use, and they function well to promote effective writing. The topics in the Thinking-Writing Model that is the foundation of this book demonstrate contemporary applications of many classical principles.

Notice how subject, purpose, audience, and writer connect in multiple ways with the concepts of *logos, pathos,* and *ethos.* If *logos* means both content and the logic of its presentation, *logos* connects with the Model's topics of subject, defining a thesis, and organizing ideas as well as with thinking critically. *Pathos* connects, of course, with the Model's audience and purpose; *ethos,* with the writer and also with the editing and proofreading stages of revising since a well-finished paper gives a good impression of its writer.

The classical concepts of *discovery* and *arrangement* are clearly connected to the Model's notions of thinking creatively, generating ideas, organizing ideas, and drafting.

Good Rhetoric   Today, the words *argument* and *rhetoric* are regularly used in conversation and in the media differently from the ways in which they are used in this chapter. Popularly, *argument* often means "a quarrel," and *rhetoric* is often used to mean "insubstantial or misleading language" (which is connected to the classical concerns about the use of rhetorical power for honorable ends). In this chapter, **rhetoric** means "the use of the best means of persuasion." We will discuss argument throughout the chapter and define the term on page 479.

MODERN CONCEPTS

In the twentieth and twenty-first centuries, much attention has been paid to argument, at least partly because both mass media and education have extended their reaches. More communication and analyses of it from different points of view continue to provide new ways of thinking about arguments. Three important modern approaches are the **Toulmin method,** analyzing the effects of electronic communication, and various consensus-building strategies.

Toulmin's Method   College composition students are often introduced to some concepts that have developed from the work of the British professor of philosophy Stephen Toulmin. Professor Toulmin's ideas about argument can be applied to almost any argument, no matter how it is constructed. Terms important to the Toulmin method are *claim* and *qualified claim, grounds, warrants,* and *backings.*

These are not strange or difficult terms. You already understand **claim** because *thesis, main point,* and *conclusion* are other ways to say it. You already understand **grounds** because it means *reasons, evidence, support, examples,* and *data*. You have established a thesis and provided support for it in most papers that you have written for this course.

As you improved your ability to develop a good thesis and studied Chapter 9's material on definition and classification, you were learning about qualified claims or qualifiers. A **qualified claim** is an accurately worded claim, one that establishes the category to be discussed. A qualified claim is not exaggerated or overly general. For example, you might not want to claim that *"Teenagers* should not be allowed to drive after midnight." Instead, you might claim that "People *under eighteen years* of age should not be allowed to drive after midnight." That way you would be acknowledging the probable differences in experience and maturity between a sixteen-year-old and an eighteen- or nineteen-year-old and showing that the overly general word *teenager* needs qualification. Properly qualified claims produce effective arguments.

Warrants are the assumptions, principles, premises, and beliefs that are the foundations of most arguments. This is an important concept to understand because warrants are not always stated. However, warrants provide the connection between a claim and its grounds, and they enable the acceptance or rejection of an argument. Here's a simple example:

Claim: People should brush and floss their teeth regularly.

Grounds: Dentists tell us that brushing and flossing will help prevent tooth decay and gum disease.

Warrants: People do not want their teeth to fall out. They do not want to have toothaches or ugly decayed teeth. People do not want drilling, fillings, and dentists' bills.

Backings are larger principles that support warrants. They are the foundations of the foundations. A backing for the warrants about brushing and flossing is the generally accepted principle of self-interest. People are concerned about their own health, appearance, and finances; people are concerned about situations that affect them. Therefore, the backing of the principle of self-interest supports the warrants about what people don't want, which support and connect the claim and grounds about dental hygiene.

This use of the word *warrant* is related to its use in law enforcement—a warrant for an arrest or a search warrant, which authorize actions. The warrants of an argument are also related to the sources of beliefs (see Chapters 2 and 10). In addition, warrants are related to the premises used in deductive reasoning, which you will study later in this chapter.

Just as you need to understand the sources of your beliefs and those of others, you need to understand the warrants behind the arguments that you make and that people present to you. You need to recognize them when they are stated as part of an argument and search for them if they are not stated.

Looking at these U.S. Army recruitment materials should help you understand warrants. Can you see some assumptions, principles, beliefs—or warrants—that are behind the approaches taken by the poster and by the web site as they try to convice young people to enlist?

I Want You *for U.S. Army*

BY JAMES MONTGOMERY FLAGG

www.goarmy.com
U.S. ARMY

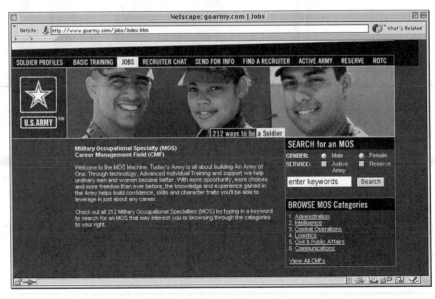

Critical Reading Questions

1. What are some assumptions, principles, beliefs—or warrants—that provide a foundation for the argument presented by the 1917 poster?

2. What are some assumptions, principles, beliefs—or warrants—that provide a foundation for the arguments presented by the 2001 web site? Visit the U.S. Army web site at www.goarmy.com to gather additional information for your analysis.

3. List the warrants that you identified for each recruiting effort. See if you and your classmates found the same ones.

4. Why are warrants about service and patriotism powerful? Why are warrants about self-development powerful? Can you identify any backings for the warrants that you found?

5. What warrants can you detect behind another advertisement that you have seen in a recent magazine or newspaper or on your computer screen?

6. After you jot down answers to questions 4 and 5, discuss them with your classmates.

Argument and Electronic Media   There is currently much speculation about the effects of electronic communication on arguments. Of course, different kinds of electronic technologies raise different questions. Obviously, radio transmits spoken arguments, and television uses both sound and visuals to produce its well-known impact on audiences. Computers do so many things that analysis is difficult—but exciting. Visuals, sounds, and texts can be combined in countless ways, so distinctions among written, pictorial, and spoken arguments are blurred.

Many characteristics of computerized communication can affect arguments. The movement of linking means that logical connections are not always made. The speed at which ideas are transmitted and the rapidity with which some information can change can cause confusion and raise questions about credibility. Many people tend to write more informally in email than on paper, and such informality can change the tone of an argument for better or for worse. The rapid transmission of email can quickly conclude an argument or cause it to go on longer.

On the other hand, many Internet texts are simply posted versions of printed material or have been composed in a traditional manner. We need to be aware of the ways in which electronic and written communications differ as well as the ways in which argumentative concepts operate similarly in various media.

More Links to the Thinking-Writing Model   Just as the concepts of classical rhetoric connect with components in the Thinking-Writing Model, so do the modern concepts. A claim, especially a qualified claim, clearly relates to defining a thesis.

Grounds are important for generating and organizing ideas. Warrants and backing connect significantly with audience, purpose, and the writer. Writers need to understand their own assumptions and basic beliefs as they develop arguments in order to think critically about what they are presenting. Also, since assumptions and basic beliefs can differ in various communities, writers need to consider how the warrants beneath an argument might affect their audiences. Consensus-building approaches relate most obviously to reaching an audience but also pertain to purposes and to organizing ideas.

Achieving Mutual Understanding Some people believe that the purpose of argument is to coerce or to "win." As we have seen in this book, though, critical thinkers strive to develop the most informed understanding, which involves trying to fully appreciate other perspectives. Instead of attempting to prove others wrong, a more desirable purpose is to arrive at a clear and mutual understanding about the issue being discussed. Sometimes people are so far apart in their convictions that agreement cannot be reached and an impasse (or worse) occurs. At other times people "agree to disagree" and work around their differences; but if agreement does come, good feelings can result in progress, problem solving, or other desired achievements. By thinking critically, you can inspire others to think critically as well so that all parties are working together to achieve the clearest understanding rather than splintering into adversarial factions. In the following cartoon, the man on the right seems to be pursuing conflict rather than mutual understanding. What are the disadvantages of such an approach? Can you think of some more constructive strategies that he could use?

"I shall now punch a huge hole in your argument."

Considering Other Points of View People do not argue about things on which they agree, nor do they argue about concepts that are accepted as facts. For example, it's not likely that an argument would arise over the relative lengths of a meter and a yard. A measuring tape takes care of the question. However, people do argue about whether the United States should adopt the metric system. Arguments develop because people have different opinions about issues.

You should not ignore opposing points of view when you are making an argument. Sometimes, people will ignore other ideas and present one-sided cases—as in most advertisements, some sermons, many political statements, and attempts at pushing proposals through. But in reasoned arguments, you should address varying ideas in order to demonstrate your grasp of the issue and also to try to achieve mutual understanding and, if possible, consensus or agreement.

Guidelines for Addressing Other Points of View

1. *Restate the other claim to show that you understand it.* This is often easier to do in a face-to-face discussion than in writing, but it is important in any argument. Sometimes misunderstandings can be uncovered by this technique. Restatements can also lead to finding common ground. A restatement should be made in a nonjudgmental, respectful tone.

2. *Find areas of agreement, or common ground, at the outset of the argument.* This, too, is sometimes easier to do in a face-to-face discussion than in writing. It is a technique often used in negotiations and mediation. However, in a written argument, you should try whenever you can to establish common ground with those who have other beliefs about the issue that you are addressing. Often identifying warrants can lead parties to find areas of agreement. When people see that they agree about some parts of an issue, they can establish mutual respect and then examine their differing opinions carefully.

3. *Identify which differences are important and which are trivial.* This, too, is more easily done when people talk with each other, but it is also something that can be attempted in written argument. Here, too, identifying warrants sometimes clarifies the significance of some parts of an argument.

4. *Concede points that you cannot uphold.* Sometimes you will have to concede that some of your opponents' ideas are so strong that you cannot counter them, even if you do not agree with them.

5. *Compromise.* At times, accepting a middle position or a partial achievement of your purpose is better than arguing for its complete achievement.

6. *Rebut.* This means to refute or to present opposing evidence. Rebuttal often seems necessary. It is part of the debate tradition and is important in legal arguments, but it maintains adversarial positions. If you have to rebut an opposing point, do so courteously.

7. *Be sensitive to different argumentative philosophies.* Some cultures, some groups, and some individuals prefer indirect methods of argumentation while others want to get to the point quickly. Sometimes a direct approach is seen as rude or overly aggressive; sometimes an indirect approach is seen as weak, sneaky, or confusing. In the United States, directness is often considered as the best approach. If your audience is from a different culture, however, be sure that you understand that culture's argumentative style.

Thinking ↔ Writing Activity

Establishing Agreement

1. Find a classmate who disagrees with you about something—for example, the quality of a specific television show, a political principle, or a controversy at your college. Each of you should then write a brief statement about your position. Next, read each other's statements.

2. See if you can establish some areas of agreement. Can you identify warrants for your position and for your classmate's? Where might you compromise? Determine whether any differences are not important. Do either of you have to concede a point?

Analyzing the Audience You learned long ago that you should speak and write differently to different audiences. You use one kind of vocabulary and tone with your friends and another with your grandparents. You write formally in a job application letter and informally in an email to your sister telling what you did last weekend.

The suggestions for completing every Writing Project in this book include some discussion of your audience because it is one of the major components of any writing situation and therefore is prominently featured in the Thinking-Writing Model. However, consideration of audience is especially important when you are writing an argumentative paper, particularly if you hope to effect some change or action. Also, remember that you may have more than one audience. Here are some questions to ask yourself about the audiences for any argument you write:

- Who is interested in this issue?
- What concerns do these interested people have?
- What is their level of education or expertise?
- What related issues interest them?
- How much time might they give to reading my argument?

- Who can do something about the situation?
- Who is opposed to my point of view?
- What are the opposing claims?
- What format, tone, or method of presentation will be effective with this audience?

Can you think of other questions to ask about audiences?

Going Too Far Paying attention to audiences does not mean telling an audience only what it wants to hear or manipulating ideas just to reach a certain audience. Some advertisers and politicians mislead audiences in such ways. Pandering to an audience is one of the ways in which rhetoric can be misused. Responsible writers and speakers accommodate their audiences honestly.

Recognizing Arguments

TWO FRIENDS ARGUE: SHOULD MARIJUANA BE LEGALIZED?

Consider the following dialogue about whether marijuana should be legalized. Have you participated in such exchanges? In what ways do dialogues like this differ from written argument? How do such dialogues provide a starting point for written arguments?

Dennis: Have you read about the medical uses of marijuana—that people who have cancer, AIDS, and some other diseases might be helped by smoking? I think some doctors are prescribing it, and some states may be changing their laws. This might change people's thinking more than all those discussions about unenforced laws, unjust punishments, and victimless crimes that have been going on since my uncles were in college.

Caroline: Well, I agree that we need to think about drug laws. But I hope you agree that we have to be careful. Drugs pose a serious threat to the young people of our country. Look at all the people who are addicted to drugs, who have their lives ruined, and who often die at an early age of overdoses. And think of all the crimes people commit to support their drug habits. So I don't know if anything that's illegal now should be legalized, . . . and the laws should be enforced.

Dennis: That's ridiculous. Smoking marijuana is nothing like using drugs such as heroin or even cocaine. It follows that smoking marijuana should not be against the law if it's harmless and maybe even helpful to some sick people.

Caroline: I don't agree. Although marijuana may not be as dangerous as some other drugs, it does affect things like a driver's ability to judge distances. And smoking it surely isn't good for you. And I don't think that anything that is a threat to your health should be legal.

Dennis: What about cigarettes and alcohol? We know that they are dangerous. Medical research has linked smoking cigarettes to lung cancer, emphysema, and heart disease. Alcohol damages the liver and also the brain. Has anyone ever proved that marijuana is a threat to our health? And even if it does turn out to be somewhat unhealthy, it's certainly not as dangerous as cigarettes and alcohol.

Caroline: That's a good point. But to tell you the truth, I'm not so sure that cigarettes and alcohol should be legal. And in any case, they are legal. The fact that cigarettes and alcohol are bad for your health is not reason to legalize another drug that can cause health problems.

Dennis: Look—life is full of risks. We take chances every time we cross the street or climb into our cars. In fact, with all the irresponsible drivers on the road, driving could be a lot more hazardous to our health than any of the drugs around. Many of the foods we eat can kill. For example, red meat contributes to heart disease, and artificial sweeteners can cause cancer. The point is, if people want to take chances with their health, that's up to them. And many people in our society like to mellow out with marijuana. I read somewhere that over 70 percent of the people in the United States think that marijuana should be legalized.

Caroline: There's a big difference between letting people drive cars and letting them use dangerous drugs. Society has a responsibility to protect people from themselves. People often do things that are foolish if they are encouraged to or given the opportunity. Legalizing something like marijuana encourages people to use it, especially young people. It follows that many more people would use marijuana if it were legalized. It's like society saying "This is all right—go ahead and use it."

Dennis: I still maintain that marijuana isn't dangerous. It's not addictive—like heroin is—and there is no evidence that it harms you. Consequently, anything that is harmless should be legal.

Caroline: Marijuana may not be physically addictive like heroin, but I think that it can be psychologically addictive because people tend to use more and more of it over time. I know a number of people who spend a lot of their time getting high. What about Carl? All he does is lie around and get high. This shows that smoking it over a period of time definitely affects your mind. Think about the people you know who smoke a lot—don't they seem to be floating in a dream world? How are they ever going to make anything of their lives? As far as I'm concerned, a pothead is like a zombie—living but dead.

Dennis: Since you have had so little experience with marijuana, I don't think that you can offer an informed opinion on the subject. And anyway, if you do too much of anything, it can hurt you. Even something as healthy as exercise can cause problems if you do too much of it. But I sure don't see anything wrong with toking up with some friends at a party or even getting into a relaxed state by yourself. In fact, I find that I can even concentrate better on my school work after taking a little smoke.

Caroline: If you believe that, then marijuana really has damaged your brain. You're just trying to rationalize your drug habit. Smoking marijuana doesn't help you concentrate—it takes you away from reality. And I don't think that people can control it. Either you smoke and surrender control of your life, or you don't smoke because you want to retain control. There's nothing in between.

Dennis: Let me point out something to you. Because marijuana is illegal, organized crime controls its distribution and makes all the money from it. If marijuana were legalized, the government could tax the sale of it—like cigarettes and alcohol—and use the money for some worthwhile purpose. For example, many states have legalized gambling and use the money to support education. In fact, the major tobacco companies have already copyrighted names for different marijuana brands—like "Acapulco Gold." Obviously they believe that marijuana will soon become legal.

Caroline: The fact that the government can make money out of something doesn't mean that they should legalize it. We could also legalize prostitution or muggings and then tax the proceeds. Also, even if the cigarette companies are prepared to sell marijuana, that doesn't mean that selling it makes sense. After all, they're the ones who are selling us cigarettes. . . .

Can you think of other views on the subject of legalizing marijuana? Can you think of other subjects about which such dialogues are taking place now?

The previous discussion illustrates two people's engaging in *dialogue*, the systematic exchange of ideas. Discussing issues with others encourages you to be mentally active, to ask questions, to view issues from different perspectives, to develop reasons that support conclusions, and to write convincingly.

This chapter focuses on the last quality of thinking critically—supporting claims with reasons—because when we offer reasons to support a conclusion, we are presenting an *argument*, the essence of most college and business writing. An **argument** is a form of thinking in which certain statements (reasons or evidence) are offered to support another statement (a conclusion or a claim).

In the dialogue, Dennis presents the following argument for legalizing marijuana:

Reason: Marijuana might help some people who have serious diseases.

Reason: Marijuana isn't dangerous like heroin and cocaine.

Reason: Governments could tax the sale of marijuana as they do cigarettes and alcohol.

Claim: Marijuana should be legalized.

Expanding the definition of *argument*, we can define the main ideas that make up an argument. **Reasons, evidence,** or **grounds** are statements that support another statement (a conclusion, claim, or thesis), justify it, or make it more probable. The **claim, thesis,** or **conclusion** is a statement that explains, asserts, or predicts on the basis of statements (known as reasons) that are offered as evidence to support it.

The type of thinking that uses argument—presenting reasons to support conclusions—is known as **reasoning,** and it is a type of thinking explained throughout this book. We are continually trying to explain, justify, and predict through the process of reasoning, and often we must present such thinking in writing.

Of course, our reasoning—and that of others—is not always correct. The reasons someone offers may not really support the claim they are intended to, a conclusion may not really follow from the reasons stated, or the reasons may be questionable or wrong. These difficulties are illustrated in a number of the arguments contained in the previous discussion on marijuana.

Nevertheless, whenever we accept a conclusion as likely or true on the basis of certain reasons, or whenever we offer reasons to support a conclusion, we are using arguments—even if our reasoning is weak or faulty and needs improvement.

Let's return to the discussion about marijuana. After Dennis presents one argument, Caroline presents another, giving reasons that lead to a conclusion that conflicts with the one Dennis has offered.

Reason: Drugs pose a very serious threat to the young people of our country.

Reason: Many crimes are committed to support drug habits.

Claim: As a result, society has to have drug laws and to enforce them to convince people of the seriousness of the situation.

Which of Dennis's or Caroline's arguments do you see as reasonable? Which seem weak or faulty?

English, like other languages, provides guidance in our efforts to identify reasons and conclusions. Certain key words, or cue words, signal that a reason is being offered to support a conclusion or that a conclusion is being drawn on the basis of certain reasons. After you read the following list, go back to the dialogue and see how and when Dennis and Caroline use these words.

On the following page are some commonly used cue words for reasons and conclusions.

Useful Words for Recognizing and Writing Arguments

Cue Words Signaling Reasons

since	in view of
for	first, second
because	in the first (second) place
as shown by	may be inferred from
as indicated by	may be deduced from
given that	may be derived from
assuming that	for the reason that

Cue Words Signaling Conclusions

therefore	then
thus	it follows that
hence	thereby showing
so	demonstrates that
(which) shows that	allows us to infer that
(which) proves that	suggests very strongly that
implies that	you see that
points to	leads me to believe that
as a result	allows us to deduce that
consequently	

Of course, identifying reasons, claims, and conclusions involves more than looking for cue words. The words and phrases just listed do not always signal reasons and conclusions, and in many cases people present arguments without using cue words. Cue words, however, do alert us that an argument is being offered. Careful use of cue words helps us to write effective arguments.

Thinking ↔ Writing Activity

Analyzing a Dialogue

Write responses to the previous dialogue. Then share your responses with classmates and note where you agree and disagree.

1. Review the discussion and underline cue words that signal when Dennis and Caroline are giving reasons or announcing conclusions.

2. Identify one argument in the dialogue that you find convincing and one that seems unconvincing. Write your reasons for your opinions, referring to specific places in the dialogue.

The following two essays discuss the issue of whether drugs should be legalized. The first passage is by essayist and novelist Gore Vidal. The second is by *New York Times* editor and columnist A. M. Rosenthal.

Drugs

BY GORE VIDAL

It is possible to stop most drug addiction in the United States within a very short time. Simply make all drugs available and sell them at cost. Label each drug with a precise description of what effect—good and bad—the drug will have on the taker. This will require heroic honesty. Don't say that marijuana is addictive or dangerous when it is neither, as millions of people know—unlike "speed," which kills most unpleasantly, or heroin, which is addictive and difficult to kick.

For the record, I have tried—once—almost every drug and liked none, disproving the popular Fu Manchu theory that a single whiff of opium will enslave the mind. Nevertheless many drugs are bad for certain people to take and they should be told why in a sensible way.

Along with exhortation and warning, it might be good for our citizens to recall (or learn for the first time) that the United States was the creation of men who believed that each man has the right to do what he wants with his own life as long as he does not interfere with his neighbor's pursuit of happiness. (That his neighbor's idea of happiness is persecuting others does confuse matters a bit.)

This is a startling notion to the current generation of Americans. They reflect a system of public education which has made the Bill of Rights, literally, unacceptable to a majority of high school graduates who now form the "silent majority"—a phrase which that underestimated wit Richard Nixon took from Homer who used it to describe the dead.

5   Now one can hear the warning rumble begin: If everyone is allowed to take drugs, everyone will and the GNP will decrease, the Commies will stop us from making everyone free, and we shall end up a race of zombies, passively murmuring "groovy" to one another. Alarming thought. Yet it seems most unlikely that any reasonably sane person will become a drug addict if he knows in advance what addiction is going to be like.

Is everyone reasonably sane? No. Some people will always become drug addicts just as some people will always become alcoholics, and it is just too bad.

Every man, however, has the power (and should have the legal right) to kill himself if he chooses. But since most men don't, they won't be mainliners either. Nevertheless, forbidding people things they like or think they might enjoy only makes them want those things all the more. This psychological insight is, for some mysterious reason, perennially denied by our governors.

It is a lucky thing for the American moralist that our country has always existed in a kind of time-vacuum: We have no public memory of anything that happened before last Tuesday. No one in Washington today recalls what happened during the years alcohol was forbidden to the people by a Congress that thought it had a divine mission to stamp out Demon Rum—launching, in the process, the greatest crime wave in the country's history, causing thousands of deaths from bad alcohol, and creating a general (and persisting) contempt among the citizenry for the laws of the United States.

The same thing is happening today. But the government has learned nothing from past attempts at prohibition, not to mention repression.

Last year when the supply of Mexican marijuana was slightly curtailed by the Feds, the pushers got the kids hooked on heroin and deaths increased dramatically, particularly in New York. Whose fault? Evil men like the Mafiosi? Permissive Dr. Spock? Wild-eyed Dr. Leary? No.

10   The Government of the United States was responsible for those deaths. The bureaucratic machine has a vested interest in playing cops and robbers. Both the Bureau of Narcotics and the Mafia want strong laws against the sale and use of drugs because if drugs are sold at cost, there would be no money in it for anyone.

If there was no money in it for the Mafia, there would be no friendly playground pushers, and addicts would not commit crimes to pay for the next fix. Finally, if there was no money in it, the Bureau of Narcotics would wither away, something they are not about to do without a struggle.

Will anything sensible be done? Of course not. The American people are as devoted to the idea of sin and its punishment as they are to making money—and fighting drugs is nearly as big a business as pushing them. Since the combination of sin and money is irresistible (particularly to the professional politician), the situation will only grow worse.

The Case for Slavery

BY A. M. ROSENTHAL

Across the country, a scattered but influential collection of intellectuals is intensely engaged in making the case for slavery.

With considerable passion, these Americans are repeatedly expounding the benefits of not only tolerating slavery but legalizing it:

It would make life less dangerous for the free. It would save a great deal of money. And since the economies could be used to improve the lot of the slaves, in the end they would be better off.

The new antiabolitionists, like their predecessors in the nineteenth century, concede that those now in bondage do not themselves see the benefits of legalizing their status.

5   But in time they will, we are assured, because the beautiful part of legalization is that slavery would be designed so as to keep slaves pacified with the very thing that enslaves them!

The form of slavery under discussion is drug addiction. It does not have every characteristic of more traditional forms of bondage. But they have enough in common to make the comparison morally valid—and the campaign for drug legalization morally disgusting.

Like the plantation slavery that was a foundation of American society for so long, drug addiction largely involves specifiable groups of people. Most of the enchained are children and adolescents of all colors and black and Hispanic adults.

Like plantation slavery, drug addiction is passed on from generation to generation. And this may be the most important similarity: Like plantation slavery, addiction can destroy among its victims the social resources most valuable to free people for their own betterment—family life, family traditions, family values.

In plantation-time America, mothers were taken from their children. In drug-time America, mothers abandon their children. Do the children suffer less, or the mothers?

10   Antiabolitionists argue that legalization would make drugs so cheap and available that the profit for crime would be removed. Well-supplied addicts would be peaceful addicts. We would not waste billions for jails and could spend some of the savings helping the addicted become drug-free.

That would happen at the very time that new millions of Americans were being enticed into addiction by legalization—somehow.

Are we really foolish enough to believe that tens of thousands of drug gang members would meekly steal away, foiled by the marvels of the free market?

Not likely. The pushers would cut prices, making more money than ever from the ever-growing mass market. They would immediately increase the potency and variety beyond anything available at any Government-approved narcotics counters.

Crime would increase. Crack produces paranoid violence. More permissiveness equals more use equals more violence.

15   And what will legalization do to the brains of Americans drawn into drug slavery by easy availability?

Earlier this year, an expert drug pediatrician told me that after only a few months babies born with crack addiction seemed to recover. Now we learn that stultifying behavioral effects last at least through early childhood. Will they last forever?

How long will crack affect neurological patterns in the brain of adult crack users? Dr. Gabriel G. Nahas of Columbia University argues in his new book, *Cocaine: The Great White Plague,* that the damage may be irreversible. Would it not be an act of simple intelligence to drop the legalization campaign until we find out?

Then why do a number of writers and academicians, left to right, support it? I have discussed this with antidrug leaders like Jesse Jackson, Dr. Mitchell Rosenthal of Phoenix House, and William J. Bennett, who search for answers themselves.

Perhaps the answer is that the legalizers are not dealing with reality in America. I think the reason has to do with class.

20   Crack is beginning to move into the white middle and upper classes. That is a tragedy for those addicted.

However, it has not yet destroyed the communities around which their lives revolve, not taken over every street and doorway. It has not passed generation to generation among them, killing the continuity of family.

But in ghetto communities poverty and drugs come together in a catalytic reaction that is reducing them to social rubble.

The antiabolitionists, virtually all white and well-to-do, do not see or do not care. Either way they show symptoms of the callousness of class. That can be a particularly dangerous social disorder.

Critical Reading Questions

1. Try to state in one sentence the thesis, conclusion, or claim of each essay. Where did each writer make his thesis clear? Did you find the placement effective? Why or why not?

2. Identify two or three specific reasons that each writer gives to support his thesis.

3. What impression does each essay convey of its writer? Why?

4. Do you agree with either writer's position? Explain. What shapes your identity as an audience for these arguments?

5. Can you connect these questions with *ethos, logos,* and *pathos* as defined on page 469?

6. Can you identify the warrants and backings for these arguments?

Arguments as Inferences

When you construct arguments, you are constructing views of the world by means of your ability to infer. As you saw in Chapter 10, inferring is a thinking process used to reason from what one already knows (or believes to be the case) to acquire new knowledge or beliefs. This is usually what you do when you construct arguments: work from reasons you know or believe to draw conclusions based on them.

Just as you can use inferences to make sense of different types of situations, you can also construct arguments for different purposes. As already noted, some people believe in using arguments to coerce or to "win." A more desirable goal is to use arguments to clarify issues, develop mutual understanding, and if possible, bring about agreement or consensus on the issue being discussed. Notice how you can work toward agreement when you construct arguments to do any of the following: decide, explain, predict, persuade.

CONSTRUCTING ARGUMENTS TO DECIDE

Reason: Throughout my life, I've always been interested in all kinds of electricity.

Reason: There are many attractive job opportunities in the field of electrical engineering.

Claim: Electrical engineering would be a good major for me.

Audience: Myself, my parents, my academic adviser, the scholarship office

An argument to decide

Reason: _____

Reason: _____

Claim: _____

Audience: _____

CONSTRUCTING ARGUMENTS TO EXPLAIN

Reason: I was delayed leaving my house because my dog needed emergency walking.

Reason: There was an unexpected traffic jam caused by motorists slowing down to view an overturned chicken truck.

Claim: Therefore, I couldn't help being late for our appointment.

Audience: The person waiting for me

An argument to explain

Reason: _____

Reason: _____

Claim: _____

Audience: _____

CONSTRUCTING ARGUMENTS TO PREDICT

Reason: Some people will always drive faster than the speed limit allows, no matter whether the limit is 55 or 65 mph.

Reason: Car accidents are more likely to occur at higher speeds.

Claim: A reinstated 65 mph speed limit will result in more accidents.

Audience: Legislators, voters, drivers

An argument to predict

Reason: _____

Reason: _____

Claim: _____

Audience: _____

CONSTRUCTING ARGUMENTS TO PERSUADE

Reason: Chewing tobacco can lead to cancer of the mouth and throat.

Reason: Young people sometimes begin chewing tobacco because they see ads that feature sports heroes they admire doing it.

Claim: Ads for chewing tobacco should be banned.

Audience: Parents, voters, legislators, advertising agencies, media executives

An argument to persuade

Reason: _____

Reason: _____

Claim: _____

Audience: _____

Evaluating Arguments

To construct good arguments, you must be skilled at evaluating the effectiveness, or soundness, of arguments already constructed. You must investigate the components of an argument to determine the soundness of the argument as a whole.

1. How true are the reasons being offered to support the conclusion?
2. To what extent do the reasons support the conclusion, claim, or thesis—or to what extent does the conclusion follow from the reasons offered?

TRUTH: HOW TRUE ARE THE SUPPORTING REASONS?

The first aspect of an argument that you must evaluate is the truth of the reasons being used to support a conclusion. Ask yourself these questions:

- What specific evidence is the writer offering to illustrate each reason?
- Are any reasons consistent with my own experience?
- Are the reasons based on reliable sources?
- Are the reasons relevant to the subject of the argument?

You use these questions and others like them to analyze the reasons offered and to determine how true they seem to be. As you saw in Chapter 10, Believing and Knowing, evaluating the kinds of beliefs used as reasons in arguments is a complex challenge.

VALIDITY: DO THE REASONS SUPPORT THE CLAIM OR CONCLUSION?

In addition to determining whether the reasons are true, evaluating arguments involves investigating the relationship between the reasons and the claim or the conclusion (which becomes the thesis of a piece of writing that argues a position on an issue).

When the reasons support the conclusion in such a way that the conclusion follows from them, you have a **valid argument.** If, however, the reasons do not support the conclusion—that is, if the conclusion does not follow from the reasons being offered—you have an **invalid argument.** Remember that the words *valid* and *true* do not have the same meaning. You must first evaluate the truth of a reason, then determine its validity.

One way to focus on the concept of *validity* is to assume that all the reasons in an argument are true, then try to determine how probable they make the conclusion. The following is an example of one type of valid argument.

Reason: Anything that is a threat to our health should not be legal.

Reason: Marijuana is a threat to our health.

Conclusion: Therefore, marijuana should not be legal.

This is a valid argument because if we assume that the reasons are true, its conclusion does necessarily follow from them.

Of course, we may not agree that either or both of the reasons are true; in that case, we would not agree with the conclusion. Nevertheless, the structure of the argument is valid. This particular form of thinking is known as *deduction*.

Here is a different type of argument:

Reason: As part of a project in my social science class, we selected one hundred students in the school to be interviewed. We took special steps to ensure that these students were representative of the student body as a whole (total students: 4,386). We asked the students whether they thought that the United States should actively try to overthrow foreign governments that it disapproves of. Of the one hundred students interviewed, eighty-eight said that the United States should definitely not be involved in such activities.

Conclusion: We can conclude that most students in this school believe that the United States should not be engaged in attempts to actively overthrow foreign governments that it disapproves of.

This is a persuasive argument because if we assume that the reason is true, that reason provides strong support for the conclusion. In this case, the key part of the reason is the statement that the one hundred students selected were representative of the entire student population at the school. To evaluate the truth of the reason, we might want to investigate the procedure used to select the one hundred students in order to determine whether this sample was in fact representative of all the students. (Notice that the conclusion carefully said "in this school." It did not imprecisely say "most students.")

This particular form of thinking is an example of *induction*.

SOUNDNESS: IS THE ARGUMENT BOTH TRUE AND VALID?

When an argument includes both true reasons and a valid structure, the argument is considered sound. When an argument has either false reasons or an invalid structure, however, the argument is considered unsound.

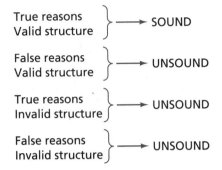

Figure 12.1 Sound and Unsound Arguments

The preceding chart (Figure 12.1) reminds us that in terms of arguments, *truth* and *validity* are not identical concepts. An argument can have true reasons and an invalid structure or have false reasons and a valid structure. In both cases the argument is unsound. Consider the following argument:

Reason: Professor Davis believes that megadoses of vitamins can cure colds.

Reason: Davis is a professor of computer science.

Conclusion: Megadoses of vitamins can cure colds.

This argument is obviously not valid: even if we assume that the reasons are true, the conclusion does not follow. Professor Davis's expertise with computers does not provide her with special knowledge about nutrition and medicine. This invalid thinking is neither structurally nor factually acceptable. It is clearly not a sound argument. Now, consider this argument:

Reason: For a democracy to function most effectively, the citizens should be able to think critically about the major social and political issues.

Reason: Education plays a key role in developing critical thinking abilities.

Conclusion: Therefore, education plays a key role in ensuring that a democracy is functioning most effectively.

A good case could be made for the soundness of this argument because the reasons are persuasive and the argument structure is valid. Of course, someone might counter that one or both of the reasons are not completely true, which illustrates an important point about the arguments we construct and evaluate. Many of the arguments we encounter in life fall somewhere between complete soundness and complete unsoundness because often we are not sure if our reasons are completely true. Throughout this book, we have found that developing accurate beliefs is an ongoing process and that our beliefs are subject to clarification and revision. As a result, the conclusion of any argument can be only as certain as the reasons supporting the conclusion.

The following two articles present different points of view about "end of life" issues. A variety of topics are now receiving attention: passive euthanasia, or nontreatment; active euthanasia or mercy killing; assisted suicide; the work of Dr. Kevorkian (nicknamed "Dr. Death"); the hospice movement (termed "Dr. Dignity"); the "right to die" laws of the state of Oregon and of the Netherlands.

These articles use different argumentative approaches. The first gives a human example, uses description, and employs *pathos*. The second, taken from the web site of the Hemlock Society, emphasizes logical argument, using many thinking patterns discussed in this book: contrast, comparison, definition, and causal analysis. It also refers to the fallacies *false dichotomy* and *slippery slope*.

In No Hurry for Next Leg of the Journey

BY DAVID GONZALEZ

The waning afternoon sunlight slipped into the rooms of Calvary Hospital in the Bronx. Outside, the trees looked like propped-up sticks, gray, crooked and ready for winter. Inside, it was warm and quiet, in anticipation of a bigger chill. Michael Burke lay in his bed, the latest stop in a medical journey that started in September with treatment at another hospital for a cancer that spread from his colon to his lung and brain.

"The doctors think I'm terminal," he said. "I think I'm terminal."

Calvary Hospital bills itself as the country's only specialty hospital for adults in the final stages of advanced cancer. It is not a hospice, since its patients require constant medical attention to stabilize them and ease their pain. Doctors tend to nearly every aspect of a patient's physical and emotional comfort as well as helping families that are emotionally battered by the disease.

Doctors at Calvary, which started almost 100 years ago in a Greenwich Village house, see their work as a counterpoint to those who advocate "a definitive medical response" to terminal illness. In plain English, they offer the dying patient an alternative to assisted suicide. It's not a place that Dr. Jack Kevorkian, who was ordered this week to stand trial on murder charges for his role in a suicide shown on television, has ever visited.

5   Mr. Burke, 45, a mechanical contractor, understands how frustration and despair drive some people to suicide, even if they have received the best care. But he does not consider that an option, and he is alarmed by Dr. Kevorkian's increasingly brazen attempts to force the issue.

"He seems seriously aggressive about it," Mr. Burke said. "But what constitutes the envelope of what he considers candidates for euthanasia would become bigger and bigger. I think people need to make it difficult for guys like that."

Calvary operates under the auspices of the Roman Catholic Archdiocese of New York, so its opposition to suicide hews to church teaching. Its patients—200 on any given day—represent many faiths. In rare cases, critically ill patients arrive at the hospital asking for a quick end. More common are feelings of depression or emotional suffering, which, if not addressed by doctors, psychiatrists and social workers, could lead to desperate yearnings.

"Depression is more painful than physical pain," said Dr. Michael Brescia, the hospital's medical director. "Emotional suffering is the absence of love. This is a time when people have to say final farewells to their children. There are no more holidays. No future. You're not in this life, you're on the outside looking in. Everybody else has a life and you don't have one. Most people, if they ask for suicide, it's from the emotional aspects of this disease."

Those emotional hardships, doctors said, aren't made any easier by the difficulties patients have in persuading their health maintenance organizations to allow them to seek appropriate care in other hospitals, or at least let them check into Calvary when death is near. Dr. James Cimino, director of Calvary's paliative care institute, said the medical run-around has been exploited by proponents of assisted suicide, who present euthanasia as a dignified response to the indignities of the health care bureaucracy.

10   "Kevorkian forced us as a society to ask why people want to die prematurely," Dr. Cimino said. "But we should have confronted it before."

He knows that other doctors—good, well-meaning ones—also support euthanasia. But each day he sees patients who resist an early demise. "Maybe it's something about the nature of the person that they have this suffering, yet they don't request suicide," he said. "I don't want to get into the philosophy of that."

But Michael Burke does.

"Kevorkian is assuming there's nothing out there after this," he said. "I assume there is. I think that's where we part company."

He said that as long as he was comfortable—and he was—he had no problem. Suicide, he said, would be unfair to his wife and two children.

15   "I wouldn't want them to believe Daddy had the option of pushing this button and leaving," he said. "I'm not trying to squeeze every last moment. But if I can live for a week and see my son one more time, I would. As opposed to seeing Kevorkian this afternoon. Not that I think they would let him in the door here."

He gave a small smile and a thumbs-up sign. The gesture was his own definitive response.

Hospice Care or Assisted Suicide: A False Dichotomy

BY JOHN L. MILLER

For the past few months, I have been reading, with great interest, the editorials and updates regarding the "Dr. Dignity" program. I would like to offer a different perspective. The view expressed here is one which comes from within the hospice movement, but which supports legal reforms to allow physician-assisted suicide.

Specifically, the legal reforms I am referring to would require many important safeguards which Dr. Kevorkian does not implement. A responsible assisted suicide would require free and repeated requests by the patient, with a substantial interval between requests. The involvement of a third party in a suicide ethically requires us to make sure the suffering is not temporary, or due to lack of information or obtainable (and desired) treatment. Informed consent, confirmed by two independent medical practitioners, would be required only after all available alternatives have been offered and explored. The fine details of these conditions are, of course, much debated. This article, however, looks not at these details, but at the ethical justification for such a position.

To begin, I applaud the promotion of hospice care in the media. Promoting compassionate palliative care to the general public is essential, especially if one believes that physician-assisted suicide should be made available in the context of offering choices.

But the "Dr. Dignity" program does not promote hospice care as just a choice. It promotes it as the only moral choice and, in doing so, sets up a false dichotomy. If one were to believe the editorials in this journal, one might mistakenly conclude that all proponents of legal reform were either historically naive, ignorant of hospice and palliative care, or both. And while some people may be guilty of this lack of information, many others are not.

5   Many people who have devoted their lives to the care of the dying are not opposed to physician-assisted suicide. Such people believe it should be available as one of several options, and, therefore, do not believe that promoting hospice[s] and advocating for the availability of regulated physician-assisted suicide are contradictory goals.

Understanding this position begins with an understanding of how and why assisted suicide and euthanasia differ. Not surprisingly, most people in the general public do not know the difference between the two terms; opponents of assisted suicide often deliberately obscure these differences by using the terms interchangeably.

But, many people support legalized assisted suicide for the same reason that they oppose euthanasia: the first offers us life choices and power over our own bodies, while the second takes control and choices away from us. Hospice care also offers people an essential choice, and so, on we campaign to make it available, and to make it better.

The problem with hospice care, however, is that in spite of our best public relations efforts, it doesn't always take away people's pain, and it isn't always wanted.

Parallels are often drawn between this debate and the one on abortion rights. These parallels are indeed apt. And since the war of words is as confusing there as it is here, let's blow away the fog: Mainstream proponents of legalized, assisted suicide advocate for its availability not because they are pro death, but because they believe in a person's right to control his/her life, and the right of a person to a death which s/he feels is dignified (even if we don't agree that it is).

10   In the assisted suicide debate, opponents sometimes use logical fallacies and historical misinformation to point fear at the wrong menace. It is easy to quell dissent in this way.

Take the argument, for instance, that assisted suicide will lead to euthanasia, eugenics, or even genocide. For a "slippery slope" argument to be valid, there must be a connection between an initial minor social ill and a potentially more serious one—an ill which, when amplified incrementally, creeps up on us and finally, has catastrophic, societal results. This connection usually exists because the minor social ill is of the same kind as the more serious one, and because taking one step makes the next one easier.

In this case, it is not valid to link assisted suicide to the more serious threat of euthanasia, eugenics, and genocide simply because they all involve third parties in the death of another person. One of these things is not like the others. To link them in this way is as ridiculous as saying that electing a government to make state decisions leads to fascism. Just because both involve state rule doesn't mean that giving a government power inevitably leads to its absolute power. A slippery slope to fascism happens when the checks which make governments representative and accountable are subtly removed, one by one.

Fear of a societal erosion of personal autonomy is a valid concern. The response must be to give people more choices, not fewer; more autonomy, not less. The legal reforms I offer for debate move us further away from fascism, not towards it.

If assisted suicide were an act, which in some small way diminished a person's power of self-determination, then one might make an argument that allowing such an act pushes us down a slippery slope towards more serious violations of this kind. The slow whittling away of self-determination can creep up on us, if we don't watch out.

15 And so, concerns should be expressed when laws which erode people's rights are created, or when existing rights legislation is revoked. Concern should be expressed when states give power to medical practitioners to override informed consent.

In remembering history, let's remember that this is exactly what occurred in Nazi-occupied Europe. Under the Nazis, "physician-assisted suicide" was never any such thing. It was always murder, the taking of someone's life against his/her will. Doctors assisted in these murders in a context where Jews and other minorities had no rights of any kind, and where neither quality of life, nor life itself were valued.

It is indeed conceivable that personal freedoms may be eroded in North America. But the top of the slippery slope is not assisted suicide. If anything, the "slope" is the loss of personal autonomy, and it exists already. We are teetering on the edge, and proponents of assisted suicide are reaching out to help pull us back up, not to push us down.

If, in North America, the right to control our bodies and our lives is further eroded in any significant way, physician-assisted suicide would certainly never become available. Women's reproductive rights would also be targets (they already are), as would informed consent in any medical decision, including one involving hospice care.

Dressing up hospice care is a panacea, and the only moral alternative to physician-assisted suicide is unhelpful, and inaccurate.

20   This issue is not simplistic. Reforms must happen in a context where we continue to promote alternatives, where we understand that several things can be true at the same time. Hospice care is wonderful for some. Physician-assisted suicide is a valid choice for others. People will always seek to influence the vulnerable and the sick. With freedoms come responsibilities.

Disabled rights activists, and indeed those of us in the hospice movement, know that it is not just the state which can coerce people to make unwanted or unnecessary choices. Family members, friends, [and] peers can also put subtle pressures on loved ones to choose a path which is better for the well person than for the sick.

But these pressures work both ways, unfortunately. Just as there are those who pressure people they love to end it all, there are also those who push people unduly to "hang on until the end." Knowing when to step back, knowing when to move forward, finding this balance in supporting the dignity of those we care for—this is the precious challenge with which we are all entrusted in hospice care.

We must be wary of the danger of falling to the extremes. At one end, are those who value life at all cost—even at the expense of quality. At this end, preventing another person from ending his/her life regardless of the circumstances is seen as acceptable. At the other end are those who put quality of life first, but who also believe that they can know how good or bad someone else's life is. People who think this way can be equally dangerous, because they feel no qualms about either pressuring us to end our life if they feel we are too miserable, or pressuring us to hang on, if they decide for us that our life is still worth living.

When we fall to the extremes, we take choices away from those who[m] we believe we are helping. But, there is a middle ground. When we aim for that middle ground, we all win.

Critical Reading Questions

1. What is the central claim or thesis of each article?

2. Identify two or three reasons that each writer gives to support his claim and evaluate these reasons.

3. Which argument seems more convincing to you? Explain why.

4. Identify the warrants for each argument. Does detecting the warrants help you to understand the differing claims?

5. Identify any qualifiers—words and phrases that keep the arguments from being simplistic.

6. Explore the web site from which the second article is taken (*www.hemlock.org*) and identify additional features that are used to support the Hemlock Society's central claim.

Forms of Argument

Arguments occur in many forms, but two major thinking methods—deduction and induction—provide the foundations for most arguments and also influence the organizational structure of arguments. They can be seen as (1) moving from general principles to specific applications and (2) moving from specific examples to general conclusions. Deduction and induction are seldom applied in "pure" or textbook ways in real-life arguments. Instead, they often are compressed or combined, so recognizing and analyzing their uses can sometimes be difficult. In fact, some teachers and students feel that studying them separately is more a mental exercise than a practical activity. However, as a critical thinker, a writer of arguments, and an analyst of arguments, you need to understand these principles.

DEDUCTIVE REASONING

The deductive argument is the one most commonly associated with the study of logic. Though it has a variety of valid forms, they all share one characteristic: if you accept the supporting reasons (also called **premises**) as true, you must also accept the conclusion as true. A **deductive argument** is an argument form in which one reasons from premises that are known or assumed to be true to a conclusion that necessarily follows from these premises. For example, consider the following famous deductive argument:

Reason/Premise: All persons are mortal.

Reason/Premise: Socrates is a person.

Conclusion: Therefore, Socrates is mortal.

In this example of **deductive reasoning,** accepting the premises of the argument as true means that the conclusion necessarily follows; it cannot be false. Many deductive arguments, like this one, are structured as **syllogisms,** an argument form that consists of two supporting premises and a conclusion. There are also, however, a large number of invalid deductive forms, one of which is illustrated in the following defective syllogism:

Reason/Premise: All persons are mortal.

Reason/Premise: Socrates is a person.

Conclusion: Therefore, all persons are Socrates.

This example is deliberately absurd, but people do shift terms in these ways and think things such as "all tall people should play basketball" just because basketball players are usually tall. Despite the variety of invalid deductive structures, once you become aware of the concept of *validity,* you should be able to detect invalidity.

One way to do this is through the application of a general rule. Whenever we reason by using the form illustrated by the valid Socrates syllogism, we are using the following argument structure:

Premise: All A (people) are B (mortal).

Premise: S is an A (Socrates is a person).

Conclusion: Therefore, S is B (Socrates is mortal).

This basic argument form is valid no matter what terms are included. For example:

Premise: All politicians are untrustworthy.

Premise: Bill White is a politician.

Conclusion: Therefore, Bill White is untrustworthy.

Notice again that with any valid deductive form, if we assume that the premises are true, we must accept the conclusion. Of course, in this case it is unlikely that the first premise is true.

Although we are not always aware of doing so, we use this basic type of reasoning whenever we apply a general rule. For instance:

Premise: All eight-year-old children should be in bed by 9:30 P.M.

Premise: You are an eight-year-old child.

Conclusion: Therefore, you should be in bed by 9:30 P.M.

Often we present this kind of reasoning in an abbreviated form called an *enthymeme,* which assumes the first premise: You should be in bed by 9:30 because you're an eight-year-old child; Bill White is a politician, so he's untrustworthy.

Describe an example from your own experience in which you use this deductive form, both as a syllogism and as an enthymeme.

OTHER DEDUCTIVE FORMS

Deductive arguments, or syllogisms and enthymemes, come in many other forms, most of which have been named by logicians. At some point in your college education, you should consider taking a course in critical thinking or logic to learn about as many kinds of reasoning as you can. This chapter provides only an introduction.

Affirming the antecedent

Premise: If I have prepared thoroughly for the final exam, I will do well.

Premise: I prepared thoroughly for the exam.

Conclusion: Therefore, I will do well on the exam.

When we reason like this, we are using the following argument structure:

Premise: If A (I have prepared thoroughly), then B (I will do well).

Premise: A (I have prepared thoroughly).

Conclusion: Therefore, B (I will do well).

Like all valid deductive forms, this form is valid no matter what specific terms are included. For example:

Premise: If the Democrats register 20 million new voters, they will win the presidential election.

Premise: The Democrats have registered more than 20 million new voters.

Conclusion: Therefore, the Democrats will win the presidential election.

As with other valid argument forms, the conclusion will be true if the reasons are true. Although the second premise in this argument expresses information that can be verified, the first premise would be more difficult to establish.

Denying the consequent

Premise: If Michael were a really good friend, he would lend me his car for the weekend.

Premise: Michael refuses to lend me his car for the weekend.

Conclusion: Therefore, Michael is not a really good friend.

When we reason in this fashion, we are using the following argument structure:

Premise: If A (Michael is a really good friend), then B (He will lend me his car).

Premise: Not B (He won't lend me his car).

Conclusion: Therefore, not A (He's not a really good friend).

Again, like other valid reasoning forms, this form is valid no matter what subject is being considered. As always, the truth of the premises must be evaluated.

Disjunctive syllogism

Premise: Either I left my wallet on my dresser, or I have lost it.

Premise: The wallet is not on my dresser.

Conclusion: Therefore, I must have lost it.

When we reason in this way, we are using the following argument structure:

Premise: Either A (I left my wallet on my dresser) or B (I have lost it).

Premise: Not A (I didn't leave it on my dresser).

Conclusion: Therefore, B (I have lost it).

This valid reasoning form can be applied to any number of situations and still yield accurate results. For example:

> *Premise:* Either your stomach trouble is caused by what you are eating, or it is caused by nervous tension.
>
> *Premise:* You tell me that you have been very careful about your diet.
>
> *Conclusion:* Therefore, your stomach trouble is caused by nervous tension.

To determine the accuracy of the conclusion, we must determine the accuracy of the premises. If they are true, then the conclusion must also be true.

All of the preceding basic argument forms can be found not only in informal daily conversations but also at more formal levels of thinking. They appear in academic disciplines, in scientific inquiry, in debates on social issues, and so on. Many other argument forms—both deductive and inductive—also constitute human reasoning. By sharpening your understanding of these ways of thinking, you will be better able to make sense of the world by constructing and evaluating effective arguments.

Thinking ↔ Writing Activity

Evaluating Deductive Arguments

Analyze the following arguments by completing these steps.

1. Summarize the reasons and conclusions given.
2. Identify which, if any, deductive argument forms are being used.
3. Evaluate the truth of the reasons that support the conclusion.

For if the brain is a machine of ten billion nerve cells and the mind can somehow be explained as the summed activity of a finite number of chemical and electrical reactions, [then] boundaries limit the human prospect—we are biological and our souls cannot fly free. —Edward O. Wilson, *On Human Nature*

The extreme vulnerability of a complex industrial society to intelligent, targeted terrorism by a very small number of people may prove the fatal challenge to which Western states have no adequate response. Counterforce alone will never suffice. The real challenge of the true terrorist is to the basic values of a society. If there is no commitment to shared values in Western society—and if none are imparted in our amoral institutions of higher learning—no increase in police and burglar alarms will suffice to preserve our society from the specter that haunts us—not a bomb from above but a gun from within. —James Billington, "The Gun Within"

To fully believe in something, to truly understand something, one must be intimately acquainted with its opposite. One should not adopt a creed by default, because no alternative is known. Education should prepare students for the "real world" not by segregating them from evil but by urging full confrontation to test and modify the validity of the good. —Robert Baron, "In Defense of Teaching Racism, Sexism, and Fascism"

The inescapable conclusion is that society secretly wants crime, needs crime, and gains definite satisfactions from the present mishandling of it! We condemn crime; we punish offenders for it; but we need it. The crime and punishment ritual is a part of our lives. We need crimes to wonder at, to enjoy vicariously, to discuss and speculate about, and to publicly deplore. We need criminals to identify ourselves with, to envy secretly, and to punish stoutly. They do for us the forbidden, illegal things we wish to do and, like scapegoats of old, they bear the burdens of our displaced guilt and punishment—"the iniquities of us all." —Karl Menninger, "The Crime of Punishment"

INDUCTIVE REASONING

The preceding section focused on deductive reasoning, an argument form in which one reasons from premises that are known or assumed to be true to a conclusion that follows necessarily from the premises. This section introduces **inductive reasoning,** an argument form in which one reasons from premises or instances that are known or assumed to be true to a conclusion that is supported by the premises but does not necessarily follow from them.

When you reason inductively, your premises, instances, or data provide evidence that makes it more or less probable (but not certain) that the conclusion is true. The following statements are examples of conclusions reached through inductive reasoning. As you read them, think about how the data might have been obtained and what arguments could be based on each statement.

1. A recent Gallup poll reported that 74 percent of the American public believes that abortion should remain legal.

2. On the average, a person with a college degree will earn over $830,000 more in his or her lifetime than a person with just a high school diploma.

3. The outbreak of food poisoning at the end-of-year school party was probably caused by the squid salad.

4. The devastating disease AIDS is caused by a particularly complex virus that may not be curable.

5. The solar system is probably the result of an enormous explosion—a "big bang"—that occurred billions of years ago.

Each of the first two statements is an example of inductive reasoning known as **empirical generalization**—a general statement about an entire group made on the basis of observing some members of the group. The final three statements are examples of **causal reasoning**—a form of inductive reasoning which claims that an event (or events) is the result of the occurrence of another event (or events).

CAUSAL REASONING

You were introduced to causal analysis in Chapter 8 and also to the fallacies that can result if causes are not analyzed logically. Review pages 284–286 to recall the characteristics of this pattern of induction.

Causal reasoning is the backbone of the natural and the social sciences. It is also central to the *scientific method,* which operates on the assumption that the world is constructed in a complex web of causal relationships that can be discovered through systematic investigation. You apply the scientific method in your science courses.

EMPIRICAL GENERALIZATION

An important tool used by both natural and social scientists is empirical generalization. Have you ever wondered how the major television and radio networks can predict election results hours before the polls close? These predictions are made possible by using **empirical generalization,** a form of inductive reasoning which is defined as "reasoning by examining a limited sample to reach a general conclusion based on that sample."

Network election predictions, as well as public opinion polls that are conducted throughout a political campaign, are based on interviews with a select number of people. Ideally, pollsters would interview everyone in the "target population" (in this case, voters), but doing this, of course, is hardly practical. Instead, they select a relatively small group of individuals from the target population, known as a "sample," who they have determined will adequately represent the group as a whole. Pollsters believe that they can then generalize the opinions of this smaller group to the target population. The results are often accurate—with a few notable exceptions (such as the 2000 presidential election in which Al Gore withdrew his concession to George W. Bush on election night, following a changed projection in the state of Florida).

There are three key criteria for evaluating inductive arguments:

- Is the sample known?
- Is the sample sufficient?
- Is the sample representative?

Is the Sample Known? An inductive argument is only as strong as the sample on which it is based. For example, sample populations described in vague terms—such as "highly placed sources" or "many young people interviewed"—provide a treacherously weak foundation for generalizing to larger populations. In order for an inductive argument to be persuasive, the sample population should be explicitly known and clearly identified. Natural and social scientists take great care when selecting members of sample groups. They also make information on members of the sample groups available to outside investigators who may wish to evaluate and verify the results.

Is the Sample Sufficient? The second criterion for evaluating inductive reasoning is to consider the size of the sample. It should be large enough to provide an accurate sense of the group as a whole. In the polling example discussed earlier, we would be concerned if only a few registered voters had been interviewed, and the results of the interviews were then generalized to a much larger population. Overall, the larger the sample, the more reliable the inductive conclusions. Natural and social scientists have developed precise guidelines for determining the size of the sample needed to achieve reliable results. For example, poll results are often accompanied by a qualification such as "These results are subject to an error factor of $\pm$ 3 percentage points." This means that if the sample reveals that 47 percent of those interviewed prefer candidate X, we can reliably state that 44 to 50 percent of the target population prefers candidate X. Because a sample is usually a small portion of the target population, we can rarely state that the two match each other exactly—there must always be some room for variation. The exceptions to this are situations in which the target population is completely homogeneous. For instance, tasting one cookie from a bag of cookies is usually enough to tell us whether or not the contents of the entire bag are stale.

Is the Sample Representative? The third crucial element in effective inductive reasoning is the representativeness of the sample. If we are to generalize with confidence from the sample to the target population, we have to be sure the sample is similar in all relevant aspects to the larger group from which it is drawn. For instance, in the polling example, the sample population should reflect the same percentage of men and women, of Democrats and Republicans, of young and old, and so on, as exists in the target population. It is obvious that many characteristics—such as hair color, favorite food, and shoe size—are not relevant to the comparison. The better the sample reflects the target population in terms of relevant qualities, however, the better the accuracy of the generalizations. On the other hand, when the sample does not represent the target population—for example, if the election pollsters interviewed only females between the ages of thirty and thirty-five—the sample is termed *biased,* and any generalizations about the target population will be highly suspect.

How do we ensure that the sample is representative of the target population? One important device is *random selection,* a selection strategy in which every member of the target population has an equal chance of being included in the sample. For example, the various techniques used to select winning lottery tickets are supposed to be random—each ticket is supposed to have an equal chance of winning. In complex cases of inductive reasoning—such as polling—random selection is often combined with the confirmation that all the important categories in the population are adequately represented. For example, an election pollster would want to ensure that all significant geographical areas are included and then would randomly select individuals from within those areas to compose the sample.

Understanding the principles of empirical generalization is crucial to effective thinking because we are continually challenged to evaluate this form of inductive thinking in our lives. In addition, when writing about political or social issues, we often use the results of inductive investigations, so we should be able to determine their accuracy and relevance.

Thinking ↔ Writing Activity

Analyzing Empirical Generalization

Review the following examples of empirical generalizing. Select two and then evaluate the quality of the thinking by answering the following questions.

1. Is the sample known?
2. Is the sample sufficient?
3. Is the sample representative?
4. Do you believe that the conclusions are likely to be accurate? Why or why not?
5. What are some arguments that might be based on your answers?

In a study of a possible relationship between pornography and antisocial behavior, questionnaires went out to 7,500 psychiatrists and psychoanalysts whose listing in the directory of the American Psychological Association indicated clinical experience. Over 3,400 of these professionals responded. The result: 7.4 percent of the psychiatrists and psychologists had cases in which they were convinced that pornography was a causal factor in antisocial behavior, an additional 9.4 percent were suspicious, 3.2 percent did not commit themselves, and 80 percent said they had no cases in which a causal connection was suspected.

A survey by the Sleep Disorder Clinic of the VA hospital in La Jolla, California (involving more than one million people), revealed that people who sleep more than ten hours a night have a death rate 80 percent higher than those who sleep only seven or eight hours. Men who sleep fewer than four hours a night have a death rate 180 percent higher, and women with less [than four hours'] sleep have a rate 40 percent higher. This might be taken as indicating that too much and too little sleep cause death.

In a recent survey, twice as many doctors interviewed stated that if they were stranded on a desert island, they would prefer X Aspirin to Extra Strength Y.

Being a general practitioner in a rural area has tremendous drawbacks—being on virtual 24-hour call 365 days a year, patients without financial means or insurance, low fees in the first place, inadequate facilities and assistance. Nevertheless, America's small-town G.P.s seem fairly content with their lot. According to a survey taken by *Country Doctor*, fully 50 percent wrote back that they "basically like being a rural G.P." Only 1 in 15 regretted that he or she had not specialized. Only 2 out of 20 rural general practitioners would trade places with their urban counterparts, given the chance. And only 1 in 30 would "choose some other line of work altogether."

More Fallacies: Forms of False Reasoning

As we pointed out in Chapter 8, certain forms of reasoning are not logical. These types of pseudoreasoning (false reasoning) are often termed *fallacies:* arguments that are not sound because of various errors in reasoning. Fallacious reasoning is sometimes used to influence others. It seeks to persuade not on the basis of sound arguments and critical thinking but rather on the basis of emotional and illogical factors. Sometimes fallacious reasoning is used inadvertently. However, it is always dangerous, so it is important to recognize it as well as to avoid using it. Detecting fallacious reasoning is a significant factor in evaluating sources of beliefs, the concept discussed in Chapter 10.

In Chapter 9, Forming Concepts, we explored the way in which we form concepts through the interactive process of generalizing (identifying the common qualities that define the boundaries of the concept) and interpreting (identifying examples of the concept). This process is similar to the process involved in constructing empirical generalizations as we seek to reach a general conclusion based on a limited number of examples and then apply this conclusion to other examples. Although generalizing and interpreting are useful in forming concepts, they also can lead to fallacious ways of thinking, including hasty generalization, sweeping generalization, and false dilemma.

HASTY GENERALIZATION

Consider the following examples of reasoning. Do you think the arguments are sound? Why or why not?

- My boyfriends have never shown any real concern for my feelings. My conclusion is that men are insensitive, selfish, and emotionally superficial.
- My mother always gets upset over insignificant things. This leads me to believe that women are very emotional.

In both of these cases, a general conclusion has been reached that is based on a very small sample. As a result, the reasons provide very weak support for the conclusions. It does not make good sense to generalize from one or a few individuals to all men or all women. The conclusion is *hasty* because the information is not adequate enough to justify the generalization.

SWEEPING GENERALIZATION

Whereas the fallacy of hasty generalization deals with errors in the process of generalizing, the fallacy of *sweeping generalization* stems from difficulties in the process of interpreting. Consider the following examples of reasoning. Do you consider the arguments sound? Why or why not?

- Vigorous exercise contributes to overall good health. Therefore, vigorous exercise should be practiced by recent heart-attack victims, people who are out of shape, and women in the last month of pregnancy.
- People should be allowed to make their own decisions, providing that their actions do not harm other people. Therefore, people who are trying to commit suicide should be left alone to do as they please.

In both of these cases, generalizations that are true in most cases have been deliberately applied to examples that are clearly intended to be exceptions to the generalizations because of their special features. Of course, the use of a sweeping generalization motivates us to clarify the generalization, rephrasing it to exclude examples, like those given here, that have special features. For example, the first generalization could be reformulated as "Vigorous exercise contributes to the overall good health of most people *except* recent heart-attack victims, people who are out of shape, and women who are about to give birth." Sweeping generalizations become dangerous when they are accepted without critical analysis.

Examine the following examples of sweeping generalizations. In each case (a) explain why it is a sweeping generalization and (b) reformulate the statement to make it a legitimate generalization.

1. A college education stimulates you to develop as a person and prepares you for many professions. Therefore, all people should attend college, no matter what career interests them.

2. Drugs such as heroin and morphine are addictive and therefore qualify as dangerous drugs. This means that they should never be used, even as painkillers in medical situations.

3. Once criminals have served time for the crimes they have committed, they have paid their debt to society and should be permitted to work at any job they choose.

FALSE DILEMMA

The fallacy of the *false dilemma*—also known as the *either/or* fallacy and the *false dichotomy* fallacy—occurs when one is asked to choose between two extreme alternatives without being able to consider additional options. For example, we may say, "You're either for me or against me." Sometimes giving people only two choices on an issue makes sense ("If you decide to swim the English Channel, you'll either make it or you won't"). At other times, however, viewing a complicated situation in such extreme terms can result in a serious oversimplification.

The following statements are examples of false dilemmas. After analyzing the fallacy in each case, suggest different alternatives than those being presented.

Example: "Everyone in Germany is a National Socialist—the few outside the party are either lunatics or idiots." (Adolf Hitler, quoted by the *New York Times*, April 5, 1938)

Analysis: Hitler was saying that Germans who were not Nazis were lunatics or idiots. By limiting the classification of the population to these three categories, Hitler was simply ignoring all the people who did not qualify as Nazis, lunatics, or idiots.

1. "America—love it or leave it!"

2. "She loves me; she loves me not."

3. "Live free or die."

4. "If you're not part of the solution, you're part of the problem."

5. "If you know about a BMW, you either own one or you want to."

FALLACIES OF RELEVANCE

Many fallacious arguments try to gain support by appealing to factors that have little or nothing to do with the arguments. In these cases, false appeals substitute for sound reasoning and a critical examination of the issues. Such appeals are known as fallacies of *relevance*.

Appeal to Authority In Chapters 2 and 10, we explored the ways in which we sometimes use various authorities to establish our beliefs or to prove our points. At that time, we noted that to serve as a basis for beliefs, authorities must have legitimate expertise in the area in which they are advising—for example, an experienced mechanic could diagnose your car's problem. However, people occasionally appeal to authorities who are not qualified to give an expert opinion. Consider the reasoning in the following advertisements. Do you think the arguments are sound? Why or why not?

- Hi. You've probably seen me out on the football field. After a hard day's work crushing halfbacks and sacking quarterbacks, I like to settle down with a cold, smooth Maltz beer.
- SONY. Ask anyone.
- Over 11 million women will read this ad. Only 16 will own the coat.

Each of these arguments is intended to persuade us of the value of a product through the appeal to various authorities. In the first case, the authority is a well-known sports figure; in the second, the authority is large numbers of people; in the third, the authority is a select few, so the appeal is to our desire to be exclusive ("snob appeal"). Unfortunately, none of these authorities offers legitimate expertise about the product. Football players are not beer experts, large numbers of people are often misled, and exclusive groups of people are frequently mistaken in their beliefs. To evaluate authorities properly, we have to ask:

What are the professional credentials on which the authorities' expertise is based?
Is their expertise in the area on which they are commenting?

Appeal to Pity Consider the reasoning in the following arguments. Do you think the arguments are sound? Why or why not?

- I know that I haven't completed my term paper, but I really think that I should be excused. This has been a very difficult semester for me. I caught every kind of flu that came around. In addition, my brother has a drinking problem, and this has been very upsetting for me. Also, my dog died.
- I admit that my client embezzled money from the company, Your Honor. However, I would like to bring several facts to your attention. He is a family man with a wonderful wife and two terrific children. He is an important member of the community. He is active in his church, coaches a Little League baseball team, and has worked very hard to be a good person who cares about people. I think that you should take these things into consideration when handing down your sentence.

In each of these arguments, the reasons offered to support the conclusions may indeed be true, yet they are not relevant to the conclusion. Instead of providing evidence that supports the conclusion, the reasons are designed to make us feel sorry for the person involved and therefore to agree with the conclusion out of sympathy. Although these appeals can often be effective, the arguments are not sound. The validity of a conclusion can only be established by reasons that support and are relevant to the conclusion.

Appeal to Fear   Consider the reasoning in the following arguments. Do you consider the arguments sound? Why or why not?

- I don't think you deserve a raise. After all, there are many people who would be happy to have your job at the salary you are currently receiving. I would be happy to interview some of these people if you really think that you are underpaid.

- If you continue to disagree with my interpretation of *The Catcher in the Rye*, I'm afraid it may affect the grade on your paper.

In both of these arguments, the conclusions being suggested are supported by an appeal to fear, not by reasons that provide evidence for the conclusions. In the first case, the threat is that if you do not forgo your salary demands, your job may be in jeopardy. In the second case, the threat is that if you do not agree with the teacher's interpretation, you may receive a low grade. In neither instance are the real issues—Is a salary increase deserved? Is the student's interpretation legitimate?—being discussed. People who appeal to fear to support their conclusions are interested only in prevailing, regardless of which position might be more justified.

Appeal to Ignorance   Consider the reasoning in the following arguments. Do you find the arguments sound? Why or why not?

- You say that you don't believe in God. But can you prove that an omnipotent spirit doesn't exist? If not, then you have to accept the conclusion that it does in fact exist.

- Greco Tires are the best. No others have been proved better.

When this argument form is used, the person offering the conclusion is asking his or her opponent to *disprove* the conclusion. If the opponent is unable to do so, the conclusion is asserted to be true. This argument form is not valid because it is the task of the person proposing the argument to prove the conclusion. The fact that an opponent cannot disprove it offers no evidence that the conclusion is justified.

Appeal to Personal Attack   Consider the reasoning in the following arguments. Do you think the arguments are valid? Why or why not?

- Senator Smith's opinion about a tax cut is wrong. It's impossible to believe anything he says since he left his wife for that model.

- How can you have an intelligent opinion about abortion? You're not a woman, so this is a decision that you'll never have to make.

This argument form has been one of the fallacies most frequently used through the ages. Its effectiveness results from ignoring the issues of the argument and focusing instead on the qualities of the person presenting it. Trying to discredit the other person is an effort to discredit the argument—no matter what reasons are offered. This fallacy is also referred to as the *ad hominem* argument (which means drawing attention "to the man" rather than to the issue) and as *poisoning the well* (since the speaker is trying to ensure that any water drawn from the opponent's well will be regarded as undrinkable).

The effort to discredit can take two forms, as illustrated in the preceding examples. The fallacy can be *abusive* by directly attacking the credibility of an opponent. In addition, the fallacy can be *circumstantial* by claiming that a person's circumstances, not character, render his or her opinion so biased or uninformed that it cannot be treated seriously. Another example of the circumstantial form would be disregarding the views on nuclear-plant safety that were presented by an owner of a nuclear plant.

Thinking ↔ Writing Activity

Analyzing Fallacies

1. Find in advertisements, political statements, or other arguments that you have encountered, examples of two or three false appeals. Write a brief explanation of why you think the appeal is not warranted. Look for the following fallacies:

   - Appeal to authority
   - Appeal to pity
   - Appeal to fear
   - Appeal to ignorance
   - Appeal to personal attack

2. Share the fallacies you have found with classmates and also examine the ones they have identified.

3. Write a few sentences explaining how you can avoid using fallacies in your own writing.

Analyzing well-known arguments to see how they use deduction, induction, evidence *(logos)*, *ethos*, *pathos*, appeals—and perhaps fallacious reasoning—is a challenging activity and one that can help you with your own arguments. Read the Declaration of Independence and the Declaration of Sentiments and Resolutions, which follow, and Martin Luther King Jr.'s speech, "I Have a Dream" (page 180 in Chapter 5). Then answer the questions that follow the readings.

The Declaration of Independence

In Congress, July 4, 1776
The unanimous declaration of the thirteen
United States of America

When in the course of human events, it becomes necessary for one people to dissolve the political bands which have connected them with another, and to assume among the powers of the earth, the separate and equal station to which the Laws of Nature and of Nature's God entitle them, a decent respect to the opinions of mankind requires that they should declare the causes which impel them to the separation.

We hold these truths to be self-evident, that all men are created equal, that they are endowed by their Creator with certain unalienable rights, that among these are life, liberty and the pursuit of happiness. That to secure these rights, governments are instituted among men, deriving their just powers from the consent of the governed. That whenever any form of government becomes destructive of these ends, it is the right of the people to alter or to abolish it, and to institute new government, laying its foundation on such principles and organizing its powers in such form, as to them shall seem most likely to effect their safety and happiness. Prudence, indeed, will dictate that governments long established should not be changed for light and transient causes; and accordingly all experience hath shown, that mankind are more disposed to suffer, while evils are sufferable, than to right themselves by abolishing the forms to which they are accustomed. But when a long train of abuses and usurpations, pursuing invariably the same object evinces a design to reduce them under absolute despotism, it is their right, it is their duty, to throw off such government, and to provide new guards for their future security. Such has been the patient sufferance of these Colonies; and such is now the necessity which constrains them to alter their former systems of government. The history of the present King of Great Britain is a history of repeated injuries and usurpations, all having in direct object the establishment of an absolute tyranny over these States. To prove this, let facts be submitted to a candid world.

He has refused his assent to laws, the most wholesome and necessary for the public good.

He has forbidden his Governors to pass laws of immediate and pressing importance, unless suspended in their operation till his assent should be obtained; and when so suspended, he has utterly neglected to attend to them.

5 He has refused to pass other laws for the accommodation of large districts of people, unless those people would relinquish the right of representation in the Legislature, a right inestimable to them and formidable to tyrants only.

He has called together legislative bodies at places unusual, uncomfortable, and distant from the depository of their public records, for the sole purpose of fatiguing them into compliance with his measures.

He has dissolved representative houses repeatedly, for opposing with manly firmness his invasions on the rights of the people.

He has refused for a long time, after such dissolutions, to cause others to be elected; whereby the legislative powers, incapable of annihilation, have returned to the people at large for their exercise; the State remaining in the meantime exposed to all the dangers of invasion from without and convulsions within.

He has endeavoured to prevent the population of these States; for that purpose obstructing the laws of naturalization of foreigners; refusing to pass others to encourage their migration hither, and raising the conditions of new appropriations of lands.

10   He has obstructed the administration of justice, by refusing his assent to laws for establishing judiciary powers.

He has made judges dependent on his will alone, for the tenure of their offices, and the amount and payment of their salaries.

He has erected a multitude of new offices, and sent hither swarms of officers to harass our people, and eat out their substance.

He has kept among us, in times of peace, standing armies without the consent of our legislatures.

He has affected to render the military independent of and superior to the civil power.

15   He has combined with others to subject us to a jurisdiction foreign to our constitution, and unacknowledged by our laws; giving his assent to their acts of pretended legislation:

For quartering large bodies of armed troops among us:

For protecting them, by a mock trial, from punishment for any murders which they should commit on the inhabitants of these States:

For cutting off our trade with all parts of the world:

For imposing taxes on us without our consent:

20   For depriving us, in many cases, of the benefits of trial by jury:

For transporting us beyond seas to be tried for pretended offences:

For abolishing the free system of English laws in a neighbouring Province, establishing therein an arbitrary government, and enlarging its boundaries so as to render it at once an example and fit instrument for introducing the same absolute rule into these Colonies:

For taking away our Charters, abolishing our most valuable laws, and altering fundamentally the forms of our governments:

For suspending our own Legislatures, and declaring themselves invested with power to legislate for us in all cases whatsoever.

25   He has abdicated government here, by declaring us out of his protection and waging war against us.

He has plundered our seas, ravaged our coasts, burnt our towns, and destroyed the lives of our people.

He is at this time transporting large armies of foreign mercenaries to complete the works of death, desolation and tyranny, already begun with circumstances of cruelty and perfidy scarcely paralleled in the most barbarous ages, and totally unworthy the head of a civilized nation.

He has constrained our fellow citizens taken captive on the high seas to bear arms against their country, to become the executioners of their friends and brethren, or to fall themselves by their hands.

He has excited domestic insurrections amongst us, and has endeavoured to bring on the inhabitants of our frontiers, the merciless Indian savages, whose known rule of warfare, is an undistinguished destruction of all ages, sexes, and conditions.

30   In every stage of these oppressions we have petitioned for redress in the most humble terms: our repeated petitions have been answered only by repeated injury. A prince whose character is thus marked by every act which may define a tyrant is unfit to be the ruler of a free people.

Nor have we been wanting in attention to our British brethren. We have warned them from time to time of attempts by their legislature to extend an unwarrantable jurisdiction over us. We have reminded them of the circumstances of our emigration and settlement here. We have appealed to their native justice and magnanimity, and we have conjured them by the ties of our common kindred to disavow these usurpations, which would inevitably interrupt our connections and correspondence. They too have been deaf to the voice of justice and of consanguinity. We must, therefore, acquiesce in the necessity, which denounces our separation, and hold them, as we hold the rest of mankind, enemies in war, in peace friends.

We, therefore, the Representatives of the United States of America, in General Congress assembled, appealing to the Supreme Judge of the world for the rectitude of our intentions, do, in the name, and by the authority of the good people of these Colonies, solemnly publish and declare, That these United Colonies are, and of right ought to be Free and Independent States; that they are absolved from all allegiance to the British Crown, and that all political connection between them and the State of Great Britain, is and ought to be totally dissolved; and that as Free and Independent States, they have full power to levy war, conclude peace, contract alliances, establish commerce, and to do all other acts and things which Independent States may of right do. And for the support of this declaration, with a firm reliance on the protection of Divine Providence, we mutually pledge to each other our lives, our fortunes, and our sacred honor.

Declaration of Sentiments and Resolutions

BY ELIZABETH CADY STANTON

When, in the course of human events, it becomes necessary for one person of the family of man to assume among the people of the earth a position different from that which they have hitherto occupied, but one to which the laws of nature and nature's God entitle them, a decent respect to the opinions of mankind requires that they should declare the causes that impel them to such a course.

We hold these truths to be self-evident: that all men and women are created equal; that they are endowed by their Creator with certain inalienable rights; that among these are life, liberty, and the pursuit of happiness; that to secure these rights governments are instituted, deriving their just powers from the consent of the governed. Whenever any form of government becomes destructive of these ends, it is the right of those who suffer from it to refuse allegiance to it, and to insist upon the institution of a new government, laying its foundation on such principles, and organizing its powers in such form, as to them shall seem most likely to effect their safety and happiness. Prudence, indeed, will dictate that governments long established should not be changed for light and transient causes; and accordingly all experience hath shown that mankind are more disposed to suffer, while evils are sufferable, than to right themselves by abolishing the forms to which they were accustomed. But when a long train of abuses and usurpations, pursuing invariably the same object evinces a design to reduce them under absolute despotism, it is their duty to throw off such government, and to provide new guards for their future security. Such has been the patient sufferance of the women under this government, and such is now the necessity which constrains them to demand the equal station to which they are entitled.

The history of mankind is a history of repeated injuries and usurpations on the part of man toward woman, having in direct object the establishment of an absolute tyranny over her. To prove this, let facts be submitted to a candid world.

He has never permitted her to exercise her inalienable right to the elective franchise.

5   He has compelled her to submit to laws, in the formation of which she had no voice.

He has withheld from her rights which are given to the most ignorant and degraded men—both natives and foreigners.

Having deprived her of this first right of a citizen, the elective franchise, thereby leaving her without representation in the halls of legislation, he has oppressed her on all sides.

He has made her, if married, in the eye of the law, civilly dead.

He has taken from her all right in property, even to the wages she earns.

10   He has made her, morally, an irresponsible being, as she can commit many crimes with impunity, provided they be done in the presence of her husband. In the covenant of marriage, she is compelled to promise obedience to her husband, he becoming, to all intents and purposes, her master—the law giving him power to deprive her of her liberty, and to administer chastisement.

He has so framed the laws of divorce, as to what shall be the proper causes, and in case of separation, to whom the guardianship of the children shall be given, as to be wholly regardless of the happiness of women—the law, in all cases, going upon a false supposition of the supremacy of man, and giving all power into his hands.

After depriving her of all rights as a married woman, if single, and the owner of property, he has taxed her to support a government which recognizes her only when her property can be made profitable to it.

He has monopolized nearly all the profitable employments, and from those she is permitted to follow, she receives but a scanty remuneration. He closes against her all the avenues to wealth and distinction which he considers most honorable to himself. As a teacher of theology, medicine, or law, she is not known.

He has denied her the facilities for obtaining a thorough education, all colleges being closed against her.

15　He allows her in Church, as well as State, but a subordinate position, claiming Apostolic authority for her exclusion from the ministry, and, with some exceptions, from any public participation in the affairs of the Church.

He has created a false public sentiment by giving to the world a different code of morals for men and women, by which moral delinquencies which exclude women from society are not only tolerated, but deemed of little account in man.

He has usurped the prerogative of Jehovah himself, claiming it as his right to assign for her a sphere of action, when that belongs to her conscience and to her God.

He has endeavored, in every way that he could, to destroy her confidence in her own powers, to lessen her self-respect, and to make her willing to lead a dependent and abject life.

Now, in view of this entire disfranchisement of one-half the people of this country, their social and religious degradation—in view of the unjust laws above mentioned, and because women do feel themselves aggrieved, oppressed, and fraudulently deprived of their most sacred rights, we insist that they have immediate admission to all the rights and privileges which belong to them as citizens of the United States.

20　In entering upon the great work before us, we anticipate no small amount of misconception, misrepresentation, and ridicule; but we shall use every instrumentality within our power to effect our object. We shall employ agents, circulate tracts, petition the State and National legislatures, and endeavor to enlist the pulpit and the press in our behalf. We hope this Convention will be followed by a series of Conventions embracing every part of the country.

Resolutions

WHEREAS, The great precept of nature is conceded to be, that "man shall pursue his own true and substantial happiness." Blackstone in his Commentaries remarks, that this law of Nature being coeval with mankind, and dictated by God himself, is of course superior in obligation to any other. It is binding over all the globe, in all countries and at all times; no human laws are of any validity if contrary to this, and such of them as are valid, derive all their force and all their validity, and all their authority, mediately and immediately, from this original; therefore,

Resolved, That such laws as conflict, in any way, with the true and substantial happiness of woman, are contrary to the great precept of nature and of no validity, for this is "superior in obligation to any other."

Resolved, That all laws which prevent woman from occupying such a station in society as her conscience shall dictate, or which place her in a position inferior to that of man, are contrary to the great precept of nature, and therefore of no force or authority.

Resolved, That woman is man's equal—was intended to be so by the Creator, and the highest good of the race demands that she should be recognized as such.

25 *Resolved,* That the women of this country ought to be enlightened in regard to the laws under which they live, that they may no longer publish their degradation by declaring themselves satisfied with their present position, nor their ignorance, by asserting that they have all the rights they want.

Resolved, That inasmuch as man, while claiming for himself intellectual superiority, does accord to woman moral superiority for it is preeminently his duty to encourage her to speak and teach, as she has an opportunity, in all religious assemblies.

Resolved, That the same amount of virtue, delicacy, and refinement of behavior that is required of woman in the social state, should also be required of man, and the same transgressions should be visited with equal severity on both man and woman.

Resolved, That the objection of indelicacy and impropriety, which is so often brought against woman when she addresses a public audience, comes with a very ill-grace from those who encourage, by their attendance, her appearance on the stage, in the concert, or in feats of the circus.

Resolved, That woman has too long rested satisfied in the circumscribed limits which corrupt customs and a perverted application of the Scriptures have marked out for her, and that it is time she should move in the enlarged sphere which her great Creator has assigned her.

30 *Resolved,* That it is the duty of the women of this country to secure to themselves their sacred right to the elective franchise.

Resolved, That the equality of human rights results necessarily from the fact of the identity of the race in capabilities and responsibilities.

Resolved, therefore, That, being invested by the Creator with the same capabilities, and the same consciousness of responsibility for their exercise, it is demonstrably the right and duty of woman, equally with man, to promote every righteous cause by every righteous means; and especially in regard to the great subjects of morals and religion, it is self-evidently her right to participate with her brother in teaching them, both in private and in public, by writing and by speaking, by any instrumentalities proper to be used, and in any assemblies proper to be held; and this being a self-evident truth growing out of the divinely implanted principles of human nature, any custom or authority adverse to it, whether modern or wearing the hoary sanction of antiquity, is to be regarded as a self-evident falsehood, and at war with mankind.

[At the last session Lucretia Mott offered and spoke to the following resolution:]

Resolved, That the speedy success of our cause depends upon the zealous and untiring efforts of both men and women, for the overthrow of the monopoly of the pulpit, and for the securing to women an equal participation with men in the various trades, professions and commerce.

Critical Reading Questions

1. What is the thesis of each of these arguments? Where is it stated in each?

2. How does the Declaration of Independence use deduction and induction? Identify the premises and the conclusion in the second paragraph. Comment on the instances that are listed beginning in the third paragraph. Comment on the effectiveness of this deliberate use of these basic reasoning methods.

3. How does the Declaration of Sentiments and Resolutions use induction to support the central claim? What are the effects of its parallels with the Declaration of Independence?

4. In your library or on the Internet, locate a copy of Martin Luther King Jr.'s "Letter from Birmingham Jail." What differences in approach do you see between it and "I Have a Dream"? What about the tone or *ethos*? Can you identify the warrants and qualifiers in King's arguments?

5. These political arguments address major human questions. What in them could be applicable to arguments that you might write about academic or business issues? What might not be applicable?

Deductive and Inductive Reasoning in Writing

As pointed out earlier in this chapter, writers and speakers seldom use deductive or inductive reasoning solely or purely. In their arguments, conclusions reached by induction become premises for deductions; statements that are premises are asserted but not demonstrated, as in the opening sentences of the Declaration of Independence. Deductively developed paragraphs interact with inductively developed ones, as in Gould's "Evolution as Fact and Theory" (see the sections Creationism Is Not Science and The Fact of Evolution) in Chapter 10.

However, deduction is used obviously when a definition or principle is established by the writer and the point of the paper or paragraph is to claim that the subject being discussed fits the definition or demonstrates the principle. If the readers agree with the definition and also agree that the subject fits it, the claim is proved for whatever purpose the writer has. Political science, literature, philosophy, theology, psychology, and law are among the many fields that employ deductive arguments in this way.

Inductive reasoning is reflected in two ways in writing. One is structural. When a writer chooses to present instances of evidence first, leading readers to the claim presented as a conclusion, the paragraph or paper is organized inductively. Composition instructors tend to steer students away from using this technique to structure entire papers since great skill is needed to keep readers with the argument. The sections Organizing Ideas and Revising in the Writing Projects have asked you to think carefully about where you state your thesis or claim for this reason. It is usually more effective to use a deductively based structure.

A reflection of inductive reasoning that is often used in writing occurs when the writer makes a claim in a topic sentence or thesis statement, then simply exemplifies it. The writer is asking the readers to re-enact the inductive process that led him or her to make the claim. Notice how the list of evils alleged to have been committed by the British government functions this way in the Declaration of Independence. Notice how regularly you use this technique, and how often much of what you read uses it, too.

In addition, deduction often appears in the abbreviated form of the enthymeme (see page 497), and induction is commonly presented through the small sample of the example, the inference, and the anecdote. These practices are neither wrong nor fallacious. Writers cannot take the time or space to state all the premises of every deduction or to give multiple instances to support each idea. However, critical thinkers need to understand these reductions so that claims and evidence can be evaluated. Deduction and induction, the basic reasoning methods, are at work in various ways in what we write and read.

Principles for Writing Responsible Arguments

The following principles for writing responsible arguments are fundamental to the Western tradition of logical, structured argument. Always be sure to follow them as well as you can.

Principles for Writing Responsible Arguments

1. Formulate and qualify the thesis statement carefully. Place it purposefully. Use deductive and inductive approaches as appropriate to develop and support the thesis.

2. Provide a context for the thesis; give reasons for its importance. These might be warrants.

3. Provide sound evidence, or grounds, presented clearly and specifically.

4. Acknowledge and demonstrate understanding of other points of view. Grant validity to any point when it is justified. To strengthen your argument, refute courteously points with which you disagree.

5. Use the thinking/organizing patterns in Part Two. Arguments often rely on definitions. Causes of a situation and the effects of a proposal are often vital to an argument. Narratives and chronologies are often effective. Contrasts, comparisons, and analogies illuminate your points.

6. Don't use fallacious reasoning.

7. Be aware of your tone. You want to sound reasonable, thoughtful, and polite as you argue your points.

8. Remember that the conclusion to an argument is extremely important. Restate the thesis or claim with a suggestion, a call for action, a decision, or further thought.

Writing Project: Arguing a Position on a Significant Issue

This chapter has emphasized the importance of the basic concepts and terminology connected with argument because reasoned argument leading to mutual understanding, concensus, or agreement is the foundation of a democratic society and also is often the key to success in personal, academic, and business activities.

Because so much college and professional writing is argumentative, this Writing Project asks you to concentrate on the two central elements of argument: establishing a clear thesis and providing sound evidence for it. In addition, you should be particularly careful to be logical, to avoid fallacious statements, to consider your audience, and to present yourself as a reasonable, well-informed proponent of your claims.

Write an essay in which you argue logically for a position on an issue that you consider significant. Use print sources, electronic sources, and—if possible—an interview with an informed individual to support your claims. Follow your instructor's directions regarding the number and range of sources, length of the paper, and academic format for citation of sources. Be sure to follow exactly the model in your handbook when you complete your paper in MLA, APA, or other appropriate format. Consult Chapter 13 in this book.

On a page separate from your paper, identify the audience to whom you are addressing your argument and explain why it will benefit from understanding your position. Also, either within the paper or in an accompanying note, explain why this issue is important to you so that your classmates and instructor, as they help you revise your drafts, can be aware of the nature of your expertise and any possible biases.

This chapter has included both readings and Thinking-Writing Activities that encourage you to think about argument. Be sure to reread what you wrote for those activities; you may be able to use some of the material for this Writing Project. Begin by considering the key elements in the Thinking-Writing Model.

THE WRITING SITUATION

Purpose Your primary purpose is to write an argument that will persuade your intended audience to agree with your claim or thesis. As you work toward that goal, you will have to think critically about a subject that you care about and clarify or modify your view of it, which is another useful purpose.

Audience The audience is a major concern in any argument. A successful writer understands the characteristics and attitudes of his or her audience. When you develop an argument, you must have a specific audience in mind. Although pandering dishonorably to the audience by distorting evidence or by using flattery is bad rhetoric, an arguer still should be aware of the makeup of the audience and accommodate its needs. Some factors to consider are knowledge (an expert audience needs less background than an uninformed one does), age (younger and older people often have different points of view), roles (people have various roles and respond differently as those roles change), relationships (an audience of peers can be approached differently than another kind of audience), and the emotional level of the issue and situation (a highly charged situation should be approached differently than a calm one would be).

Your classmates, as always, will be a good audience for this assignment as expert reviewers of your drafts and also, if you are dealing with an issue at your college or one pertaining to students, as an affected group.

Finally, your instructor remains the audience who will judge how well you have planned, drafted, and revised. As a writing teacher, your instructor cares about a well-formulated thesis, use of logic and evidence, clear organization, and accepted usage. Keep these factors in mind as you revise, edit, and proofread.

Subject Whenever you argue for a position about which you are concerned, you are addressing an important subject. In addition, the techniques of argument themselves constitute a subject that merits much attention because argument has such importance in people's lives.

Writer As you work on this Writing Project, you should be excited about the subject since you are writing about something that you consider important. Also, if you have been using sources for other projects, you should be comfortable incorporating other people's ideas into your writing and documenting them appropriately. A new role for you may be that of the good rhetorician, the responsible arguer; but if you use your developing critical thinking abilities, you will manage that role well.

THE WRITING PROCESS

The following sections will guide you through the stages of generating, planning, drafting, and revising as you develop your argument.

Generating Ideas

- You may be involved with an issue because of your sex, ethnicity, or field of study or through some organization in which you participate. Or you may be concerned about a problem at your college, in your community, in your country, or elsewhere in the world. If so, you should have no problem deciding what to write about.
- If no issue comes quickly to mind, look around your campus and community to see what problems exist or what changes could be made.
- Watch the news and read the local paper and national publications such as the *New York Times*, the *Wall Street Journal*, *Newsweek*, and *Time*. Talk with friends, family members, and professors about significant issues.
- Think about questions in your areas of interest: your favorite college subjects, sports, entertainment, food, cars, the environment, architecture. Some of these questions may pertain to serious issues; some might be more lighthearted; many will merit a reasoned argument.
- Freewrite about one or two of your concerns. See how many issues or positions you can come up with in five minutes.

Defining a Focus   After selecting an issue to write about, draft a thesis statement that describes the position which you will argue. Be sure that the statement states your points accurately; it may be a complex sentence. Then share it with classmates to profit from their responses. Revise it on the basis of their feedback.

Organizing Ideas   Your argument should probably be set up in the traditional "no-fail" structure: introduction, thesis, evidence, handling of other views, summing up, conclusion/recommendation for action. However, you may be able to use some other arrangement effectively.

Notice how your material adapts itself to various thinking patterns. Use them firmly to clarify your points.

Select and place material from your sources carefully. Connect source material smoothly with your ideas by introducing and commenting on it.

Drafting   Begin with the easiest part to write, which for this paper might be the beginning since you have been thinking so much about your thesis and its context.

However, never get stymied by trying to compose a beginning. Draft sections in any order that works for you. You might want to draft the paragraphs that present your evidence, then consider what inductive or deductive methods you should use.

Be sure to use word processing effectively as you draft your argument. Since writers draft and revise differently, you need to identify ways that your computer can help you produce better versions of drafted papers.

- Sometimes copying a draft or parts of it and revising one version while retaining another is productive. That way, if a revision is not satisfactory, you have preserved the earlier version.

- Sometimes writers need to start over by making a new file for a revised version.

- Sometimes it helps to scroll down or up and to rewrite a paragraph or section. Then you can use the better version and delete the weaker one.

Be sure to keep track of publication information for all sources. Note abbreviated titles, authors, and pages in your draft. Then, when you revise, you can cite the sources in the required format. Be sure to use quotation marks or indenting in your draft whenever you quote.

Revising If you can review drafts with classmates, use one of the peer review methods on pages 65–66 and 105–107 or follow your instructor's directions. After using classmates' suggestions to improve your draft, you will be ready to work through the following revision concerns. If you did not have the chance to work with classmates, let your draft sit for a while and then look at it with the questions to guide you toward presenting your argument well.

1. **Think big.** Look at your draft as a whole.

   - Does it fulfill the assignment? Does it present an argument about an issue that is important to you?

   - Could your claim or thesis be stated more clearly? Is it appropriately qualified?

   - Is your evidence good? Do you provide sufficient grounds for your claim?

   - Have you used sources well to establish the validity of your claim?

   - Is there material in your draft that does not support your argument?

   - Do you need to be more logical? Have you avoided making fallacious statements?

   - Did you state any of the warrants for your argument? Should you include warrants or leave them unstated?

   - Is the tone appropriate for establishing your desired *ethos* (the audience's impression of you) and *pathos* (the argument's effect on your audience)?

2. **Think medium.** Look at your draft paragraph by paragraph.

   - First consider your introduction. How can you rewrite your opening paragraph to draw your audience into your argument?

   - Then look at each of the body paragraphs. Does each support the thesis? Which paragraphs have effective topic sentences that develop the argument? Which paragraphs do not have topic sentences? Do they need them?

   - Which paragraphs present solid evidence for your claim? Do any contain weak support? Do any lack specific examples?

- Do you use transitional words and phrases that help your readers follow your argument?

3. **Think small.** Look at your draft sentence by sentence.

- Which sentences do not present your claim or grounds clearly? How can you rewrite them?

- Which sentences are too long or too short? How can you revise them?

- Do any sentences contain errors in Standard English grammar? How can you correct them?

4. **Think "picky."** Look at your draft as the fussiest critic might.

- Which words are unclear or do not promote your argument? Which words could be used instead?

- Are any words misspelled? Run your spell checker, but don't rely on it alone to detect errors.

- Is the form of your documentation correct? Did you introduce all sources effectively?

- Are the pages numbered? Is your name on all pages?

- Will your finished paper make a good impression by being nicely presented in the format that your instructor requires?

- Is there anything else that you can do to improve your draft?

Editing and Proofreading After you prepare the final draft, check again for typographical errors, omitted words, punctuation mistakes, grammatical problems, and misspellings. If you can, ask a friend to proofread your paper. Sometimes we can't see mistakes in our own writing.

The following essay shows how one student responded to the assignment of arguing a position on a significant issue.

STUDENT WRITING

Cellular Phones in Public Schools

BY JOSEPHINE R. CIMINO

As one half of a two-income domestic partnership, I find it very difficult to keep track of my son's, my husband's and my own activities. I can only imagine how much harder it is for families with more children. My husband's job requires him to travel, often out of state. As a very concerned and involved parent, I am left with the task of keeping track and assuring the safety of our child. My son is now in high school, and his day is filled with school, sports, and other extracurricular activities.

He went to a high school football game not too long ago, and I did not have to worry about him because one of his friend's parents was going to give him a ride home. When he got home, he said one of his other friends was caught using a cellular phone to call his parents to pick him up. Unfortunately, the assistant principal saw and confiscated the phone. The student was automatically suspended for ten days for violating Maryland law and school policy. I was so perturbed by this incident that I spoke with a school administrator, Mrs. Shenk, who stated she agreed that the law should be changed. In fact, she had given her daughter, a senior in high school, a cell phone to keep in her car. The administrator admitted that her daughter kept the cellular phone hidden at all times to avoid detection by other school administrators or teachers.

A law was enacted in Maryland in 1989 banning cellular phones and pagers from school grounds and school-related activities (Shen M3). According to a Montgomery County Public Schools regulation, if a student is caught using a cellular phone, the phone is confiscated, and the student is automatically suspended for ten days. In addition, for a second offense, the school is obliged to notify the police. Further, the student can also be expelled if the use of the cell phone was related to any criminal activity (Regulation). According to Shen, violation of the law is a misdemeanor, punishable by a fine of as much as $2500, and a maximum six-month imprisonment (M1).

Various news reports state that some educators and lawmakers have been opposed to the use of cellular phones on school grounds and at school-related activities due to the perception in the late 1980's and early 1990's that cellular phones were used for drug and other illegal activities. According to Mrs. Shenk, some educators and opponents of cellular phones think that cell phones will cause undue disruption in the schools because of the ringing of phones and kids talking on the phones inappropriately. She further states that another argument against cell phones is the possible loss or theft of cell phones by other students. Further, she states, cell phones can also distract students from their school-related activities and their studies.

I do not agree with the current Maryland law. I believe that this law has been surpassed by the electronic age and the availability of cellular phones. I believe that students in the middle schools and high schools should be allowed to carry cellular phones on school grounds and be allowed to use them before and after classes. Further, I believe that students should be allowed to carry and use cellular phones at school-related activities as long as the use is not related to something illegal.

The reasons for having cell phones available to students in schools are compelling. First of all, cell phones are a real time-saver for busy working parents with several children who need to be in several places. Parents do not have to wait around for activities to finish. The children can call when they are ready to be picked up, or to say that they are staying longer and need to be picked up later. Parents still spend an inordinate amount of time in their cars waiting for their children to finish their activities. If children are allowed to have cell phones, parents can use their time more productively. An example is my son's friend at the football game. His parents were probably doing errands or eating dinner, rather than waiting in the parking lot. They probably used their time for something they wanted or needed to do, other than just waiting for their son.

The availability and accessibility of regular pay phones in schools and on school grounds are sadly lacking. There is only one pay phone outside of my son's high school building, and there are no pay phones available near the football field, the basketball courts, or the soccer field. The school is often closed when games are played during the evening hours; therefore, the pay phones inside cannot be accessed. The students often have to wait in long lines to use the one pay phone available on school grounds to call their parents.

Another reason why students should be allowed to have cell phones is so parents can keep track of their children. Parents like me want to know what their children are doing at all times. I, for one, want to know where my son is so that I can be assured that everything is going the way it should. If he tells me he is going home with another child, I want to know for sure that this is what he is doing and that there are no hitches in the plans. I do not want him to be stranded somewhere because his plans fell apart. Parents should be able to call their children after school is over to confirm their schedules and activities.

Finally, students should be allowed to have cellular phones for safety reasons. With the current prevalence of abductions, kidnappings, and school violence, students should be allowed the safety net of having a cellular phone. It would be easy to dial 911 in case of an accident, or if the safety of the child was in question. Students should be able to call parents in case of a dead car battery after a school activity, or if a ride home fell through, or they are separated from friends during a football game. Numerous news reports said that some students were able to call their parents during the Columbine shooting in Colorado. Parents were assured that their children were still alive and able to talk to them about what was happening.

Incidents like the Columbine shooting and other reports of abductions and kidnappings on the way to and from school force parents to think of safety first and to minimize the consequences if a child is caught using the cell phone during school-related activities. Most parents would rather have their kids safe than take the risk of their being harmed.

Earlier this year, a bill was introduced unsuccessfully to change the current laws regulating cellular phones in public schools (Shen M1). However, on April 26, 2000, the School Board of Montgomery County gave the principals in all Montgomery County public schools the discretion of suspending students from one to ten days, instead of the previous automatic ten-day suspension (MCPS–Board). Obviously educators and school administrators agreed that the law needed changing by this revision of county policy. This is a good start, but is not enough to keep our children safe.

Parents, as advocates for the safety of children, should continue efforts to convince lawmakers to change the current law. Students should be allowed to use and carry cell phones in schools and during school activities under strict guidelines. If these guidelines are not followed, then those students should suffer the consequences. Students should not be punished for wanting to be safe and to be in contact with their parents. The safety of our children should be our foremost priority.

Works Cited

Montgomery County Public Schools. "Board Endorses Reduced Penalty for Use of Cellular Phones, Approves Non-Recommended Reductions to FY2001 Operating Budget Request." MCPS Media Announcement. 26 April 2000 <http/filemaker.mcps.k12. md.us>.

———. "Regulation—Portable Communication Devices COG-RA." 26 April 2000 <http/ www.mcps.k12.md.us>.

Shen, Fern. "Rules on Cell Phones Decried." <u>Washington Post</u> 17 February 2000: M1+.

Shenk, Susan. Personal interview. 2 January 2000.

13

"If we would have new knowledge, we must get a whole world of new questions." —Susanne K. Langer

Thinking About Research

Writing About Investigations

Critical Thinking Focus: Deciding what information to look for, what to use, and how to present it

Writing Focus: Completing a researched paper

Writing Project: A research project

Rewards of Research

The *Oxford English Dictionary* gives the year 1593 as the earliest written use of the word *research* to mean "to investigate or study closely." Of course, men and women all over the world had investigated and studied for thousands of years before that word came into use. Thus, when you work on your college research projects, you are participating in one of humanity's oldest and most productive efforts.

You can easily come up with an endless list of scientific, technical, historical, and social investigations that have made our lives richer and safer. Then, thinking personally, you can come up with a shorter list of the ways in which doing good research can be rewarding for you. It can contribute to your success in college and, often, to your progress in a career. And although research can be hard work and can be frustrating when answers don't come, completing a project will usually give you much satisfaction.

As you continue your studies, you will do several kinds of research, including retrieving and understanding what others have discovered, synthesizing and connecting others' discoveries, connecting others' discoveries with your own ideas, and formulating new concepts and theories yourself. Each of these activities is rewarding in itself, and each is also an important component in research as an extensive human activity.

Critical and creative thinking are parts of all aspects of research. The concepts discussed in every chapter of this book also pertain to research. As people seek information, they constantly deal with *perceptions, beliefs, perspectives, processes, causes, comparisons, contrasts, analogies, definitions,* and *arguments.* Research often involves *making decisions* and *problem solving.* Researchers present *reports, inferences,* and *judgments.*

In addition, like writing, research is often a recursive process rather than a linear one. One source will lead to another, new questions will arise, a creative insight will illuminate a topic, or a critical analysis will change the direction of a project.

This chapter emphasizes some of the logic behind using researched information in academic papers. Your handbook will give you full explanations of various formats and techniques, as will guides to writing research papers that you can find in your college bookstore. Your bookstore will also have publications that provide detailed instructions for using the Internet.

An appendix to this book provides guidelines for using the Modern Language Association (MLA) documentation style, which is the style used in this book's student papers. Since the philosophy of documentation is similar in all academic fields, much of what is said about the MLA style can be applied to any method of documentation, such as those established by the American Psychological Association (APA) or the Council of Biology Editors (CBE).

Starting with Questions

The starting point in research is usually a question. When people do research, they are looking for answers. Even when an instructor assigns a topic, asking questions about it is usually an effective approach because questions can help you find a focus and can stimulate inquiry. Questions can help you in various ways.

QUESTIONS THAT IDENTIFY YOUR TOPIC

If you are choosing your own topic, you can ask questions like these:

- What interests me most within the guidelines for this project?

- What within the guidelines pertains to my college major or my future career?
- What affects my life or the lives of people close to me?
- What affects my community?
- What topics can I find material about in my college library and on the Internet?

QUESTIONS THAT NARROW YOUR TOPIC

After you have selected a broad topic, or if your instructor has assigned a topic, you can use questions to narrow it into a manageable and interesting focus. Ask questions like the following. (Notice how many of these questions use the thinking patterns discussed in previous chapters of this book.)

- What are the issues involved in a topic? How are they defined? (Chapter 9)
- What are some different perspectives on the issues? (Chapter 7)
- What did people believe about it in previous historical periods? (Chapter 10)
- How have theories about it changed? (Chapter 10)
- What caused it? (Chapter 8)
- What problems are connected with it? How might they be solved? (Chapter 11)
- What are future concerns about it likely to be?

The specific question that you want to investigate can be called a **research question.**

Can you formulate the questions that might have inspired some of the student papers in this book? Perhaps they were the following:

What caused a flood in a park or the congregating of birds in a mall's parking lot? (Chapter 8)

Why did my father treat me as he did? (Chapter 6)

How can college drinking be reduced? (Chapter 10)

What influences youth violence? (Chapter 13)

Most major discoveries have begun with a question. Do you think that some famous people might have asked these?

How can a European find a short ocean route to India?

Why do birds on the Galapagos Islands look different than those on the mainland?

How can large numbers of automobiles be produced and sold at affordable prices?

Thinking ↔ Writing Activity

Developing Research Questions

1. Identify a field of study which interests you. Then write two or three questions about specific issues in that field.

2. If you can, show your questions to a professor or graduate student in the field. Ask her or him if these questions have been answered or if researchers are still working on them.

3. Share your questions with classmates. See if they have additional questions that pertain to this field of study.

Searching for Information

FINDING ELECTRONIC AND PRINT SOURCES IN THE LIBRARY

Finding information is easier now than it was in the past simply because of computers. Indeed, it sometimes seems as if too much data is available when the entry of a key word brings up a hundred (or more) possible matches! You are probably accustomed to asking an online service or a search engine to connect

you with all kinds of information. However, if you are not yet comfortable online, you should take a class, find some up-to-date instructional books, have a skilled friend teach you, or get help at your college's computer center or library.

Your college library is designed to assist you, your classmates, and your professors. Your library has a collection of books, magazines, journals, newspapers, pamphlets, and other print material that has been assembled for you and your fellow students. The librarians are specially trained to guide students and faculty to material for their work.

Also, your library uses computers in at least four ways to direct you to source material:

1. The library's holdings are *cataloged* via a computer program, so the best way for you to find books, articles, and videos is to learn to use the terminals in your library.

2. Most college libraries subscribe to *databases* such as Expanded Academic ASAP and National Newspapers which contain whole texts of articles from newspapers, magazines, and specialized journals, so a good way for you to find solid information is to learn to use whatever service your library has. The library provides databases that cannot be accessed on most home computers.

3. Your library probably has a *collection of CD-ROMs* containing encyclopedias, books, poems, and visuals.

4. Your library probably has computer terminals through which you can access the Internet and use various search engines to find an infinite variety of material.

Most college libraries provide guides to their resources. Some instructors or departments require completion of a workbook or physical or online attendance at library orientation sessions. You should take every opportunity to improve your ability to use your college library and the Internet.

Thinking ↔ Writing Activity

Learning About Your Library

1. Go to your college library. Find out how to access its holdings and learn what Internet services it provides.

2. Write a paragraph explaining what your library can do for you and how to use its computers. Also, explain how you would go about obtaining print sources.

COLLECTING INFORMATION FROM PEOPLE AND FROM THE FIELD

In addition to obtaining material from print and electronic sources, you can get information from people who have expertise on your subject. Also, you can go to places or events that are important to your research questions and observe what goes on.

Interviews Conducting an interview can be a valuable way to obtain information. Your creativity and critical abilities will be well used in an interview. Here are some guidelines for interviewing:

1. Identify the person with whom you wish to talk and then make an appointment with her or him.

2. Carefully develop—and write out—the questions you will ask. You might want to email them to the interviewee ahead of time so that he or she will be able to prepare thorough responses.

3. Be careful as you record the interview. If you want to tape the interview, you must ask permission. If you are writing down the responses or keying them into a laptop computer, you must be sure to be accurate.

4. Do not take up too much of your interviewee's time, and—of course—give appropriate thanks.

5. Use and cite the material from an interview as you would any other source. It should be effectively integrated into your paper where it works best to develop the points that you are making. Often information from an interview can be used in several sections of a paper; occasionally, the interview can be presented as a feature.

6. If you can, give your interviewee a draft of your paper to show how you have presented the material and be willing to heed suggestions if any are offered.

7. Provide the person interviewed with a copy of the completed paper and thank him or her again.

Questionnaires Using questionnaires is another way to obtain information from people, but they are difficult to design well. If you want to gather information with a questionnaire, you should review the material on inductive reasoning and empirical generalization in Chapter 12 on pages 500–503. As a beginning researcher, you should only ask a few questions, perhaps no more than three or four.

Also, think about these concerns:

1. What exactly is the issue about which you want people's opinions? Define it very clearly.

2. How can you state questions to obtain unambiguous information? Sometimes "yes-no" or "two-way" questions are best since they elicit

specific responses. However, sometimes yes-no questions are frustrating because people do not want to respond in such a limited way.

3. If you do not ask yes-no questions, how can you obtain possible responses in a small number of consistent categories that pertain to the information you want? Do you want choices? Do you want to construct a scale?

4. Can the responses be easily tabulated?

5. How many people can you poll in the time that you have and with the methods that you want to use? Will that group provide a representative sample appropriate for the scope of your project?

6. How will you use the results? How can you report them accurately, clearly identifying the characteristics and numbers of those who responded?

7. How can you use caution when drawing conclusions?

Questionnaires can be administered in several ways: by face-to-face polling; by mailing forms with a stamped, addressed return envelope; or by email. Practically speaking, a first attempt should focus on a small group—for example, asking the people on your block about a community issue or asking the students in one of your classes about a campus or political issue.

 If you know someone experienced in questionnaire use—such as a social science professor, a math whiz, or a journalism major—you might ask that person to help you craft your instrument. Also, test your questions on a few close friends or family members to see what kinds of answers you get. Then, after revising any questions that need adjusting, pose them to your selected group.

Observations, or Field Research Observations provide firsthand data and are often used in art history, sociology, education, environmental studies, medicine, and other branches of science. If you want to conduct an observation, you should review Chapter 6 to remind yourself about factors that might affect your perceptions and Chapter 7 to recall different perspectives that you might take as an observer, either consciously or unconsciously. You should consider the following principles when you conduct an observation.

1. Identify a place, situation, or object that pertains to your research question.

2. Ask permission from an appropriate person if the site is reserved for use by a specific group such as a class, a club, or a religious assembly.

3. Select a good time to go to your observation site.

4. Do not become involved in any of the activities that you have come to observe.

5. Be as unobtrusive as possible. The presence of an observer often alters the dynamics of a situation.

6. If you are observing an object such as a painting, statue, building, or element of nature, try to study it at different times of day or under varying circumstances. In your write-up, accurately report the circumstances under which you made your observations.

7. Note your observations carefully.

8. Present your observations as objectively as possible. State any inferences and judgments carefully and separate them from your reporting of information obtained through your senses.

Thinking ↔ Writing Activity

Interviews, Questionnaires, and Observations

1. Interview one of your instructors about using firsthand sources of information. Ask him or her about how observations, questionnaires, and interviews are used in his or her field. Ask how these instruments should be designed and what pitfalls to avoid.

2. Write a paragraph or two about what you have learned from the interview.

Using Information

Finding material is relatively easy. Dealing with it is the challenging part. First, you must evaluate what you've found. Then, you must select what you will use, a process which involves thinking critically, and you must write your paper, a process which involves all the interrelated elements of the Thinking-Writing Model. In addition, you must integrate and cite source materials in a prescribed academic format, a process which may at first seem difficult. A goal of this chapter is to help you to do all these things by showing you some of the thinking that directs the research and writing of academic papers.

EVALUATING SOURCES FOR A RESEARCH PROJECT

All material found during research has to be evaluated. Sometimes evaluation is easy—a source may be so obviously good that you know you will use it, or it may be so clearly weak or irrelevant to your inquiry that you know you will not need it.

Here are some guidelines for deciding whether material will be useful to you. These guidelines are an abbreviated version of the material on pages

373–375. You may want to review those pages. Also, you may want to consult Chapters 2 and 10 to think again about some of the ways in which your beliefs have been formed since beliefs have a strong influence on evaluation.

These basic questions can help to judge information and sources:

1. *How reliable is the source?* Some sources, such as advertising, can be unreliable. Some that are clearly presenting a particular point of view, such as political campaign material or a newspaper editorial, can be one-sided. Some might be outdated. In order to identify solid, well-informed, current, and balanced material, ask yourself:

   - What kind of text is this? an editorial, a report, an advertisement?
   - Who is its intended audience? Is this audience important to the text's point of view?
   - When was it written? Is the date relevant to my research question?

2. *How knowledgeable or experienced is the author?* Some people of authority or recorded references offer stronger information than others. Scholars, scientists, and people whose lives have been devoted to any field can usually give broad and deep coverage of their areas of expertise. On the other hand, personal experience can often provide intense accounts of a situation, so sometimes an inexperienced observer can present a fresh point of view. Ask yourself:

   - What credentials does the person who provided this information have?
   - If the person is not an expert, under what circumstances did she or he provide the information?

3. *What specific ideas are being presented?* Ask yourself these questions about any material that you find:

   - What is the main point, claim, or thesis?
   - What reasons or evidence support the information? Does anything about it seem false?
   - Does anything seem to have been left out?
   - Are interests, purposes, and intended audiences apparent?
   - If an argument is presented, can you identify its warrants?

Material found on the Internet needs to be carefully evaluated. Online texts of articles from well-known publications have some built-in reputation since they have undergone a review process before being printed and posted online. If a newspaper, magazine, or journal is known for publishing sound material, then an article from it is probably reliable. However, if the publication is considered biased or shallow, then you must examine the article more carefully.

Material from individual web sites needs special scrutiny. The following checklist will help you develop a healthy skepticism.

Tips for Evaluating the Reliability of a Web Site

Criterion 1: Authority

❑ Is it clear who sponsors the site and what the sponsor's purpose is in maintaining it?

❑ Is it evident who wrote the material and what the author's qualifications for writing on this topic are?

❑ If the material is protected by copyright, is the name of the copyright holder given?

❑ Is there a way to verify the legitimacy of the page's sponsor; that is, is there a phone number or postal address to contact for more information? If there is, don't hesitate to send a letter or email or to phone. You may even end up with more information for your project.

❑ If you recognize the source and are sure that it is operating the site, you are likely to be on solid ground. But don't forget that some of the people running sites are trying to confuse you, that sites on a particular topic often carry opposing messages, and that hackers can sometimes commandeer legitimate sites.

❑ A *tilde* in the web site's address (as in ~jdoe) often indicates a personal home page, not one sponsored by an organization or institution. Another clue that a site is a personal page is when the address includes the name of a common Internet service provider—such as *geocities, tripod,* or *members.aol.com.*

❑ If you come across unfamiliar topics or web site authors, run their names through a search engine to see what other people have said about them.

Criterion 2: Accuracy

❑ Are the sources of any factual information clearly listed so that they can be verified in another source?

❑ Has the sponsor provided a link to other sites and sources—such as product reviews or reports filed with government organizations— that can be used to verify the sponsor's claims? Even better, does the site contain some references to print and other offline sources?

❑ Is statistical data in graphs and charts well labeled and easy to read?

❑ Is the information free of grammatical, spelling, and typographical errors? These kinds of errors sometimes indicate a lack of quality control and can also produce inaccuracies in the information.

Criterion 3: Objectivity

❑ For any given piece of information, is the sponsor's motivation for providing it evident?

❑ Is the information content obviously separated from any advertising or opinion content?

❑ Is the sponsor's point of view presented in a clear manner with well-supported arguments?

❑ If the site is not objective, does it at least take opposing points of view into account?

Criterion 4: Currency

❑ Is the material recent enough to be relevant to your project?

❑ Are there any indications that the material is kept up-to-date? On a browser such as Netscape Navigator, you can click on View and Page Info to see when the site was last revised.

❑ If the site contains charts and graphs, do you see statements indicating when the data were gathered?

❑ Is there an indication that the site has been completed and is not still being developed?

Thinking ↔ Writing Activity

Evaluating Print and Web Sources

1. After you have found a print source, ask the evaluative questions above and then write your answers.

2. Go to an Internet site and evaluate it according to the web checklist. Then write your answers.

3. Examine your answers to the previous two questions. How will they influence your possible use of these sources?

MOVING FROM QUESTIONS TO FOCUS

At some point, you will move from your research questions to a focus for the paper in which you will write about your findings. Sometimes this happens very quickly; at other times, it takes a while. The guidelines for all of this book's Writing Projects include suggestions for identifying a focus and defining a thesis. Reviewing these suggestions will help you when you are writing a research paper.

Some research papers take an informative position; others are strongly argumentative. This distinction will depend on your purpose, the traditions of the discipline in which you are writing the paper, and your instructor's goals for the assignment. Be sure that you understand whether your instructor wants your paper to be informative or argumentative.

Thinking ↔ Writing Activity

Going from Questions to Thesis

1. Select one of the questions that you wrote for the Thinking-Writing Activity: Developing Research Questions on page 529. Then find or imagine some answers to it. Next, write at least one thesis statement that answers it or makes a claim about an answer to it.

2. Look at the questions and statements that two or three of your classmates created for this Thinking-Writing Activity. Identify the statements that seem most clear and have the most potential to be developed into solid papers.

Taking Notes

Although photocopying and downloading have made note taking less necessary than it was in previous eras, researchers still need to have methods for deciding what to note, highlight, or underline; for accurately recording content and bibliographic information; and for placing source material into the parts of a paper where it belongs.

DECIDING WHAT TO NOTE

Sometimes you can easily see that certain parts of an article, book, or web site relate to your research question or working thesis. Naturally, in such cases, you will then note the material or photocopy, highlight, or download it. However, at other times, you may not be sure what to select from a source. Of course, one way to avoid making selections for a while is to photocopy the entire article or to check the book out of the library for the longest time possible. But eventually you will have to decide what material you want to use in your paper in order to answer your research question or to support your thesis.

Your critical reading abilities will come into play here. Before you even think about taking notes, you should read an entire article. If you are consulting a book, read the whole book— if possible—or skim it, consult the index, and read the chapters that contain information related to your topic. Look for headings, topic sentences, chapter titles—all the elements that point out what the writer is discussing. As you read through, jot down page numbers or mark passages that strike you in some way, but you really should not take notes until you have a grasp of the entire piece.

After getting an overview of the work, you need to go back and select specific points that pertain to your question or thesis. If you're not sure how the material relates, note it! You want too much information instead of too little. Highlighting and underlining are forms of note taking because you are choosing information.

QUOTING OR PARAPHRASING

Another decision that you have to make while taking notes is whether to quote (using exact words) or to paraphrase (restating). Highlighting and underlining are forms of quoting. There are only two rules:

1. When you quote, put all of the quoted material inside quotation marks in your notes so that you will never forget that these are the author's exact words. Then you will know that anything else in your notes that is not in quotation marks is paraphrased.

2. Be accurate.

The following are some guidelines.

- If the author has said something in a distinctive way, quote or highlight it.
- If the author has said something complicated and/or technical, quote or highlight it.
- If the author has said something controversial, quote or highlight it.
- When in doubt, quote the author's words in your notes. You can decide if you would rather paraphrase them later when you are writing your paper.
- If you know that you only want a summary of a source or an indication of what it says, paraphrase it.

Here are examples of a full note and the paraphrased version:

Quoted note:

Parker—p. 348. "Poverty is dirt. You say in your clean clothes . . . 'Anybody can be clean.' Let me explain about housekeeping with no money. . . . I wash in cold water with no soap. Even the cheapest soap has to be saved for the baby's diapers. . . . Look at my hands, so cracked and red. Fuel costs money. . . . Hot water is a luxury. . . . Every night I wash every stitch my school age child has on and just hope her clothes will be dry by morning."

Paraphrased note:

Parker—p. 348. Reminds people who think that poor people can at least be clean that soap and hot water cost money. Tells of washing her daughter's clothes (by hand) every night and hoping they'll dry in time for her to go to school.

CHARACTERISTICS OF EFFECTIVE NOTE-TAKING SYSTEMS

Good note-taking systems include

- accuracy in recording material
- accuracy in recording full bibliographic information
- differentiation between quoted and paraphrased material
- indication of the source from which a specific note is taken
- indication of the section of a paper to which a specific note pertains
- capacity to rearrange notes to put material into the appropriate sections of a paper

The old-fashioned technique of using note cards has all of these characteristics. Other methods can accomplish the same tasks, but researchers need to use care to separate noted items and to find a way to sort information in order to insert it in its logical place in the paper. If, like many students today, you only use note cards when you cannot photocopy or download a source, you need to think carefully about ways to develop a method that will provide you with the benefits of the note-card system.

The old system has two parts: a note card for each piece of information and a bibliographic card for every source.

Note Cards A note card contains only one item of information. The act of selecting specific items motivates you to think carefully about what *you* are looking for in order to present your ideas in the paper. Figure 13.1 shows an example of a note card.

Kosmin, Lachman   history

"America's religious history began on October 12, 1492, when Christopher Columbus... took possession of an island in the New World, which he names San Salvador (Holy Saviour)... and his mission was to convert the Native Americans who inhabited the island to Christianity... and many of them adopted the Christian faith as their own.

                          pp. 18–19

Figure 13.1
Note Card

You indicate clearly on the card whether the material is quoted by using quotation marks or whether it is paraphrased by not using the marks. You also briefly identify the source on the card and note the section or subtopic of your paper to which the information pertains. As you begin drafting, arrange the cards in groups according to the places in the paper where that information will be used. Citation of sources is easy because each card records its source.

Think about these questions as you look at Figure 13.1: Did this student quote or paraphrase from her source? How do you know? Did she omit some words that were in the original? Who are the authors? To what section of her paper does this material pertain? What pages did this information come from? Why will this material be easy for this student to use when she writes her paper?

Bibliographic Cards A good note-taking system includes a set of bibliography cards (or a list) which provides the full publication information for each source. You arrange the cards alphabetically by author or title when preparing your Works Cited list.

Figure 13.2 shows the bibliography card for the source of the quotation illustrated in Figure 13.1.

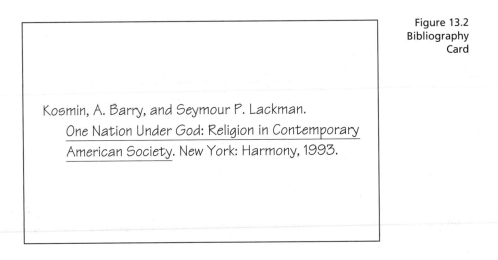

Figure 13.2
Bibliography
Card

Kosmin, A. Barry, and Seymour P. Lackman.
    *One Nation Under God: Religion in Contemporary
    American Society*. New York: Harmony, 1993.

Look at the Works Cited list for one of the documented student papers in this book or consult your handbook. Then ask yourself: Is this source recorded in the MLA Works Cited–list format? Is it a book, a periodical, or an Internet source? Why will it be easy for this student to insert this source into her Works Cited list?

Using Your Computer to Take Notes Computers can be used in many ways for note taking. Simply by using a word-processing program, you can enter notes in appropriate files or under specific headings, and by pasting, copying, or using other combining methods, you can put the information into the part of your paper where you want it. You should double- or triple-space so that you can see items clearly, write changes interlinearly on printouts, and cut pages up to rearrange material. You can compile a Works Cited list by using an alphabetizing program or simply by copying or pasting.

Computer programs have been developed that produce virtual note cards, sort material into outlines, and print Works Cited, Reference, or Bibliography lists. In addition, database programs, scanners, and other electronic tools can help you to record information and incorporate it wherever you want it.

Printouts and photocopies can be cut up (always note the source on each piece) so that you can sort highlighted material as you would note cards.

Most students today are likely to use combinations of note taking and recording methods—card- or paper-based systems when necessary, electronic-based ones when possible. Probably the most unwieldy system—and one to avoid—is writing page after page of notes in a notebook, on both sides of the paper, without leaving spaces for notes to be annotated or cut apart and rearranged. You should avoid using any technique that does not allow you to review and organize material easily.

Thinking ↔ Writing Activity

Learning About the Methods of Experienced Note Takers

1. Ask one of your instructors or a successful upper-division student how he or she takes notes, keeps records of sources, and arranges source material for use in a paper. Ask her or him about the advantages and/or disadvantages of the system.

2. Write a paragraph summarizing what you have learned. Then share what you have written with classmates and see what systems they have learned about.

Thinking ↔ Writing Activity

Creating Your Own Methods

1. If you have previously worked on research projects, write an explanation of your own note-taking and record-keeping processes. How do you use your computer to complete tasks? What do you do that is effective? What do you need to improve?

2. Share your system with your classmates and learn about their systems. Does a classmate have a technique that you would like to adopt?

SUMMARIZING

You will often need to summarize what a source says, either as a way of taking notes or as a way of inserting information into your paper. Your critical reading abilities will serve you well when you write a summary. Here are some guidelines:

- A summary is by definition short. An article or book chapter might be summarized in five or six sentences.

- A summary presents major points, not introductory material or multiple examples. It might give one necessary example.

- A summary should state the main point or the thesis clearly, probably at the beginning.

- A summary does not include your commentary on or evaluation of the material. You can comment later as you introduce summarized material into your paper or after you have included it

  Comment or evaluation: "This article discussed a major breakthrough. . . ."

  Summary: "It says . . ."

  Comment or evaluation: "This book takes a stand that is no longer accepted. . . ."

  Summary: "It claims . . ."

- Signal that you are presenting summarized material. One way to begin a summary is to state the main point. Signal words such as "The article says . . ." "He points out . . ." or "She concludes . . ." are helpful throughout a summary.

- Usually a summary paraphrases a source, but if you quote special words, graceful phrases, or entire sentences, be sure to use quotation marks.

- A summary is accurate.

The following is a professionally written summary of the article "Hospice Care or Assisted Suicide: A False Dichotomy" that appears in Chapter 12 on pages 492–495.

In this paper, the author argues that making assisted suicide available is not a contradictory position to espousing hospice care. He draws on historical and political examples to explain the ethical basis for this assertion. By defining the issue at stake as one of personal autonomy (the loss or gain thereof), the author challenges the argument that making assisted suicide available leads to a slippery slope toward euthanasia, eugenics, or genocide. He asserts that narrowing choices by preventing people from seeking assistance in suicide is more likely to lead us down the slippery slope toward coercive medical and state intervention in our lives.

Thinking ↔ Writing Activity

Learning to Summarize

1. Write a four- or five-sentence summary of one of the sources that you evaluated for the Thinking-Writing Activity: Evaluating Print and Web Sources on page 536.

2. If you can, ask a classmate to read the source and then comment on whether your summary seems accurate.

Preparing an Annotated Bibliography

One technique that can help you evaluate your sources is writing an annotated bibliography. Annotated bibliographies have been printed about many subjects, either as books or as indexes. Perhaps one of the librarians can direct you to such a bibliography so that you can see how useful annotation can be.

Sometimes instructors will ask students to create such a bibliography as a part of a research project. An **annotated bibliography** is simply a list of sources with a brief summary of and some evaluative comments about each one. An instructor might ask you to write one or two sentences about each source's potential value in a paper.

A student who was researching the role of religion in United States politics made the entries shown in the example in Figure 13.3 on page 544. Her instructor had required students to prepare an annotated bibliography of several sources before drafting their research papers.

Thinking ↔ Writing Activity

Creating an Annotated Bibliography

1. Find three sources that pertain to one of the questions that you used in a previous Thinking-Writing Activity or to a paper that you are writing.

2. After you have read the sources carefully, create an annotated bibliography in which you list full bibliographic information. Also, summarize each source in one or two sentences and comment in one or two sentences about what each source's value would be in a paper about the subject.

Lessner, Lori. "A Passionate Political Embrace of Faith."
   Philadelphia Enquirer 8 Nov 1999: A1+.

This article says that many of the current presiden
tial candidates have been vociferous in talking about
their religious beliefs. Lessner explains that this religious
openness could affect these candidates' campaigns
because some analysts say that candidates could lose
votes from differing religious groups.
   I will use this article to show how religion can help
or harm a candidate's campaign.

Rosen, Jeffery. "Is Nothing Secular?" New York Times
   Magazine 30 Jan 2000: 40–45.

This article explains how religion is playing an
important part in the 2000 presidential primary campaign.
Rosen says that most of the religiously outspoken
candidates of the past have been from the South. He
also explains how religion has been a part of American
politics since the Revolutionary War.
   I will use this article to provide some historical
background.

Figure 13.3 Annotated Bibliography

Integrating Source Material: Being a Good Host

The most important part of any research project is writing up the findings. Of
course, there are many forms for presenting research findings, such as laboratory reports and government documents. However, since this book focuses on
undergraduate-level research essays, especially those written for English classes
and courses in other disciplines, we will examine formats appropriate for such
writing.

Research has often been described as an endless conversation. The formats
in which academic work is presented reflect the metaphor of research as conversation by indicating who is saying what.

The most important point to remember is that *you* are the person presenting
the information in your paper. You are, in effect, participating in a conversation

with your sources and your readers. Your paper is not just a series of quotations and paraphrases from sources; instead, it is a presentation of your ideas about the issue and your thinking about what your sources have said.

SEEING YOUR PROJECT AS A TALK SHOW

An extension of the notion of research as conversation is seeing a research paper as analogous to a dignified television or radio talk show or a panel discussion about a current issue. Think of yourself as a talk-show host as you write a paper that uses source material. Just as the host sets up the discussion, you will provide a context and purpose for presenting the material that you have found. Just as the host introduces each guest to the audience, you will introduce each source into your paper. Just as the host helps the guests interact, you will point out the connections and oppositions between and among your sources. And just as the host wraps the show up, you will conclude your paper in an effective manner.

To be a good host, you will need to know how academic writers signal that a source is coming into a paper. Here are some techniques:

- *Use the name of the author, especially a significant writer or scholar:*
  "Elizabeth Cady Stanton wrote that 'it is the duty of the women of this country to secure to themselves their sacred right to the elective franchise.'"

- *Use the name of the publication:*
  "A *New York Times* article provides guidelines for evaluating information found on the Web. It says . . ."

- *Establish a context:*
  "Students now receive much advice about how to decide whether information found on the internet is likely to be good or useless. For example, an article in the *New York Times* provides a list of hints and warnings. This article says . . ."

- *Indicate why you are presenting the information.* This is part of the research conversation. You are talking about the source. In the following passage, a student has commented in his own voice both before and after paraphrasing from a source.

Student { Clearly, the political events of the past century, as well as current events, show a need for real and comprehensive reform in the campaign finance system.

Source { Sabato and Simpson say that influence peddling and other forms of corruption are now worse than they ever have been because they are part of a political tradition that has been institutionalized (7).

Student

{ The question remains: What is the best approach for achieving meaningful

reform, given the realities of the American political and electoral system?

ESTABLISHING YOUR VOICE

You will use your own voice in your research writing to fulfill several purposes. First, as just explained, you will always signal in some way that you are introducing source material into your paper. In addition, as the author of a paper, not just a compiler of other people's ideas, you might

- *Comment on what sources say.* You should indicate why you have included the source material in the paper. You could express agreement or disagreement with particular sources. You might explain which sources you consider most important to the points you are making in the paper. Providing such commentary is an important part of your role as "host."

- *Synthesize what sources say.* You should discuss ways in which sources relate to each other. You might point out a chronological sequence of concepts or explain how theories differ from each other. You could show how sources agree.

- *Present your own thinking.* You have established a thesis for your paper, and, of course, you will present ideas to support it. You might explain why you agree with one source or a group of sources or why you differ from them all and have your own claim to put forth. You might present ideas that have come from your experiences, your observations, your interpretations, or your creative thinking.

You need to clarify when you are speaking in order to be credited for your ideas and comments, just as you must indicate when your sources are speaking so that proper credit is given to them.

Your voice should be easily identifiable as long as you have indicated where all source material begins and ends. Then everything else is either your commentary, your synthesis, or your own thinking. Often, you will want to use words or phrases to show that you are commenting—such as "Therefore," "A consideration of these concepts shows . . . ," or "Another significant idea is . . ."

CHOOSING PRONOUNS

If your instructor agrees, you could simply present some of your comments and ideas as first-person statements: "I want to suggest . . ." ; "After analyzing these reports, I decided . . ."; "I believe . . ." However, some instructors are not comfortable with the use of *I*. There is an academic tradition that discourages the use of the first person singular pronoun (*I*) in order to suggest an objective and impersonal point of view. This tradition is stronger in some disciplines than in others. You should ask your instructors about the preferred pronoun use in research papers and also look at pronoun use in academic journals in the fields in which you are studying.

Also be careful about using *we*. Be sure you identify who "we" is—people sometimes use the word to mean society at large, the citizens of a particular country, or the readers of a particular newspaper or magazine. However, your readers should never have to assume. In addition, *you* is rarely used in academic writing.

Thinking ↔ Writing Activity

Clarifying Who Is Talking

1. Look at the student paper at the end of this chapter, at other documented papers in this book, or at a research paper in your handbook. Notice how the student writers introduce other people's ideas into their papers. Then write a paragraph about what you have observed. Quote some different ways in which these student writers bring sources into their papers.

2. Notice how the writers clarify what their own thinking is about the source material or about the point that the source is being used to support. Identify two specific places where student writers are speaking in their own voices.

Think about how this activity might help you to write your next documented paper and to avoid creating a paper that is just a string of quotations and paraphrases of others' ideas.

The Logic Behind Documentation Formats

REASONS FOR DOCUMENTATION

Two principles underlie academic documentation formats:

- Readers have to know *who* says something.
- Readers have to know *where* something is said.

All academic formats provide this information in logical systems whether they use parentheses, endnotes, or footnotes. Different disciplines use different formats, but they are all based on these two principles. Your handbook or guide to research will explain most of the formats, such as those adopted by the American Psychological Association (APA), the Council of Biology Editors (CBE), and the Modern Language Association (MLA). Also, these associations maintain web sites on which you can find the most current format models. Guidelines to the MLA style are in this book's appendix.

Researchers clarify who said something and where it was said for a number of reasons:

- *To give credibility to a paper.* The strength or weakness of source materials helps readers judge the strength or weakness of a research project and its presentation.

- *To help readers and other researchers learn more.* Proper documentation can direct readers to sources so that they can find out more about a subject than what is presented in a paper.

- *To give credit where credit is due.* Research papers combine many people's ideas. Democracy tells us that each person is important. Giving appropriate credit shows respect for the human being who expressed the idea being used. Further, out of self-respect, researchers and writers want their own ideas to be credited to them just as much as they want to acknowledge others' ideas.

- *To observe the courtesies of conversation.* If research is a millennia-long conversation, the courtesies of conversation are in order. People take turns speaking during a conversation; sometimes points are recapped; often questions are asked and answered. It is usually important to identify who is speaking in a conversation.

- *To avoid plagiarism.* **Plagiarism** is presenting another person's ideas or words as your own. There are two good reasons not to plagiarize. The first is honesty. Most people do not want to be fakes; they want to be honest, so they do not want to use others' ideas without giving them credit. The second is that plagiarism can bring penalties, both in college and in the workplace.

In college studies, two kinds of plagiarism are possible. One is deliberate and dishonorable—the intentional copying of another student's paper, part of a paper, or a source. Buying a paper from a service is a form of plagiarism because a student who does this is taking credit for someone else's words and ideas. Unfortunately, the easy accessibility of all kinds of texts on the Internet make plagiarism technically easy.

The other kind of plagiarism is accidental and happens when a student does not know how to document properly. Once you understand that you must always signal the points at which sources enter and leave your paper and that you must always clarify who said something and where it was said, you should be able to avoid accidental plagiarism.

THE LOGIC OF MLA STYLE

The MLA system is used in this book because it is widely used in English classes. To understand how it works, look at the paper at the end of this chapter or at a model in your handbook or guide to research.

1. First, note that at the end of a paper, there is a list of Works Cited, with the sources listed alphabetically according to *author*, or if no author is given, according to the *title* of the source. Full bibliographic information is given in this list so that it does not have to be provided in the parenthetical citations within the body of the paper.

2. Next, look at the places within the paper where sources are cited. Note that when material has been taken from a source, the last name or an abbreviated title under which it is listed in Works Cited is given— either when the material is introduced or in parentheses at the end of its use. The number of the page on which the material can be found is given in parentheses at the end of the quotation or paraphrase. The parentheses signal the end of the source material.

3. If a source does not have a page number, then a number cannot be given, so you must otherwise signal that use of the source has ended. Many documents downloaded from the Internet do not show page numbers, so you must be careful to indicate where your use of such a source ends. One way to do this is to end a paragraph. You must clearly signal the place at which the next source comes into the paper or comment so that readers know that you or another source is now contributing information and that the use of the unpaginated source has ended. You need to signal the end of material from an interview in the same manner.

Thinking ↔ Writing Activity

Explaining the MLA System

1. Look again at the documented paper in this chapter or in your handbook. Then write an explanation of how the MLA system works as illustrated in that paper. Explain the relationship between the Works Cited list and the parenthetical citations.

2. Next, explain the MLA system to a classmate. Then tell your classmate why you believe the reasons for documentation are important. See if she or he agrees.

Working Thoughtfully on Research Projects

Much of the work you do to produce a research paper is similar to what you do when you write from your own resources. However, research projects often involve some special steps and concerns, including scheduling a significant amount of time, planning your paper carefully, using a specified academic format, and, often, consulting with librarians and with your instructor.

TIME

No one needs to tell you that you cannot just sit down and write up the results of a research project in a short hour spent at your keyboard. Indeed, you know from experience, from this book's advice, and from your writing instructors that you seldom can write a personal piece without spending time thinking, drafting, and revising. However, a researched piece of writing demands a great deal of time.

Doing the research itself is time-consuming. The Internet has made it easy to locate some sources, and the miracle of electronics can quickly bring sources to computer screens. Yet reading, evaluating, selecting, noting, commenting on, and arranging material demands the use of critical and creative thinking processes that usually cannot be hurried.

Using a library can involve waiting for help from a librarian, learning to use the computerized catalog, searching the shelves for material, seeing interesting material that doesn't pertain to your paper, and, of course, having to read, evaluate, copy, take notes, and think about what you've found. College libraries are pleasant places where time is usually well spent—and where you will spend much time while working on a research project.

Deciding on the scope of a project, working though research questions, narrowing a topic, interviewing knowledgeable persons, and revising and qualifying a thesis all take time.

Therefore, you should make a schedule when you begin a research project. You must complete the project within the time frame that your instructor allows. Instructors usually give weeks or months for research projects, but it is amazing how quickly that time evaporates and how suddenly deadlines are staring you in the face. Start as soon as you are given the assignment. Block out time to work on it regularly. Be sure to follow any time line that your instructor establishes for topic selection, working on drafts, and conferences.

PLANNING AND OUTLINING

Since research papers are often longer than essays or reports, planning and outlining are important steps. You will probably have to gather information before you can see what shape your paper will take, but as soon as you can, you will want to block out the sections of the paper and make a working outline (to be changed as the paper develops). If your instructor requires that a formal outline be submitted with your finished paper, look at the paper at the end of this chapter or consult your handbook for a model. Some word-processing programs include formal outlines in their formatting options, so your computer might help you with an outline.

FORMATS AND MODELS

You must use an accepted academic documentation format when you write a research paper for a college class. You cannot be creative about documentation. You must follow the models exactly.

COLLABORATION

The research conducted in business, at large laboratories, and by think tanks and professional organizations is often done by teams. Therefore, to give students this experience, some instructors may assign team projects in college classes. But even if the project that you will be working on will be an individual effort, other people can provide much help. You will want to work with your instructor, the librarians, computer experts, and your classmates as much as you can as you complete your research.

As tempting as this "mental blender" approach to research might appear, there is at this time no substitute for research based on thoughtful exploration, effective planning, productive collaboration, and above all, critical thinking. © Reprinted with special permission of King Feature Syndicate.

Writing Project: A Research Project

This chapter emphasizes the reasoning behind many of the activities that occur while you are engaged in research. The Thinking-Writing Activities should help you find and use information. Be sure to reread what you wrote for those activities.

> Following all instructions given by your instructor, complete a research project and write a well-documented paper in which you report and discuss your findings.

Begin by considering the key elements in the Thinking-Writing Model on page 31.

THE WRITING SITUATION

Purpose Of course, your two major purposes here are to learn as much as you can about the issue that you are researching and then to present your thinking about your findings in an effective paper. Also, you can improve your ability to use your college library and the Internet. You can also become more skilled at using and better understanding academic formats. In addition, you will further develop your critical and creative thinking abilities as you apply almost every concept presented in this book to your research project.

Audience If your classmates are working on similar projects, they will be an excellent audience for your finished paper as well as for drafts. If your research topic is about a social or political issue, your audience might include people beyond your college. Perhaps you can find a way to share what you've learned at a community forum; in a newspaper, newsletter, or listserv; or on a web site. Naturally, your instructor remains the audience who will judge how well you have shaped your research question, investigated possible answers, discussed what you have found, and documented your paper in the required academic format.

Subject Obviously, you should be interested in the subject of your research so that your work will be a pleasure rather than a chore. If the subject is significant in your life or connected with one of your favorite academic fields, you should be able to think of a stimulating research question. If the subject has been assigned and, perhaps, is not among your interests, do everything you can to connect it to your interests. Ask questions about it, read as widely as you can, and consult web sites. You will almost surely find issues within any subject that you can relate to your own concerns.

Writer If you've already worked on research projects in previous classes, you should feel confident as you undertake this one, but you should be willing to improve your abilities throughout the entire process. If you have not done research before, jump in and swim as well as you can. Be your most efficient self by setting up a schedule, working steadily, and meeting all deadlines. Don't hesitate to ask for help from librarians, computer room staff, and your instructor.

Remember the talk-show analogy presented in this chapter: you are the host, in charge of the paper. Comment on what you discover during your investigation; present your own thinking and keep yourself in the paper as much as is appropriate to the subject, to the traditions of the discipline in which you are working, and to your assignment.

THE WRITING PROCESS

Much of the material already presented in this chapter relates to generating ideas, finding a focus, and defining a thesis as you work on a research project. You should review it before you begin your paper.

Generating Ideas

- As you use the technique of asking questions about your subject, look again at the questions presented in Chapter 3 (pages 75–77). Apply as many of those questions as you can.

- Brainstorm and freewrite as you begin your research project, just as you would do when writing a paper from your own experience. "Talk to yourself" on paper about what you want to investigate and what you want to say about the topic.

- Use the thinking patterns discussed in Chapters 6, 7, 8, and 9 as ways to find ideas. Ask yourself about any processes involved in your subject. Describe important objects connected with it. Think about similarities and differences within it. Identify causal relationships. Define important terms. And be sure to write down what the thinking patterns show you.

- Before you decide on a limited focus, read widely about your subject. Consult encyclopedias and web sites to get background information and ideas.

Defining a Thesis As you turn your research question (or questions) into a tentative thesis statement, you need to be sure that your thesis reflects the rhetorical purpose of your paper. Are you explaining, presenting different points of views, or arguing for a specific position?

Notice how the documented student papers in Chapters 8 and 9 explain their topics. Notice how Joshua Bartlett's paper in Chapter 11 and the paper in

Chapter 12 argue for specific changes. Notice how the paper in this chapter argues for a claim.

Draft more than one possible thesis statement and then decide which one best serves your purposes. Remember that you may refocus your paper as you draft and revise it, so you should be open to reshaping your thesis statement as you rework the paper.

Organizing Ideas Research papers, especially those longer than three or four pages, are usually divided into logically distinguished sections. As you organize your paper, you need to think about how the material that you have found pertains to different aspects of the topic. And in an interactive process, as your research develops, the material you find will suggest different points that you may want to develop.

For example, if you are researching changes in beliefs about healthy diets, you might divide your paper chronologically or according to food groups, depending on what you decide to emphasize. If you are researching homelessness in a community in order to present an overview of it to an audience of relatively affluent young people, your paper might include almost equally developed sections on the estimated numbers of homeless people, the causes of homelessness, and the programs to help the homeless. If your purpose is to argue for improved programs, your paper might have a short introductory section on the numbers and causes and well-developed sections on various options for helping the homeless.

If you have used note cards and classified them according to the aspect of your topic to which they contribute, you can easily arrange and rearrange them as you incorporate information into your draft. If you have taken notes on paper, you can cut up the pages to arrange information. If you have taken notes on your computer, you can print files and/or copy and organize. If you have assembled printouts and photocopies of articles and pages, you'll need to identify the parts of your paper where this information belongs and sort it appropriately. If you have a combination of downloaded material, photocopies, and written notes—which is likely—you will need to put them in logical piles or arrange them near your keyboard in a way that will help you to incorporate information and keep track of where every item came from.

Outlines are usually necessary planning tools for long research papers. You should create rough, working outlines several times during your research process. If your instructor requires a formal outline, you can write one at the end of your planning, after you have completed a good draft, or after you finish the paper. A formal outline will provide a good measure of the organization of your paper. See your handbook or your word processor's outline format option or consult with your instructor.

Drafting Drafting a research paper differs from drafting a personal paper in one important way: you must remember to indicate within the draft where source material begins, where it ends, where it is from, and whether it is quoted or paraphrased. In a draft, citation formats and wordings of the signals that indicate a source do not have to be perfect. You can polish these up when you revise and edit, but you must keep track of this material as you draft.

One decision you will have to make during drafting is whether to quote, paraphrase, or summarize source material. This is not always an easy choice. You do not want to quote too much, yet you do need to report what sources say. You should read documented papers and articles in your fields of interest in order to develop a sense of how experienced academic writers use their sources. Notice how these writers use short quotations, long quotations, paraphrases, and summaries.

The following are some guidelines for deciding what to quote, paraphrase, or summarize.

- You probably should quote if what a source has said is worded in a special way, is complicated or technical, or is controversial.

- If you are still learning about the field that your sources are discussing, you might need to quote more than an expert would.

- You should not use many long quoted passages. If you include a lot of lengthy quotations, you may end up compiling a small anthology instead of writing a paper.

- Remember that you do not have to quote whole sentences; often a few words will suffice. Example: In contrasting facts and theories, Stephen Jay Gould calls facts "the world's data," and theories "structures of ideas that explain and interpret facts" (400).

- You might want to quote fairly extensively in an early draft and then ask your classmates, writing center tutors, or instructor for help with shortening quotations and paraphrasing.

- **Paraphrasing**, or restating another's ideas in your own words, requires a good vocabulary and well-developed critical reading skills. Ask yourself as you are drafting: "Let's see. What is this source saying? How do these ideas help develop my paper?" Then write your answers and see how they might help you to incorporate the source into your paper.

- You use **summaries** to show the main points of an article, section, chapter, book, or Internet source. Remember to explain the significance of the summarized material.

Remember that you must always signal the beginning and end of source use and cite appropriately, whether you are quoting, paraphrasing, or summarizing.

You should remain aware of your talk-show host role as you comment on what you have used from your sources. You will probably need to draft your statements several times as you reread your notes and sources and rethink what you want to say.

Revising One of the best revision strategies is to get an audience's reactions to your draft. Your classmates, or peers, can help you see where your draft is already successful and where it needs improvement. If your instructor allows class time for peer review, be sure to have a draft ready. Be ready to help your classmates and to be helped.

Reading your draft aloud or having a classmate read it aloud is a most effective way to start a review session. The instructions given on pages 65–66 and 105–107 include that step. However, since research papers are sometimes long, you and your classmates might want to read each other's drafts silently before class or at the beginning of the review session.

Follow your instructor's directions as you look at your classmates' drafts and also think about how these instructions can provide you with some useful suggestions for your own draft. After your classmates have given you suggestions, work through the following revision questions.

If you do not have an opportunity for a peer review of your draft, put it aside for a day or two and then work through the revision questions.

1. **Think big.** Look at your draft as a whole.

   - Does it fulfill the assignment as to topic, number and types of sources used, and length?
   - Does your thesis reflect the results of your research? Can you word it more effectively?
   - Does your thesis reflect the rhetorical purpose of your paper by presenting a claim for an argument or a statement for an investigation?
   - Can you make the organization more logical?
   - Are there ways to improve the connections between sections and paragraphs?
   - Look at every place where source material is used. Is it always clear where this material begins and ends?
   - Have you interpreted the information adequately rather than just stringing quotations together?
   - Can you make your introductions of sources more effective?
   - Look at the quotation marks and indentations. Is every quoted passage punctuated or formatted so that your audience knows that it is being quoted?
   - How do you indicate when *you* are talking?
   - Do you need to do more research to provide more evidence or information?

2. **Think medium.** Look at your draft paragraph by paragraph.

   - Can your first paragraph do a better job of introducing your research?

   - Is there any paragraph lacking a topic sentence that needs one?

   - Can you make any of the topic sentences more specific? Which ones introduce sources? Which ones present your ideas?

   - Can you make any paragraph more unified?

   - How can your use of transition words and phrases be improved?

   - What improvements does the concluding paragraph need? Does it do a good job of wrapping things up? Does it end your argument well or explain your investigation well?

3. **Think small.** Look at your draft sentence by sentence.

   - Be sure that any quotations blended into a sentence fit smoothly into the syntax of the sentence. Read these sentences aloud to be sure that they sound natural.

   - Find any sentences that are too long, too short, or not clearly written. Then divide, expand or rewrite them as necessary.

   - Do you need to correct any sentences for Standard English grammar and usage?

4. **Think "picky."** Look at your draft as your fussiest critic might.

   - Double-check your academic formatting with the models in your handbook, guide to research, or this book's MLA appendix. Look carefully at your Works Cited or References list. Are the punctuation marks and margins completely consistent with those in the models?

   - Can you find better words to express any of the ideas that you are presenting?

   - Are any words misspelled?

   - Are there any punctuation errors?

   - Can your draft be finished as a neatly presented paper?

   - Is there anything else you could do to improve your draft?

 Editing and Proofreading After you have prepared your final draft, edit and proofread it carefully. Run your spell checker program, but remember that it cannot detect all errors.

If you can, ask a friend who is a good detail person to read your paper to spot any grammatical or punctuation errors.

Annotated Student Research Paper with Outline and Drafts

The paper on pages 563–574 was written for an English composition course that emphasizes argument and research. Dr. Michael Eckert taught the course; Reuben Smith is the student author. A sequence of reading and writing assignments led up to the paper assignment. Students wrote short papers exploring the issue that they had selected and papers analyzing arguments about various aspects of violence. Students responded to each other's drafts during two Writers' Circle Workshops (peer review sessions) held two weeks and one week before the paper was due. Reuben Smith discussed his work on this paper in an interview with one of this book's authors.

REUBEN'S WRITING SITUATION

Purpose The course concluded with this paper in which the students were to apply what they had learned about argument and research. The paper had to be based on research, and it had to argue for a position on an issue concerning violence, a reading theme for the semester. Students had to decide whether to use an adversarial or consensus-building approach. Reuben chose consensus building.

Audience Reuben identified his classmates as his primary audience, although he realized that parents of young children would be a good audience, too. He described his classmates as "a small group of college students from various ethnic and cultural backgrounds. The readers are all under the age of 25 and not yet parents. Some may have come from broken, neglectful, or abusive homes and may know the effects of such an atmosphere firsthand." Dr. Eckert advised the students to consider their classmates and him as their audience. Reuben said that Dr. Eckert reassured them by saying that they weren't writing for publication, so they shouldn't have stage fright. (Now Reuben laughs: "And here my paper is—in a book!")

Subject Reuben said that at first he was not enthusiastic about the assigned subject. He said, "Sure, violence is bad, but I didn't have any other strong opinions about it. So I had to connect it with things that I am interested in. I'm a young person, and I really care about children. It pains me to think about children being abused and young people in big trouble. So I decided to focus on youth violence. And I got more interested as I got into it." Reuben said that he came to be "appreciative of the focus" that Dr. Eckert had established because it provided direction for the entire class.

Writer Reuben described himself as "an 18-year-old college freshman who has explored the issue of youth violence in considerable detail over the semester."

He said that he "writes from the position of having been raised in a loving and supportive family environment." Reuben likes to write, can use a word processor pretty well, and has a good computer and printer at home.

REUBEN'S WRITING PROCESS

As he thought about drafting, organizing, revising, and collaborating, Reuben made the following observations.

- Dr. Eckert's clear instructions and the sequence of assignments made drafting easy. Much of what was in the preliminary exploratory and analytical writings could fit into the paper (and was supposed to). Working "piece by piece" helps, Reuben said.

- Reuben liked the Writers' Workshops (peer review sessions) which were similar to those in which he had participated in high school. His classmates' responses helped him to see where his drafts needed more work. He also regarded these sessions as establishing "three due dates," which forced him to finish his drafts promptly instead of writing them at the last minute.

- Reuben's sources were books from the college library, an anthology of essays that was assigned for the course, downloaded Internet articles, and interview notes. He likes to spread his material around him on a table and go from source to source to find useful information to put into his word-processed drafts. He said that he handwrote some notes from the books on pieces of paper in order "to see what I had." Using bookmarks confused him, so he found that he needed to take notes.

- Reuben knew that he had to identify sources carefully as he inserted material from them into a draft. He said, "I don't trust myself to put in names and pages later. If you mess up, it shoots the paper!"

- Reuben was surprised that some of his classmates seemed "scared of sources." He wanted to tell them, "Sources are our friends. They'll write the paper for you, just about. They are the experienced voices."

- Reuben writes on his computer. He made rough outlines of his paper on the computer several times. He said that he's not much of a freewriter. He likes to try to get drafts on the screen in fairly good shape, but he rewrites sentences and paragraphs as he goes. He prints out drafts in order to revise. He explained that he "has to see the whole thing on paper" because he's "big on flow." Moving readers from source to source with comments helps a research paper flow, he said.

One version of his outline follows.

Addressing the Issue of Violence by Young People

<u>Claim:</u> In an aggressive world of broken families, media violence, and school shootings, it is crucial that a child has the guidance of an involved parent to help him or her sort out these influences and respond to them in a healthy way.

I. Youth violence—a disturbing fact of life

II. Debate over causes

    A. Breakdown of the two-parent family

    B. The individual

    C. The media

    D. Child abuse

    E. Strongest influence—family life

III. Breakdown of the two-parent family

    A. Divorce rate

    B. Violent teenage crime and absent fathers

    C. Single-parent pressures

    D. Unsupervised children

IV. Violence in the Media

    A. Extent

    B. Possible influence

V. Many factors—role of parenting

VI. Dysfunctional families

    A. Definitions

    B. Abuse

        1. Crawford example

        2. Thornberry study

    C. Parental neglect

VII. Parents' responsibilities

    A. Fulfilling needs

    B. Constructive discipline

VIII. Steps to reduce juvenile violence

    A. Reclaiming the children

    B. Programs

<u>Conclusion:</u> Full statement of claim, thesis, conclusion

Reuben made three drafts of his paper before writing the final draft. He participated in a peer review session and a meeting with a writing center tutor, and he conducted an additional interview that reminded him of the recent decrease in crime rates. After getting all this input, Reuben felt that he should rethink the beginning of his paper.

The following is the third draft of his beginning, marked with his notes about what he decided to change.

On April 20, 1999, eighteen-year-old Eric Harris

and his friend and cohort, seventeen-year-old Dylan

One event not enough   Klebold, opened fire on their fellow classmates and

teachers in Littleton, Colorado. For nearly five hours,   *Change this*

the two teenaged gunmen methodically killed or

wounded thirty-five students and one teacher before

ultimately taking their own lives (Breggin 1).

The debate over what causes youth violence has

escalated in recent years, perhaps reaching an apex

repeat   after the ~~recent~~ shootings at Columbine High School.

Toll and effect not   ~~Those who feel youth violence is a serious issue that~~
discussed in paper

~~must be addressed point to such instances as devast-~~

~~ing testimonies to the toll youth violence can take on~~

~~a nation.~~ The issues surrounding the cause ~~and effect~~   *many causes*

of violence in this country are vast and numerous. As

more and more people become aware of the ~~rising~~   *Not rising now*

problem of youth violence, many are scrambling to

find some institution on which to place the blame.

Some point to the breakdown of two-parent families

as the root cause of juvenile aggression, while others

blame the individual who committed the crime. There

are those who hold the media responsible, while still

others link youth violence to child abuse within the

Not clear: factors? traced?

family. There may indeed be many factors that con-

tribute to the development of violence in a person, but

nearly each one can be traced back to what a child is   *Qualify more*

exposed to in the home.

This final draft of Reuben's beginning is annotated to point out the improvements he made:

Television newscasts, web sites, and newspapers regularly give reports of

violent actions committed by young people. A headline says "Teen Convicted

of First-Degree Murder." An Internet search produces many items, including a

"fact sheet" titled "Youth Violence: A Public Health Concern." The murderous

Revised paragraph

assault by two teenaged gunmen at Columbine High School in Colorado horri-

fied the nation in April 1999. Even though there has been a recent decrease in

crime, including juvenile crime, youth violence is widely considered to be one

of the most disturbing facts of life in the United States today.

The debate over what causes youth violence has escalated in recent years,

perhaps reaching an apex after the shootings at Columbine. The issues sur-

rounding the causes of violence in this country are vast and numerous. As

More accurate wordings more and more people become aware of the problem of youth violence, many

are looking for some institution on which to place the blame. Some point to the breakdown of two-parent families as the root cause of juvenile aggression, while others blame the individual who committed the crime. There are those who hold the media responsible, while still others link youth violence to child abuse within the family. There may indeed be many factors that contribute to the development of violence in a person, but probably the strongest influence is a child's family life.

Clearer statement; better qualification of partial thesis

Here is Reuben's complete, final paper. The annotations indicate format requirements and point out Reuben's opening and closing strategies as well as the ways in which he introduces and cites sources.

As you read this paper, observe how topic sentences and transitional words help the flow. Notice where the student writer is speaking and think about his abilities as a host. Consider the support or grounds that he offers for his claim. Also, decide whether the tone and approach encourage agreement.

STUDENT WRITING:

REUBEN SMITH, "ADDRESSING THE ISSUE OF VIOLENCE BY YOUNG PEOPLE"

1"

½"
Smith 1

Reuben Smith

English 102   *Double space*

Dr. Michael Eckert

December 1, 2000

Addressing the Issue of   *center title*

Violence by Young People

Indent five spaces Television newscasts, web sites and newspapers regularly give reports of violent actions committed by young people. A headline says "Teen Convicted of First-Degree Murder." An Internet search produces many items, including a "fact sheet" titled "Youth Violence: A Public Health Concern." The murderous assault by two teenaged gunmen at Columbine High School in Colorado horrified the nation in April 1999. Even though there has been a recent decrease in crime, including juvenile crime, youth violence is widely considered to be one of the most disturbing facts of life in the United States today.

Introduction of the subject; warrants for the argument

1"   1"

The debate over what causes youth violence has escalated in recent years, perhaps reaching an apex after the shootings at Columbine. The issues surrounding the causes of violence in this country are vast and numerous. As more and more people become aware of the problem of youth violence, many are looking for some institution on which to place the blame. Some point to the breakdown of two-parent families as the root cause of juvenile aggression, while others blame the individual who committed the crime. There are those who hold the media responsible, while still others link youth violence to child abuse within the family. There may indeed be many factors that contribute to the development of violence in a person, but probably the strongest influence is a child's family life.

Preview of specific topics; more warrants

Partial statement of thesis or claim

1"

Smith 2

Some argue that the breakdown of stable, two-parent families is directly responsible for youth violence. They claim that without the dual influence and provision of two parents during a child's early years, youngsters are more likely to turn to destructive substitutes such as gangs, drugs, and violent crime. In the U.S. today the divorce rate continues to mount. In his book <u>Coping in a Dysfunctional Family,</u> Raymond Jamiolkowski reports that "[56] percent of all children in America live or will live in a family that has gone through a divorce. This is more than 10 million people. Sixty percent of all single-parent families are created through divorce" (124). Patrick F. Fagan, a senior policy analyst at the Heritage Foundation in Washington, D.C., points to social science studies that show how "over the past thirty years, the rise in violent teenage crime has paralleled the number of homes abandoned by fathers" (86).

Book title and author introduce quoted material; page number in parentheses before period

While Jamiolkowski concedes that "a family is not dysfunctional simply because it is headed by a single parent," he observes that single parents face unique pressures and greater demands that might otherwise be shared (120). For example, without the additional support of a husband, a single mother must often juggle multiple jobs on top of rearing her children. This leaves less time to spend with her children and puts a strain on the family. As a result, Fagan concludes, children are left in the care of others or merely left to themselves with weaker feelings of connection to their parents (90). Making a similar point in an interview, a professor of criminal justice at Montgomery College, Vicky Dorworth, said that a major source of serious problems is that too many children are unsupervised.

Interview

Still others argue that regardless of the situation at home, the family is being attacked by a barrage of violence in the media. Gruesome acts of hostility that a child may never be exposed to in the home or the community can be vividly

Smith 3

portrayed on the TV screen. In many families today, according to Mortimer B. Zuckerman, the editor-in-chief of U.S. News and World Report, children are spending far too much time in front of the television. Zuckerman explains, "It has become the nation's mom and pop, storyteller, baby sitter, preacher and teacher. Our children watch an astonishing 5,000 hours by the first grade and 19,000 hours by the end of high school—more time than they spend in class" (53). With all the time children spend in front of the tube, many have questioned just how much violence they are being exposed to. Zuckerman says that TV Guide did a study on this in which it looked at ten channels during a regular 18-hour day and was able to identify 1,846 individual acts of violence (53). Whether or not children are becoming more aggressive by viewing violence on TV, it is difficult to dispute that a considerable amount of violence is indeed being portrayed on TV daily.

Holding that children are imitative by nature, many claim that by viewing violent acts played out on television, youngsters could respond to what they see by mimicking it and perceiving it as acceptable behavior. Barbara Hattemer, the president of the National Family Foundation, observes that "two- to six-year-old children cannot evaluate the messages they receive from the media they watch. . . . Six- to twelve-year-olds imitate what they see and hear without fully understanding the consequences of what they are doing" (63). While children may not immediately put what they see into action, what they are exposed to may resurface again down the road. An article from the Ann Arbor News reports that experts have found that "children who are exposed to significant amounts of TV violence at the age of 8 are consistently more likely to commit violent crimes, abuse their spouses, or abuse their children later in life" (Disher).

After observing these statistics, it seems fair to conclude that children growing up in single-parent households and

Marginal notes:

Author identified

Fewer than four lines quoted within text, with quotation marks

Author using a source

Author's name in parentheses; single-page article

Smith 4

those exposed to significant amounts of violence are in fact
more likely to turn to destructive crime. However, these factors
alone are not necessary requisites for juvenile violence.
Experts agree that there are many facets to this complex
problem. Writes Madeline Levine in her book <u>Viewing Violence</u>:

> The fact remains that no one theory of aggression
> is able to make sense of all acts of aggression.
> Furthermore, no individual factor, by itself, is a
> good predictor of aggressive behavior. When look-
> ing at the factors that contribute to aggression we
> would do well to think in terms of "all the above"
> rather than "either/or." (53)

The question then might be asked: How many of these contributing factors are strengthened or nullified by the influence of a child's parents? How pivotal is the role of
parenting in the development of juvenile violence? Might the
example set by parents in the home be either one of the
greatest weapons against violence or one of the strongest
enforcements of it?

Before moving on, it is important to define a couple of
key terms. In <u>Coping in a Dysfunctional Family,</u> Raymond
Jamiolkowski provides a definition: "A dysfunctional family
is one that fails to meet the basic needs of its members.
These basic needs are survival, safety and security, love and
belonging, self-esteem, growth, and development of skills
needed for independent living" (120). He goes on to say
that the structure of a family does not determine dysfunc-
tion. Regardless of the family dynamics, Jamiolkowski
claims that most obstacles can be overcome in a functional
family where each member's needs are being met (123). In
this respect, dysfunctional or poor parenting will be defined
as parental behavior that hinders a child's basic needs.
Whether it manifests itself in the form of neglect, physical

Four lines or more quoted; indented; no quotation marks; page number in parentheses after period

Source quoted and cited; then paraphrased and cited

Smith 5

or emotional abuse, brutal discipline or no discipline at all, poor parenting can greatly intensify the effects of violent influences from the outside.

Christina Crawford, who wrote the poignant autobiography <u>Mommie Dearest</u> in 1978, knows firsthand the pain caused by an abusive parent. In her recent book entitled <u>No Safe Place,</u> Crawford speaks of her own childhood experience:

> My body was physically hurt, punished, and
> ridiculed. My mind was programmed for servitude
> and made susceptible to manipulation. . . .
> Instead of being protected, guided, and loved, I
> was taught to be ashamed, alone, frightened, sus-
> picious, enraged, and empty, that I didn't belong
> anywhere and that nothing belonged to me. . . . As
> a small child, I was beaten with objects, threat-
> ened, deprived of basic necessities such as food
> and sleep, ignored, abandoned, disrespected, sex-
> ualized, and manipulated . . . convinced that I was
> a fundamentally flawed human being and that
> probably nothing would set me right. (12)

Crawford explains how she would regularly engage in violent activities such as schoolyard fistfights and verbal shouting matches as a child. Because physical and emotional abuse was the only life she knew at home, her behavior became a reflection of this (3). Asserting that violence begets vio-lence, Crawford predicts that the epidemic of violence in this country will continue to surge out of control: "If vio-lence within the family is not addressed, we as a society will never be able to stop the violence in streets [and] between races, nations, and religions, which creates the feeling that there is no safe place for anyone, anywhere, anytime" (10).

Extensive research has been conducted in order to confirm the correlation between parental violence and

Smith 6

youth violence. In his essay "Family Violence Causes Youth Violence," Terence P. Thornberry, a professor, highlights the results of an ongoing study of delinquency called The Rochester Youth Development Study. In this study, young students from seventh to twelfth grade were interviewed along with their primary caretakers every six months. They were asked to personally report any involvement in delinquent behavior defined under six categories ranging from simple assault to armed robbery. Thornberry explains that information from schools, police, social services, and other relevant agencies was also taken into account during the study (109). According to the results, children who had experienced multiple forms of family violence—ranging from violence between parents to violence against the child or another sibling—were much more likely to turn to violent crime:

> While 38 percent of the youngsters from non-violent families reported involvement in violent youth delinquency, this rate increased to 60 percent for youngsters whose family engaged in one of these forms of violence, to 73 percent for those exposed to two forms of family violence, and further increased to 78 percent for adolescents exposed to all three forms of family violence. (Thornberry 111)

Drastic instances of physical and verbal abuse are not the only sort of harm parents can inflict upon their children. Many claim that the act of neglecting children is far more common than overt abuse and can have just as destructive results. John J. DiIulio Jr., a professor of politics and public affairs at Princeton University, claims that many children live in a state of moral poverty without the presence of positive adult influence. DiIulio says, "Moral poverty is the poverty of being without loving, capable, responsible

Material omitted; pages given

adults who teach you right from wrong. . . . It is the poverty of growing up in the virtual absence of people who teach morality by their everyday example . . ." (111–112).

As has already been stated, parental neglect can do much to push children toward violent activity. A family does not need to be broken to be neglectful. Two-parent families can be just as neglectful to children. Delbert S. Elliott is the director of the Institute of Behavioral Science's Center for the Study and Prevention of Violence at the University of Colorado in Boulder. Writes Elliott:

> Even if violence is not modeled in the home,
> research suggests that the absence of effective
> social bonds and control, together with failure of
> parents to teach (and children to internalize) con-
> ventional norms and values, puts children at risk of
> later violence. In fact, parental neglect may have
> an even stronger effect than the physical abuse on
> later violence, as it appears to be more damaging
> to the subsequent course of youth development
> and involves three times as many youth. (85)

Considering all this, it is important to keep in mind that parents have a far greater responsibility than simply paying attention to their children and avoiding maltreatment. A loving, healthy, and functional family environment is one in which each child's primary needs are met within the home. "Needs, however," writes Jamiolkowski on the subject, "are not the same as wants, wishes, or desires. Being a part of a family means cooperating so that every member is able to have his needs fulfilled" (3). Jamiolkowski stresses the importance of active, loving parenting in developing healthy children (3–4).

Even though the harmful effects of physical abuse have been clearly demonstrated, experts agree that functional parenting requires enforcing some form of constructive

Smith 8

discipline. While there is considerable disagreement as to what this discipline ought to look like specifically, experts in child development emphasize the need for caring, rational discipline that is bathed in communication, respect, and love. James Dobson, who holds a Ph.D. in child development and wrote the best-selling book <u>The New Dare to Discipline,</u> comments on the need for active parents who will love their children enough to train them:

> Children thrive best in an atmosphere of genuine
> love undergirded by reasonable, consistent disci-
> pline. In a day of widespread drug usage,
> immorality, sexually transmitted diseases, vandal-
> ism, and violence, we must not depend on hope
> and luck to fashion the critical attitudes we value
> in our children. (7)

Parents who do not lovingly work to foster their child's physical, emotional, and moral well-being will only worsen the ever-growing problem of youth delinquency in this nation. If in fact parents do have a lasting impact on their children's lives for the better or for the worse, it seems the logical first step in undermining the potency of juvenile violence would be to strengthen and improve the family. This calls for a change in how seriously a person views the role of parenting. In his book <u>Reclaiming Our Children,</u> Peter R. Breggin writes: "Reclaiming our children and rescuing them from violence and despair requires a change of heart not in our children but in ourselves. Our children will then manifest the effect of our good efforts in their own improved lives" (282). Breggin drives home the point that parents must place a higher prior-ity on nurturing the children they bring into this world:

> Our children need more of us—our unconditional
> love and unambiguous caring, our serious attention,

First statement of conclusion and claim

our moral leadership, our precious time, our economic resources. Whether we are parents, teachers,
counselors, ministers, police officers, mentors,
politicians, government administrators, or leaders of
great corporations and universities, we must make
children a higher priority in our personal lives and in
our social and economic policies. (283)

These arguments are based on the warrant that children
learn primarily by example; the qualities to which children
are exposed during their early years of development will
usually be reflected in their lives later on.

On the positive side, Criminal Justice Professor Dorworth
said that she believes youth violence has been reduced as
the result of programs that she hopes will continue. She
points to an increase in after-school activities for unsupervised children. She also said that many agencies and
groups are doing more to encourage good parenting.

Conclusion; claim; thesis

If poor parenting marked by physical, emotional, and neglectful maltreatment is a compelling factor of youth violence,
then it stands to reason that good parenting marked by loving and supportive nourishment can do much to prevent it.
This world into which children are born is not a perfect one,
and no parents can hope to protect their children from every
violent influence to which they may be exposed. No matter
how nourishing and active parents may be in the lives of their
children, they will never be able to keep their lives entirely
untouched by the scope of violence. In an aggressive world of
broken families, media violence, and school shootings, it is

Conclusion

crucial that a child has the guidance of an involved parent to
help him or her sort out these influences and respond to
them in a healthy way. Though the negative effects of these
factors can be strong, a stronger bond of family love can
greatly reduce the destructive forces of violence.

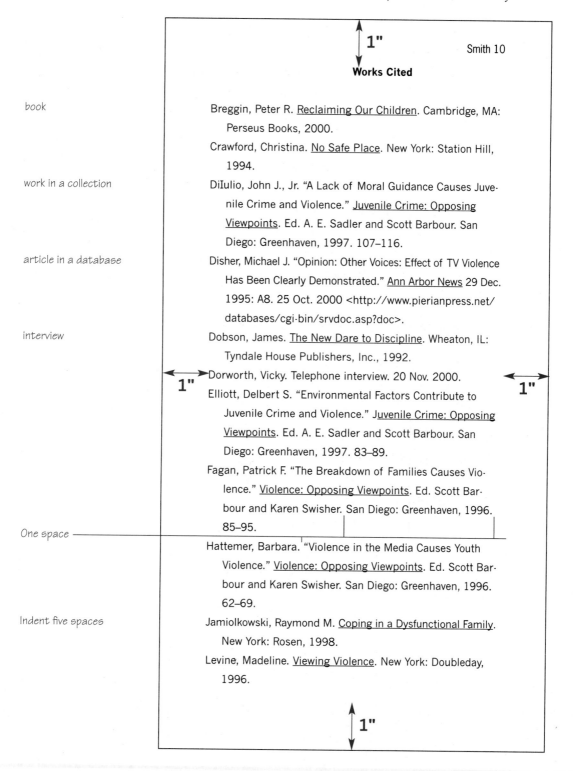

Smith 10

Works Cited

book

Breggin, Peter R. <u>Reclaiming Our Children</u>. Cambridge, MA: Perseus Books, 2000.

Crawford, Christina. <u>No Safe Place</u>. New York: Station Hill, 1994.

work in a collection

DiIulio, John J., Jr. "A Lack of Moral Guidance Causes Juvenile Crime and Violence." <u>Juvenile Crime: Opposing Viewpoints</u>. Ed. A. E. Sadler and Scott Barbour. San Diego: Greenhaven, 1997. 107–116.

article in a database

Disher, Michael J. "Opinion: Other Voices: Effect of TV Violence Has Been Clearly Demonstrated." <u>Ann Arbor News</u> 29 Dec. 1995: A8. 25 Oct. 2000 <http://www.pierianpress.net/ databases/cgi-bin/srvdoc.asp?doc>.

interview

Dobson, James. <u>The New Dare to Discipline</u>. Wheaton, IL: Tyndale House Publishers, Inc., 1992.

Dorworth, Vicky. Telephone interview. 20 Nov. 2000.

Elliott, Delbert S. "Environmental Factors Contribute to Juvenile Crime and Violence." <u>Juvenile Crime: Opposing Viewpoints</u>. Ed. A. E. Sadler and Scott Barbour. San Diego: Greenhaven, 1997. 83–89.

Fagan, Patrick F. "The Breakdown of Families Causes Violence." <u>Violence: Opposing Viewpoints</u>. Ed. Scott Barbour and Karen Swisher. San Diego: Greenhaven, 1996. 85–95.

One space

Hattemer, Barbara. "Violence in the Media Causes Youth Violence." <u>Violence: Opposing Viewpoints</u>. Ed. Scott Barbour and Karen Swisher. San Diego: Greenhaven, 1996. 62–69.

Indent five spaces

Jamiolkowski, Raymond M. <u>Coping in a Dysfunctional Family</u>. New York: Rosen, 1998.

Levine, Madeline. <u>Viewing Violence</u>. New York: Doubleday, 1996.

Smith 11

Thornberry, Terence P. "Family Violence Causes Youth Violence." <u>Violence: Opposing Viewpoints</u>. Ed. Scott Barbour
and Karen Swisher. San Diego: Greenhaven, 1996.
108–112.

"Youth Violence: A Public Health Concern." CSVP Fact Sheet
No. 9. <u>Center for the Study and Prevention of Violence</u>.
1998. 30 Nov. 2000 <http://www.colorado.edu/cspv/
factsheets/factsheet9.html>.

Zuckerman, Mortimer B. "Television Violence Contributes to
Juvenile Crime." <u>Juvenile Crime: Opposing Viewpoints</u>.
Ed. A. E. Sadler and Scott Barbour. San Diego: Green-
haven, 1997. 52–55.

Modern Language Association Style

Careful documentation and a complete works-cited list provide readers with full information on sources cited in the paper. (See "The Logic of MLA Style," Chapter 13, page 549 for information on in-text citations.)

To be useful to readers, citations must be clear and consistent. Therefore, very specific rules of documentation have been devised and must be applied.

Quick Reference for Basic Entries

Using the following formats, begin preparing your works-cited entries as soon as you begin taking notes. Use a new 3-by-5-inch card for each entry or create a works-cited file on your word processor.

❑ A book by one author

Author's last name, first name. <u>Book title</u>. Additional information.
City of publication: Publishing company, publication date.

❑ An article by one author

Author's last name, first name. "Article title." <u>Periodical title</u> Date:
   inclusive pages.

Guidelines for preparing entries for other types of sources appear on the
pages that follow.

Citation Format

Most research writing in English and other humanities courses uses the documentation format described in Joseph Gibaldi's *MLA [Modern Language Association] Handbook for Writers of Research Papers,* fifth edition (New York: MLA, 1999). This documentation format, known as MLA style, is simple, clear, and widely accepted.

Other subjects, however, may require other styles of documentation, so always ask instructors, especially in nonhumanities courses, whether MLA style is acceptable. In addition to the *MLA Handbook,* a number of other style guides are frequently used.

FREQUENTLY USED STYLE GUIDES

The Chicago Manual of Style. 14th ed. Chicago: U of Chicago P, 1993.

Publication Manual of the American Psychological Association. 4th ed. Washington, DC: APA, 1994.

Scientific Style and Format: The CBE [Council of Biology Editors] Manual for Authors, Editors, and Publishers. 6th ed. Chicago: Cambridge UP, 1994.

Turabian, Kate L. *A Manual for Writers of Term Papers, Theses, and Dissertations.* Rev. John Grossman and Alice Bennett. 6th ed. Chicago: U of Chicago P, 1996.

The most widely used of these alternate styles is that of the American Psychological Association (APA), often the preferred style for writing in the social sciences.

Accuracy and Completeness

Because works-cited entries direct readers to sources used in research writing, they must be as complete as possible and presented in a consistent and recognizable format. If the following guidelines do not cover a source you want to use, consult the *MLA Handbook.*

To complete a citation, leaf through the following samples until you find the one that most closely corresponds to your source, remembering that some citations combine information according to the guidelines that follow.

INFORMATION FOR MLA CITATIONS

MLA citations present information in an established order. When combining forms (to list a translation of a second edition, for example), follow these guidelines to determine the order of information:

1. *Author(s).* Use the name or names with the spelling and order shown on the title page of books or on the first page of articles, without degrees, titles, or affiliations. If no author (individual or organization) is named, list the work by title in the works-cited entry.

2. *Title.* List titles from part to whole: the title of an essay (the part) before the book (the whole), the title of an article before the periodical title, an episode before the program, or a song before the compact disc. Use complete titles, including subtitles, no matter how long they are.

3. *Additional information.* In the order noted next, include any of the following information listed on the title page of the book or on the first page of an article: editor, translator, compiler, edition number, volume number, or name of series.

4. *Facts of publication.* For books, find the publisher's name and the place of publication on the title page and the date of publication on the copyright page (immediately following the title page). Use the publisher's name in abbreviated form, use the first city listed if more than one is given, and use the most recent date shown. When a city is unfamiliar, abbreviate the state by using two capital letters without a period. For periodicals, find the volume number, issue number, and date on the masthead (at the top of the first page of newspapers or within the first few pages in journals and magazines, often in combination with the table of contents).

5. *Page numbers.* When citing a part of a book or an article, provide inclusive page numbers without page abbreviations. Record inclusive page numbers from one to ninety-nine in full form (8–12, 33–39, 68–73); inclusive numbers of one hundred or higher require at least the last two digits and any other digits needed for clarity (100–02, 120–36, 193–206).

MLA STYLE

FORMAT FOR MLA CITATIONS

MLA citations follow these general formatting guidelines:

- Begin the first line of each entry at the left margin and indent subsequent lines one-half inch (five spaces).
- Invert the author's name so that it appears with the last name first (to alphabetize easily). If sources are coauthored, list additional authors' names in normal, first-then-last order.
- Italicize or underline titles of full-length works (the meaning is the same), but do not underline the period that follows the title. Be consistent throughout the paper.
- Separate major sections of entries (author, title, and publication information) with periods and one space, not two. When other forms of end punctuation are used (when titles end with question marks or exclamation points, for example), the period may be omitted. Punctuation that is part of a title must be italicized (or underlined).
- Double-space all entries.

Books

A Book by One Author   Freemuth, John C. <u>Islands under Siege: National Parks and the Politics of External Threats</u>. Lawrence: UP of Kansas, 1991.

[The period with the author's middle initial substitutes for the period that normally follows the author's name. The letters UP, without periods or a space, abbreviate *University Press*.]

A Book by Two or More Authors   Authors' names appear in the order in which they are presented on the title page, which may or may not be alphabetical. A comma follows the initial author's first name; second and third authors' names appear in normal order.

Scott, John Paul, and John L. Fuller. <u>Genetics and the Social Behavior of the Dog</u>. Chicago: U of Chicago P, 1965.

When a book has four or more authors, include only the first author's name in full form; substitute *et al.* (meaning "and others," not italicized or underlined) for the names of additional authors.

Gershey, Edward L., et al. <u>Low-Level Radioactive Waste: From Cradle to Grave</u>. New York: Van Nostrand, 1990.

A Book with No Author   When no author is named, list the work by title. Alphabetize books listed by title using the first important word of the title, not the articles *a, an,* or *the.*

> United Press International Stylebook: The Authoritative Handbook for Writers, Editors, and News Directors. 3rd ed. Lincolnwood, IL: Natl. Textbook, 1992.

[Because the city of Lincolnwood is not commonly recognized, the state abbreviation is required. Note that *national* is abbreviated when it is part of a publisher's name.]

Multiple Works by the Same Author   When citing multiple works by the same author, present the first citation completely. Subsequent entries, alphabetized by title, are introduced by three hyphens and a period and alphabetized by title. Coauthored works require full names and are alphabetized after those with single authors.

> Ehrenreich, Barbara. "Battered Welfare Syndrome." Time 3 Apr. 1995: 82.
>
> ---. Fear of Falling: The Inner Life of the Middle Class. New York: Pantheon, 1989.
>
> Ehrenreich, Barbara, Elizabeth Hess, and Gloria Jacobs. Re-Making Love: The Feminization of Sex. Garden City, NY: Anchor-Doubleday, 1986.

[Notice that the publisher of the last selection includes a two-part name: the imprint and the major publisher (see An Imprint, page 582, for an additional sample).]

A Book with an Organization as Author   When an organization is both the author and the publisher, present the name completely in the author position and use an abbreviation in the publisher position.

> Gemological Institute of America. The Diamond Dictionary. Santa Monica, CA: GIA, 1977.

An Edition Other than the First   The edition number, noted on the title page, follows the title of the book. When a book also has an editor, translator, or compiler, the edition number follows that information. Edition numbers are presented in numeral-abbreviation form (*2nd, 3rd, 4th*).

> Mano, M. Morris. Digital Design. 2nd ed. Englewood Cliffs, NJ: Prentice Hull, 1991.

A Reprint A reprint, a newly printed but unaltered version of a book, is identified as such on the title page or copyright page. The original publication date precedes the facts of publication, and the date of the reprinted edition follows the publisher's name.

Palmer, John. <u>The Comedy of Manners</u>. 1913. New York: Russell, 1962.

A Multivolume Work A multivolume work may have one title, or it may have a comprehensive title for the complete work and separate titles for each volume. When you use the entire set of volumes, use the collective title and note the number of volumes. If volumes are published over several years, provide inclusive dates (1993–95); if the work is still in progress, include the earliest date, a hyphen, one space, and the closing period (1996– .).

<u>Perspectives on Western Art: Source Documents and Readings from the Renaissance to the 1970s</u>. Ed. Linnea H. Wren. 2 vols. New York: Icon-Harper, 1994.

To emphasize a single volume, first cite the volume as a separate book. Then add the volume number, the collection title, and the total number of volumes.

<u>Direct Solar Energy</u>. Ed. T. Nejat Veziroglu. New York: Nova, 1991. Vol. A of <u>Energy and Environmental Progress</u>. 7 vols.

[Volumes identified by letters should be presented that way in the citation.]

A Work in a Collection To cite a work in a collection, include the name of the selection's author, the title of the specific selection (appropriately punctuated), the collection title, publication facts, and the inclusive page numbers for the selection (without page abbreviations). To cite more than one selection from the collection, prepare separate citations (see Multiple Selections from the Same Collection, page 581).

Modelski, George, and William R. Thompson. "Long Cycles and Global War." <u>Handbook of War Studies</u>. Ed. Manus I. Midlarsky. Ann Arbor: U Michigan P, 1993. 23–54.

A Previously Published Work in a Collection To indicate that a selection has been previously published, begin the citation with original facts of publication. *Rpt.*, meaning "reprinted," begins the second part of the citation, which includes information about the source you have used.

Wallace, Mike. "Mickey Mouse History: Portraying the Past at Disney World." <u>Radical History Review</u> 32 (1985): 33–55. Rpt. in <u>Customs in</u>

Conflict: The Anthology of a Changing World. Ed. Frank Manning
and Jean-Marc Philbert. Peterborough, ON: Broadview, 1990. 304–32.

Multiple Selections from the Same Collection To cite several selections from the same collection, prepare a citation for the complete work—beginning either with the editor's name or with the collection title. Additional references begin with the author of the individual selection and its title. However, instead of providing full publication information, include the editor's name or a shortened version of the title; provide inclusive page numbers for the selection. Notice that all citations are alphabetized.

Gilbert, Sandra, and Susan Gubar. "The Parable of the Cave." Richter
1119–26.

James, Henry. "The Art of Fiction." Richter 420–33.

Richter, David H., ed. *The Critical Tradition: Classic Texts and Contemporary Trends*. New York: Bedford, 1989.

An Article in an Encyclopedia or Other Reference Work Use an author's name when it is available. If only initials are listed with the article, match them with the name from the list of contributors. Well-known reference books require no information other than the title, edition number (if any), and date. Citations for less well-known or recently published reference works include full publication information. Page numbers are not needed when a reference work is arranged alphabetically.

Angermüller, Rudolph. "Salieri, Antonio." *The New Grove Dictionary
of Music and Musicians*. 1980 ed.

**[This twenty-volume set is extremely well known and consequently
needs no publication information.]**

Gietschier, Steven. "Paige, Satchel." *The Ballplayers: Baseball's Ultimate Biographical Reference*. Ed. Mike Shatzkin. New York:
Arbour, 1990.

**[Since this source is relatively new, full publishing information is
required.]**

When no author's name or initials appear with an article, begin with the title, reproduced to match the pattern in the reference book. Other principles remain the same.

"Glenn, John Hershel, Jr." *Who's Who in Aviation and Aerospace*. US
ed. Boston: Natl. Aeronautical Inst., 1983.

A Work in a Series Names of series (collections of books related to the same subject, genre, time period, and so on) are typically found on a book's title page and should be included just before the publishing information. Abbreviate the word *Series* (Ser.) if it is part of the series title.

> Morley, Carolyn. <u>Transformation, Miracles, and Mischief: The Moun-</u>
> <u>tain Priest Plays of Kyogen</u>. Cornell East Asia Ser. Ithaca, NY:
> Cornell UP, 1993.

When volumes in a series are numbered, include both the series name and number, followed by a period.

> Forster, E. M. <u>Passage to India</u>. Everyman's Library 29. New York:
> Knopf, 1992.

An Imprint An imprint is a specialized division of a larger publishing company. When an imprint name and a publisher name both appear on the title page, list them together (imprint name first), separated by a hyphen and no additional spaces.

> <u>African Rhapsody: Short Stories of the Contemporary African Experi-</u>
> <u>ence</u>. Ed. Nadezda Obradovic. New York: Anchor-Doubleday, 1994.

> **[Anchor is the imprint; Doubleday is the publisher.]**

A Translation A translator's name must always be included in a citation for a translated work because he or she prepared the version that you read. To emphasize the original work (the most common pattern), place the abbreviation *Trans.* (for "translated by," not italicized) and the translator's name after the title (but following editors' names, if the translator translated the entire work).

> Esquivel, Laura. <u>Like Water for Chocolate: A Novel in Monthly Install-</u>
> <u>ments, with Recipes, Romances, and Home Remedies</u>. Trans. Carol
> Christensen and Thomas Christensen. New York: Doubleday, 1992.

If selections within a collection are translated by different people, then each translator's name should follow the appropriate selection.

> Salamun, Tomaz. "Clumsy Guys." Trans. Sonja Kravanja. <u>The Push-</u>
> <u>cart Prize XVII: Best of the Small Presses</u>. Ed. Bill Henderson et
> al. New York: Pushcart, 1993. 443.

A Government ***Congressional Record***
Document

Citations for *Congressional Record* are exceedingly brief: the italicized and abbreviated title, *Cong. Rec.*, the date (presented in day-month-year order), and the page number. Page numbers used alone indicate Senate records; page numbers preceded by an *H* indicate records from the House of Representatives.

<u>Cong. Rec</u>. 15 June 1993: 7276+.

[This simple citation is for a Senate record. The plus sign (+) following the page number indicates that the discussion continues on several pages.]

<u>Cong. Rec</u>. 7 Oct. 1994: H11251.

[Note the page reference, with the H indicating that this citation is for a House record.]

Committee, Commission, Department

Information to describe government documents is generally presented in this order: (1) country, state, province, or county; (2) government official, governing body, sponsoring department, commission, center, ministry, or agency; (3) office, bureau, or committee; (4) the title of the publication, italicized; (5) if appropriate, the author of the document, the number and session of Congress, the kind and number of the document; (6) the city of publication, the publisher, and the date.

When citing more than one work from the same government or agency, use three hyphens and a period to substitute for identical elements.

United States. Commission on Migrant Education. <u>Invisible Children:</u>
    <u>A Portrait of Migrant Education in the United States</u>. Washing-
    ton: GPO, 1992.

[The Government Printing Office, the publisher of most federal documents, is abbreviated to save space.]

---. Cong. Budget Office. <u>An Analysis of the Managed Competition</u>
    <u>Act</u>. Washington: GPO, 1994.

---. ---. ---. <u>Federal Financial Support for High-Technology Indus-</u>
    <u>tries</u>. Washington: GPO, 1985.

[The three sets of three hyphens indicate that this source also was prepared by the United States Congressional Budget Office.]

---. ---. Senate. Committee on Aging. <u>Hearings</u>. 101st Cong., 1st
    sess. 1989. Washington: GPO, 1990.

[The use of only two sets of hyphens indicates that only the first two elements correspond to the preceding citation: this source was

prepared by the United States Congress, but the Senate affiliation requires the introduction of new, clarifying information in the third position.]

A Preface, Introduction, Foreword, Epilogue, or Afterword To cite material that is separate from the primary text of a book, begin with the name of the person who wrote the separate material, an assigned title (if applicable) in quotation marks, a descriptive title for the part used (capitalized but not punctuated), the title of the book, the name of the book's author (introduced with *By*, not italicized), publication facts, and inclusive page numbers for the separate material. Note that most prefatory or introductory material is paged using lowercase roman numerals.

Dabney, Lewis M. "Edmund Wilson and The Sixties." Introduction. The Sixties: The Last Journal, 1960–1972. By Edmund Wilson. New York: Farrar, 1993. xxi–xlvii.

Finnegan, William. Epilogue. Crossing the Line: A Year in the Land of Apartheid. New York: Harper, 1986. 401–09.

A Pamphlet When pamphlets contain clear and complete information, they are cited like books. When information is missing, use these abbreviations: *N.p.* for "No place of publication," *n.p.* for "no publisher," *n.d.* for "no date," and *N. Pag.* (with a space between the abbreviations) for "no page."

Adams, Andrew B. Hospice Care. New York: American Cancer Soc., 1984. 9–16.

America's Cup? The Sober Truth about Alcohol and Boating. Alexandria, VA: Boat/U. S., n.d.

A Dissertation A citation for an unpublished dissertation begins with the author's name, the dissertation title in quotation marks, the abbreviation *Diss.* (not italicized), the name of the degree-granting school (with *University* abbreviated as *U*), and the date.

Stevenson, David Stacey. "Heat Transfer in Active Volcanoes: Models of Crater Lake Systems." Diss. Open U, UK, 1994.

[When the university's location is unfamiliar, include the state, province, or country.]

A published dissertation is a book and should be presented as such. However, include dissertation information between the title and the facts of publication.

Salmon, Jaslin U. <u>Black Executives in White Businesses</u>. Diss. U of
Illinois-Chicago, 1977. Washington, DC: UP of America, 1979.

Sacred Writings Citations for sacred writing follow patterns similar to those of other
books, with several notable variations. First, titles of sacred writings
(the parts or the whole) are neither placed in quotation marks nor italicized; they are capitalized only. Second, full facts of publication are not
required for traditional editions. When appropriate, include additional
information according to the guidelines for the element.

The Bhagavad Gita. Trans. Juan Mascaró. New York: Penguin, 1962.

[Include translators when appropriate.]

The Holy Bible.

**[This citation is for the King James version of the Bible, the tradi-
tional edition.]**

The New Oxford Annotated Bible. Rev. Standard Version. Ed. Herbert
G. May and Bruce M. Metzger. New York: Oxford UP, 1973.

**[This citation provides full information, highlighting a version other
than the King James and the editorial work that it includes.]**

Periodicals

An Article in a To cite an article in a monthly magazine, include the author's name, the
Monthly Magazine article's title in quotation marks, the magazine's name (italicized), the
month (abbreviated) and year, and the inclusive pages of the article
(without page abbreviations).

Frosch, Robert A. "The Industrial Ecology of the Twenty-First Century."
<u>Scientific American</u> Sept. 1995: 178–81.

**[Note that the period comes before the closing quotation marks of the
article's title, that one space (but no punctuation) separates the periodical title and the date, and that a colon separates the date and the
pages.]**

An Article in a Citations for articles in weekly magazines are identical to those for
Weekly Magazine monthly magazines, with one exception: the publication date is presented in more detailed form, in day-month-year order (with the month
abbreviated).

Morrow, James. "Watching Web Speech." <u>U.S. News and World Report</u> 15 Feb. 1999: 32.

[Even though magazines often use special typography (as in *U.S. News & World Report*), such material is standardized in citations.]

An Article in a Journal with Continuous Paging Journals with continuous paging number the issues sequentially for the entire year. For this kind of journal, place the volume number after the journal title, identify the year in parentheses, follow it with a colon, and then list page numbers.

Enstad, Nan. "Fashioning Political Identities: Cultural Studies and the Historical Construction of Political Subjects." <u>American Quarterly</u> 50 (1998): 745–82.

An Article in a Journal with Separate Paging For journals that page each issue separately, follow the volume number with a period and the issue number (without spaces).

Hardy, Janice V. "Teacher Attitudes toward and Knowledge of Computer Technology." <u>Computers in the Schools</u> 14.3–4 (1998): 119–36.

[When issues are combined, list both numbers separating them with a hyphen without additional spaces.]

An Article in a Newspaper Citations for newspapers resemble those for magazines: they include the author's name, article title (in quotation marks), newspaper title (italicized), the date (in day-month-year order, followed by a colon), and inclusive pages.

However, when newspapers have editions (*morning, evening, national*), they must be identified. After the year, place a comma and describe the edition, abbreviating common words.

When sections of newspapers are designated by letters, place the section letter with the page number, without a space (*A22, C3, F11*). If sections are indicated by numerals, place a comma after the date or edition (rather than a colon), include the abbreviation *sec.* (not italicized), the section number, a colon, a space, and the page number (*sec. 1: 22, sec. 3: 2, sec. 5: 17*).

When an article continues in a later part of the paper, indicate the initial page, use a comma, and then add the subsequent page. If the article appears on more than three separated pages, list the initial page, followed by a plus sign (*22+, A17+, sec. 2: 9+*).

Weekly newspapers are cited just like daily newspapers.

Brody, Jane E. "Americans Gamble on Herbs as Medicine." <u>New York Times</u> 9 Feb. 1999: D1, 7.

Snyder, Jeffrey B. "<u>Star Wars</u> Toys: A Force to Reckon With." <u>Antique</u>
<u>Week</u> 25 Jan. 1999: A1, 43-44.

An Editorial The citation for an editorial resembles that for a magazine or newspaper
article, with one exception: the word *Editorial* (not italicized), with a
period, follows the title of the essay.

McCormick, David M. "The Draft Isn't the Answer." Editorial. <u>New</u>
<u>York Times</u> 10 Feb. 1999: A31.

A Letter to the Editor Letters to the editor follow a very simple format. Include the author's
name, the word *Letter* (not italicized), the name of the publication (magazine, journal, or newspaper), and appropriate facts of publication. Do
not record descriptive, attention-getting titles that publications, not
authors, supply.

Trivedi, Apaar. Letter. <u>Business Week</u> 25 May 1998: 12.

**["Counting Chickens before They Hatch" served as the functional
title of this letter to the editor, but it is not used in the citation.]**

A Review A citation for a review begins with the author's name and the title of the
review (if one is provided). The abbreviation *Rev. of* (not italicized) follows, with the name of the book, film, recording, performance, product,
or whatever is being reviewed, followed by clarifying information. Publication information ends the citation, incorporating elements required
for different kinds of sources.

Siegel, Lee. "A Writer Who Is Good for You." Rev. of <u>Jane Austen: A</u>
<u>Biography</u> by Claire Tomalin and <u>Jane Austen: A Life</u> by David
Nokes. <u>Atlantic Monthly</u> Jan. 1998: 93-98.

Nonprint Sources Finding documentation information for nonprint sources is usually easy
but sometimes requires ingenuity. Compact disc booklets provide the
manufacturers' catalog numbers and copyright dates. Printed programs
for speeches or syllabuses for course lectures provide names, titles, locations, and dates. Information about films or television programs can be
obtained from opening or closing credits or from reference books such as
Facts on File or web sites such as *All-Movie Guide* (<http://allmovie.com>).
If you have difficulty finding the information to document nonprint
sources clearly, ask your instructor or a librarian for help.

A Lecture or Speech A citation for a formal lecture or speech includes the speaker's name,
the title of the presentation (in quotation marks), the name of the lecture
or speaker series (if applicable), the location of the speech (convention,
meeting, university, library, meeting hall), the city (and state if necessary), and the date in day-month-year order.

Branch, Tayler. "Democracy in an Age of Denial." Humanities on the Hill Ser. Washington, DC, 7 May 1992.

Mitten, David M. "Greek Art and Architecture in the West: Southern Italy, Sicily, and Campania." Class lecture. Harvard University. Cambridge, 15 May 1989.

[For class lectures, provide as much of this information as possible: speaker, title of lecture (in quotation marks), a descriptive title, the school, the city (and state if necessary), and the date.]

Quayle, J. Danforth. "The Most Litigious Society in the World." American Bar Assn. Annual Meeting. Atlanta, 13 Aug. 1991.

A Work of Art When artists title their own work, include this information: artist's name; the title (italicized); the museum, gallery, or collection where the work of art is housed; and the city (and state, province, or country if needed for clarity).

Cézanne, Paul. Houses along a Road. The Hermitage, St. Petersburg, Russia.

When an artist has not titled a work, use the title that art historians have given to it (without quotation marks), followed by a brief description of the work. The rest of the citation is the same as those for other works of art.

Amateis, Edmond Romulus. Jonas Edward Salk. Sculpture in bronze. Natl. Portrait Gallery, Washington, DC.

[*Jonas Edward Salk* is the attributed title of the statue of this famous scientist.]

A Map, Graph, Maps, graphs, tables, and charts are treated like books. If it's known,
Table, or Chart include the name of the author, artist, designer, scientist, person, or group responsible for the map, graph, table, or chart. Then include the title (italicized), followed by a separately punctuated descriptive title. Also include any other necessary information.

Lewis, R. J. [Noninteractive and Interactive] Telecommunication Technologies. Table. Meeting Learners' Needs through Telecommunication: A Directory and Guide to Programs. Washington, DC: American Assn. for Higher Education, 1983. 75.

[Clarifying information can be added within brackets.]

A Cartoon Begin with the cartoonist's name, the title of the cartoon in quotation marks, and the word *Cartoon* (not italicized), followed by a period. Then include the citation information required for the source.

> Davis, Jack, and Stan Hart. "Groan with the Wind." Cartoon. <u>Mad</u>
> Jan. 1991: 42–47.

[This cartoon appeared in a monthly magazine.]

A Film To cite a film as a complete work, include the title (italicized), the director (noted by the abbreviation *Dir.*, not italicized), the studio, and the date of release. If you include other people's contributions, do so after the director's name by using brief phrases (*Screenplay by, Original score by*) or abbreviations (*Perf.* for "performed by," *Prod.* for "produced by") to clarify their roles.

> <u>On the Waterfront</u>. Dir. Elia Kazan. Perf. Marlon Brando and Eva
> Marie Saint. Horizon-Columbia, 1954.

To emphasize the contribution of an individual (rather than the film as a whole), place the person's name first, followed by a comma and a descriptive title (beginning with a lowercase letter). The rest of the citation follows normal patterns.

> Coppola, Francis Ford, dir. <u>Apocalypse Now</u>. Perf. Martin Sheen, Marlon Brando, and Robert Duvall. United Artists, 1979. Suggested
> by Joseph Conrad's <u>Heart of Darkness</u>.

A Television Broadcast List a regular program by the title (italicized), the network (CBS, CNN, Fox), the local station (including both the call letters and the city, separated by a comma), and the broadcast date (in day-month-year order).
Include other people's contributions after the program title, using brief phrases (*Written by, Hosted by*) or abbreviations (*Perf.* for "performed by," *Prod.* for "produced by") to clarify their roles.

> <u>X-Files</u>. Perf. Gillian Anderson and David Duchovny. Fox. WXIN, Indianapolis. 20 June 1999.

To cite a single episode of an ongoing program, include the name of the episode in quotation marks before the program's title. Other elements are presented in the same order as used for a regular program.

> "The Understudy." <u>Seinfeld</u>. Perf. Bette Midler. NBC. WTHR, Indianapolis. 18 May 1995.

List special programs by title, followed by traditional descriptive information. If a special program is part of a series (for example, Hallmark

Hall of Fame, Great Performances, or American Playhouse), include the series name without quotation marks or italics immediately preceding the name of the network.

The Sleeping Beauty. Composed by Peter Ilich Tchaikovsky. Choreographed by Marius Petipa. Perf. Viviana Durante and Zoltan Solymosi. Great Performances. PBS. WFYI, Indianapolis. 24 Dec. 1995.

A Radio Broadcast A citation for a radio broadcast follows the same guidelines as those for a television broadcast.

The War of the Worlds. WCBS, New York. 30 Oct. 1938.

A Recording Citations for recordings usually begin with the performer or composer, followed by the title of the recording (italicized except for titles using numerals for musical form, key, or number), the recording company, the catalog number, and the copyright date.

List other contributors after the title, using brief phrases or abbreviations (*Cond.*, the abbreviation for conductor; *Perf.* for "performed by"; *Composed by*) to clarify their roles. Orchestras (abbreviated *orch.*) and other large musical groups are listed without clarifying phrases, usually following the conductor's name.

When appropriate, include recording dates immediately following the title. Compact discs (CDs) are now the standard recording format; indicate other formats, when necessary, after the title.

Notation of multidisc sets, similar to the pattern for multivolume books, appears immediately preceding the record company.

The Beatles. Live at the BBC. 2 discs. Capital, C2-31796-2, 1994.

Mahler, Gustav. Symphony no. 1 in D major. Record. Cond. Georg Solti. Chicago Symphony Orch. London, 411731-2, 1984.

[Since this selection is titled by musical form and key, it is not italicized. As noted after the title, this is a record, not a CD.]

To cite a single selection from a recording, include the selection title in quotation marks followed by the title of the complete recording. All else remains the same.

Clapton, Eric. "Tears in Heaven." Eric Clapton Unplugged. Reprise, 9 45024-2, 1992.

To cite liner notes, the printed material that comes with many recordings, list the name of the writer and the description *Liner notes* (not italicized), followed by a period. The rest of the citation follows normal patterns.

McClintick, David, and William Kennedy. Liner notes. <u>Frank Sinatra:</u>
<u>The Reprise Collection</u>. 4 discs. Reprise, 020373, 1990.

An Interview Citations for personally conducted interviews include the name of the
person interviewed, the type of interview (personal or telephone), and
the interview date.

Otwell, Stephen. Personal interview. 11 Nov. 1998.

Citations for broadcast or printed interviews include the name of
the person interviewed, the descriptive title *Interview* (not italicized),
and information necessary to describe the source.

Stewart, Jimmy. Interview. <u>Reflections on the Silver Screen</u>. A&E. 5
Nov. 1994.

A Transcript Transcripts of programs are presented according to the source of the
original broadcast, with clarifying information provided. The entry
ends with information about availability.

Watkins, Terri, et al. "McVeigh Said to Have Mentioned Other Bombings
in Letter." Transcript. <u>Daybreak</u>. CNN. 28 Apr. 1995. Available:
Journal Graphics Online.

Electronic Sources

Electronic sources, including Internet sources and CD-ROMs, provide a wide
array of materials for current researchers. However, because of their variety,
providing clear documentation for electronic sources can be a challenge. It is,
nevertheless, a challenge worth meeting.

Be both resourceful and patient as you gather citation information for electronic sources. Information does not always appear in the same place in each
source, a situation which can be confusing, and some sources do not provide
all of the information you might want, a situation which can be frustrating. Provide as much information as possible on each source, following the patterns
described in this section.

INTERNET SOURCES

Internet sources exist in widely varied forms, from online books to personal web
sites, making the process of citing them complicated. However, using the following list, you should be able to provide the information necessary to complete

an accurate and helpful citation for each of your Internet sources. Provide, in this order, all information pertinent to your source:

1. Author (or editor), last name first
2. Title (of article, poem, and so on) from a scholarly project, database, or periodical, in quotation marks; title of discussion-group posting, in quotation marks (followed by the phrase *Online posting,* not italicized); title of book, italicized (underlined)
3. Additional information: editor, compiler, or translator, preceded by the appropriate abbreviation
4. Facts of publication for material available in print form
5. Date of electronic publication (or most recent updating or posting)
6. Name of subscription service (or listserv or forum)
7. Number of pages or paragraphs when they are identified (7 pp. or 36 pars.)
8. Name of sponsoring institution or organization
9. Date you gained access to the source
10. Electronic address enclosed in angle brackets

A Professional Site Law Student Division. American Bar Association. 11 Feb. 1999 <http://www.abanet.org//lsd/home.html>.

An Article in a Magazine Begley, Sharon, and Martha Brant. "The Real Scandal." Newsweek 15 Feb. 1999. 16 Feb. 1999 <http://www.newsweek.com/nw=srv/ printed/int/socu/sp0107_7.htm>.

An Article in a Journal Miller, Donald E. "Experiencing Homelessness." Journal of Contemporary Ethnography 27 (1998): 5 pp. 13 Feb. 1999 <http:proquest.umi.com/pqdweb>.

An Article in a Reference Database "Expenditures for Health Care Plans by Employers and Employees." Bureau of Labor Statistics. 7 Dec. 1998. Bureau of Labor Statistics. 17 Feb. 1999 <http://stats.bls.gov/pub/news.release/nce.txt>.

A Book Lofting, Hugh. The Voyages of Doctor Dolittle. Project Gutenberg. Jan. 1998. U of Illinois. 2 Feb. 1999 <ftp://uiarchive.cso.uiuc.edu/ pub/etext/gutenberg/etext98/vdrdl10.txt>.

A Poem Dickinson, Emily. "I felt a funeral in my brain." Emily Dickinson: Poems. Project Bartleby Archives. Columbia U. 31 Jan. 1999 <http://www.columbia.edu/acis/bartleby/dickinson4.html#30>.

A Scholarly Project   Austen, Jane. <u>Sense and Sensibility</u>. Project Gutenberg. Sept. 1994.
U of Illinois. 4 Feb. 1999 <ftp:/uiarchive.cso.uiuc.edu/pub/
etext/gutenberg/etext94/sense11.txt>.

A Posting to a   Dungarvin Parent Association of Delaware. "Developing Programs for
Discussion Group   Adults with Autism." Online posting. 14 June 1998. 3 Feb. 1999
<grnlks@alltell.net>.

CD-ROM SOURCES

Although CD-ROMs are being phased out in many libraries because Internet
sites provide more easily updated materials, it is possible that you will still need
to cite a CD-ROM source.

If a CD-ROM source reproduces material available in print form, begin the
citation with full print information: author (or editor), title, and facts of publication (see pages 578–591 for complete citation patterns). If the material is not
available in print form, begin the citation with identifying information: author
(if given), title (in quotation marks), and the date of the material (if appropriate).
Citations for both kinds of materials then include information about the CD-
ROM source in this order:

1. The title of the database, italicized

2. The description *CD-ROM,* not italicized

3. The city (if known) and the name of the company that produced the
CD-ROM

4. The date of electronic publication

Available in Print Form   "On the Brink: An Interview with Yitzhak Rabin." <u>Jerusalem Post</u> 23
Apr. 1994: 16. <u>PAIS International</u>. CD-ROM. Silverplatter, 1995.

Electronic Only   "National Rifle Association of America (NRA)." <u>Encyclopedia of
Associations</u>. CD-ROM. Detroit: Gale, 1994.

If a CD-ROM source is not regularly revised or updated, the citation
follows a pattern similar to that for a book, with one exception: the
description *CD-ROM* (not italicized) precedes the publishing information.

Welmers, William E. "African Languages." <u>The New Grolier Multi-
media Encyclopedia</u>. 1994 ed. CD-ROM. New York: Grolier, 1994.

Credits

Chapter 1: Page 9: Reprinted by permission of International Creative Management, Inc. Copyright © 1987 by Toni Morrison; page 21: Excerpt pp. 18–26 from *How a Writer Works*, revised edition by Roger Garrison. Copyright © 1985 by The Estate of Roger H. Garrison. Reprinted by permission of Pearson Education, Inc.; page 30: From John Chaffee, Ph.D., *Thinking Critically*, 6/e, pp. 77–78. Used by permission of Houghton Mifflin Company.

Chapter 2: Page 40: © The New Yorker Collection. 1998 Frank Cotham from cartoonbank.com. All rights reserved; page 49: Excerpt from *An American Childhood* by Annie Dillard. Copyright © 1987 by Annie Dillard. Reprinted by permission of HarperCollins Publishers, Inc.; page 51: N. Scott Momaday, "The End of My Childhood" from *Names: A Memoir*, Harper & Row, 1976. © N. Scott Momaday. Reprinted by permission of the author; page 53: "Independence and the Inward 'I'" by Peter J. Rondinone. Reprinted by permission of the author; page 58: From Edwidge Danticat, "We Are Ugly, But We Are Here," Caribbean Writers Online. Reprinted by permission of the authors.

Chapter 3: Page 78: Reprinted by permission of the author and Story Line Press from *Writing Without the Muse: 50 Beginning Exercises for the Creative Writer* (1995). www.storylinepress.com; page 86: *Boston Globe* (staff produced copy only) by David L. Chandler. Copyright 2000 by Globe Newspaper Co. (MA). Reprinted with permission of Globe Newspaper Co. (MA) in the format Textbook via Copyright Clearance Center ;page 93: Excerpt from *Pizza Tiger* by Tom Monaghan with Robert Anderson, pp. 241–243, 1986, Random House. Reprinted by permission of Domino's Pizza, Inc.; page 95: Reprinted with permission from *Psychology Today Magazine*, Copyright © (1989) Sussex Publishers, Inc.

Chapter 4: Page 117: "The Red Candle" from *The Joy Luck Club* by Amy Tan, copyright © 1989 by Amy Tan. Used with permission of G. P. Putnam's Sons, a division of Penguin Putnam, Inc.; page 134: Donald M. Murray, "The Maker's Eye: Revising Your Own Manuscripts." Reprinted by permission of the author; page 138: "How to Say Nothing in Five Hundred Words" from *Understanding English* by Paul Roberts. Copyright © 1958 by Paul Roberts. Reprinted by permission of Addison-Wesley Educational Publishers, Inc.

Chapter 5: Page 168: From *The Autobiography of Malcolm X* by Malcolm X and Alex Haley, copyright © 1964 by Alex Haley and Malcolm X. Copyright © 1965 by Alex Haley and Betty Shabazz. Used by permission of Random House, Inc.; page 170: From *Blue Highways* by

Index

Tips for Evaluating the Reliability of a Web Site

This method is presented in more detail in Chapter 13.

1. **Authority**
   - ❑ Are the sponsor's identity and purpose clear?
   - ❑ Are the author's identity and qualifications evident?
   - ❑ If the material is copyrighted, who is the copyright holder?
   - ❑ Is there a way to verify the legitimacy of the site's sponsor?
   - ❑ Don't forget that some of the people running sites are trying to confuse you.
   - ❑ Look for clues that indicate a personal home page.
   - ❑ Run unfamiliar topics or author names through a search engine.

2. **Accuracy**
   - ❑ Are sources of factual information clearly listed?
   - ❑ Has the sponsor provided links that can be used to verify the sponsor's claims?
   - ❑ Is statistical data well labeled and easy to read?
   - ❑ Is the information free of grammatical errors, spelling errors, and typos?

3. **Objectivity**
   - ❑ Is it evident why the sponsor is providing each piece of information?
   - ❑ Is the information content separate from advertising or opinion?
   - ❑ Is the sponsor's point of view presented clearly with well-supported arguments?
   - ❑ If the site is not objective, does it account for opposing points of view?

4. **Currency**
   - ❑ Is the material recent enough to be relevant to your project?
   - ❑ Are there any indications that the material is kept up to date?
   - ❑ Do you see statements indicating where data for charts and graphs were gathered?
   - ❑ Is there an indication that the site is complete and not still being developed?